Cultural Crossroads in the Ancient Novel

Trends in Classics – Supplementary Volumes

Edited by
Franco Montanari and Antonios Rengakos

Associate Editors
Evangelos Karakasis · Fausto Montana · Lara Pagani ·
Serena Perrone · Evina Sistakou · Christos Tsagalis

Scientific Committee
Alberto Bernabé · Margarethe Billerbeck
Claude Calame · Jonas Grethlein · Philip R. Hardie
Stephen J. Harrison · Richard Hunter · Christina Kraus
Giuseppe Mastromarco · Gregory Nagy
Theodore D. Papanghelis · Giusto Picone
Tim Whitmarsh · Bernhard Zimmermann

Volume 40

Cultural Crossroads
in the Ancient Novel

Edited by
Marília P. Futre Pinheiro, David Konstan
and Bruce Duncan MacQueen

DE GRUYTER

ISBN 978-1-5015-1942-0
e-ISBN (PDF) 978-1-5015-0398-6
e-ISBN (EPUB) 978-1-5015-0402-0
ISSN 1868-4785

Library of Congress Cataloging-in-Publication Data
A CIP catalog record for this book has been applied for at the Library of Congress.

Bibliographic information published by the Deutsche Nationalbibliothek
The Deutsche Nationalbibliothek lists this publication in the Deutsche Nationalbibliografie;
detailed bibliographic data are available in the Internet at http://dnb.dnb.de.

© 2019 Walter de Gruyter GmbH, Berlin/Boston
This volume is text- and page-identical with the hardback published in 2018.
Editorial Office: Alessia Ferreccio and Katerina Zianna
Logo: Christopher Schneider, Laufen
Printing: CPI books GmbH, Leck
♾ Printed on acid-free paper
Printed in Germany

www.degruyter.com

Acknowledgements

This volume is the eighth in a series of thematically organized papers, presenting to an international academic public a selection from the 280 papers originally delivered at the Fourth International Conference on the Ancient Novel (ICAN IV), which was held at the Fundação Calouste Gulbenkian, in Lisbon, in July 2008. The papers assembled in this volume reflect the accelerated pace of scholarly research in one of the most innovative and fast-growing fields of study in classical and comparative studies. The ancient novel has increasingly become a crucial element in the interpretation of ancient culture, identity, reading practices, and the history of the modern genre as well. Focussing on the crossing of cultures, languages, races and mentalities, this volume introduces a wide array of topics that characterize the novelistic genre and are simultaneously at the centre of contemporary cultural debates: spaces, frontiers, and intersections, which serve as metaphors for a host of questions, concerns and issues.

A special word of recognition goes to all those who have generously contributed their time and effort to bring about this publication. First, I want to offer my warm gratitude to my fellow editors, David Konstan and Bruce MacQueen, to whom this publication owes so much. Without their friendly and continuous support, careful reading and editing of the papers, and generous commitment, it would not been possible to bring this project to completion.

The editors are particularly grateful to the contributers themselves, who exhibited exemplary patience during the long process of editing and revising. The staff at De Gruyter also deserves a special mention for their precise professional work and support during the publication process: Dr. Serena Pirrotta, Editorial Director Classical Studies & Philosophy, Olena Gainulina and Florian Ruppenstein, Production Editors, and Marco Michele Acquafredda, Project Editor.

We are also indebted to the two PhD students at Brown University: Christopher Ell and Sam Caldis, for their invaluable assistance in the final stages of copy-editing (Chris) and preparation of the indices (Sam).

Finally, a special word of gratitude is due to Professors Antonios Rengakos and Franco Montanari, editors-in-charge, for kindly including this volume in their monograph series, *Trends in Classics*.

Marília P. Futre Pinheiro

Table of Contents

David Konstan
Introduction —— 1

Mapping the World in the Ancient Novel

Gottskálk Jensson
Sailing from Massalia, or Mapping Out the Significance of Encolpius' Travels in the *Satyrica* —— 7

Andrea Capra
Xenophon's 'Round Trip': Geography as Narrative Consistency in the *Ephesiaka* —— 17

Dimitri Kasprzyk
Permeable Worlds in Iamblichus's *Babyloniaka* —— 29

Catherine Connors
Babylonian Stories and the Ancient Novel: Magi and the Limits of Empire in Iamblichus' *Babyloniaka* —— 39

Ashli Jane Elizabeth Baker
Theama Kainon*: Reading Natural History in Achilles Tatius' *Leucippe and Clitophon —— 51

The Dialogic Imagination

Shannon N. Byrne
Fortunata and Terentia: A Model for Trimalchio's Wife —— 65

Christoph Kugelmeier
Elements of Ancient Novel and Novella in Tacitus —— 79

Sophie Lalanne
'A mirror carried along a high road'? Reflections on (and of) Society in the Greek Novel —— 93

Francesca Mestre and Pilar Gómez
The *Heroikos* of Philostratus: A Novel of Heroes, and more —— 107

Janelle Peters
Springs as a Civilizing Mechanism in *Daphnis and Chloe* —— 123

Martina Meyer
Arcadia Revisited: Material Gardens and Virtual Spaces in Longus' *Daphnis and Chloe* and in Roman Landscape Painting —— 143

H. Christian Blood
Narrating Voyages to Heaven and Hell: Seneca, Apuleius, and Bakhtin's Menippea —— 163

Turning Points in Scholarship on the Ancient Novel

Manuel Sanz Morales
Copyists' Versions and the Readership of the Greek Novel —— 183

Marina F. A. Martelli
Clues from the Papyri: Structure and Style of Chariton's Novel —— 195

Nicola Pace
New Evidence For Dating The Discovery At Traù Of The Petronian *Cena Trimalchionis* —— 209

Robert H. F. Carver
Bologna as Hypata: Annotation, Transformation, and Transl(oc)ation in the Circles of Filippo Beroaldo and Francesco Colonna —— 221

Saiichiro Nakatani
The First Japanese Translation of *Daphnis & Chloe* —— 239

Boundaries: Geographical and Metaphorical

Ellen Finkelpearl
Refiguring the Animal/Human Divide in Apuleius and Heliodorus —— 251

Mary Jaeger
Eros the Cheese Maker: A Food Studies Approach to *Daphnis and Chloe* —— 263

Jason König
Rethinking Landscape in Ancient Fiction: Mountains in Apuleius and Jerome —— 277

John Bodel
Kangaroo Courts: Displaced Justice in the Roman Novel —— 291

Character and Emotion in the Ancient Novel

David Konstan
Pity vs. Forgiveness in Pagan and Judaeo-Christian Narratives —— 305

Michael Cummings
The Interaction of Emotions in the Greek Novels —— 315

Cristiana Sogno
A Critique of Curiosity: Magic and Fiction in Apuleius' *Metamorphoses* —— 327

Vered Lev Kenaan
Spectacles of a Dormant Soul: A Reading of Plato's Gyges and Apuleius' Lucius —— 341

Edmund P. Cueva
Why doesn't Habrocomes run away from Aegialeus and his Mummified Wife?: Horror and the Ancient Novel —— 361

List of Contributors — 377

Index nominum et rerum — 381

Index locorum — 389

David Konstan
Introduction

The papers collected in this volume were originally delivered as oral presentations at the Fourth International Conference on the Ancient Novel (ICAN IV), held in Lisbon in July 2008 under the generous sponsorship of the Fundação Calouste Gulbenkian, to which all participants hereby express their deep gratitude. The conference was remarkable for including 280 papers on a wide variety of topics, from ancient texts to modern reception, and from the latest theoretical approaches to the detailed study of manuscripts and papyri; the range extended from classical Greek and Roman fiction and related genres to Jewish and Christian novelistic writing. The umbrella theme of the conference was "Crossroads in the Ancient Novel: Spaces, Frontiers, Intersections," but its canopy was broad enough to include sessions dedicated to such topics as archaeology and the novel, the novel as a world map, boundaries of gender and sexuality, the organization of space, the porous frontiers between history and literature, turning points in scholarship on the novels, questions of empire and self, memory, intertextuality, literature as resistance, the novel and myth, mystery cults, philosophy, critical theory, the Menippean satire and the picaresque, and more.

The present volume gathers papers from several of these sessions under the heading, "Cultural Crossroads in the Ancient Novel," a topic at the heart of the overarching theme of the conference. For the protagonists of the ancient novels wandered or were carried off to distant lands, from Italy in the west to Persia in the east and Ethiopia in the south; the authors themselves came, or pretended to come, from remote places such as Aphrodisia and Phoenicia; and the novelistic form had antecedents in a host of classical genres, but also in narrative traditions far and wide. The very range of intersections means that any cross-section of papers will have something of the quality of a potpourri or medley, and the present volume indeed brings together a wide sampling of approaches and topics. But this is all to the good, since one of the lessons of the conference was that approaches to the novels cannot be constrained by a single method or focus.

Papers in the first section of this volume deal with the topic of "mapping the world." GOTTSKÁLK JENSSON tracks the travels of Encolpius, the narrator of Petronius' *Satyrica*, who derives from Marseilles and makes his way south across Italy; Jensson succeeds in filling in some missing elements in the story, which he connects with the Greek tradition of the Milesian tale. ANDREA CAPRA examines the geography of Xenophon of Ephesus' *Ephesiaca*, revealing a circular pattern that underscores the coherence of the novel and gives the lie to the idea that its present from is an epitome of a lengthier original. DIMITRI KASPRZYK explores the mixture of times and places in Iamblichus' *Babyloniaka*, creating a world of multiple and permeable identities and indeed genres that reflects the geographically hybrid world of the novel. Iamblichus' novel is also the subject of CATHERINE CONNORS' chapter, which relates the narrator's professed expertise in the arts of the Magi to his specialized knowledge of geography. Finally, ASHLI BAKER looks at Achilles' Tatius' digressions on natural history, such as the motion of the Nile or the nature of the Phoenix, thereby taking in a wide range of geographical locales.

The second section examines the notion of the dialogic imagination, and more particularly the conversation between history and literature. SHANNON BYRNE shows how Petronius' Fortunata, the wife of Trimalchio, is modeled on Terentia, the wife of Maecenas, who was himself caricatured by Seneca as effeminate and uxorious. CHRISTOPH KUGELMEIER turns the mirror around, and suggests that Tacitus' account, in the *Annals*, of Nero's reign exploits novelistic motifs, for example in his description of Nero's relationship to his mother, Agrippina. SOPHIE LALANNE relates the Greek novels to the realities of social life in the Greek-speaking provinces of the Roman Empire, particularly in relation to the social stratification of the times. FRANCESCA MESTRE and PILAR GÓMEZ investigate the relationship between fiction and society in Philostratus' *Heroikos*, as reflected in the two narrative levels of the text; Homeric epic is thereby adapted to contemporary religious feeling and the revitalization of hero cults. JANELLE PETERS relates how a spring that runs through the ideal garden described in the proem to Daphnis and Chloe stands for "real" springs located on the island of Lesbos; at the same time it establishes gender equality by providing a location for alternative cultural definitions of civilization. In her examination of gardens and the construction of pastoral space in Longus' *Daphnis and Chloe*, MARTINA MEYER reveals correspondences with Roman landscape painting, thus bringing the ancient novel into dialogue with the pictorial arts. Lastly, CHRISTIAN BLOOD shows how the final book of Apuleius' *Metamorphoses* is indebted to Seneca's *Apocolocyntosis*, and that both reflect the Menippean tradition highlighted by Bakhtin, the granddaddy of the dialogical approach to the novel.

Section three treats changes in the way ancient fiction has been transmitted and perceived. Chapters single out some pivotal moments in reception of the novel, from antiquity, at the time when the novels were first being transcribed, to the Renaissance in the West and modern Japan. MANUEL SANZ MORALES notes that several of the Greek novels survive in multiple versions, and he relates this phenomenon to the question of the readership of the Greek novel: ancient copyists regarded the novel mainly as entertainment, which gave them license to introduce modifications into the text; this in turn suggests that the novels appealed not only to the educated elite but also to lower strata of society. MARINA MARTELLI compares the surviving codex of Chariton's novel with papyrus fragments, and suggests that Chariton's text might have been adapted at a certain point for a less cultivated public. NICOLA PACE focuses on the moment when the manuscript of the *Cena Trimalchionis* was first discovered, and shows that the delay in its publication was due to severe doubts among scholars of the time concerning its authenticity. ROBERT CARVER looks at Beroaldo's commentary on Apuleius' *Metamorphoses* (1500) and the *Hypnerotomachia Poliphili* ascribed to Francesco Colonna (1499); taken together, the edition and the imitation shed new light on the reception of the novel, which was seen as a metaphor for Renaissance humanism's own promise of renewal and transformation. SAIICHIRO NAKATANI discusses the first Japanese translation of Longus' *Daphnis and Chloe*, by Gen'ichi Yanome in 1925, and records how the translator dealt with the perceived "pornographic" elements in the novel.

Space, as the locus of cultural interaction and exchange, is the topic of the next part. ELLEN FINKELPEARL looks at the ways in which Apuleius and Heliodorus disrupt the boundaries between humans and animals, Apuleius by transforming a man into an ass that is nevertheless rational, and Heliodorus by placing in the mouth of a vegetarian priest a critique of the division into god, human, and animal; the collapse of these distinctions is mirrored in the complex intersection of ethnic identities. MARY JAEGER considers the function of milk and cheese in *Daphnis and Chloe:* here too the relationship between man and animal is subtly questioned, while cheese is also a metaphor for sexual maturation and for Chloe's transformation from a child into a commodity exchanged between men. JASON KÖNIG examines the metaphorical role of mountains in Apuleius' *Metamorphoses*, as regions of fear and pain, and Jerome's *Life of Hilarion*, where they stand for the capacity of Christianity to transform marginal spaces into places of holiness; in both, nevertheless, mountains represent the possibility of transcending the physical world. JOHN BODEL brings this section to a close with a look at mock trials in Petronius's *Satyrica* (Eumolpus's defense of Encolpius and Giton aboard Lichas's ship) and in Apuleius's *Metamorphoses* (the Risus festival); both display the collapse of order when justice is displaced from its proper setting and becomes subject to the whim of authority and emotive rhetoric.

The fifth and final section is devoted to character and emotion, and how these are perceived or constructed in ancient fiction. DAVID KONSTAN contrasts the way the heroes and heroines of the Greek novels beg pity from the gods but do not regard themselves as having done anything wrong, whereas in the Judeo-Christian *Life of Adam and Eve* the entire emphasis is on sin (especially Eve's), and the protagonists seek God's forgiveness rather than his pity. MICHAEL CUM-

MINGS exploits Lakoff and Johnson's theory of conceptual metaphor to explain how characters experience conflicting emotions simultaneously in the Greek novels, while also advancing an alternative model of emotion that is not predicated on conflict. CRISTIANA SOGNO shows how magic operates as a metaphor for fiction in Apuleius' *Metamorphoses*, thereby offering a perspective on how to interpret character in the novel. VERED LEV KENAAN compares Plato's account of Gyges' ring with Lucius' metamorphosis in Apuleius' novel to show how in both authors dreams and fantasy open a window onto the realm of the unconscious. Finally, EDMUND CUEVA invokes Noel Carroll's investigation of horror movies to show that horror, and the revulsion and shudders that it occasions, was a feature too of the ancient Greek and Roman novels.

Mapping the World in the Ancient Novel

Gottskálk Jensson
Sailing from Massalia, or Mapping Out the Significance of Encolpius' Travels in the *Satyrica*

Abstract: The aim of this paper is to suggest a way of reading the severely fragmented text of the *Satyrica* by investigating the literary and cultural significance of the Massaliotic identity of Encolpius, the narrator and fictional author of this ancient Graeco-Roman traveler's tale by Petronius. I argue that, even if we are missing many details of the plot, we are still able to draw important conclusions about the basic purpose and artistic aim of the original full-text *Satyrica*, which was most likely designed as an entertaining satire on the sorry state of Greek cities under Roman rule. Accordingly, the underlying story can hardly have been conceived by a member of the Roman senatorial aristocracy; rather, the *Satyrica* appears to be a Roman adaptation, however freely made, from an otherwise lost Milesian novel in Greek.

This paper argues that, despite the fragmentary condition of its text, it remains possible to reconstruct usefully the plot of the *Satyrica* and map out Encolpius' travels based on the evidence of the preserved text and some fragments, particularly fragments I and IV (Bücheler). As I shall attempt to show, we do not need to have every single plot detail in place to be able to draw important conclusions about the basic purpose and artistic aim of the original full-text *Satyrica*.

The geographical signposts for reconstructing the travels of Encolpius are simple enough. In chapter 99 of the extant text, when Eumolpus leads Encolpius and Giton on board the ship of Lichas in the *urbs Graeca* (*Sat.* 81,3), a city much like the quintessential Greek colony of Neapolis ('New City'), it soon becomes clear that the boys have been on that very ship before, and fled from it in another port in the Bay of Naples. The flight is related to their complicated erotic relationships with a luxury-loving passenger, Tryphaena, who is being transported to Tarentum 'as an exile' (*Sat.* 100), and with the captain, Lichas, and not least with his wife (*Sat.* 113,3 *libidinosa migratio*). The ship is carrying goods to be sold in Tarentum (*Sat.* 101). Although the ship is a large merchantman built for long-distance voyaging, ships in those days sailed along the coast and rarely ventured out into the open sea. The passenger Tryphaena claims she has been in

Gottskálk Jensson, University of Copenhagen

https://doi.org/10.1515/9781501503986-002

Baiae (*Sat.* 104,2), according to our slightly emended text, just north of Puteoli and Neapolis. Besides Baiae, the ship has likely already been in Ostia further north, since Encolpius has seen things in Rome during the Saturnalia (*Sat.* 69.9, *vidi Romae*). Encolpius and Giton left the ship in the Bay of Naples, but not in the *urbs Graeca* itself, since they are newcomers there, and very surprised at their accidental reencounter with the ship in this city. This part of the route of Lichas' ship, both actual and intended, can therefore be established with probability as Ostia-Baiae-Neapolis-Tarentum, although, as it happens, the ship is wrecked before it reaches Tarentum.[1]

As for reconstructing further the route of the ship, a legal signpost for this is hidden in the information provided about the passenger Tryphaena; namely, that she is going into 'exile' in Tarentum. This home port of Lychas and his ship was, like Neapolis, originally a Greek city, although by this time it had been Romanized to a far greater extent. Founded as a Spartan colony in the 8th century BCE, it led Magna Graecia militarily for an extended period until, after several defeats by the Romans, its population was granted *ius Latii* and citizenship in 89 BCE, when Tarentum was made a Roman *municipium*. The fact that Tryphaena is going into exile in Tarentum tells us that she is not a Roman citizen.

As it turns out, Tryphaena shares her legal status as an exile with Giton (*Sat.* 100,4), and Encolpius (*Sat.* 81,3), who have therefore arrived in Roman territory with the ship from beyond the borders of Rome. It is not surprising that Encolpius and Giton share this fate, since they evidently have a long-standing relationship (*vetustissima consuetudo*, *Sat.* 80,6). The *urbs Graeca* is to Encolpius a *locus peregrinus* (*Sat.* 80,8), a foreign city. Although Greek, it is not *his* Greek city. Ethnicity and citizenship are not identical. By virtue of being exiles in Italy, these three characters, Tryphaena, Giton and Encolpius, are clearly characterized as the former-citizens of a foreign state (from the Roman perspective), which in the first century CE, the apparent dramatic date of the story, had a reciprocal *ius exulandi* with Rome. As I have shown elsewhere, this is the only

---

1 Some scholars prefer to identify ancient Puteoli as the *Graeca urbs*, and some doubt that the ship was ever in Baiae, but even if the protagonists are meant to have boarded the ship in Puteoli for the last time, it seems clear that at least one other Campanian city was involved, and it is not unlikely that two were (e.g. Baiae or Neapolis). If one prefers to see historical Puteoli as the model for the 'Greek' city of the *Satyrica*, one should also accept the implications of this Greek ethnicity for the overall design of the *Satyrica*. For a detailed discussion of the textual passages used in reconstructing the plot of the missing early books of the *Satyrica*, see Jensson 1997, 97–160 (revised in Jensson 2004, 96–173) and Courtney 2001, 43–49, who accepts the main points of the reconstruction.

sense *exul* can have in this context.² Taken together with their legal status as *exules*, the Greek names of these characters most obviously betray a Greek origin and prior Greek citizenship. We may use this information to extend the route of Lichas' ship beyond Rome and beyond the main body of the preserved text.

There is reliable evidence in fragments I and IV (Bücheler) of the *Satyrica* to locate the beginning of the *Satyrica* in the Greek city of Massalia, ancient Marseille. Encolpius, the narrator and main character, is a young man and needs to leave his hometown in order for his adventures to commence. Such is the invariable beginning of ancient fictions involving the adventure stories and travelers' tales of young people: Ninos, Metiochus, Callirhoë, Dinias from the *Wonders beyond Thule*, Sinonis and Rhodanes from the *Babyloniaca*, Habrocomes and Anthia, Clitophon, Theagenes and Charikleia, the narrating 'I' of Lucian's *A True Story*, the kings Alexander and Apollonius, all start by leaving home – even the Greek Ass-Story begins with Loukios having just left his hometown Patrai for Thessaly on business for his father. Only Daphnis and Chloë never journey from Lesbos, although they are exposed by their parents from Mytilene, and their adventures involve his being kidnapped by pirates and her being kidnapped by a Methymnian fleet.

In fragment I of the *Satyrica*, derived from Servius' commentary of on the *Aeneid* (3,57), an attempt is being made to explain Virgil's use of the adjective *sacer*, meaning *execrabilis*, in the phrase *auri sacra fames*, 'accursed hunger for gold'. The phrase is uttered by Aeneas in outrage upon recalling how King Lycurgus of Thrace had slain a young Trojan, Polydorus, whom King Priam of Troy had given into his care with a great quantity of gold: 'This sense of the word', reads the commentary of Servius, 'derives from a custom of the Gauls, for whenever the Massaliots suffered from a pestilence, one of the poor citizens [*unus... ex pauperibus*] offered himself to be fed for a whole year on public and pure food. This individual was then equipped with branches and dressed in sacred attire [*vestibus sacris*] and led around the whole city with curses [*execrationibus*], so that on him would descend the evils of the whole city, and thus he was banished. This is, moreover, found/read in Petronius [*hoc autem in Petronio lectum est*]' (Serv. ad Aen. 3,57).³

---

2 Jensson 2004, 110–112.
3 Anton Bitel (Bitel 2006), in his review of my book, *The Recollections of Encolpius* (Groningen 2004), doubts that Servius is referring to a lost episode in the *Satyrica*, because the language of the note is cast in imperfects and has other frequentative markers like '*more Gallorum*' and '*quotiens*'. However, an annual ritual providing the background for a novelistic episode is necessarily both a recurrent event (in historical fact) and a singular episode (in the novelistic account),

In offering this explanation, Servius assumes that, since Virgil was a Mantuan and thus from Cisalpine Gaul, he was employing the Latin adjective *sacer* in a sense derived from a Gallic custom, where an individual is accursed during a sacred ritual of cleansing. It is possible that the name and disposition of King Lycurgus of the Virgilian passage has triggered Servius' association with the *Satyrica* of Petronius, where an equally barbaric Lycurgus played an important role in a lost episode (cf. *Sat. 83,6*; 117,3). In any case, Servius attempts to support his reading of Virgil's Gallic-Latin usage of *sacer* by borrowing material from Petronius, another author presumed to be of northern Italian or semi-Gallic origins. The late ancient commentator is interested in the regional differences of Latin, and while he knows that Petronius wrote in Latin, he does not care, or know, that Massalia was a Greek-speaking city in the first century. What seems evident is that Servius believed that Massalia was as much Petronius' birthplace as Mantua was Virgil's, and he was not the only author of late antiquity to hold this opinion.

A ritual or a religious festival is used in three of the five fully extant erotic fictions (Chariton, Xenophon and Heliodorus) to get the plot going. Much in the spirit of the *Satyrica*, Servius elaborates on the immoral mixture of the sacred with greed in the phrase 'the sacred/accursed hunger for gold', and to explain it he relates an outlandish story read in Petronius, involving a greedy participant in a sacred ritual, a poor citizen who accepts this ultimate one-year civil service to satisfy his hunger/greed, and after the final ceremony is cast out, exiled from his city. The religious context of this 'Gallic' custom is almost entirely eclipsed by the scandalous ethical paradox. To supply such a context from elsewhere, an ancient account of a Greek scapegoating ritual is found in the poems of Hipponax (*Frs.* 5–11 [West]). In threatening his enemies with destruction, Hipponax provides a description of how the φαρμακός should be dealt with: A deformed and repulsive male is selected and force-fed with figs, barley broth, and cheese, before being whipped with fig branches and sea onions, and then struck seven times on his *membrum virile*. According to Walter Burkert: 'This is not active killing, but simply a matter of offscourings which must be thrown across the boundaries or over the cliffs, never to return.'[4]

In the extant *Satyrica*, religious cults and rituals are represented as little more than pretexts for exploitation – sexual, financial or otherwise. Encolpius, who is poor and needy (in *Sat. 125,4*, he is happy about his *tandem expugnata*

---

while at the end of his note Servius states directly: 'This is, moreover, found/read in Petronius' (*hoc autem in Petronio lectum est*).
4 Burkert 1985, 83.

paupertas), fits the profile of the Massaliot scapegoat in another way. We know that, of the characters in the extant *Satyrica*, he is most susceptible to sexual humiliation. The possibility that the branches mentioned in the account of Servius have to do with the beating of the scapegoat on his penis, and, in any case, the general prominence of Encolpius' male member in the extant story make him well suited to play the φαρμακός in such a ritual. Like Lichas in *Satyrica* 105,9, we too may recognize Encolpius by his *mentula*. Encolpius' humiliating procession through the streets of Massalia would have a partial but striking resemblance to the *Risus*-festival in Apuleius (*Met.* 3,1–12), where Lucius is made the butt of the citizenry of Hypata.

More information can be gleaned from the fragments of the *Satyrica*. Fragment IV, a few lines from a poetic eulogy by Sidonius Apollinaris (*Carm.* 28,145–7), also places Petronius and the *Satyrica* in Massalia. The late fifth-century Christian bishop here apostrophizes three Roman worthies (Cicero, Livy and Virgil) by noting only their birthplaces (Arpinum, Patavium, Mantua). He goes on to address others and amongst them 'Arbiter', who is presented as a Massaliot: 'and you, Arbiter, worshipper of the holy trunk, throughout the gardens of Massalia, on a par with Priapus of the Hellespont?' (*et te Massiliensium per hortos / sacri stipitis, Arbiter, colonum / Hellespontiaco parem Priapo?*, *Carm.* 28,155–7). Sidonius was from Lugudunum (Lyons) in Gaul, a city associated with Massalia through traffic on the Rhône, and he clearly read the *Satyrica* as the story of Petronius the Massaliot. Sidonius has modeled his lines on the words of Encolpius in *Satyrica* 139,2,14–15: 'me, too, through lands, over hoary Nereus' surface, / haunts the heavy wrath of Hellespontiac Priapus' (*me quoque per terras, per cani Nereos aequor / Hellespontiaci sequitur gravis ira Priapi*).[5]

On Sidonius' reading of the *Satyrica*, it is 'Arbiter' who is the speaker of the imitated lines in *Satyrica* 139,2,14–15, and 'Arbiter' is a Massaliot. Thus the bishop deflates Encolpius' fabulous hyperbole, *per terras, per cani Nereos aequor*, by redefining the speaker's relationship with the grotesque pagan deity and putting it in its proper ambiance in Massalia. What Sidonius says about Petronius recalls in form and content what Encolpius says about himself, but more obviously the detail about Petronius' supposed phallic looks betrays the identity of Encolpius, or Mr. Incrotch, the narrator of the *Satyrica*.

It was Bücheler, the first modern editor of the *Satyrica*, who explained the biographical fallacy in Sidonius' reading of Petronius by noting that the poet 'thought, evidently, that Petronius was the same as Encolpius' (*ratus uidelicet eu-*

---

5 The last line is in turn a reworking of Virgil *G.* 4,111, *Hellespontiaci servet tutela Priapi*.

ndem esse Petronium atque Encolpium).[6] St. Augustine, another learned interpreter of the same critical school as Sidonius, shows some doubt as to whether one should believe Apuleius' statement 'about himself' (August. *C.D.* 18,18, *inscribit sibi ipsi accidisse*) in the *Metamorphoses*, to the effect that he changed into an ass, but he does not hesitate to apply Lucius' statement to the author, Apuleius. Fulgentius, likewise, is convinced that it was Petronius himself and not Encolpius who drank the aphrodisiac (Fragment 7). Late antiquity consistently confused Petronius with the fictional narrator of the *Satyrica*. Autobiography was a rare form of literature, and even more so fictional autobiography, an artistic concept apparently incomprehensible to these learned men. On this reading, any autodiegetic statement had to be reliable information about the author. So the fact that Servius and Sidonius both knew Petronius to have been a native of Massalia simply informs us that this was the identity of the narrator of the *Satyrica*, Encolpius.

Fragments I and IV together thus support the narrator Encolpius' citizenship in Massalia, his poverty, his voluntary assumption of the degrading role of phallic scapegoat for financial gain, and his final expulsion from the city. This information is confirmed by the extant text of the *Satyrica*, where Encolpius refers to himself as *exul* (*Sat.* 81,3), as I mentioned previously, and not least where Lichas, the captain of the ship, refers to Encolpius directly with the Greek word for scapegoat (*pharmace*): 'What do you have to say for yourself, you thief? ... Answer me, you scapegoat!' (*quid dicis tu latro? [...] pharmace, responde!*, 107,15,). Lichas, on whose ship Encolpius had traveled from Massalia, knew how he had earned his exile. Significantly, the narrator Encolpius immediately acknowledges the truth of Lichas' accusations, adding 'and I couldn't invent anything to say against such manifestly accurate statements' (*nec quid in re manifestissima dicerem inveniebam*, 108,1).

In Roman literature, the name of Massalia (or Massilia as the Romans spelled it) was loaded with political and cultural significance. The Massaliots were praised for having preserved the old Greek civilization in barbarian territory (e. g. Cic. *Flacc* 63; Liv. 37,54; Sil. 15,168–72), and the city's destiny was perceived as intimately connected with that of Rome from its very foundation. Legend had it that in the times of king Tarquinius the youthful settlers from Phocaea, which is sometimes portrayed as another sacked Troy (Luc. 3,340), had sailed up the Tiber and made friends with the Romans before continuing on their journey to found Massalia in the midst of barbaric nations. Massalia, moreover, was believed to have provided financial aid after the sack of Rome by Gauls, and like

---

6 Bücheler 1862, *ad Fr.* IV.

Rome it fought against the Carthaginians. It had the reputation of a faithful friend and ally to Rome in war and peace (Just. 43,5,3). Accordingly, the siege and subsequent capitulation of Massalia to Caesar during the civil war was viewed as symbolic of the irreparable harm and madness of that conflict. Massalia, like Troy in the poem of Eumolpus (*Sat.* 89), might be presented as a projection of Rome herself with respect to her fate in the civil war, the subject of another of Eumolpus' poems.

Greek writers, on the other hand, had a very different story to tell about the Massaliots, one that, indeed, resonates better with the tenor of the *Satyrica*. They describe the Massaliots as wearing richly embroidered tragic robes with floor-length tunics, being effeminate, soft of character and passive like women, which gave rise to the Greek saying 'you might sail to Massalia' (Ath. 12,25; Ps.-Plutarch *Proverb. Alex.* 60). This saying is explained in the late tenth-century Byzantine lexicon, the Suda, in the following way: 'Used of those living an effeminate and soft life, since the people of Massalia used to live rather effeminately, wearing fancy long robes and perfumes' (Suda, epsilon 3161). In the same fashion, the phrase 'you are coming from Massalia' gets the gloss: 'Used of effeminate and luxury-loving people, inasmuch as the men of Massalia are said to wear effeminate clothing and perfume, and tie their hair up, and are a disgrace because of this softness' (Suda, epsilon 499). One wonders what the source of this information might be. The Younger Seneca wrote to Nero about a father who had shown his clemency to a son who had made an attempt on his life: 'satisfying himself with exile—and a luxurious exile—he detained the parricide at Massalia and gave him the same liberal allowance that he had before' (*Cl.* 1,15,2). Although a Greek *Satyrica* could possibly be the source of late testimonies, such as the Suda, Massalia's bad reputation dates to much earlier times, e.g. Plautus lets a character refer to effeminacy as 'practicing the morals of the Massaliots' (*Cas.* 963), in a play he adapted from a work by Diphilus of Sinope, a contemporary of Menander.

Massalia prided itself on having a port of major commercial importance in the western Mediterranean, and the city was famous for its Atlantic explorers, Pytheas and Euthymenes, whose travelogues were nevertheless considered untrustworthy and fictitious by most ancient authorities. Antonius Diogenes parodied Pytheas of Massalia in his *The Wonders beyond Thule*, and Euthymenes of Massalia is called a braggart by the sophist Aelius Aristides and his *Periplous* nothing but an 'account for Alkinous' (Aristid. *Aeg.* p.354 [Jebb], ἀπόλογος Ἀλκίνου), i.e. of the same type as the lying fables told by Odysseus to the gullible king of the Phaeacians. Because of such incredible travelers' tales connected with the city of Massalia, Aelius Aristides uses the term 'Massaliotic fables' (*Aeg.* p.353 [Jebb], μῦθοι Μασσαλιωτικοί) to cover this type of travelogue. Whether the Massaliots Pytheas and Euthymenes were mere liars or misunderstood explorers far ahead of their time is difficult to ascertain, but it is certain that they were known to later authors as Odyssean spinners of yarns, which makes their city especially appropriate as the home of Encolpius, the narrator of the travelogue we know as the *Satyrica*.

Encolpius is, in several ways, the archetypal Massaliot. His education fits the image of this Greek university town in imperial times, his sexual preferences are stereotypical for Massaliots in Greek literature, and his travelogue may be read as a parody of the Odyssean yarns of his fellow citizens. In the *Satyrica*, allusions to the Odyssey evoke a Homeric frame of reference, making Encolpius into a sort of Odyssean traveler, moving from city to city, becoming acquainted with the minds of many men. As such Encolpius is also an ideal vehicle for an entertaining satire on the state of literature and morals in Greek communities under Roman rule. The image or reputation of cities is of major importance in the *Satyrica*, just as the association of Hypata and Thessaly with magic is of major importance in the *Metamorphoses* of Apuleius. The plan of Encolpius and Ascyltos to earn a living from their knowledge of letters (*Sat*. 10,4–6), a plan which they undoubtedly formed prior to arriving to Naples, thus seems to spring from the reputation of *docta Neapolis*, in the same manner that the conception of Eumolpus' profitable *mimus* arises from information about the reputation of the ghost-town of Croton, the adoptive city of Pythagoras, now become obsessed with legacy hunting. Encolpius' visit to Rome, which apparently fell during the Saturnalia, presumably defined the character given to that city in a lost episode.

Rather than voyaging to the fabulous edges of the world, the overeducated but unheroic Encolpius heads to the heart of civilization, to face moral and aesthetic monstrosities of no less fabulous proportions. This movement inwards to the ordinary (and prosaic) and away from the mythical (and poetic) is probably related to the moral therapy of Greek Cynic satire, which ridiculed scholars for studying in detail the errors of Odysseus while being ignorant of their own. For Petronius the effeminate Massaliot provided, additionally, a platform from which to deflate Roman delusions about the empire under the Julio-Claudian dynasty. However, when one keeps in mind the manifest Greekness of the *Satyrica*, especially the bitter ideological worries concerning the humiliating state of Greek communities under Roman rule – in comparison with the grandeur that was Greece – it seems impossible that Petronius, who is most often thought to have been a member of the Roman senatorial aristocracy, conceived the idea of this entertaining text without having recourse to a Greek original, perhaps by the same Greek title, Σατυρικά. There is certainly no lack of parallels in Roman literature for this method of writing, while the genre of Milesian fiction was certainly of Greek origins, and considerably older than the *Satyrica*.

Bibliography

Bitel, A. 2006. 'Gottskálk Jensson, The Recollections of Encolpius' [a book review]. *Bryn Mawr Classical Review* 2006.01.33. Available online at: http://bmcr.brynmawr.edu/2006/2006-01-33.html
Bücheler, F. 1862. *Petronii Arbitri Satirarum reliquiae. Adjectus est liber priapeorum*, Berlin: Weidmanni.
Courtney, E. 2001. *A Companion to Petronius*, Oxford: Oxford University Press.
Hodge, A. T. 1998. *Ancient Greek France*, London: Duckworth.
Jensson, G. 2004. *The Recollections of Encolpius: The* Satyrica *of Petronius as Milesian Fiction*, ANS 2, Groningen: Barkhuis Publishing & Groningen University Library.
Romm, S. J. 1992. *The Edges of the Earth in Ancient Thought: Geography, Exploration, and Fiction*, Princeton: Princeton University Press.

Andrea Capra
Xenophon's 'Round Trip': Geography as Narrative Consistency in the *Ephesiaka*

Abstract: A careful examination of Xenophon's geography reveals a circular pattern and a neat if rudimentary technique of *entrelacement*. Such an arrangement (i.e. the characters' 'round trip') squares well with Xenophon's orali(istic) style and accounts for its open-ended structure: far from being a shortcoming, this feature is best interpreted in the light of ancient poetics, and helps us to understand a number of alleged problems in this novel, such as the difference in style between the first (extra-circular, in fact) scene and the frantic adventures forming the core of the story. The circular pattern thus reinforces the case against the epitome theory in books 2–5.

Xenophon of Ephesus is notorious for overwhelming his (modern) readers with both geographical and personal names. He seems to suffer from a severe form of *horror vacui*, which in turn is responsible for the breathless pace of his narration. Thus, to quote from Brian Reardon's classic book, 'Miracles accumulate, each more lurid than its predecessor; Xenophon can think of no very effective means of conducting the parallel actions, and ends up moving his characters more and more wildly around the Mediterranean, like demented chessmen. It all ends happily, of course – if only from sheer exhaustion, for there seems little reason in the action itself why it should ever end at all. In this respect too Xenophon cannot match Chariton, who carefully builds his action to a crisis that must be resolved, be it only by chance or war'.[1]

Reardon's words are quite typical of a certain way of approaching the *Ephesiaka*: in a similar vein, Rohde described Xenophon's characters as 'blosse Mari-

---

Warm thanks to P.A. Agapitos for his useful and encouraging comments. I submitted an almost finalized version of this paper in June 2011. References to more recent bibliography are brief and limited to a few footnotes that I had the opportunity to integrate in May 2015.

1 Reardon 1991, 36.

Andrea Capra, Università degli Studi di Milano

https://doi.org/10.1515/9781501503986-003

onetten, welche dieser stümperhafte Poet vor uns tanzen lasst',[2] and equally unflattering comments are fairly common among other scholars as well. To be sure, any modern reader of the *Ephesiaka* is likely to feel puzzled by the frantic pace of Xenophon's narration. Moreover, it would not be difficult to prove that the seemingly endless series of episodes which take place in the novel are somehow unnecessary: as Reardon implies, nothing crucial would change if some of them were crossed out, nor – conversely – if someone decided to cram even more episodes and names into the plot. But why is this so? It may be possible that Xenophon is just 'incompetent', but before we accept such a facile explanation it is worth trying to get a fuller picture of his novel. Could it not be the case that some hidden threads, scarcely visible for the modern reader, keep the story together? And what if there are some centripetal factors, obvious enough for Xenophon's contemporaries, to counterbalance the centrifugal forces that we modern readers are so ready to notice?

Xenophon and his modern readers

We may begin by reviewing – very briefly – previous attempts to 'rescue' Xenophon as a consistent writer. By far the commonest explanation for his alleged shortcomings is the so-called 'epitome' theory. According to it, the central books of the *Ephesiaka* have survived in an abridged version. Besides explaining Xenophon's 'incompetence', the theory is designed to account for the slower rhythm of much of the first and last books. It is no surprise, then, that the theory has been – and still is in some quarters – very popular. Considerations of space prevent me from discussing this issue at length, but it may be worth recalling that the most thorough version of the theory, namely Bürger's,[3] has been discussed and, by fairly general consensus, refuted by Thomas Hägg.[4]

By 'most thorough' I simply mean that Bürger has set himself the task of producing literary and linguistic evidence in support of the theory, such as a close examination of the particles (*men, de*), patterning most of the episodes of the novel. The evidence has proven inconclusive, but Bürger must be credited with leaving aside the aprioristic approach so typical of scholars such as Erwin Rohde and – much more recently than Rohde and Bürger himself – Reinhold Merkelbach.[5] According to the latter, Greek novels, almost by definition, conceal

---

2 Rohde 1914, 426.
3 Bürger 1892. For new arguments, cf. Borgogno 1985 and Bianchi 2011.
4 Hägg 1966.
5 Rohde 1914 (first ed. 1876), Merkelbach 1962.

a mystic meaning to be grasped by the initiated. Since Xenophon's novel does not seem to measure up to this theory, it must be 'wrong'. So, for instance, Merkelbach notices that most of Xenophon's references to the divine revolve around one of two principles: the one is feminine and lunar (Artemis, Isis…), the other is masculine and solar (Apollo, Helios…).[6] As a consequence, the novel as we read it must be a conflation between an original *Isisredaktion* and a later *Heliosredaktion*, although there is hardly any philological evidence for such an astonishing conclusion.

My reason for lingering a bit on Merkelbach's theory is that it will come in handy later. For the time being, however, I would like to add that, although hardly anyone has espoused Merkelbach's theory, many scholars implicitly agree that religion is indeed an important factor in the Greek novel (including Xenophon's).[7] The 'miracles' and wanderings of the characters, however 'lurid' and 'wild', are the product of divine will, and the predictions of Apollo's oracle are fairly accurate. Thus, Xenophon's references to the divine can be construed as a promising, if thin, thread keeping the story together.[8]

The most recent and sustained attempts to defend Xenophon's novel as good narrative are those by Marcelle Laplace, James O'Sullivan, Consuelo Ruiz-Montero, Konstantin Doulamis, Anton Bierl and Jason König.[9] At the end of the novel, the lovers set up 'an inscription in honour of the goddess commemorating all their sufferings and all their adventures'.[10] According to Laplace,[11] this fascinating remark can be construed as a kind of a posteriori explanation for the frantic pace of the narration, the 'inscription' (*graphe*, i.e. the novel itself) being necessarily brief and desultory, and König takes this as a sign of the increasing textualisation/monumentalisation of the text, self-consciously shifting from an oral to a literary mode for artistic purposes. O'Sullivan, as is well known, has made a strong case for an altogether new appreciation of the *Ephesiaka*.[12] The

---

6 One may of course argue that in the *Ephesiaka* Isis is a more prominent deity than Helios: cf. Enermalm 1997.
7 See Bierl 2007, esp. 249, with ample bibliography. Merkelbach himself subsequently modified his position: 'In einer monotheistischen Religion aufgewachsen, hatte ich mir nicht klar gemacht, dass Isis und Sarapis-Helios ein Ehepaar sind und dass Helios-Re, der Nil, Isis und Osiris die Hauptgoetter Aegyptens waren. – Meine Hyopthese ist widerlegt worden von H. Gaertner, R.E. IXA 2074–2080' (Merkelbach 1995, 348 n. 1).
8 Cf. Chew 1997–1998.
9 The list is now enriched by Tagliabue 2012, who construes Xenophon's novel as a Bildungsroman leading to the foundation of a new community based on spiritual love.
10 5,15,2.
11 Laplace 1994; cf. Bierl 2007, 310.
12 O'Sullivan 1995.

idea that Xenophon's novel might be an oral (or 'transitional') text, complete with a formulaic system, is groundbreaking, and has important consequences for its overall evaluation. Needless to say, if we accept such a theory traditional notions of literary criticism can hardly apply, and the very idea of an 'incompetent' author should, at the very least, be revised according to a wholly different set of aesthetic principles. Ruiz-Montero, too, has carefully analysed the 'oral story-telling features' of Xenophon's novel,[13] but according to her such features are artfully contrived, so that 'Xenophon is another face or aspect of the Second Sophistic'.[14] For his part, Konstantin Doulamis builds on Ruiz-Montero's thesis and argues for Stoic echoes as a unifying factor in the *Ephesiaka*.[15] According to Bierl,[16] finally, the first and last sections of the novel respectively, before the lovers' separation and after their reunion, are clearly distinct from the central part, crammed with fantastic adventures. The lovers' separation that is the beginning of the fabulous adventures, is marked by the dream of Habrocomes,[17] whose vision – a purple (*phoinix*) woman – clearly foreshadows the assault of the Phoenician (*phoinikes*) pirates. Thus, according to Bierl the rationale of the narration changes abruptly, because from now on the frantic adventures of the lovers follow a symbolic and associative pattern. The many episodes are linked to one another by associations of words (as in the case of the adjective 'purple'), so as to form a '*Signifikantenkette*' alluding to the symbolic logic of dreams, as if the lovers' adventures were nothing but a kind of temporary nightmare.

The ingenious explanations put forward by Laplace and Bierl may lack significant parallels in Greek literature and culture, yet they seem to shed new light on the structure and inner logic of Xenophon's novel. As will become clear, my own explanation is not incompatible with theirs, yet it follows a completely different track. Moreover, it would square very well with O'Sullivan's oral approach as well as with the more or less 'oralistic' readings by Ruiz-Montero, Doulamis

---

[13] Ruiz-Montero 2003, 44.
[14] Ruiz-Montero 2003, 60. Cf. Shea 1998, claiming that Xenophon's novel can be construed as a series of *ekphraseis* . and Temmermann 2014, 118–51, with excellent points on Xenophon's apheleia.
[15] Doulamis 2007, who concludes by saying that 'the combination of simplicity and subtle rhetoric in certain sections of this novel provides a suitable stylistic environment for, and at the same time helps to bring out, the Stoic echoes in the discourse of certain characters' (172).
[16] Bierl 2006 (cf. http://chs.harvard.edu/CHS/article/display/5637 for an updated 2014 version in English). According to König 2007, the obsessive repetitiveness of Xenophon's oral style contributes to the nigthmarish atmosphere of the heroes' adventures.
[17] 1,12,4.

and König, although it is by no means based or dependent on them.[18] My own approach may be labelled as *geographical*, inasmuch as it starts from an examination of the geography of the *Ephesiaka* within the frame of oral(istic) poetics.

A geographical approach

The importance of space in the Greek novel has long been recognised, and, more to our point, David Konstan has argued that 'Xenophon's spatial arrangements are as complex as they are because he is expressing by means of them one aspect of his theme', namely the symmetry between male and female heroes, as expressed by parallel movements.[19] I fully share this view, but here I would like to focus on the actual places covered by the travelling heroes, rather than on space as an abstract dimension. Is there any meaning in Xenophon's choice of his novel's geographical settings?

Although the lovers' adventures are consistently narrated in external focalisation, whereas Hippothoos' story is partly delivered by himself as a 'first-person narrator-participant', it is noticeable that the three main characters share the same travel pattern, covering four areas clockwise: Ionia, Asia, Egypt, Italy, and – again – Ionia. The characters' movements can be easily arranged in a synoptic table:

	Anthia	Habrocomes	Hippothoos
1 Ionia	Ephesus Ephesus-Samos (1,11) Samos-Rhodes via Kos-Knidos (1,11-2)	Ephesus Ephesus-Samos (1,11) Samos-Rhodes via Kos-Knidos (1,11-2)	Perinthus (*flashback*) Perinthus-Byzantium (*flashback*) Byzantium-Lesbos (*flashback*)
2 Asia	Egyptian sea-Tyre (1,14) Tyre-Antiochia (2,9) Antiochia-Cilicia (2,11) Cilicia-Tarsus (2,13)	Egyptian sea-Tyre (1,14) Tyre-Antiochia (2,12) Tyre-Cilicia (2,14) Cilicia-Cappadocia-Cilicia (3,1-3)	Lesbos-Phrygia (*flashback*) Phrygia-Pamphylia (*flashback*) Pamphylia-Cilicia (*flashback*) Cilicia-Cappadocia-Cilicia (3,1-3)
3 Egypt	Tarsus-Alexandria (3,8) Alexandria-Ethiopia (via Memphis) (4,3)	Cilicia [Alexandria] Pelusium (3,12) Around the Nile delta (4,2)	Tarsus-Syria-Phoenicia-Egypt (4,1) Ethiopia via Pelusium, Hermoupolis, Schedia [Alexandria], Mem-

---

18 I shall be using the term 'oralistic' to describe a narration that, while consciously adopting oral techniques, is the product of literacy.
19 Konstan 2002, 9. On Xenophon's treatment of space see also Temmerman 2012.

Continued

	Anthia	Habrocomes	Hippothoos
			phis, Mende, Taba, Leontopolis (4,1)
	Ethiopia-Alexandria-(via Memphis) (5,4)	Northern Egypt	Ethiopia-Alexandria, Nile, Schedia (5,2–3)
4 Magna Graecia	Alexandria-Italy (Tarentum) (5,5)	Egypt [Italy] Syracuse (5,1)	Alexandria [Syrac.] Taormina (5,6)
	Tarentum	Syracuse-Italy (Nucerium) (5,8)	Taormina-Italy (Tarentum) (5,9)
1 Ionia	Italy-Rhodes (5,11)	Italy-Rhodes via Sicily, Crete, Cyprus[20] (5,10)	Italy-Rhodes (5.11)
	Rhodes-Ephesus (5,15)	Rhodes-Ephesus (5,15)	Rhodes-Ephesus (5,15) Lesbos

Table 1, the wanderings of the three main characters. Square brackets indicate that the character does not succeed in reaching a given place. The colours indicate that two or three characters are together in a given moment.

Xenophon shares with other Greek novelists the basic notion of a happy *nostos* after some dangerous travelling through faraway lands. However, other novels feature mostly linear travels, whereas Xenophon's are circular, as is obvious from the table (1–2–3–4–1).[21] Rather than *nostoi*, we may thus call them jokingly 'round trips', taking our cue from travel agents. This peculiarity has a number of consequences for the interpretation of the novel. To begin with, the circular pattern brings about a sense of completion somewhat at odds with Xenophon's notoriously openended style. In some respects, Xenophon's novel threatens to become an endless catalogue of unnecessary episodes, yet this impression is counterbalanced by the circular pattern.

Xenophon's travels, as we have seen, are arranged into geographical units, which are introduced clockwise and are at times so frantic as to look like a catalogue of names. Such an arrangement is immediately reminiscent of a strategy as old as Homer, which can be seen at work whenever the poet launches into one of the so-called epic catalogues. The technique is a well-known feature of epic poetry, so a couple of scholarly quotes – on Homer's Catalogue of Ships and Hesiod's Catalogue of Suitors respectively – will suffice:

---

20 Crete-Cyprus is the only sea-route in the novel that does not seem to make sense. The mention of Aphrodite's island is arguably due to the copyist's intervention (see Capra 2012).
21 See in general Morgan 2007.

For all this catalogue is long and detailed, we can deduce the singer's overall strategy for retrieving it from memory. It resembles all Homer's lists in that it is constructed from material which is connected thematically. But what is more important in this case is that the material is connected spatially also: the catalogue is organised and presented as a kind of circuit around Greece and the islands, broken only at 2, 645–80 to include Crete, Rhodes and the islands close by. This arrangement is not, I believe, the result of happy chance. I suggest that the content of the Catalogue had long been structured in this way so that it might be formatted in any bard's memory as a 'cognitive map', a kind of schema which preserves information about places and the relationships between places. The sequential order of the 'map' directs search in memory. It assists in the recall of the principal regions and the peoples who dwelt there. It acts as a kind of check: it attempts to guard against the unintentional omission of items (as indeed may have happened in this case – the Cycladic group of islands is, by accident or design, omitted from the Catalogue).[22]

With regard to place of origin – and no differently from the Homeric Catalogue of Ships – The Catalogue of Suitors seems to follow a geographical spiral oriented clockwise, starting from the Peloponnese, where Tyndareus' palace was located (at Lacedaemon), and ending with Crete and possibly Rhodes (Tlepolemos?).[23]

To the surprise of modern readers, epic catalogues were a highly praised form of poetry, as is precociously testified by Homer's elaborate invocation to the Muses, and geographical thoroughness was clearly an important aesthetic principle. This is obviously one point where modern taste is not in tune with ancient perceptions, something that can help account for scholarly dissatisfaction with Xenophon's novel as well. It will be obvious that such a conclusion squares very well with O'Sullivan's oral theory, but even if O'Sullivan were wrong, there is a growing consensus that Xenophon's style is – more or less self-consciously – 'popular' and designed to please large audiences.[24] These people were likely to share in such an 'aesthetics of thoroughness', with its reassuring circular pattern.

In a way, Rohde was right when he noticed that 'Sobald die Liebenden erst einmal auseinander gerissen sind, beginnt das zweckloseste Hin- und Herfahren im Zickzack'.[25] To be sure, the three main characters have not the slightest clue as to where they should go, and the narrator himself somehow adopts their perspective:[26] from this limited point of view the heroes' wanderings are indeed 'zwecklos'. However, the circular pattern of the *Ephesiaka* makes it clear that from the vantage point of the listener/reader their travels are hardly aimless: there is little room for zigzagging, and notions of authorial incompetence or tex-

---

22 Minchin 1996, 12.
23 Cingano 2005, 128.
24 See e.g. Ruiz-Montero 1994, with further bibliography.
25 Rohde 1914, 426.
26 As is argued by Chew 1998.

tual conflation seem to be out of the question. Far from being an element of weakness, the structure of the *Ephesiaka* was probably perceived by ancient audiences as Xenophon's 'forte', as is suggested by Theodorus Prodromus' reworking. In his 12th century novel, *Rhodanthe and Dosikles*, Theodorus draws heavily on Heliodorus, but he turns to Xenophon for points of structure. Like Xenophon, Theodorus resorts to Apollo's oracle as a pivotal element, and – what is more – textual echoes make it clear that he is openly drawing on the *Ephesiaka*.[27] Moreover, Theodorus follows in Xenophon's footsteps in making Rhodes, as it were, the *omphalos* of the story: the Island of the Sun is again the first stop after the lovers' departure and the last one before their final *nostos*, which recreates, albeit in a simplified form, the circular pattern of the *Ephesiaka*. Theodorus' reworking is likely to reflect Xenophon's ability in creating a well-rounded story.

Amorous *entrelacement*

As we have seen, well-rounded completeness is a key factor. Moreover, a sense of order is generated by the characters' mutual quest, complete with missed encounters (see square brackets in the table) and unexpected couples sharing stages of their circular journey (see coloured areas in the table).[28] After the lovers' separation, Habrocomes, while looking for Anthia, meets Hippothoos in Asia, and the latter is with Anthia in Egypt and Italy while looking for Habrocomes, who is in turn always a step late in his search for his wife. In the end, all possible encounters between the three main characters have been experienced: Xenophon's novel thus reveals a neat, if rudimentary, *entrelacement* technique.

The very notion of '*entrelacement*' may be useful to revise the widespread idea that Xenophon's novel lacks unity on the ground that the story would stand even if entire episodes were added or crossed out. Such an approach, it seems to me, rests upon an ultimately romantic notion of unity. According to such a view, great masterpieces are governed by a sort of intrinsic necessity that makes it impossible to alter a single detail without spoiling the ineffable beauty of the whole. However, an undisputed masterpiece such as Ariosto's *Orlando Furioso* might help question this notion of unity. Like the *Ephesiaka*, his poem is largely built along the lines of amorous quest and *entrelacement*, and

---

[27] Cf. the persuasive parallels detected by Borgogno 1985. However, I do not agree with Borgogno's attempt to reconstruct Xenophon's allegedly original text on the basis of Theodorus' novel.
[28] Some good points in Lowe 2000, 230–231.

we happen to know that Ariosto added various episodes over the years. Moreover, further additions are perfectly conceivable, because the poem has an obviously open structure. Needless to say, this is not to suggest that Xenophon's simple novel can match Ariosto's exquisite poem, but merely that romantic notions of unity as necessity are not very useful when evaluating pre-romantic romances.[29]

The narrative circle of the *Ephesiaka* has its focal point in Rhodes, where Anthia and Habrocomes last taste their love 'feast' before their separation, only to reunite on the island after their adventures, ready to enjoy their lifelong 'feast'.[30] Such a pattern leaves out the initial scenes on Ephesus, arguably the most polished of the novel, and the moving *nostos* of the lovers to their hometown.[31] It may be argued that Xenophon's 'round trip' gives a satisfactory explanation for such a difference in style. The first 'extracircular' Ephesian scenes feature the crucial events for the psychological and divine background of the story, namely the *coup de foudre*, Eros' intervention, and the ominous oracle.[32] After that, the circular pattern sets in and, quite naturally, stylistic embellishments become less pronounced, giving place to what O'Sullivan calls an oral technique. The circular pattern, then, reinforces the case against the epitome theory in books 2–5.

Finally, and rather more tentatively, I would like to argue that Xenophon's references to the divine may be seen as yet another instance of 'round' structure. Lunar-feminine and solar-masculine elements alternate, as Merkelebach noticed. However, far from being the result of textual conflation, such a pattern of alternating divine elements might be seen in an altogether different perspective. As Thomas Hägg has observed, the lovers' adventures would likely have lasted several years, and yet the only time-lag recorded in the novel is the alternation of night and day, which is explicitly and repeatedly mentioned.[33] In a somewhat similar way, Xenophon's narration is built as a kind of ping-pong between Anthia and Habrocomes. Thus, the alternation of the two astral siblings, the Sun (Helios-

---

[29] On ancient notions of artistic unity as *poikilia* rather than intrinsic necessity, see e.g. Heath 1989, maintaining that only neo-Platonic thinkers came close to modern notions of unity. Nimis 1999 has some good points on open-endedness as an intrinsic feature of Xenophon. Aristotle's notion of unity (*Poetics*, ch. 8) allows for the multiplication of episodes (ch. 17).
[30] Compare *heorte* at 1,10 and 5,15, forming a neat ring composition emphasising the reestablishment of the lovers' happiness.
[31] Whitmarsh 2011, 45–50, construes this opposition in terms of centre vs. periphery.
[32] The same is true of the final 'extracircular' scenes, which abound in emphatic forms of closure: see Nimis 2004.
[33] Hägg 1971.

Apollo: masculine principle) and the Moon (Artemis-Isis: feminine principle), seems to reflect the simple structure of the story, and the circular pattern of the narration might even be ultimately due to a kind of naïve 'astral' conception:[34] it may not be coincidental that two extremes of the circle, namely Rhodes and Ethiopia, are celebrated residences of the Sun. Needless to say, such imagery is simple as well as vague. I am afraid that there is no mystery to be decoded by the initiated, either ancient believers or over-subtle modern scholars, as opposed to *hoi polloi*.

Conclusion

In this paper, I have tried to suggest that Xenophon's novel should be evaluated on the basis of some very simple aesthetic principles – oral(istic) ones, as it were – which were commonplace in the Greek world: geographical thoroughness, a technique going back to Homeric epics, is a crucial strategy by which Xenophon made his novel palatable and entertaining to his contemporary audiences.[35] Seen in this light, Xenophon is far from an incompetent story-teller, and his novel is not the result of posthumous abridgment or textual conflation. By and large, Xenophon's (modern) critical misfortunes rest on an ultimately romantic notion of unity as intrinsic necessity, a principle that can hardly be applied to ancient narrative. By removing the dust of modern prejudices, a new picture is revealed, and – I dare say – it is a beautiful one.

Bibliography

Bianchi, N. 2011. 'A Neglected Testimonium on Xenophon of Ephesus: Gregory Pardos', in M.P. Futre Pinheiro, S.J. Harrison (eds.), *Fictional Traces: Receptions of the Ancient Novel*, vol. 1, Groningen: Barkhuis & Groningen University Library. 83–92.

Bierl, A. 2006. 'Räume im Anderen und der griechische Liebesroman des Xenophon von Ephesos. Träume?' in: A. Loprieno (ed.), *Mensch und Raum von der Antike bis zur Gegenwart*, München/Leipzig: Saur. 71–103.

Bierl, A. 2007. 'Mysterien der Liebe und die Initiation Jugendlicher. Literatur und Religion im griechischen Roman', in: A. Bierl, R. Lämmle, K. Wesselmann, *Literatur und Religion 2*.

---

[34] For a similar point, see Bierl 2007, 311. It is worth noticing that the four areas covered by the lovers can be easily construed as standing for the cardinal points.

[35] The naming of characters and a net of allusions to well-known tragic plots are two additional strategies: cf. Capra 2009, with bibliography.

Wege zu einer mythis-rituellen Poetik bei den Griechen, Berlin: Walter de Gruyter. 239–334.
Borgogno, A. 1985. 'Senofonte Efesio e Teodoro Prodromo', *AFLS* 6, 221–226.
Bürger, K. 1892. 'Zu Xenophon von Ephesos', *Hermes* 27, 36–67.
Capra, A. 2009. 'The (Un)happy Romance of Curleo and Liliet'. Xenophon of Ephesus, the Cyropaedia and the Birth of the 'Anti-tragic' Novel', *AN* 7, 29–50.
Capra, A. 2012. 'Detour en route in the Aegean sea? Xen. Eph. 5.10.2', *CPh* 107, 70–74.
Chew, K. 1997–1998. 'Inconsistency and Creativity in Xenophon's Ephesiaka', *CQ* 91, 203–213.
Chew, K. 1998. 'Focalization in Xenophon of Ephesus' Ephesiaka', in: R. Hock, J. Chance, J. Perkins (eds.), *Ancient Fiction and Early Christian Narrative*, Atlanta: Scholars Press. 47–59.
Cingano, E. 2005. 'A catalogue within a Catalogue: Helen's suitors in the Hesiodic Catalogue of Women (frr. 196–204)', in: R. Hunter (ed.), *The Hesiodic Catalogue of Women. Constructions and Reconstructions*, Cambridge: Cambridge University Press. 118–152.
Doulamis, K. 2007. 'Stoic Echoes and Style in Xenophon of Ephesus', in: J.R. Morgan, M. Jones (eds.), *Philosophical Presences in the Ancient Novel*, ANS 10, Groningen: Barkhuis & Groningen University Library. 151–175.
Enermalm, A. 1997. 'An Ephesian Tale. Prayers to Isis and Other Gods', in: M. Kiley (ed.), *Prayer from Alexander to Constantine. A Critical Anthology*, London/New York: Routledge. 176–180.
Gärtner, H. 1967. *Xenophon von Ephesos*, RE IX A 2, 2055–2089.
Hägg, T. 1966. 'Die Ephesiaka des Xenophon Ephesios – Original oder Epitome?', *Cl & M* 37, 118–161.
Hägg, T. 1971. *Narrative Tecnhinque in Ancient Greek Romances. Studies on Chariton, Xenophon Ephesius, and Achilles Tatius*, Stockholm: Svenska Institutet i Athen; Uppsala: Almqvist and Wiksell boktryckeri.
Heath, M. 1989. 'The Unity of Plato's Phaedrus', *OSAP* 7, 151–173 and 189–191.
König, J. 2007. 'Orality and Authority in Xenophon of Ephesus', in: V. Rimell (ed.), *Seeing Tongues, Hearing Scripts: Orality and Representation in the Ancient Novel*, ANS 7, Groningen: Barkhuis & Groningen University Library. 1–22.
Konstan, D. 2002. 'Narrative Spaces', in: M. Paschalis, S. Frangoulidis (eds.), *Space in the Ancient Novel*, ANS 1, Groningen: Barkhuis Publishing & The University Library Groningen. 1–11.
Laplace, M. 1994. 'Récit d'une éducation amoureuse et discours panégirique dans les Éphésiaques de Xénophon d'Éphèse', *REG* 107, 440–479.
Lowe, N.J. 2000. *The Classical Plot and the Invention of Western Narrative*, Cambridge: Cambridge University Press.
Merkelbach, R. 1962. *Roman und Mysterium in der Antike*, München/Berlin: Beck.
Merkelbach, R. 1995. *Isis regina – Zeus Sarapis, Die griechisch-aegyptische Religion nach den Quellen dargestellt*, Stuttgart/Leipzig: Teubner.
Minchin, E. 1996. 'The Performance of Lists and Catalogues in the Homeric Epics', in: I. Worthington (ed.), *Voice into Text. Orality and Literacy in Ancient Greece*, Leiden: Brill. 3–20.
Morgan, J.R. 2007. 'Travel in the Greek Novels: Function and Interpretation', in: C. Adams, J. Roy (eds.), *Travel, Geography and Culture in Ancient Greece, Egypt and the Near East*

(Leicester-Nottingham Studies in Ancient Society 10), Leicester-Nottingham: Oxbow Books. 139–60.
Nimis, S. 1999. 'The Sense of Open-endedness in the Ancient Novel', *Arethusa* 32, 215–238.
Nimis, S. 2004. 'Oral and Written Forms of Closure in the Ancient Novel', in: C. Mackie (ed.), *Oral Performance and Its Context*, Leiden: Brill. 179–194.
O'Sullivan, J. 1995. *Xenophon of Ephesus: His Compositional Technique and the Birth of the Novel*, Berlin: Walter de Gruyter.
Reardon, B.P. 1991. *The Form of Greek Romance*, Princeton: Princeton University Press.
Rhode, E. 1914. *Der Griechische Roman und seine Vorläufer*, Leipzig: Breitkopf und Hartel.
Ruiz-Montero, C. 1994. 'Xenophon von Ephesos: Ein Überblick', in: *Aufstieg und Niedergang der römischen Welt* II, 34.2, Berlin: Walter de Gruyter. 1088–1138.
Ruiz-Montero, C. 2003. 'Xenophon of Ephesus and Orality in the Roman Empire', *AN* 3, 43–62.
Shea, C. 1998. 'Setting the Stage for Romances: Xenophon of Ephesus and the Ecphrasis', in: R. Hock, J. Chance, J. Perkins (eds.), *Ancient Fiction and Early Christian Narrative*, Atlanta: Scholars Press. 61–76.
Schmeling, G. 1980. *Xenophon of Ephesus*, Boston: Twaine.
Tagliabue, A. 2012. 'The Ephesiaca as a Bildungsroman', *AN* 10, 17–46.
Temmerman K. de, 2012. 'Xenophon of Ephesus', in: I.J.F. de Jong (ed.), *Space in Ancient Greek Literature. Studies in Ancient Greek Narrative*, Leiden/Boston: Brill. 503–516.
Temmerman K. de, 2014. *Crafting Characters. Heroes and Heroines in the Ancient Greek Novel*, Oxford: Oxford University Press.
Whitmarsh, T. 2011. *Narrative and Identity in the Ancient Greek Novel. Returning Romance*, Cambridge: Cambridge University Press.

Dimitri Kasprzyk
Permeable Worlds in Iamblichus's *Babyloniaka*

Abstract: In his *Babyloniaka* (second century CE), Iamblichus devotes an important part of the narration (as it is summarized by Photius) to events occurring in a very particular place: an unnamed island formed by the Tigris and the Euphrates. This paper aims to show how Iamblichus has intermingled times, places, identities and genres to create a permeable world which reflects the pluricultural identity of the author. The island concentrates levels of reality which are usually separated to construct a geographically and ontologically hybrid world, which is enigmatic and paradigmatic of the novel as a whole. In accordance with a permeable genre, Iamblichus has constructed a permeable world, which seems to be characteristic of an author who has several geographical and cultural roots.

This paper[1] concerns a place which is apparently insignificant in Iamblichus's *Babyloniaka:* a small Mesopotamian island where the main characters stay for a while after being set free by Soraichos. This island is a refuge and a break in the middle of their adventures. In this respect, Iamblichus is not different from other novelists, since the heroes of Chariton or Xenophon stop off in Arados or Rhodes, which are important stages in the geographical, dramatic and symbolical structure of their stories. These islands are situated on the threshold of adventures, or they are a place for reunion – in any case, a good place for a pause in the action. But in the *Babyloniaka*, the situation is somewhat peculiar: the island is not only isolated or remote, but a world apart, where several dimensions coexist, from a geographical, temporal, and narrative point of view. I shall try to show that, by bringing together elements which are usually incompatible, but here interpenetrate, Iamblichus makes the island a symbol of a sort of permeability which is inherent in the novelistic genre.

---

[1] A modified version of this paper has been published under the title 'L'île entre les fleuves : géographie symbolique des Babyloniaka de Jamblique', *Hermes* 138, 2010, p. 216–229.

Dimitri Kasprzyk, Université de Bretagne Occidentale, Brest

https://doi.org/10.1515/9781501503986-004

It is difficult to have an idea of the island's shape because, from a geographical and syntactical point of view, Photius's summary[2] is far from clear. The island, which the fragments do not describe, appears in two stages. First it is mentioned casually when the heroes are delivered by Soraichos:

> ὑποδείκνυσι τὸ τῆς Ἀφροδίτης ἱερὸν ἐν τῇ νησῖδι, ἐν ᾧ ἔμελλε καὶ τὸ τραῦμα ἡ Σινωνὶς θεραπευθήσεσθαι. (75a34)
>
> he shows them the temple of Aphrodite on the island, in which Sinonis would be cured of her wound.

Then the summary is more precise:

> Ὡς ἐν παρεκβολῇ δὲ διηγεῖται καὶ τὰ περὶ τοῦ ἱεροῦ καὶ τῆς νησῖδος, καὶ ὅτι ὁ Εὐφράτης καὶ ὁ Τίγρις περιρρέοντες αὐτὴν ποιοῦσι νησῖδα. (ibid.)
>
> As a digression, the story is told of the temple and the island: how the Euphrates and the Tigris run on either side and so make it an island...

The last sentence, if examined closely, looks strange for two reasons. On the one hand, if we consider that the rivers form an island, in other words a stretch of land surrounded by water, there should only be one river, just as the Seine, in Paris, surrounds the so-called *Île de la Cité*. So should we define the little Mesopotamian island as a real island? In fact, it looks as if the novelist had wanted this place to be an island and had wanted to keep both rivers. Now (and this is my second point) the letter of the text is disconcerting in itself since, according to the summary, the rivers flowing around *it* (that means *around the island*) make it an *island*.[3] The expression is somewhat awkward, verging on tautology; but it looks as if the difficulty was introduced by the novelist, who seems to deny us the possibility of picturing the island. Some texts evoke islands located on the Tigris or the Euphrates,[4] but what Iamblichus says does not refer to any known place – which is itself uncommon in Greek novels – or even to any possible place.

The fact that it is located in Mesopotamia both increases and explains the difficulty in representing the island. Ancient authors naturally defined Mesopotamia as the country between the Tigris and the Euphrates (cf. Arr. *An.* 7,7,3): now, around the country of Meroe, Strabo writes that, since it is delimited by

---

[2] Photius' summary of Iamblichus' *Babyloniaka* is cited from the Budé edition of Henry (Paris 1960).
[3] ὁ Εὐφράτης καὶ ὁ Τίγρις περιρρέοντες αὐτὴν ποιοῦσι νησῖδα.
[4] Plb. 5,46,9 (τινα νησίζοντα τόπον, 'a place forming an island' on Tigris); D.C. 68,28,4 (Mesene, on Tigris); St.Byz. *Ethnica*, s.v. Syrbanè (an island on Euphrates)

two tributaries of the Nile, it forms an island (17,1,2; cf. Hld. 10,5,1); in the same way, according to a division criticized by the geographer Eratosthenes, rivers can be used to outline continents, which are islands from this point of view. Nowhere is Mesopotamia defined in such a way; but its form fits in with this theory. Mesopotamia is both mainland and island, and through a reduplication which is typical of the global structure of the novel, it encloses an island which is surrounded by the two rivers. Thus the same place (the same island) appears twice, on two different scales. The fact that the island is inhabited by a young girl called Mesopotamia reinforces the effect of a nesting-structure. The island has a temple whose priestess has three children, called Tigris, Euphrates and Mesopotamia. Since the rivers give their names to the brothers, one can infer that the same thing happens to the girl. But is it the whole country that gives her a name? I wonder if the young Mesopotamia does not live on an island called Mesopotamia, a miniature Mesopotamia, situated in the centre of Mesopotamia.[5]

The outline is hazy because an island lying in the middle of a river may look a little strange. It is not that an island located on a river is an extraordinary geographical fact;[6] however, it should be noted, for instance, that Arrian relates that Alexander, after crossing an Indian river, lands on an island located on this river (5,13,2), thinking he has arrived on the other side. This example (which is not unique) suggests that the perception of a river-island is not entirely natural and straightforward.[7] The islands which are evoked in the other novels are always located in the sea, so that our Mesopotamian island, by contrast, looks like a hybrid place, lending itself to an ambiguous representation.

Rivers are naturally a frontier (at least symbolically), as indicated by the famous episode where Callirhoe laments before crossing the Euphrates, because she feels she is really going into a barbarian country.[8] Crossing a river, generally speaking, has a considerable symbolic force; besides, an island is a peculiar place, isolated from the rest of humanity. Consequently, coming onto an island across a river suggests in a redundant way a removal from the ordinary world.

---

5 On the island as a miniature world, an image of the *oikoumene*, see Borca 2000, 40.
6 In general, the writers do not comment upon river-islands. On this sort of island, see Plb. 3,42,7 (about the Rhone which forms an island by dividing into two arms); D.S. 3,8,1 (islands on the Nile); Plu. *Ant. 19*,1 (an island where Octavius, Lepidus and Antony prepare the proscriptions; D.C., 46,55 writes that they meet on this island for privacy).
7 Cf. Borca 2000, 95 : ' sono le isole "di terra" – fluviali o lacustri –a suscitare uno speciale interesse : spazi continentali circondati e protetti dall'acqua, e perciò stesso anomali, tali isole realizzano sulla terraferma cio chè è tipico di un contesto marino'.
8 On the river as a frontier, see Braund 1996.

Indeed, our island is a hallowed place, with a temple dedicated to Aphrodite.⁹ On the island, the goddess acts concretely: the priestess's daughter is an ugly girl whom Aphrodite makes beautiful (75a41).¹⁰ It is in fact the only episode (at least in the summary) where a god is mentioned as intervening actively in this novel: no doubt this is no coincidence.

Since the island is a place where some mortals may have contact with a deity, it is not surprising that life and death should be so closely linked on it. Whereas Sinonis heals from her wound,¹¹ the physician who treated her dies while crossing the river after denouncing the protagonists to Garmos: may we see in this a divine intervention, the goddess protecting her priest by killing the messenger?¹² Anyway, entering the island is not allowed to all people, as the access to certain sacred islands is neither easy nor permitted to everyone. Another character dies on the island, in circumstances in which death is closely bound up with religion. Tigris perishes by swallowing a rose. This episode has been explained as a sequence of death and mystical rebirth, since one of the verbs referring to Tigris's fate is τελειοῦσθαι, which expresses improvement or perfection.¹³ The young man disappears altogether, however, as though he were really dead. His mother tries to bring him back to life through magical practices, but the experiment fails and only the arrival of Rhodanes, who is Tigris's look-alike, makes her believe that it was a success:

καὶ βοᾷ ἡ μήτηρ τὸν τεθνηκότα αὐτῆς υἱὸν ἀναβιῶναι, εἰς τὸν Ῥοδάνην ὁρῶσα, καὶ Κόρην αὐτῷ ἐκεῖθεν ἕπεσθαι. (76a4)

And when their mother saw Rhodanes, she cried out that her dead son had returned to life and that Kore had come with him.

Humorously treated by the novelist, the episode reverses the topos of the apparent death by narrating instead an apparent resurrection.¹⁴

---

9 In Greek culture, islands seem to be naturally sacred places: cf. Peyras 1995.
10 This miraculous intervention, which does not seem to have any parallel, can be compared to episodes where a deity enhances the beauty of a hero she protects (cf. *Od.* 6,229–235: after Odysseus has washed himself in a river, Athena makes him look taller and gives him beauty, χάρις).
11 Jones 2005, 21 remarks that the Romans, when introducing Asclepius in Rome, placed his sanctuary on the Tiber island.
12 Aphrodite seems to be the goddess of the river: indeed, her mysteries are connected with those of Aphrodite Tanaitis (see below), identified with Anahita, protectress of the river; cf. Merkelbach 1962, 185 and Ustinova 1999, 149–151.
13 Cf. Trencsényi-Waldappfel 1969, 515.
14 We may notice that the character who ate a rose is symbolically replaced by a man whose name contains the word ῥόδον, 'rose'.

I will not insist upon this use of doublets which, as is well known, is an essential feature in the novel's dramatic structure.[15] I only note here that this feature appropriately makes its first appearance on the island. Indeed, ontologically speaking, it is an ambiguous place, where identities and categories are not clearly separated. That is why there is no clear-cut distinction between waking and sleeping, as can be seen from an isolated fragment of the novel, which is preserved in two manuscripts. According to Photius,

Λέγει οὖν ὡς ἐν παρενθήκῃ περὶ τοῦ τῆς Ἀφροδίτης ἱεροῦ, καὶ ὡς ἀνάγκη τὰς γυναῖκας ἐκεῖσε φοιτώσας ἀπαγγέλλειν δημοσίᾳ τὰ ἐν τῷ ναῷ αὐταῖς ὁρώμενα ὄνειρα. (75b8)

[Soraichos] tells as a digression about Aphrodite's temple how women who went there must publicly announce the dreams that they have in the temple.

Now, the fragment contains a speech (strongly inspired by declamation) which a man delivers, accusing his wife of adultery with a slave because she had dreamt she was sleeping with him. According to the speaker, the wife's dream is a memory, or an image (εἴδωλον), of reality: the dream becomes the proof of a supposed crime because real life seems to invade the dreamworld. Again, it is remarkable that, in the *Babyloniaka*, the continuity between two different dimensions appears on the island. It is a place where characters pass through different physiological and ontological states, whose borderlines are not hermetic anymore.

From a narratological, and from a generic, point of view, the island episodes are a sort of hybrid whose outlines are blurred. Just as the island is an enclave between two rivers, the narratives concerning it form a big enclave in the main narrative, a digression – παρεκβολή, 75a36 – whose boundaries are not clear throughout. Digressions multiply inside the main digression (which deals with the island in general): Soraichos speaks about the island and some of its inhabitants; a specific account is devoted to them (for example in the story of Bochorus's judgement, 75b1). Then the custom of recounting one's dreams is reported in a παρενθήκη (75b8). This digression on Aphrodite's temple leads to a further narrative, which was apparently rather long (λεπτομερῶς διεξέρχεται), about a country where the action does not seem to take place, but where Aphrodite's mysteries come from: the Tanais-country.[16] Then, since the narrator speaks

---

15 Cf. Stephens-Winkler 1995, 184–186.
16 τὰ περὶ τὸν τόπον καὶ τὴν χώραν τοῦ Τανάϊδος τοῖς κατοικοῦσιν Ἀφροδίτης μυστήρια Τανάϊδος καὶ Φαρσίριδός εἰσιν (other interpretation in Ustinova 1999, 150: 'the mysteries of Aphrodite, that are celebrated by the people living in the place and its vicinity, are in honor of Tanais and Pharsiris').

about magical practices operated by the priestess, 'Iamblichus goes through various types of magic' (75b20), which leads him, apparently by association of ideas, to give some information about himself, since he has studied magic himself (75b28). Only after this autobiographical digression, at the end of several boxed accounts, does the narrative return to the main characters.

It is not clear exactly where the island digression begins. According to Photius, Soraichos mentions the island and then relates what he knows about it. As the arrival on the island is not related here, does the digression, the secondary narrative, begin some time before, on the road before crossing the river?[17] The arrival is summarized after the digression about the author, when the priestess, seeing Rhodanes, believes her son has come back (76a3–6). Her mistake is first evoked when Photius speaks about the priestess's magic, in the middle of the series of digressions (75b19). In this case, we would have the following sequence: arrival and the sighting of the island; digressions about the island; arrival on the island; digression about Tigris's death. In any case, on this reconstruction the digression and the main narrative are intimately interlaced. It seems that the novelist has blurred, or intertwined, two narratological levels, no doubt changing the chronological order of the reported events, a feature which, as is well known, troubled Photius when he summarized Heliodorus's novel.[18] It is possible too that all the adventures narrated up to then were actually reported by the heroes since, according to Photius, they tell Soraichos their story. The simple verb ἀπαγγέλλουσι (75a34) used by Photius possibly conceals a huge secondary narrative, equivalent to that by Calasiris's in Heliodorus.

The status of the episodes is not stable from a generic point of view either; we cannot examine in detail each narrative category exploited by the novelist in this sequence, but what must be noticed is their juxtaposition at a place which intertwines apparently incompatible kinds of data, not only geographical and ontological but generic and chronological as well, all interlinked.

The digression begins with the presentation of the main inhabitants of the island, the priestess and her three children. They have geographical names, which is characteristic of mythographical texts,[19] in which characters are eponymous of lands, rivers or springs. Of course, Photius's summary says nothing of the kind plainly, and we may suppose that places inspired the characters' names;[20] but we may notice that, in the digression about Tanais, which is very

---

17 This is a sample of the *topos* of the narrative on the road.
18 Cf. Danek 2000, 121–122.
19 For instance, according to the Ps.-Apollodorus (3,10,3), Taygete had a son, Lacedemon, who gave his name to the land of Lacedemon.
20 Herodotus speaks about a man named Thessalos, who is actually a Spartan (5,46).

brief in Photius's account, but may have been far more developed in the original novel, the narrator speaks about a character called Tanais, saying that he gave his name to the river (75b12). Given that the Tanais-land is connected with Mesopotamia, it is possible that, in the same way, the novelist established a clearer relationship between Mesopotamian places-names and those of the island-dwellers. In that case, Iamblichus's characters would seem to belong to the category of mythological heroes. The presentation of the characters is followed by an anecdote centered on Mesopotamia, involving a judge named Borochus or Bochorus (75b1–8): his name is undoubtedly borrowed from the Egyptian king Bochoris mentioned by Diodorus. If this is not the same person, the homonymy was certainly deliberate, so that the novelistic fiction includes a pseudo-historical digression with this anecdote on Bochorus, which reminds us, for example, of the Egyptian tales narrated by Herodotus (2,121–123). It transports us, within a novelistic plot, into a remote past, a time which is historically datable (under the Assyrian empire), legendary (under the reign of Bochoris) and, in a way, mythical.

Shortly afterwards, when the heroes are still on the island, we read an autobiographical account by the novelist, which he connects with the recent history of the Roman Empire (75b27–41); I cannot analyse its content here,[21] but it should be noted that such a short autobiography within a novel creates a second level of reality, heterogeneous both from an ontological and a generic point of view, not to mention the fact that this autobiography might be fictitious too.[22] The Babylonian origin of a novelist who relates Babylonian stories could be merely an argument of authority on the part of an author aiming to gain credibility.[23] But if this is the case, the allusion to the Greek education which Iamblichus claims to have received (75b29)[24] underscores, in my opinion, the fictitious character of the story: indeed it is precisely this education, this *paideia*, which allows him to write in a Greek literary genre whose main characteristic is to relate fictitious events. It means that the autobiography serves both to display the fictitious character of the novel and to warrant its truthfulness, thanks to the coincidence between the subject and the ethnic origin of the author.

Moreover, the novelist's autobiography is anchored in reality thanks to references to the political and military situation of the region at this time (75b36). The evocation of the Parthian war, whose length in the original novel is hard to es-

---

21 I do not discuss the information given in the margin of manuscript A.
22 See *contra*, Di Gregorio 1964, 3, and Ramelli 2001.
23 Actually, if Iamblichus really is a Babylonian, the point of this detail may be the same.
24 Another aspect of the permeability of the Babyloniaka (cf. Ramelli 2001, 453: *'forte permeabilità culturale dell'autore'*).

timate, belongs to historiography. At around the same time period, Lucian's treatise *How to Write History* censures novice or bad historians who think they are authorized to write it. I wonder whether Iamblichus may not have been a target of Lucian, who criticizes a writer for presenting his history as a prediction, whereas Iamblichus says that he had predicted the war and its end (75b37–38).[25] In any case, this historical digression enhances the effect of generic mixture which is characteristic of the narrative – introduced, as it is, by an arrival at an island. This mixture implies a juxtaposition, in the same geographical and textual place, of different temporal frames:[26] the fiction is located in the past (a Babylonian king belonging to the period preceding the Persian Empire, before the middle of the 6th century[27]), but the autobiographical passage refers to the present, whereas the events which have occurred recently are partly related as pertaining to the future, since Iamblichus supposedly predicted (before it took place, of course) that this war would occur (γενήσεται).

With this historical and autobiographical account, we have left the island for some time; but actually, this digression only exists through a system of successive digressions whose core is the island. Being an isolated place, geographically hybrid, the island is a melting-pot in which several temporal layers (whose juxtaposition is natural in a timeless place), different levels of reality (that of the author and that of the characters, which is manifold, between life and death, waking and dreaming), different narratological levels, and various patterns of narratives all mingle. The island is a microcosm, reflecting the land which surrounds it,[28] about which we would like to know if the novelist called it Mesopotamia or Babylonia; in the same way, the sequence on the island may be seen as a microcosm of the novel as a whole, or even of the genre itself, reflecting its formal and generic multiplicity, its status apart, absent from the literary canons of the time, but, just like Iamblichus's island, certainly more trodden upon than one may have supposed.

---

25 See however Di Gregorio 1964, 5.
26 Cf. Schneider-Menzel 1948, 90.
27 Things were perhaps clearer in the original text; but, after all, Heliodorus's, Tatius's and Xenophon's novels are located in a time which is not indicated precisely; in Photius's summary, the intervention of the Alanoi, Garmos's mercernaries, complicates the situation since they belong to a time contemporary of Iamblichus's (78a15).
28 On the island as a microcosm, see Borca 2000, 40.

Bibliography

Borca, F. 2000. *Terra Mari Cincta. Insularità e Cultura Romana*, Roma: Carocci.
Braund, D. 1996. 'Rivers frontiers in the environmental psychology of the Roman world', in:
 D. L. Kennedy (ed.), *The Roman Army in the East*, Ann Arbor: *Journal of Roman Archaeology Supplementary Series* no. 18. 43–47.
Danek, G. 2000. 'Iamblichs Babyloniaka und Heliodor bei Photios: Referattechnik und Handlungsstruktur', WS 113, 113–134.
Di Gregorio, L. 1964. 'Sulla biografia di Giamblico e la fortuna del suo romanzo attraverso i secoli ', *Aevum*, 38, 1–13.
Henry, R. (ed. and trans.) 1960. *Photius, Bibliothèque*, vol. II, Paris: Les Belles Lettres.
Jones, P. J. 2005. *Reading Rivers in Roman Literature and Culture*, Lanham: Lexington Books.
Merkelbach, R. 1962. *Roman und Mysterium in der Antike*, München/Berlin: Beck.
Morales, H. 2006. 'Marrying Mesopotamia : female sexuality and cultural resonance in Iamblichus' *Babylonian Tales*', Ramus 35, 78–101.
Peyras, J. 1995. 'L'île et le sacré dans l'Antiquité', in: J.-C. Marimoutou, J.-M. Racault (eds.), *L'Insularité. Thématique et représentations*, Paris: L'Harmattan. 27–35.
Ramelli, I. 2001. 'I Babyloniakà di Giamblico e la cultura plurietnica dell'impero fra II e III secolo', Athenaeum 89, 447–458.
Schneider-Menzel, U. 1948. 'Jamblichos' Babylonische Geschichten', in: F. Altheim (ed.), *Literatur und Gesellschaft im ausgehendem Altertum*, I, Halle/Saale: Niemeyer. 48–92.
Stephens, S. and Winkler, J. 1995. *Ancient Greek Novels: the Fragments*, Princeton: Princeton University Press.
Trencsényi-Waldappfel, I. 1969. 'Das Rosenmotiv ausserhalb des Eselromans', in: R. Stiehl, H. E. Stier (eds.), *Beiträge zur alten Geschichte und deren Nachleben. Festschrift für Franz Altheim*, Berlin: de Gruyter. 512–517.
Ustinova, Y. 1999. *The Supreme God of the Bosporan Kingdom*, Leiden: Brill.

Catherine Connors
Babylonian Stories and the Ancient Novel: Magi and the Limits of Empire in Iamblichus' *Babyloniaka*

Abstract: This paper compares Iamblichus' representation of Mesopotamia to Greek and Latin historical and geographical discourse about Mesopotamia. Magi and their powers are a regular part of Greek and Latin geographical and historical discourse about Mesopotamia. Against this historical background, Iamblichus' narrator claims some expertise in the arts of the Magi, and the powers of the Magi were referred to explicitly and, I argue, implicitly throughout the novel. The non-fiction historical narratives of Herodotus, Strabo, Diodorus, Pliny and Arrian, offer an essentialized view of what being a magus entails – you either are born one or you are not. By contrast, in Iamblichus' Babylonian landscapes, the knowledge of the Magi is something that can be acquired even if one is not born into it. Iamblichus creates a Babylonian world where those who pay attention can use their knowledge to make things come out the way they want, at least for a while.

Three ancient Greek novels present Babylonian stories. During the period in which the Greek novels were written, lucrative trade was practiced along routes from Antioch via Parthia to points east, including the distant land of the Seres (source of silk). Diodorus Siculus says about the Tigris and Euphrates:

> [in addition to founding Babylon] Semiramis established other cities along the Euphrates and the Tigris rivers, and in them she established market centers (emporia) for merchants who bring goods from Media, Paraetacene and all the region nearby.... They provide many advantages to men who engage in merchant trade, and for this reason the areas along their banks are filled with prosperous market centers which add much to the fame of Babylonia' (Diod. 2,11,1–3).

These trade routes were also powerful incentives for Rome's commercial and military actions in relation to Parthia.[1]

---

[1] For an overview of Roman interventions in Mesopotamia, see Ball 2000, 8–19; in more detail

Catherine Connors, University of Washington, Seattle, USA

https://doi.org/10.1515/9781501503986-005

Chariton's *Callirhoe* represents the Persian King and his court at Babylon in splendid detail, and Jean Alvares and Saundra Schwartz have persuasively argued that Chariton's Babylon can be interpreted as a figure for the Roman Empire. Indeed, the Romanness of the Persian court at Babylon provides an imaginative space in which to explore ways elite Greeks might interact with the Roman government. The fragments of the so-called *Ninus Romance* reach further back in time to invent episodes from the life of Babylon's legendary founder Semiramis. David Braund has argued that when Ninus goes to the river Hippos on the Black Sea, the novel is writing a prehistory of Black Sea trade routes to points east.[2] It may also be the case that Greek stories touching on eastern trade routes via Antioch and the Euphrates were among Ovid's sources for the notably novelistic story of Pyramus and Thisbe at Babylon in *Met.* 4.[3] It may even be that Ovid's novelistic Greek source presented the Pyramus and mulberry tree story as an *aition* of the silk trade, but detailed consideration of these Ovidian (and botanical and entomological) issues will fall outside my discussion here, which focuses on Iamblichus' *Babyloniaka*.

Iamblichus' vigorous story of adventure and intrigue has an exceptionally resourceful and fierce heroine in Sinonis. Her passions – love for her husband Rhodanes, hatred for Garmos king of Babylon, and jealousy of a farmer's daughter twice found in a compromising position with Rhodanes – relentlessly drive the plot. While the main story is set in what seems in some ways a rather vague Babylonian past, some features (crucifixion, for example) reflect a conceptual framework based in the Roman Empire. Iamblichus' narrative frame referred explicitly to Roman campaigns against Parthia in 115–116 CE and in 162–166 CE. According to the scholion in one MS of Photius' epitome of the novel, the narrator identifies himself as a Syrian by birth and says that a Babylonian taken into slavery in Trajan's Parthian campaign (115/116) was one of his teachers; this would be where he learned what he says here that he knows about the Magi. He had a Greek education; he is living during the time of Sohaimos, a Persian-Parthian who was a Roman senator and king of Armenia (164–172; cf. Dio 71,3). The narrator's claim to have accurately foretold the result of Verus' campaign in 162–166 – the defeat of the Parthian king Vologaeses and the annexation of Mesopotamia as a Roman province – is proof of his mastery of the techniques of Babylonian divination. At first glance this might imply that Iamblichus had a pro-Roman attitude. Stephens and Winkler see the literary sophistication of Iambli-

---

Millar 1993. For ancient places discussed in this paper see Talbert *et al.* 2000. All translations are my own unless noted otherwise.
2 Braund 2002.
3 On the novelistic qualities of *Met. 4* see Holzberg 1988.

chus' vibrant narrative as evidence that he 'moved, or hoped that he might move, in the high circles of the Greek-speaking social elite in the eastern Roman empire.'[4] Fergus Millar argues that the text's representations of Syrian, Babylonian, Greek, and Roman identities raise complex and hard to answer questions about the nature of cultural interaction in this area during Iamblichus' period. Helen Morales goes further than Millar in proposing that the text may incorporate perspectives that are not merely local but indeed resistant to Roman rule.[5] I want to bring even more geographic and cultural specificity to the reading of Iamblichus, or in other words, to consider what exactly might be 'Babylonian' about his novel. To do this I will examine the ways in which Iamblichus' novel – especially its representation of Magi and their expertises – relates to geographical, historical, and ethnographic accounts of its setting in Greek and in Latin.

Magi and their esoteric knowledge are a regular part of geographical and historical discourse about Mesopotamia (Strabo 15,1,68; 15,3,13–15; Diod. Sic. 2,29–31; Ammianus 23,6,32–6; cf. Pliny *Nat.* 30,1).[6] Magi are called 'native philosophers' of Babylonia (Strabo 16,1,6); sometimes they are called Chaldaeans.[7]

They are said to live in their own districts in the marshy areas near Babylon and south toward the Persian Gulf. The powers of the Magi are directed toward managing the interaction of people with land across the interrelated spheres of political organization, agriculture and ritual. They have close connections to the royal household, and they have expertise in writing; astronomy and mathematics; sacrifice and fire; divination via birds and other media; astrology and the casting of horoscopes (esp. political ones); management of crops via manipulating weather, insects, pests, and blight; medicinal and poisonous uses of plants, insects, animals and minerals; topography of marshy delta regions and routes; ritual handling of the dead and necromantic summoning of the dead. This list certainly does not exhaust the potential areas that Magi might be thought to control. Their powers could be thought to lurk anywhere in the landscape: Ammianus reports in his ethnography of Persia that Persians do not touch anything while marching through enemy gardens and vineyards, 'on account of their fear of poisons and esoteric arts' (*venenorum et secretarum artium metu*, Am. 23,6,78). When Greeks and Romans want to talk about the difficulty of ach-

---

4 Stephens and Winkler 1995, 184.
5 Millar 1993, 489–511; Morales 2006.
6 den Boeft et al. 1998, 168–76 on Amm. 23,6,32–33.
7 On the terminology see Ogden 2002, 33. The sources on Magi collected and annotated by him (33–55) offer a useful overview of qualities attributed to Magi in Greek and Latin texts.

ieving and maintaining imperial mastery over Mesopotamia, they tell stories about Magi and their powers.

Arrian tells a story of how 'Chaldaean seers' (*logioi*) met Alexander as he returned from India to Babylon in 323 and advised him not to enter the city because they had an oracle from Baal that it would not go well for him there. When that ploy fails they advise him to approach it from a different, much marshier direction.[8] Alexander suspects their motives, thinking they want to keep him out of Babylon to ensure their control of the revenues of the temple of Baal, but follows the route they indicate: their knowledge of the marshy landscape is superior to his and only with difficulty does he make his way into the city where he is shortly to die (Arrian *Anabasis* 7,16,5–17,6; cf. Plut. *Alex.* 73,1). At the end of the fourth century, Seleucus I Nicator founded the new city of Seleucia, where the Euphrates is joined to the Tigris via canal. The location took advantage of connections to the river route south via the Tigris to the Persian Gulf, north via canal to the Euphrates and east via land routes. Highly dramatic – novelistic – stories told that Seleucia was founded when Seleucus' wise physician cleverly managed events after Seleucus' son Antiochus fell in love with Seleucus' wife (Antiochus' stepmother) Stratonice.[9] According to Appian, Magi tried to sabotage the foundation of Seleucia: they knew the most propitious time to break ground, but they told Seleucus a different time. Still, Seleucus' soldiers seemed to hear a voice urging them on at exactly the right time and set to work immediately. The Magi subsequently confessed all (Appian *Syr.* 11,58). In 53 BCE the Roman general Crassus had ambitions to extend Rome's rule beyond the Euphrates all the way to India. Plutarch tells of how Crassus was misled by 'an Arab chieftain' Ariamnes into taking an overland route instead of going to Seleucia via the Euphrates route (Plut. *Crass.* 21). One of Crassus' officers, the quaestor Cassius (Plut. *Crass.* 18,4), becomes suspicious and berates the 'barbarian': With what drugs (φαρμάκοις) and sorcery (γοητείας) did you convince Crassus to pour out his army into a vast and deep desert?' Ariamnes encourages the men by joking 'Do you think you are traversing Campania, wishing for its springs and streams and shady places, and of course baths and inns?' and Plutarch comments: 'So the barbarian played the role of paedagogos (διεπαιδαγώγησε) to the Romans' (Plut. *Crass.* 22,4–6).

During the reign of Nero, Corbulo's military and diplomatic missions in the East eventually yielded the arrangement under which the Parthian prince Tiri-

---

[8] Babylon protected by marshes: Diod. Sic. 2,7,5; Strabo 16,4,1; Pliny *Nat.* 6,27.
[9] Stratonice: Plut. *Demetrius* 38, App. *Syr.* 59–61; Lucian *De Dea Syria* 17–18; Val. Max. 5,2,7, ext. 1.

dates agreed to travel to Rome to be crowned by Nero as king of Armenia. Champlin emphasizes the degree to which Tiridates, who was himself a Magus, used this status to dictate the terms on which he met Nero.[10] Because Magi were forbidden to pollute the sea in any way, Tiridates insisted on travelling overland at huge expense to Nero. Pliny criticizes Nero's infatuation with Tiridates and Magi in general in no uncertain terms: 'in these men the arts of poisoning are more powerful than the magical arts' (*Nat.* 30,16–17).

Trajan moved aggressively against Parthian targets in the second century CE. His advance beyond the Euphrates and sacking of Seleucia in 115/116 culminated in the annexation of Mesopotamia as a new Roman province (Dio 68,26–30). Dio's account (perhaps based on Arrian's *Parthica*) contains several highly dramatic episodes. After Trajan's Parthian conquests he made his way south to Spasinou Charax, a fortified settlement on an island in the Tigris near the Persian Gulf that was founded by Alexander the Great and rebuilt several times after flooding. He took possession of the island without difficulty, Dio says, but he was then endangered because of a storm, the current of the Tigris, and the rising ocean tide. Dio says that while Trajan was near the Persian Gulf, the places he had conquered revolted and drove out or killed the garrisons he had put in place: 'all the Parthian campaign had been for nothing.' Seleucia was sacked and burned for its rebelliousness. Trajan made his way to Babylon, where he visited the room in which Alexander had died. At Hatra the whole army including Trajan was besieged at every meal by flies; when Trajan fell ill shortly after departure (68,31,4), he suspected that he had been poisoned (68,33,2). He continued on his way to Rome, but died while still in Asia Minor in 116 (Dio 68,28–31; 68,33). While Magi are not mentioned explicitly here, their powers are suggested by the disturbing flies and the suspicions of poisoning.

In 162–166 Verus, co-emperor with Marcus Aurelius, headed a military campaign against the Parthians. His forces sacked Seleucia and once again Rome laid claim to Mesopotamia as a province (Dio 71,2). Iamblichus' narrator predicts the success of this campaign. The *Scriptores Historiae Augustae* says of Verus' Parthian campaigns of 162–166: 'It was his fate that he seemed to bring pestilence with him to the provinces through which he passed even all the way to Rome. The plague originated in Babylonia, when a pestilent vapor arose in a temple of Apollo from a golden casket which a soldier had broken open by accident and from there it spread through the Parthians and the world' (*SHA Verus* 8,1–2). In Ammianus Marcellinus' slightly different account, after the

---

[10] Tacitus *Ann.* 15,28–30; Dio 63,1–6; Suet. *Nero* 13, Pliny *Nat.* 30,16–17; Champlin 2003, 221–229.

sack of Seleucia, soldiers broke open a crack into a space where plague had been walled up 'by Chaldaeans' (23,6,24). The effects of this plague (perhaps smallpox) are recorded as devastating at Rome (*SHA Marcus Antoninus* 13,3). Marcus Aurelius himself fell victim to it.[11]

Against this historical background, Iamblichus' narrator claims some expertise in the arts of the Magi, and the expertises of the Magi were referred to explicitly and – I want to argue – implicitly throughout the novel. The setting of the novel in itself is an indication that Magi and their powers will be a presence in the narrative. From what we can gather two specific places are mentioned by Iamblichus: Babylon and the island sacred to Aphrodite. There are no indications in the surviving evidence that the characters ventured outside of Mesopotamia, aside from the fact that Sinonis marries the king of the Assyrians. When Strabo and Diodorus (and later Ammianus) talk about Babylon, they feel the need to explain the customs of the Magi. Iamblichus too can count on his readers to expect Magi and their powers in a Babylonian story.

About the powers of Magi in the initial scene in a meadow, I do not have much to say except to point out that Rhodanes finds out about a treasure from an inscribed lion-stele. Does this imply that other people did not know how to read the stele? That Rhodanes had some specialized knowledge allowing him to decipher the inscription? This would be the sort of knowledge that Magi had. One of the types of Magi that the narrator later says he knows about is the magus of lions. But we will return to the meadow at the end.

When Rhodanes and Sinonis escape from a cave after their hiding place has been discovered by Damas' soldiers, the soldiers are fatally overcome by poisonous honey while our heroes are merely laid low enough to look like corpses by the roadside. Iamblichus recalls historical incidents from Xenophon's *Anabasis* (4,8,20–21) and Pompey's war with Mithridates (Strabo 12,3,18) in which invading soldiers were overcome by poisonous honey in Pontus near Trapezus. Of course Iamblichus has to (rather implausibly) explain that his pursuing solders had the honey drip on to them, since (unlike Xenophon's tired men and Pompey's greedy ones) in the heat of pursuit they would not stop to consume it! Strabo's account of the maddening honey near Trapezus has several interesting features. 'Chaldaeans and Sanni' live in the neighborhood, and one of the settlements near the Black Sea is named Pharnakia, a name which seems connected to the story of Pharnouchos that Iamblichus includes while narrating the episode on the island (Str. 12,3,18). Pliny too mentions maddening honey

---

[11] See the full and fascinating account of Mayor 2003, 118–143 and 152; den Boeft, Drijvers, den Hengst, Teitler 1998, on Ammianus 23,6,24.

as occurring in this locality. Pliny says that one type of poisonous honey occurs when bees feed on the plant *aigolethron* ('fatal to goats') (at Heracleia in Pontus, *Nat.* 21,74) while another kind comes from the *flore rhododendri* in the region of the Sanni in Pontus (*Nat.* 21,77). The key here is that poison honey is understood as traceable to a shrub, most often called the nerium / rhododendron / rhododaphne (note the 'rose' element in those names). Indeed, modern pharmacology documents the existence of toxic honey derived from some varieties of rhododendron in this area and elsewhere.[12] Perhaps this explanation of mad honey is part of why the mouth of Iamblichus' cave is blocked by a shrub. The snakes are rather puzzling: Photius says 'the bees in fact have distilled their honey like a drug from the plants eaten by serpents' (αἱ δὲ μέλλισαι καὶ τὸ μέλι ἐξ ἑρπετῶν πεφαρμακευμέναι τροφῆς, 74b1, trans. Stephens and Winkler). A line attributed to Iamblichus in the Souda says 'since the honey was neither pure nor from ancanthus but gathered from <the nurturing of> snakes it upset their insides' (τὸ δὲ μέλι, ἅτε οὐκ ἀκέραιον οὔτε ἀπὸ ἀκάνθων, ἀλλ' ἀπὸ ἑρπετῶν <τροφῆς> συμπεπορισμένον, ἀνέστρεφε τὰ σπλάγχνα, fr. 16 Habrich). The problem with these quotations is that snakes do not eat plants and bees do not eat snakes. However, the same plant from which bees make poison honey is elsewhere said to be a remedy for snakebite. So Pliny says: 'the "rhododendron", as is clear in its name, comes from the Greeks (others have called it "nerium", others "rhododaphne"); it is evergreen and similar to a rose bush; the shoots grow out from the stem; it is poison to cattle, goats and sheep, and the same thing is for men a remedy for the poison of snakes' (*Nat.* 16,79, and cf. *Nat.* 24,90). Lucian tells an amusing story of a Chaldaean who cures a bad snakebite and summons snakes and kills them with his breath at *Philopseudes* 11–13. Perhaps someone in Iamblichus was cultivating snakes and has the (mad-honey producing) shrub as a ready source of antidote. Knocked out by the poison honey, Rhodanes and Senonis are treated as corpses that have been exposed, a practice associated with Magi by Herodotus (1,140).[13]

After Rhodanes and Sinonis escape from the soldiers they stop at an inn. As Schneider-Menzel points out, the fact that there is an inn means that they are travelling on an established trade route.[14] They proceed to another inn where they are tried for murder and then acquitted after the real perpetrator commits suicide. Their next stop is the house of a cannibal brigand; when this house is

---

12 See the excellent discussion of Mayor 2003, 145–154 and, for the pharmacology Koka and Koka 2007.
13 Cf. de Jong 1997, 400–441.
14 Schneider-Menzel 1948, 91.

burned they manage to pass as the ghosts of his victims. Successfully handling fire is one of the things Magi are good at.[15] Sinonis and Rhodanes encounter a funeral procession, at which point a Chaldaean old man (that is, a Magus) presides over the raising of a girl from the dead and makes a prophecy that Rhodanes will be king (74b42–75a4). In terms of the plot this gives Sinonis and Rhodanes a place for the night in the empty tomb and it contributes to an overall pattern in which Sinonis is identified with Kore / Persephone and her return from the dead.

Sinonis and Rhodanes next pass the special river whose waters are reserved for the king of the Babylonians (75a16; cf. Pliny *Nat.* 31,36 and Strabo 15,3,22). This is the Choaspes, also called the Eulaeus, (modern Karkheh).[16] Sinonis tries to sell some of the valuable grave offerings from the tomb and is arrested as a grave robber and handed into the care of Soraichos the just, son of Soraichos the tax collector. The couple try to commit suicide, unaware that Soraichos has substituted a sleeping potion for the fatal poison that Rhodanes pocketed at the public house where they were tried for murder. It is probably fair to say that in Babylonia, a man good at pharmacology has Magi-like qualities, or access to Magi-quality information. Soraichos puts the sleeping Sinonis and Rhodanes in a cart to bring them to Garmos. When they awaken and realize what has happened, Sinonis tries to commit suicide. Her determination impresses Soraichos and he arranges for them to go to 'a small island that the Euphrates and Tigris made by flowing around it' (Photius 94,75a37–8). Morales understands the island as a geographically vague way of referring to Mesopotamia, the land between the rivers, and there is truth in this (Strabo 16,1,21 and Diod. Sic. 2,11). Readings of the symbolic power of the island landscape are also persuasive. But why call it a '*small* island' (νησῖδος)? Could it be a recognizable place? Rohde surveys the possibilities in a lengthy footnote.[17] One ancient passage that he does not cite actually gives the clearest indication, I think, of how Iamblichus might have thought about the location. Pliny quotes rather extensively from the account of Onesicritus, describing his sea voyage on Alexander's orders from India to the Persian Gulf; it ends as follows: *ostium Euphrates; lacus quem faciunt Eulaeus et Tigris iuxta Characen, inde Tigri Susa*, (*Nat.* 6,96; cf. 6,135) ('here is the mouth of the Euphrates, then the lake which the Eulaeus and the Tigris make next to Charax, then Susa, by way of the Tigris'). This is the geo-

---

15 de Jong 1997, 343–350.
16 Hansman 1967. The water was said to be lighter in weight than other water; this would result from having a lower concentration of salt. On the significance of Spasinou Charax see Potts 1990, 145–146.
17 Rohde 1974, 369 n. 1.

graphical understanding that Iamblichus is working with, the zone comprising Euphrates, Tigris, the Eulaeus, and the island of Spasinou Charax. The treacherous doctor who tries to bring a letter from Garmos to the island drowns for his trouble (he had put the letter into the ear of a camel and tied himself onto the camel for the trip across the river). The drowning recalls Trajan getting in trouble at Spasinou Charax amid rising tides and flood waters, or an ill-omened accident when Crassus was about to cross the Euphrates and one of Crassus' horses dragged his groom into the water whereupon both drowned (Plut. *Crass.* 19,4).

The Aphrodite cult on the island is referred to relatively briefly, but it might be thought of as analogous to the cult of the Syrian goddess upriver at Hierapolis–Bambyke on the Euphrates. The fact that women must recount the dreams they had in the temple parallels narratives of sacred prostitution[18] and may connect to ideas about Magi as interpreters of dreams (cf. Herod. 1,108). The priestess and priest have a daughter, Mesopotamia, and two sons (who look like each other), Tigris and Euphrates. Tigris has recently died, having 'eaten for dessert' (ἐντραγών) a rose that had a cantharis (Spanish fly) hidden within it. The bug was used as a cure for impotence, though it could be deadly; it was said to breed on roses (Pliny *Nat.* 29,93–94). The sexual symbolism of the insect cantharis nestled within the bloom of the rose is worth considering. And the Rhod- in Rhodanes' name makes Greek puns on the word *rhodos* a possibility. Certainly Rhodanes brings a lot of unexpected trouble to the island. The rose + cantharis problem on the island re-iterates the deadly rose + insect problem implicit in the account of the poison honey (from what I think must be a rhododendron / oleander) back at the cave. In this connection it is an interesting fact that Pliny mentions poisonous honey immediately after his discussion of the cantharis, in a section of the *Natural History* peppered with references to Magi (*Nat.* 29,93–97).[19] Pliny remarks elsewhere that cantharis eats away at crops (*Nat.* 18,152) – Magi should be good at managing this kind of bug. Tigris's death seems to result from a failure or absence of the botanical and entomological lore associated with Magi. But some magic is afoot on the island: it is striking that when the priestess performs

---

[18] On the controversial evidence for sacred prostitution see Herod. 1,199, Strabo 16,1,20 with Lightfoot 324–326.
[19] Pliny cites (critically) 'the Magi' as sources for various remedies (29,53, 59, 66, 68, 76, (78 'the Parthians'), 81, 83, 117, 138), and at the beginning of book 30 he makes an overall attack on 'the worthless arts of the Magi' (*Nat.* 30, 1). Pliny mentions elsewhere (*Nat.* 25,5) that Mithridates' writings on toxicology and medicine and his collection of works from his subjects were translated by the freedman Lenaeus after Pompey defeated the king and took possession of his library: thus 'that victory benefited life no less than it benefited the republic' (*Nat.* 25,7).

magical rites over her dead son and comes to believe that Tigris 'has become a hero' the verb in Photius is ἐκμαγεύσασα.

The Tigris and Euphrates flow together today in Shatt al-Arab, near Basra. In the ancient Greek and Latin sources the actual course of the Euphrates through the marshy delta regions is described in various ways and the confluence is put in various places; it is usually the Euphrates that is said to disappear or become obscure (Mela 3,78 and Pliny *Nat.* 6,130; cf. Ammianus 23,6,11). Perhaps Iamblichus' story of the death of one of the brothers gives narrative form to the hydrological transformation of two into one at the confluence of the Tigris and Euphrates: both Tigris and Euphrates approach the 'small island' but only one can leave it behind.

The remainder of the novel unfolds bloodily at a farmer's house and the 'deserted lodging' that is nearby, at the house of Sinonis' unfortunate victim Setapos, and at Babylon. Back at the meadow near Babylon, where Rhodanes and Soraichos are to be executed on the order of Garmos, Soraichos seems to know where the gold is that Rhodanes learned about in the beginning. Soraichos convinces a group of 'Alanoi,' mercenary soldiers currently working for Garmos, that his knowledge of the gold is divine, and he further convinces the Alanoi to fight under him and defeat Garmos. The implication is clearly that the Alanoi see Soraichos as a Magus. Soraichos' divine-looking prediction of success for the Alanoi (he must have convinced them a fight against Garmos would succeed) parallels Iamblichus' own prediction of success for the campaign of Verus. If you are waging a military campaign in Mesopotamia and someone claims to use the practices of the Magi to tell you it will go well for you, would you be well advised to believe him?

Babyloniaka, the title given for Iamblichus' work by the *Suda* (2,603,18 s.v. Iamblichos), is analogous to the titles of works such as the *Persika* and *Indika* by the historian Ctesias. We can see the analogy at work in some sequences that emerge in Photius' collection of epitomes. Photius says in his prefatory letter addressing the *Bibliotheca* to his brother that he has not arranged the collection systematically but 'the summaries will be treated in whatever order memory presents each of them.'[20] Photius' codex 72 gives a long summary of Ctesias' *Persika*, while codex 73 summarizes Heliodorus' *Aethiopika*. The sequence in which the *Babyloniaka* is embedded is even more striking. Codex 91 is a summary of Arrian's *Anabasis of Alexander* (ending with his death at Babylon); codex 92 is Arrian's *Events after the death of Alexander* (this ends with very high praise for Arrian as a writer: Photius 91,68b28–29); Codex 93 is the *Bithyniaka* of Arrian,

---

20 Treadgold 1977, 345.

a fairly brief overview, but Photius notes that the work covered the period from the time of myth to the death of the last Nicomedes, who bequeathed the kingdom to Rome. It makes perfect sense then for Photius to turn next (codex 94) to Iamblichus' *Babyloniaka*, whose scope extends from Babylon's past to Verus' campaigns in Parthia. Photius is also aware of another work by Arrian, *On the battle order against the Alanoi*, about a campaign he himself commanded against the Alanoi in 135 CE (and Arrian's *Parthica* is summarized in codex 58). Photius sees a significant relationship I think between the works of Arrian and Iamblichus' *Babyloniaka*. By the time Photius read the *Babyloniaka* in the 9th century, the eventual results of Roman campaigns in the east looked quite different from the Parthian flight back east of the Tigris that Iamblichus' narrator claims to have predicted.

For all the parallels between Iamblichus and the historians, there remain some striking differences. The non-fiction historical narratives of Herodotus, Strabo, Diodorus, Pliny and Arrian offer a very essentialized view of what being a Magus entails – you either are born one or you are not. Diodorus, for example, contrasts the wisdom of the Chaldaeans, handed on intact from father to son, with what he describes as a Greek wisdom practice characterized by individuals constantly striving as for innovation (Diod. 2,29,4 – 6). Iamblichus' handling of the wisdom of the Magi falls somewhere between these two extremes. In Iamblichus' Babylonian landscapes, the knowledge of the Magi is something that can be acquired even if one is not born into it. Clever people can strategically deploy the kinds of things Magi know how to do. In the space of fiction, Iamblichus creates a Babylonian world where those who pay attention can use their knowledge to make things come out the way they want, at least for a while.

Bibliography

Alvares, J. 2001–2002. 'Some political and ideological dimensions of Chariton's *Chaireas and Callirhoe*', *CJ* 97, 2, 113–144.
Ball, W. 2000. *Rome in the East: The Transformation of an Empire*, London: Routledge.
Braund, D. 2002. 'Indian Traders at Phasis: Neglected texts on ancient Georgia', in: *Pont-Euxin et commerce: la genèse de la 'route de la soie'*, Actes du IXe Symposium de Vani (Colchide) – 1999. Paris: Presses Universitaires Franc-Comtoises. 287–295.
Champlin, E. 2003. *Nero*, Cambridge/London: Harvard University Press.
de Jong, A. 1997. *Traditions of the Magi: Zoroastrianism in Greek and Latin Literature*, Leiden: Brill.
den Boeft, J., Drijvers, J. W., den Hengst, D., and Teitler, H. C. 1998. *Philological and Historical Commentary on Ammianus Marcellinus xxiii*, Groningen: E. Forsten.
Habrich, E. 1960. *Iamblichi Babyloniacorum Reliquiae*, Leipzig: Teubner.

Hansman, J. 1967. 'Charax and the Karkeh', *Iranica Antiqua* 7, 21–58.
Henry, R. (ed. and trans.) 1959–1977. *Photios, Bibliothèque*, Paris: Les Belles Lettres.
Holzberg, N. 1988. 'Ovids *Babyloniaka* (*Met.* 4.55–166)', *WS* 101, 265–77.
Koka, I. and Koka, A.H. 2007. 'Poisoning by Mad Honey: A brief review', *Food and Chemical Toxicology* 45, 1315–1318.
Mayor, A. 2003. *Greek Fire, Poison Arrows and Scorpion Bombs: Biological and Chemical Warfare in the Ancient World*, Woodstock/New York/London: Overlook Duckworth Press.
Millar, F. 1993. *The Roman Near East 31 BC- AD 337*, Cambridge/London: Harvard University Press.
Morales, H. 2006. 'Marrying Mesopotamia: Female sexuality and cultural resistance in Iamblichus' *Babylonian Tales*', *Ramus* 35, 78–101.
Ogden, D. 2002. *Magic, Witchcraft, and Ghosts in the Greek and Roman Worlds*, Oxford: Oxford University Press.
Potts, D. T. 1990. *The Arabian Gulf in Antiquity, vol. 2: From Alexander the Great to the Coming of Islam*, Oxford: Oxford University Press.
Rohde, E. 1974. *Der griechische Roman und seine Vorläufer*, Hildesheim: Georg Olms. (Original Work Published 1876)
Schneider-Menzel, U. 1948. 'Jamblichos' Babylonische Geschichten', in: F. Altheim (ed.), *Literatur und Gesellschaft im ausgehenden Altertum*, I, Halle/Salle: Niemeyer. 48–92.
Schwartz, S. 2003. 'Rome in the Greek Novel? Images and Ideas of Empire in Chariton's Persia', *Arethusa* 36, 375–394.
Stephens, S., and Winkler, J.J. 1995. *Ancient Greek Novels: The Fragments*, Princeton: Princeton University Press.
Talbert, R.J.A. et al. 2000. *The Barrington Atlas of the Greek and Roman World*, Princeton: Princeton University Press.
Treadgold, W. T. 1977. 'The Preface of the *Bibliotheca* of Photius: Text, Translation, and Commentary', *Dumbarton Oaks Papers* 31, 343–349.

Ashli Jane Elizabeth Baker
Theama Kainon: Reading Natural History in Achilles Tatius' *Leucippe and Clitophon*

Abstract: The Nile, a *theama kainon*, winds its convoluted path through Achilles Tatius' *Leucippe and Clitophon*, defying characterization. So too do the novel's natural history descriptions. This paper examines how the internal and external signification of these natural histories constructs and deconstructs meaning, perhaps even subtly alluding to the emperor Hadrian.

In Book Four of Achilles Tatius' *Leucippe and Clitophon*, Clitophon describes the Nile's movements through Egypt:

Ὁ Νεῖλος ῥεῖ μὲν ἄνωθεν ἐκ Θηβῶν τῶν Αἰγυπτίων καὶ ἔστιν ἐς τοσοῦτον ῥέων ἄχρι Μέμφεως...Ἐντεῦθεν δὲ περιρρήγνυται τῇ γῇ καὶ ἐξ ἑνὸς ποταμοῦ γίνονται τρεῖς, δύο μὲν ἑκατέρωθεν λελυμένοι, ὁ δὲ εἷς καὶ τὴν γῆν εἰς τὰ σχήματα Δέλτα ποιῶν, ὥσπερ ἦν ῥέων πρὶν λυθῇ. Ἀλλ' οὐδὲ τούτων ἕκαστος τῶν ποταμῶν ἀνέχεται μέχρι θαλάσσης ῥέων, ἀλλὰ περισχίζεται ἄλλος ἄλλῃ κατὰ πόλεις, καὶ εἰσὶν αἱ σχίσεις μείζονες τῶν παρ' Ἕλλησι ποταμῶν. Τὸ δὲ ὕδωρ πανταχοῦ μεμερισμένον οὐκ ἐξασθενεῖ, ἀλλὰ καὶ πλεῖται καὶ πίνεται καὶ γεωργεῖται. Νεῖλος ὁ πολὺς πάντα αὐτοῖς γίνεται, καὶ ποταμὸς καὶ γῆ καὶ θάλασσα καὶ λίμνη. καὶ ἔστι τὸ θέαμα καινόν...(4,11,3 – 4,12,1)[1]

The Nile flows down from Egyptian Thebes, and continues to flow as before as far as Memphis...Thereupon it fragments around the land and three rivers are born from one, two of which spread out on either side, while the remaining one continues to flow as it did before it was divided, forming the land into deltoid shapes. Not even one of these rivers manages to flow all the way to the sea: they bifurcate variously around cities (and these offshoots are bigger than Greek rivers). Although the water is everywhere diffused, it does not lose its

---

I would like to take this opportunity to thank those who made ICAN IV in Portugal such a wonderful forum for conversations about the Ancient Novel (and beyond), particularly Marília Futre Pinheiro. I would also like to acknowledge those who gave me critical feedback before, during, and after the conference which has shaped this paper and continues to shape my work, especially Catherine Connors, Stephen Hinds, Alain Gowing, Ewen Bowie, Lucia Athanassaki, Stephen Nimis, Tim Whitmarsh, and Silvia Montiglio.

[1] The Greek text of *Leucippe and Clitophon* is taken from the Budé 1991 edition; translations are those of Whitmarsh 2001.

Ashli Jane Elizabeth Baker, Bucknell University

https://doi.org/10.1515/9781501503986-006

capacity to be sailed on, drunk, and farmed. The mighty Nile is everything to the locals: river, land, sea, and lake. What a novel spectacle!

This passage brings to mind Nile narratives by authors from Herodotus to Pliny and, together with Achilles' countless descriptions of plants and animals, displays his preoccupation with natural history. Yet this description of a river which becomes increasingly diffuse, appearing now as sea, now as land, a θέαμα καινόν, also reveals nuances of Achilles' writing and, particularly, his use of natural histories. Achilles' Nile spreads into smaller and smaller streams, growing ever weaker and increasingly difficult to identify – the river defies characterization. It is simultaneously different bodies of water – in its various incarnations as river, sea, and lake – and its complete opposite, land. Like the river, Achilles' natural history descriptions defy interpretation as the narrative advances, seeming now one thing, now another, a true θέαμα καινόν.²

It is important to note that natural histories, such as the description of the Nile above, are not the only type of pause in the narrative of the novel. Achilles' text is interspersed with a variety of debates, *ekphraseis*, and other seemingly discursive miscellany. Although there is a long history of marginalizing Achilles' narrative detours as either irrelevant or mere stalling tactics, it is now, thanks largely to the work of three scholars, Bartsch, Morales, and Nimis, no longer acceptable to read such pauses as evidence of Achilles' incompetence.³ Contrary to debasing the narrative, these (and other) scholars argue, Achilles' digressions contain material that is vital to any interpretation of the larger work.

Building on the work of these scholars, I discuss the multifarious quality of Achilles' natural history descriptions, specifically those of the peacock, date-palm, and phoenix. These natural histories, I suggest, echo, reflect, or generate

---

2 Thanks to Stephen Nimis for referring me to Plazenet 1995 who also discusses the Nile's shifting significance, particularly in the novels of Xenophon of Ephesus, Achilles Tatius, and Heliodorus, concluding: 'Les romanciers grecs ne nourrissent aucune intention descriptive pour elle-même. Le Nil et l'espace qu'il modèle, en tant que décor, ne sont pas signifiants. Le Nil joue un rôle essentiel dans les romans grecs à partir de Xénophon d'Éphèse parce que, riche d'une tradition littéraire bien connue, il permet aux romanciers de signifier par décalages leurs intentions. Il témoigne de l'investissement narratologique auquel sont soumises, dans les romans grecs, des données apparemment référentielles. Leur étude en termes de réalisme, ou une analyse de type linéaire, compromettent la compréhension des œuvres en cause.' (22)
3 Bartsch 1989, Morales 1995 and 2004, Nimis 1998. For a selection of criticism of Achilles' digressions, see: Reardon 1969 and Perry 1967. Perry 1967, 118–119 states, 'Iamblichus, Achilles Tatius, and Heliodorus seek to entertain their readers with disquisitions on a variety of topics which they regard as edifying or instructive, but which contribute nothing to the artistry of the main story, either outwardly as drama or inwardly as psychological experience.'

themes throughout the novel, while simultaneously frustrating a unified reading of those themes and opening the text to various simultaneous interpretive possibilities. Additionally, I hope to shed some light on the extra-textual significance of these descriptions. In other words, I seek to answer the questions: Why does Achilles choose *this particular* plant or animal to describe in his text? What external, pre-existing associations would it have brought to the novel?

Achilles first incorporates natural history into his narrative in the middle of Book One when Clitophon rushes away from the funeral of his cousin's boyfriend, Charicles, and into his family's garden in order to spy on and woo his new-found love, Leucippe (1,15). Clitophon takes this opportunity to describe the household garden in detail. The *ekphrasis* that follows comprises highly sexualized images of the garden that remind the reader of the errand that Clitophon is on, namely to convince Leucippe to sleep with him. Achilles writes:

"Ἔθαλλον οἱ κλάδοι, συνέπιπτον ἀλλήλοις ἄλλος ἐπ' ἄλλον· αἱ γείτονες τῶν πετάλων περιπλοκαί, τῶν φύλλων περιβολαί, τῶν καρπῶν συμπλοκαί. Τοσαύτη τις ἦν ὁμιλία τῶν φυτῶν. (1,15,2)

Branches abounded, interlocking, one on top of another: leaf caressed leaf, beside frond embracing frond, beside fruit coiling around fruit, so intimate was this kind of mingling of trees.[4]

In addition to the sexualized account of the plants in the garden, Clitophon also describes the birds that inhabit it, noting especially the peacock, which 'trailed his fan among the flowers.'

This type of *ekphrasis*, a description of a place which is 'before the eye' of the narrator, is extremely common in literature of the Second Sophistic and in the Greek novel particularly.[5] Achilles' novel, which opens with an *ekphrasis* of a painting of Europa that includes a meadow in full flower, shows a preoccupation with *ekphrasis* throughout. Achilles, however, employs this *ekphrasis* differently than other novelists.

---

4 Besides the generally erotic tone of the description of the intertwining plants and the fertility they evoke, the meaning of ὁμιλία can be read in a more explicitly sexual way, not simply 'a being together' but also 'sexual intercourse.'

5 For more on ancient and modern concepts of *ekphrasis*, see Webb 1999. She writes, '[Ekphrasis] is a form of vivid evocation that may have as its subject-matter anything – an action, a person, a place, a battle, even a crocodile. What distinguishes *ekphrasis* is its quality of vividness, *enargeia*, its impact on the mind's eye of the listener who must, in Theon's words, be almost made to see the subject.' (13)

First, his narrator recognizes the sexual potential of the garden and makes it explicit when, immediately following the description of the garden, he says:

Βουλόμενος οὖν ἐγὼ εὐάγωγον τὴν κόρην εἰς ἔρωτα παρασκευάσαι, λόγων πρὸς τὸν Σάτυρον ἠρχόμην, ἀπὸ τοῦ ὄρνιθος λαβὼν τὴν εὐκαιρίαν. Διαβαδίζουσα γὰρ ἔτυχεν ἅμα τῇ Κλειοῖ καὶ ἐπιστᾶσα τῷ ταῷ καταντίον. Ἔτυχε γὰρ τύχῃ τινὶ συμβὰν τότε τὸν ὄρνιν ἀναπτερῶσαι τὸ κάλλος καὶ τὸ θέατρον ἐπιδεικνύναι τῶν πτερῶν. (1,16,1–2)

Now, since I was keen to break the girl into the ways of desire, I struck up a conversation with Satyrus, taking advantage of the opportunity afforded by the bird; for, as it happened, Leucippe was strolling with Clio and had come to a halt in front of the peacock, since, again by chance, at that time the bird had fanned out his glory and staged a show of his feathers.

Clitophon directly connects the scene before him to erotic persuasion and uses the peacock, displaying τὸ θέατρον of his feathers, to display himself to Leucippe and win her. In fact, once he realizes that Leucippe is near enough to hear him, Clitophon begins not simply to describe the garden or the peacock but also to interweave observations about the peacock and peahen with a description of the sexual behavior of the species. He supplants a purely visual and *ekphrastic* account of the peacock with a narration that blends eye-witness account and natural history.

As Clitophon begins to describe the peacock to Satyrus and an eavesdropping Leucippe, he says:

'Τοῦτο μέντοι οὐκ ἄνευ τέχνης ὁ ὄρνις,' ἔφην, 'ποιεῖ· ἀλλ' ἔστι γὰρ ἐρωτικός. Ὅταν ἐπαγαγέσθαι θέλῃ τὴν ἐρωμένην, τότε οὕτως καλλωπίζεται. Ὁρᾷς ἐκείνην τὴν τῆς πλατάνου πλησίον;' δείξας θήλειαν ταῶνα· 'ταύτῃ νῦν οὗτος τὸ κάλλος ἐπιδείκνυται λειμῶνα πτερῶν. Ὁ δὲ τοῦ ταῶ λειμὼν εὐανθέστερος· πεφύτευται γὰρ αὐτῷ καὶ χρυσὸς ἐν τοῖς πτεροῖς, κύκλῳ δὲ τὸ ἁλουργὲς τὸν χρυσὸν περιθέει τὸν ἴσον κύκλον, καὶ ἔστιν ὀφθαλμὸς ἐν τῷ πτερῷ.' (1,16,2–3)

'The bird's actions, you know, are not without design. He is in love, you see: whenever he wishes to seduce his beloved, he glorifies himself like this. Do you see that hen near the plane tree?' I pointed out the female. 'She is the one to whom he is displaying his glory, his feathery meadow. The male's meadow is the more florid, for nature has sown gold on his feathers, and deep purple runs in a circle around an identical circle of gold, forming an eye on the plumage.'

Clitophon's language shows that he is simultaneously pointing out the birds before them and giving a general description of peafowl behavior. Rather than simply describing the physical appearance of the birds, Clitophon employs his knowledge of natural history to reveal the reasons for the behavior of the peacock and peahen.

Several clues about how to read the natural histories that are sprinkled throughout Achilles' text can be gleaned from this first example. Not only does this passage reflect generally on and refer to the novel's erotic theme; the reader is also encouraged to associate these animals with characters in the story. Clitophon states that the peacock, being ἐρωτικός, woos his ἐρωμένη with τέχνη, a characteristic of human, not animal behavior. In addition, just as the peacock displays τὸ θέατρον of his feathers in order to seduce his onlooker, the peahen, Clitophon performs his natural history in order to seduce his own observer, Leucippe. The link between the peacock and Clitophon is made even more explicit through Achilles' choice of language. The verb δείκνυμι is used twice in connection with the peacock's behavior, first when the peacock shows his feathers to the peahen – ἐπιδεικνύναι, ἐπιδείκνυται – and then when Clitophon points out the peahen – δείξας. Clitophon has effectively become the peacock, displaying his skills to Leucippe in order to win her.

As often, however, Achilles does not produce a one-to-one relationship between his natural histories and the plot of the novel. Although initially Clitophon is associated with the peacock and Leucippe with the peahen, Achilles immediately inverts the symbolism. After his long account of natural history, of which more will be said below, Clitophon reveals that he looked to Leucippe to see her reaction to his exposition and that she 'seemed to be signaling that the experience was not without a certain pleasure' (1,19). Just as the peahen will eventually be won over by the peacock's display, so too Leucippe seems won over by Clitophon's. Suddenly, however, Leucippe changes roles and is no longer the peahen; instead, Clitophon says, she is more beautiful than the peacock.

> τὸ δὲ κάλλος ἀστράπτον τοῦ ταῶ ἧττον ἐδόκει μοι τοῦ Λευκίππης εἶναι προσώπου. τὸ γὰρ τοῦ σώματος κάλλος αὐτῆς πρὸς τὰ τοῦ λειμῶνος ἤριζεν ἄνθη…. τοσοῦτος ἦν Λευκίππης ἐπὶ τῶν προσώπων ὁ λειμών. (1,19,1–2)
>
> The effulgent beauty of the peacock seemed to me a lesser thing than Leucippe's countenance, for the beauty of her form was vying with the flowers of the meadow….such was the brilliant meadow that lay on Leucippe's face.

In Clitophon's comparison, he has become the peahen, attracted to Leucippe's display of beauty. Achilles uses the word κάλλος here as a trait shared by Leucippe and the peacock, whose colorful tail is called τὸ κάλλος in 1,16,1–2 above. The language of this passage also refers back to the moment when Leucippe first drew Clitophon to her with her beauty at the beginning of the story, where he says, 'the vision of her face struck my eyes like lightning – καταστράπτει' (1,4,2), using language similar to the passage above, where again beauty acts like lightning (τὸ δὲ κάλλος ἀστράπτον). Finally, the beauty of the peacock and peahen are described as a meadow – λειμών – in 1,16,2–3, and the peacock's meadow in particular is described as εὐανθέστερος. Similarly, in 1,19,1–2 Leucippe's beauty is described as a meadow and is said to 'vie with the flowers' (τὸ γὰρ τοῦ σώματος κάλλος αὐτῆς πρὸς τὰ τοῦ λειμῶνος ἤριζεν ἄνθη), language that directly links Leucippe with the peacock. This language also recalls the highly sexualized description of the garden only moments before, connecting both the peacock and Leucippe to the fertile and erotic qualities of the space in which they are standing. This natural history, then, seems both to reflect on and to generate themes for the text without insisting upon one particular interpretation and perhaps even discouraging such a reading.

After describing the peacock's behavior, Clitophon says that the erotic performance of these birds is the least miraculous display of desire in the natural world. He then gives an account of four different examples of passion which are not present before them but exist only in his narrative. Eros, he says, 'can reach snakes, plants, and (in my opinion) stones' (1,17,1). Clitophon goes on to speak about the male date-palm, called φοῖνιξ in Greek, and its love for the female date-palm:

> Ὁ δὲ λόγος· ἄλλο μὲν ἄλλου φυτὸν ἐρᾶν, τῷ δὲ φοίνικι τὸν ἔρωτα μᾶλλον ἐνοχλεῖν. Λέγουσι δὲ τὸν μὲν ἄρρενα τῶν φοινίκων, τὸν δὲ θῆλυν. Ὁ ἄρρην οὖν τοῦ θήλεος ἐρᾷ· κἂν ὁ θῆλυς ἀπῳκισμένος εἴη τῇ τῆς φυτείας στάσει, ὁ ἐραστὴς ὁ ἄρρην αὐαίνεται. Συνίησιν οὖν ὁ γεωργὸς τὴν λύπην τοῦ φυτοῦ, καὶ εἰς τὴν τοῦ χωρίου περιωπὴν ἀνελθὼν ἐφορᾷ ποῦ νένευκε· κλίνεται γὰρ εἰς τὸ ἐρώμενον. Καὶ μαθὼν θεραπεύει τοῦ φυτοῦ τὴν νόσον· πτόρθον γὰρ τοῦ θήλεος φοίνικος λαβὼν εἰς τὴν τοῦ ἄρρενος καρδίαν ἐντίθησι. Καὶ ἀνέψυξε μὲν τὴν ψυχὴν τοῦ φυτοῦ, τὸ δὲ σῶμα ἀποθνῆσκον πάλιν ἀνεζωπύρησε καὶ ἐξανέστη, χαῖρον ἐπὶ τῇ τῆς ἐρωμένης συμπλοκῇ. Καὶ τοῦτό ἐστι γάμος φυτοῦ. (1,17,3–5)

> They say that there are various instances of plant desiring plant, but this desire particularly afflicts the palm tree. There are, they say, male and female palms. The male lusts after the female, and if the female is uprooted from the patch where the male is planted, the lusting male pines. The countryman understands what is upsetting the plant. He goes up to a point of vantage over the land and looks in the direction in which the palm has bowed (for it inclines towards its beloved). When he has ascertained this, he treats the plant's malady: he takes a shoot from the female palm and grafts it into the heart of the male. Thus he revives the soul of the plant, and life is breathed into its dying body, which recuperates, rejoicing in the embrace of its beloved. It is botanical marriage.

This anthropomorphic description of the date-palm reflects elements of the larger story in multiple ways. First of all, although Clitophon claims that many different plants experience this type of passion, he focuses on the φοῖνιξ. It is no coincidence that Clitophon finds the date-palm to be a particularly good example, considering that the name for this plant echoes the very first detail the narratee learns about Clitophon, namely that he is Phoenician (Ἐμοὶ Φοινίκη γένος,

Τύρος ἡ πατρίς, ὄνομα Κλειτοφῶν, 1,3,1). The moment that Clitophon speaks of the date-palm, the reader realizes that Clitophon is also speaking about himself.

And, in fact, Clitophon's plight and that of the male date-palm, abandoned by the female, show many similarities. First of all, Achilles -or Clitophon- has changed the traditional story of the date-palm. In Pliny it is the female who pines after and wilts towards the male (*NH* 13,7). By changing the gender of the lover and beloved, Clitophon makes this description of the date-palm reflect his own experience. He is drawn toward Leucippe and will perish without her. This moment will be recalled when Leucippe is repeatedly taken from Clitophon and he grieves for her loss. In addition, in the natural history of the date-palm, Clitophon explains that a portion of the female must be grafted into the heart of the male in order to remedy his illness. This echoes Clitophon's nightmare at the beginning of Book One in which he is fused to his half-sister and betrothed, Calligone, and then severed from her by a menacing woman wielding a weapon (1,3). In his nightmare, he has been grafted to a woman from whom he wishes to be parted and ultimately is, when Calligone is kidnapped. In his story about the date-palms, however, the negative idea contained in the nightmare is made right as the desired female is grafted into the male. The ever-changing internal associations generated by the descriptions of the peafowl and the date palms demonstrate the many ways in which Achilles' natural histories signify. While there are echoes and connections that can be made across the text to these descriptions, the signifiers perpetually fluctuate in meaning and open the text to different interpretations.

The natural history of the phoenix bird at the end of Book Three functions in a similar way. As Clitophon and his friend Menelaus are meeting with an Egyptian general, a messenger arrives to inform him that the troops he has been waiting for are delayed because of the arrival of a holy bird 'bearing its father's tomb' (3,24). Clitophon, ignorant of the bird about which the messenger speaks and wanting more information, asks what type of bird it is and what it means that it bears its father's tomb. By way of explanation, the general gives a complete natural history of the phoenix from birth to death:

> Φοῖνιξ μὲν ὁ ὄρνις ὄνομα, τὸ δὲ γένος Αἰθίοψ, μέγεθος κατὰ ταῶνα· τῇ χροιᾷ ταὼς ἐν κάλλει δεύτερος. Κεκέρασται μὲν τὰ πτερὰ χρυσῷ καὶ πορφύρᾳ· αὐχεῖ δὲ τὸν Ἥλιον δεσπότην, καὶ ἡ κεφαλὴ μαρτυρεῖ· ἐστεφάνωσε γὰρ αὐτὴν κύκλος εὐφυής· ἡλίου δέ ἐστιν ὁ τοῦ κύκλου στέφανος εἰκών.... Ἐνθεὶς δὲ καὶ ἐναρμόσας τὸν ὄρνιν τῇ σορῷ κλείει τὸ χάσμα γηΐνῳ χώματι, ἐπὶ τὸν Νεῖλον οὕτως ἵπταται τὸ ἔργον φέρων. Ἕπεται δὲ αὐτῷ χορὸς ἄλλων ὀρνίθων ὥσπερ δορυφόρων, καὶ ἔοικεν ὁ ὄρνις ἀποδημοῦντι βασιλεῖ καὶ τὴν πόλιν οὐ πλανᾶται τὴν Ἡλίου· ὄρνιθος αὕτη μετοικία νεκροῦ. (3,25,1–6)

The bird is called the phoenix, although it comes not from Phoenicia but from Ethiopia. It is as big as a peacock; as far as complexions go, though, a peacock would come in second in a beauty contest. Its wings are a combination of gold and purple. It boasts of being the servant of the Sun; and its head proves it, crowned as it is with a handsome ring, this circular crown being the very image of the sun.... It commits [its parent] to the coffin and fixes it there, sealing the gap by plugging it with clay. Then it flies along the Nile bearing this fabrication. Other birds follow in a troupe, looking like sentinels, and the [phoenix] resembles a king on a state visit. They fly straight to Heliopolis without deviation, the goal of the dead bird's migration.

While much could be said about Achilles' description of the phoenix – and has been in an excellent article by Helen Morales – there is time for only a few points in this paper. Morales argues that the phoenix symbolizes Leucippe in multiple ways – from their shared comparison to the peacock to the fact that both publicly expose their genitalia.[6]

Considering Achilles' tendency, however, to resist writing one-to-one correspondences between his descriptive passages and the characters and action of the plot, perhaps this is not the only way to read the phoenix. As Morales herself points out, 'animals often stand in metonymic relation to the countries which they represent…Although the phoenix is said to come from Ethiopia, it also represents Phoenicia, as its etymological root makes clear.'[7] Although Morales suggests that the phoenix, and therefore Leucippe, is associated with the Phoenicians and their sexually licentious reputation, there is a yet more apparent connection, namely between the phoenix and Clitophon.

Both Clitophon and the phoenix are introduced into the story using remarkably similar language – Clitophon, in the beginning of Book One, is introduced with the phrase ἐμοὶ Φοινίκη γένος and the phoenix, in the passage above, with Φοῖνιξ μὲν ὁ ὄρνις ὄνομα – and the fact that both are in some way Phoenician, although the bird only in its name, is relevant to the plot which begins and ends in Phoenicia. In addition, Clitophon's association with the date-palm, called φοῖνιξ in Greek, as previously noted, makes it difficult not to connect him with another φοῖνιξ, the bird. In fact, Pliny believes that the name of the bird derives from the name of the tree because both die and return to life (*NH* 13,9).[8] Although the phoenix may indeed be a symbol of Leucippe as Morales argues, it is best not to insist that it refers only to her. Here, again, Achilles employs a natural history description that resists identification with only one character or moment in the plot. Rather, he generates a multivalent symbolism that keeps the text open to interpretation. In fact, this fluctuation continues through-

---

6 Morales 1995.
7 Ibid., 44.
8 Isidore, in contrast, believes the name of the tree derives from the bird (*Orig.* 17,7,1).

out the novel in the natural histories of the eel and viper, the hippopotamus, the Egyptian ox, the rose, and more.

Not only does Achilles manipulate the internal signification of his natural histories, he also brings the extra-textual associations of the plants and animals he describes into the text. While it is beyond the scope of this paper to discuss in detail all of the extra-textual associations of the natural histories in Achilles' novel, several of these associations reinforce themes already discussed. Many of the animals described in the novel are associated with fecundity, death, and rebirth. One of these is the peacock which, although male, represents Juno particularly in her incarnation as the goddess of child-birth and, like the phoenix, symbolizes immortality.[9] The extra-textual associations of these animals reinforce themes present in other ways in the novel.

Many of the animals in Achilles' novel also seem to draw Rome allusively into the matrix of symbolic associations. Animals, often brought to the City from distant places, were an integral part of spectacle, whether in the arena or as static displays in Rome. Exhibiting these animals illustrated both the foreignness of the places from which they came and the tremendous size of Rome's dominion, which stretched to the homelands of these exotic beasts. Most inhabitants of Rome probably had seen first-hand many of the animals – elephants, crocodiles, and hippopotami – which Achilles presents in his natural histories. These three animals were also featured on Roman coins and art representing Africa.[10] Even the phoenix is said to have appeared in Rome, although Pliny expresses skepticism about this account (*NH* 10,5). In this way, these animals simultaneously represent the world beyond Rome and Rome itself.[11]

There is, however, another – if you will – 'elephant in the room' of this novel. Many of these animals are associated not only with general Roman *imperium* but also more directly with the imperial household. The phoenix and peacock were both emblazoned on Roman coins. The phoenix appears on coinage for the first time under the rule of Hadrian, representing a Golden Age utopia and the immortality and 'filial *pietas*' of the emperor himself.[12] And the peacock too is seen on coins picturing Hadrian although it is most closely identified with

---

9 Toynbee 1973, 250–253.
10 See Toynbee 1973, 32–54 (on elephants), 218–220 (on crocodiles), 128–130 (on hippopotami).
11 As the source of many of the exotic animals, Egypt functions in a similar way. Cf. Takacs 1995, 268: '…The exotic land *beyond*, which provided an imaginary escape from the accepted and enforced norms, was at the same time *within* the Roman sphere, within its realm of activity and control.'
12 Evans 2003, 289 and van Den Broek 1972, who includes plates picturing phoenix coinage.

the women of the imperial house.[13] It appears on coins also depicting these royal women, including the wife of Hadrian.

In addition, animals and plants throughout the novel are described using the word βασιλεύς or one of its derivatives. The rose is likened to a king when Leucippe sings, 'If Zeus had wished to set a king over the other flowers, the rose would have been king of the flowers' (Εἰ τοῖς ἄνθεσιν ἤθελεν ὁ Ζεὺς ἐπιθεῖναι βασιλέα, τὸ ῥόδον ἂν τῶν ἀνθέων ἐβασίλευε, 2,1,2). The Egyptian ox in a religious procession in Book Two parades 'as if this performance displayed its kingship over the other beasts' (βαδίζει δὲ ταῦρος ὑψαυχενῶν καὶ ὥσπερ ἐπιδεικνύμενος ὅτι τῶν ἄλλων βοῶν ἐστι βασιλεύς, 2,15,4). Finally, the phoenix, associated with the emperor through its extra-textual associations, is said to fly down the Nile resembling a 'king on a state visit' (ἔοικεν ὁ ὄρνις ἀποδημοῦντι βασιλεῖ) in 3,25,1–6 (quoted above). Is it possible to use the word βασιλεύς in the second century CE without conjuring thoughts of the emperor?[14] In this same passage the phoenix also boasts gold and purple wings, is crowned, and surrounded by 'bodyguards', called δορυφόροι, the Greek word used for the Latin *praetoriani*.[15] And the piety of this bird in deposing the body of its parent and its succession to the role of its father also call to mind the transfer of imperial power. While this is highly speculative, I do wonder if the Roman emperor is, in some small way, the 'elephant' in the novel. Perhaps it is even Hadrian specifically, who was known as one of the most widely traveled emperors, spending ten of his twenty-year reign abroad. Hadrian did travel to Egypt in 130 CE. Could Achilles' repeated references to the 'king,' particularly the king traveling down the Nile on a state visit, refer to Hadrian's trip down the Nile during his time in Africa?[16] Without insisting that these references to the king and kingship signify Hadrian, or even more generally, the Roman emperor, it is interesting that

---

13 Toynbee 1973, 251.
14 Cf. Mason 1974: 120–121: 'βασιλεύς and related words begin to occur in inscriptions, though not yet in formal titulature, about the time of Hadrian. Notable examples are a dedication to Σαβεῖνα βασίλισσα from Megara (*IG* 7,73)…and a dedication naming Hadrian δεσπότης βασιλεύς ἐπιφανέστατος νεὸς Ἀσκληπιός (*IGRom.* 4,341). Examples gradually increase during the second century…'
15 Ibid, s.v. δορυφόρος.
16 There is not complete agreement on the date of *Leucippe and Clitophon*. Winkler dates it between 150–175 CE, whereas Bowie dates it to earlier in the second century, 'perhaps…nearer to 120 than 150CE' (Winkler 1989, 170; Bowie 2008, 23). Hadrian's presence in the background of *Leucippe and Clitophon* may help date the novel to late in his reign or shortly after. This would also offer historical context for Clitophon's statement near the end of Book 2 that 'desire for males is all the rage these days' (2, 35), which could be read as a reference to Hadrian's high-profile relationship with Antinous (thanks to Ewen Bowie for the suggestion).

the text remains open to the possibility, imbuing the narrative with Rome and the emperor while simultaneously suppressing any overt reference to the empire.

Achilles Tatius' use of natural histories is one way in which he displays his craftsmanship, opening his novel to countless interpretations which echo, reflect, or generate meaning in the text, meaning that refuses to remain static, constantly fluctuating and defying interpretive finality. While the text initially appears to use symbolic language in a unified way, on closer inspection, just like the Nile, the novel continually deconstructs, giving the reader the sense of knowing less about the narrative as it progresses. It is this multivalence which allows and, in fact, insists that *Leucippe and Clitophon* be read in myriad ways. Achilles' manipulation of symbols and deconstruction of meaning are the novel's true θέαμα καινόν.

Bibliography

Anderson, G. 1982. *Eros Sophistes: Ancient Novelists at Play*, Chico: Scholars Press.
Bartsch, S. 1989. *Decoding the Ancient Novel*, Princeton: Princeton University Press.
Beagon, M. 1992. *Roman Nature: The Thought of Pliny the Elder*, Oxford: Oxford University Press.
Bowie, E. 2008. 'Literary Milieux', in: T. Whitmarsh (ed.), *The Cambridge Companion to the Greek and Roman Novel*, Cambridge: Cambridge University Press. 17–38.
Chew, K. 2000. 'Achilles Tatius and Parody', *CJ* 96, 57–70.
Chowen, R.H. 1954. 'Traveling Companions of Hadrian', *CJ* 50, 122–124.
Evans, R. 2003. 'Searching for Paradise: Landscape, Utopia, and Rome', *Arethusa* 36, 285–307.
Gabba, E. 1981. 'True History and False History in Classical Antiquity', *JRS* 71, 50–62.
Fowler, D.P. 1991. 'Narrate and Describe: The Problem of Ekphrasis', *JRS* 81, 25–35.
French, R. 1994. *Ancient Natural History*, London: Routledge.
Mason, H.J. 1974. *Greek Terms for Roman Institutions: A Lexicon and Analysis*, Toronto: Hakkert.
Meyboom, P.G.P. 1995. *The Nile Mosaic of Palestrina. Early Evidence of Egyptian Religion in Italy*, Leiden: E. J. Brill.
Moffitt, J.F. 1997. 'The Palestrina Mosaic with a "Nile Scene"; Philostratus and Ekphrasis; Ptolemy and Chorographia', *Zeitschrift für Kunstgeschichte* 60, 227–247.
Morales, H.L. 2004. *Vision and Narrative in Achilles Tatius' Leucippe and Clitophon*, Cambridge: Cambridge University Press.
Morales, H.L. 1995. 'The Taming of the View: Natural Curiosities in *Leucippe and Clitophon*', *Groningen Colloquia on the Novel* 6, 39–50.
Nimis, S. 1998. 'Memory and Description in the Ancient Novel', *Arethusa* 31, 99–122.
Perry, B.E. 1967. *The Ancient Romances: A Literary-Historical Account of their Origins*, Berkeley/Los Angeles: University of California Press.
Plazenet, L. 1995. 'Le Nil et Son Delta Dans les Romans Grecs', *Phoenix* 49, 5–22.

Reardon, B.P. 1994. 'Achilles Tatius and Ego-Narrative', in: J. R. Morgan, R. Stoneman (eds.), *Greek Fiction: The Greek Novel in Context*, London/New York: Routledge. 80–96.

Smith, E.M. 1928. 'The Egypt of the Greek Romances', *CJ* 23, 531–537.

Takacs, S. 1995. 'Alexandria in Rome', *HSPh* 97, 263–276.

Toynbee, J.M.C. 1973. *Animals in Roman Life & Art*, Ithaca: Cornell University Press.

van Den Broek, R. 1972. *The Myth of the Phoenix according to Classical and Early Christian Traditions*, Leiden: Brill.

Webb, R. 1999. '*Ekphrasis* Ancient and Modern: The Invention of a Genre', *Word and Image* 15, 7–18.

Whitehouse, H. 1985. 'Shipwreck on the Nile: A Greek Novel on a "Lost" Roman Mosaic?', *AJA* 89, 129–134.

Whitmarsh, T., and Morales, H. (trans. and introd.) 2001. *Achilles Tatius' Leucippe and Clitophon*, Oxford and New York: Oxford University Press.

Winkler, J. 1989. *Achilles Tatius. Leucippe and Clitophon*, in: B.P. Reardon (ed.), *Collected Ancient Greek Novels*, Berkeley: University of California Press. 170–284.

Zeitlin, F. 1994. 'Gardens of Desire in Longus's *Daphnis and Chloe*', in: J. Tatum (ed.), *The Search for the Ancient Novel*, Baltimore: Johns Hopkins University Press. 148–172.

The Dialogic Imagination

Shannon N. Byrne
Fortunata and Terentia: A Model for Trimalchio's Wife

Abstract: One of the analogues for Trimalchio is Maecenas, both the historical figure and the decadent caricature criticized by Seneca in the *Epistles*. This paper looks at Trimalchio's wife, Fortunata, for whom Maecenas' wife, Terentia, serves as an analogue. What little we know about Terentia are things Petronius' contemporaries would have known and enjoyed seeing in Fortunata: for example, both women married high-maintenance men, both behave questionably with a family friend, both have a sharp eye for finances, and both like to dance. Endowing Fortunata with Terentia's characteristics made the Trimalchio/Maecenas connection all the more amusing for Petronius' audience.

In a previous paper I argued that Maecenas was the main analogue for Petronius' Trimalchio largely because of Seneca, whose recent and devastating criticisms of Maecenas provided an opportunity for topicality and parody in the hands of a current favorite against a rival who had fallen into disfavor.[1] Maecenas was not the only model Petronius used to flesh out Trimalchio: part of the fun for Nero's crowd was identifying references of all sorts in Petronius' work,[2] and it is not surprising that the character of Trimalchio is packed with allusions to literary and historical figures that are intelligible on several levels.[3] But Senecan thought and imagery, above all in the *Epistles*,[4] were especially on Petronius' mind, which is why he endowed Trimalchio with characteristics found in Sene-

---

[1] Byrne 2007, 31–50. For citations of parodies of Seneca in Petronius, see Studer 1843, 89–91; Rose 1971, 69–74; Sullivan 1968b, 453–467 and 1985, 172–179.
[2] Many allusions in the *Satyricon* seem to have been intended for Nero's crowd; see Rose 1971, 41–43 and 75–81; Sullivan 1968a, 255; Sullivan 1968b, 467; Sullivan 1985, 159–161; Bagnani 1954a, 34–35; Bodel 1999, 43; Schmeling 1996, 480.
[3] For literary antecedents such as Horace's *Satire* 2,8 and Plato's *Symposium* see, for example, Bodel 1999, 39–40; Petersmann 1998, 269–277; Cameron 1969, 367–370; Shero 1923, 126–143, esp. 134–139; Révay 1922, 202–212; for mime and comedy (with bibliography) see Panayotakis 1995 and Preston 1915, 260–269; other sources that deal with the characterization of Trimalchio and his guests include Boyce 1991, 95–102 and Steele 1920, 279–293.
[4] See Sullivan 1985, 172–79 and 1968b, 453–467.

Shannon N. Byrne, Xavier University

https://doi.org/10.1515/9781501503986-007

ca's depictions of Calvisius Sabinus, Pacuvius, and, of course, Maecenas.[5] Hence, both Seneca's Maecenas and Trimalchio share a desire for bizarre dress and ostentation, overindulgence, fondness for eunuchs, and a fear of death.

Detecting allusions to recent imagery culled from a former favorite's works would have amused Petronius' more sophisticated audience, but once the connection was made, Petronius did not stop there: he had at his disposal a wealth of information about the real Maecenas, things his educated audience would have known in addition to what Seneca had singled out for criticism, and this sort of information also made its way into the picture of Trimalchio. Hence, both Trimalchio and Maecenas avoid high honor, build massive homes, have an interest in wine, own vast estates and countless slaves, and write bad poetry. Most importantly for the purposes of this paper, both Trimalchio and Maecenas had difficult wives. Due to the similarities between Maecenas and Trimalchio, R. B. Steele some 90 years ago had suggested a comparison between Terentia, Maecenas' wife, and Trimalchio's wife Fortunata, but only in a superficial way, as the focus of his paper was literary adaptation in Petronius in general.[6] Based on my research showing Maecenas as the primary analogue for Trimalchio, it is fitting to return to Steele's idea and explore it in more depth. Admittedly, Terentia is a shadowy figure, but the few things that we know about her are things that Petronius and his educated contemporaries would have known, and writing Terentia's characteristics into Fortunata would have made the Trimalchio/Maecenas connection all the more amusing.

Maecenas' wife Terentia, described by one scholar as 'beautiful, but morose and haughty,'[7] has been identified as the aunt of L. Seius Strabo, father of Sejanus.[8] She was either the full sister of an A. Terentius Varro Murena, or became his sister by adoption when, as Licinius Murena, he was adopted by her father, A. Terentius.[9] The identity of Murena itself raises questions: was he the mysterious consul of 23 BCE and the Licinius warned by Horace in *Odes* 2, 10 to keep to

---

5 For all three see Sullivan 1985, 175 and n. 33; 1968b, 463 and n. 29; 1968a, 132–133. For Petronius' echoes of Seneca's Calvisius Sabinus and his malapropisms (*Ep.* 27,5–8) and Pacuvius' mock funeral (*Ep.* 12,8) see Maiuri 1945, 19–20 and 23–24.
6 Steele 1920, 279–293.
7 Arkenburg 1993, 348.
8 For her kinship with Sejanus, see Sumner 1965, 134. Sealey 1961, 105–106 argues that from this connection Sejanus and his father belonged to a political party headed by Maecenas, which opposed Agrippa's party in the 20s and lost power temporarily, only to regain it later.
9 Treggiari 1973, 255 suggests that she was Murena's full sister, while Sumner 1978, 192 is more certain; Stockton 1965, 22 raises the possibility that they were related by adoption, while Paturzo 1999, 71 is more certain.

the golden mean?¹⁰ We know for sure he was the conspirator of late 23 or early 22 BCE: according to Dio (54,3) when M. Primus was on trial for an unauthorized attack on the Odrysae, Murena as Primus' advocate criticized Augustus for appearing in court and butting in without cause. When Augustus brushed aside the criticism he won the undying hatred of Murena and other independent-minded senators like Fannius Caepio, who formed a conspiracy against Augustus on the grounds that he had overstepped his authority. Dio leaves Murena's actual complicity in the plot unresolved,¹¹ as he relates that the conspirators were tried *in absentia* and convicted, and that Maecenas, despite his influence with Augustus, could not save his brother-in-law from death (54,3,5). What assistance Maecenas might have attempted to provide is uncertain. Suetonius (*Aug.* 66,3) writes that Maecenas revealed to Terentia that the conspiracy had been detected, and Strabo (14,5,4) mentions that Murena took flight and was captured. We assume, therefore, that Murena tried to escape because Terentia, forewarned by Maecenas, had informed her brother of Augustus' intentions, allowing him an opportunity to try to escape. In any case she knew about her brother's plight before he was captured because of Maecenas, and Maecenas' lack of discretion tested Augustus' patience (Suet. *Aug.* 66,3).

It is possible Terentia was born in the late 50s BCE, if she was in fact the full sister of the conspirator, who is thought to have been born c. 56.¹² Her marriage to Maecenas has been dated to sometime in the early 30s or just before 23 BCE, with no evidence to support any date with certainty.¹³ Horace says that he and his group of travelers on the way to Brundisium passed the night in the house of a Murena (*Sat.* 1,5,38), who may be the future conspirator. Perhaps Maecenas met Terentia at this time and married her soon after. In an attempt to justify his union with Cleopatra, Antony accuses Octavian of numerous extra-marital affairs; in a letter he names four women, among whom is found a Terentilla,

---

10 For the confusing matter of Murena's identity and family connections, see Sumner 1978, 187–195; Treggiari 1973, 253–261; Swan 1966, 235–247; Stockton 1965, 18–40; Atkinson 1960, 440–473; Hanslik 1953, 282–287. For a review of the diverse points of view and bibliography, see Arkenberg 1993.
11 Dio 54,3,4. Velleius Paterculus 2,91,2 and Suetonius *Aug.* 19,1 name Murena as co-founder of the conspiracy without reservation. Dio 54,3 provides the fullest account of the Primus trial and subsequent conspiracy. See also Strabo 14, 5, 4; Suet. *Aug.* 19,1; 56,4; 66,3; *Tib.* 8; Vell. Pat. 2,91,2; Sen. *Brev.Vit.* 4,5; *Clem.* 1,9,6; Macrob. *Sat.* 1,11,21; Tac. *Ann.* 1,10,4.
12 Treggiari 1973, 255–256.
13 For the earlier date, see Treggiari 1973, 256; for the later, see Atkinson 1960, 472.

which some believe could be a diminutive for Maecenas' Terentia.[14] Dio (54,19,1–3) states that in 16 BCE Augustus decided to leave Rome in Solon-like fashion to give the city a reprieve from his onerous presence and to avoid resentment for recently enacted laws. Dio adds, however, that some people suspected Augustus' real reason for leaving was to avoid public criticism concerning his affair with Terentia, with whom he planned to live openly while away from prying eyes at Rome.[15] This was not a bad idea considering Augustus' attempt at regulating adultery just two years earlier. Some suggest that Augustus and Terentia had been having an affair since the 30s, referencing the 'Terentilla' of Antony's letter. Such is the opinion of Raoul Verdière, who believes that among Terentia's many lovers for the period around 25 BCE we should include a young Ovid, who proclaimed his infatuation for Terentia under the pseudonym 'Corinna,' thereby keeping the identity of his tempestuous mistress a secret from posterity.[16]

It is also possible Terentia's affair with Augustus began after the Murena conspiracy on the grounds that if she had been intimate with Augustus at the time of the conspiracy, she might have saved her brother's life.[17] On the other hand, an affair with Augustus six years after her brother's execution suggests a curiously forgiving nature on her part. We simply do not have enough information to draw any conclusions as to when the affair between Augustus and Terentia started or how long it lasted. We have the beginning of a letter Augustus wrote to Maecenas that contains a series of playful epithets and includes the designation *malagma moecharum*, 'mattress of adulteresses' (Macrob. *Sat.* 2,4,12); this could refer to Maecenas' own womanizing behavior,[18] for which there is some evidence: Plutarch (*Mor.* 759–760 f) relates that a certain Gabba who was hosting a dinner party pretended to fall asleep during a banquet so that Maecenas could

---

14 Suet. *Aug.* 69; cf. Syme 1939, 277 n. 2: 'The women alluded to may be the wives of certain associates of Octavianus – at least Terentilla is presumably Terentia, the wife of Maecenas, not unknown to subsequent scandal.' See also André 1967, 40.
15 Dio also relates (54,19,3–4) that Augustus had Livia and Terentia compete in a beauty contest.
16 Verdière 1971, 623–648 builds on the observation of Thibault 1964, 44–46 and 115, that the *Caesarea puella* mentioned by Sidonius Apollinarus (*Carm.* 23,157–160) as the cause of Ovid's exile was more likely a reference to a mistress of Augustus rather than to a member of the imperial household. Verdière considers possible candidates for the *Caesarea puella* and settles on Terentia. Even though Ovid's affair with Terentia had occurred 33 years in the past, Verdière suggests that this *error* contributed to the harshness of his exile. Verdière defends and further explicates the identification in 1983, 619–624, and finds support in Paturzo 1999, 170–171.
17 Gardthausen 1896, 2,2,440 n. 46.
18 Martini 1995, 184–185.

make time with his wife,[19] and Dio (54,30,4) notes that in 12 BCE Maecenas defended a man on trial for adultery. However, Augustus might have been referring to Maecenas' own bizarre marital circumstances, in which he was serving as the mattress for an adulteress whose pleasures Augustus himself enjoyed.[20]

Although ancient sources reveal little about Terentia, they are in agreement that she could be difficult, proof of which survives in a court case regarding a gift reported in the *Digest* 24,1,64:

> Trebatius inter Terentiam et Maecenatem respondit si verum divortium fuisset, ratam esse donationem, si simulatum, contra. sed verum est, quod Proculus et Caecilius putant, tunc verum esse divortium et valere donationem diuortii causa factam si aliae nuptiae insecutae sunt aut tam longo tempore vidua fuissel, ut dubium non foret alterum esse matrimonium: alias nec donationem ullius esse momenti futuram.
>
> Trebatius responded in the case of Terentia and Maecenas that if there had been a real divorce, it was considered a gift, if the divorce was not real, the contrary. But it is true, as Proculus and Caecilius think, that then a divorce is real and a gift made for the sake of divorce is valid if another marriage followed or if the woman had been alone for a long time, so that there would be no doubt that there was a second marriage: at another time a gift would be of no importance.

The point of the case is that during the period of separation and reconciliation, Maecenas and Terentia were not technically divorced, and since gifts between spouses have no legal basis, whatever Maecenas gave to Terentia to win her back before the final divorce ought to be returned to him.[21] The divorce must have occurred sometime after her affair with Augustus in 16 BCE. Possibly Maecenas first divorced Terentia because of the affair, changed his mind and won her back with the gift in question in the *Digest*, but then Terentia divorced him, causing Maecenas to try to reclaim the gift by arguing there had been no legal divorce when it was made.[22] Franco Paturzo posits that the lawsuit in the *Digest* was instigated by Terentia, who wanted to hold on to property that Maecenas had given to her as a gift when, as she claimed, they were legally divorced.[23] Antonio Guarino dates the case in the *Digest* to shortly after Maecenas' death in 8 BCE, and

---

19 The story about a host feigning sleep to allow his wife freedom to practice adultery is found as early as Lucilius (frag. 251) and seems to be a fairly well-known yarn among Romans; cf. Cic. *Fam.* 7,24,1 and *Att.* 13,49,2.
20 Billerbeck 1990, 193.
21 The explanation presented above is from J.E. Spruit, 'Een aniteke huwelijkstwist: de casus van D. 24, 1, 64', *Romeinsrechtelijke ramesken* (Deventer 1979) 73–85, as summarized by Evenpoel 1990, 105–106.
22 Martini 1995, 178–185.
23 Paturzo 1999, 172.

suggests that the instigator of the suit was Augustus himself, heir to most of Maecenas' estate, which included gifts Terentia had wrongly kept because, as he claimed, she and Maecenas were not legally divorced when the gifts had been given.[24] It is unfortunate that Seneca weighs in on the marital strife that afflicted Maecenas, for as I have shown elsewhere, Seneca is hardly a fair judge of anything concerning Maecenas.[25] Seneca says that Maecenas suffered from insomnia because Terentia daily denied him sex (*Prov.* 3,10), and claims that Maecenas was married a thousand times but only had one wife (*Ep.* 114,6).[26] With typical exaggeration Seneca denigrates Maecenas' attempts at reconciliation with his wife and passes on slander about his sex life that befits an effeminate, uxorious man. In the second poem of the anonymously composed *Elegiae in Maecenatem*, Maecenas mourns the untimely death of Drusus in comparison to his own long life, then abruptly breaks off a thought that starts '*discidio vellemque prius*': '"I would have wished before the discord/divorce" – he did not say everything and modesty cut off what his love almost said' (7–9). A note in the Loeb text states that Maecenas was thinking about the past hostilities (*discidium*) between Octavian and Antony, a subject still too recent to talk about directly.[27] But *discidium* according to the *OLD*³ more often means 'divorce,' and right after these lines Maecenas started seeking the embraces and kisses of his wife (*moriens quaerebat amatae / coniugis amplexus oscula verba manus*); the final two thirds of the poem are Maecenas' good wishes for Augustus and we hear absolutely nothing about his wife in the poem except for this brief mention. Perhaps the poet envisioned a later period of reconciliation between husband and wife, however long that took to happen, and had Maecenas almost mention their divorce, a thought he wisely cuts short in view of the fact that he is addressing the man responsible for it.[28]

At the end of his obituary for Maecenas Dio (55,6,5) mentions that Augustus was moved upon learning that Maecenas made him heir to most of his estate despite his involvement with Terentia. The will suggests that Maecenas and Terentia had no children and ancient writers mention no offspring. Her absence from

---

24 Guarino 1992, 137–146.
25 Byrne 2006, 83–111.
26 Guarino 1992, 137 suggests it was her insistence on the divorce that disturbed Maecenas, not her withholding of sex.
27 Duff and Duff 1935, 135.
28 Ellis 1907, 15 writes that Maecenas' last thoughts are partly on his wife Terentia and partly on Augustus 'whose intimacy with Terentia could not but disturb the last moments of her husband.' But his deathbed words (lines 11–34) are strictly addressed to and concern Augustus. Ellis does not connect *discidium* with divorce.

Maecenas' will could mean that Terentia predeceased him, or that the divorce between them had at last become final and she had no legal claim to his estate, or that she was alive but had enough money of her own and did not need to inherit more.[29] A marble columbarium that dates to the end of first century BCE bears the inscription for one of its members 'Eros Senecio of Terentia and Maecenas.' The inscription seems to be later than 8 BCE, which would indicate that Terentia survived Maecenas, since Senecio was still in her possession and had not become part of Augustus' property along with Maecenas' other slaves that were willed to the emperor in 8 BCE.[30] If Guarino is correct that Augustus initiated the lawsuit in the *Digest*, then Terentia outlived both Maecenas and her appeal.

We first meet Fortunata in the *Cena* when Encolpius notices a woman bustling about and asks a fellow guest who she is (*Sat.* 37).[31] The freedman Hermeros provides an answer: she is Fortunata, Trimalchio's wife, and the first thing he highlights is her great wealth: she measures coins by the bushel (*nummos modio metitur*).[32] At one time you wouldn't have wanted to take bread from her hand, though now she's on top of the world, and from this we start to gather that Fortunata is not unlike the goddess 'Fortuna,' complete with highs and lows.[33] She is Trimalchio's 'everything' (*topanta*), able to convince him that it is nighttime in the middle of the day. Trimalchio has no clue how much he's worth, but this *lupatria*, 'she wolf,' provides for everything.[34] She is *sicca*, 'dry,' and *sobria*, 'sober,' the same adjectives Seneca uses twice with the implication that to be *siccus* and *sobrius* was good,[35] though Hermeros' use of the words is not as flattering.[36] Hermeros continues that Fortunata has a bad tongue

---

29 Hammond 1980, 270–271.
30 Hammond 1980, 270–271 is hesitant to fix too firm a date on the inscription, and acknowledges Terentia may have predeceased Maecenas, though Senecio's inscription could indicate she outlived him; cf. 271–272 on the possibility that others of the deceased in the columbarium belonged to Terentia and Maecenas.
31 For interpretations on Fortunata as a character in the *Satyricon*, see Malone, Regúnaga, and Rivara 2001, and Cicu 1991.
32 Smith 1975, 79–82 notes that this is one of many proverbial expressions used in this introductory description.
33 Malone, Regúnaga, and Rivara 2001, 118 state that Fortunata is hardly 'fortunate,' her name instead signaling the precariousness of life for women like her bound in a sort of servitude to their husbands.
34 The word seems to be a hybrid of Latin *lupa* with a Greek suffix; Smith 1975, 81. Neumann 1980 argues for the reading *lupatris* and not a hybrid.
35 Cf. *Ep.* 18,4 describing a man of self-control amid the drunken populace, and *Ep.* 114,3 describing the *ingenium* of the man who is *sanus*, *compositus*, *gravis*, and *temperans*.
36 Smith 1975, 81 notes the references in Seneca without noting the positive implications of the context or that the phrase occurs just before Seneca begins his most scathing tirade against the

with a tendency to gossip.[37] Before abruptly switching to Trimalchio's good fortune, Hermeros concludes his description of Fortunata by saying 'whom she loves, she loves, whom she does not love, she does not love.' The goddess Fortuna stands with the three *Parcae* at the end of Trimalchio's success story in the picture that engrosses Encolpius upon entering the house (*Sat.* 29,6), and Trimalchio isn't the only freedman at the *Cena* to enjoy her favor (cf. *Sat.* 43,7). But she is not always favorable – even Trimalchio failed in his first business venture, and all ancients knew Fortuna was fickle and unpredictable, a point Trimalchio himself makes in an epigram (*Sat.* 55,3). The same unpredictability applies to Fortunata.

Foreign freedmen sought out Roman women to marry because of their knowledge of Roman household management and because they carried a higher social status and greater respectability.[38] Fortunata displays the good qualities of a Roman matron most of the time, as when we first meet her in *Sat.* 37,2: despite Hermeros' unflattering portrait, Fortunata is deeply engaged in tending to the banquet operations (*huc atque illuc discurreret*). She is busy doing the same thing when Habinnas asks after her at *Sat.* 67,1–3, and Trimalchio comments on her need to take care of business before she can relax. At *Sat.* 73,5 she has prepared the next spread for the drunken guests after a much needed bath, and she grinds pepper at *Sat.* 74,1 for the rooster that was about to be cooked. She is first to grieve openly, cup in hand, at the mere idea of her husband's death (*Sat.* 54,2), and she is first to weep, this time following her husband's cue, after Trimalchio recited his own epitaph (*Sat.* 72,1). Good household management and devotion to her husband are the main qualities of a Roman wife, and Fortunata has a right to brag about her *diligentia* as *mater familias* to her friend Scintilla (*Sat.* 67,11).

Fortunata nevertheless sometimes makes life difficult for her husband, the first of many qualities she shares with Terentia. It is interesting that Trimalchio is especially sensitive to Fortunata's disdain or criticism: sometimes, presumably in more sober moments, she could persuade Trimalchio to behave better, though

---

intemperate Maecenas; Smith also cites Martial 12,30 for the collocation of the same adjectives, but does not note that Martial's use of the adjectives is more like Petronius' than Seneca's in that the words are not meant to be flattering. Smith concludes that the expression is proverbial, but the sense is not the same in all three authors. Salanitro 1990 focuses on the adjectives in Petronius with Martial's use because in both instances the words occur together without a conjunction, and she argues that they are designed to convey a sense of avarice, not sobriety.
37 If Smith 1975, 81 has correctly interpreted the words *pica pulvinaris* ('magpie on the couch').
38 Salonius 1927–1929, 7.

just as often he reverted to his true nature.[39] Trimalchio is not offended when Ascyltus and Giton titter at the lowbrow ways of freedmen (*Sat.* 57,1 and 58,1), but he reacts sharply to Fortunata's laughter at his candor regarding his stomach ailment (*Sat.* 47,5). This occurs when Trimalchio returns from using the facilities and regales his guests with philosophical and practical toilet talk: he tries to treat a distasteful subject with gentlemanly tact,[40] and when Fortunata laughs at his mention of bowel troubles, he announces to the guests that her own problems strike at night and render him sleepless (*rides, Fortunata, quae soles me nocte desomnem facere?*). Her criticism hits a nerve at *Sat.* 74,10–12: Trimalchio openly displays affection for a young slave boy, and Fortunata explodes with cursing and insults. His reaction to her displeasure is so violent that divorce seems imminent.[41] He hits her in the face with a cup, and recalls her unseemly past and current respectability, which she owes to his goodwill; he claims that he remains childless despite other marriage offers out of loyalty to her, sticking an ax in his own leg (*ipse mihi asciam in crus impegi*).[42] Her criticism makes him so angry he no longer wants her statue on his monument, and he announces that she is not allowed to attend his funeral (*Sat.* 74,13). But after all these harsh words, he recalls a *rem piam* of Fortunata (*Sat.* 76,7), namely, her willingness to sacrifice her own possessions for him when an early business venture failed. Even when he is most angry with her, Trimalchio cannot help but recall her sense of duty to him, which exceeds her duties as *mater familias*. He continues to seethe, referring to her twice as a viper (*Sat.* 77,2 and 4), but at this point he is venting in general: by including Fortunata's act of devotion in his autobiography and acknowledging the sacrifice of childlessness that he made for her, he reveals that his union with Fortunata is firm, their loyalty mutual.[43] He had complained earlier that she was self-inflated like the proverbial frog (*at inflat se tanquam rana*, *Sat.* 74,13), but he acknowledges that he was a frog once himself (*sic vester amicus, qui fuit rana, nunc est rex*, *Sat.* 77,6): they are two of a kind. She might drive him to distraction, but he stays with her.

---

39 Cf. *Sat.* 52,10: Trimalchio almost joined the pantomimes until Fortunata reminded him that such behavior was beneath him; *nihil autem tam inaequale erat; name modo Fortunatam suam revertebatur modo ad naturam.*
40 See Castorina 1973, 26 and Maiuri 1945, 37–38 for Trimalchio's sincerity on the subject.
41 Tandoi 1970, 452. For the intensity of Fortunata's reaction, see Schievenin 1976, 299.
42 The childless marriage is another negative feature of *liberti* as a social class; see Malone, Regúnaga, and Rivara 2001, 123. Cicu 1991, 99 speculates from *Sat.* 74,13 ('*quid enim' inquit 'ambubaiam non meminisse! de machina illam sustuli'*) that Fortunata was probably put up for sale near the end of her career as a flute player because her former owner wanted to get rid of her.
43 Schievenin 1976, 302; cf. Tandoi 1970, 443–452; Cicu 1991 deals specifically with the way Petronius gradually reveals Fortunata's *humanitas* over the course of the *cena*.

Nevertheless, the marriage has its ups and downs, which, as we have seen, also describes the marriage of Terentia and Maecenas. Romeo Schievenin makes an interesting argument that Fortunata misunderstood the nature of Trimalchio's affection for the slave mentioned above, that Trimalchio did not have erotic feelings for a boy, as Fortunata assumed, but rather fatherly feelings for a youth whose native intelligence was leading him on the same path to success that Trimalchio once followed: the slave was the closest thing Trimalchio would have to a real son in view of his admitted childlessness.[44] But Schievenin still has to admit that boy favorites bothered Roman wives, especially when it came to public displays of affection for them, as seen in Scintilla's annoyance at Habinnas' praises for his *deliciae* (*Sat.* 69,1–2). Perhaps Terentia felt similar jealousy and humiliation regarding Maecenas' very public love for Bathyllus, the Alexandrian freedman and famous pantomime. Dio (54,17,5) relates that Bathyllus won a dispute with a fellow actor because Maecenas, infatuated with his former slave, used his influence with Augustus.[45] Horace perhaps alludes to Maecenas' passion for Bathyllus in *Epod.* 14, where he tells Maecenas that he cannot finish his iambics because he has been afflicted by a love no less powerful than the love for the Samian Bathyllus that afflicted Anacreon.[46] Trimalchio's household abounds in pantomimes and panotmime-like displays, not to mention boys from Alexandria (cf. *Sat.* 31,7; *Sat.* 68,7–8).[47] Alexandrian boys are recognizable signs of decadence and luxury,[48] but they are not generally connected with pantomime, and Petronius' use of pantomime imagery on the two occasions he mentions Trimalchio's Alexandrian boys could stem from a sly desire to reference the relationship between Maecenas and Bathyllus, a recherché treat for the learned. The relationship was still the subject of discussion a century after Maecenas'

---

44 Schievenin 1973, 295–302.
45 The elder Seneca, *Contr.* pf. 10,8, and Dio 54,17, 5 indicate that Bathyllus was a freedman of Maecenas; see Grysar 1834, 76. For Bathyllus' fame long after his death see Macrob. *Sat.* 2,7; for his Alexandrian origins see Ath. 1,20d; for Maecenas' fondness for Bathyllus see Tac. *Ann.* 1,54,2 and Dio 54,17,5.
46 Hor. *Epod.* 14,9–10. Griffin, 1984, 194: 'The spicy underlying hint is of Maecenas' scandalous intrigue with an actor named Bathyllus. Horace slyly introduces the name, but as if it were only that of the beloved of a long-dead Greek poet.'
47 See Panayotakis 1995, 76 on the beautiful boy who distributes grapes to the guests while singing and impersonating Dionysus (*Sat.* 41,6): 'The boy must have been performing three variations on the pantomime-theme of Dionysus (cf. Luc. *De Salt.* 39), whereby the slave has been playing the part of both the dancer and the chorus who accompanied with his song the gestures of the silent pantomime.'
48 Smith 1975, 65.

death (cf. Tac. *Ann.* 1,54 and Dio 54,17,5): what must the gossip have been like for Terentia to bear?

There are more obvious similarities between the two women besides childlessness, an unstable marriage, and rivalry with young boys. Steele stopped short at pressing the fact that both names have four syllables since there is no metrical correspondence.[49] I would like to point out that there is a metrical correspondence if and when Terentia is the Terentilla of Antony's letter. If Antony could refer to Terentia as Terentilla, then perhaps in later periods educated men recalled the diminutive form of her name alongside the more proper form: the play on an alternate form was another clue for his audience as they followed Petronius' narrative.

Like Terentia, Fortunata seems to have aroused the passion of a man who is not her husband: when the jovial Habinnas barges into the *Cena* he is overly concerned to see Fortunata and threatens to leave if she does not appear immediately (*Sat.* 67,1–3). As Fortunata chatters with Habinnas' wife Scintilla, Habinnas stands up and with too great familiarity tosses Fortunata's legs onto the couch, exposing her knees (*Sat.* 67,12); this scene may depict the spontaneously good-natured, lowbrow antics of freedmen,[50] but Habinnas is altogether too free with his attention to another man's wife, and perhaps we are to assume there is something going on between Trimalchio's good friend and his wife, just as there was something going on between Maecenas' good friend and his wife.[51]

Fortunata likes to dance and not in a very lady-like way (*cordacem nemo melius ducit*, *Sat.* 52,8; cf. *Sat.* 70,10).[52] A note in the Ps. Acro commentary claims that the dancing *domina Licymnia* in Horace *Odes* 2,12 is really Maecenas' wife Terentia.[53] Scholars are not entirely convinced the claim is true,[54] but Petronius

---

49 Steele 1920, 284.
50 Schievenin 1976, 300–301; see also Malone, Regúnaga, and Rivara 2001, 123, who note that this sort of behavior would have been unacceptable in higher circles.
51 Preston 1915, 262–263 briefly refers to this episode as an example of 'out-and-out buffoonery' for comic effect, and the cry Fortunata utters (*au au*) is reminiscent of comedy (cf. Smith 1975, 189 for Donatus on Ter. *Eun.* 899: '*au interiectio est perturbatae mulieris*'). But the familiarity Habinnas displays with Trimalchio's wife is itself eye-catching.
52 Smith 1975, 141: 'the precise nature of this dance is more doubtful than its obscenity.' Cicu 1991, 80 observes that Petronius leaves it to the reader to figure out that such a sexy dance was a bad choice for a fat, graceless freedwoman.
53 For the text, which occurs as a note with *Sat.* 1,2,64, see Davis 1975, 71.
54 Syme 1939, 342 once accepted that Terentia was the Licymnia of *Odes* 2,12, but later (1986, 390) he changed his mind: 'Scholiasts are often bold or silly in their assertions.' Davis 1975, 70–83 offers a vigorous argument against the identification, but West 1998, 83–86 uses what is known about Maecenas to argue that Horace may well have had Terentia in mind in this

could have been aware of the rumored identification when filling in the details of his portrait of Fortunata. Horace's popularity under Nero had reached an all-time high, as seen in Persius' imitation of his satires and Caesius Bassus' imitation of his lyrics.[55] Petronius might have known about the identification of Horace's Licymnia and used it along with Terentia's mercurial temperament as an analogue for Fortunata. Such a connection would add a new dimension to the humor in Fortunata's fondness for dancing. A Fortunata-Terentia identification would likewise enhance the episode mentioned previously at *Sat.* 47,5 when Fortunata laughed at Trimalchio's detailed discussion about his bowels: Seneca claims that Terentia kept Maecenas from sleeping by denying him sex and forcing him to seek relief in wine and calming sounds (*cui [Maecenati] amoribus anxio et morosae uxoris cotidiana repudia deflenti somnus per symphoniarum cantum ex longinquo lene resonantium quaeritur? Prov.* 3,10); Trimalchio says Fortunata keeps him sleepless at night not from spite but from her need to seek release from her own stomach problems (*rides, Fortunata, quae soles me nocte desomnem facere? Sat.* 47,5). The implication of a loss of sleep connected to a need for release would have been significant to anyone who was aware of Seneca's original criticism.

I realize that the Terentia/Fortunata connection rests on a lot of 'what ifs' and that this thesis is hardly likely to persuade everyone. But if we agree that Trimalchio is endowed with characteristics that Seneca had used to describe Maecenas, and that Petronius' audience would have read or heard the *Epistles* in which Seneca vehemently criticized Maecenas, then it is not too far of a stretch to assume that Petronius would not stop at Senecan imagery in producing a character with clear attachments to Maecenas. He would test his audience's awareness of the real Maecenas, and this would include allusions to Maecenas' difficult marriage and scandalous wife. Fortunata is a true type, a shrewish and frugal wife, but she finds a suitable analogue in Terentia, so much so that the result suggests an intentional parallel.

---

poem. For other opinions see Nisbet and Hubbard 1978, 180–182 and 185; André 1967, 25 n. 4; Williams 1962, 36–38. Cicu 1991, 79–80 takes the scholiast at his word as support that dancing had become respectable for upper-class women by Horace's time, a change in attitude since Sallust's slur on Sempronia. It may be relevant that Maecenas' Bathyllus helped turn the *cordax* into an Italian dance (Ath. 1,20e).

55 Such imitation inspired scholarly commentaries on Horace in the next generation; see Mayer 1982, 313–315 and Lo Monaco 1995, 1211–1212.

Bibliography

André, J.-M. 1967. *Mécène: Essai de biographie spirituelle*, Annalues Littéraires de l'Université de Besançon 86, Paris: Les Belles Lettres.
Arkenburg, J.S. 1993. 'Licinii Murenae, Terentii Varrones, and Varrones Murenae', *Historia* 42, 326–351 and 471–491.
Atkinson, K.M.T. 1960. 'Constitutional and Legal Aspects of the Trials of Marcus Primus and Varro Murena', *Historia* 9, 440–473.
Bagnani, G. 1954a 'The House of Trimalchio', *AJP* 75, 16–39.
Bagnani, G. 1954b. 'Trimalchio', *Phoenix* 8, 77–91.
Bodel, J. 1999. 'The *Cena Trimalchionis*', in: H. Hofmann (ed.), *Latin Fiction: The Latin Novel in Context*, London/New York: Routledge. 38–51.
Boyce, B. 1991. *The Language of the Freedmen in Petronius' Cena Trimalchionis*, Leiden et al.: Brill.
Billerbeck, M. 1990. 'Philology at the Imperial Court', *G&R* 37, 191–203.
Byrne, S. 2006. 'Petronius and Maecenas: Seneca's Calculated Criticism', in: S. Byrne, E. Cueva, J. Alvares (eds.), *Authors, Authority, and Interpreters in the Ancient Novel. Essays in Honor of Gareth L. Schmeling*, ANS 5, Groningen: Barkuis Publishing & Groningen University Library. 83–111.
Byrne, S. 2007. 'Maecenas and Petronius' Trimalchio Maecenatianus', *AN* 5, 31–50.
Cameron, A. 1969. 'Petronius and Plato', *CQ* 19, 367–370.
Castorina, E. 1973. 'La lingua di Petronio e la figura di Trimalchione', *SicGymn* 26, 18–40.
Cicu, L. 1991. 'Fortunata', *Sandalion* 14, 63–102.
Davis, G. 1975. 'The Persona of Licymnia: A Revaluation of Horace, *Carm*. 2.12', *Philologus* 119, 70–83.
Duff, J.W., and Duff, A.M. 1935. *Minor Latin Poets*. Loeb Classical Library, Cambridge: Harvard University Press.
Ellis, R. 1907. *The Elegiae in Maecenatem*, London: Oxford University Press.
Evenepoel, W. 1990. 'Maecenas: A Survey of Recent Literature', *AncSoc* 21, 99–117.
Gardthausen, V. 1896. *Augustus und seine Zeit*, Vol. 2, Leipzig: Scientia Verlag Aalen.
Griffin, J. 1984. 'Augustus and the Poets: *Caesar, qui cogere posset*', in: F. Millar, E. Segal (eds.), *Caesar Augustus: Seven Aspects*, Oxford: Clarendon Press. 189–218.
Grysar, P. 1834, 'Über den Pantomimus der Römer', *RhM* 2, 30–80.
Guarino, A. 1992. 'Mecenate e Terenzia', *Labeo* 38, 137–146.
Hammond, M. 1980. 'An Unpublished Latin Funerary Inscription of Persons Connected with Maecenas', *HSCP* 84, 263–277.
Hanslik, R. 1953. 'Horaz und Varro Murena', *RhM* 96, 282–287.
Lo Monaco, F. 1995. 'Note sull' esegesi oraziana antica', in: L. Belloni, G. Milanese, A. Porro (eds.), *Studia classica Iohnanni Tarditi oblata*, Milan: Vita e pensiero. 1203–1224.
Maiuri, A. 1945. *La Cena di Trimalchione*, Naples: Casa editrice Raffaele Pironti.
Malone, P., Regúnaga, A., and Rivara, C.. 2001. '*Noluisses de manu illius panem accipere*. Fortunata en el Satyricon', *Circe* 6, 111–128.
Martini, R. 1995. 'Di una causa giudizaria, inter Terentiam et Maecenatem', *RSA* 25, 178–185.
Mayer, R. 1982. 'Neronian Classicism', *AJP* 103, 305–318.
Nisbet, R.G.M., and Hubbard, M.. 1970 and 1978. *A Commentary on Horace Odes*, 2 vols, Oxford: Clarendon Press.

Neumann, G. 1980. 'Lupatria in Petron c.37,6 und das Problem der hybriden Bildungen', WJA 6:173–180.
Panayotakis, C. 1995. *Theatrum Arbitri: Theatrical Elements in the Satirica of Petronius*, Leiden et al.: Brill.
Paturzo, F. 1999. *Mecenate: il ministro d'Augusto*, Cortona: Calosci Ediore.
Petersmann, H. 1998. 'Maecenas, Nasidienus, und Trimalchio', in: A. E. Radke (ed.), *Candide Iudex: Beiträge zur augusteischen Dichtung. Festschrift für Walter Wimmel zum 75. Geburtstag*, Stuttgart: Franz Steiner. 269–277.
Preston, K. 1915. 'Some Sources of Comic Effect in Petronius', CP 10, 260–269.
Révay, J. 1922. 'Horaz und Petron', CP 17, 202–212.
Rose, K. F. C. 1971. *The Date and Author of the Satyricon*, Leiden: Brill.
Salanitro, M. 1990. 'La moglie di Trimalchione e un amico di Marziale', A&R 35, 17–25.
Salonius, A.H. 1927–1929. 'Trimalchio und seine Gäste', in: *Commentationes Humanarum Litterarum II*, Helsingfors: Akademische Buchhandlung. 5–38.
Schievenin, R. 1976. 'Trimalcione e il *puer non inspeciosus* (Petron. 75,5)', BStudLat 6, 295–302.
Schmeling, G. L. 1996. 'The *Satyrica* of Petronius', in: G. Schmeling (ed.), *The Novel in the Ancient World*, Leiden et al.: Brill. 457–490.
Sealey, R. 1961. 'The Political Attachments of L. Aelius Seianus', Phoenix 15, 97–114.
Shero, L. R. 1923. 'The *Cena* in Roman Satire', CP 18, 126–43.
Smith, M. S. 1975. *Petronii Artbitri Cena Trimalchionis*, Oxford: Clarendon Press.
Steele, R. B. 1920. 'Literary Adaptions and References in Petronius', CJ 15, 279–293.
Stockton, D. 1965. 'Primus and Murena', Historia 14, 18–40.
Studer, G. 1843. 'Über das Zeitalter des Petronius Arbiter', RhM 2, 89–91.
Sullivan, J. P. 1968a. *The Satyricon of Petronius: A Literary Study*, Bloomington: Indiana University Press.
Sullivan, J. P. 1968b. 'Petronius, Seneca, and Lucan: A Neronian Literary Feud?' TAPA 99, 453–467.
Sullivan, J. P. 1985. *Literature and Politics in the Age of Nero*, Ithaca: Cornell University Press.
Sumner, G. V. 1965. 'The Family Connections of L. Aelius Seianus', Phoenix 19, 134–145.
Sumner, G. V. 1978. 'Varrones Murenae', HSCP 82, 187–195.
Swan, M. 1966. 'The Consular *Fasti* of 23 B.C. and the Conspiracy of Varro Murena', HSCP 71, 235–247.
Syme, R. 1939. *The Roman Revolution*, Oxford: Clarendon Press.
Syme, R. 1986. *The Augustan Aristocracy*, Oxford: Clarendon Press.
Tandoi, V. 1970. 'Una proposita di matrimonio per Trimalchione (Petr., Satyr. 74,15)', in: *Studia Florentina Alexandro Ronconi Sexagenario Oblata*. Rome, Edizioni dell'Ateneo. 431–453.
Thibault, J. C. 1964. *The Mystery of Ovid's Exile*, Berkeley/Los Angeles: University of California Press.
Treggiari, S. 1973. 'Cicero, Horace, and Mutual Friends: Lamiae and Varrones Murenae', Phoenix 27, 245–61.
Verdière, R. 1971. 'Un amour secret d'Ovide', AC 40, 623–648.
Verdière, R. 1983. 'Caesarea puella', Helmantica 34, 619–624.
West, D. 1991. '*Cur me Querelis* (Horace, *Odes* 2.17)', AJP 112, 45–52.
West, D. 1998. *Horace Odes II: Vatis Amici*, Oxford: Clarendon Press.
Williams, G. 1962. 'Poetry in the Moral Climate of Augustan Rome', JRS 52, 36–38.

Christoph Kugelmeier
Elements of Ancient Novel and Novella in Tacitus

Abstract: This paper aims to examine the way in which Tacitus in the books of his *Annals* concerning the reign of Nero makes use of ancient novelistic literature and to what purpose he employs novelistic motifs in writing history. The hypothesis that he does indeed make use of such means is confirmed by many instances; examples include certain passages from the books concerning the reign of Nero (13–16), especially his relationship with his mother Agrippina. This method of writing appears to be typical of Tacitus, who in this respect stands for a great part of ancient historiography. In writing history, dramatization is achieved not only by means of the writer's art but frequently also by direct recourse to the features not only of fictional literature and dramatic poetry, but also of novels and novellae.

Only with the greatest caution may we construct an image of the Roman emperors of the 1st c. CE. In a popular view of this era, often shaped by modern films and historical novels, individuals like Caligula or Nero are conceived of as beasts in human form. Neither may the influence be ignored which derives from the images of the despotic *principes* created by ancient historiographers like Tacitus, an influence felt strongly even today. After centuries of historical criticism and the revision of older views, what we nevertheless find upon opening any schoolbook are the historians and biographers of antiquity cited as evidence for historical facts which their authority serves to establish once and for all. One gets the impression that, while historical and philological research may have expressed many doubts for some time now, and in great detail, it must still struggle to make itself heard, even though it has long been apparent that caution is very appropriate in this case. There is not only the fair judgement of long deceased persons that is at the stake, but much more, and that is knowing whether or not the image we get of these persons is part of a skilful strategy of historical narrative which in turn serves the biases of various authors, either political-ideological or personal. To put it more exactly, we should not ask ourselves nowadays so much whether in drawing a picture of the epoch of Nero we can believe without reservation Tacitus, Suetonius or Cassius Dio (the third of our principal literary sour-

Christoph Kugelmeier, Universität des Saarlandes (Saarbrücken)

ces for this period). As I have already said, it is apparent that we have every reason for doubt. Rather, we should pose the question of why we still feel in a certain sense *obliged* to believe the words of historiographers who seem to fulfil their task so well, why it is so difficult for us to free ourselves from the effects of a well-written narrative which pretends to narrate only real facts. As far as Cassius Dio's totally negative description of the reign of Nero is concerned, the gap of time alone between his lifetime and the events he describes suffices to warn us against being too credulous; Suetonius raises doubts by the sheer quantity of anecdotical material obviously brought together tendentiously.[1] The problem, however, becomes most delicate in the case of Tacitus. After all, he is widely considered to be the most important Roman historian just because of his self-professed fidelity to acknowledged facts.[2] And no less a scholar than Ronald Syme, in his standard study on Tacitus, maintains that 'distrust' (namely in respect to unwarranted rumours) is 'the prime quality of Cornelius Tacitus'.[3] It may be then cause for some disquiet to find that the Roman historian himself exploits rather a lot of unwarranted rumours as a main ingredient of his narrative.

Admittedly, the *principles* of his composition have often been described as 'dramatic', without meaning that Tacitus shifted deliberately to another literary genre. Which effect is meant can be clearly seen at the very beginning of the Nero books of the *Annals*:

prima novo principatu mors Iunii Silani proconsulis Asiae ignaro Nerone per dolum Agrippinae paratur. (13,1)

The first death under the new emperor, that of Junius Silanus, proconsul of Asia, was, without Nero's knowledge, planned by the treachery of Agrippina.[4]

This passage (so Erich Koestermann maintains in his commentary ad loc.)[5] is marked 'with emphasis and significance as the beginning of a new *dramatic*

---

[1] The most recent state of the question is given by Wallace-Hadrill 1995, Pausch 2004 and Power / Gibson 2014.
[2] Tacitus himself emphasizes impartiality as his programme for writing history at the very beginning of the *Annals*, 1,1, when he claims to write *sine ira et studio*. In a recent survey Schmal 2016, 116 offers (rightly) just the opposite conclusion: 'Tacitus ist alles andere als ein objektiver Historiker'. The artificial shaping of Tacitus' 'subtle subjectivity' (and that of other historians as well) still demands systematical study. Cf. also Edwards 1993, 28.
[3] Syme 1958–1959, 398.
[4] English translations from Tacitus' Annals are by Church and Brodribb 1888.
[5] Koestermann 1963–1968: 'markant und bedeutungsschwanger als Beginn einer neu einsetzenden, dramatischen (tragischen) Entwicklung gekennzeichnet'. See also Mendell 1986, 460.

(tragic) development'. In particular, the conflict already hinted at here between Agrippina, the mother, and Nero, her son, rises in Tacitus' narrative to a tragic tension, finally to erupt in a murderous explosion. At this crucial part of his story, the murder of Agrippina in book 14, Tacitus not only composes in a dramatic style but quotes a piece of literature that we actually know to be a drama: the *praetexta Octavia* attributed to Seneca[6]. This fact is important for the present theme, as the undoubtedly deliberate recourse to a drama leads us to consider whether Tacitus borrows from fictional literature in other passages of his narrative, too. And indeed, we do not have far to go to recognize, precisely in the narrative concerning Agrippina, the influence of ancient fictional literature, and more particularly of the ancient Greek novel and novella.

In dealing with the relationship between Nero and Agrippina, Tacitus more often than usual applies his method of insinuation, of inserting *rumores* into an apparently objective rendering of different opinions.[7] In the present case he would be particularly justified in that, because naturally there were no witnesses to the private dealings between mother and son. The historian's authority was so successful that even so monstrous a charge stuck in the memory of posterity, namely that a mother, plotting to secure her influence, was willing to seduce her own son.[8] It is true that some commentators (e.g. Koestermann at 13,13,2) recognize that the limits of credibility are being transgressed here. But Koestermann only notes that Tacitus was struggling with this 'problem'. The real problem consists in the use of such slanderous *topoi* often enough to raise suspicion about their credibility. Doubts of this sort are stirred when these *topoi* are used for *political* defamation – the sort of slander easily uttered because no one will be able to test it.

Reproaches of this kind are directed already against Caligula (cf. Suetonius *Cal.* 23–24), who himself abuses Augustus. So we already see three emperors who have allegedly committed such monstrosities, 'good ones' (like Augustus) and 'bad ones' (like Caligula and Nero) – not to speak of the almost identical stories the *Historia Augusta* tells about such events in the families of Marcus Aurelius and Septimius Severus. We find astonishing parallels to the description of Nero's life also in other respects (fratricide, debaucheries at night in ill-famed

---

[6] See my forthcoming article (2017) 'Tacitus und die Macht der Nerobilder', in: T. Blank, F. K. Maier (eds.), Die sinfonischen Schwestern. Narrative Konstruktionen von 'Wahrheit' in der nachklassischen Geschichtsschreibung, Stuttgart: Franz Steiner Verlag, 327–344.
[7] For the important function of rumours in forming popular opinion at this time cf. Flaig 2003.
[8] *Ann.* 14,2.

taverns, incest).⁹ And this parallelism of narrative is taken as convincing proof of the credibility of these reproaches!¹⁰

But these are not the only such parallels. It has long been recognized, but not sufficiently appreciated, that a half-legendary person from Greek history shows a remarkable likeness to Nero.¹¹ Diogenes Laertius gives a βίος of Periander, the Corinthian tyrant (beginning of the 6th c. BCE), who was one of the Seven Sages as well as an archetype of the despotic ruler. There we read of him:

φησὶ δὲ Ἀρίστιππος ἐν πρώτῳ Περὶ παλαιᾶς τρυφῆς περὶ αὐτοῦ τάδε, ὡς ἄρα ἐρασθεῖσα ἡ μήτηρ αὐτοῦ Κράτεια συνῆν αὐτῷ λάθρα· καὶ ὃς ἥδετο. φανεροῦ δὲ γενομένου βαρὺς πᾶσιν ἐγένετο διὰ τὸ ἀλγεῖν ἐπὶ τῇ φωρᾷ. (D. L. 1,96)

Aristippus in the first book of his work *On the Luxury of the Ancients* accuses him of incest with his own mother Crateia, and adds that, when the fact came to light, he vented his annoyance in indiscriminate severity.¹²

---

9 HA 7,5,8–11 (on Commodus) *sororibus dein suis ceteris, ut dicitur, constupratis, consobrina patris complexibus suis iniuncta uni etiam ex concubinis matris nomen inposuit. uxorem, quam deprehensam in adulterio exegit, exactam relegavit et postea occidit ... nec inruentium in se iuvenum carebat infamia, omni parte corporis atque ore in sexum utrumque pollutus* (After debauching his other sisters, as it is said, he formed an amour with a cousin of his father, and even gave the name of his mother to one of his concubines. His wife, whom he caught in adultery, he drove from his house, then banished her, and later put her to death ... and he was not free from the disgrace of intimacy with young men, defiling every part of his body in dealings with persons of either sex; English translation by Magie 1979); cf. also 7,3,7 *vespera etiam per tabernas ad lupanaria volitavit* (in the evening he would ramble through taverns and brothels; the same translation), 10,21,7 (on Caracalla) *qui novercam suam – et quid novercam? matrem quin immo, in cuius sinu Getam filium eius occiderat, uxorem duxit* (who took his own stepmother to wife – stepmother did I say? – nay rather the mother on whose bosom he had slain Geta, her son; the same translation) and 13,10,1 (on Caracalla) *interest scire, quemadmodum novercam suam Iuliam uxorem duxisse dicatur. quae cum esset pulcherrima et quasi per neglegentiam se maxima corporis parte nudasset dixisset Antoninus 'vellem, si liceret', respondisse fertur 'si libet, licet. an nescis te imperatorem esse et leges dare, non accipere?'* (It is of interest to know the way in which they say he married his stepmother Julia. She was a very beautiful woman, and once when she displayed a considerable part of her person, as it were in carelessness, Antoninus (Caracalla) said, 'I should like to, if I might,' whereupon, they relate, she replied, 'If you wish, you may; are you not aware that you are the emperor and that you make the laws and do not receive them?'; the same translation). So here too the tyrannical, transgressive aspects of incest are emphasized; the sexual reproach becomes a means of political propaganda.
10 Cf. the many examples in Krenkel 1980 (2006). For the more general political implications see also Dorey 1962.
11 Cf. Champlin 2003, 107–110.
12 English translation by Hicks 1925.

The similarity to the rumour about Nero and Agrippina is evident; and Diogenes himself tells us where he has got this anecdotal material: it is from the author of a polemical book against the Academics by Aristippus of Cyrene, a pupil of Socrates and founder of the hedonistic Cyrenaic school; he presents an anecdote which he obviously has shaped in order to discredit the so-called 'wise' Periander as a tyrant.[13] The story recurs in the 17th tale of the Ἐρωτικὰ παθήματα ('Love Romances') of Parthenius.[14] If the anecdote about the incest in Aristippus' version, as known from Diogenes, bears obvious features of the 'wandering novel' (to use the title of an article by Ludwig Radermacher),[15] Parthenius further embellishes the legend with novelistic details:[16] Periander's mother, Crateia, falls in love with her son and indeed succeeds in starting an erotic relationship with him by pretending to be a *postillon d'amour* for a woman who, she says, is in love with Periander but unwilling to reveal her identity. When they have met in secret several times Periander at last discovers the truth. How widespread this novelistic incest-motif was is shown by the fact that the famous Babylonian queen Semiramis is said to have attempted a very similar relationship with her son Ninyas. This too ended in the violent death of the temptress at the hand of her son, as we are told by Justin, *Epitome* 1,12: *ad postremum, cum concubitum filii petisset, ab eodem interfecta est* (at last, when she sought to sleep with her son, she was kil-

---

13 Wilamowitz-Moellendorff, U. von 1914, 48: 'es ist die alte tyrannenfabel, das μητράσι μίγνυσθαι (a quotation from the mythographer Conon, see below p. 84), von Periandros mit novellistischem detail erzählt'.
14 Also in Plutarch *De septem sapientium convivio*, *Mor.* 146d. For a list of acts of incest, see Hyginus *Fab.* 253. With regard to the novel, cf. e.g. Achilles Tatius *Leucippe and Clitophon*, where cousins fall in love with each other. Lightfoot 1999 ad loc. notes a parallel between Tacitus and Parthenius: compare *Ann.* 14,2,1 *comptam et incesto paratam* (she (Agrippina) presented herself attractively attired ... and offered him (Nero) her person) with Parthenius 17,4 ὡς ὅτι κράτιστα αὐτὴν ἀσκήσασα εἰσέρχεται παρὰ τὸν παῖδα (she (Crateia) decked herself out as well as she could and went in to her son; English translations from Parthenius always according to the edition of Lightfoot).
15 Radermacher 1942.
16 The following novelistic motifs can be recognized (according to Lightfoot 1999, 483): 1.) 'the tale of the unknown lover' 2.) 'unknown (clandestine) paramour', 3.) 'mother-son incest', 4.) 'boy unwittingly commits incest with his mother'. This method of narrative is typical for the sort of biography that ultimately stems from Peripatetic tradition; cf. Momigliano 1993, 79 on Hermippus, a contemporary of Callimachus and an important source for Diogenes' narrative on the Seven Sages: 'His interest in the frivolous, the morbid (death scenes), the paradoxical is well established: he went all out to captivate his readers by learned sensationalism'; 84: 'basic interest in discovering a variety of human characters had a philosophic root, but the wealth of strange details, of piquant anecdotes, was ultimately meant to satisfy the curiosity of the common reader.'

led by him).[17] As parallel versions recorded by Diodorus Siculus show (2,7 and 2,20,1–3), the legend of Semiramis goes back at least to Ctesias, a contemporary of Xenophon and himself a novelist in the guise of a historiographer.[18] But both he[19] and the mythographer Conon (living about the turn of the 1st c. BCE/CE)[20] make Ninyas, the son, attempt to lay hands on his mother, not in a sexual but in a political sense, by means of a political conspiracy. What has obviously happened is that Justin has combined in a novelistic manner the sexual assault on the mother with the (attempted) political assault on the kingdom, understood as 'Mother Earth' (for more examples see below p. 86 with n. 28).

An interesting political reason for inserting the scandal story about Periander into anti-Neronian historiography is that Parthenius offers a psychological explanation, as it were, for the later cruelty of the tyrant. According to Parthenius (17,1), Periander at the beginning of his rule had been quite 'mild and gentle' (ἐπιεικής τε καὶ πρᾶος; the terms ἐπιείκεια[21] and πραότης are equivalent to the Latin *clementia*,[22] by which the ideal ruler differs from the tyrant); after this incident (κἀκ τούτου), however,

παραπλὴξ ἦν νοῦ τε καὶ φρενῶν κατέσκηψέ τε εἰς ὠμότητα καὶ πολλοὺς ἀπέσφαξε τῶν πολιτῶν. (17,7)

he was stricken in mind and soul, plunging into savagery and murdering many of the citizens.

Herodotus characterizes in very similar language (but with a different motif) the radical change in the rule of Periander:

---

17 The parallel is first shown by Krappe 1940, 468. – My translation.
18 Cf. Högemann 1999.
19 *FGrHist* 688 F 1,20.
20 *FGrHist* 26 F 1,9 = Photius *Bibl.* 186 p. 132 a f. (where Photius' interesting remarks shed light on how interchangeable are legends of this kind).
21 Defined by Aristotle *MM* 2,1,1 (1198b26): ἔστιν δὲ ἡ ἐπιείκεια καὶ ὁ ἐπιεικὴς ὁ ἐλαττωτικὸς τῶν δικαίων τῶν κατὰ νόμον (now Equity, and the equitable or considerate man, are distinguished by readiness to take less than their just legal right; English translation by Armstrong 1947).
22 On ἐπιείκεια cf. Dio 44,6,3 (consecration of the temple of the *Clementia Caesaris*) καὶ ναὸν αὐτῷ τῇ <τ'> Ἐπιεικείᾳ αὐτοῦ τεμενισθῆναι ἔγνωσαν ([they] ordered a temple to be consecrated to him and to his Clemency; English translation by Cary 1961); both terms appear combined in Plutarch *Caes.* 57,4 (referring to the same consecration) καὶ τό γε τῆς Ἐπιεικείας ἱερὸν οὐκ ἀπὸ τρόπου δοκοῦσι χαριστήριον ἐπὶ τῇ πραότητι ψηφίσασθαι (and certainly it is thought not inappropriate that the temple of Clemency was decreed as a thank-offering in view of his mildness; English translation by Perrin 1919); cf. Dahlmann 1970, 130.

ὁ τοίνυν Περίανδρος κατ' ἀρχὰς μὲν ἦν ἠπιώτερος τοῦ πατρός, ἐπείτε δὲ ὡμίλησε δι' ἀγγέλων Θρασυβούλῳ τῷ Μιλήτου τυράννῳ, πολλῷ ἔτι ἐγένετο Κυψέλου μιαιφονώτερος. (Hdt. 5,92 ζ 1)

> Now Periander was to begin with milder than his father, but after he had held converse by messenger with Thrasybulus the tyrant of Miletus, he became much more bloodthirsty than Cypselus.[23]

The passage from Herodotus clearly points to a long tradition of legendary biography concerning the Corinthian tyrant.[24]

We may feel here an anticipation, moreover, of the usual division of the rule of Nero in two parts, one before and one after the murder of his mother, the event that is always regarded as the crucial turning point for the worse.[25] If so, we might interpret Tacitus' reminiscence of the Periander legend via Parthenius as follows: From this time on the young *princeps*, gifted but easily led astray, once and for all enters upon the downward sloping path to despotism, and his personality can be analysed in terms of the traditional negative image of the typical tyrant, that is, of the gifted but unstable young ruler whose character deteriorates. For Periander is not without reason numbered among the Seven Sages; like Nero, he was regarded as a patron of fine arts and as a far-sighted ruler. Among other things he planned to dig a canal through the Isthmus of Corinth (according to Diogenes Laertius 1,99). As we know, several centuries later a Roman *princeps* took up this idea anew – Nero.[26] Here too the negative view of

---

23 English translation by Godley 1922.
24 For the obviously tragical elements in Herodotus' account of the Cypselid dynasty (generation curse, parallels with Orestes and Polynices) cf. Vernant 1982, 26–33.
25 It is true, however, that the concept of a relatively good *quinquennium Neronis* first appears at a later time; the term occurs in Aurelius Victor (relating the opinion of Trajan!) in his *Libellus de vita et moribus imperatorum* 5,2 (written about 360 CE): *procul differre cunctos principes Neronis quinquennio* (that all princes differed much from the five-year period of Nero; my translation); cf. Murray 1965. But Tacitus makes it clear that he regards all the events in connection with the year 59 as leading to the fatal break in Nero's life and reign. Already the passion for Poppaea, according to Tacitus the main motif for murdering Agrippina, is introduced by the ominous word: *non minus insignis eo anno [58] impudicitia magnorum rei publicae malorum initium fecit*, 13,45,1 (a profligacy equally notorious in that same year proved the beginning of great evils to the State), and surely not by accident the 13th book closes with an ill omen (the dying Ficus Ruminalis, 13,58; cf. the sensible explanation of the effect of this ending by Wuilleumier 1964, 104). After that the 14th book relates the never-ending chain of tragedies caused by the increasing *vitia* in Nero's personality. Tacitus finally frames his narrative of the fated disaster by noting that after the death of Burrus in 62 the political influence of Seneca, the third figure involved in the murder, is also broken and by remarking about Nero: *ad deteriores inclinabat*, 14,52,1 (began to lean on worse advisers). Cf. Syme 1958–1959, 262.
26 Suetonius *Nero* 19, Dio 63,16.

this plan does not come as a surprise. Economically it surely was sensible, but the anti-Neronian Roman authors represent it as an attack on nature. Both rulers, Periander as well as Nero, had already been the objects of allegations that they had broken the laws of nature by incest with their mothers, and with that, as it were, the subsequent violation of 'Mother Earth' by technical means had been ominously predicted.[27] Thus it seemed appropriate to connect the canal project too with the Periander tradition.[28]

Parthenius was far from unknown to the Romans of the 1st c. CE: Apart from his dedication of the 'Love Romances' to Cornelius Gallus and the notice that he was the teacher of Greek of no less a figure than Vergil,[29] we learn that the Emperor Tiberius in person favoured including the work in public libraries and thus made it possible for the Roman public to read and study this author more intensely.[30] Admittedly, we could also assume a direct influence of Herodotus on

---

27 It does not matter in this context whether Nero had been seduced by Agrippina or himself had made approaches to her, which Tacitus gives as an alternative (*Ann.* 14,2 *Fabius Rusticus non Agrippinae, sed Neroni cupitum id memorat* 'Fabius Rusticus tells us that it was not Agrippina, but Nero, who lusted for the crime'; cf. Koestermann 1963–1968, a.l.: ‚Dahinter steht offenbar das Bemühen, Seneca von jeder Mitverantwortung für den Muttermord zu entlasten') and Suetonius as the only version (*Nero* 28,2 *matris concubitum appetisse ... nemo dubitavit* 'that he entertained an incestuous passion for his mother ... was universally believed'; English translation by Rolfe 1959). The monstrous thing is in any case the involvement in the incest as such.

28 Related is the idea of having intercourse with or even raping the earth, conceived of as 'Mother Earth', which leads to the dominion over her. Plutarch *Caes.* 32 and Suetonius *Jul.* 7 tell about a dream of this kind Caesar had before crossing the Rubicon; already Plato *R.* 9 p. 571 c f. regards such a dream as a sign of the development of a tyrant. Cf. Delcourt 1944, 202–204 and my comments above, p. 83–84 with regard to the Semiramis legend. All this must be seen in the context of the typical image of the tyrant which in Tacitus' time was current in historiography; cf. Gernet 1968, 354 and Vernant 1982, 33: 'In rejecting all the rules which, for the Greeks [and Romans, we may add], are the foundation of communal life, the tyrant puts himself socially out of play. He is external to the network of relations which unites citizens, man with woman, father with son according to precise norms'.

29 Macrobius 5,17,18 = Parthenius test. 9 (a) Lightfoot; this testimony, however, is not above suspicion (cf. Lightfoot 1999, 15).

30 Suetonius *Tib.* 70 = Parthenius test. 3 Lightfoot *fecit et Graeca poemata imitatus Euphorionem et Rhianum et Parthenium, quibus poetis admodum delectatus scripta omnium et imagines publicis bibliothecis inter veteres et praecipuos auctores dedicavit; et ob hoc plerique eruditorum certatim ad eum multa de his ediderunt* '(Tiberius) composed Greek verse in imitation of Euphorion and Rhianus and Parthenius. He took great delight in these poets, collected all their writings, and consecrated their statues among the ancient classic authors in the public libraries; and for this reason many learned men vied with each other to publish long commentaries on their works'. Hadrian too was an admirer of Parthenius (test. 4 Lightfoot). For Parthenius' influence on Roman literature see Lightfoot 1999, 76–96.

the anti-Nero historians. The *pater historiae* was eagerly read in the time between Nero and Tacitus, according to Quintilian *Inst.* 9,4,18. We must, however, exclude the possibility that Tacitus in the passage we have discussed directly adopts his theme from the Greek historiographer, because in Herodotus no trace can be found of the incest-motif. Most probably Tacitus' narrative method can be interpreted as follows: He connected the Periander legend, already well known to the Greek historians, with his description of the life of Nero because it offered a striking parallel to the catastrophic change he saw in Nero's reign. In order to paint this in still stronger colours and to let the rumours about Nero which circulated during the lifetime of the emperor form part of his characterization, he combined this political analysis with the novelistic incest-motif which he took from Parthenius and which, as I have said, fit very well with the image of the typical tyrant applied to Nero.

The next link in this chain of novelistic reminiscences is the gloomy story about the death of the pregnant Poppaea, whom Nero is said to have killed by kicking her in the belly in a fit of rage.[31] As we find the same story in almost the same words in Diogenes Laertius (1,94) and again in the novelist Chariton (*Chaireas and Callirhoe* 1,4,12),[32] I am inclined to say, in the words of Roland Mayer:[33] 'we are asked to believe that history repeats itself' – or rather: that stories repeat themselves. Again the antiquity of the legend is testified to by Herodotus (3,50,1);[34] but here too a direct reception must be excluded, inasmuch as the Greek historian does not offer the decisive element, namely the method of killing (Tacitus also shows that there was another variant of the event). Herodotus tells the same story about the Persian king Cambyses, who he says killed his

---

31 Tacitus *Ann.* 16,6,1.
32 The date of *Chaireas and Callirhoe* is controversial. Müller 2006, 450 n. 19 with cogent (above all linguistic and stylistic) arguments pleads for the late Hellenistic period, possibly as early as the 1st c. BCE.
33 Mayer 1982; in this exemplary short paper he comes to the conclusion: 'If someone wanted to make of Nero the Roman Periander, it may be that poor Poppaea, without her husband's help, miscarried and died'.
34 Ἐπείτε γὰρ τὴν ἑωυτοῦ γυναῖκα Μέλισσαν Περίανδρος ἀπέκτεινε, συμφορὴν τοιήνδε οἱ ἄλλην συνέβη πρὸς τῇ γεγονυίῃ γενέσθαι (For after killing his own wife Melissa, Periander suffered yet another calamity on top of what he had already suffered; English translation by Godley 1922); cf. Suetonius *Nero* 35,3 *ictu calcis occidit, quod se ex aurigatione sero reversum gravida et aegra conviciis incesserat* (he caused her death too by kicking her when she was pregnant and ill, because she had scolded him for coming home late from the races; English translation by Rolfe 1959) = Dio 62,27,4 κυούσῃ γὰρ αὐτῇ λάξ, εἴτε ἑκὼν εἴτε καὶ ἄκων, ἐνέθορεν (either accidentally or intentionally he had leaped upon her with his feet while she was pregnant; English translation by Cary 1968).

own wife because he was angry about reproaches (3,32,4); he too is a paradigm of the type of the mad tyrant.

After Nero one more prominent person is rebuked for the same misdeed: Herodes Atticus is numbered among the company of those who are said to have planned to build a canal through the Isthmus! This story is told by Philostratus.[35]

Thus a wandering motif, taken not alone from the novelistic passages of earlier historiography but, as substantial correspondences show, from novelistic literature itself forms the basis of the rumours about Nero's private life. The fact that Tacitus gives room to these rumours at important places in his narrative must therefore be regarded not as proof for their historical credibility but just the other way round, as an indication of how he strove to confer as much as possible the image of the traditional tyrant upon his object, with the help of the *rumores*.

This method of writing appears to be typical of Tacitus, who in this respect is representative of a great deal of ancient historiography. In writing history, dramatization is achieved not only by means of the writers' art but frequently also by direct recourse to fictional literature, dramatic poetry as well as the novel. Thus Eduard Schwartz was able to call Tacitus 'nicht den letzten großen antiken Historiker, wohl aber den letzten großen antiken Dichter'.[36] This casts a somewhat dubious light on the authority of the Roman historiographer as a historical source. What is more, in ancient historiography emotional responses of the characters toward one another and toward the powers of fate are given priority over

---

[35] *Vitae sophistarum* 2,1,8 πληγεῖσαν δὲ ἐς τὴν γαστέρα τὴν γυναῖκα ἀποθανεῖν ἐν ὠμῷ τῷ τόκῳ (the woman died in premature childbirth from a blow in the belly; English translation by Wright 1921). Cf. Champlin 2003, 109; Ameling 1986; Fairweather 1974, 231–275, e.g. 270: 'We quite often find in the *Lives* [of Greek poets] stories for which there are close parallels in heroic mythology and romantic fiction' and 272: 'Popular legend, throughout the Hellenistic period and right into the time of the Roman Empire, liked to surround the lives of men of genius with marvels'. Fraenkel 1935, 625, 27–39 (quoted by Mayer and Ameling) hits the nail on the head: 'Es ist durchaus denkbar, daß das wirkliche Leben einmal die Tücke begeht, einen τόπος der konventionellen Literatenbiographie auch seinerseits hervorzubringen. Im Falle eines so boshaften Zusammentreffens würde der kritischen Methode bedauerlicherweise die Verifizierung einer interessanten Begebenheit unmöglich gemacht. Diese Gefahr ist aber bei der Natur unserer Überlieferung hundertmal geringer als die andere, daß wir auch das trivialste Cliché gläubig als Faktum buchen, weil wir jeden Zweifel von vornherein mit der Frage abwehren: warum soll es denn nicht so gewesen sein? Der Gewinn, daß man auf diese Art sogar eine farbige Homerbiographie schreiben kann, ist denn doch etwas teuer erkauft'. It seems, however, that ancient authors and readers were especially interested in this sort of colourfulness, even at the expense of historical truth.

[36] 'Not the last of the great historians, but of the great poets of antiquity,' Schwartz 1943, 125.

rational analysis of political, social or economic matters, which are the centre of attention in modern historical research. Carl Werner Müller rightly concludes: 'Dieser grundlegende Unterschied zur Geschichtsschreibung der Neuzeit rechtfertigt die Anwendung des Novellenbegriffs auf entsprechende historiographische Texte der Antike'.[37] To examine further the close relation between historiography and fictional literature, the novel but also tragedy, remains a task for the future, especially where motifs of this kind can be shown to have been adopted directly from such literature. This is a separate enterprise from the use of historical sources which themselves present novelistic motifs, above all Herodotus and the 'tragic historiography' of the Hellenistic period.[38] A critical examination of the strategies of writing used by the ancient historians may help to sharpen our awareness of certain distortions of historical truth, and to discover the instances in which narrating history becomes the telling of stories – then and now.

Bibliography

Aly, W. 1969. *Volksmärchen, Sage und Novelle bei Herodot und seinen Zeitgenossen. Eine Untersuchung über die volkstümlichen Elemente der altgriechischen Prosaerzählung*, Göttingen: Vandenhoeck & Ruprecht. (Original work published 1921)

Ameling, W. 1986. 'Tyrannen und schwangere Frauen', *Historia* 35, 507–508.

Armstrong, G. C. (ed. and trans.) 1947. *Aristotle. Oeconomica, Magna Moralia*, Cambridge: Harvard University Press; London: Heinemann.

Barrett, A.A. 1996. *Agrippina, Mother of Nero*, London: Batsford.

Barrett, A.A. 1996. *Agrippina. Sex, Power, and Politics in the Early Empire*, New Haven: Yale University Press. Reprinted 2001.

Cary, E. (ed. and trans.) 1961. *Dio's Roman History*, vol. I, Cambridge: Harvard University Press; London: Heinemann.

Champlin, E. 2003. *Nero*, Cambridge: Belknap Press of Harvard University Press.

Church, A. J., and Brodribb, W. J. (trans.) 1888. *Annals of Tacitus*, London/New York: MacMillan.

Cizek, E. 1997. *Néron*, Paris: Fayard. (Original work published 1982)

Dahlmann, H. 1970. 'Clementia Caesaris', in: *Kleine Schriften*, Hildesheim: Olms. 116–131. (Original work published 1934).

---

37 'This fundamental difference from modern historiography justifies the application of the term 'novelistic' to historiographical texts of this sort in antiquity', Müller 2006, 54.

38 Even here fictional sources can sometimes be recognized, cf. Aly 1921, and the important remarks by Moles 1993, 97: 'If a historian imitates a non-historian (as, in one sense, Herodotus regards Homer), whether for purposes of homage, rivalry, evocative effect, or supplementation of deficient material according to received stereotypes, factual distortion is certain, though it may vary greatly according to circumstances'.

Delcourt, M. 1944. *Oedipe ou la légende du conquérant*, Liège: Faculté de philosophie et lettres. (Reprinted Paris 1981)

Dorey, T. A. 1962. 'Adultery and Propaganda in the Early Roman Empire', *University of Birmingham Historical Journal* 8, 1–6.

Edwards, C. 1993. *Politics of Immorality in Ancient Rome*, Cambridge: Cambridge University Press. Reprinted 2002.

Fairweather, J. 1974. 'Fictions in the Biographies of Ancient Writers', *Ancient Society* 5, 231–275.

Flaig, E. 2003. 'Wie Kaiser Nero die Akzeptanz bei der Plebs urbana verlor. Eine Fallstudie zum politischen Gerücht im Prinzipat', *Historia* 52, 351–372.

Fraenkel, E. 1935. 'Naevius', in: *RE, Suppl.* VI, Stuttgart: Metzler. 622–640.

Gernet, L. 1968. *Anthropologie de la Grèce antique*, Paris: Maspero.

Ginsburg, J. 2006. *Representing Agrippina. Constructions of Female Power in the Early Roman Empire*, Oxford: Oxford University Press.

Godley, A. D. (trans.) 1922. *Herodotus. The Persian Wars*, vol. III, Cambridge: Harvard University Press; London: Heinemann.

Grant, M. 1989. *Nero*, New York: Dorset Press. (Original work published 1970)

Griffin, M. 1984. *Nero. The End of a Dynasty*, London/New York: Routledge. (Reprinted 2016).

Hicks, R. D. (ed. and trans.) 1925, Diogenes Laertius, *Lives of Eminent Philosophers*, 2 vols., Cambridge: Harvard University Press; London: Heinemann.

Högemann, P. 1999. 'Ktesias', in: *Der Neue Pauly*, vol. 6, Stuttgart/Weimar: Metzler. 874–875.

Holland, R. 2000. *Nero. The Man behind the Myth*, Stroud: Sutton. Reprinted 2006.

Krappe, A.H. 1940. 'La fin d'Agrippine', *Revue des Études Anciennes* 42, 466–472.

Krenkel, W. A. 1980. 'Sex und politische Biographie', *Wissenschaftliche Zeitschrift der Universität Rostock* 29, 65–76 = *Naturalia non turpia. Sex and Gender in Ancient Greece and Rome. Schriften zur antiken Kultur- und Sexualwissenschaft.* Ed. by C. Reitz and W. Bernard, Hildesheim: Olms, 2006. 233–263.

Koestermann, E. 1963–1968. *Cornelius Tacitus, Annalen. Erläutert und mit einer Einleitung versehen*, 4 vols., Heidelberg: Winter.

Lightfoot, J. L. (ed.) 1999. *Parthenius of Nicaea. The Poetical Fragments and the Ἐρωτικὰ παθήματα. Ed. with introd. and comm.*, Oxford: Oxford Classical Press.

Magie, D. (ed. and trans.) 1979. *Historia Augusta*, vol. I, Cambridge: Harvard University Press; London: Heinemann.

Mayer, R. 1982. 'What Caused Poppaea's Death?', *Historia* 31, 248–249.

Mendell, C. W. 1986. 'Der dramatische Aufbau von Tacitus' Annalen', in: V. Pöschl (ed.), *Tacitus*, Darmstadt: Wissenschaftliche Buchgesellschaft. 449–512. (Original work published 1935)

Moles, J. L. 1993. 'Truth and Untruth in Herodotus and Thucydides', in: C. Gill, T. P. Wiseman (eds.), *Lies and Fiction in the Ancient World*, Exeter: University of Exeter Press. 88–121.

Momigliano, A. 1993. *The Development of Greek Biography*, Cambridge: Harvard University Press.

Müller, C. W. 2006. *Legende – Novelle – Roman. Dreizehn Kapitel zur erzählenden Prosaliteratur der Antike*, Göttingen: Vandenhoeck & Ruprecht.

Murray, O. 1965. 'The *Quinquennium Neronis* and the Stoics', *Historia* 14, 41–61.

Pausch, D. 2004. Biographie und Bildungskultur. Personendarstellungen bei Plinius dem Jüngeren, Gellius und Sueton , Berlin / New York: De Gruyter.
Perrin, B. (trans.) 1919. *Plutarch. Lives*, vol. 7, Cambridge: Harvard University Press; London: Heinemann.
Power, T., Gibson, R. K. (eds.) 2014. Suetonius, the Biographer. Studies in Roman Lives, Oxford / New York.
Radermacher, L. 'Eine wandernde Novelle und Aristippos Περὶ παλαιᾶς τρυφῆς', *RhM* 91, 181–185.
Rolfe, J. C. (ed. and trans.) 1959. *Suetonius. The Lives of the Caesars*, 2 vols., Cambridge: Harvard University Press; London: Heinemann.
Schmal, S. 2016. *Tacitus*, Darmstadt: Wissenschaftliche Buchgesellschaft. Fourth edition.
Schwartz, E. 1943. *Fünf Vorträge über den griechischen Roman. Das Romanhafte in der erzählenden Literatur der Griechen*, Berlin: de Gruyter.
Shotter, D. 2005. *Nero*, London/New York: Routledge.
Syme, R. 1958–1959. *Tacitus*, Oxford: Oxford Classical Press.
Treu, K. 1984. 'Roman und Geschichtsschreibung', *Klio* 66, 456–459.
Vernant, J. 1982. 'From Oedipus to Periander. Lameness, Tyranny, Incest in Legend and History', *Arethusa* 15, 19–37.
Wallace-Hadrill, A. 1995. Suetonius. *The Scholar and His Caesars*, Bristol: Bristol Classical Press.
Warmington, B. H. 1969. *Nero: Reality and Legend*, London: Chatto and Windus.
Wilamowitz-Moellendorff, U. von 1914. *Antigonos von Karystos*, Berlin: Weidmann.
Wright, W. C. (ed. and trans.) 1961. *Philostratus, Lives of Sophists*, Cambridge: Harvard University Press; London: Heinemann.
Wuilleumier, P. 1964. *Tacite, Annales, livre XIII. Ed., introd. et commentaire*, Paris: Presses Universitaires de France.

Sophie Lalanne
'A mirror carried along a high road'? Reflections on (and of) Society in the Greek Novel

Abstract: The relationship between the Greek novel and the 'real world' deserves reconsideration. Because the Greek-speaking provinces of the Roman Empire have recently inspired a large number of publications, this paper aims at delivering some remarks relative to the sort of historical informations which can be drawn from these texts, so far improperly characterized as 'ideal novels'. Concerning elite, for instance, wealth appears to be more important than *eugeneia*, even if it allows to perform prestige through the same social practices of differentiation than before. Secondary roles and even groups of ordinary people (sailors, goatherds) display a large description of Greek civic societies, not restricted to the elite.

The relationship between fiction and reality has long been a concern among literary scholars. The image of the mirror, proposed by the French novelist Stendhal,[1] a precursor of the realist movement of the 19th century, has often been used to conceptualize the connection between the imaginary world of a novel and the real life, sometimes even the ordinary life, it was dealing with. The image of the mirror is a convenient *medium* to study various phenomena as reflection, recreation, misrepresentation, or distortion. In the case of the ancient novel, especially the Greek novel, suspicion has affected several decades of investigation.[2]

Three reasons can explain this reluctance. First of all, since B. Perry,[3] Greek novels were renowned for their 'ideal' representation of the world, as opposed to the comic realism of Latin novels which seemed more relevant to historians of

---
[1] Stendhal, *Le Rouge et le Noir*, epigraph to the chapter 13, developed in chapter 49.
[2] Some publications have been like milestones along the route, see Bowie 1977; Saïd [1987] 1999; Futre Pinheiro 1989; Baslez-Trédé-Hoffmann 1992; Bowersock 1994; Scarcella [1996] 2003; Bertrand 1998; Rife 2009. Recently, the 7th Rethymnon International Conference on the Ancient Novel dealt on 'slaves and masters' (May 27–28, 2013).
[3] Perry 1967, Preface VI-VII.

Sophie Lalanne, University of Paris 1 Panthéon-Sorbonne, ANHIMA

https://doi.org/10.1515/9781501503986-009

antiquity.[4] One may wonder how this 'ideal' quality of the Greek novels could go further than the supreme form of love shared by the protagonists (mutual love at first sight) and the perfection that they embody according to Greek standards (youth, beauty, courage, temperance, etc.). For pirates, brigands, shipwrecks, rapists, and executioners can hardly be part of an 'ideal' world, even if the heroes' misadventures always lead the action to a happy ending.

A second reason is that it was difficult until recently to locate Greek novels in time, in respect of their date of composition and, sometimes also, of their historical setting. Stylistic considerations were then major arguments in favour of a location in the Hellenistic period. Because Greek novels were supposed to be deeply rooted in an 'idealized' classical world, this made them useless for any knowledge of *realia*. More recently, the same texts were located in the first three centuries CE and, except *Callirhoe*, their plot was clearly set in a contemporary time. Still, novelists and their public were still supposed to use their imagination to escape from the real world, i.e. from their ordinary life in a quiet province of the Eastern Roman Empire in a period described as the Empire's 'Golden Age', and to dream with pure nostalgia of a world full of wars, kidnappings, attempted rapes, tyrannical abuse, etc.

One can add to this short list a third objection which is that the social background of the novelists themselves was far from clear,[5] an argument which evidently diminished the reliability of their account in historians' opinion. But it is now admitted that the authors of Greek novels belonged to the highly educated Greek-speaking society of the Eastern provinces, as demonstrated by their own level of literacy.[6] If they were not sophists themselves (a term which includes after all rhetorical performers at different social levels), they were sophists' personal assistants, as Chariton claims to be to Athenagoras of Aphrodisias, some time before the major cultural phenomenon of the Second Sophistic which gave birth to the novels of Longus, Achilles Tatius, and Heliodorus.

These significant evolutions lead me to think that Greek novels deserve to be considered in a new way as far as history of ancient societies is concerned. This contribution will attempt, very modestly, to lay some elements of foundation and to display some very preliminary remarks with the aim of a more general study of society in the Greek fiction of the Roman period.

---

4 For instance, among the most convincing interpretations, Veyne 1961; Millar 1981.
5 For a quick survey on this topic, Whitmarsh 2008.
6 Bowie 1994; Stephens 1994; Bowie 2003; Hunter 2008.

My first observations will be, in some way, reading against the grain. As a matter of fact, the social setting of the novels, in which heroes and heroines are presented as the sons and daughters of the first citizens of their mother-city, induce the reader to believe that aristocratic origin is a regular attribute in the world of the novel. However, this is, in my view, a sort of mirage produced by the novels and we should not allow the glitter of the elite to outshine society as a whole. If secondary characters can be heroes' social peers, they are also domestic slaves, servants, or eunuchs. This vivid depiction of the human world at large offers more than a mere glance at Greek society, predominantly in the form of Greek civic societies, and it also offers glimpses of local communities like the village of *boucoloi* in the Nile delta.[7] Of course, the historian of antiquity is now much better equipped with definitions and concepts to analyse an elite than any other part of society. After the flood of social studies produced in the seventies, which foregrounded oppositions between mass and elite, a historiographical revival during the last two decades has generated many conferences on the subject,[8] as well as monographs.[9] But this focus must not prevent us from seeing the wood for the trees.

Moreover, the heroes and heroines of the Greek novels are generally identified in modern scholarship specifically as the members of an aristocracy relying on noble birth and social prestige.[10] For many readers of the Greek novels, this *eugeneia* appears to be the culmination of a long list of physical and social features and, as such, the first and highest quality that a hero must be endowed with. Nevertheless, heroes and heroines are less often said by the novels to be aristocrats than members of citizen families which dominate society through wealth, power, and prestige. In archaic Greek society or in the early part of the classical period, the distinction between aristocracy and these three qualities might have appeared to be irrelevant,[11] but this is not the case in the Roman Empire where social mobility (climbing as well as descending the social ladder) is an important phenomenon that must be taken into consideration.

---

[7] Bertrand 1998.
[8] Some are more relevant than others to a study of the Greek novels: Demougin, Devijver, Raepsaet-Charlier 1999; Salzman and Rapp 2000; Cébeillac-Gervasoni, Lamoine, Trément 2003; Cébeillac-Gervasoni, Lamoine, Trément 2005; Los and Nawotka 2005; Rizakis and Camia 2008; Capdetrey et Lafond 2010.
[9] Ober 1991; Aurell 1996; Fouchard 1997; Salzman 2002; Badel 2005; Duplouy 2006.
[10] Baslez 1990, 120–122.
[11] Nagy 1996 insists on birth, wealth and power as the major criteria defining an aristocracy in the archaic and classical era.

The presentation of the main characters is interesting from this point of view. Callirhoe is the daughter of the famous *strategos* Hermocrates of Syracuse (*Callirhoe* 1,1,1), living in the second half of the 5th century. So her *eugeneia* is beyond all doubt, and she never misses an opportunity to mention it. Chaereas is the son of a man who is not said to be an aristocrat, but who holds the second position after Hermocrates (πατρὸς Ἀρίστωνος τὰ δεύτερα ἐν Συρακούσαις μετὰ Ἑρμοκράτην, 1,1,3). So he too must be of noble birth at a time, the classical period when, even in a democratic regime, highest public offices were shared by a small number of men. But aristocracy is not so prominent in other novels: wealth overshines it. Habrocomes' father is among the most powerful citizens of Ephesos (ἀνὴρ τῶν τὰ πρῶτα ἐκεῖ δυναμένων, *Ephesiaca*, 1,1,1) in the Roman province of Asia, while Anthia's parents only 'live nearby' (θυγάτηρ Μεγαμήδους καὶ Εὐίππης ἐγχωρίων, 1,2,5), i. e. in the most prosperous neighbourhood. Aigialeus' family in Sparta is also described in terms of fortune at a time when the famous Peloponnesian city is no longer an exception: 'my family was among the most powerful and was extremely rich' (τῶν τὰ πρῶτα ἐκεῖ δυναμένων, καὶ περιουσίαν ἔχων πολλήν, 5,1,4). Dionysophanes, Daphnis' natural father, is characterized only by his fortune and his civic virtue (ἀλλὰ καὶ πλούσιος ἐν ὀλίγοις καὶ χρηστὸς ὡς οὐδεὶς ἕτερος, *Daphnis and Chloe*, 4,13,2), even if the term χρηστός often denotes aristocratic status in the classical period and even if Dionysophanes invites to his son's wedding all the aristocrats of Mitylene (πάντας τοὺς ἀρίστους Μιτυληναίων ποιεῖται συμπότας, 4,34,2). Among these, Chloe's natural parents must be counted. Leucippe's father, Sostratos, is a *strategos* of Byzantion in charge of the war (*Leucippe and Cleitophon*, 2,4,2), and one of the first things we learn while reading Achilles Tatius' novel is that Sostratos was living in this city because he had inherited a considerable fortune from his mother (ὁ μὲν οὖν τὸν πάντα χρόνον εἶχεν ἐν Βυζαντίῳ· πολὺς γὰρ ὁ τῆς μητρὸς κλῆρος ἦν αὐτῷ· 1,3,1). Thus, wealth is the major criterion of a high and prestigious social status. Leucippe's mother is a tall woman dressed in rich garments and surrounded by a crowd of servants (ἐν μέσοις δὲ ἦν γυνὴ μεγάλη καὶ πλουσία τῇ στολῇ, 1,4,1). The reader is given no information about the status of Cleitophon apart from the description of his father's wealthy house in Tyre (1,5,1) and Cleitophon's rank as 'the first of the Tyrians' (Τυρίων οὐδενὸς δεύτερος, 6,9,2).

So again, wealth prevails over aristocratic origin, when this quality is mentioned, and is most often the major element of social characterization. Thus the novel's elite society relies more on fortune than birth to establish social predominance. The role of euergetism, liturgies, and expensive offices, which were very often hold by the same individuals, may explain this special attention paid to economic power in the novels' presentation of societies in the Eastern provinces of the Roman Empire. Thus, trying to establish if the novelists understood or not the society that they strove to describe when this one was remoted in time as in the case of *Callirhoe* is not a relevant point here: what matters to us is that these men living in the Eastern provinces of the Roman Empire concentrate their attention on what appears to them to be the very basis of a high social status, it is to say fortune, and power.

For power is the second attribute that a novel's hero or heroine (as well as their family) must possess. A major characteristic of the elite in the Greek novels is that they hold all sorts of power. Political power first: they hold the highest public offices in their city or in their province as *strategoi* or governors; they are the only ones who can summon the *ecclesia* at any time; they lead embassies on behalf of their city; they behave as *proxenoi* toward some protagonists. Their religious power resides in the fact that they hold the most prestigious priesthoods (mainly in the cult of Artemis); they lead *theoriai* (during the Delia, for instance, or to the Artemision of Ephesos); they lead processions in civic festivals; they take part in the most famous Panhellenic games. Nevertheless, even if all major characters are to be counted among the first citizens of their city, little information is given about their actual behaviour as public officers, members of the *boule*, priests, ambassadors, *euergetai*, *leitourgoi*, etc. The *strategia* is the only office which is described in some detail. Moreover, the same characters hold economic power: they assume the cost of liturgies, in particular the most expensive like *choregia* or *trierarchia*; as *euergetai*, they offer sacrifices and banquets (but, generally, for private occasions). But cultural power is also their privilege: the ability to read, to write, to send letters, the knowledge of myth, skills in rhetoric – members of the elite in the novels are almost the only characters to give speeches – and *paideia* in general are characteristics common to all the novels' protagonists, women as well as men.

Heliodorus' novel displays a slightly different variation of this general pattern. Theagenes, an Aenianian from Thessaly, claims that he descends from Achilles, a far more prestigious ancestor than his own father who is never mentioned; though even Calasiris expresses some doubts about this ancestry (*Aithiopica* 2,34,4–7), it gives him prestige.[12] At this time, historical and mythical genealogy is a major element in historical Greek cities' and individuals' creation of their identity. As for Charicleia, she appears first as a member of the highest sacerdotal class as the supposed daughter of Charicles, priest of Apollo in Delphi, and later as the spiritual daughter of Calasiris, priest of Isis in Memphis; still later it is revealed that she is the daughter of the king and queen of Meroe in Aethiopia, Hydaspes and Persinna, who are also respectively priest

---

[12] On Miltiades descending from Ajax for instance, see Duplouy 2006, 61–64.

of Helios and priestess of Selene. No Greek aristocracy here either, but the prestige attached to a highly prestigious descent according to the criteria of the imperial period.

Thus heroes and heroines are born into the richest, most powerful and most prestigious families of their city. This does not of course prevent them being true members of aristocracy: but after this quick survey it becomes obvious that, for instance, far from being another 'signe extérieur de noblesse', wealth outshines *eugeneia* as a criterion of social predominance and their behaviour highlights their social status more than their birth. This is an interesting aspect of Greek society as depicted in the novels which corresponds to a real, historical evolution in the late Hellenistic and Roman period.

Belonging to the elite depends not only on economic or political status, but also on patterns of social and cultural behaviour. What are, in the Greek novels, these social practices of differentiation which indicate that this or that character belongs to the elite? Important events in human life give a good opportunity for upper-class families to behave differently, to express their 'habitus' in Bourdieu's words. Elite express their superiority through ancestry, marriage, funerals, offerings to gods and monuments.[13]

The Greek novel abounds in these social markers. We have mentioned the importance of genealogy in the case of Theagenes. We can add now a quick survey of other elements: marriage, which is the very centre of the plot in the five complete novels, a marriage preferably endogamous between two adolescents of almost the same age; funerals, whose pattern is given by Callirhoe's *pompe*; offerings, such as the beautiful golden armour that Anthia and Habrocomes dedicate to Helios in Rhodes; monuments, like Callirhoe's tomb and Chaireas' cenotaph, standing on the highest coasts within the cities of Syracuse and Miletos, visible from all directions and facing each other... These are examples of social practices through which an elite can distinguish itself from the mass. They are also examples of the general desire of members of the Greek elite to compete with each other in a permanent *agôn* which is one of the major features of Hellenic culture, allowing a permanent reconfiguration of a city's internal hierarchies. In the Greek novels, there is not only a first citizen in each city. There is a second too, and probably a third and a fourth, as there were a first, a second, and a third city in the province of Asia. Thus, Hermocrates is said to be the first citizen in Syracuse, ranking before Ariston, Dionysophanes the first before Chloe's father in Mytilene, Cleitophon the first of the Tyrians, and Callisthenes before all others in Byzantion.

---

13 Duplouy 2006.

Within this social category, designed by the broad term of 'elite' which covers economic, political, and cultural elites, it turns out that, perhaps surprisingly, heroes and heroines do not have the most characteristic careers. As a matter of fact, the novel is a better source of information if one steps away from the major strands of the plot. Some characters, perhaps because they are older than the heroes, display a more interesting pedigree: such is the case of Dionysios in *Callirhoe*, Dionysophanes in *Daphnis and Chloe*, Sostratos, Thersander and Melite in *Leucippe and Cleitophon*. Some of them have already attracted scholarly attention like Dionysophanes[14] or Dionysios,[15] others have not. We will see that Callisthenes in *Leucippe and Cleitophon* or Astylos, the son of Dionysophanes in *Daphnis and Chloe*, share common features with the heroes but, because they are not confronted by ordeals and exile, they live the ordinary life of young members of a Greek elite.

Callisthenes, who has a secondary role in *Leucippe and Cleitophon*, may be the best example of the first stage of a public officer's career. Callisthenes belongs to the first family of Byzantion and is a young aristocrat – something that this time the novelist explicitly has him claim (ἀλλὰ γάρ εἰμι τῶν εὖ γεγονότων, γένει Βυζάντιος, δεύτερος οὐδενός, 8,17,3). In order to carry off Calligone, whom he believes to be Leucippe, he takes part in a *theoria* sent to Tyre by Byzantion to honour Heracles (2,15,1); to do so he fits out a ship (2,17,1) and hires men (2,16,2). Callisthenes does just what a rich citizen would have done for his city as recorded in honorific decrees and statue bases of the Hellenistic and Roman periods. Later, we learn that not only he has respected Calligone's chastity, but he has given her, even before the marriage itself, a beautiful dowry and, as a wedding present, gorgeous clothes, gold jewels and other goods characteristic of a rich woman (8,17,4). Marriage creating a bond with another elite family is an important step in such a career. With this in mind, Callisthenes does his best to please the man whom he expects to have as a stepfather, Sostratos, *strategos* of Byzantion. To do so, he accompanies him to the *agora*, performs military exercises, rides horses, gives large amounts of money to the city and, thanks to his *euergesiai*, is elected *strategos* along with Sostratos (8,17,8 – 10). This was the typical path of young Greek aristocrats since the beginning of the classical (if not the archaic) period: a military training, a political career, a good network of relationships among the first citizens and a good mar-

---

14 For instance Saïd 1999, 93 – 94.
15 See, for example, Jones 1992, 164 – 165.

riage in the same *milieu*.[16] This is exactly the career that the heroes would have followed if they had not been victims of misfortune or if they wished to integrate themselves properly in Greek society.[17]

As for Astylos, the young landlord of *Daphnis and Chloe*, he arrives at the countryside before his father, Dionysophanes, apparently with time for leisure while his father takes care of the family property. He rides a horse, which in the novels is a social privilege related to the historical institution of the *ephebeia*, as does his parasite, Gnathon, which reinforces this distinguishing feature (4,10,1; 4,11,2). He doesn't drive a carriage (*ochêma*) as is usual for aristocrats, probably because he is a young man and a keen hunter. He comes to the countryside for pleasure, like the young Methymnians who sail along the beautiful coasts of Lesbos (2,12,1), especially to enjoy the landscape and to hunt (οἷα πλούσιος νεανίσκος καὶ τρυφῶν ἀεὶ καὶ ἀφιγμένος εἰς τὸν ἀγρὸν εἰς ἀπόλαυσιν ξένης ἡδονῆς, 4,11,1). He is used to spending (or, at least, is ready to spend) large amounts of money for, when his father's garden is vandalised by Lampis, he immediately offers to pay for the devastation. Of course, we can hardly imagine that his father would take any money from him, but it means anyhow that he knows how much the reimbursement would cost Lamon, and it seems to be a good opportunity for him to prove and to exercise his generosity. Later, when Gnathon asks for Daphnis as his slave, he immediately takes steps to give his parasite what he wants. At the end of the novel, when Dionysophanes has recognized Daphnis as his son and heir and gives him his villa in the countryside, including lands, slaves, and herds (4,23,3–4), Astylos expresses no feeling of worry, jealousy or envy. After all, this villa is only a part of Dionysophanes' property (4,24,4) and Astylos can evidently expect to come into the rest of his fortune. In the Greek novels, the main hobby of this sort of character, obviously borrowed from New Comedy, is to spend their father's money and to wait for their inheritance in utter tranquillity.

My last point will be that, even in the Greek novels, the elite forms only a part of society as a whole. Even if the elite draws most of the reader's attention, nevertheless ordinary people like peasants, sailors, fishermen, quarry-workers, and servants are, as it should be, far more numerous. Some information can be drawn from the mention of those categories which form part of the general setting of the novels. From the *Ephesiaca*, for instance, we learn some information

---

[16] These are the major steps that Pauline Schmitt Pantel 2009 picks out in her analysis of the biographies of famous politicians of the fifth century BCE.
[17] On Cleitophon as a 'Black hunter', cf Lalanne 2006, 168–173.

about the ordinary people of Ephesos. Many of them come to the city from the *chôra*, along with inhabitants of nearby cities, to attend the festival of the Artemision sanctuary (1,2,3). They are attracted by the spectacle of the *pompe* which is the highlight of the day, but also by the *panegyris* and the encounters it allows, especially among marriageable young people. It is possible to deduce from this information, given by Xenophon to his reader in order to set up the meeting between Anthia and Habrocomes, that all girls, at least the daughters of Ephesian citizens, marched in this procession. But the Ephesian people also came from all over the city's territory to worship the goddess Artemis: that is what they do by entering the sanctuary and taking part in sacrifices (1,3,1) before going back home. This manifestation of public piety can be compared to the offerings that Anthia and Habrocomes make to the gods, for instance the golden armour they dedicated to Helios in Rhodes and the stele inscribed in golden letters that Leucon and Rhode offered in the same sanctuary in favour of their young masters.

The Ephesian sailors whose ship takes Anthia and Habrocomes away from the city are other members of this large part of society. They appear as the crew of a big ship (1,10,4) that the heroes' fathers have chartered or set at their disposal – for we cannot know if one of them owns the ship or not, as is most often the case in a society where being a shipowner or a merchant is less honorable than owning property.[18] The sailors and their steersman take their positions amid orders and shouts as the ship sets sail (1,10,8). They then ask for a short stop over at Rhodes before embarking for the long trip (1,11,6). It is during a period of windless calm that they begin to drink and then sleep, which make them an easy prey for Phoenician pirates. What is interesting for us, then, is the considerable risk that sailors could take on long voyages: for them being attacked by pirates meant being killed as they fought back, or jumping in the sea and getting drowned, or perishing on their ship when it was set on fire (1,13,5 – 1,14,3). No hope is left for ordinary people: only members of the elite can expect being sold or exchanged for a ransom, which requires their being left alive.

The goatherd Lampon is another interesting character in the *Ephesiaca*. He is said to be an οἰκέτης (2,9,1), a servant of Moeris, Manto's husband, which does not imply necessarily that he is a slave, but more probably means that he is a peasant attached to the land located around Antioch, probably Antioch on the Orontes. He is poor, too poor to have a wife (Anthia is given to him as to the lowest of all the men working in the estate) or even to have a hut (he is only men-

---

18 Sartre 1991, 170 – 171.

tioned as going back to his land, χωρίον (2,9,1 and 9,4) or ἀγρός (2,11,9)). But what makes difficult to believe that he is a slave is the fact that both his master Moeris (2,11,1) and his mistress Manto (2,11,3) promise him money, in particular a *misthos* or payment, when they give him their orders. A slave would not have to be paid, especially when he is so clearly afraid of his masters (2,11,2 and 11,4). Besides, he can go freely to the harbour to sell Anthia to Cilician merchants – does he go as far as Seleucia Pieria ? or, more probably, to a river port in town ? – and can make the transaction in his own name, without even having to give any title deed (2,11,9). We have here a vivid portrait of a miserable peasant attached to the land in Syria as described by historical sources since the Seleucid reform in land-management.[19]

Next to these two groups of poor and ordinary people, we find farmers, merchants (among whom I include brothel-keepers), doctors, and rhetors whose status is obviously higher, but who still have to work to earn their living: this has led some scholars to identify this group, in a problematic way, as a 'middle-class level'.[20] It is true that even if all of these characters live a quite comfortable life, and even if some of them have benefited from a good *paideia*, they nevertheless have to work, while members of the elite live a life of leisure and manage their property. As for priests, they probably belong to the upper class, for this office usually requires a high level of personal wealth. In this broad social spectrum, the elite draw the focus of the reader's attention as if they represented the most important part of Greek society, which is evidently not the case. One could consider this fact as merely a characteristic of the 'ideal' novel, but it is a feature which is common to all sorts of sources of the imperial period such as honorary decrees, funeral orations, statue bases, letters or speeches, and also to the material culture recovered by archaeology as necropoleis, houses, villas, and public buildings. All this historical material throws a brighter light on the elite than on the mass of people. This is of course a perspective error, due to the fact that the information derived from these sources is limited to a small part of the real world, indeed to its glamorous part. An elite cannot be an elite without an effective system of self-representation; and the Greek novels may be part of this system.

---

19 Capdetrey 2007, 59–73, 96–101, 135–157.
20 Scarcella [1996] 2003.

In conclusion,[21] this quick survey may give a foretaste of the sort of social and historical information that can be drawn from the Greek novels. It is certainly more than usually believed. It shows also that a certain distance has to be maintained between the texts themselves and the idea that we have of ancient society: the glitter of the elite may obscure or distort simple facts. To offer support to our imagination, the novel scatters tiny details that are aimed at producing an *'effet de réel'* (to quote from Roland Barthes): it is in these details that we might find unique material for the study of society in the Greek-speaking part of the Roman Empire.

Bibliography

Aurell, M. 1996. La *Noblesse en Occident*, Paris: Armand Colin.
Badel, C. 2005. *La noblesse de l'Empire romain: les masques et la vertu*, Seyssel: éditions Champs Vallon.
Baslez, M.-F. 1990. 'L'idée de noblesse dans le roman grec', *DHA* 16.1, 115–128.
Baslez, M.-F., Hoffmann P., Trédé M. (eds.) 1992. *Le monde du roman grec*, Paris: Presses de l'Ecole Normale Supérieure.
Bertrand, J.-M. 1998. 'Les *Boucôloi* ou le monde à l'envers', *REA* 90, 139–149.
Bowersock, G. W. 1994. *Fiction as history, from Nero to Julian*, Berkeley: University of California Press.
Bowie, E. L. 1977. 'The novels and the real world', in: B. Reardon (ed.), *Erotica Antiqua*, Bangor, 91-96.
Bowie, E. L. 1994. 'The readership of Greek novels in the ancient world', in: J. Tatum (ed.), *The search for the ancient novel*, Baltimore–London: Johns Hopkins University Press. 435–459.
Bowie, E. L. 2003. 'The ancient readers of the Greek novels' , in: G. Schmeling (ed.), *The novel in the Ancient world*, revised edition, Boston–Leiden: Brill, 87–106.
Capdetrey, L. 2007. *Le pouvoir séleucide. Territoire, administration, finances d'un royaume hellénistique (312–129 avant J.-C.)*, Rennes: Presses Universitaires de Rennes.
Capdetrey, L., and Lafond, Y. (eds.), 2010. *Pratiques et représentations des formes de domination et de contrôle social dans les cités grecques (VIIIe av.-Ier ap. J.-C.)*, Bordeaux: Ausonius.
Cébeillac-Gervasoni, M., Lamoine L., Trément F. (eds.) 2003. *Les élites et leurs facettes. Les élites locales dans le monde hellénistique et romain*, Rome–Clermont-Ferrand: Ecole Française de Rome.

---

21 I would like to express my deep gratitude to the professor E. L. Bowie for both his careful reading of this article's content and for his invaluable friendship. I accept full responsibility for any errors which may remain in this text.

Cébeillac-Gervasoni, M., Lamoine L., Trément F. (eds.) 2005. *L'autocélébration des élites locales dans le monde romain. Contexte, textes, images (IIe s. av. J.-C.-IIIe s. ap. J.-C.)*, Clermont-Ferrand: Presses Universitaires Blaise Pascal.

Demougin, S., Devijver H., Raepsaet-Charlier M.-T. (eds.) 1999. *L'ordre équestre : histoire d'une aristocratie (IIe s. avant J.-C.-IIIe s. après J.-C.)*, Rome: Ecole Française de Rome.

Duplouy, A. 2006. *Le prestige des élites. Recherches sur les modes de reconnaissance sociale en Grèce entre les Xe et Ve siècles avant J.-C*, Paris: Les Belles Lettres.

Fouchard, A. 1997. *Aristocratie et démocratie. Idéologies et sociétés en Grèce ancienne*, Besançon: Presses Universitaires de Franche-Comté.

Futre Pinheiro, M. 1989. 'Aspects de la problématique sociale et économique dans le roman d'Héliodore' in: P. Liviabella Furiani and A.M. Scarcella (eds.), *Piccolo mondo antico: le donne, gli amori, i costumi, il mondo reale nel romanzo antico*, Naples: Ed. scientifiche italiane, 15–42.

Hunter, R. 2008. 'Ancient readers', in: T. Whitmarsh (ed.), *The Cambridge companion to the Greek and Roman novel*, Cambridge: Cambridge University Press, 261–271.

Jones, C. P. 1992. 'La personnalité de Chariton', in: M.-F. Baslez, P. Hoffmann, M. Trédé (eds.), *Le monde du roman grec*, Paris: ENS, 161–167.

Lalanne, S. 2006. *Une éducation grecque. Rites de passage et construction des genres dans le roman grec ancien*, Paris: La Découverte.

Los, A., and Nawotka, K. (eds.) 2005. *Elite in Greek and Roman Antiquity*, Antiquitas XXVIII, Wroclaw.

Millar, F. 1981. 'The World of the *Golden Ass*', *JRS* 71, 1981, 63–75.

Nagy, G. 1996. 'Aristocrazia: caratteri e stili di vita' in: S. Settis (ed.), *I Greci. Storia, cultura, arte, societa. 2. Una storia greca. 1. Formazione*, Turin: Einaudi, 577–598.

Ober, J. 1989. *Mass and elite in democratic Athens: Rhetoric, ideology, and the power of the people*, Princeton: Princeton University Press.

Perry, B. E. 1967, *The ancient romances. A literary-historical account of their origins*, Berkeley/Los Angeles: University of California Press.

Rife, J. L. 2009, 'The deaths of the sophists: biography, funerary practice, and elite social identity', in: E. L. Bowie and J. Elsner (eds.), *Philostratus*, Cambridge: Cambridge University Press, 100–129.

Rizakis, A. D., and Camia, F. (eds.) 2008. *Pathways to power : civic elites in the Eastern part of the Roman Empire*, Athens: Scuola Archeologica Italiana.

Saïd, S. 1999. 'La société rurale dans le roman grec ou la campagne vue de la ville', in: E. Frézouls (ed.), *Sociétés urbaines, sociétés rurales dans l'Asie Mineure et la Syrie hellénistique et romaine*, Strasbourg 1987, published in English translation: 'Rural society in the Greek novel, or the country seen from the town', in: S. Swain (ed.), *Oxford readings in the Greek novel*, Oxford: Oxford University Press, 82–107.

Salzman, M. R., and Rapp, C. (eds.) 2000. *Elites in Late Antiquity*, Arethusa 33.3.

Salzman, M. R. 2002. *The Making of a Christian Aristocracy. Social and Religious Change in the Western Roman Empire* (IVe et Ve siècles), Cambridge: Harvard University Press.

Sartre, M. 1991. *L'Orient romain. Provinces et sociétés provinciales en Méditerranée orientale d'Auguste aux Sévères (31 avant J.-C.–235 après J.-C)*, Paris: Seuil.

Scarcella, A.M. 2003. 'Social and economic structure of the ancient novels', in: G. Schmeling (ed.), *The novel in the ancient world*, revised edition, Boston–Leiden: Brill, 221–276.

Schmitt Pantel, P. 2009. *Hommes illustres. Mœurs et politique à Athènes au Ve siècle*, Paris: Flammarion.

Stephens, S.A. 1994. 'Who read ancient novels ?', in: J. Tatum (ed.), *The search for the ancient novel*, Baltimore–London: Johns Hopkins University Press, 405–418.

Veyne, P. 1961. 'Vie de Trimalchion', *Annales* 16, 213–247.

Whitmarsh, T. 2008. 'Class', in: T. Whitmarsh (ed.), *The Cambridge companion to the Greek and Roman novel*, Cambridge: Cambridge University Press, 72–87.

Francesca Mestre and Pilar Gómez
The *Heroikos* of Philostratus: A Novel of Heroes, and more

Abstract: This paper aims to analyze why the *Heroikos* puts together, in a fictional work, local heroes – and their real cults – and pan-Hellenic heroes of epic: two aspects belonging, apparently, to different domains. In this work, in a very complex way, the author offers the reader a range of highly significant elements, in the fields of both literature and of 'reality', taking into account, however, that both are fictional. Our approach, then, is to establish two separate levels in this narration: first, the narrative about heroes (in this sense we could consider the *Heroikos* 'a novel of heroes'); secondly, the description of the framework in which the dialogue takes place, and of the characters in it; that is, primarily the vinedresser and the Phoenician in person, and the absent Protesilaos. In the end this reading shows that, among other things, one of Philostratus' goals in writing the *Heroikos* is to show that the figure of the hero is a central point of Greek identity within the Roman Empire, because it *both* covers the everyday life of belief *and* the mythical life of relevant heroic 'history'.

The *Heroikos*[1] of Philostratus is a very complex piece of literature. This is perhaps the reason why it has received less attention from scholars than other works under the name of Philostratus,[2] though in recent years a range of interesting approaches have emerged, largely due to the translation of Philostratus' text into various modern languages.[3] Naturally, one of these approaches focuses on the literary techniques displayed in the *Heroikos*, and their proximity to all the narrative forms of the imperial period, especially the novel.

E. Bowie wrote of the *Heroikos* that the boundaries between fact and fiction were less contentious in this work than in *The Stories* (or *The Life*) *of Apollonius of Tyana*: 'The *Heroicus*, then, lures the reader through a landscape where some of the illusions will be familiar from incursions into the romantic novel, but

---

[1] Quotations in this paper are from Maclean and Aitken 2001.
[2] On the identities under the name of Philostratus and the attribution of works, cf. Flintermann 1995, 5–14; De Lannoy 1997, with previous bibliography.
[3] Translations, apart from the English one mentioned in n. 1, include: Grossardt 2006b (German); Rossi 1997 (Italian); Mestre 1996 (Spanish).

Francesca Mestre – Pilar Gómez, University of Barcelona

many will not. But illusions there are: this can hardly be doubted.'⁴ And this 'luring' of the reader is something that even modern readers can appreciate. Certainly, when reading the *Heroikos* ourselves, even if we are not absolutely fascinated from the beginning to the end, we can understand how, and through what resources, it would have captured the attention of readers of Philostratus' times.

Just as we assume the romantic novel won over its readers – with its stories of voyages around the Mediterranean Sea, erotic attraction, kidnappings, shipwrecks, separations, recognitions, dangers of all kinds, the whole concentrated in the vicissitudes of two main characters, a boy and a girl, paradigms of beauty, innocence, naivety and pure love – in a similar way the *Heroikos* offered, probably to a similar readership, an array of epic heroes, recalling Homeric poetry and all the tradition that followed it: their physiques, their deeds, the war at Troy, the relationships between them, love stories, everyday life; the whole is located within a sort of *locus amoenus*, a haven of peace, harmony, wisdom and spirituality: a vineyard in the country, in the present day, in real places. There, two unnamed, fictitious characters, a vinedresser and a Phoenician, converse about heroes and their cult on the one hand, and about their mythical deeds on the other.

At first sight, then, though the literary genre is not formally the same (the *Heroikos* is a dialogue),⁵ though the framework is different and the characters do not present erotic attraction, and even though for the ancient Greeks the Homeric narrative was not the same kind of fiction, the work bears similarities to ancient novels and has a clear fictional component. However, a deeper analysis suggests that the text is far more than escapist entertainment; therefore, our doubts about its true literary nature and the author's main aim make it difficult to situate it in the written production of the Roman Empire. Some questions arise immediately: is it a simple – and innovative – way of conveying a classical revival, like the discourses of the sophists?⁶ Has it something to do with the historical background, assuming that the *Heroikos* was composed during the reign of Alexander Severus?⁷ Does the author intend to present, or foster, some aspects of religious belief and initiation?⁸ And finally, does the text have other dimen-

---

4 Bowie 1994, 187.
5 Cf. Whitmarsh 2009, 208 on Platonic dialogue as an 'important hypotextual resource for *Heroicus*'.
6 Reardon 1971, 185–198; Anderson 1986, 13, 283–289, 241–257.
7 Aitken 2004, 280–284; Bonner 1937, 131–133; Mantero 1966, 45–47; Kim 2010, 175.
8 Eitrem 1929; Betz 2004; Pache 2004; Koester 2001.

sions, other than the literary; if so, of what kind, and to what extent?⁹ As a matter of fact, none of these possibilities excludes the others. However, scholars have usually stressed one of them over the others, in order to explore the true implications of the work.

Our aim in this paper is to argue that the *Heroikos* has a very important religious element, if we understand religion in a broad sense to include and touch upon various aspects of culture, literature, and everyday life. In short, it pursues a full program of Hellenic attitudes, where hero cult as well as epic heroes represent, in contrast to the beliefs of other religions or other sacred literary writings, the stable core of Hellenicity.

It has been established that there are two separate levels in the *Heroikos*' narration.[10] The first is the description of the framework in which the dialogue takes place, and of the characters in it, specifically the vinedresser and the Phoenician in person, and the absent Protesilaos, whose tales of the heroes are repeated by the vinedresser. The second is the narrative about heroes – it is in this sense that we could consider the *Heroikos* 'a novel of heroes'. Of course, the narrative about Homeric heroes takes epic poems as its main reference, but some modifications are introduced in order to make them more human, that is to say, more representative of then-contemporary values than of those of the epic world: therefore, for instance, Odysseus is strongly criticized,[11] while his counterpart, Palamedes, becomes necessary,[12] regardless of whether he is Homeric or not. Even so, the mere mention of the names and features of these heroes, with all that they evoke – because they are the *imaginaire* of Greek identity – provide ἡδονή (25,2),[13] at least, to the Phoenician, who is the fictional addressee, and to the potential reader as well.

On the other hand, the discussion between the vinedresser and the Phoenician could be an instance of allegorical reality. The author presents an ideal life model which involves a sort of transcendental attitude, a religious devotion and conversion. Not far from the shrine dedicated to Protesilaos in Elaious, the vine-

---

9 Anderson 1986, 241–248; Billault 2000, 126–136. We should not forget the tradition of corrections of Homer broadly cultivated at the time, cf. Billault 2000, 130–138; Zeitlin 2001, 195–266; Betz 2004, 38–44; Mestre 2004, 129; for the dependence of the *Heroikos* on the *Ephemereis* of Dictys, cf. Grossardt 2006a; Champlin 1981, 210–212; Mantero 1966, 198–224; in general, on all these questions and others, cf. also Whitmarsh 2009, 206–211 (with bibliography).
10 Bowie 1994, 184.
11 Cf. especially *Her.* 34; 43,10–16.
12 He becomes necessary because he is a civilizing hero; therefore, for Philostratus, his features are more heroic than those of Achilles or Odysseus; cf. *Her.* 33–34.
13 On the use of this word applied to the effect of Homeric poetry, cf. also 26,1; 29,6; 34,4; 43,2.

dresser tends the crops and is an already-initiated witness of the powers of Protesilaos; and when the Phoenician, by chance or not,[14] comes to the vineyard, the vinedresser begins the process of his initiation. We see then a rhetorical process of persuasion, which ends with the Phoenician's conversion: πίστις, πιστεύω, πιθανός, and their opposites, are the main words exchanged for this process. Moreover, Protesilaos provides another level of persuasion, as well as of pleasure, by putting the truth of heroes into words, rhetorically, but, at the same time, indicating that all of them, like himself, fulfil a similar function, in the real world. However, apart from the two levels of fiction, Philostratus wisely organises his work into three parts, with a specific goal: to put heroes at the centre of religious belief, as men who are divine, and make possible a sort of intercourse between divinity and mankind.[15] How is this goal to be achieved? First of all, it is necessary to set out the evidence for Philostratus' method. The first part, then, is the part of πίστις.

At the beginning, we find an apparently incidental interaction between the two characters, which functions to give an account of the vinedresser's initiated status and of the Phoenician's skepticism. The vinedresser then proceeds step by step. By talking about his intercourse with Protesilaos, he achieves the first two objectives: to prove that Protesilaos 'exists', and thus that other heroes exist, too, and to establish a clear difference between what Protesilaos says – which is the truth – and other tales told by nurses, poets, and similar sources. At this point Protesilaos is trustworthy simply because, as a hero who went to Troy, he knows what happened there. But, as far as the Phoenician is aware – because his single source till now has been Homer – Protesilaos died at the very beginning of the war and did not participate in it. How can Protesilaos have known the truth if he was dead?[16]

The answer is clear and takes us to the next step: the Phoenician is told that death, for a hero, implies becoming a soul, free of the body. In this state heroes take their place as assistants of the gods, that is to say, they live with them, associate with them; and, like gods, heroes' souls observe the affairs of mortals:

θεούς τε γάρ, ὧν ὀπαδοί εἰσι, γιγνώσκουσι τότε οὐκ ἀγάλματα θεραπεύουσαι καὶ ὑπονοίας, ἀλλὰ ξυνουσίας φανερὰς πρὸς αὐτοὺς ποιούμεναι, τά τε τῶν ἀνθρώπων ὁρῶσιν ἐλεύθεραι νόσων τε καὶ σώματος. (7,3)

---

14 Cf. the Phoenician's dream, 6,3–7.
15 Heroes are ὀπαδοί of the gods, cf. 7,3.
16 Cf. 7,2. On Protesilaos death, Il. 2,695–702.

For the gods, whose attendants they are, they then know, not by worshipping statues and conjectures, but gaining visible association with them; and free from the body and its diseases, souls observe the affairs of mortals.

This explanation is particularly interesting from the religious point of view. In no more than two sentences, the vinedresser has solved the difficult point about the divine or semi-divine nature of heroes, and furthermore he has excluded worshipping statues and suppositions (ἀγάλματα θεραπεύουσαι καὶ ὑπονοίας) from the real sense of religion;[17] the relationship established between men and gods via cult ritual is not all there is: there is something more authentic than this, the 'real' interaction with divinity (ξυνουσίας φανερὰς), which is achieved by heroes after their death.

If this is true, the real person Protesilaos, as a warrior of Troy, is no longer needed as a witness: any hero – or hero's soul – can be a reliable informant about people and deeds in Troy. But Protesilaos is needed as a source of knowledge for the initiated, since there is no other way to share life with the vinedresser than to have a real appearance. Nonetheless, the Phoenician needs something more as evidence: the words of the vinedresser, as well as those of Protesilaos – even if he were speaking to a human being – are only words, like the tales of nurses.[18] The Phoenician remains skeptical: he does not accept the tales of others without question (8,10).

The next step, then, is physical evidences, bones.[19] The vinedresser runs through different places of the Greek world where known heroes (Orestes, Hyllos, Alkyoneus) or even anonymous giants have been seen, near their tombs, and in some cases their bones, of extraordinary size, are still visible: κἂν ἀπιστῇς, πλεύσωμεν· πρόκειται γὰρ γυμνὸς ἔτι..., 8,12 (If you disbelieve me, let us set sail. The corpse still lies exposed...).[20] After this physical evidence, the Phoenician acknowledges his ignorance:

---

17 This is a Christian argument as well; cf., for instance, *Act. Ap.* 17,22–31.
18 But see further on 43,3 (τὸν μὲν γὰρ Πρωτεσίλεων δαίμονα ἤδη ὄντα).
19 On the physical evidence of bones and their use in politics, Plutarch also provides an evidence concerning Theseus, whose remains were taken to Athens by Cimon (*Thes.* 36,2 and *Cim.* 8, 5–7), cf. McCauley 1999. On hero cult, cf. Hughes 1999; Alcock 2004; Nagy 2013, 169–234.
20 Cf. Lucian *VH* 1,26, where, at the end of his account of the life on the moon, the narrator uses a similar expression, challenging the reader to test the accuracy of his statements, following the idea of Herodotean *autopsia*, in order to make credible what might seem hard to believe; on Greek historiography as hypotext of the *Heroikos*, cf. Whitmarsh 2009, 209–211.

ἐγὼ δὲ μεγάλα μὲν ἠγνόουν, ἀνοήτως δὲ ἠπίστουν. ἀλλὰ τὰ τοῦ Πρωτεσίλεω πῶς ἔχει; καιρὸς γάρ που ἐπ' ἐκεῖνα ἥκειν μηκέτ' ἀπιστούμενα. (8,18)

I was ignorant of such great bones, and out of ignorance I disbelieved. But what about the stories of Protesilaos? It is time, I suppose, to come to those, since they are no longer unbelievable.

This profession of belief constitutes the transgression of the threshold of πίστις, where the Phoenician has crossed from incredulity to unbelief, making his forthcoming 'initiation' possible.

Secondly, in order to strengthen all the evidence provided, the vinedresser has to insist on the absolute reliability of the main witness, Protesilaos. We must take into account that, for the moment, the evidence of the bones has only proved the real existence of heroes once upon a time, and the explanation given by the vinedresser of the divine nature of the hero might have been accepted by the Phoenician, but that does not mean that he has accepted the actual existence of them, nor the truth of the accounts of the hero, nor even the reliability of the vinedresser himself. Now the challenge for the vinedresser is to confront the nature of Protesilaos' knowledge with another kind of knowledge; that is, the knowledge transmitted by Homer.

Homer narrated stories about heroes, and what he said is indeed accepted knowledge, but at a different level: from the point of view of the factual framework, where we find the Phoenician and the vinedresser and even the ghost of Protesilaos, Homer is only fiction.[21] What strategies will the vinedresser use to prove the difference between the fiction of Homer and the reality of Protesilaos? In the end he does this by introducing certain things which Homer does not mention, and which, for the Greek mentality of the Empire, deserve the most attention, such as hero cults – an everyday activity for ordinary people – and other features of heroes that are close to ordinary people's lives: their physical appearance, their romances, their private lives.[22] The vinedresser draws attention to real places, and describes the holy place where Protesilaos' sanctuary, destroyed by the sacrilegious acts of the Persian Artyactes,[23] once stood, visible from the vineyard. As a continuity of this reality, he recalls the beauty of the hero's face, his physique and his love for Laodameia. He then answers the Phoenician's questions: where the hero lives, how long he spends with the vinedresser, whether they eat together, whether they kiss, what kind of activities the hero carries

---

21 On Homer between history and fiction, cf. Kim 2010, 1–18.
22 Cf. Whitmarsh 2005, on ancient novels' interest in the private lives of their characters.
23 As narrated in Hdt. 7,33 and 9,120; cf. a detailed analysis in Nagy 1990, 268–273.

out, what he thinks about his premature death, and so on. With this kind of gossiping about the hero, it is as if the Phoenician wanted to get to know a new acquaintance, to make a new friend. There are, obviously, references to the stories Protesilaos tells, not known by ordinary people, as they cannot be found in Homer:

> τὸν μὲν δὴ Ἀχιλλέα φησὶν ἐπαξίως ὑμνῆσθαι, τὸν δὲ Ὀδυσσέα μειζόνως. καὶ ὁπόσα δὲ Σθενέλου τε καὶ Παλαμήδους καὶ τῶν τοιῶνδε ἀνδρῶν παραλέλειπται, δίειμί σοι μικρὸν ὕστερον, μὴ γὰρ ἀγνοήσας γε ἀπέλθοις τι τούτων. (14,2–3)
>
> He says that Achilles is celebrated in song worthily but Odysseus at too great a length. But I shall tell you a little later whatever was left untold of Sthenelos, Palamedes, and other such men, lest you go away knowing nothing about them.

A digression follows on Protesilaos' athletic achievements,[24] his advice to well-known athletes of the past and present, and his healing abilities. The important feature here is the hero's everyday association with people: in sport, when they are sick, and so on. By this point, the Phoenician is completely convinced; he says:

> Πείθομαι, νὴ τὸν Πρωτεσίλεων, ἀμπελουργέ· καλὸν γάρ, ὡς ὁρῶ, καὶ ὀμνύναι τοιοῦτον ἥρω. (16,6)
>
> By Protesilaos, I am convinced, vinedresser. It is good, I see, to swear by such a hero.

The vinedresser goes on to offer other examples of the cult of the heroes and proofs of their appearances to human beings, in Cilicia and in Thrace: Amphiaraos, Amphilokhos, Marôn, Rhêsos. Just then, the Phoenician says:

> Μετὰ σοῦ λοιπόν, ἀμπελουργέ, τάττω ἐμαυτὸν καὶ οὐδεὶς ἔτι τοῖς τοιούτοις ἀπιστήσει. (18,1)
>
> Finally I am on your side, vinedresser, and no one hereafter will disbelieve such stories.

It is done: the vinedresser has achieved his first goal; from here on, the Phoenician wants to find out the truth about something thought to be untrue without questioning the reliability of it: he himself wishes to enter into a new kind of knowledge, he needs it. Therefore he asks the vinedresser to speak about recent appearances of heroes on the plain of Troy (a phenomenon which is not related

---

24 This subject is certainly, familiar to Philostratus, and a feature of Hellenic identity, as his work *Gymnasticus* shows; for a recent analysis of *Gymnasticus*, cf. König 2007; Mestre 2007, 542–553; and Mestre 2014a, 287–299.

to Homer's poetry – on the contrary, it is still evidence for πίστις); the vinedresser, again, speaks at length and in great detail about the cults of several heroes: Ajax, Hektor, Achilles, Antilokhos, and Palamedes. The latter and his otherwise unknown participation with Achilles and Protesilaos at the Battle of Mysia opens up another section, which is not found in Homer, either; these are splendid events that Homer omitted!

It is certainly very interesting to see how Philostratus explains Homer's omissions and apparent mistakes.[25] In this case, only Protesilaos knows the reason: again, his prophetic voice makes it clear why the facts, what really happened, differ somewhat from what Homer told in his poems; it is not the same and can never be the same, because, as Protesilaos says, Homer is an extraordinary poet, the best:

> Τὸν Ὅμηρον φησί, ξένε, καθάπερ ἐν ἁρμονίᾳ μουσικῇ πάντας ψῆλαι τοὺς ποιητικοὺς τῶν τρόπων καὶ τοὺς ποιητάς, ἐφ' οἷς ἐγένετο, ὑπερβεβλῆσθαι πάντας, ἐν ὅτῳ ἕκαστος αὐτῶν ἦν κράτιστος· μεγαλορρημοσύνην τε γὰρ ὑπὲρ τὸν Ὀρφέα ἀσκῆσαι ἡδονῇ τε ὑπερβαλέσθαι τὸν Ἡσίοδον καὶ ἄλλῳ ἄλλον. (25,2)

> My guest, he says that just as Homer, in terms of musical harmonics, sang every poetic pitch, he also surpassed all the poets whom he encountered, each in the area of his expertise. For example, he fashioned verses more solemnly than Orpheus, excelled Hesiod in providing pleasure, and outdid other poets in other ways.

But he had to choose a subject, a plot, its main characters, their extraordinary deeds, which is to say, he had to invent his story, to build his tale:

> καὶ λόγον μὲν ὑποθέσθαι[26] Τρωικόν, ἐς ὃν ἡ τύχη τὰς πάντων Ἑλλήνων τε καὶ βαρβάρων ἀρετὰς ξυνήνεγκεν, ἐσαγαγέσθαι δὲ ἐς αὐτὸν πολέμους τοὺς μὲν πρὸς ἄνδρας, τοὺς δὲ πρὸς ἵππους καὶ τείχη, τοὺς δὲ πρὸς ποταμούς, τοὺς δὲ πρὸς θεοὺς καὶ θεάς, καὶ ὁπόσα κατ' εἰρήνην εἰσὶ καὶ χοροὺς καὶ ᾠδὰς καὶ ἔρωτας καὶ δαῖτας ἔργα τε, ὧν γεωργία ἅπτεται, καὶ ὥρας, αἳ σημαίνουσιν, ὁπόσα ἐς τὴν γῆν δεῖ πράττειν, καὶ ναυτιλίας καὶ ὁπλοποιίας τὰς ἐν Ἡφαίστῳ, εἴδη τε ἀνδρῶν καὶ ἤθη ποικίλα. πάντα ταῦτα τὸν Ὅμηρον δαιμονίως ἐξειργάσθαι φησὶ καὶ τοὺς μὴ ἐρῶντας αὐτοῦ μαίνεσθαι. (25,3–4)[27]

> He took the story of the Trojan War as his subject, in which fate brought together the excellent deeds both of all the Hellenes and of the barbarians. Homer introduced into the story battles involving men, horses and walls, rivers, as well as gods and goddesses. Protesilaos says that Homer also included all matters pertaining to peace: choral dances,

---

25 Cf. Mestre 2004.
26 The verb ὑποτίθημι, with the same meaning, is used elsewhere in the *Heroikos* to show where Homer 'invented' a story on the Trojan deeds, confronted with the 'truth' we know from Protesilaos; cf. 25,13; 27,12; 43,4; 43,16.
27 Cf. further on 43,3–44,4.

songs, erotic encounters, and feasts; he touched on agricultural tasks and the appropriate seasons for performing them. He also described sea voyages, the making of arms in the 'Hephaistos', and especially men's appearances and their various characteristics. Protesilaos says that Homer accomplished all these things with divine power and that those who do not love him are mad.

It is obvious, then, says Protesilaos, that a *hypothesis* implies making choices, for the sake of an engagement and for coherence; thus, some aspects of truth must be left aside. In a word: fiction is the main affair of the poet, not truth.

Moreover, it has become clear that there are two different kinds of knowledge, placed at different levels: the world of Homer, a construction whose realm is entertainment, artistic skills and pleasure; and another universe, related to spirituality, a world that makes sense and is useful for everyday life: in other words, a frame for religious feeling. Now, from this new standpoint concerning heroes, the third part of the *Heroikos* may start: the Phoenician is on the way to being initiated: he now believes. So only now, and not before, is he ready to listen to what he most wished to hear: true tales about heroes. This is, in our opinion, the way to connect religious hero and literature hero: initiation.[28] But in the setting we have just described, the question is: what kind of religion is this? And how does it make sense in the time of Philostratus?

Scholarship on the religious realm of the *Heroikos* has stressed the attempt to revive hero cults, encouraged by the emperor Caracalla, who in CE 214 went to Troy to honour the tomb of Achilles.[29] It appears to have been a revival similar to that of the Olympic Games after Nero's visit to Olympia,[30] or Plutarch's accounts of the cults in Delphi.[31] However, things changed between the first and third centuries CE. All kinds of mystery cults spread throughout the Empire, and, moreover, the emergence and diffusion of Christianity at almost all levels of Roman society took on real significance. It is true that we have no evidence of any acquaintance or contact between Philostratus and the Christians: he never mentions them in his works, unlike other pagan authors of the Empire, such as Tacitus, Lucian, Pliny the Younger, Galen and Celsus. However, he may well have been aware of at least some of the main stories about Jesus and his prominent followers, and he may well have been aware of, or even have read, certain New Testament or early Christian texts.

---

28 Cf. Mestre 2014b, 427–430.
29 Cf. D.C. 78,16,7; Hdn. 4,8,3; Eitrem 1929; Mantero 1966; Jones 2001. Philostratus, then, could have composed this dialogue in order to please the emperor, cf. Kim 2010, 196 n. 60.
30 Cf. Paus. 5,12,8; 5,25,8; 5,26,3.
31 Cf. Plu. *Moralia* 384d-394c (*E ap. Delph.*); 394d-409d (*Pyth. or.*); 409e-438d (*Def. orac.*).

Many possible coincidences between aspects of Philostratus' works and of Christian writings have been emphasised:[32] there are clear similarities between heroes, as presented in the *Heroikos*, and Christian martyrs and saints (although when Philostratus composed his *Heroikos*, formal procedures of sanctification or official declarations of sainthood presumably did not yet exist[33]) or even the profile of Jesus and the apostles from the narratives in the New Testament. Moreover, it has been suggested that local martyrs may have taken on the role of the old protecting heroes, so this is not only a matter of narratives, but also a matter of religious practice and ritual, during the late antique evolution of which we know that Christian and non-Christian practitioners often interacted.[34]

We do not intend to say that the *Heroikos* is merely a *Mysterientext*,[35] a defence of ancient Hellenic cults against Christianity or other superstitions. It is hard to determine how the cultural developments of ways of conceiving of divinity and of expressing religious feeling in Philostratus' time and society might have influenced him to produce a literary work such as the *Heroikos*. But what we can safely assume is that such discussions were taking place in Philostratus' social, historical context and that such discussions therefore provide important context for the *Heroikos*' religious terminology and perspectives.

Philosophy, culture, and *paideia* led little by little in antiquity to an idea of divinity related with good and a sort of transcendentalism. Besides, popular pagan religion in the Roman Empire did not have an intellectual expression, only practices: cults, rituals, feasts, executed as a part of the social and political programme. Myth remained predominantly a matter of literary construction and not a source of embodied religious or spiritual significance.[36]

Within such a cultural religious context, Christianity aimed to develop its new knowledge (καινὴ διδαχή)[37] against other ancient knowledge with their own practices, many of which had certain 'Jewish' or 'pagan' antecedents. Christian belief therefore needs to be declared, and this public declaration signifies adherence to a group. This is why Christian religion is a mark of identity, although declaring oneself a Christian could mean a variety of things, since nothing resembling a Christian orthodoxy existed at least until the 4th century. Furthermore, they also needed to establish their own personality within and apart

---

[32] And not only in the *Heroikos*, but especially in *VA*; cf. Brown 1995, 57–78; Cameron 1997. See above n. 17.
[33] On these procedures, cf. Hershbell 2004, 176; Van Uytfanghe 2009, 347.
[34] Cf. Koester 2001, 258–259.
[35] In the sense of Merkelbach's theory (cf. Merkelbach 1962); cf. also Hägg 1983, 101–104.
[36] Cf. Veyne 2005, 507–509: even if it is exaggerated, the tendency is well described.
[37] As in *Act. Ap.* 17,19 or *Ev. Marc.* 1,27.

from Judaism, basically by reinterpreting Jewish writings and by placing more stress on the personality and the meaning of their unique figurehead, Jesus.

How would pagans receive this? In fact, early Christians systematically adopted the habits and the language of Greek philosophy, pagan models and techniques, and invaded schools, temples and all the places where intellectual and more popular influence could be exerted. One can suppose that it was as difficult to ignore them if they evinced such a cultural presence. It is safe to assume, therefore, that Philostratus and his entourage were familiar with the main arguments of the Christians: a man, son of God, poor, wise and humble, performing miracles, who died a victim of injustice, but came back to life to protect and save his adherents, who lived in a very special relationship of love with him, and suffered and died for him. A champion of Hellenism like Philostratus might have regarded this astonishing kind of religious sentiment with its accompanying action as exportable to his own *milieu*, richer than Christians' in all its facets except spirituality and religious feeling.[38]

The *Heroikos*, then, is not a text of conversion, nor merely a device of self-affirmation, but a proposal for the revision of the Hellenic tradition along religious lines, similar to those of Christians, taking hero cult and hero tradition as the basis for transmitting the possibility of a new spiritual knowledge for pagans, which should co-exist with literary and mythological tradition. The main features for this new spiritual world are, on the one hand, the belief in the proximity of heroes as mediators of divinity – so their cult must become a truly religious one – and, on the other, the establishment of a new model of holy man, whose morality has to correspond to the ideals of the time.

Thus, the centrality of Palamedes in the *Heroikos* has an important meaning, Palamedes is the only non-Homeric hero who has a major role in the work of Philostratus.[39] We are told (21), nevertheless, that he was worshipped, in Troy, by hero cults, and he converses with a farmer in the same way as Protesilaos speaks to the vinedresser in Thracian Chersonesus. Moreover, the farmer in Troy feels a deep love for the hero: 'φιλῶ σε, ὦ Παλάμηδες', εἶπεν, 'ὅτι μοι δοκεῖς φρονιμώτατος ἀνθρώπων γεγονέναι..., 21,6 ('I love you, Palamedes, because you seem to me to be the most sensible of all...'), a love mixed with piety, derived from the awareness that Palamedes has suffered and died unfairly, misunderstood by his peers, Odysseus and the other heroes.[40]

---

38 Cf. Hershbell 2004, 172.
39 Cf. the important role of Palamedes in *VA* (4,13) as well; cf. Woodford 1994.
40 Tradition on Palamedes, cf. Mestre 2015.

The qualities of Palamedes, a good adviser for Achilles and Diomedes at war (23,20–23), are, above all, intelligence, wisdom in all fields, and modesty. Homer obviously had to ignore him, because it was impossible to give Odysseus a heroic role if he also introduced Palamedes. But as we have seen before, the tales of Homer were a literary construction, where the author had to choose, and Homer chose Odysseus, as was his right.[41] The factual truth, that of belief (πίστις), nonetheless, is rather different, so it is necessary to restore Palamedes to his rightful place (25,13–17). This place is Philostratus' catalogue of heroes,[42] as the positive counterpart of the villain Odysseus: a simple reading of the pair Palamedes-Odysseus (33,1–34,7) shows that the latter is absolutely subsidiary to the former, albeit necessary as a Homeric hero. Philostratus represents Palamedes as a sophist figure in the most positive sense of the word. He stands in contrast with his rival Odysseus, whose ingenuity is linked with all the most negative aspects of rhetorical identity.[43]

Now, we shall focus only on the episode of the betrayal, which leads to what we could call Palamedes' martyrdom: he is summoned by the leader Agamemnon, and, in the absence of Achilles who would not tolerate such an injustice, Palamedes is found guilty of betraying the Achaeans and is stoned to death by the Peloponnesians and Ithacans.[44] Only Ajax objected to Agamemnon's prohibition of an honourable burial, and performed funeral rites for him (33,31–33). Palamedes was put to death like a martyr,[45] and far from seeking revenge,[46] he

---

[41] The word that Protesilaos uses twice to mean that Odysseus was the subject matter of Homer is παίγνιον (24,14): a sophistic term to indicate that literary composition is a sort of game, cf. Demetr. *Eloc.* 120.

[42] From 25,18 onwards; the catalogue is organized as follows: Nestor and Antilokhos; Diomedes and Sthenelos; Philoktêtês; Agamemnon, Menelaos and Idomeneus; Ajax the Locrian; Palamedes and Odysseus; Ajax the Telamônian; the Trojan heroes; and, at the end, separately, Achilles. The organization of the catalogue does not seem to correspond to a particular plan; the only thing worth noting is that Palamedes is not an epic hero like all the others, and so he appears paired with Odysseus. Philostratus is a sophist, and, though he may focus on non-literary areas, as we argue in this paper, his composition of the *Heroikos* takes into account sophistic laws and techniques, deriving from the *progymnasmata*: the catalogue includes only Homeric heroes, so the presence of Palamedes needs to be justified as the counter-part of a Homeric hero; as for the narrative on Achilles, it should be understood as an autonomous piece, formally not included in the catalogue.

[43] Cf. Hodkinson 2011, 79–101, on the analysis of Palamedes' rivalry with Odysseus in Platonic terms.

[44] Interestingly, this kind of execution is common to the Archaic periods in the Greek tradition to purify the community, and to the Jewish tradition to punish impiety and blasphemy.

[45] Like, for instance, Stephen, the first martyr in the *Book of Acts* (*Act. Ap.* 7,54–60).

offered his head to the stones, knowing that justice was in his favour (33,37). And so, though other heroes were responsible for Palamedes' death, the first hero cult he received was from his hero friends: Ajax who honoured his tomb, and Achilles who created a song for the lyre for him, and praised him in song 'as much as he did the earlier heroes' (33,36).[47] The example of Palamedes is useful to our aim: he is presented as a martyr, in many aspects very similar to Jesus or to the Christian martyrs, but he is also a pagan hero, deserving a prominent place among the Homeric frame of heroes, because, in Philostratus' and probably his contemporaries' minds, Odysseus' heroicity requires some justification. As we underlined at the beginning, not all the levels of meaning of the *Heroikos* are easy to understand. Hero cults certainly constitute one of the central points of the text, but it is extended to pan-Hellenic heroes, giving a greater scope to what were very often local practices. The other point is, in our opinion, a sort of adaptation to the new religious feelings spread in the time of the Severans, which can be related to the Christian messages stressing love for divinity, intercourse with a sort of transcendent spiritualism, the quest for a simple, natural life, and a sense of engagement in a collective identity.

Philostratus was fully aware that, in the *Heroikos*, he was presenting a pagan, Hellenic programme of religious spirituality; but, by choosing not to look only to the past – the vinedresser, the Phoenician, and other 'real' people who have intercourse with heroes, are to be considered of the present day – he cannot avoid the influence of other approaches to religious feeling, which were so much present in the world around him – a world where both groups, pagans and Christians, express their distinctive beliefs in common popular practices.[48] All this is presented in the construction of a very complex fiction which combines two levels: the literary fiction of myth, and the 'truthful fiction'[49] of belief.

Bibliography

Aitken, E.B. 2004. 'Why a Phoenician? A proposal for the historical occasion', in: E.B. Aitken, J.K.B. Maclean (eds.), *Philostratus' Heroikos. Religion and Cultural Identity in the Third Century C.E.*, Atlanta: SBL. 267–284.

---

46 He does not even agree with his father Nauplios who avenged him by destroying the Greek fleet when it returned from Troy (33,47), cf. E. *Hel.* 767; 1122–1131.
47 Cf. Pache 2004, 215.
48 Cf. Skedros 2004, 193.
49 Cf. Francis 1998.

Aitken, E.B., and Maclean, J.K.B. (eds.). 2004. *Philostratus' Heroikos. Religion and Cultural Identity in the Third Century C.E.*, Atlanta: SBL.

Alcock, S.E. 2004. 'Material Witness: An Archaeological Context for the *Heroikos*', in: E.B. Aitken, J.K.B. Maclean (eds.), *Philostratus' Heroikos. Religion and Cultural Identity in the Third Century C.E.*, Atlanta: SBL. 159–168.

Amato, E. (ed.). 2006. *Approches de la Troisième Sophistique*, Bruxelles: Latomus.

Anderson, G. 1986. *Philostratus. Biography and Belles Lettres in the Third Century*, London: Croom Helm.

Betz, H.D. 2004. 'Hero Worship and Christian Beliefs: Observations from the History of Religion on Philostratus' '*Heroikos*, in: E.B. Aitken, J.K.B. Maclean (eds.), *Philostratus' Heroikos. Religion and Cultural Identity in the Third Century C.E.*, Atlanta: SBL. 25–47 (= 'Heroenverehrung und Christglaube: Religionsgeschichtliche Beobachtungen zu Philostrats *Heroicus*' in: H. Cancik (ed.). 1996. *Griechische und Römische Religion*, Tübingen: Mohr Siebeck.)

Billault, A. 2000. *L'univers de Philostrate*, Bruxelles: Latomus.

Bonner, C. 1937. 'Some Phases of Religious Feeling in Later Paganism', *The Harvard Theological Review* 30.3, 119–140.

Bowie, E. 1994. 'Philostratus: Writer of Fiction', in: J.R. Morgan, R. Stoneman (eds.), *Greek Fiction: the Greek Novel in Context*, London/New York: Routledge. 181–199.

Bowie, E., and Elsner, J. (eds.) 2009. *Philostratus*, Cambridge/New York: Cambridge University Press.

Brown, P. 1995. *Authority and the Sacred. Aspects of the Christianisation of the Roman World*, Cambridge/New York: Cambridge University Press.

Cameron, A. 1997. "Eusebius' *Vita Constantini* and the Construction of Constantine", in: M.J. Edwards, S. Swain (eds.), *Portraits: Biographical Representation in the Greek and Latin Literature of the Roman Empire*, Oxford: Clarendon Press. 145–174.

Champlin, E. 1981. 'Serenus Sammonicus', *HSCP* 85, 189–212.

De Lannoy, L. 1977. *Flavii Philostrati Heroicus*, Leipzig: Teubner.

De Lannoy, L. 1997. 'Le problème des Philostrate. État de la question', *ANRW* II.34.3, 2362–2449.

Demoen, K., and Praet, D. (eds.) 2009. *Theios Sophistes. Essays on Flavius Philostratus' Vita Apollonii*, Leiden/Boston: Brill.

Eitrem, S. 1929. 'Zu Philostrats *Heroikos*', *Symbolae Osloenses* 8, 1–56.

Flintermann, J.-J. 1995. *Power, Paideia & Pythagoreanism. Greek Identity, Conceptions of the Relationship between Philosophers and Monarchs and Political Ideas in Philotratus' Life of Apollonius*, Amsterdam: G.C. Gieben.

Francis, J.A. 1998. 'Truthful Fictions: New Questions to Old Answers on Philostatus' *Life of Apollonius*', *AJPh* 119, 419–441.

Goldhill, S. (ed.). 2001. *Being Greek under Rome: a Cultural Identity, the Second Sophistic and the Development of Empire*, Cambridge/New York: Cambridge University Press.

Grossardt, P. 2006a. 'Die Kataloge der troischen Kriegsparteien. Von Dares und Malalas zu Isaak Porphyrogennetos und Johannes Tzetzes – und zurück zu Dictys und Philostrat', in: E. Amato (ed.), *Approches de la Troisième Sophistique*, Bruxelles: Latomus. 449–457.

Grossardt, P. 2006b. *Einführung, Übersetzung und Kommentar zum Heroikos von Flavius Philostrat*, Basel: Schwabe.

Hägg, T. 1983. *The Novel in Antiquity*, Berkeley: University of California Press.
Hägg, R. (ed.). 1999. *Ancient Greek Hero Cult*, Stockholm: Åströms Förlag.
Hershbell, J.P. 2004. 'Philostratus' *Heroikos* and Early Christianity: Heroes, Saints, and Martyrs', in: E.B. Aitken, J.K.B. Maclean (eds.), *Philostratus' Heroikos. Religion and Cultural Identity in the Third Century C.E.*, Atlanta: SBL. 169–179.
Hodkinson, O. 2011. *Authority and Tradition in Philostratus' Heroikos. Satura, 8.* Lecce: Pensa Multimedia
Hughes, D.D. 1999. 'Hero Cult, Heroic Honors, Heroic Dead: Some Developments in the Hellenistic and Roman Periods', in: R. Hägg (ed.), *Ancient Greek Hero Cult*, Stockholm: Åströms Förlag. 167–175.
Jones, C.P. 2001. 'Philostratus' *Heroikos* and its setting in reality', *JHS* 121, 141–149.
Kayser, C. L. 1870–1871. *Flavii Philostrati opera*, Leipzig: Teubner.
Kim, L. 2010. *Homer Between History and Fiction in Imperial Greek Literature*, Cambridge: Cambridge University Press.
Koester, H. 2001. 'On Heroes, Tombs, and Early Christianity: An Epilogue', in: J.K.B. Maclean, E.B. Aitken (eds.), *Flavius Philostratus. Heroikos*, Atlanta: SBL. 257–264.
König, J. 2007. 'Greek athletics in the Severan period: literary views', in: S. Swain, S. Harrison, J. Elsner (eds.), *Severan Culture*, Cambridge/New York: Cambridge University Press. 135–145.
Maclean, J.K.B., and Aitken, E.B. 2001. *Flavius Philostratus. Heroikos*, Atlanta: SBL.
Mantero, T. 1966. *Ricerche sull'Heroikos di Filostrato.* Genova: Università di Genova, Istituto di Filologia Classica e Medioevale.
McCauley, B. 1999. 'Heroes and Power: The Politics of Bone Transferal', in: R. Hägg (ed.), *Ancient Greek Hero Cult*, Stockholm: Åströms Förlag. 85–98.
Merkelbach, R. 1962. *Roman und Mysterium in der Antike*, München: Beck.
Mestre, F. 1996. *Filóstrato, Heroico, Gimnástico, Descripciones de cuadros; Calístrato, Descripciones*, Madrid: Gredos.
Mestre, F. 2004. 'Refuting Homer in the *Heroikos* of Philostratus', in: E.B. Aitken, J.K.B. Maclean (eds.), *Philostratus' Heroikos. Religion and Cultural Identity in the Third Century C.E.*, Atlanta: SBL. 127–141.
Mestre, F. 2007. 'Filóstrato y los *progymnasmata*', in J.A. Fernández Delgado, F. Pordomingo, A. Stramaglia (eds.), *Escuela y literatura en Grecia antigua*, Cassino: Edizioni dell'Università degli Studi di Cassino. 523–556.
Mestre, F. 2014a. 'La *sophia* de Philostrate. Quelques idées sur le *Gymnastikos*', in: F. Mestre, P. Gómez (eds.). *Three centuries of Greek culture under the Roman Empire*, Barcelona: Edicions i Publicacions de la Universitat de Barcelona, 287–299.
Mestre, F. 2014b. 'Héroes de Culto y Héroes del Mito, en el *Heroico* de Filóstrato', in: A. Pérez Jiménez (ed.), *Realidad, Fantasía, Interpretación, Funciones y Pervivencia del Mito Griego. Estudios en Honor del Profesor Carlos García Gual*, Zaragoza: Libros Pórtico, 423–436.
Mestre, F. 2015. 'Odiseo y Palamedes: historia de una rivalidad', in: C. Fernández, J. Nápoli, G. Zecchin (eds.), *AΓΩN: competencia y cooperación. de la antigua Grecia a la actualidad*, La Plata.
Nagy, G. 1990. *Pindar's Homer. The Lyric Possession of an Epic Past*, Baltimore: Johns Hopkins University Press.

Nagy, G. 2013. *The Ancient Greek Hero in 24 Hours*, Cambridge/London: Cambridge University Press.

Pache, C.O. 2004. 'Singing Heroes. The Poetics of Hero Cult in the *Heroikos*', in: E.B. Aitken, J.K.B. Maclean (eds.), *Philostratus' Heroikos. Religion and Cultural Identity in the Third Century C.E.*, Atlanta: SBL. 3–24.

Reardon, B.P. 1971. *Courants littéraires grecs des IIè et IIIè siècles après J.C*, Paris: Belles Lettres.

Rossi, V. 1997. *Filostrato. Eroico*, Venice: Marsilio.

Skedros, J.C. 2004. 'The *Heroikos* and popular Christianity in the Third Century C.E.', in: E.B. Aitken, J.K.B. Maclean (eds.), *Philostratus'* Heroikos. *Religion and Cultural Identity in the Third Century C.E.*, Atlanta: SBL. 181–193.

Van Uytfanghe, M. 2009. 'La *Vie d'Apollonios de Tyane* et le discours hagiographique', in: K. Demoen, D. Praet (eds.), *Theios Sophistes. Essays on Flavius Philostratus'* Vita Apollonii, Leiden/Boston: Brill. 335–374.

Veyne, P. 2005. *L'empire gréco-romain*, Paris: Seuil.

Whitmarsh, T. 2005. 'The Greek Novel: Titles and Genre', *AJPh* 126, 587–611.

Whitmarsh, T. 2009. 'Performing heroics: language, landscape and identity in Philostratus' Heroicus, in: E. Bowie, J. Elsner (eds.), *Philostratus*, Cambridge/New York: Cambridge University Press. 205–229.

Woodford, S. 1994. 'Palamedes seeks revenge', *JHS* 114, 164–169.

Zeitlin, F. 2001. 'Visions and Revisions of Homer', in: S. Goldhill (ed.), *Being Greek under Rome: a cultural Identity, the Second Sophistic and the Development of Empire*, Cambridge: Cambridge University Press. 195–266.

Janelle Peters
Springs as a Civilizing Mechanism in *Daphnis and Chloe*

Abstract: In Longus' *Daphnis and Chloe*, springs are a central motif of the Prologue and the novel as a whole. This motif counters male domination, since it is associated with Chloe, while the flowers watered by springs in this novel are identified with Daphnis. This study will examine how the motif of springs reflects the resistance of Daphnis and Chloe to pervasive cultural constructions of gender, creating individuals who participate in the larger society without reproducing its structures.

Given the progression of Longus' novel toward a normative marriage of a heterosexual couple of the same socioeconomic status, interpreters of *Daphnis and Chloe* have often focused on the motifs that teach the characters how to comport themselves according to societal expectations. Epstein stresses the narrative's association of Daphnis, Pan, and goats.[1] Morgan suggests that Longus 'naturalizes' gender inequalities by depicting males as promiscuous and females as submissive in a pastoral setting.[2] As Chalk and Winkler have noted, Longus evinces a realistic awareness about the dangers of both the patriarchal and pastoral.[3] Indeed, this might be seen in the narrative's concern for the voices of the nightingales and the echo, originally women who suffered male violence. I will propose, however, that the social critique of *Daphnis and Chloe* continues past identifying the consequences of gender-based violence and into providing an erotic alternative to the sexual relationships that disenfranchised Procne, Philomela, and Echo. Throughout the novel, Longus' healing of the relations between the sexes is associated with springs. In the ideal grove of the Prologue, a single spring sustains the whole complex, and this presages the function of 'real' springs – that is, springs located on the island of Lesbos – in the novel as a whole. The spring establishes gender equality by providing a location for alternative cultural definitions of 'civilization': it is the site where Daphnis and

---

1 Epstein 2002, 72.
2 Morgan 2004, 12.
3 Chalk 1960, 46; Winkler 1990.

Janelle Peters, University of St. Francis (Illinois)

https://doi.org/10.1515/9781501503986-011

Chloe begin and defend their reciprocal relationship against threats from romantic rivals and militaristic invaders. Chloe, who thinks her ablution of Daphnis in the spring of the Nymphs has rendered him *kalos*, successfully avoids having either Dorkon or Daphnis abduct her or take her virginity, and in each instance this happens beside a spring in the woods. Daphnis, as Epstein has stated, learns to avert his animalistic impulses in a way that his rival Dorkon does not.[4] After the relationship is ratified by the ruling elite of Mitylene, Daphnis and Chloe ground their relationship in the spring and the goats that nourished them in their youth: they decorate the spring of the Nymphs and introduce the cult to their children. Through their connection with the spring, Daphnis and Chloe live *in* the city without being *of* the city.

In proposing that the spring provides *Daphnis and Chloe* with an enfranchising but still alternative romantic relationship, I posit that Longus pushes against patriarchal hegemony both within his social context and within his choice of narrative mode. The Second Sophistic was a time of cultural flux, latent with possibilities for alternate social constructions, as society was changing.[5] Moreover, Konstan has shown that the ancient Greek novel differentiates itself from New Comedy in terms of romantic relationships: whereas New Comedy reinscribes patriarchal control over would-be adulterous wives and men of lower social status, the ancient Greek novel champions the passive hero in order to create sexual symmetry.[6] In constructing his novel, then, Longus uses a sexually symmetrical pair whose innocence enables them to critique literary commonplaces – they are too naïve to know that they should be taking rhetorical tropes seriously, and so the unnaturalness of Greek cultural attitudes is revealed. De Certeau has labeled this type of literary phenomenon 'social delinquency' and sees it as a strategy of cultural critique:

> Social delinquency consists in taking the story literally, in making it the principle of physical existence where a society no longer offers to subjects or groups symbolic outlets and expectations of spaces, where there is no longer any alternative to disciplinary falling-into-line or illegal drifting away, that is, one form or another of prison and wandering outside the pale.[7]

It is precisely the text's ridiculous demand to take cultural conventions literally – as though they really were natural – that allows Longus to construct a romantic

---

4 Epstein 1995.
5 Goldhill 1995, 2; Perkins 1995, 124; Boyarin 1997, 7.
6 Konstan 1994, 7.
7 De Certeau 1984, 130.

novel that extricates its protagonists from the *maenad/basilinna* (anti-wife/ queen) dichotomy inherent in Dionysiac rituals in ancient Greek society.[8]

Longus chooses the spring of the Nymphs in particular to create an alternate Dionysiac religious practice: the spring creates a local idiom through such *praxis* as the offerings of first fruits of wine and of the syrinx. These rituals restore the songs of the nightingales, who perfect their laments. From Ovid's description of the myth of Philomela and Procne, we know that this was already connected with Dionysiac ritual.[9] Longus' novel reconfigures the Dionysiac symbolic universe to highlight the voices in society that need to be tuned after neglect and abuse. This can be seen again in Philetas' garden, when the god Love possesses a silvery laugh like 'no swallow, no nightingale, no swan grown old' (2,5,1), thus encompassing both women and men. The religious matrix of Longus' novel seeks to give a voice to the vulnerable couple and, presumably, the vulnerable reader.

Though the prologue has begun with a pleasure garden, the *incipit* of Book One centers on the city: Πόλις ἐστι τῆς Λέσβου Μιτυλήνη. This sets the scene for a tension between spring and city throughout the novel. As MacQueen has argued more broadly of the pastoral setting, the spring acts as a 'buffer'.[10] Ultimately, no broad social reform will be effected, but Daphnis and Chloe will experience a reciprocal relationship through ethics flowing from the springs of the novel. Their relationship will be sanctioned through the approval of the entire elite in Mitylene. Since the elite are summoned to recognize Chloe's birth tokens in response to Dionysophanes' dream, Daphnis and Chloe's relationship may be assumed to be authorized at both divine and mortal levels (4,34,1–2).

1 Springs

Springs feature prominently in *Daphnis and Chloe,* as they do on the island of Lesbos.[11] In the Prologue, Longus describes the *historia* of the scene in a painting as being dependent upon the spring: 'a single spring sustained everything, flow-

---

[8] For recent discussions on the pervasiveness of these dichotomies in Greek culture, see Seaford 1995, 301–11; Goff 2004, 278; Gilhuly 2009, 185. Social delinquency is a different notion than Bakhtin's novelistic hybridity that exists where different languages are brought together in order to critique each other. In Longus's *Daphnis and Chloe,* the same language, that of conventional erotic imagery, is consistently misread or not perceived. On novelistic hybridity, see Bakhtin 1981, 361; Burrus 1995, 51.
[9] Ovid, *Met.* 6,587–605; 6,645–646; Burkert 1983, 181.
[10] MacQueen 1990, 166.
[11] Mason 1995, 263; Vieilleford 1987, 200.

ers and trees alike'. The repetition of features from the Prologue's garden portrait communicates the pastoral message of *Daphnis and Chloe*. Froma Zeitlin has argued that the gardens of rustic scholar Philetas and urban elite Dionysophanes 'are precisely situated at crucial moments in the narrative as sequential models of the children's erotic development'.[12] As the site of Eros, springs are at the center of the gardens of the novel and the heart of the relationship of the young lovers. The spring in the grotto of the Nymphs, where Chloe was abandoned as an infant, is the primary spring of the novel. This spring permits Daphnis and Chloe to bathe in each other's sight (1,12–13; 1,32). Chloe washes Daphnis in the spring after the Methymnean raid (2,18). Moreover, the trees and the vegetation of gardens can be taken elsewhere – for triumphal processions, for example – in ways that springs cannot.[13] When Chloe is abducted by pirates beside the spring, Daphnis falls asleep at the spring and receives a dream revelation from the Nymphs (2,23,1).[14] At their transition from pastoral to civilized life, Daphnis and Chloe dedicate their most prized possessions at the spring.[15] Daphnis drinks from the spring, and Chloe pours wine into it (4,32,3).

Other springs in the novel reinforce the civilizing associations of the spring in the Grotto of the Nymphs. First, the lovers wash Dorkon in the spring where the goats drink after his attempted rape of Chloe (1,21,4). Second, the garden of Philetas has three springs that sustain it and cleanse him (2,3,4; 2,5,4). Third, Lykainion leads Daphnis to a spring hidden in the woods (3,17,1). She suggests that Chloe should bathe in the spring after Daphnis takes her virginity. The narrative then skips to the virgin Chloe bathing in springs while Daphnis swims in rivers (3,24,2). Fourth, when Lamon receives word that his master will be coming at the beginning of Book Four, his first act is to clean the springs in the park (4,1,3). The authorial voice proceeds to describe the abundance of flowers supported by the spring and the Dionysiac temple at the center of the *paradeisos* (4,2,6).[16] This repeats the association of spring, garden, and Nymphs at the beginning of the novel. A spring reserved for flowers is deemed Daphnis' spring (4,4,1).

---

[12] Zeitlin 1990, 421.
[13] Kuttner 1999a, 345.
[14] Dream revelations in Second Temple period Jewish literature often occur while the prophet is asleep at the river (*Dan.* 10,9; *1 Enoch.* 13,7–8). See Peters 2009, 133. In *Daphnis and Chloe*, the first dream revelation (that of the parents) envisages the spring (1,7,2), the second (that of Daphnis) occurs at the spring, and the third (that of captain Bryaxis) is near the sea (2,27–28). Beginning with the third book, the dream revelations come in response to conscious anxieties of the dreamers and use legitimating description that convinces the dreamer to act unconventionally (e.g., abandoning refined education for shepherding).
[15] Zeitlin 1990, 443.
[16] Zeitlin 1990, 451.

Longus' motif of the spring subverts the natural landscapes, the *loci amoeni*, found in critics of luxury. In authors such as Horace and Lucretius, these idyllic environments are minimally defined by elements of water, trees, and song.[17] Horace sets such places of natural beauty in opposition to the perversion of nature in the Roman villa. The Epicurean landscape, for Lucretius, symbolizes the correct way of living, free of *luxuria*.[18] Ann Kuttner has written on the purpose of the frescoes of the Roman garden room to domesticate – and, consequently, dominate – nature.[19] Longus, though, notes the many problems of pastoral life, beginning with the potential wolves (1,20,4) and biting flies (1,23,3). *Technē*, as when Chloe becomes more beautiful with make-up, will ultimately be preferred to *phusis*.[20] At the same time, Longus concludes the novel by refusing fully to authorize civilization, as Daphnis and Chloe bring their goats into the city, much to the consternation of their neighbors (4,38,4). Daphnis and Chloe not only continue in their cultic devotion to the ritual site of the spring, but they emulate their own upbringing in having goats suckle their children.

2 The Spring as Egalitarian Motif

A Chloe's Association with the Spring

As the prologue establishes that the spring sustains everything in the idealized garden of Longus, Chloe's association with the motif of springs serves as the mechanism by which Longus destabilizes and reconfigures gender roles throughout the novel. The spring is a liminal space in which she can explore the bodies of both herself and Daphnis outside normal gender expression. It creates a reciprocal relationship between Chloe and Daphnis. The spring's constancy in its connection with her resists the competing demands from the pastoral and civilized spheres, bringing forth the imaginative space in which a less patriarchal union can be created and nurtured.

The spring by which Chloe was abandoned witnesses the beginning of *erōs* when Chloe gazes on Daphnis' bathing body in the Nymphs' cave.[21] This devel-

---

17 *Saec.* 4,2,27–32 and 4,3,10–12; Lucr. 2,20–33.
18 Newlands 2002, 130.
19 Kuttner 1999b. See also Mittelstadt 1967.
20 Goldhill 1995, 64, 107, discusses Roman moralists' excoriation of women for wearing make-up. In Xenophon *Oic.* 10, the new bride is chided for wearing make-up and high heels like a slave. See Goff 2004, 135.
21 Goldhill 1995, 9–11.

opment has been presaged in the novel in the dream revelation received by both Lamon and Dryas depicting Daphnis and Chloe being handed over by the Nymphs to an unidentified winged boy – the site is the spring 'where Dryas had found the baby' (1,7,2). In order to avoid parental censure for having a minor escapade in their pastoral duties that involved Daphnis falling into a pit, the pair go to the Nymphs in order to wash the mud off Daphnis' body (1,12–13). As Chloe watches Daphnis bathe, he seems beautiful to her for the first time. She thinks the bath must be the cause of his newfound beauty, and she tests her hypothesis as she washes his back. Longus suggests her desire is one of similarity in body: Chloe feels Daphnis' skin to see if it is softer than hers (1,13,2). Longus departs from such marital models as the Homeric like-minded marriage between Odysseus and Penelope, where Penelope's bed-trick forces Odysseus to reveal his identity. Longus instead emphasizes that the basis of the erotic relationship between Daphnis and Chloe is the tactile similarity of their bodies, empirically discovered by Chloe as she touches Daphnis.[22] Where Penelope waits for epistemological enlightenment from Odysseus, Chloe actively constructs her fields of knowledge scientifically.

The idyllic setting prevents Daphnis and Chloe from questioning the appropriateness of their actions. Social anxieties concerning the bath were manifested in myriad myths concerning violations of female bathing: the violation of Susanna's bath by two prominent men in Susanna and the Elders; the unintended disturbance of Artemis' bath by Aktaion; the blinding of Erymanthos, son of Apollo, for chancing upon Aphrodite in the bath; the lusting of Hermas after his mistress Rhoda bathing in the Tiber in the *Shepherd of Hermas*. The thrust of these myths, though, is not to restrict women's mobility by implying that they are under constant threat from male sexuality. Instead, in each of these stories, the sanctity of a woman's bath, even when it is in the public sphere, such as a river or a spring, is upheld. Such is the assessment of Quintilian, who acknowledges the potential for misunderstanding mixed bathing – men and women bathing together – as promiscuous behavior liable to result in adultery. He dismisses this line of reasoning on the grounds that if mixed bathing were considered promiscuous behavior, then so too could reveling with youths and having intimate friendships with men be considered grounds of adultery (*Inst. Orat.* 5,9,14). Some of this salacious activity might have involved prostitutes, but there are also sources such as Martial's epigram relating Galba's desire to marry Martial (11,19). Juvenal's satire of the practice of mixed bathing as a venue for the genital stimulation of ma-

---

22 For the problematic nature of touching in Greek literature, see Carson 1990, 135.

trons is further confirmation of its popularity as a healthy activity bordering between the respectable and the risqué.[23]

Premarital mixed bathing, of course, is not perceived as a problem in *Daphnis and Chloe*. Chloe's empowerment over traditional gender performance continues in her subsequent ablutions of Daphnis. After the burial of Daphnis' rival Dorkon, Chloe takes Daphnis to the Nymphs and bathes him. Chloe keeps her kiss with Dorkon secret. She re-establishes a unique erotic relationship with Daphnis by bathing in front of him for the first time. In both the contemporary Christian text of Ephesians and Ovid's version of the festival of Venus, Verticordia, a bath functions to wash blemishes off the body of the woman in the eyes of a man – in Ephesians, the husband washes the blemishes off his wife (5,26 – 27); in the cult of Venus Verticordia, the women wash the blemishes off themselves and adorn the cult statue with garlands (Ov. *Fast.* 4,133 – 160). Chloe, naturally, does not need the bath to remove blemishes – the bath made Daphnis *kalos* to Chloe, and it was a kiss that enflamed the heart of Daphnis. The pair offers flower garlands for Dorkon to the Nymphs. Chloe's character seems to have derived some of the benefits associated with female bathing rituals and customs, while escaping such potential pitfalls as the imputed presence of blemishes.

The flow of Longus' narrative places Chloe's bath, a significant development in Daphnis and Chloe's relationship, between two narrative events connected with Daphnis' dead rival (1,32,1). Chloe does not go as far as Daphnis will go with Lykainion, but she has a sexual secret of her own, one that she has made consciously. Moreover, this incident follows Chloe's removal of her breastband to give to a cowherd recruited from a neighboring farm (1,12,4). The breastband is charged with eroticism, particularly since a series of erotic representations found among Fourth Style wall-paintings (62–79 CE) feature women naked save for a breastband.[24] On the one hand, Chloe's removal of her breastband prepares her for a sexual relationship with Daphnis in a manner that reminds one of Martial's comment to his wife that 'a girl cannot be naked enough' (11,104,7–8). This is a play on the motif of Aphrodite/matron (un)tying her breastband at her bath, found from the Hellenistic to imperial Roman periods.[25] On the other hand, Chloe hands the breastband not to Daphnis, but to a cowherd, who extends it to Daphnis. Theorizing on the nature of striptease, Barthes has observed that removing elements of clothing reinscribes 'nakedness as a *natural* vesture of woman, which amounts in the end to regaining a perfectly chaste

---

[23] Ward 1992, 134–138.
[24] Stafford 2005, 106.
[25] Stafford 2005, 107.

state of the flesh'.²⁶ Here, Chloe's action of removing her breast-support highlights the artifice and *technē* that it is, as the strip of cloth can also literally serve as a hoisting device. One wonders about the identity of Longus' intended audience: would elite male readers really be consoled at the thought of their female counterparts sharing kisses with their romantic rivals and, as Dorkon is a cowherd rather than a mere goatherd, social betters?

But the spring does not only enhance Chloe's agency; it also constructs Daphnis as a passive hero, the fundamental protagonist of the Greek novel.²⁷ During the Methymnean raid, Chloe takes Daphnis to the Nymphs 'very quietly' (*pollēn hēsuxian*) in order that she may wash the blood off his face, feed him, and kiss him (2,18). In contrast, Daphnis looks for Chloe in the 'quiet' (*hēsuxias*) of the post-raid plain (2,21,2). Upon discovering she has been taken as booty, he resolves either to die or to wait until the next war.²⁸ He then visits the spring to accuse the Nymphs, who offer to intercede for him with Pan (2,23,4). Similarly, after the flowers of Daphnis' spring have been destroyed in the wake of Lamon's cleaning of them, the family mourns his impending punishment by the master, and Chloe envisions him already being flogged (4,9,1). Daphnis' encounters with springs underscore his social vulnerabilities.

Chloe, of course, shares these vulnerabilities. The springs of the novel do not act as a utopian or apotropaic refuge for her—after all, she is abducted by pirates at the Grotto of the Nymphs. As Daphnis must succeed where Pan has failed, by getting the girl, Chloe must learn to choose more strategic geographic locations than Syrinx when in duress. In Book Two, after Lamon's story about Pan and Syrinx and Philetas' song, Longus' narrative tells us that all syrinxes are represented by one syrinx (2,35,4). Chloe then enacts the role of Syrinx to Daphnis' Pan, but, instead of fleeing to a marsh, she hides in the woods (2,37,2). The importance of this innovation does not become clear until Book Four, in the scene where Daphnis entertains the large crowd, including Gnathon, by playing the syrinx. Chloe, upon seeing the crowd approach, has already fled into the woods. Perhaps this timidity is an illustration of Bourdieu's argument that women, of necessity, are better than men at reading non-verbal, non-explicit cues.²⁹ Chloe has never been completely protected from the dangers of the opposite sex in Longus' ideal landscape. During the pirate raid of the first book, Chloe is safe because she was driving Dryas' sheep out more slowly, due to her fear of the headstrong shepherds (1,28,2).

---

[26] Barthes 1972, 85.
[27] Konstan 1994, 15–36.
[28] Iamblichos' *Babyloniaka* features men who kill themselves freely.
[29] Bourdieu 2001, 31.

In any event, Chloe's response contrasts with the uncharacteristic boldness of Daphnis, who here manages to play an aggressive, masculine role in entertaining the crowd in the hopes of being rewarded with marriage to Chloe. He will later emulate her approach—albeit in his own suicidal manner, by running toward the sea to cast himself off a cliff—when Astylus and a large crowd run toward him to give him the glad tidings that he is the son of Dionysophanes and the brother of Astylus (4,22,2). Hiding in the woods, of course, would have been the wiser action for Daphnis, as the woods would have concealed him from Gnathon's gaze and taken him back to the site where he learned how to perform the 'work of love' from Lykainion. Paradoxically, the woods are a site of agency as much as they are the site of hiddenness.[30] The ideal spring in the novel is a site of civilization, which is a negotiated space and, as such, never a safe haven.

Though both Daphnis and Chloe interact with the spring, the narrative codes the spring as Chloe's. Chloe is the only one of the pair to be nursed in the Nymphs' cave. When Daphnis and Chloe dedicate their pastoral items at the cave at the conclusion of their pastoral life, Daphnis takes a drink from the spring because he had often done so on his outings with Chloe. Longus thus portrays Daphnis as the object of Chloe's gaze at the spring both literally and in remembrance (1,12–13; 4,26,4). Chloe pours wine into the spring because she had been nursed by it and bathed in it (4,26,4; 4,32,3). Lykainion's instruction to have Chloe bathe in the spring to remove the blood of defloration is thwarted when the narrative progresses to Daphnis swimming in rivers and Chloe bathing in springs (3,24,2).

B Daphnis' Association with Flowers

To complement Chloe's connection with the spring, Daphnis is associated with flowers. The metaphors of the novel thus take 'literally', in the manner of de Certeau's notion of social delinquency, the worries of Chloe's mother that Chloe will give up her virginity for apples or roses.[31] In the Prologue, the flowers are subordinated to the sustaining spring. Likewise, Daphnis' association with the flowers watered by the spring in the subsequent narrative serves to subordinate him to Chloe.[32]

---

30 Kestner 1973, 171.
31 For Greek cultural associations of maidens with fruit, see Carson 1990, 145–148.
32 Daphnis also assumes other typically feminine imagery, such as being a talkative cricket (1,17,4).

Daphnis' floral connection is made clear first by the comparisons of the novel. When Chloe laments her lovesickness after seeing Daphnis in his bath, she compares Daphnis to flowers. In the contest with Dorkon for a kiss from Chloe, Daphnis himself compares himself to flowers. To win his suit, Dorkon has claimed that Daphnis is 'beardless like a woman' (1,16,2). Daphnis is at a disadvantage against Dorkon in age, since Dorkon used to shepherd with Chloe's adopted father. Daphnis therefore likens both his beardlessness and his skin to the hyacinth and announces that Dionysos shares this attribute. Moreover, there is a hierarchy of flowers – the hyacinth is better than the lily, for example – and so Daphnis' perceived softness is of the very best kind. Chloe crowns Daphnis' head with violets and kisses his hair, which she thinks is better than the violets. This might be a literary allusion to Odysseus' hair when he woos Nausikaa and his own wife Penelope.[33] In Roman literature, violets symbolize beautiful yet fragile virginity and love.[34] In the *Lament for Bion*, the hyacinth chatters in sorrow at the death of the beautiful flute-player. The resemblance of Daphnis to flowers both underscores his heroic beauty and threatens to tear the lovers apart.

As the narrative progresses, Daphnis soon becomes quite literally and inextricably linked with the fate of flowers. When Lampis realizes that Daphnis will be the one to wed Chloe if the master consents, Lampis ruins the flowers in Daphnis' master's park in an attempt to implicate Daphnis in the crime. Daphnis' father, Lamon, has just cleaned the springs for his master's arrival. The family proceeds to mourn for the flowers, 'a novelty' (4,8,1). Throughout the novel, Daphnis' association with flowers endows him with a vulnerability corroborated by his near abduction by a socially superior suitor and his helpless weeping at Chloe's actual abduction by a rival.

C The Spring in Relation to the Development of the Novel

Daphnis' dominance is often seen to develop as the novel progresses to the normative urban marriage at its conclusion. Two aspects in particular have been interpreted as introducing Daphnis to his proper patriarchal moment as a man. First, Daphnis' education of Chloe places him in the husbandly role of instructor established since Xenophon's *Oikonomikos*, though Chloe is, unusually, only two years younger than Daphnis. Second, the apple-picking scene, where Daphnis re-

---

[33] *Od.* 6,231; *Od.* 23,157–162.
[34] Cf. Ovid *Met.* 5,392; Pliny *Hist. Nat.* 21,38,4.

trieves an apple for Chloe against her wishes, confirms him as the dominant, decision-making patriarch. I will suggest that these scenes give Chloe agency: she initiates kisses beyond Daphnis' requests, and she demands that Daphnis pay her due attention. They do not establish a patriarchal, asymmetrical relationship between Daphnis and Chloe.

D Daphnis' Education of Chloe

At the conclusion of the novel, Daphnis 'does Chloe some of what Lykainion had taught him'. This is often taken by interpreters to signify Daphnis' assumption of the traditional pedagogic role of the husband.[35] However, the verbs applied to Daphnis and Lykainion differ – Daphnis does (*edrase*), but Lykainion originally taught (*epaideuse*) the act (4,40,3). Thus, Daphnis does not become the teacher any more than he has truly become the wolf after a lupine liminal experience from childhood into adulthood. Up to this culminating point, the narrative has consistently undercut the reader's perception of Daphnis' exclusive knowledge.

The introduction of the *erotodidaskalos* Philetas near the beginning of the second book is one of the fundamental moments of pedagogy. Longus' Philetas shares his name with the grammarian who penned *Akatoi glōssai*. It is from Philetas that the young couple acquires a name to apply to *Erōs*: 'they heard for the first time the name of Love' (2,8,1). The concern for the name of *Erōs* is as much semiological as it is religious and practical.[36] Indeed, Daphnis' and Chloe's adopted parents have already had dreams with Love in them, and, though the pair is still entrusted to Love, they will not need to pay the god any type of obeisance. Their lexical education will not produce enlightenment as to how to satisfy their desire for one another. Daphnis and Chloe instead emulate in their confusion the example of Philetas the grammarian, who wasted away in a search for the 'fallacious *logos*'. The scene establishes Philetas as the teacher.

The novel's conclusion gives Chloe knowledge superior even to the authorial voice, which informs the reader that Daphnis and Chloe stayed up as late as owls in the wedding chamber. Longus' choice of the owl comparison is curious, for it resumes the description of the couple in pastoral language that the authorial voice has declared to be over. Even more peculiar is that Chloe learns that what had happened in the woods (τὰ ἐπὶ τῆς ὕλης γενόμενα) were mere shepherd's games. As the majority of Daphnis and Chloe's romantic activity has oc-

---

35 Winkler 1990, 124; Epstein 1995, 70; Morgan 2004, 12.
36 Whitmarsh 2005, 147.

curred in the fields and the Grotto of the Nymphs, the woods should be taken as the site of the romantic overtures of Dorkon and Lykainion. In the winter, Daphnis makes the same request of Chloe that the dying Dorkon did: to remember him. Chloe reassures Daphnis by swearing that she does remember him, swearing by the Nymphs of the Grotto, where they will return once the Scythian snow melts.

Civilization and cultivation are signified by the marriage – Chloe and Daphnis entered the wedding chamber to an *epithalamium* that sounded as though the singing wedding party were breaking the ground with pitchforks. Greek literature typically presents the bride as a wild location that needs to be cultivated by the husband and the coital act as corresponding to the verb 'to hoe' (σκαλεύειν).[37] Accordingly, the reader may think of the tryst between Lykainion and Daphnis as a 'mere shepherd's game', a game that is not appropriate to Daphnis' newly elevated social status. Chloe's own perspective on the loss of her virginity contradicts Lykainion's prognostication. With her new education, Chloe has triumphed over Daphnis' would-be ἐραστής.

3 Springs as Symbols of Hospitality and Civilization

Ultimately, Chloe and Daphnis mature from country- to urban-dwellers through the tutelage of the text. So, too, do springs expand into a symbol of broader hospitality and civilization. Five characters have a connection with bathing in springs in the novel: Daphnis, Chloe, Philetas, Dorkon, and Lykainion. Daphnis and Chloe are the chosen pair of Eros, whose shepherding role is embodied by Philetas. After the initial she-wolf encounter leads Chloe to bathe Daphnis in the spring, the two human 'wolves' in the story, Dorkon and Lykainion, challenge this arrangement. The spring develops the generosity of hospitality, as Dorkon is rehabilitated, and the values of civilization, as Lykainion is not.

A Dorkon's Redemption

Dorkon is redeemed authorially by being washed in the spring by the lovers, who remain unaware of his transgression. As his dying act, Dorkon saves the life of

---

[37] For betrothal formulas, see Clement of Alexandria *Strom.* 2,23, and Menander *Pk.* 435. For sexual intercourse, see Aristophanes *Pax* 440 and *Ec.* 611. See Carson 1990, 149.

his romantic rival in exchange for a kiss and a promise to remember him. Daphnis and Chloe proceed to pay homage to his memory at the spring in the Nymph's cave. Thus, the spring sustains Dorkon's rehabilitation into society and worship of the gods. Since other incidents, such as the Methymnean driving of Chloe and goats from the cave, seem to indicate a choice in piety, the novel represents an optimistic viewpoint on human relations: enemies need not remain so in light of the civilizing influence of the spring (2,20).

B Lykainion's Pedagogy

Lykainion does not bathe in the spring nor is she redeemed as the male characters Dorkon and Gnathon are. She is present at Daphnis and Chloe's wedding with her husband, but this is inconclusive as evidence of her character, since Lampis is also present (4,38,2–3). Interpreters such as Konstan and May have taken Lykainion to be a sympathetic character.[38] However, Epstein observes that Lykainion's teaching has an element of Pan.[39] She is a stock character also found in *Leucippe and Clitophon*, where Clitophon tells Melite that it would be unsuitable to consummate their marriage on a moving bed (5,16), a clear play on the trope of Odysseus' famously immovable bed. Lykainion and Melite belong to the long-established tradition of the predatory woman, well known since Euripides' treatment of Phaedra and Hippolytos.[40] However, in Daphnis' case, Lykainion represents real danger, as she, an elite woman, is asking a slave to commit adultery with her, an offense which in plays such as *Miles gloriosus* carries threats of castration (1398–1399). Though a woman, Lykainion has a class advantage on Daphnis that far outweighs Dorkon's superiority over Daphnis and Chloe, due to his shepherding of cows instead of goats. This makes her analogous to the upper-class wives in Juvenal's sixth satire who have affairs with men of lower classes.[41] She should not be sexually available to the slave Daphnis. Nonetheless, despite her privileged social and sexual positions, the novel gives Lykainion an advantage over neither Daphnis nor Chloe.

True to her 'little wolf' moniker, Lykainion suggests that Daphnis bring Chloe to the spring, take her virginity where no one can hear her screams, and have her bathe the blood off in the spring. Such an action would transpire outside of the community. Daphnis, who has previously insisted to Chloe that

---

[38] Konstan 1994, 54; May 2005, 132.
[39] Epstein 1995, 70; Epstein 2002, 72.
[40] For Phaedra, see Zeitlin 1996, 219–284.
[41] On Juvenal, see Smith 2005, 119.

doing 'everything he wanted' would 'conquer the bitterness of love' (3,14,3), now cringes at the thought of Chloe bleeding and yelling at him as if he were an enemy (3,24,3). If, as Carson notes, civilization is a function of boundaries and anthropologists have correctly observed that 'every touch is a modified blow', then Daphnis is reassessing the norms of civilization and the violence therein.[42] Pain, as evidenced by the Spartan practice of commemorating by tomb inscription only male death on the battlefield and female death in childbirth, was culturally perceived as inevitable and even beneficial.[43] It is the thought of turning Chloe into an enemy that gives Daphnis real distress.

Lykainion's proposal inhabits the marginal spatiality of maenadism, which is a state diametrically opposed to marriage in ancient Greek consciousness.[44] The maenad is akin to the sanctioned female ἐραστής; the Dionysiac priestess pays to initiate worshippers 'in the city, in the country, in the islands' (*LSAM* 48,18–19, an early third-century inscription from Miletos on the priestess' responsibilities). Lykainion is behaving as a maenad in the no-man's-land territory of a maenad, and she has used gifts to initiate Daphnis in order to induce him to induct Chloe likewise into maenadism, outside the conventions of marriage.

The patriarchal message undergirding Lykainion's admonition – that male desire is a desire to harm, to conquer – is particularly dire in the opinion of Winkler: 'Nevertheless, the content of Lykainion's warning, even if the context shifts it into an ironic mode, is grim'.[45] In response to Winkler, Goldhill suggests Daphnis' naivete erects him as a positive exemplum: 'Is not part of the joke precisely that Daphnis *does* take the message to heart and that *that* is a sign of pastoral innocence, his ποιμενικὴ γνώμη?' Whereas the medical writer Soranus finds evidence of the voracious female sexual appetite even in the instance of rape, in Goldhill's reading, Daphnis interrogates his masculine desire lest it be deleterious to the object of his desire. Love, for Daphnis, seeks what is best for the beloved.[46]

In Daphnis' aversion to conceptualizing Chloe in violent metaphors, Longus presents a subtle critique on the warfare *topoi* prevalent across genres, including that of the ancient novel, with a focus on love.[47] The sensuality of Callirhoe's bathing body is indicated by the fear that touching her might inflict a 'bad

---

42 du Bois 1988; Carson 1990, 135.
43 Plutarch *Lyc.* 27,2–3; King 1999, 274–276.
44 Seaford 1995, 301–11; Goff 2004, 278.
45 Goldhill 1995, 35.
46 Goldhill 1995, 39.
47 Smith 2005, 82, provides an overview of warfare imagery in Roman erotic literature.

wound'.⁴⁸ Lucretius compares the attraction one feels toward a beautiful body with falling toward a wound.⁴⁹ Ovid declares 'every lover is a warrior' and depicts the sleeping husband as the enemy.⁵⁰ In *Ninos,* the eponymous protagonist protests to his beloved's mother that her daughter has made him a 'prisoner of war—an honorable captivity, of course'.⁵¹ Daphnis is so steadfast in his desire not to hurt Chloe that he stops seeking to have her lie next to him naked, and finally pursues her hand in marriage only when it becomes apparent that her parents will marry her off to another who will have no such qualms.⁵² The relationship of a man and woman, for Longus, can be positively expressed through fruit metaphors, but not through warfare metaphors. A man and a woman are not enemies; they are partners against life's real threats.

The spring thus represents Chloe's privileged status as a protagonist of the novel. Daphnis' mother Myrtale is persuaded that Chloe might want a handsome young husband rather than a rich one (3,26,4). Lykainion is in an unequal marriage: her aged spouse has come to farm his own land in the country, while she is still young and pretty. Lykainion does not obtain a lengthy, torrid love affair but a 'one-spring stand'. If she wants to continue to supplement her elderly husband's deficiencies, she will have to repeat the process of investigation and outlay of economic goods in exchange for sensual pleasures.⁵³

Chloe is privileged again by the novel when Lykainion's plan for Chloe to have a singular sexual encounter with Daphnis – as opposed to the coveted marriage to an equal – is thwarted by the progression of the narrative toward aquatic recreation. Daphnis proceeds to swim in the rivers, while Chloe proceeds to bathe in the springs. From the first book of the novel, we know that the only difference between these two actions is the topographical feature: Daphnis bathes (and incidentally hunts circularly swimming fish) when he is swimming in rivers. Interpreting these through the narrative framework, there could be a seasonal aspect and an implication of the cycle of life, recurring motifs in the novel (cf. 2,3,4). From an anthropological vantage point, swimming in rivers is part of an initiation ritual in a report by Euanthes, read by Varro and found in Pliny.⁵⁴ In an Arcadian family descended from Anthos, a young boy, selected by lot, had to re-

---

48 Hunter 1993, 1074–5.
49 Lucr. 4,1049–1057.
50 *Am. 1,*9,1; 1,9,25–26.
51 A, II,27–31.
52 Konstan 1994, 88.
53 Stephen and Winkler 1995, 347, correlate Lykainion's behavior with that of Persis in *Phoinikika.*
54 *Nat.* 8,81.

move his clothes, swim across a lake, and become a wolf for eight years. If he successfully managed to avoid eating human meat, he was allowed to swim back and resume his human existence, now as a grown man. Epstein has posited that the liminal period suggested by this Spartan myth serves to form the ephebe into a new *corps* for the Spartan military corporate body.[55] By contrast, Daphnis, by swimming circularly, is not orienting himself in the normal expansiveness of ancient men. He masters the circular fish within the river without needing to cross over to the other side to become a wolf.

Longus' thwarting of Lykainion also reverses associations found in other second century myths. Pausanias recounts a story with the same association of rivers as male and springs as female. In it, the hunter Alpheus falls in love with the huntress Arethusa. Unwilling to marry, Arethusa swims to the island Ortygia and turns into a spring in order to escape Alpheus' advances. However, the outcome of Pausanias' tale is entirely different. Alpheus wins in the romantic struggle, since he is able to turn into a river which can mingle with Arethusa's spring.[56] The geographical consequences of unrequited love in Pausanias' version are almost identical to Ovid's tale of the river-god Acheloos' lapping his streams against a nymph-turned-island. A recognition of the danger for the female in this motif can be found in the Greek novel *Leucippe and Cleitophon*, where the hero Cleitophon enumerates four examples of *eros* in nature. After deeming the flowing together of Alpheus and Arethusa a marriage (*gamos*), the hero explains that in the mating of the land-snake and the water-snake, 'the continental lover and the island beloved', the land-snake must eject the poison from his fangs before kissing the water-snake (1,7). Through the motif of the spring, Daphnis and Chloe subvert both the asymmetrical relationships of wealthy women and slave found in the satirists and New Comedy, and of victorious man and conquered woman related by Ovid and Pausanias.[57]

4 Politics of the Spring

The final moral of the novel is: live in the city, but be not 'of the city'. The idealized bucolic values are connected to the cave, the nymphs, and the spring. This may be seen in the scene where Daphnis dedicates his pastoral items, speaks

---

[55] Epstein 1995, 72.
[56] Paus. 5,7,2–3.
[57] Konstan 1994, 85.

with the goats, and drinks from the spring. The narrative function of the spring is to critique the value-system of civilization traditionally defined.

Militaristic and imperialistic *topoi* saturate Longus' *historia*. The novel commences with a suckling she-wolf, traditionally a symbol for Rome, destroying livestock. The central political incident is the Methymnean invasion, where the militaristic trumpet plays on pastoral pipes. Daphnis initially believes that doing 'everything he wanted' would 'conquer the bitterness of love' (3,14,3), though he desists from this pursuit because he does not want Chloe to look at him as though he were an 'enemy'. Warfare imagery also features in Lykainion's instructions to Daphnis. Captain Bryaxis' dream from Pan rescues the captured Chloe. Militaristic intervention is necessary again when Gnathon has a 'great victory' rescuing Chloe and is eager to tie up Lampis as a 'prisoner of war' (4,29,3). After refusing to employ the warfare metaphors common in erotic literature, Longus suggests the juxtaposition of political and pastoral by the new titles of 'Soldier' for Pan and 'Shepherd' for Eros at the end of the novel.

Ultimately, this division is not a dichotomy. Pan, with his theriomorphism and war, does not exist in isolation from the Nymphs, with their spring and civilization. Daphnis and Chloe demonstrate the pedagogic value of the interplay of the spring and the flock by using sheep and goats to nurse their children, Philopoemen and Agele, in the city (4,39,2). The Temple of Pan appears to be unique to Longus, and indicates bringing Pan in from the periphery.[58] In the protagonists' mutual negotiation of a socially acceptable relationship in which the male is modeled on Pan/Dionysos and the female is modeled on the Nymphs, both husband and wife gain authority in the socioreligious order of Longus' moral vision. As in the Roman notion of *emulatio*, the young lovers improve on the examples of Pan and the Nymphs in their mimesis.

5 Conclusion

In *Daphnis and Chloe*, the phrase '*philesai philousan*' ('to love a woman who loves in turn') is paradigmatic.[59] Given the gender inequalities pervading the contemporary culture, Longus' technique for effecting mutuality in desire and its expression is to create a relation of motifs that privilege the female in order to resist cultural impulses toward patriarchy. Longus highlights the vestiges of the voices belonging to those dismembered by patriarchy: the nightin-

---

58 Morgan 2004, 248.
59 Konstan 1994, 35.

gale, the swallow, and Echo. Men and women, however, need not be at war even metaphorically; they may partner together against actual threats from pirates, Methymneans, and even their own neighbors. Thus, Chloe is associated with the central motif of the spring and the Nymphs, and Daphnis is allied with the flowers sustained by the spring and Pan/Dionysos. Participation of parental figures such as Lamon and Philetas in the maintenance and enjoyment of the spring sanction the marital and civic valences of the *topos*. Chloe and Daphnis utilize the spring to circumvent and rehabilitate rivals, occasionally with negotiation of *topoi* associated with Pan. Raising their children at the spring, they attempt to replicate their own liberating education in order to have people with whom to grow old. This mimesis does not include their neighbors, who remain rehabilitated by the spring but not initiated into and sustained by it. In these ways, the symbolism of the spring occupies the interstices of narratological relations and Longus' timeless message.

Bibliography

Anagianou, A. 1991. *Sacred Marriage in the Rituals of Greek Religion*, Berne: Peter Lang.
Barthes, R. 1972. *Mythologies* (A. Levers, trans.), New York: Hill and Wang.
Bourdieu, P. 2001. *Masculine Domination* (R. Nice, trans.), Stanford: Stanford University Press.
Bowie, E. 2005. 'Metaphor in *Daphnis and Chloe*', in: S. Harrison, M. Paschalis, S. Frangoulidis (eds.), *Ancient Narrative: Metaphor and the Ancient Novel*, Groningen: Barkhuis. 68–86.
Boyarin, D. 1997. *Unheroic Conduct: The Rise of Heterosexuality and the Invention of the Jewish Man*, Berkeley: University of California Press.
Brethes, R. 2007. *'Poiein Aischra Kai Legein Aischra*, Est-ce Vraiment La Même Chose ? Ou la bouche souillée de Chariclée', in: V. Rimell (ed.), *Seeing Tongues, Hearing Scripts: Orality and Representation in the Ancient Novel*, Groningen: Barkuis, 223–256.
Burkert, W. 1983. *Homo Necans: The Anthropology of Ancient Greek Sacrificial Ritual and Myth* (P. Bing, trans.), Berkeley: University of California Press.
Burrus, V. 2005. 'Mimicking Virgins: Colonial Ambivalence and the Ancient Romance', *Arethusa* 38, 49–88.
Carson, A. 1990. 'Putting Her in Her Place: Woman, Dirt, and Desire', in: D.M. Halperin, J.J. Winkler, F.I. Zeitlin (eds.), *Before sexuality: the construction of the erotic experience in the ancient Greek world*, Princeton: Princeton University Press. 135–169.
Chalk, H.O. 1960. 'Eros and the Lesbian Pastorals of Longos', *JHS* 80, 32–51.
Chew, K. 2007. 'Divine Epistemology: The Relationship Between Speech and Writing in the *Aithiopika*', in: V. Rimell (ed.), *Seeing Tongues, Hearing Scripts: Orality and Representation in the Ancient Novel*, Groningen : Barkuis, 279–298.

D'Ambra, E. 1996. 'The Calculus of Venus: Nude Portraits of Roman Matrons', in: N.B. Kampen (ed.), *Sexuality in Ancient Art: Near East, Egypt, Greece, and Italy*. Cambridge: Cambridge University Press. 219–232.
de Certeau, M. 1984. *The Practice of Everyday Life*, Berkeley: University of California Press.
du Bois, P. 1988. *Sowing the Body: Psychoanalysis and Ancient Representations of Women*, Chicago: University of Chicago Press.
Epstein, S. 1995. 'Longus' Werewolves', *Classical Philology* 90, 58–73.
Epstein, S. 2002. 'The Education of Daphnis: Goat, Gods, the Birds, and the Bees', *Phoenix* 56, 25–39.
Faraone, C. 1990. 'Aphrodite's *KESTOS* and Apples for Atalanta: Aphrodisiacs in Early Greek Myth and Ritual', *Phoenix* 44, 219–243.
Gilhuly, K. 2009. *The Feminine Matrix of Sex and Gender in Classical Athens*, Cambridge: Cambridge University Press.
Goff, B. 2004. *Citizen Bacchae: Women's Ritual Practice in Ancient Greece*, Berkeley: University of California Press.
Goldhill, S. 1995. *Foucault's Virginity*, Cambridge: Cambridge University Press.
Hawkins, T. 2009. 'This is the Death of the Earth: Crisis Narratives in Archilochus and Mnesiepes', *TAPA* 139, 1–20.
Hunter, R. 1993. 'History and Historicity in Chariton', *ANRW* II.43.2, 1055–1086.
Kestner, J. 1973. 'Ekphrasis as Frame in Longus' *Daphnis and Chloe*,' *Classical World* 67, 166–171.
King, H. 1999. 'Chronic Pain and the Creation of Narrative', in: J.I. Porter (ed.), *Constructions of the Classical Body*, Ann Arbor: University of Michigan Press. 269–286.
Konstan, D. 1994. *Sexual Symmetry: Love in the Ancient Novel and Related Genres*, Princeton: Princeton University Press.
Kuttner, A. 1999a. 'Culture and History at Pompey's Museum', *TAPA* 129, 343–373.
Kuttner, A. 1999b. 'Looking Outside Inside: Ancient Roman Garden Rooms', *Studies in the History of Gardens and Designed Landscapes* 19.1 [special issue, J. D. Hunt (ed.), *The Immediate Garden and the Larger*], 7–35.
Lissarrague, F. 1990. 'The Sexual Life of Satyrs', in: D.M. Halperin, J.J. Winkler, F.I. Zeitlin (eds.), *Before sexuality: the construction of the erotic experience in the ancient Greek world*, Princeton: Princeton University Press. 53–81.
Littlewood, A.R. 1968. 'The Symbolism of the Apple in Greek and Roman Literature', *HSPh* 72, 147–181.
Luginbill, R.D. 2002. 'A Delightful Possession: Longus' Prologue and Thucydides', *CJ* 97, 233–247.
MacQueen, Bruce. 1990. *Myth, Rhetoric, and Fiction*. Lincoln: University of Nebraska Press.
Marinelli, P.V. 1971. *Pastoral*, London: Methuen.
Mason, H.J. 1995. 'Romance in a Limestone Landscape,' *Classical Philology* 90, 263–266.
Mattingly, D. 2011. *Imperialism, Power, and Identity: Experiencing the Roman Empire*, Princeton: Princeton University Press.
May, R. 2005. 'Chaste Artemis and Lusty Aphrodite: The Portrait of Women and Marriage in the Greek and Latin Novels', in: W.S. Smith, (ed.), *Satiric Advice on Women and Marriage: From Plautus to Chaucer*, Ann Arbor: University of Michigan Press. 129–153.
Mittelstadt, M. 1967. 'Longus: *Daphnis and Chloe* and Roman Narrative Painting', *Latomus* 26, 752–761.

Morgan, J.R. (trans.) 2004. *Longus: Daphnis and Chloe*, Oxford: Oxbow.
Newlands, C.E. 2002. *Statius' Silvae and the Poetics of Empire*, Cambridge: Cambridge University Press.
Newlands, C.E. 1987. "*Technē*' and '*Tuchē*' in Longus' *Daphnis and Chloe*', *Pacific Coast Philology* 22, 52–58.
Nickau, K. 2002. 'Zur Epiphanie des Eros im Hirtenroman des Longos', *Hermes* 130, 176–191.
Pandiri, T.A. 1985. '*Daphnis and Chloe*: the Art of Pastoral Play', *Ramus* 14: 116–141.
Peters, J. 2009. 'Hellenistic Imagery and Iconography in Daniel 12.5–13', *Journal for the Study of the Pseudepigrapha* 19, 127–145.
Pratt, L. 1994. '*Odyssey* 19.535–50: On the Interpretation of Dreams and Signs in Homer', *CPh* 89, 148–153.
Richlin, A. 1983. *The Garden of Priapus: Sexuality and Aggression in Roman Humor*, New Haven: Yale University Press.
Seaford, R. 1995. *Reciprocity and Ritual*, Oxford: Oxford University Press.
Smith, W.S. 2005. 'Advice on Sex by the Self-Defeating Satirists', in: W.S. Smith (ed.), *Satiric Advice on Women and Marriage: From Plautus to Chaucer*, Ann Arbor: University of Michigan Press. 111–128.
Smith, W.S. 2005. "The Cold Cares of Venus': Lucretius and Anti-Marriage Literature', in: W.S. Smith (ed.), *Satiric Advice on Women and Marriage: From Plautus to Chaucer*, Ann Arbor: University of Michigan Press. 129–153.
Stafford, Emma J. 2005. 'Viewing and Obscuring the Female Breast', in: L. Cleland, M. Harlow, and L. Llewellyn-Jones (eds.), *The Clothed Body in the Ancient World*, Oxbow: Oxbow. 96–112.
Stephen, S., and Winkler, J.J. (eds. and trans.) 1995. *Ancient Greek Novels: The Fragments*, Princeton: Princeton University Press.
Takács, S.A. 2008. *Vestal Virgins, Sibyls, and Matrons: Women in Roman Religion*, Austin: University of Texas Press.
Turner, P. 1960. 'Daphnis and Chloe: An Interpretation,' *G&R*, 117–123.
Vieillefond, J.-R. (ed. and trans.) 1987. *Longus: Pastorales*, Paris : Société d'Édition Les Belles Lettres.
Ward, R.B. 1992. 'Women in Roman Baths', *HThR* 85, 125–147.
Whitmarsh, T. 2005. 'The Lexicon of Love: Longus and Philetas Grammatikos', *JHS* 125, 145–148.
Winkler, J.J. 1990. 'The Education of Chloe: Hidden Injuries of Sex', in: J.J. Winkler (ed.), *Constraints of Desire: The Anthropology of Sex and Gender in Ancient Greece*, New York. 101–126.
Wouters, A. 1987. 'Irony in Daphnis' and Chloe's Love Lessons', *QUCC* 55, 111–118.
Zeitlin, F.I. 1996. *Playing the Other: Gender and Society in Classical Greek Literature*, Chicago: University of Chicago Press.
Zeitlin, F.I. 1990. 'The Poetics of *Erōs*: Nature, Art, and Imitation in Longus' *Daphnis and Chloe*', in: D.M. Halperin, J.J. Winkler, F.I. Zeitlin (eds.), *Before sexuality: the construction of the erotic experience in the ancient Greek world*, Princeton: Princeton University Press. 417–464.

Martina Meyer
Arcadia Revisited: Material Gardens and Virtual Spaces in Longus' *Daphnis and Chloe* and in Roman Landscape Painting

Abstract: The interplay between wild nature and artfully constructed space is the focal point for this discussion of the relationship between Longus' *Daphnis and Chloe* and Augustan landscape painting. The combined effect of nature and artifice affects the perceptual and conceptual reaction of the viewer to both both real and imagined space. The goal of Longus' art lies in imitating the skill with which a painted image can project a convincing sensation of pastoral harmony, where the deception of the senses is more pleasing than the materiality of the real. In the discussion that follows I shall explore the correspondence between material space and imagined space by identifying the characteristics of painting that produce the effect of 'Golden Age' reality, upon which the reader's emotional experience of Longus' novel depends.

Longus begins *Daphnis and Chloe* by establishing, in the opening sentences of the Prologue (I,1–4) the interdependence between wild nature and painted picture. While hunting, the narrator wanders into a grove sacred to the Nymphs, where, in a delightful space, thick with trees and flowers and watered by fountains and streams, he finds a work of art that is, to his mind, even more pleasing than the grove, as it not only imitates nature convincingly, but also introduces human emotion into nature's solitude. This admiration for imitative realism is well articulated in Pliny the Elder's story of two rival painters, Zeuxis and Parrhasius, who were competing to see who could produce the most realistic painting.[1] Zeuxis painted a picture of grapes so convincing that birds were deceived into pecking at the fruit. Parrhasius then invited Zeuxis to his studio to examine his contribution to their contest. Zeuxis tried to lift the curtain from the panel to see the painting underneath. To his surprise, the panel was a painting of a curtain. Zeuxis conceded that Parrhasius was the better painter: whereas he had deceived only birds, Parrhasius had fooled a human being. To the mind of Longus'

---

[1] Plin. *Nat.* 35.

Martina Meyer, Stanford University

https://doi.org/10.1515/9781501503986-012

narrator, the painted picture is similarly more wondrous than the sacred grove in which he stands. The verisimilitude and exactitude of the painting's deceptive imitation commands greater admiration than the reality that it recreates. It is as if, while remaining a product of human creation, the painting reproduces nature exactly, but within a language and imbued with a coherence that reflects what the human mind wants to see and feel, in contradistinction to what it actually experiences.

The painting is the idyllic and deceptively natural environment within which the romance will occur, suggesting that the novel may be as much indebted to the models and structures of Roman painting as it is to narrative tales of love and poetic celebrations of nature. The argument that Longus deliberately modeled his novel, *Daphnis and Chloe*, upon Roman narrative painting opens up many avenues of comparison between literary work and image.[2] While our understanding of the relationship between the novel and Roman narrative painting benefits from comparisons between the genres, re-directing the focus from narrative to painted landscape can expand our insights into the Augustan vision of a 'Golden Age' and the nostalgia it reflected. This nostalgia is evident in the affective, or psychological, response to the fictive landscapes created by panel paintings, represented for the purposes of this discussion by Livia's Garden Room, a sacro-idyllic landscape from the north wall at Boscoreale, and a mythic romance from Boscotrecase. At the heart of these fictive settings are the cultivated gardens and wild landscapes that inspired the artistic imagination. Fresh critical analyses of the Roman *experience* of the garden and the larger landscape have contributed greatly to our understanding of the construction and meaning of space.[3] Katharine von Stackelberg concentrates her recent investigation of gardens and their social function upon the centrality of an experience that involves memory and intellect. She reveals how gardens, whether designed for production or display, were multivalent spaces. They could signify idyllic nature, nostalgia, isolation or degeneracy, or any combination of these associations.[4] The painting Longus says he found 'in a grove of the Nymphs', recast as a four-book narrative, produces similar multivalent spaces by its emphasis on setting, exploiting the construct of an idealized environment in which man co-exists in harmony with nature, and revels in its own ability to draw the reader into experiencing real pleasure in its deceptions.

---

2 Mittelstadt 1967, 752–761; Nagy 2001.
3 von Stackelberg 2009; Pagán 2006; Bowe 2004. De Jong, ed. (2012), adopts the view that space reflects the feelings of a character and spatial surroundings provide a psychological insight.
4 von Stackelberg 2009, ch.1.

The mechanism by which an idyllic symbiosis between humans and their environment is created has been the object of much debate. Anthony Blunt once defined the genre of pastoral painting as an expression of polarity, a polarity he described as two extremes of reason – on the one side, the harmonies of nature, and on the other, the virtues of man.[5] By identifying the dichotomy inherent in the genre, Blunt emphasized the essential spirit of the pastoral tradition in the visual arts as being derived from, and therefore dependent upon, tension, a viewpoint that contrasts sharply with the notion that the 'pastoral' signifies serenity, security and visual pleasure.[6] If we accept the argument that tension underlies the pastoral, it follows that fictive pastoral landscapes are founded upon and are attempts to reconcile conflicting principles. On the one hand, the natural environment arises spontaneously; human intervention may be in evidence, but its transient materiality, manifest in the simple construction of rustic shelters and modest woodland shrines, underscores the dominance of nature. On the other hand, the technologies civilization imposes on nature in essence recreate it, leaving a permanent and indelible record in an environment so modified that intervention is required to recapture the experience of the 'natural'.[7] While the pastoral world is undeniably a fiction, its affective properties are indebted to the real; the sensation of harmony that makes this imagined, or virtual, space so compelling depends upon a credible union of the actual and the idealized. This inter-dependent relationship lies at the heart of John Dixon Hunt's observation, when speaking of approaches adopted by gardeners and architects to landscape design, that 'the very hold a designed landscape has on the imagination derives, paradoxically, from the solid materiality of its invented sceneries'.[8]

This paradox, namely an idealized love story taking place in a setting that imitates the real but shapes and tames it, takes hold of the imagination by its reliance on solid materiality in order to produce delight through deception. *Daphnis and Chloe* has been described by Paul Alpers as the only 'pastoral' work among several extant romances written in the early Christian era.[9] It is my view that the novel's pastoralism is achieved by its imitation of painted pastoral landscapes – images that rely upon the memory of the palpable and haptic in order to reinforce the deception that the imagined environment can be a gen-

---

5 Blunt 1995, 285. See also David Halperin 1983 whose definition of 'pastoral' focuses on the significance of opposition within the genre. Similarly, Bettina Bergmann 1992.
6 Pugh 1990, 1.
7 Appleton 1996, 168–9.
8 Hunt 1996, 37.
9 Alpers 1996, 324.

uine space to inhabit, even as such spaces remain an invention and, however convincing, are always shaped, edited, and fictive.[10] Augustan panel painting creates the longed-for but lost natural environment by relying upon the familiarity of the real, combined with the verisimilitude and materiality of its representation, to authenticate imagined space, and thus opens a path towards transcendence.[11] Accordingly, the designed landscape, actual or painted, projects, simultaneously, a sense of a tangible real nature, and a coherent, organized virtual reality. If we apply this observation to *Daphnis and Chloe*, we realize that much of the seductive allure of Longus' *pastoralism* lies in the narrative's ability to unite real and imagined spaces in ways that promise all the delights of a return to a 'Golden Age' of harmonious coexistence of man and nature, in a manner that disguises the fundamental fiction of the pastoral construct.[12]

How is that nostalgia achieved? What kinds of constructions draw the viewer into the experience of the spaces represented by literary description? How do fabricated landscapes, symbolic gardens, rustic deities and themes of courtship and sexual awakening represent an idyllic relationship between nature and human beings?[13] In her discussion of the power images exert upon one's memory of text or performance, Bettina Bergmann concludes that image has an independent, and sometimes even insidious influence on memory, in its exceptional ability to complement, amplify, distort and corrupt textual narrative.[14] The function of paintings, as well as other decorative objects, such as free-standing sculpture, relief carvings and mosaics, by setting an 'associative mood', has been thoroughly investigated. Von Stackelberg concludes, further, that the combined effect of nature and reality, through artifice, affects the viewer's experience with both real and imagined space.[15] It is this combination of real and imagined that produces the emotional response that is the focus of my investigation of the relationship between *Daphnis and Chloe* and panel paintings, which offered the novelist not only a narrative framework, as he explicitly states in the Prologue, but also, more importantly, a mood to emulate.

---

[10] Hunt 2004 33–56.
[11] Appleton 1996, 168, rightly describes the success and allure of this experience as being dependent upon vicarious involvement or participation by proxy.
[12] The pastoral operates upon a perceptible conflict between nature and civilization that finds resolution through representation, Bergmann 1992, 44.
[13] Alpers 1996, 326.
[14] Bergmann 1994.
[15] Von Stackelberg 2009, 27.

Longus and Painted Spaces

Images of Daphnis and Chloe are unknown in ancient art, leading many Longus scholars to propose primarily verbal antecedents. Eleanor Winsor Leach observed that the scholarship on the subject focuses first on Longus' debt to the pastoral poetry of Theocritus, which is then 'filtered through Virgilian pastoral, imitations thereof, and, finally, Virgilian commentary'.[16] Certainly, the influence of a variety of literary genres can be observed throughout the narrative in the form of numerous allusions, an important feature of the erudition espoused by the Second Sophistic, but the novel's descriptive passages and the particular emotional reactions they produce are also found in the visual tradition. This overall effect has led Thalia Pandiri to observe that Longus presents the pastoral scene as 'an artifact, a crafted view to be seen and admired by the connoisseur.'[17] The feeling that the novel is itself an object is heightened by the fact that the pastoral landscape provides both the foundation and the structure for human activity, acting as a framework to which the narrative events are firmly attached. So realistic are the author's descriptive passages detailing the features of landscapes and gardens that there has been considerable debate about the author's familiarity with the island of Lesbos.[18] However, the question of whether or not Longus had first hand experience of Lesbos, in my view, fails to confront the more salient issue: Longus is describing a painting, and treats his reader as a viewer of that painting.[19] In both arts – that is, the literary pastoral and pastoral painting – the binary opposition between town and country, civilization and nature achieves balance and harmony, with each polarity sharing authority to shape and influence the other. The artificiality of such a balance between opposites has led to the view that the author's presentation of his text as an expanded description of a painting emphasizes the essential artifice of both genres from the start.[20] Is it the author's intention to emphasize artifice? Are the two genres truly presented as equivalent?

---

16 Leach 1992, 65. Publications on the intertextuality of the ancient novel is lengthy and the following provide something of a history of the scholarship: Valley 1926; Rhode 1937; Mittelstadt 1970; Cresci 1981; Effe 1982; Hunter 1983 and 1997; Cozzoli 2000; di Marco 2000; Czapla 2002; Luginbill 2002; Morgan and Harrison 2008.
17 Pandiri 1985, 116. See also, Newlands 1987, 53.
18 Naber 1877; von Gärtingen 1934–6; Mason 1979; Green 1982.
19 Kuttner 2003, 106, takes the view that landscape sensibility was acculturated and that acculturated above all is an understanding of the relationship with nature: philosophically, religiously, and historically. See also Kuttner 1999 for a recent survey of Roman painted gardens.
20 Newlands 1987, 53.

The text begins with a description of a painting described as a 'miracle of skill' that inspired the narrator with a 'longing to write down what the picture told'.[21] Paul Alpers describes Longus' *Daphnis and Chloe* as a series of 'little pictures'.[22] The inspirational painting is broken down into a series of 'little pictures' that concretely establish the setting. These 'miracles of skill' inspire Longus to contrive for his reader a similar emotional experience, with the result that, even as the text presents a 'crafted view to be admired', it actually, like the wall paintings, de-emphasizes artifice in favor of plausibility, and so is able to make real the pastoral experience of the 'Golden Age'.[23]

Longus draws his audience into the pastoral world through verbal images that mimic the evocative emotional properties of Roman landscape painting. For example, Longus' literary landscape, like a painting, is viewed from without; the reader's progress into its spaces is guided first to an image whose setting, complete in every detail, exemplifies all that is foreign, and yet is simultaneously, comfortably familiar. The verbal image mimics reality so as to become a gateway into imagined space, space that the ensuing narrative inhabits and could not survive without. Consider again the model of historical, contemporary landscape design – itself no stranger to paradox. Hunt has observed that among the least analyzed paradoxes is precisely this sense of 'virtual reality' projected by the designed landscape or garden – 'this combination of a felt experience of both organic and inorganic materials with a deliberate creation of fictive worlds into whose inventions, systems and mythological or metaphorical languages we allow ourselves to be drawn.'[24] Grounded in the real, the virtual space of the pastoral world transcends the Cartesian distance between the subject viewer and the object illusion. Instead of the act of writing or painting reinforcing distance by drawing one's attention to the craft of illusion, Longus' 'painted' garden establishes a foundation that is literally 'grounded' in the concrete and material, allowing one to 'suspend reality' and so participate within this imagined landscape with an active intellectual and emotive involvement.[25]

An example of this idea can be found in the Salon de Musique in the Hôtel de Lauzon on the Île Saint Louis in Paris. This ornate room, typical of the tastes of the 1660s, is a locus for sensual pleasure. The plaster, paint, gilt, and marble of the graceful, spacious, carefully proportioned and highly ornamented archi-

---

21 Longus, *Daphnis and Chloe*, preface, translated by R. McCail 2002, 3.
22 Alpers 1996, 327.
23 Alpers 1996, 327.
24 Hunt 2004, 37–8.
25 Newlands 1987, 52, takes the opposite view and argues that Longus keeps his reader distanced from the pastoral world by deliberately reminding him that it is an illusion.

tectural space seems to be at odds with the painted panels illustrating the romance of Daphnis and Chloe decorating the walls. These contradictions underscore the dependence of the pastoral upon the real and the tangible.[26] The practical physical comforts of the actual space do not reinforce psychological distance from the rustic herdsmen pictured, but encourage an imaginative escape from reality reinforced by the auditory pleasure of music and by the seemingly uncomplicated romance played out within that idyllic landscape. What is striking about this juxtaposition (the literal and the allegorical) is the sensation of harmony that exists despite the obvious contradictions between the room's civilized artifice and painted nature. The salon incorporates this duality, and the result is, undoubtedly, a contrivance; still, the delight offered by this artificial space works precisely because it unites the real and the virtual. The comforts of the physical environment are complemented, expanded and reinforced by the virtual, introduced by pastoral landscape, and culminating in the ultimate experience of human art – the entirely subjective experience of music. For its part, the emotional success of the painted pastoral landscape depends not on its unrestrained invention, but on its materiality. The painted pastoral world is no less real than the grandiose architecture it ornaments. The experience is similar to contemporary 'cyberspace', whose allure is also, rather paradoxically, derived from the very immaterialities of the literal and tangible world that inspire it, bearing out David Rosand's argument that, in gazing at pastoral landscapes, we willingly ignore the art and make it transparent.[27] Pastoral landscape painting produces a world that is always artful; its function is not the production of an artificial construct to be admired for its aesthetic virtuosity, or appreciated for its intellectual pedigree, but the articulation of an invented, or special place, whose true appeal lies in the promise of a richer, or fuller, or more intense experience than would be possible if it were a real place, not a construct.[28]

The achievement of this particular kind of emotional experience inclines me to suggest that Longus' novel is also involved in a similar construction of space – specifically, the narrator's invention of an allegorical landscape inspired by a pastoral painting, which, like painting, relies on materiality for its success. Longus himself emphasizes two kinds of *techne*: in the Prologue, he states that he wishes to emulate a painting that combines great artistic skill with an erotic subject while at the same time, in the highly significant descriptions of the literary environment, he acknowledges the influence of the material landscape and gar-

---

[26] The ceiling is attributed to Michel Dorigny, but the panels lack attribution.
[27] Rosand 1992.
[28] Hunt 2004, 37, argues that 'invented' landscapes offer the imagination a greater sense of intensity.

den.²⁹ For example, he describes Dionysophanes' garden as a marvel of cultivation that unites the works of artistic skill and nature, which the servant Lamon, when he arrives to tend the plants and trees, is dismayed to discover vandalized.³⁰ It is no surprise to learn that the pastoral garden can be vandalized. Even this imagined space is fragile. The fact that nature can be wantonly destroyed suggests that Longus is not merely conscious of the tensions between nature and culture, but effectively uses it to reinforce the reality of the fictive space he creates.³¹ His literary garden, like any actual garden, is vulnerable, and even the fictive world of the pastoral is not immune to human caprice or malice. Various formal principles, such as the cycle of the seasons, the framing structure of ecphrastic scenes, and corroborating patterns of repetition offer a sense of spatial wholeness and real time to the story's linear unfolding, thereby authenticating the fictive construct. Material landscapes present the painter with models from which to create a virtual reality that promises a richer experience than that offered by prosaic country excursions, and forms the foundation for the essential tripartite interdependence (landscape – painting – novel) perceptible in the text.

Roman landscape paintings present two divergent, but concurrent visual approaches that create this fictive space. The *trompe-l'oeil* 'Garden Room' at the Villa of Livia depicts a pastoral paradise in which man is not represented, although his incursions are made manifest by a series of gates and fences that organize the space, and a gilded birdcage that speaks eloquently to human control (Fig. 1).³² In their survey of classical art, Mary Beard and John Henderson describe the 'Garden Room' as:

> … an impossibly utopian mixture of bright flowers beside laden fruit trees, tidy shrubs before a receding woodland vista, planned garden display within a surround of Italian trees, as if in their natural habitat. But this is not nature reproduced; instead, a world specially made for us – yet made to do without us. Beyond the balustrade, as no wild birds ever could, these pay not the slightest attention to anyone in the room, impossibly ignoring our proximity. Emblematized by the songbird in its golden cage, art here *creates* nature, beyond anything you could find in the real world.³³

---

29 Newlands 1987.
30 Book 4,2–3, 7–8.
31 See Alpers 1996, 331, for a discussion of Dionysophanes' garden as a locus of tension.
32 South Wall, Garden Room, Prima Porta. Ca. 40 BCE, MNR Palazzo Massimo alle Terme, inv. 12637. Photo: https://upload.wikimedia.org/wikipedia/commons/6/65/Villa di livia52C affreschi di giardi no%2C parete corta meridionale 01.jpg. Via Wikimedia Commons.
33 Beard and Henderson 2001, 55. For interpretations of Livia's garden room see also Kuttner 1999 and Mazzoleni and Pappalardo 2005.

Fig. 1: Livia's 'Garden Room'

The image projects real and imagined space. Bergmann describes such imagined space as 'ideal realities' that are sustained and augmented by the apprehension of design, order and purpose.[34] Wild birds are the counterpoint to the caged bird, and the spontaneous plants that crowd the borders of the composition likewise draw attention to demonstrations of human control. While humans are not pictured, suggesting that this particular world can do without us, the inclusion of the birdcage suggests otherwise, so reinforcing our participation in this 'ideal reality'. The fences and hedges, practical architectural devices, serve equally practical painterly purposes as compositional devices that create perspective and depth, and heighten the realism of the illusion while, like the birdcage, underscoring man's presence. These architectural inclusions also act as 'guides' that encourage the viewer's emotional response by compelling the eye to seek a route of entry, or some other signs of human presence (a caged bird does, after all, require feeding) with the result that the viewer ceases to be a passive observer, and becomes an active participant – the transition from passive to ac-

---

34 Bergmann 1992.

tive concretizing the success of the virtual experience. Together nature and artifice eradicate psychological distance even as they define it, allowing the viewer to participate in the space and in the illusion of harmony between nature and culture.

Barbara Kellum positions Livia's 'Garden Room' within the wider context of Augustan Rome and observes a connection between the painted space and the political agenda. She notes that 'the emperor was quick to establish an arboreal mythology' and the city was punctuated with plants and trees that 'were as protean and multivalent in their structures and meanings as the contemporary poetry of Virgil, Horace and Ovid.'[35] The murals of Livia's 'Garden Room' are structured around regularly placed oak, pine and spruce trees, but with a profusion of wild plants in between, order and disorder complimenting each other in a way reminiscent of Virgil's *Georgics*. According to Kellum, this juxtaposition of the wild and the cultivated harmonizes the beneficent world of nature and that of the state under a common rule of organic order.[36] Landscape, real and imagined, reinforced Augustan social identity – in which the real functions as the device by which the ideal is made both accessible and credible. The distribution of plants and trees throughout the urban space of Rome employed nature as a building material, with the result that nature itself functions as architecture. Trees can be fences; likewise, plants can be organized in ways that direct and guide human movement throughout urban space as successfully as any human guides or written signposts might.

Not all landscape paintings rely solely on indications of human presence as a means of access to the viewer; some actually introduce human activity into the painted landscape. In her analysis of representations of the 'grove' on Roman walls, Bettina Bergmann observes two distinct artistic approaches: there are those paintings that venerate natural sites, while, in others, human technology triumphs over land and sea.[37] Such opposition reinforces the polarity inherent in the relation of civilization and nature; that, however, is where the polarity breaks down. We 'willingly ignore the art' in depictions of the sacro-idyllic landscape. It is in this environment that the illusion of harmony between nature and civilization is indispensable. The many extant paintings that focus on sacro-idyllic landscapes are witness to the popularity and success of such imagined spaces. One such landscape decorates the north wall of the 'Red Room' at Bosco-

---

[35] Kellum 1994, 211; Reeder 2001.
[36] Kellum 1994, 217.
[37] Bergmann 1992, 23. For a discussion of the manipulation of the landscape to produce a virtual experience, see Kuttner 2003.

Fig. 2: North Wall of the 'Red Room', Boscotrecase

trecase (Fig. 2).[38] In this image, goats graze while shepherds rest within sight of rustic shrines. Human enterprise is evident not just in the construction of shrines in honor of simple country gods, but also in the more sophisticated monumental architecture barely glimpsed in the distance. While uninhabited landscapes like that which ornaments Livia's Garden Room merely suggest human activity in the cultivation and organization of nature, the sacro-idyllic landscape takes human engagement further by introducing the human psychological response to nature

---

[38] North Wall of the 'Red Room' (cubiculum 16 of the Villa of Agrippa Postumus, Boscotrecase, ca. first quarter of the first century CE). Museo Archeologico Nazionale, Naples, 147501.
  Photo: Harald Mielsch: Römische Wandmalerei, Wissenschaftliche Buchgesellschaft, Darmstadt, 2001. https://en.wikipedia.org/wiki/Roman_art#/media/File:Pompejanischer_Maler_-um_10_20_001.jpg. Via Wikimedia Commons.

into the image with evidence of the activities surrounding its worship.[39] Accordingly, such landscapes stimulate a sensation of participation that introduces an increasingly more complex emotional response.[40] While there is no perceptible sensation of conflict or tension between the real and the imagined, that polarity pervades the subject at hand. Bergmann observes that 'monument and vegetation intersect in ways that bring linear and historical time into the cycles of nature', thus drawing our attention, rightly, to the fact that natural and constructed objects of worship, a tree, a statue or a monument, share the identical ritual decorations.[41] The egalitarian nature of their veneration is an overt mark of congruence, while the signs of distant civilization suggest a co-existence between nature and culture without the fear of technological annexation that is so much a part of reality. Taken as a whole, these visual devices provide the underlying sense of reality that reinforces the plausibility of the harmony depicted and before which we, through a longing for this union between man and nature, willing make the fiction transparent.

At this point it may be worthwhile to look more closely at two opposing arguments concerning the influence of literature upon the representation of the landscape in these paintings. Elfride Knauer has proposed that in the Red Room at Boscotrecase, sacro-idyllic landscape paintings take precedence over the rest of the decoration, but that the real achievement of the images results from the fact that the viewer's delight must have been enhanced when they perceived the felicitous references to literature, and especially bucolic poetry.[42] Her argument – that the artist of the Red Room turns sacred landscapes into 'easel paintings' that are intentionally at one remove from reality – privileges the perspective that literary allusion is the primary goal of the artist and of the genre of mythological painting, and that these images are carefully constructed to demonstrate the sophistication of the viewer.[43] I suggest that the illusion created may be in and of itself the goal, and, if it is not, that the emotional response that the image produces takes precedence and can only be restrained when sacred land-

---

39 Zeitlin 2008, 91, observes that 'the topography of any ancient city, for example, would be unrecognizable without its temples and shrines, its statues and votive offerings, its frequent public festivals and processions, and its generally familiar modes of worship'. For the role of religion in the ancient novel see also: Chalk 1960; Alperowitz 1992; Hunter 2003.
40 Von Stackelberg 2009.
41 Bergmann 1992, 23.
42 Knauer 1993, 26–7.
43 Knauer 1993, 28. The connection between painting and literature as a source of information for Roman social attitudes and practices has been extensively explored, see Blankenhagen and Alexander 1990 Laurence 1994. More recently, Leach 2004 also emphasizes the function of paintings in the creation of status and the role that textual allusion plays therein.

scapes are presented as easel paintings. The success of the illusion created by painted space necessitates some distancing device, such as easel painting provides, in order for the viewer's literary sophistication to be appreciated. In his analysis of Longus' text, Stephen Nimis stresses the importance of 'presence' and argues for a reading of the text as a discourse that de-emphasizes the effects of literacy.[44] To Nimis' careful and perceptive analysis I would add that such a de-emphasis is accomplished precisely by the author's sustained imitation of landscape painting in order to underscore the emotional responses characteristic of visual art.

Painted landscapes in which pastoral gods inhabit rustic shrines, enjoying the veneration of shepherds who guard their flocks to the accompaniment of bucolic musical instruments, are not the final means of access into the imagined landscape. Panel painters provided another means of access into the pastoral landscape by making it the setting for courtship – a powerfully real, and simultaneously liminal experience.[45] The Villa at Boscotrecase provides examples of mythological romances in panels that represent Andromeda's rescue by Perseus, and Polyphemus' wooing of Galatea (Fig. 3).[46] Surely in representations of such subjects one might expect to observe a straightforward relationship between the visual and the textual. However, Eleanor Winsor Leach has called that relationship an 'oblique dialogue between literature and the visual arts.'[47] In her discussion of the 'pastoral courtship' of Polyphemus and Galatea, Leach points out that in art historical terms, the visual tradition is 'mysterious and lacunate'.[48] She questions the indebtedness of the Boscotrecase painting to Theocritus, and her analysis of the ways in which image diverged from text leads her to conclude that 'under the influence of popular mimic performances, depictions of the subject have departed further and further from their literary sources and assumed their own independent shape, whose direction answers to the culture in which it participates'.[49] Once more the purely literary is de-emphasized in favor of the emotional response. I would enlarge upon Leach's argument by adding that the pictorial representation of 'pastoral' mythological subjects has its own

---

44 Nimis 2001, 185.
45 See Helen Morales 2008, 39–55 for a recent discussion of the erotic in the ancient novel. Her bibliography is especially inclusive. Also, Alpers 1996, 321–347.
46 'Polyphemus and Galatea in a landscape,' from the imperial villa at Boscotrecase, last decade of first century B.C., Metropolitan Museum of Art, New York, 20.192.17. Photo: Metropolitan Museum of Art, New York.
47 Leach 1992, 66.
48 Leach 1992, 70.
49 Leach 1992, 74.

Fig. 3: 'Polyphemos and Galatea in a Landscape', Boscotrecase

particular momentum, and that the structure of the image is only slightly dependent on literary association, not necessarily because it is more indebted to mime, but because it is essentially pictorial. Leach observes that the Polyphemus landscape may not represent a generically conceived pastoral landscape; instead, it is 'a setting that becomes pastoral by association'.[50] The imaginative sphere of the pastoral is a liminal or mediating realm. The delight the viewer gains is not the result of the image's connection with literature or performance, although these associations can certainly enhance the experience, but with the image's creation of imagined space, the pastoral world. The transference of erotic

---

50 Leach 1992, 72.

myth and, by extension, the erotic experience itself to the pastoral landscape unites the actual and the virtual to produce the emotional experience that Longus masterfully evokes in his novel.

So far I have focused on some of the ways in which paintings permit the viewer to enter into virtual spaces. The 'Garden Room' is an example of paintings that offer the viewer a liminal experience that is achieved and heightened by some impression of human presence within and manipulation of the environment – the virtual footprint.[51] In contrast, sacro-idyllic landscapes and painted mythological narratives do not require the viewer to seek entry: humanity is depicted and the viewer is caught up in an imagined experience of reality. In the case of sacro-idyllic landscapes, the sensation of participation is achieved by the viewer's ability to identify with others who are not similarly deprived of the pastoral experience, while mythological courtships exploit the real and liminal experience of eroticism. The relationship between the real and the virtual takes a fascinating turn if we revisit the role of display and consider how iconography and architecture together determine the viewer's experience. Shelley Hales argues that wall painting and other elements of home décor, including architectural elements and especially gardens, highlight the ways in which 'the whole house acts as a threshold between different long-established rhetorical *topoi*: public and private, town and country, mortal and divine, Roman and alien.'[52] Thus the real and the imagined mediate between the materiality of the everyday world and the attitudes that underlie Roman social identity with the result that the combined experience of architecture and iconography reconciles the polarity of the *topoi*. Domestic space becomes a place of transcendence, as real space co-exists with imagined space. In a similar manner, Timothy O'Sullivan in his investigation of the cultural and artistic context of the 'Odyssey Landscapes' observes that the fictive portico frame in which the images are situated would have evoked in the Roman viewer the experience of *ambulatio*, the act of walking for leisure and contemplation that came to be an essential element of the properly Hellenized *otium*. He proposes that 'the viewer walks with Odysseus on a parallel journey of philosophical reflection.'[53] Even as he acknowledges the importance of the material architectural setting to the success of the fictive experience, he denies the painted virtual world its full impact by priv-

---

[51] Reeder 2001 connects the garden room, its decoration, and the rest of the villa with emphasis on the laurel grove.
[52] Hales 2003, 162.
[53] O'Sullivan 2007, 497–532. The relationship between real space and the virtual space created by painting are the subject of a recent investigation of the frescoes at Boscoreale, see Bergmann, de Caro and Mertens 2010.

ileging the role of architecture over painting in the creation of the viewer's experience. It is, I believe, equally possible to argue that the architectural framework, like the easel approach to the sacro-idyllic landscapes at Boscotrecase, a device equally vital to the creation of the sensation of harmony between the material and the illusory.

In the case of *Daphnis and Chloe*, the text achieves its particular 'pastoralism' by producing an emotional response that allows the reader to realize the interplay between interior and exterior space and consequentially the sensation of harmony by inversion. The miraculous painting to which the narrative is indebted and the 'little pictures' created by the descriptive passages are the architectural framework, and function, as it were, as material architecture does for the display of wall paintings, guiding the reader into an experience of the virtual space, while the novel's narrative events assume the role of decorative wall paintings. Such a view credits the author not just with imitation of the formal characteristics of landscape painting, but also with the creation of a similar emotional experience. Longus' romance fully participates in this painted pastoral world, already a familiar and a nostalgic theme in the decoration of domestic settings.

The old man, Philetas, who was instrumental in teaching Daphnis and Chloe about love and how to enjoy its beauties, articulates what is, perhaps, one of the most significant passages in *Daphnis and Chloe*, for the present purposes:

> I have a garden that I made with my own hands:
> If you took away the fence, my garden would look exactly like a small wood...(*Daphnis and Chloe* 2,3)

The landscape Philetas's description presents to the reader is an organized space that, despite all human contrivance, is only one remove from nature. Its survival relies upon harmony between polarities. Philetas' garden, too, fully participates in the materiality that is foundational for pastoral landscape painting to communicate its emotional experience and appeal. Longus' pastoralism results from his imitation of art to recreate the same virtual experience communicated by landscape painting. The novel's emotional experience is founded upon the real and familiar, which invites the viewer to enter into the virtual world by promising the creation of a special space, with the same enrichment and harmony that pastoral landscape painting offers. The novel appropriates painting's sensation of liminality, even as it is firmly situated within and authenticated by the erudite literary conventions of the Second Sophistic. Longus' literary sophistication underscores the seeming simplicity and innocence of the painted pastoral world in which his charmingly naïve romance is played out, and nowhere is his skill more evident than in his ability to compel the reader to 'willingly make art transparent' through the conscious de-emphasis of artifice. His 'little pictures' produce in the reader an emotive engagement at once intellectual and sensual – and the success of the text in producing such engagement is deeply indebted to the landscape painter's production of imagined spaces founded in the material, yet creating an experience of delicate balance between the contradictions and polarities of the pastoral world.

Bibliography

Alperowitz, M. 1992. *Das Wirken und Walten der Götter im griechischen Roman*, Heidelberg: C. Winter.
Alpers, P. 1996. *What is Pastoral?*, Chicago: University of Chicago Press.
Appleton, J. 1996. *The Experience of Landscape*, New York: Wiley.
Beard, M., and Henderson, J. 2001. *Classical Art: From Greece to Rome*, Oxford: Oxford University Press.
Bergmann, B. 1992. 'Exploring the Grove: Pastoral Space on Roman Walls,' in: J.D. Hunt (ed.), *The Pastoral Landscape*, Studies in the History of Art 36, Washington DC: National Gallery of Art. 21–46.
Bergmann, B. 1994. 'The Roman House as Memory Theater: The House of the Tragic Poet in Pompeii.' *Art Bulletin*, 76 (2), 225–256.
Bergmann, B., S. et al. (eds.) 2010. *Roman Frescoes at Boscoreale: The Villa of Publius Fannius Synistor in Reality and Virtual Reality*, New Haven: Yale University Press.
Blankenhagen, P. van and C. Alexander. 1990; *Roman Art in the Private Sphere: New Perspectives on the Art and Architecture of the Roman Domus, Villa and Insula*, edited by E.K. Gazda and assisted by A.E. Haekel, Ann Arbor: University of Michigan Press.
Blunt, A. 1995. *Nicholas Poussin*, London: Pallas Athene.
Bowe, P. 2004. *Gardens of the Roman World*, Los Angeles: Getty Publications.
Chalk, H.H.O. 1960. 'Eros and the Lesbian Pastorals of Longus,' *JHS* 80, 32–51.
Clarke, J.R. 1991. *The Houses of Roman Italy, 100 B.C.-A.D. 250: Ritual, Space, and Decoration*, Berkeley/Oxford: University of California Press.
Cole, S. 2004. *Landscape, Gender and Ritual Space: the Ancient Greek Experience*, Berkeley/Los Angeles/London: University of California Press.
Cozzoli, A.T. 2000. 'Dalla poesia al romanzo: motivi poetici nella rielaborazione narrativa di Longo sofista', *SemRom* 3, 295–312.
Cresci, L.R. 1981. 'Il romanzo di Longo Sofista e la tradizione bucolica', *A&R* 26, 1–25.
Czapla, B. 2002. 'Literarische Lese-, Kinst- und Liebesmodelle: eine intertextuelle Interpretation von Longos' Hirtenroman', *A & A* 48, 18–42.
de Jong, I.J.F. (ed.) 2012 *Space in Ancient Greek Literature. Studies in Ancient Greek Narrative*, vol. 3. Mnemosyne supplements. Monographs on Greek and Latin language and literature, 339. Leiden/Boston: Brill.
di Marco, M. 2000. 'Fileta praeceptor amoris: Longo Sofista e la correzione del modello bucolico', *SCO* 47, 9–35.
Effe, B. 1982. 'Longos: Zur Funktionsgeschichte der Bukolik in der römischen Kaiserzeit', *Hermes* 110, 65–84.

E. K. Gazda (ed.) 1991. *Roman Art in the Private Sphere: New Perspectives on the Art and Architecture of the Roman Domus, Villa and Insula*, Michigan: University of Michigan Press.

Green, P. 1982. 'Longus, Antiphon and the Topography of Lesbos', *JHS* 102, 210–214.

Hales, S. 2003. *The Roman house and Social Identity*, Cambridge: Cambridge University Press.

Halperin, D. 1983. *Before Pastoral: Theocritus and the Ancient Tradition of Bucolic Poetry*, New Haven: Yale University Press.

Hardin, R. F. 2000. *Love in a Green Shade: Idyllic Romances Ancient to Modern*, Lincoln: University of Nebraska Press.

Hunt, J.D. 2004. *The Afterlife of Gardens*, London: Reaktion Books.

Hunter, R.L. 1983. *A Study of 'Daphnis and Chloe'*, Cambridge: Cambridge University Press.

Kellum, B. 1994. 'The Construction of Landscape in Augustan Rome: The Garden Room at the Villa ad Gallinas', *Art Bulletin* 76.2 (June 1994): 211–224.

Knauer, E. 1993. 'Roman Wall Paintings from Boscotrecase: Three Studies in the Relationship between Writing and Painting', *Metropolitan Museum Journal* 28, 13–46.

Kuttner, A. L. 2003. 'Delight and Danger in the Roman Water Garden: Sperlonga and Tivoli,' in: M. Conon (ed.), *Landscape Design and the Experience of Motion. Dumbarton Oaks Colloquium on the History of Landscape Architecture* 24, Washington, DC: Dumbarton Oaks. 103–156.

Kuttner, A. L. 1999. 'Looking Outside Inside: Ancient Roman Garden Rooms,' *Studies in the History of Gardens and Designed Landscapes* 19, 7–35.

Laurence, R. 1994. *Roman Pompeii: Space and Society*, London: Routledge.

Leach, E.W. 1992. 'Polyphemus in a Landscape: Traditions of Pastoral Courtship', in: J.D. Hunt (ed.), *The Pastoral Landscape*, Studies in the History of Art 36, Washington DC: National Gallery of Art. 63–72.

Leach, E.W. 2004. *The Social Life of Painting in Ancient Rome and on the Bay of Naples*, Cambridge: Cambridge University Press.

Luginbill, R.D. 2002. 'A Delightful Possession: Longus' Prologue and Thucydides', *CJ* 97.3, 233–247.

Mason, H. J. 1979. 'Longus and the Topography of Lesbos', *TAPA* 109, 149–63.

Mazzoleni, D., Pappalardo, U., Romano, L. 2004. *Domus: Wall Painting in the Roman House* (A.L. Jenkins, trans.), Los Angeles: J. Paul Getty Museum.

Mittelstadt, M.C. 1967. 'Longus: *Daphnis and Chloe* and Roman Narrative Painting', *Latomus* 26, 752–761.

Morales, H. 2008. 'The History of Sexuality', in: T. Whitmarsh (ed.), *The Cambridge Companion to The Greek and Roman Novel*, Cambridge: Cambridge University Press. 39–55.

Morgan, J., and Harrison, S. 2008. 'Intertextuality', in: T. Whitmarsh (ed.), *The Cambridge Companion to The Greek and Roman Novel*, Cambridge: Cambridge University Press. 218–236.

Naber, S.A. 1877. 'Adnotationes criticae ad Longi Pastoralia', *Mnemosyne* 5, 199–220.

Newlands, C. 1987. 'Techne' and 'Tuche' in Longus' *Daphnis and Chloe*', *Pacific Coast Philology* 22, No. 1/2 (Nov.), 52–58.

Nimis, S. 2001. 'Cycles and Sequence in Longus' *Daphnis and Chloe*,' in: J. Watson (ed.), *Speaking Volumes: Orality and Literacy in the Greek and Roman World*, Mnemosyne Supplement 218, Leiden: Brill. 187–200.

O'Sullivan, T. 2006. 'The Mind in Motion: Walking and Metaphorical Travel in the Roman Villa,' *CP* 101(2), 133–152.

O'Sullivan, T. 2007. 'Walking with Odysseus: The Portico Frame of the Odyssey Landscapes,' *AJP* 128 (4), 497–532.

Pagán, V. E. 2006. *Rome and the Literature of Gardens*, London: Duckworth.

Pandiri, T. A. 1985. 'Daphnis and Chloe: The Art of Pastoral Play,' *Ramus* 14, 116–141.

Panofsky, E. 1955. 'Et in Arcadia Ego: Poussin and the Elegiac Tradition', in: E. Panofsky, *Meaning in the Visual Arts*, Garden City: Doubleday Books. 295–320.

Pugh, S. (ed.) 1990. *Reading Landscape: Country, City, Capital*, Manchester: Manchester University Press; New York: St. Martin's Press.

Reeder, J.C. 2001. *The Villa of Livia Ad Gallinas Albas. A Study in the Augustan Villa and Garden*, Archaeologica Transatlantica XX, Providence: Center for Old World Archaeology and Art.

Rohde, G. 1937. 'Longus und die Bukolik', *RhM* 86, 23–49 [repr. in H. Gärtner (ed.) 1984. *Beiträge zum griechischen Liebesroman*, Hildesheim, Zürich, New York: Georg Holms Verlag. 361–87].

Rosand, D. 1988. *Places of Delight*, Washington, DC: The Phillips Collection and the National Gallery of Art.

Rosand, D. 1992. 'Pastoral Topoi: On the Construction of Meaning in Landscape', in: J.D. Hunt (ed.), *The Pastoral Landscape*, Studies in the History of Art 36, Washington DC: National Gallery of Art. 160–177.

Rosenmeyer, T. G. 1969. *The Green Cabinet: Theocritus and the European Pastoral Lyric*, Berkeley/Los Angeles: University of California Press.

Valley, G. 1926. *Über den Sprachgebrauch des Longus*, Uppsala: E. Berlings Nya.

von Blankenhagen, P.H., and Alexander, C. 1990. *The Augustan Villa at Boscotrecase*, Mainz am Rhein: P von Zabern.

von Gärtringen, F.H. 1934. 'Neue Forschungen zur Geschichte und Epigraphie von Lesbos,' *Nachrichten von der Akademie der Wissenschaften in Göttingen. Philologisch-Historische Klasse. Fachgruppe* 1, 107–119.

von Stackelberg, K.T. 2009. *The Roman Garden: Space, Sense and Society*, Routledge Monographs in Classical Studies, London/New York: Routledge.

Zeitlin, F. I. 1990. 'The Poetics of Eros: Nature, Art and Imitation in Longus' *Daphnis and Chloe*,' in: D. M. Halperin, J. J. Winkler, F. I. Zeitlin (eds.), *Before Sexuality: The Construction of Erotic Experience in the Ancient Greek World*, Princeton: Princeton University Press. 417–464.

Zeitlin, F. 2008. 'Religion', in: T. Whitmarsh (ed.), *The Cambridge Companion to The Greek and Roman Novel*, Cambridge: Cambridge University Press. 91–108.

H. Christian Blood
Narrating Voyages to Heaven and Hell: Seneca, Apuleius, and Bakhtin's Menippea

Abstract: According to Bakhtin's *Problems of Dostoevsky's Poetics*, Seneca's *Apocolocyntosis* is 'classical' Menippean satire (which critics support) and Apuleius' *Metamorphoses* is 'full-blown' menippea (which critics almost always reject). With an eye toward shedding new light on the problem of Book XI, I offer parallel readings, showing that *Metamorphoses* could a 'rewriting' of *Apocolocyntosis*. As menippea, *Metamorphoses*' contested ending is not an ambiguous horse-race between humor *or* piety. Rather, as Bakhtin's menippea turns on *syncrisis*, the rhetorical figure of juxtaposition, the Isis Book is an authorized menippean mixture of humor *and* piety in which indeterminacy is hard-wired into the novel's poetics.

M.M. Bakhtin is notorious for outrageous, apparently untenable enunciations. In his alternate history of the novel, *Problems of Dostoevsky's Poetics*, he proclaims that Seneca's *Apocolocyntosis* is 'a classical Menippean satire', and Apuleius' *Metamorphoses* is 'a full-blown Menippean satire'.[1] The first assertion is easy enough to deal with; almost everyone agrees that *Apocolocyntosis* is Menippean satire.[2] The second, however, is more troublesome; almost no one agrees with Bakhtin that the *Metamorphoses* is Menippean satire.[3] How are students of ancient prose fiction to understand Bakhtin's conclusions? Is Bakhtin worth the trouble?[4] R. Bracht Branham has noted that Bakhtin's declarations often appear 'arguably false', and yet they 'telegraph a lot of truth'.[5] With that telegraphing in mind, I wish to offer a short parallel reading of *Apocolocyntosis* and *Metamorphoses*, showing how Apuleius' novel may read as *menippea*.

---

[1] Bakhtin 1984, 113. He also says that *Satyrica* is 'nothing other than a Menippean satire extended to the limits of the novel'. Unfortunately, this short discussion will not address Petronius.
[2] On *Apocolocyntosis* as Menippean satire: Courtney 1962, 91; Bakhtin 1984, 101–137; Riikonen 1987, 41–50; Relihan 1993, 75–90; Weinbrot 2005, 46–50.
[3] For discussions of *Metamorphoses* and Menippean satire: Riikonen 1987, 12 and 15; Relihan 1993, 21; Weinbrot 2005, 7–8; Zimmerman 2006, 87–104.
[4] Weinbrot 2005, 11–16.
[5] Branham 2005, 3.

H. Christian Blood, Yonsei University

https://doi.org/10.1515/9781501503986-013

The consensus that Apuleius did not write a Menippean satire owes much to that genre's received definition, prosimetric composition, of which *Apocolocyntosis* has much, while *Metamorphoses* has very little. Bakhtin, however, defines Menippean satire to include, but radically supersede prosimetry; he instead conceives of the genre through fourteen interrelated characteristics, ranging from the privileged role of comedy, to obscenity mixed with philosophical seriousness, and most of all the ubiquity of carnival.[6] Most important of these is *menippea*'s programmatic reliance on *syncrisis*, the rhetorical figure of juxtaposition, of which prosimetry is but one of many manifestations. Recent criticism would seem to suggest that Bakhtin's concept of *menippea* is more trouble than it is worth.[7] Bakhtin's synchronic analysis is unverifiable; just about any narrative displays some of the fourteen characteristics; sometimes the whole thing looks less like a heuristic than an arbitrary laundry list. These objections being noted, I argue that Bakhtin's strategy for reading ancient prose fiction on its own terms, rather than through frameworks we have inherited from Aristotle, Huet, or Romanticism, is valuable on its own, and is potentially revolutionary for Apuleius. I see almost all Bakhtin's characteristics of *menippea* at work in *Metamorphoses*, but due to constraints of space, I will limit the current discussion to two that are most visible in both *Metamorphoses* and *Apocolocyntosis*: first, *syncrisis*,[8] and secondly, the three-tiered geographical and thematic schematization, featuring voyages to Olympus and the netherworld.[9] Bakhtin constructs his alternative history of the novel on Seneca's foundation, and what is essential to *Apocolocyntosis* is therefore paradigmatic to the genre of Menippean satire as a whole. Here, I argue that it is helpful to think of *Metamorphoses* as a rewriting of *Apocolocyntosis*, even if direct influence cannot be established. Since it is indeed a Menippean satire, the *Metamorphoses*' contested ending is not an ambiguous horse race pitting humor *against* piety. Rather, as a *syncrisis*, the ending is an authentic commixture of humor *and* piety. *Metamorphoses* mobilizes Menippean poetics as a strategy to problematize the contested Isis Book.

* * *

Seneca wrote *Apocolocyntosis* not only to disparage the emperor he despised, but also to consolidate the poetic program of a protean sub-genre, Menippean satire. In turn, the text's programmatic double duty shows itself as an extended series of over-the-top formal and thematic mismatches of verse and prose, Greek and

---

6 The full list of 14 characteristics may be found at Bakhtin 1984, 114–119.
7 Weinbrot 2005, 15.
8 Bakhtin 1984, 118, Point 10.
9 Bakhtin 1984, 116, Points 6 and 7.

Latin, character assassination and apotheosis, toilet humor and moral messages, where the sutures show and the author's strategic seams are not smoothed over.

That the *Apocolocyntosis* is a Menippean satire built around *syncrisis* can be seen in its first line:

> Quid actum sit in caelo ante diem III idus Octobris anno nouo,
> initio saeculi felicissimi, uolo memoriae tradere. (*Apoc.* 1,1–2)[10]

This incipit brings into play more than one *syncrisis:* verbal motifs from history collide with elements of the marvelous, while prepositional phrases turn out to anticipate the narrative's key motifs, *katabasis* and *katascopia*. This schematization isolates the prepositional phrase *in caelo:*

quid actum sit]	in caelo	[uolo memoriae tradere
what was done	in heaven	I want to hand over to memory

This representation reveals Seneca's use of syntagmatic and paradigmatic *syncrisis:* across the unfolding sentence, Seneca juxtaposes *historia* in a parody of *res gestae*, only to be interrupted by something *other than* history, since it occurs *in caelo.*

Tradere, used here to mean 'to hand over', a favorite verb for Livy, Pliny, and Suetonius, covers a range of meanings, from 'to surrender troops to an opponent' to 'to hand over to posterity'. Edward Courtney notes that the 'incongruous' *in caelo* disrupts the historical flavor;[11] as Timothy Robinson observes, a straightforward narrative is disrupted by 'temporal transitions and periphrases that lend a peculiar distortion'.[12] As if anticipating the image of *redimita comas* (braided hair) of Lachesis,[13] the opening line intertwines conventions from historic discourses together with disruptive marvelous elements, simultaneously inhibiting yet augmenting the parody of history, so that – from its very beginning – the text sutures disparate elements and thus confounds generic logic. Caught between disruption and integration, Menippean satire reveals ruptures and highlights these seams. If the function of annalistic Roman history on its own is to purvey a Roman ideology, the *Apocolocyntosis* interrupts ideological coherence, and Menippean satire is therefore a parody of history's ideological work of consolidation.

---

10 All *Apocolocyntosis* citations and translations refer to Eden's 1984 Cambridge text.
11 Courtney 1962, 91.
12 Robinson 2005, 224.
13 *Apoc.* 4,3.

Using Bakhtin's scheme to align the *Apocolocyntosis* with the *Metamorphoses*, we discover that both tell the same story: a man becoming a donkey rather than a bird parodies a man becoming a 'pumpkin' rather than a god. Seneca depicts Claudius' literal journeys up and down, and the narrative traces time on earth, time in heaven, and time in Hades. Apuleius deploys the same structure, but he depicts ascents and descents that are figurative, set amongst literal physical transformations. The figurative three-tiered geography of the *Metamorphoses* maps directly onto Lucius' somatic transformations from man to beast to convert: the first section of *Metamorphoses* depicts a human Lucius on earth,[14] the second shows a donkey Lucius in a figurative *katabasis*,[15] the third portrays a human convert in a figurative *katascopia*.[16] The *Metamorphoses* is a symbolic *Apocolocyntosis*. From one perspective, the *Metamorphoses* allegorizes curiosity and conversion. From another, it interrogates Roman identity by positing an analogy: the cosmic relationship inscribed in the Menippean tripartite schematization duplicates the relationship between the empire's center and its multiple peripheries. How do the parts relate to the whole? How does multiplicity yield unity? How is a North African magician a Roman? In *menippea*, humans travel among three tiers, yet are paradoxically not fully at home in any of them (unlike epic, which privileges *nostoi*).

A Menippean reading of the *Metamorphoses* displaces Lucius' most famous attribute, curiosity, to focus upon its central ideological problem, that of the interloper, in the term's etymological sense of a misplaced, unauthorized presence. At the narrative's outset, Apuleius mobilizes Roman anxieties about magic and sex, and from the Roman perspective, the magic that Lucius seeks in the provinces is a 'bastard antireligion', at once exotic, rebellious, and dangerous.[17] However, Lucius' quest itself is transgressive only from the perspective of the Roman center. In Apuleius studies, un-challenged occidental readings have re-inscribed the hierarchical valuations of curiosity and piety, *eros* and *philos*, philosophy and magic, civilized and barbarian, East and West, center and margin. From a de-centered, provincial perspective, *Metamorphoses* is less a critique of curiosity than of the contradictions of Roman citizenship. Lucius' voyage tests how imperial culture thrives or fails at the edges of the empire, where competing *epistemes* face off.

---

14 *Met.* 1,1–3,24. All *Metamorphoses* citations and translations refer to the 1989 Hanson Loeb text.
15 *Met.* 3,25–11,13.
16 *Met.* 11,14–11,30.
17 Tatum 1979, 22.

The first sections of the *Apocolocyntosis* and the *Metamorphoses* unfold on earth. Here, I compare Claudius' death scene in the former[18] with the Risus Festival in the latter. Both depict liminal moments when boundaries between realms are breached, and 'low things' and 'high things' are re-conceptualized without hierarchies or binaries, so that all forms of knowledge, from philosophy to pornography, and all contexts, central and marginal, are given equal footing. The climax of the earthly portion of *Metamorphoses* is the Risus Festival, which I see as a counterpart to Claudius' death scene in *Apocolocyntosis*. Seneca reveals the breakdown of that which is autonomous and properly political through Menippean transgression, and this scene is foundational to Menippean satire, since in Menippean satire, lofty subject matter confronts 'degraded and obscene' realism.[19] Claudius, watching a troupe of mimes, starts performing, *cum maiorem sonitum emisisset illa parte qua facilius loquebatur*, 4,39–4 (after he let loose a great sound from that part whence he more easily spoke). The juxtaposition of an emperor and his flatulence is emphasized when Seneca puns on the double meaning of *maior*, which here refers to the larger degree of sound produced by his farts. The term is closely connected with *mos maiorum*, the common Roman term for 'the ways of our ancestors', and its presence in the text inevitably taps into the Roman ideological fixation upon ancestors and *mos maiorum*, from which governmental power and legitimacy derived. Doubtless, Seneca's audience would ponder the implication: Claudius' only *maius* action was his farting. In the *Apocolocyntosis*, the emperor and the mimes are metonyms for the conflict between the political and the aesthetic, and their encounter yields a foul and overflowing excess. If we believe Suetonius,[20] then Seneca wholly fabricated this scene, but the fantasy gains traction from the fact that in life Claudius was notoriously unable to maintain the autonomy and integrity of his rule against the interference of freedmen and other interlopers. In the *Apocolocyntosis*, the mime show, which *should* be the focus of all attention, is unable to compete with Claudius' 'performance'. Roman ideology assumed a continuity between the body's insides and its outsides, so that a physically deformed man was presumed to be internally deficient, too.[21] Seneca seizes the inside / outside dichotomy, transmogrifying the former into the latter: as Claudius' insides become outsides, he simultaneously transforms from spectator to spectacle, symbolizing how his rule dissolved boundaries between master and slave, insider and outsider, and effectively transformed the court into the arena.

---

18 Sen. *Apoc.* 3–4.
19 Bakhtin 1984, 115.
20 *Cl.* 44.
21 Braund and James 1998, 295.

While there is no farting in the *Metamorphoses*, the narrator's time in Thessaly on the earthly tier[22] is similarly dominated by flowing fluids and violated bodies in settings that are sexual, juridical and homicidal, especially when Lucius stumbles back to Milo's house and 'murders' a group of 'robbers'.[23] In the *Metamorphoses* 'there is no reluctance...to exploit all the available tropes of sexuality', and even here, sexual imagery is striking.[24] Lucius pulls aside his cloak to reveal his *gladium* (sword), an unavoidably sexual term,[25] which he *demergit altissime* (plunges most deeply) into each body. Phallic, penetrative, and bellicose language collapses sex and death into one another, and Lucius' description of the bodies becoming *perforati* (pierced) under his sword echoes Claudius' violable body in the *Apocolocyntosis*,[26] and at the moment of the robbers' death, each *spiritus efflaverint* (the spirits will have exhaled; breathed out), echoing the moment of Claudius' death, *ille...animam ebulliit* (4,37). Further, blood and wine are rendered equivalent in the *Metamorphoses*, just as the *Apocolocyntosis* displayed excrement, so that in both texts bodily wastes are fused into a rich symbolic matrix of death and degradation whirled with elements of play.

The next day, while on trial for murder, Lucius uncovers the bodies before the throng in the theater. Lucius tears away the covering, and finds a terrifyingly incoherent surprise: rather than three bodies, three wineskins are upon the bier. The Risus Festival 'is clearly a study in misinterpretation as well as uninterpretability',[27] in which Apuleius instigates a 'collapse of cause and effect'.[28] Enigmatic elements are vital to the narrative's dialectic between plausible and implausible. While some see a breakdown of social structure, or even of the narrative itself, Bakhtin allows for a dialogue of clashing social codes and speech genres, and consequently the Risus Festival depicts carnival chaos intruding upon decorous institutional procedures. These transformations are staged in a theatre, so this trial is no straightforward juridical procedure.[29] The forum and theater are distinct, discrete spaces, placed in opposition to facilitate carnival inversions. The trial in the theater is neither a theatrical trial nor a judicial spectacle, but rather an unmeshed mixture of the theatrical fiction and proper jurisprudence.

---

22 *Met.* 1,2–3,24.
23 *Met.* 2,32.
24 Winkler 1985, 175.
25 Adams 1982, 20.
26 4,37–42.
27 Finkelpearl 1998, 90.
28 Shumate 1996, 82.
29 For discussions of the theater setting: Tatum 1979, 42; Habinek 1990, 54; Shumate 1996, 80–85; Finkelpearl 1998, 88; Frangoulidis 2001, 50; Slater 2003, 87–93.

The juxtaposition illustrates how indecorous behavior and violations of establishment etiquette (such as we saw in Claudius' death scene in the *Apocolocyntosis*) reconfigure decorous officialdom.

The disclosure that Lucius had not murdered robbers, but was instead the butt of some bizarre, intricate joke associated with a local festival, exacerbates rather than disambiguates the strangeness of Hypata. The festival's carnival mystification hinges upon laughter, which may be difficult to decode due to the sequence's focalization through Lucius, who is ignorant of the mores and manners of Thessaly and thus unable to comprehend the semiotics of this laughter. As Shumate notes, 'that the crowd should be rendered helpless with laughter at the sight of Lucius' *dolor* is baffling to both victim and reader'.[30] Taken from the point of view of the audience, the laughter appears to be of a different character, positive and generous. The festival, then, imposes upon an ignorant 'victim' a transformative rebirth, from condemned murderer to hero. Bakhtin theorizes laughter to be fundamental to Menippean carnival as an excess of language, a purely phonic phenomenon outside and beyond *logos*. Through the din of Hypata's cacophonous laughter, Lucius is reborn a native. Blood and wine are rendered equal; the murderer becomes the savior. Lucius, however, is a stranger in a strange land, unable to understand festivals in Thessaly. This failure of comprehension reflects the tensions between the imperial center and provincial customs. For their part, the people of Thessaly seek to incorporate Lucius, but he turns down their offer of a statue.

After Lucius has fully recovered from being the butt of the Risus Festival, he asks Photis to transform him into a bird. Here he is not immature, foolish or tragically curious. Rather, he is finally at home in Hypata. The narrative has repeatedly warned Lucius about the danger of witches, but the more time he spends in the provinces, the more he deems Aristomenes and Thelyphron to have been wayward Romans suffering from witch panic. The process of integration that commences with the Risus Festival continues, and when Lucius seeks out a further rebirth from Photis, we should understand that Lucius has, at least for one moment, bridged the gap between his Roman subject position and the alternative orientation of the provinces. What is usually read as Lucius' failure is instead his moment of social and intellectual triumph: he gets Hypata, he understands Thessaly, and having left his Roman world behind, he is ready to transition from one cultural orientation to another as a reverse Aeneas. Of course, what the narrative gives us is not a full assimilation. Trying to become a bird *and* a citizen of Hypata, Lucius becomes neither. Photis makes a mistake, changing Lucius in-

---

30 Shumate 1996, 83.

stead into a donkey, sending him on an extended *katabasis*, and the *Metamorphoses* thus illustrates the imperial subject's inevitable alienation.

★ ★ ★

Having discussed the earthly tiers of the *Apocolocyntosis* and the *Metamorphoses*, I now turn to their middle sections. In the *Apocolocyntosis*, when the dead emperor Claudius is ejected from Olympus, Mercury accompanies him, *dum descendunt per uiam Sacram* to Hades (11,1). They come upon Claudius' funeral, and Claudius finally realizes that he is dead. This is a pivotal moment in the text's revision of history. Here, the *Apocolocyntosis* intersects with its antecedent, the elegy that Seneca wrote for Nero to read at Claudius' funeral, insofar as the *via sacra*, the location of funeral processions, 'would also have been the most convenient route for Claudius' mortal remains from the Palatium to the Forum, where the *laudatio funebris* for Claudius would have been delivered'.[31] For the duration of the funeral scene, the *turba* can barely contain its elation, acting out grief while barely concealing its delight. Nauta (1987, 69–73) has argued that Seneca wrote the *Apocolocyntosis* to be read to a small group of friends at the Saturnalia of 54 CE. In this way, the *Apocolocyntosis* can be regarded as a second draft of the *laudatio funebris*, as though writing fawning propaganda left such a bad taste in Seneca's mouth that only something as scurrilous as the *Apocolocyntosis* could cleanse it. The party-goers on the *via sacra* may have been the original audience of the *Apocolocyntosis*. Making fun of Claudius watching his own funeral, Seneca depicts a man who is literally of two minds, and asks, 'What kind of a man would voyage to Olympus and seek divination, and not realize he is dead?'

In the second section of the *Metamorphoses* (3,25–11,13), Lucius ceases to coincide with himself, as his donkey self seems to descend to a Hades-like world in an extended *katabasis*. From a Roman orientation, Lucius rejected the best of human society, and is now bought, sold and kidnapped by the criminals, thugs, and sadists who populate the imperial underside. Usually, this part of the novel is seen as allegorical punishment for excessive curiosity and prurience: the beastly somatic form fits the crime. The narrative itself is also transformed. Despite a little danger and a lot of confusion, Hypata was a nice place. Now, danger prevails. Magic, frequent in the earthly portion of the narrative, recedes until Book 9, as degradation and violence overtake festivals and laughter.

---

31 Eden 1984, 128.

Lucius travels through the 'subcultures of the countryside',[32] and the climactic *volta* of his *katabasis* comes when he sticks his nose where it does not belong and discovers half-dead donkeys and humans in a mill, in a moment of identification and split subjectivity, which reminds one of the *Apocolocyntosis* roadside funeral. Others have argued that this episode is a figurative *katabasis*, replete with Hades symbolism: slaves and animals are 'living ghosts', night never ends,[33] and the husband and wife who own the mill are figured as the king and queen of the underworld.[34] Indeed, the mill is the nadir of Lucius' long descent, the point after which things can only get better. Having spent a day blindfolded and tethered to an ever-revolving millstone—itself symbolic of the dead center of hell within the Ptolemaic cosmos—Lucius discovers the mill's dark secret: *homunculi vibicibus lividis totam cutem depicti*, Met. 9,12 (shrunken little men with all the surface of their skin discolored by angry welts). Then, looking past the humans, Lucius sees his *contubernales*, the donkey counterparts to the mill's human slaves (*Met.* 9,13). The image of half-dead humans and donkeys adjacent to one another merges humans and animals in Lucius' mind: *talis familiae funestum mihi etiam metuens exemplum*, Met. 9,3 (the deadly example of my family had me really scared) and viewing this ecphrasis leads Lucius to a double-identification with who he has been, and what he is now. As Claudius was confronted with himself at his funeral, in the mill in *Metamorphoses* Lucius, too, sees himself. Once he leaves the mill, Lucius seems to pick up where he left off in Hypata before Photis' mistake, in the midst of a process of integration, even if he remains donkified. With Thiasos, Lucius rehearses 'his forthcoming re-humanization'[35] in a process that has been characterized as 'a veritable checklist of differences between culture and nature'.[36] As if a child, Lucius masters table manners and sign language; as if a young man, he is initiated sexually by the Corinthian *matrona*.[37] Lucius' affair has divided critics, some concluding that it is a further punishment,[38] others detecting emotional authenticity during the interspecies coitus.[39] Bakhtin never addresses Lucius' tryst with the Corinthian matron. Despite his silence, I argue that within Bakhtin's framework, the human and the donkey in congress is another figure of *syncrisis*.

---

[32] Habinek 1990, 55.
[33] *Met.* 9,11.
[34] Sabnis 2013.
[35] Frangoulidis 2001, 150.
[36] Habinek 1990, 55.
[37] *Met.* 10,22.
[38] Mason 1971, 162; Schlam 1996, 125.
[39] Shumate 1996, 125; Finkelpearl 1998, 154–155.

Throughout the *Metamorphoses*, Apuleius strategically combines sexuality with arenas, courts and festivals. After his affair with the matron, Lucius finds himself in a lamentable bind at the Corinthian *munus*, a festival that both recalls the Risus Festival and anticipates Book 11's conversion sequence. Just as Hypata's citizens mixed the theatrical and juridical, so too does Thiasus in Corinth: to celebrate his promotion to local magistrate, he stages three days of spectacles, including gladiatorial games, a pantomime of the Judgment of Paris, and a climactic *voluptarium spectaculum*.[40] Both Risus and this *munus* are held on stage, and both precipitate physical changes for Lucius. As in *Apocolocyntosis*, all three tiers of *Metamorphoses* are governed by similar legalistic procedures. What is abhorrent is that within the logic of an extended *katabasis*, an act of love is eventually transmogrified into an act of death, once Lucius is employed as part of the machinery of Roman execution to kill the murderess. The *munus* illustrates the alienation of the provinces, as provincial subjects seem to be chewed up and spit out by the machinery of the empire.

The final episode in Lucius' extended *katabasis* is the *anteludia*.[41] While this parade and procession are in Book 11, I locate the division between the *katabasis* and *katascopia* portions of the narrative at Lucius' return to human form.[42] This has two notable consequences. First, the Isis Book is not a unified whole: it has its feet in *both* heaven *and* hell. Second, the *anteludia* is liminal, as it takes place on the cusp between tiers and physical states. Its motley, rag-tag parade is composed of numerous people in costume: a pretend soldier, hunter, gladiator, magistrate, philosopher, she-bear-cum-socialite, monkey dressed as Ganymede, donkey with Pegasus wings, and a man with cheap jewelry and a bad wig as a 'counterfeit woman'.[43] These counter-culture elements, the sacrosanct religious process for which the procession makes way, point directly to carnival. While all mediated through Lucius' awestruck voice, the whole procession is not integrated. Instead, the carnival parade followed by the religious procession is the final *syncrisis* Lucius encounters while a donkey.

* * *

Having discussed earth and hell in the *Apocolocyntosis* and the *Metamorphoses*, now let us turn to heaven. In the *Apocolocyntosis*,[44] Claudius ascends to heaven, and when he arrives, Hercules cannot determine whether he is man

---

[40] *Met.* 10,35.
[41] *Met.* 11,8.
[42] *Met.* 11,13.
[43] *Met.* 11,8.
[44] *Apoc.* 5,1–11,6.

or beast. They fail to communicate, and descend into parody when Claudius quotes the *Odyssey* to (falsely) demonstrate his Greek pedigree. This exchange exhibits all the flourishes of Menippean *syncrisis:* prose and verse, Greek with Latin, high literature mixed with low, gods confronting humans, earth abutting Olympus. Claudius quotes Homer, asserting to Hercules that he hails from Troy. Claudius presents himself as Aeneas, the mythopoetic founder of Rome, but it is unclear whether he seeks to inscribe himself as the new Aeneas, and therefore that his voyage to heaven represents an attempt to expand empire upward, or whether Claudius just happens to be quoting the only thing he can think of. The narrator undercuts Claudius through parody. Therefore, this moment creates *syncrisis* by juxtaposing two disparate, contradictory notions of Claudius, the fool, and the savvy, politic leader who feigned stupidity for political preservation.

The centerpiece of the *Apocolocyntosis* in heaven is the council of the gods.[45] Unfolding from an elevated perspective, its philosophical and moral judgments carry special weight. The council is called to determine whether Claudius will be deified; notably, only Janus, the two-faced, and Diespiter, who would have been at best obscure to a Roman audience, speak on behalf of Claudius. Janus asserts that because gods are great, great men should be honored as gods, but none after today, lest the honor of deification become mere *fabam mimum* (bean farce).[46] Diespiter ventriloquizes a real argument made by Nero, that because Claudius was related to Augustus, and because Augustus had himself been deified, Claudius should receive the same honors. In Roman politics, it was to Nero's advantage that Claudius be deified, as Nero was Claudius' adoptive son and would gain legitimacy if directly descended from a god. Seneca obliterates this claim by arguing through Augustus that he did not bring peace to Rome to honor murderers in heaven, least of all the murderer of his family. Seneca's political critique, when placed in the mouth of Augustus, is apparent: Claudius claimed to be Augustus' heir, but in the *Apocolocyntosis*, he is proved unfit for that title. The gods summarily expel him to Hades, and the divine council parodies legalistic officialdom on earth to demystify and debunk apotheosis.

In the *Metamorphoses*, Apuleius also gives us a vision of heaven similarly marked by legalism. High religiosity and a sacrosanct tone seem to replace scandalous humor, and the narrative appears to stage an authentic account of spiritual awakening. And yet, readers cannot help but think that somehow the book must be putting us on, if all that burlesque scandal is suddenly shut off to serve

---

45 *Apoc.* 4–11.
46 *Apoc.* 9,3.

piety. While debate between 'enlightenment' and 'entertainment' readings is ongoing, I think Apuleius authorizes, even encourages, contradictory yet equally sustainable readings. Enlightenment versus entertainment is a false dichotomy; rather, *Metamorphoses* insists that piety itself is parodic, and parody has some piety to it. Further, Apuleius mobilizes Menippean poetics to inscribe a poetics of ambivalence into his narrative. The final, the greatest *syncrisis* is the very fact that conversion follows everything else.

Since the three-tiered figuration of geography and metaphysics – foundational in Seneca's *Apocolocyntosis* – is appropriated to the rewriting of the *Metamorphoses*, the tripartite structure governs this novel, and once Lucius has 'descended' into the 'Netherworld', a parallel 'ascent' is to be expected. In Menippean satire, what goes down must come up. The figurative *katascopia* is bolstered by a surfeit of sidereal symbolism. Stars, planets, and even gleaming bald heads swirl around Lucius as if he himself has ascended to some heavenly vantage point; most strikingly, Lucius twice shaves his head as if he himself is becoming a heavenly body like Isis.[47] Further, his gleaming dome is another intercultural trope. From the naturalized Roman perspective, a bald head harks back to stock characters from Old Comedy and mime, in which to be bald is to be a fool. Also, as devotees of the Isis cult were known for their baldness, the exposed scalp is a semiotic signpost for exoticism and ancient wisdom, but paradoxically also suggests that the convert is ill-informed, trendy, and false. Winkler concludes that the shaved head forces us to 'see Lucius two ways – as a redeemed Isiac and as a dupe'.[48] The sense that Lucius is a dupe is nowhere as strong as in Book 11's treatment of money. The basic conflict critics have seen regarding the pecuniary aspects of the Isis Book arise out of the supposed incompatibility of religiosity and expenditure. And Lucius' conversion does not come cheap: his family must fund his initial conversion,[49] while later he is forced to sell his clothes to finance subsequent initiations.[50] Various demands weigh on Lucius, who feels *religiosum scrupulum* (religious anxiety) and *ambiguitatis caligo* (dark uncertainty),[51] and Lucius' misgivings reach a fever pitch as he prepares for his third and final initiation. Readers face the 'inescapable suggestion that Lucius is a dupe'.[52]

---

47 *Met.* 11,28; 11,30.
48 Winkler 1985, 216.
49 *Met.* 11,18.
50 *Met.* 11,28.
51 *Met.* 11,27.
52 Shumate 1996, 325.

Carnival elements have been present throughout *Metamorphoses*, and their continued role in the concluding sections of the novel account for the mixture of enlightenment and entertainment, for the nagging doubts and authorized confusions. After Lucius begins his initiation, erotic encounters are transformed into religious ecstasies, and rather than finding love and delight in Photis or the matron in Corinth, Lucius affirms: *inexplicabili voluptate simulacri divini perfruebar*, Met. 11,24 (revealing in the inexpressible pleasure of the divine likeness). *Eros* has not been extirpated but sublimated, and desiderative quests now turn toward the divine.

Partway through his initiation, Lucius travels to Rome,[53] and the 'implied location' turns out to be Rome's temple precinct.[54] Isis worship in Rome was a highly visible cultural movement with its own architecture and institutions, and its *Iseum Campense* was a large, imposing structure in the city center, the Campus Martius, its surroundings punctuated by imposing foreign objects—sphinxes, obelisks, lion and crocodile statues—where autochthonous and foreign festivals were held.[55] Further, the site of the *horologium Augusti*, whose gnomon was an Egyptian obelisk, shared physical space with the *Iseum Campense*, so that urban geography stages intercultural interactions between imperial Rome and occupied Egypt.[56] The Campus Martius signified within the Roman imagination a site of religious and cultural displays: the Campus is the carnival's address. Yet the Roman Isis cult was always a product of counterculture, always carnivalizing. For Romans, regardless of whether they understood the cult or not, its physical situation must have had symbolic significance, representing an inexplicable *otherness*, neither naturalized nor assimilated, and yet physically inserted into the midst of daily life. *Metamorphoses* culminates within the confines of the Campus, and this geographical detail reveals an important intertext between the *Metamorphoses* and the *Apocolocyntosis:* they cross paths here. Seneca's Claudius stumbles upon his funeral while descending from Olympus to Hades right here, and the *Metamorphoses* mobilizes this precedent to inject carnival into the Isis Book, which otherwise could be a monologic account of religious piety.

* * *

The Menippean tripartite schematization of geography accounts for the narrative's structure, designed to illustrate competing drives toward sameness and

---

53 *Met.* 11,26.
54 Winkler 1985, 233.
55 Griffiths 1975, 19; Durant 1972, 65.
56 Beck 2004, 316.

difference in *Metamorphoses*. All three realms are fungible: what happens in one is equivalent to what happens in the others, but with varying degrees of corruption or decadence. Moreover, the tripartite Menippean pattern, *earth → heaven → hell*, reveals another pattern, a carnival sequence: *ius → eros → transformation*. Here, I am greatly indebted to T.N. Habinek's article on 'Lucius' Rites of Passage'. Using cultural anthropology to organize Apuleius' narrative, Habinek argues that the stages of Lucius' 'rite of passage' correspond to Greco-Roman civic festivals, which are 'rituals of community identity'.[57] Lucius is alienated from or integrated into a larger community. I wish to expand this framework by considering the events that precede or follow each festival. For instance, Lucius' affair with Photis is part of the larger series of events related to the Risus Festival, and Lucius' affair with the *matrona* relates to the *anteludia*, each part of a larger sequence, which encapsulates sexuality, legalism, and transformation. Seneca's strict constructionist Menippean satire travels to Olympus and Hades in its quest; Apuleius' 'full-blown' novelistic expansion of *menippea* utilizes carnival not to traverse geographic space, but instead to traverse institutional and social spaces as if they were geographic. *Metamorphoses* resolves fantastic journeys back into daily imperial problems, as Apuleius harnesses Menippean satire's truth-seeking function, transposing its ascents and descents onto earth to shine a bright light upon the empire's dark corners.

The carnival sequence, *eros → ius → transformation*, is repeated on each geographic plane in both texts: Seneca's satire exhibits uncannily similar trials on Olympus and in Hades, with great comic effect, and the parodic legalism is not an innovation of the upper and lower realms, but rather a recapitulation of elements initiated upon the terrestrial tier. Likewise, Apuleius repeats the motif of the outsider in a strange land who first discovers *eros*, then finds himself enmeshed in a juridical situation that is foreign or illegible. The *Apocolocyntosis* renders throne rooms and courtrooms as essentially similar sites of authority, defaced by Claudius, or used to rein him in. The *Metamorphoses* presents official courts and theaters in a similar manner, as spaces where the world is turned upside down: laughter transforms a supposed murderer into a hero; interspecies intercourse becomes a means to homicide; finally, Lucius' conversion is undermined. Involvement with an Eastern cult leaves him paradoxically poorly integrated into Roman society, socially marginalized as an Isiac devotee, just as he was as a donkey. Being employed by the Roman court – a reversion back to his former livelihood – highlights not only the tenuous nature of his conversion, but also his subject position in Rome. Although the *Metamorphoses* is often

---

[57] Habinek 1990, 53.

seen as a two-part narrative, pre- and post- initiation, the Menippean character of *Metamorphoses* reveals itself in the narrative's structure of three repetitions of a carnival sequence. The final effect of a figurative presentation of these three realms reveals less about metaphysics—that is, the relationship between an afterlife and this life, or even the particular character of Isis worship—than it does about the relationship between disparate areas of human daily life *on earth*. Apuleius deploys *katascopia* and *katabasis* to deconstruct the naïve distinction between nature and culture.

Pivotal to Apuleius's narrative is the role of error in the carnival sequence. The *Metamorphoses* is a book of mistakes as much as it is a book of changes. Photis fails to transform Lucius into a bird, and her error creates the plot of the rest of the novel. Accordingly, the carnival sequence may be revised: *eros* → *ius* → *error* → *transformation*. The events in Corinth also turn on error and interruption: Lucius is supposed to copulate with a condemned woman, but instead escapes. What was supposed to be a sequence of two events—the copulation and then the execution—is transformed into two other events, the *anteludia* and *peculiaris pompa* in Cenchreae, which yield Lucius' re-humanization and Isis' appearance. To shed light on error in the Isis Book, I refer to Relihan's discussion of the 'typical Menippean ending', in which 'the lessons preached and learned in the body of the text are negated', thwarting the narrative's intention to end.[58] No tying up of loose ends, no purification, no closure: conclusion is offered, only to be negated. Had the *Apocolocyntosis* ended at the dice game, the logic of *contrapasso* would have afforded the narrative a pleasing symmetry. The ending of the *Metamorphoses* is another Menippean ending, authorizing sincerity and skepticism, consistently offering evidence to bolster both views. In the final chapters, money, doubt, and an endless series of initiations, all complicate the reader's apprehension of the sincerity of Lucius' religious experience. A great irony throughout *Metamorphoses* is the alacrity with which Lucius changes from man to beast, *gratis*, while religious initiation is protracted and costly.

Although the structurally requisite error in Book 11 does not belong to Lucius, as it has earlier, I wish to propose, alternatively, that in the Isis Book the trope of error is displaced out of the narrative, away from Lucius, and onto the reader. The reader who seeks to settle whether *Metamorphoses* is pious *or* parodic is following in the footsteps of Photis rather than Lucius. The fact that the end of *Metamorphoses* can neither be settled nor solved reveals something important about the genre: Menippean satire is anti-intellectualism for and by

---

[58] Relihan 1993, 22.

intellectuals.[59] It presents the limits of what a thinker can think through, what a philosopher may know, or what a narrative can reveal. Book 11's refusal to conclude transcends thematics to become an issue of poetics, and an issue of reading itself. Aristotle's and Huet's readers expect answers to their questions about Book 11; Bakhtin's do not.

Bibliography

Bakhtin, M.M. 1984. *Problems of Dostoevsky's Poetics* (C. Emerson, trans.), Minneapolis: University of Minnesota Press.

Beck, R. 2004. 'Lucius and the Sundial: A Hidden Chronotopic Template in *Metamorphoses* 11', in: M. Zimmerman, R. Van der Paardt (eds.), *Metamorphic Reflections: Essays Presented to Ben Hijmans at his 75th Birthday*, Dudley: Peeters. 308–318.

Branham, R.B. 2005. 'The Poetics of Genre: Bakhtin, Menippus, Petronius', in: R.B. Branham (ed.), *The Bakhtin Circle and Ancient Narrative*, ANS 3, Groningen: Groningen University Library. 3–31.

Braund, S.M., and James, P.. 1998. '*Quasi Homo*: Distortion and Contortion in Seneca's *Apocolocyntosis*', *Arethusa* 31.3, 285–311.

Courtney, E. 1962. 'Parody and Literary Allusion in Menippean Satire', *Philologus*, 106, 86–100.

Empson, W. 1935. *Some Versions of Pastoral*. Norfolk: New Directions.

Finkelpearl, E. 2004. 'The Ends of the Metamorphoses: Apuleius *Met.* 11.26.4–11.30,' in: M. Zimmerman, R. van der Paardt (eds.), *Metamorphic Reflections: Essays Presented to Ben Hijmans at his 75th Birthday*, Dudley: Peeters. 331–342.

Frangoulidis, S. 2001. *Roles and Performances in Apuleius'* Metamorphoses. Stuttgart: JB Metzler.

Habinek, T. 1990. 'Lucius' Rites of Passage', *Materiali e discussioni per analisi dei testi classici* 25, 40–69.

Hanson, J. A. 1989 (ed. and trans.). *Apuleius, Metamorphoses*, 2 vols. Cambridge: Harvard University Press.

Harrison, S. 2000. *Apuleius: A Latin Sophist*. Oxford: Oxford University Press.

Hunink, V. 2006. 'Some Cases of Genre Confusion in Apuleius' in: R.R. Nauta (ed.) *Desultoria Scientia: Genre in Apuleius'* Metamorphoses *and Related Texts,* Dudley: Peeters. 33–42.

Nauta, R.R. 1987. 'Seneca's *Apocolocyntosis* As Saturnalian Literature.' *Mnemosyne*, 40,1–2, 69–96.

Relihan, J. 1993. *Ancient Menippean Satire*. Baltimore: Johns Hopkins University Press.

Riikonen, H.K. 1987. *Menippean Satire as a Literary Genre, with special reference to Seneca's Apocolocyntosis*. Helsinki: Societas Scientiarum Fennica.

Robinson, T.J. 2005. 'In the Court of Time: The Reckoning of a Monster in the *Apocolocyntosis* of Seneca', *Arethusa* 38, 223–257.

---

59 This formulation is indebted to Empson 1935 and Blanchard 1995, 27.

Sabnis, S. 2013. 'Donkey Gone to Hell: A *katabasis* Motif in Apuleius', in: M. Futre Pinheiro, A. Bierl, R. Beck, (eds.) *Intende, Lector – Echoes of Myth, Religion and Ritual in the Ancient Novel*, MythosEikonPoiesis 6, Berlin/Boston: De Gruyter. 177–199.

Schlam, C.C. 1992. *The* Metamorphoses *of Apuleius: On Making An Ass of Oneself*, Chapel Hill: University of North Carolina Press.

Selden, D.L. 1994. 'Genre of Genre', in: J. Tatum (ed.), *Search for the Ancient Novel*, Baltimore: Johns Hopkins University Press. 39–64.

Eden, P.T. (ed. and trans.) 1984. *Seneca. Apocolocyntosis*. Cambridge: Cambridge University Press.

Shumate, N. 1996. *Crisis and Conversion in Apuleius' Metamorphoses*, Ann Arbor: University of Michigan Press.

Slater, N.W. 2003. 'Spectator and Spectacle in Apuleius', in: S. Panayotakis, M. Zimmerman, W. Keulen (eds.), *The Ancient Novel and Beyond*, Boston: Brill. 85–100.

Tatum, J. 1979. *Apuleius and The Golden Ass*, Ithaca: Cornell University Press.

Weinbrot, H. 2005. *Menippean Satire Reconsidered*, Baltimore: Johns Hopkins University Press.

Winkler, J. 1985. *Auctor and Actor: A Narratological Reading of Apuleius's* The Golden Ass, Berkeley: University of California Press.

Zimmerman, M. 2006. 'Echoes of Roman Satire in Apuleius' *Metamorphoses*', in: R.R. Nauta (ed.), *Desultoria Scientia: Genre in Apuleius'* Metamorphoses *and Related Texts*, Dudley: Peeters. 87–104.

Turning Points in Scholarship on the Ancient Novel

Manuel Sanz Morales
Copyists' Versions and the Readership of the Greek Novel

Abstract: This paper has two goals: first, it shows the existence of multiple versions in the textual transmission of several of the preserved Greek novels and considers the reasons behind this; second, it relates this phenomenon to the problem of the readership of the Greek novel. It is suggested that copyists considered the ancient novel mainly as entertainment and a non-prestigious genre, which gave them more leeway to introduce modifications into the text. This can only be explained if there was a reading public formed by not only the *pepaideuménoi* but also the less educated.

1 Preliminaries

The concept of 'multiplicity of versions' is now sufficiently well established in the field of textual criticism, and has been applied to different periods and to diverse literary traditions.[1] This paper will deal with multiple versions in the ambit of the Greek romantic novel, and will be divided into two parts. In the first I will show that in the Greek novels there are cases of multiple versions and that, with one insignificant exception, this occurs whenever the medieval manuscripts are accompanied by ancient witnesses. In the second part I will refer to what I consider to be a basic cause of this phenomenon, the intervention of the scribes, in order to help clarify the educational and cultural level of the readers of the novel genre. I am therefore attempting to introduce a new element into the debate on this complex subject, which, even in the absence of conclusive answers, establishes new and important questions for understanding the reception histories and readerships of ancient novels.

English translation by J.J. Zoltowski.

1 An example is issue 5 of the journal *Variants* (2006), which the European Society for Textual Scholarship devoted to this phenomenon in different literatures and periods. For the first part of this article, referring to multiple versions in the Greek novel and other works of fiction, I reproduce in abbreviated form some ideas or details taken from a paper of mine published in that volume (Sanz Morales 2006).

Manuel Sanz Morales, Universidad de Extremadura (Cáceres)

https://doi.org/10.1515/9781501503986-014

Of the five Greek romantic novels that have come down to us in their entirety,[2] two show signs of having witnessed multiple versions in their respective transmissions: the novels of Chariton and Achilles Tatius. However, I think it is necessary first of all to refer to the novel by Xenophon of Ephesus, at least in order to recall the hypothesis according to which the text, consisting of five books and transmitted by a *codex unicus*, the *Laurentianus Conv. Soppr. 627*, was probably an epitome of the original work. This work is assumed to have been made up of ten books, according to the figure given to us by the Byzantine lexicon Suda (s.v. Ξενοφῶν, III 495, ed. Adler 1971). It is well known that the epitome hypothesis was predominant for some time,[3] but in recent decades it has been questioned by several major specialists[4] and is now seriously challenged, although it still has its supporters.[5] Whatever the truth may be, I believe that it is essential to mention the hypothesis here.[6] It is not my intention here to come down on one side or the other, but I do wish to point out that, for the purposes of the present paper, the whole debate is faced with the considerable difficulty that it is not possible to compare two texts. But if a novel such as Xenophon's existed in such dramatically different forms at different periods, it is plausible that other novels too may have been altered in the course of their reception. The cases of Achilles Tatius and Chariton are special, since for them we do have more than one witness, as we shall see below.

---

[2] I use this term to refer only to the genre *sensu stricto*, that is, to amatory novels (cf., for example, Ruiz Montero 2006, 15–18 and 61–148); I therefore leave aside other related types of narrative, although I will refer to some of these works later.
[3] cf., for example, Gärtner 1967.
[4] Hägg 1966; Ruiz Montero 1982; O'Sullivan 1995, 100–139.
[5] Swain 1998, 104; See the comprehensive *status quaestionis* in Ruiz-Montero 1994, 1094–1095.
[6] In the hypothetical case of the transmitted text being in fact an epitome, one explanation might be that there was presumably a deliberate intervention on the part of scholars or copyists, but perhaps more plausible is the possibility that the author produced two different versions, a short one and a longer one (perhaps the longer one for a more learned public and the shorter one for a wider public that had no knowledge of, nor wished to know anything about, literary refinement or complications), and that the vicissitudes of the transmission have left us with only the shorter version. The absence of internal inconsistencies (pointed out by Hägg 1966) would seem to be more favourable to this second possibility. In this connection it is worth mentioning the brief debate on the possible existence of authorial variants in the novel by Longus. Young 1968 defended this thesis; in his opinion, of the two independent codices that have come down to us, "A [F in Reeve's Teubner edition, Leipzig, 1994] represents a first draft or first edition by Longus, and B [V in Reeve] derives from his second thoughts, as set out in a text emended by himself" (Young 1968, 74). This thesis was immediately rebutted by Reeve 1969. I am grateful to my colleague Bruce D. MacQueen for the references to Longus.

2 Chariton of Aphrodisias and Achilles Tatius

Chariton's novel has come down to us in its entirety thanks to the fact that the same medieval codex contains that of Xenophon. Yet, unlike the case of the latter, we also have some fragments of Chariton, thanks to the remains of a manuscript from the sixth or seventh century (the so-called *codex thebanus*, now lost) and to three papyri from the end of the second century or the beginning of the third. The relationship between the two manuscripts has already been studied,[7] and it can be stated without fear of contradiction that the two witnesses do not contain the same text; the Theban codex, in spite of being much older, seems to offer an inferior version,[8] with deliberately introduced textual modifications.[9]

But the question goes further than this. In a study published in 2009[10] I have attempted to demonstrate that the papyri preserve a text whose discrepancies with the medieval manuscript contain inferior readings that cannot all be explained as mechanical errors on the part of the copyist. It is true that the divergences do not in the end make for such a different version as that of the Theban codex. These are slight verbal differences, which in my opinion might have been due to a rough copy in the papyri, a copy not intended to be faithful letter for letter, but at the same time one which did not attempt to alter a model in order to make it more interesting, to 'improve' it. Moreover, given that the text of the papyri appears on the whole to be superior to the medieval text,[11] and in view of the fact that these papyri are probably between a half century and one century later than the author, two centuries at the most,[12] we might consider the possibility that the papyri contain the original text, though disfigured to a certain extent by the above-mentioned rough copy (we could consider it a first alternative version of Chariton's novel). This same original text would then be the one offered by the medieval manuscript,

---

[7] Wilcken 1901, Zimmermann 1923, Sanz Morales 2006.
[8] Zimmermann 1923; Sanz Morales 2006. On the other hand, Conca 2010 has tried to give new value to the Theban codex.
[9] Reardon 2003, 315, neatly sums up this fact and points to the conclusion to be drawn regarding the readership of the novel: 'The scribe has clearly made alterations and additions of his own, which suggests that the story had passed into the public domain, like the Alexander Romance, and was considered fair game for rewriting in the process of transmission.'
[10] Sanz Morales 2009.
[11] This conclusion is already to be found in Zimmermann 1928 and Lucke 1985; and I subscribe to it: Sanz Morales 2002 and 2009.
[12] If Chariton lived around the first half of the 2nd c. AD, a fairly generally accepted hypothesis but by no means an unchallengeable one, since the author could date from around a century or century and a half before this; in the latter case, the distance between author and papyri would be around two centuries.

but with the textual corruptions resulting from the transmission: a somewhat inferior text in general, but superior in more than one passage. On the other hand, we would then have another version: a deliberately modified text that is clearly distinguishable from the original one and presents clear signs of being inferior to it, a text that already existed between the sixth and seventh centuries and which we know to some small extent thanks to the *codex thebanus*.

Unlike the above-mentioned novels, that of Achilles Tatius has a large number of witnesses.[13] The one of most interest to us is a papyrus, probably dating from the third century[14] and published in 1914,[15] to which a new fragment was added in 1989.[16] This fragment contains an extract of the text from 8,6,14 to 8,7,6, which is not in itself of particular importance, since it could simply be an extract for an anthology. However, the first and longer part presents a different order for a number of the chapters of book II; in addition, the text has some slight changes in the transitional segments that signal an attempt to avoid breaks in continuity. One possibility, already suggested by the authors of the *editio princeps*,[17] is that there was large-scale corruption, for example with a page from the archetype from which the medieval manuscripts descend being copied in the wrong place. But what seems much more likely is the possibility, mentioned by the editors themselves, that there were previously two versions of the novel; on this point see the indispensable study by Laplace.[18]

I believe that these points are sufficiently clear to enable us to reach a first conclusion: for at least two of the five novels preserved there are multiple versions. But there is one interesting fact that should be stressed: this occurs in the only two novels that have ancient witnesses, with the exception of a tiny piece of parchment with some lines of Heliodorus (sixth to seventh century).[19] We might ask ourselves:

---

13 Vilborg 1955 is the editor who includes the greatest number, 23 to be exact; Garnaud 1995 uses 7 manuscripts and the 6 extant papyri; some fragments of these papyri had not yet been identified when Vilborg published his edition.
14 Grenfell and Hunt were inclined to date it to the 4th c., but opinion today tends to attribute it to the 3rd c. (Parsons 1989, 66; Garnaud 1995, XXIII).
15 *P. Oxy. 1250*, ed. Grenfell-Hunt 1914.
16 *P. Oxy. 3837*, ed. Parsons 1989.
17 Grenfell and Hunt 1914, 136.
18 Laplace 1983. Laplace comes out in favour of the text of the papyrus, both in a specific and difficult passage (2,2,2) and in the important question of the narrative order. As regards the condensed text offered by the other part of the papyrus (*P. Oxy. 3837*), there is a possibility that we are dealing with two parts of an alternative version to that contained in the medieval codices.
19 A fragment (proceeding from a parchment manuscript) of the *Aethiopica* of Heliodorus dated to the 6th-7th c., which contains a small part of book 8 (8,16,6–7; 8,17,3–4); as we know, there

What would happen if there were papyri or ancient codices of the other novels that have come down to us? Would they also offer an 'irregular' text?[20] It is impossible to answer these questions with complete certainty, but I feel it is worth pointing out this fact here as far as the witnesses we have are concerned.

3 Other narrative works of fiction

The Greek novel (or some Greek novels, at least) share this characteristic we have mentioned with other works which, while not belonging to the genre of the romantic novel, are obviously related to it.[21] Suffice it to offer a very brief summary here. The anonymous and popular *Life of Aesop* presents two clearly differentiated versions,[22] in one of which it is even possible to discern two different drafts.[23] The also anonymous *Alexander Romance*, a novelized biography of the great conqueror, has an extremely complicated transmission, but what is of most interest to us is that it is possible to distinguish up to five different versions from the proto-Byzantine period.[24] Another complicated case is that of *Lucius or The Ass*, a work attributed by the tradition to Lucian. There seems to be agreement among scholars that this pseudo-Lucianesque text was probably an epitome of a Greek novel on the ass, identifiable with the *Metamorphoses* of one Lucius of Patras (a work mentioned by Photius, *Bibliotheca*, cod. 129), as well as a source for the Latin novel by Apuleius.[25] Here we would have another possible case of a work that had been 'simplified' with the idea of reaching a less-demanding audience. Finally, mention should be made of the *Story of Apol-*

---

are no ancient testimonia of Xenophon of Ephesus or Longus. I have consulted the *Leuven Database of Ancient Books*.
20 These are questions I have already posed in a previous work, cited above (Sanz Morales 2006, 139). Another possible question is: What would happen if novels had been transmitted of which we have papyri?
21 It is obvious that the debate on what the novel in Greece is or is not presents numerous complications, perhaps as many as the definition of the novel in general, and it is also obvious that it is not necessary for the purpose of the present paper to enter into questions pertaining to the theory of the novel. Concerning the works that 'accompany' the Greek novels, cf. Perry 1967, 84–85; Ruiz Montero 2006, *passim*.
22 Perry 1936, 1–2 *passim*; Ferrari 1997, 41–44; Karla 2001, 10–11.
23 For an overall view of the research into the transmission of this work and a list of editions and translations, cf. Karla 2001, 12–17 and 241–246.
24 Jouanno 2002, 5 and *passim*. In her comprehensive study of the transmission of the Greek text of this work she works on the basis of the classification proposed by Merkelbach 1977. For the editions of the different versions, both in Greek and in other languages, cf. Jouanno 2002, 467–469.
25 See, for example, Fusillo 1994, with bibliography in n. 94.

lonius, King of Tyre, of which we have at least two versions attested in manuscripts from as early as the second half of the ninth century.[26] It is even thought that the versions we have can be traced back to a version from the second or third century CE, that is, the *floruit* of the Greek novel.[27]

It is true that other factors may have been at play in influencing the fluctuations in the text of the above-mentioned works. For the *Life of Aesop*, for example, an oral origin has been posited, with different strata and influences present until a text was fully shaped in the first century CE.[28] Something similar occurs with *Apollonius, King of Tyre*, in which orality must have had an influence, not only as regards transmission and reception, but also in its composition.[29] Be that as it may, the intervention of the copyists has given rise to a multiplicity of versions, or at least helped to spread them around.

The brief account of Chariton and Achilles Tatius in this paper shows that the existence of multiple versions does not only *not* set the Greek romantic novel apart, but that it brings it in line with other narrative works of fiction which do not strictly belong to the same genre. In stating this, I do not wish to claim that the erotic novels had the same degree of textual instability as the other narrative works mentioned; for one thing, the testimonia of the former are too fragmentary to enable a firm conclusion to be drawn on the matter. The main point is that, with the features that will later characterize each particular

---

[26] According to Kortekaas 1984, 132–134, with *stemma*; in contrast, Schmeling 1988, VI-VII and *stemma* on p. XXXI, supports the separate existence of a third version. Whether there were two or three versions does not affect my line of argument. See also Panayotakis 2007, 299–300, with further recent bibliography.

[27] Kortekaas 1984, 132, believes that the original text was in Greek; Schmeling 1988, VI, is of the opinion that it was in Latin, although the mark left on it by the genre of the Greek novel must have been very deep. Finally, it is worth mentioning the possibility that the original version of the novel circulated for some time in the form of an epitome, which brings to mind the cases of other novels or narrative works of fiction mentioned above. This is the opinion of Kortekaas 1984, 132 and 134, although he himself admits that this point is 'highly hypothetical'.

[28] Ruiz Montero 2006, 193–194; Ruiz-Montero, forthcoming, section II.

[29] Panayotakis 2007, 300–301, with bibliography. In the novels of romance and adventure there is, in all probability, originally oral material that has been reworked. As far as the subject dealt with in this paper is concerned, I believe the question should be whether the orality is present only in the original material, which is subsequently given a literary reworking by the author but remains visible in the resulting product, or whether it goes beyond this and is also present in the form of an oral performance, which might imply the existence of alternative versions to the 'official' one. On the presence of orality in the early Greek novel, the fully documented overview offered by Ruiz Montero (forthcoming) should be consulted; for Chariton, see section III of her work, which concludes: 'Nonetheless, a dual transmission, both oral and written, cannot be ruled out' (I am grateful to the author for kindly having allowed me to consult this work).

case, our information permits us to argue that the phenomenon of the multiplicity of versions occurs across the board in ancient Greek narrative fiction.[30]

4 Multiple versions and the type of reading public

Before I go any further, I think it is necessary to stress a point made at the time by Hägg,[31] who argued for the existence of a popular readership for the Greek novel, a point later accepted by Bowie,[32] who had previously defended the opposite option: that is, that the existence of positive proof of a certain type of readership, a learned public (which is what several scholars have stressed), does not imply the non-existence of the opposite type, the unlearned reader. A literary work can indeed entertain at different levels: literary adornments (allusions, intertextuality with classical works, etc.) were directed at an educated public, but suspense, emotional impact, etc., could reach a less well-educated audience, which does not mean that the first type of public could not also be entertained by it.[33] Or to express the argument the other way round, in view of what I have to say below: the existence of modified versions, aimed at a wider and less learned public, does not imply the non-existence of a learned public capable of appreciating elements of greater literary substance.[34]

---

30 In connection with the narrative works of fiction I have mentioned, Fusillo 1994, 239, states: 'La scarsa elaborazione formale, la fluidità della trasmissione testuale, l'apertura strutturale e la libertà stilistica ... fanno comunque pensare ad una letteratura "popolare" dalla circolazione ampia e sotterranea (un po' come accade per la novellistica): assai lontana quindi all'idea di creazione individuale e di testo chiuso che domina nella letteratura "alta"'.
31 Hägg 1994.
32 Bowie 2003.
33 Hägg 1994, 54: 'the narrative suspense, the emotional impact, the escapist function were there for all, the rhetorical and classicizing embellishment for some'. It may be of interest to refer here to the reflections of Umberto Eco 2005, 222. (I am grateful to B. D. MacQueen for the reference) on how a text (particularly a text with an aesthetic aim) tends to construct two model readers: 'to put it bluntly, the first-level model reader wants to know what happens, while the second-level model reader wants to know how what happens has been narrated' (p. 223).
34 In the ambit of the physical artifact, it is of interest to underline that in relation to the novel Cavallo 1986, 146–150, points to the existence at a technical level of both good and bad copies, which would seem to indicate the existence of different types of public.

Let us now see whether we can draw a lesson from the points we have made concerning the problem of the readership of the novel.[35]

It may well be that there is more than one reason for the multiple versions, but it is clear that the involvement of copyists and scholars is fundamental for the creation of new versions.[36] This is undoubtedly the case in the works of narrative fiction to which I have referred above. In the case of the romantic novels, this factor might explain anything from slight, possibly unintentional modifications to the text, as I have suggested happens with the papyri of Chariton, to far-reaching interventions, as with the alternative version that appears in Achilles Tatius, not to mention a version such as that of Chariton in the *codex thebanus*.

It is very difficult to ascertain exactly what the conditions were that impelled the copyists to create alternative versions of a particular text. However, there is one that I believe is certain: multiple versions arise because the modified work does not belong to a prestigious literary tradition, those works we tend to categorize as 'classical'. It is true that this is a very general term and that it does not correspond to any criteria of ancient poetics, but it is real and effective in practice, since the narrative works referred to were 'marginal' in terms of literary precepts. It is well known that the Greek novel, unlike other genres considered 'serious', was never submitted to rhetorical categorization. It is also true that we find no quotations of the novelists in other authors. These were readings for 'entertainment' (*Unterhaltungslektüre*), not for educational purposes, and as such, in the dichotomy between 'classical' and 'non-classical' (in other words 'prestigious' and 'non-prestigious') works, they were categorized in the latter group, as were the other narrative works mentioned above. And as a result certain copyists or compilers felt free to rework these texts in order to 'improve' them or make them more 'attractive', adapting the wording and even the plots to what were assumed to be the preferences of a wide audience, to whom literary refinement was of no interest or too difficult to appreciate.[37]

---

[35] It is well known that for some years there has been a heated debate among specialists on whether the novel was a popular genre or not. I limit myself here to mentioning the main supporters of each stance: in favour of the existence of a 'popular' audience, Perry 1930, Egger 1988, and Hägg 1994; and against, Wesseling 1988, Stephens 1994, and Bowie 1994 and 2003, in the latter case with qualifications. Very recently, Hunter 2008, 270, has emphasized the variety in the Greek novel, which in his view allowed the novelists 'to exploit the expectation of a diverse and complex audience response', which 'in turn might suggest a diverse and complex audience for the novels themselves', an opinion I consider to be compatible with the conclusion I reach in these pages.
[36] For a general view, see Canfora 2002.
[37] Fusillo 1994, 272, has pointed to this in relation to the Alexander novel, but I believe that the assertion can be extended, *mutatis mutandis*, for each individual work, to the romantic novels: 'È un'opera assai lontana dall'idea di testo chiuso, oggetto finito e compiuto una volta per

On this point I consider it necessary to introduce a methodological distinction proposed by Bowie,[38] namely, between 'intended readership' and 'actual readership'. It is the latter type of readership to which I refer in this paper. I do not believe that the existence of multiple versions enables us to know what the intended readership of this or that novel was, unless we can be certain that the author himself has produced more than one version.[39] However, I do think that the existence of such versions suggests that the actual readership went considerably beyond the reading circles, which were not limited to the well-educated reader. Certain copyists or compilers presumably saw that it was desirable to adapt works in novel form in order to aim them at a wider audience, which would necessarily have to be less demanding, if we accept that the 'official' texts we have seem to have been written with a learned readership in mind. And if this is how they saw things, it is because such an audience existed. This is one reason, for instance, why there are epitomes, that is, simplifications of the original work: by means of the elimination of dialogues, descriptions, the odd minor adventure, etc., the reader can enjoy the same plot but in a shorter time. And this is a literary phenomenon that is present in all periods.

Therefore, while the lack of rhetorical categorization and the absence of literary quotes from the novels, which demonstrate the lack of literary prestige of the genre, do not demonstrate absolutely the existence of a popular readership, I believe that the multiple versions do in fact prove the latter, since they are based on the existence of a type of actual readership, that is, they are not conceivable without the existence of readers who were being offered a more attractive, 'improved' text.

To conclude, and in no way claiming to have exhausted or resolved the hotly debated issue of the type of readership at which the ancient novel was aimed, I believe that the phenomenon of the multiplicity of versions deserves to be taken into account as an argument in favour of the theory that the genre of the Greek novel reached a wide audience, and not only an audience made up of people from a culturally sophisticated and literary background.

---

sempre', where there are 'vari rimaneggiamenti e attualizzazioni, probabile effetto di un pubblico crescente e diversificato'. The text, so to speak, thus became an object in the public domain: see n. 9.

38 Bowie 2003, 89.

39 This has been posited for Xenophon, but in that case we would have to accept a double hypothesis: that the text as preserved is an epitome, and that this epitome was the work of the author himself (see n. 6). For possible authorial variants in Longus, see also n. 6.

Bibliography

Bowie, E. 1994. 'The Readership of Greek Novels in the Ancient World', in: J. Tatum (ed.), *The Search for the Ancient Novel*, Baltimore: The Johns Hopkins University Press. 435–459.

Bowie, E. 2003. 'The Ancient Readers of the Greek Novels', in: G. Schmeling (ed.), *The Novel in the Ancient World*, Boston and Leiden: Brill, 87–106 (Original Work Published 1996).

Canfora, L. 2002. *Il copista come autore*, Palermo: Sellerio Editore.

Cavallo, G. 1986. 'Conservazione e perdita dei testi greci: fattori materiali, sociali, culturali', in: A. Giardina (ed.), *Società romana e impero tardoantico, IV. Tradizione dei classici, trasformazione della cultura*, Roma, Bari: Editori Laterza. 83–172 and 246–271.

Conca, F. 2010. 'Il Codex Thebanus e i papiri: suggestioni sul testo di Caritone', in: G. Bastianini, and A. Casanova (eds.), *I papiri del romanzo antico: atti del convegno internazionale di studi, Firenze, 11–12 giugno 2009*, Firenze: Istituto papirologico G. Vitelli. 139–152.

Eco, U. 2005. *On Literature*, London: Secker & Warburg (Italian ed., 2002).

Egger, B. 1988. 'Zu den Frauenrollen im griechischen Roman: Die Frau als Heldin und Leserin', in: H. Hoffmann (ed.), *Groningen Colloquia on the Novel* 1, Groningen: Egbert Forsten. 33–66.

Ferrari, F. 1997. *Romanzo di Esopo. Introduzione e testo critico*, Milano: Biblioteca Universale Rizzoli.

Fusillo, M. 1994. 'Letteratura di consumo e romanzesca', in: G. Cambiano, L. Canfora, D. Lanza (eds.), *Lo spazio letterario della Grecia antica*, I.3 (*La produzione e la circolazione del testo. I Greci e Roma*), Roma: Salerno. 223–273.

Gärtner, H. 1967. 'Xenophon von Ephesos', *RE* IX A 2, 2055–2089.

Garnaud, J.-P. (ed. and trans.) 1995. *Achille Tatius d'Alexandrie. Le roman de Leucippé et Clitophon*, Paris: Les Belles Lettres (Original Work Published 1991).

Grenfell, B.P., and Hunt, A.S. (eds. and trans.) 1914. '1250. Achilles Tatius', in: B. P. Grenfell and A. S. Hunt (eds.), *The Oxyrhynchus Papyri X*, London: The Egypt Exploration Society. 135–142 and pl. VI.

Hägg, T. 1966. 'Die Ephesiaka des Xenophon Ephesios – Original oder epitome?', *C&M* 27, 118–161.

Hägg, T. 1994. 'Orality, Literacy, and the 'Readership' of the Early Greek Novel', in: R. Eriksen (ed.), *Contexts of Pre-Novel Narrative: the European Tradition*, Berlin/New York: de Gruyter. 47–81.

Hunter, R. 2008. 'Ancient readers', in: T. Whitmarsh (ed.), *The Cambridge Companion to the Greek and Roman Novel*, Cambridge: Cambridge University Press. 261–271.

Jouanno, C. 2002. *Naissance et métamorphoses du Roman d'Alexandre. Domaine grec*, Paris: CNRS Éditions.

Karla, G. A. 2001. *Vita Aesopi. Überlieferung, Sprache und Edition einer frühbyzantinischen Fassung des Äsopromans*, Wiesbaden: Reichert.

Kortekaas, G. A. A. (ed.) 1984. *Historia Apollonii regis Tyri*, Groningen: Bouma's Boekhuis.

Laplace, M. 1983. 'Achilleus Tatios, Leucippé et Clitophon: P. Oxyrhynchos 1250', *ZPE* 53, 53–59.

Lucke, C. 1985. 'Zum Charitontext auf Papyrus', *ZPE* 58, 21–33.

Merkelbach, R. 1977. *Die Quellen des griechischen Alexanderromans*, 2. Neubearbeitete Aufl. unter Mitw. von J. Trumpf, München: C. H. Beck. (Original Work Published 1954)

O'Sullivan, J. N. 1995. *Xenophon of Ephesus. His compositional technique and the birth of the novel*, Berlin/New York: de Gruyter.
Panayotakis, S. 2007. 'Fixity and Fluidity in *Apollonius of Tyre*', in: V. Rimmell (ed.), *Seeing Tongues, Hearing Scripts. Orality and Representation in the Ancient Novel*, ANS 7, Groningen: Barkhuis & Groningen University Library. 299–320.
Parsons, P.J. (ed. and trans.) 1989. '3837. Achilles Tatius', in: M. G. Sirivianou (ed.), *The Oxyrhynchus Papyri LVI*, London: The Egypt Exploration Society. 66–69.
Perry, B.E. 1930. 'Chariton and His Romance from a Literary-Historical Point of View', *AJPh* 51, 93–134.
Perry, B.E. 1936. *Studies in the Text History of the Life and Fables of Aesop*, Haverford: American Philological Association; Oxford: Blackwell.
Perry, B.E. 1967. *The Ancient Romances. A Literary-historical Account of Their Origins*, Berkeley/Los Angeles: University of California Press.
Reeve, M.D. 1969. 'Author's variants in Longus?', *PCPhS* 15, 75–85.
Reardon, B.P. 2003. 'Chariton', in: G. Schmeling (ed.), *The Novel in the Ancient World*, Leiden, 309–335. (Original Work Published 1996)
Ruiz Montero, C. 1982. 'Una interpretación del "estilo καί" de Jenofonte de Éfeso', *Emerita* 50, 305–323.
Ruiz-Montero, C. 1994. 'Xenophon von Ephesos: Ein Überblick', *ANRW* II 34.2, Berlin/New York: de Gruyter, 1088–1138.
Ruiz Montero, C. 2006. *La novela griega*, Madrid: Editorial Síntesis.
Ruiz-Montero, C. 'Between Rhetoric and Orality: Aspects of the Spread of the Earliest Greek Novels', in: J. R. Morgan (ed.), *A Tribute to B. P. Reardon* (forthcoming).
Sanz Morales, M. 2002. 'Textkritische Bemerkungen zum Chariton-Text auf Papyrus', *ZPE* 141, 111–115.
Sanz Morales, M. 2006. 'Multiple Versions in the Greek Novel', *Variants* 5, 129–146.
Sanz Morales, M. 2009. 'Testimonio de los papiros y tradición medieval: ¿una versión diferente de la novela de Caritón?', in: M. Sanz Morales, M. Librán Moreno (eds.), *Verae lectiones. Estudios de crítica textual y edición de textos griegos*, Huelva, Cáceres: Universidad de Huelva; Universidad de Extremadura. 203–226.
Schmeling, G. (ed.) 1988. *Historia Apollonii Regis Tyri*, Leipzig: Teubner.
Stephens, S. A. 1994. 'Who Read Ancient Novels?', in: J. Tatum (ed.), *The Search for the Ancient Novel*, Baltimore: The Johns Hopkins University Press. 405–418.
Swain, S. 1998. *Hellenism and Empire. Language, Classicism and Power in the Greek World A.D. 50–250*, Oxford: Clarendon Press.
Vilborg, E. (ed.) 1955. *Achilles Tatius, Leucippe and Clitophon*, Studia Graeca et Latina Gothoburgensia, 1., Stockholm: Almqvist & Wiksell.
Wesseling, B. 1988. 'The Audience of the Ancient Novels', in: H. Hofmann (ed.), *Groningen Colloquia on the Novel*, vol. I, Groningen: Egbert Forsten. 67–79.
Wilcken, U. 1901. 'Eine neue Romanhandschrift', *APF* 1, 227–272.
Young, D.C.C. 1968. 'Author's variants in the manuscript tradition of Longus', *PCPhS* 14, 65–74.
Zimmermann, F. 1923. 'De Charitonis Codice Thebano', *Philologus* 78, 330–381.
Zimmermann, F. 1928. 'Zur Überlieferung des Chariton-Romanes', *Hermes* 63, 193–224.

Marina F. A. Martelli
Clues from the Papyri: Structure and Style of Chariton's Novel

Abstract: Through a collation of codex **F** with papyrus fragments, I advance a suggestion about Chariton's style (use of compound verbs, syntax, introduction of direct speeches). The papyrus fragments are valuable to the *constitutio textus*, sometimes supplying what is evidently a better reading. Then, I consider the time and manner of textual transmission. The text of **F** diverges considerably from the lost fragment of a palimpsest parchment codex, Thebanus, preserved in a partial transcription by Wilcken. Thebanus is also evidence for the circulation of books in late antiquity: the text of Chariton could have been adapted for a less cultivated public.

The text of Chariton's *Callirhoe* survives in only one late thirteenth-century manuscript,[1] known as **F**, and in four short papyrus fragments.[2] However, the first direct textual evidence – first according to the chronology of discovery – was the codex Thebanus, deperditus (MP^3 244). Its history is as colorful as the ancient novel's adventures: six leaves were bought in November 1898 by Ulrich Wilcken at Luxor, and were destroyed shortly after, in spring 1899, when the ship burned in a Hamburg dock. The codex was a palimpsest of parchment written in Greek and Coptish, dated from the late Byzantine period (6th/7th century). Under the Coptic text, the concluding parts of *Callirhoe* (Char. 8,5,9–8,6,1 and 8,6,8–8,7,3) were detected, and, in two sheets, the beginning of the Chion Novel.[3] Each sheet, 20 x 15 cm, had two columns, written in small letters inclined to the right, perhaps ogival capitals, as in a fragment[4] of Heliodorus, P.Amh. 160. The flesh-sides, more legible, were deciphered by Wilcken in person during the

---

1 F = Florentinus Laurentianus Conventi Soppressi 627, ca. 1270–1280.
2 Π^1 = P.Fay. 1 = MP^3 243, discovered at 1900, dated at 2nd.–3th. century: Char. 4,2,3–4,3,2; Π^2 = P.Oxy. 1019 = MP^3 241, discovered at 1910, dated at late 2nd. or beginning 3th. century: Char. 2,3,5–7; 2,3,10–2,4,2 and Π^{2bis} = P.Oxy. 2948 = MP^3 241, discovered at 1972: Char. 2,4,5–9; 2,4,10–2,5,1; Π^3 = P.Mich. 1 = MP^3 242, discovered at 1955, dated at second half of 2nd. century: Char. 2,11,4; 2,11,5–6.
3 Cf. P.Berol. inv. 10535 and P.Berol. inv. 21234.
4 Gronewald 1979, 19–21.

Marina F. A. Martelli, Università degli Studi di Milano

journey, with the Hirschig[5] edition to hand. Thus only Wilcken's partial transcription remains of Thebanus. Yet a textual discussion can be based even on this much: not to think *perditum quod periit* should be specific to philologists.[6]

On the other hand, the other papyrological discoveries are still available to us, and give some clues to the language and style of Chariton, rather different from the language attested by **F**, the unreliable *codex unicus*. A comprehensive analytical study will serve to reveal these clues. As shown in recent studies by Christina Lucke[7] and Manuel Sanz Morales,[8] a sense of Chariton's can be garnered by collating the text of the codex with the papyrus fragments. There are opportunities here to correct some places where **F** clearly presents a bad text (which critics had noticed even before the papyrus discoveries): they sometimes supply what is evidently a better reading. And they promise a sounder text, more vivid than the vulgate.

First, which is the best source of Chariton's text, **F** or the papyri? That varies, of course, from case to case. The value of **F** is rightly debated. As everybody admits, **F** was rather negligently produced, and the papyrus fragments, which cover just under six percent of the novel, have come to be very valuable for the *constitutio textus*. **F** is full of errors, an average of 25 per sheet, both trivial and serious: in other words, as Bryan Reardon estimates,[9] there is a mistake every two lines. Nunzio Bianchi, who studied the history of the codex,[10] remarks that the scribal interventions seem to be intentional choices rather than oversights. However, the contribution from the papyri is quantitatively slight: about 140 lines from papyri and 80 lines from the codex Thebanus, out of more than 4000 lines of text. It should always be asked whether or not the papyri preserve the original reading, while whatever is nearer to the author in date is not necessarily more faithful. On the one hand, there are the mistakes of **F**; on the other side, there are those of the papyri. Should editors then contaminate two traditions with their choices? The ratio between correct readings and presumed errors is different every time. Caution is required: as Renata Roncali[11] points out, the codex could represent a less corrupted branch of the manuscript tradition. In other terms, *recen-*

---

5 Hirschig 1853.
6 La Penna 1957, 3.
7 Lucke 1985, 21–33.
8 Sanz Morales 2002, 111–15; 2006b, 51–56; 2007, 95–104.
9 Reardon 1982, 157–173.
10 Florentinus was collated in 1725 by Antonio Salvini and again in 1727–28 by Antonio Cocchi. In 1843 Cobet used chemicals which have now impaired legibility.
11 Roncali 1999, 38.

tiores non deteriores. The variants are more or less significant: transpositions, omissions or additions, writing errors, verbal tenses, synonyms.

We shall follow the studies of Lucke and Sanz Morales on the papyri and linger over the codex Thebanus, which diverges so much from **F** that it is seen as less useful for the *constitutio textus*. The value of Theb. is in general questioned. Goold writes: "All agree, however, that while Theb. corrects **F** on several occasions and gives the correct spelling of Καλλιρόη and Συρακόσιοι (-ρρ- and -ρρακουσ- **F** throughout), it purveys a capricious text much inferior to **F**'s".[12] And Reardon, too: "It offers a 'rogue' text, clearly less good than that of **F** and the papyri".[13] Furthermore it has been supposed that all these mistakes could reflect an open text, which has changed during the process of transmission.

Though rogue, Theb. offers many good readings, and provides there are other linguistic and stylistic elements that can be used to reconstruct Chariton's text. Here I propose a comparison between Theb. and **F**, and distribute the different readings on the basis of a typology of errors: inversions and transpositions, omissions, writing variants, verbs and preverbs, moods, tenses, persons, alternative lexical options, and syntax.

In first position we have the reading of Theb. (using Reardon's line numbers), and in second position, **F**. The choice is in certain cases apparently *adiaphoron*: [οὐ]δὲ[ν ἠπί]σ[τατο (Theb.) and ἠπίστατο οὐδέν (**F**) are equivalent, but many other examples support[14] Theb. as the better reading. Editors are divided: Molinié and Reardon tend to follow Theb., while Blake, Goold, Borgogno, Meckelnborg-Schäfer follow **F**.

In the list of variant readings that follows, unless otherwise indicated, the editors have preferred **F**.

1) Inversions and transpositions

Theb. col. 1,4–5 = r. 343 [οὐ]δὲ[ν ἠπί]σ[τατο (Molinié, Reardon): **F** ἠπίστατο οὐδέν (Blake, Goold, Borgogno, Meckelnborg-Schäfer).

Theb. col. 1,17–20 = rr. 347–348 Διονύσιος ἐπεδείξατο παιδίαν τε καὶ φρόνησιν ἐξαίρετον: **F** φρόνησιν Διονύσιος ἐπεδείξατο καὶ παιδείαν ἐξαίρετον.[15]

---

[12] Goold 1995, 18.

[13] Reardon 1996, 315.

[14] Zimmermann 1922, 333–334: 'Utrum verborum collocatio sit genuina, non facile diiudicatur propterea quod utriusque collocationis numeri apte cadunt'; about rhythmical sentence endings cf. Heibges 1911, 51–52.

[15] However Zimmermann 1922, 337: 'Clausula φρόνησιν ἐξαίρετον melior est quam Florentini παιδείαν ἐξαίρετον'.

Theb. coll. 1,28–2,1 = rr. 350–351 ἀπάγει Καλλιρόη(ν) εἰς Συρακούσας (Reardon): **F** Καλλιρρόην εἰς Συρρακούσας ἀπάγει (Blake, Goold, Borgogno, Meckelnborg-Schäfer).

Theb. col. 2,8–9 = r. 353 ἀπέ]δωκα ἄ[ν σοι: **F** ἂν ἀπέδωκά <σοι>.

Theb. col. 2,25–27 = r. 359 ἡ]συχῇ τὴν ἐπ[ιστο]λὴν ἐπιδ[ίδωσιν]: **F** τὴν ἐπιστολὴν ἡσυχῇ δίδωσιν. According to Wilamowitz,[16] ἐπιστολὴν ἐπιδιδόναι is a technical expression, but the simple verb is also used, and the closure of **F** seems better (see point 4 below).

Theb. col. 3,12–13 = r. 365 κατεφίλησε τοὔνομα: **F** τοὔνομα κατεφίλησεν.

Theb. col. 3,18–19 = rr. 366–367 ἐμὸς εὐεργέτης: **F** εὐεργέτης ἐμός.

Theb. col. 5,7–8 = rr. 417–418 'ζῇς, τέκνον' εἶπε 'καί…' (Reardon): **F** εἶπε 'ζῇς, τέκνον, ἦ καί…' (Blake, Goold, Borgogno, Meckelnborg-Schäfer). In Theb. εἶπε is put in the direct speech, interposed, as often in Chariton.

Theb. col. 5,12–13 = r. 419 με<τ>ὰ <χ>α[ρᾶς] ἐξεχεῖτο: **F** ἐχεῖτο μετὰ χαρᾶς. Editors adopt here the simple verb and follow **F**. Chariton seems to prefer compound verbs with prefixes,[17] but perhaps the usual expression prevails as in this case, as before: Theb. col. 2,25–27 = r. 359 ἡ]συχῇ τὴν ἐπ[ιστο]λὴν ἐπιδ[ίδωσιν]: **F** τὴν ἐπιστολὴν ἡσυχῇ δίδωσιν.

Theb. col. 5,20–23 = rr. 422–423 δύνασθαι σχολάζειν πλὴν μόνῳ τῷ Καλλιρόης συνεῖναι κάλλει (Molinié): **F** σχολάζειν δύνασθαι πλὴν Καλλιρρόῃ μόνῃ (Blake, Goold, Borgogno, Reardon, Meckelnborg-Schäfer).

Theb. col. 8,6–7 = r. 446 καὶ πάντες καὶ πᾶσαι: **F** πᾶσαι καὶ πάντες.[18]

2.1) Omissions of F

Theb. col. 1,7–8 = r. 344 ἐδόκει καὶ Καλλιρόην (Blake, Molinié, Borgogno, Meckelnborg-Schäfer): **F** ἐδόκει Καλλιρρόην (Goold, Reardon). Also in Theb. col. 2,8 = r. 353 καὶ Κ[αλλιρόην (Blake, Molinié, Borgogno): **F** Καλλιρρόην (Goold, Reardon, Meckelnborg-Schäfer). Instead, in Theb. col. 3,9–10 = rr. 362–363 ἐπὶ πολὺ(ν) δὲ χρόνον: **F** καὶ ἐπὶ πολὺν χρόνον, the conjunction καί is in **F**, not δέ.

Theb. col. 1,14 = r. 346 ἐξ ἀρχῆς. Blake, Molinié, Borgogno, and Reardon accept the temporal expression. It is absent in Goold and Meckelnborg-Schäfer.

---

[16] Wilamowitz 1901, 250.
[17] Cf. Papanikolaou 1973, 49–60. Other examples come from the papyri: in Π¹ col. 2,12–13 = Char. 3,2,10 (r. 98) the papyrus' reading σ[υ]ν [απαγό]μενος is better than οὖν ἀπαγόμενος of **F**, perhaps due to aplography for the exchange between οὖν and συν – in capital writing.
[18] **F** avoids the hiatus, cf. Reeve 1971, 514–539.

Theb. col. 1,17 = r. 347 μάλιστα. All editors accept Theb. In Char. 2,4,1 (r. 155) **F** offers an analogous omission: μᾶλλον, which is read in Π² col. 2,50.

Theb. col. 1,21 = r. 348 εἴ. The editors are all in agreement with Theb.

Theb. col. 1,24 = r. 349 ταραχθῇ οὕτως: **F** ταραχθείη. Goold prints ταραχθείη, οὕτως, contaminating the two readings; Reardon writes ταραχθείη, οὕτω (iam coniecit Hercher).

Theb. col. 4,22 = r. 376 πολλῶν πόλεων: **F** πόλεων Theb. has the correct reading; **F** has a mistake due to homeoacrus.

Theb. col. 5,1–2 = r. 416 φιλαργ[υρ........ ca. 8 letters
περημ[......... ca. 9 letters

Theb. col. 5,9 = r. 418 εἶπεν is interposed, as often in Chariton.

Theb. col. 5,10 = r. 419 σε ζῶντα (Blake, Molinié, Borgogno, Reardon): **F** σε (Meckelnborg-Schäfer, following Zimmermann).[19]

Theb. col. 6,13–14 = r. 429 μεταξὺ φερόμενο[ς]. All editors accept Theb.

Theb. col. 7,16–18 = r. 440 καὶ [ε]ὐνούχους καὶ παλ[λ]ακίδας. The reading of Theb. is in general discarded.

2.2) Omissions of Theb.

Theb. col. 2,10–11 = r. 354 εὔνοι]αν καὶ πίστιν: **F** εὔνοιαν εἰς ἐμὲ καὶ πίστιν.

Theb. col. 2,20–21 = r. 357 ὁμολογήσας [ἔσπευδεν: **F** ὁμολογήσας ἔχειν ἔσπευδεν. Theb. is better, without redundance. Hercher already deleted ἔχειν.

Theb. col. 3,27 = r. 369 αὐτὸν.

Theb. col. 4,19 = r. 375 εἰς Ἰωνίαν, μέγα.

Theb. col. 5,3 = r. 416 Ἑρμοκράτης: **F** Ἑρμοκράτης δέ. The omission of δέ occurs again in Theb. col. 8,5 = rr. 445–446 εἰ[σ]ελθόντος: **F** εἰσελθόντος δέ. Vice versa, Theb. col. 7,13 = r. 439 ἐπιδεῖξαι δέ: **F** ἐπέδειξε.

Theb. col. 5,10 = rr. 418–419 ἀληθῶς: **F** νῦν ἀληθῶς.

Theb. col. 5,17–18 = r. 421 τὸν στόλον: **F** τὸν ἄλλον στόλον.

Theb. col. 6,12–13 = rr. 428–429 καὶ εὐχα[ὶ πρὸς] ἀλλήλους: **F** καὶ συνευχαὶ πυκναὶ παρ' ἀμφοτέρων πρὸς ἀλλήλους.

Theb. col. 8,2 = r. 444 ἐπὶ δέ: **F** λόγου δὲ θᾶττον.

Theb. col. 8,27 = r. 454 ὡς: **F** ὡς ἄν.

---

[19] Zimmermann 1922, 354: 'supervacaneum'.

2.3) Omissions of articles

Theb. col. 2,16–18 = r. 356 εἰ[ς] τὸν οἶκον τοῦ βασιλέως (Blake, Borgogno, Reardon, Meckelnborg-Schäfer): **F** εἰς οἶκον βασιλέως (Goold). Zimmermann was in agreement with the omission of the article.[20]

Vice versa, Theb. col. 2,19 = r. 356 προσεκύνησε Διονύσιος: **F** προσεκύνησε ὁ Διονύσιος. Editors prefer **F**.

At Char. 2,3,10 (r. 145) Reardon accepts the reading of Π² συνῆκεν ὁ Λεωνᾶς, while Blake chose **F**: συνῆκε Λεωνᾶς: the papyrus reading is better. Indeed, we can deduce a tendency, if not an actual rule: in Chariton proper nouns, when preceded by a verbal construction, usually have the article.

3) Writing variants

Theb. presents many itacism errors, but it maintains the correct reading twice:

Theb. col. 4,15–16 = r. 374 καινὴ ζηλοτυπεία: **F** κενὴ ζηλοτυπία manus prima and Molinié. Other editors follow Theb. and the manus secunda of **F**.

Theb. col. 6,16 = r. 430 λιποψυχῶν: **F** λειποψυχῶν. Reardon follows Theb., as Cobet had already done.

4) Verbs and prefixes

Theb. col. 1,12–13 = r. 342 ἦλθεν: **F** εἰσῆλθε.

Theb. col. 2,27 = r. 359 ἐπιδίδωσιν (Blake, Borgogno): **F** δίδωσιν (Zimmermann, Goold, Reardon, Meckelnborg-Schäfer).

Theb. col. 4,18–19 = rr. 374–375 παρεσκευάζετο (Reardon): **F** συνεσκευάζετο.

Theb. col. 5,12–13 = r. 419 ἐξεχεῖτο: **F** ἐχεῖτο.

5) Moods, tenses, persons

Theb. col. 1,24 = r. 349 ταραχθῇ (Goold, Reardon): **F** ταραχθείη. Zimmermann prefers the subjunctive because the optative is rare in Chariton.[21] Cobet[22] proposed ταραχθείς.

Theb. col. 2,18 = r. 356 ἀναγραφῆναι (Blake, Borgogno, Reardon): **F** ἀναγραφήσῃ (Goold, Meckelnborg-Schäfer).

---

[20] Zimmermann 1922, 342: 'Apud Charitonem saepius et nomen, a quo genetivus pendet, et genetivum ipsum articulo carere'.
[21] 55 times, oblique optative 3 times.
[22] Cobet 1859, 302.

Theb. col. 3,10 = r. 363 κατέχω(ν): **F** κατεῖχεν.
Theb. col. 3,21 = r. 367 Ἡσ ετο: **F** Ἥσθη. Zimmermann[23] suggested ᾖσθετο, Wilcken ᾖσχετο.
Theb. col. 3,27 = r. 369 κα]τέλιπεν: **F** καταλίποι.
Theb. col. 7,3 = r. 436 φησίν: **F** ἔφη.
Theb. col. 7,13 = r. 439 ἐπιδεῖξαι δέ: **F** ἐπέδειξε.
Theb. col. 8,1–2 = 444 βλέπειν καὶ ἀκούειν (Borgogno, Reardon, Meckelnborg-Schäfer): **F** ἰδεῖν καὶ ἀκοῦσαι (Zimmermann).
Theb. col. 8,11 = r. 448 εἰσαγαγὼν τήν (Blake, Borgogno, Reardon): **F** εἰσάγων καὶ τήν (Meckelnborg-Schäfer).
Theb. col. 8,19–20 = 451 ἐσχίζετο: **F** ἐσχίζοντο. Reardon chooses the reading of **F**, as an Atticism.[24] A singular collective subject in classical prose has a plural verb; in Chariton such subjects have singular verbs 22 times, the exceptional occurring at 1,1,15 (r. 71, τὸ πλῆθος...ἀνέλιπον) and 5,4,2 (r. 177–178). In 1,1,15 the scribe, under the influence of the preceding plural ἐκόσμησαν, could have made a small error.[25] Shortly after, at Char. 1,1,16, we read τὸ πλῆθος κατέλαβεν.

6) Alternative lexical variants

Theb. col. 1,15 = r. 346 ἅπαντα (Blake, Molinié, Borgogno, Reardon): **F** πάντα (Goold, Meckelnborg-Schäfer). Zimmermann[26] says this about the genesis of this mistake: 'Etiam ampliorem formam ἅπαντα breviori πάντα praeferam, quod illa multo facilius in breviorem potuit abire quam haec in ampliorem'.
Theb. col. 1,16 = r. 347 δή: **F** δέ. Editors prefer Theb. The interplay of δέ, the reading of **F** followed by Reardon, and δή, written by Borgogno,[27] occurs at Char. 1,6,4 (r. 271).
Theb. col. 3,6 = r. 361 καί: **F** εἶτα. Editors prefer **F**. Likewise, Theb. col. 7,9 = r. 438 καί: **F** εἶτα.

---

[23] Zimmermann 1922, 354.
[24] The language is an educated κοινή, showing no trace of the Atticist movement, according to Papanikolaou 1973. But Hernández Lara 1994 demonstrated that 300 of 500 analysed words are apparently genuine Atticisms (out of 3000 words of vocabulary). On the base of Ruiz Montero 1991, two-thirds of them occur in the New Testament and papyri.
[25] Sanz Morales 2007, 96.
[26] Zimmermann 1922, 337.
[27] Borgogno 2005, 116–117 n. 41.

Theb. col. 3,25 = r. 368 [κα?]τὰ τὰ ῥήματα: **F** ταῦτα τὰ ῥήματα. Blake, Borgogno, Reardon agree with **F**, whereas τὰ αὐτά is the correct reading according to Molinié and Goold.

Theb. col. 3,26 = r. 369 ὅτι: **F** ὡς

Theb. col. 5,19 = r. 422 μή: **F** μηκέτι.

Theb. col. 5,23 = r. 423 οὖν (Reardon): **F** δέ.

Theb. col. 6,7 = r. 427 ἐπὶ γῆς: **F** ἀπὸ γῆς.

Theb. col. 6,17–18 = r. 431 ἐπεκυλίοντο (Reardon): **F** ἐπεκλύοντο. Theb. is preferred by Reardon (as by D'Orville before him); the reading of **F** was corrected by Reiske and Hercher to ἐπεκελεύοντο.

Theb. col. 7,7 = 437 ἄργυρόν τε καί: **F** ἀργύριον καί. Editors are in agreement with Theb. The codex confirms Hercher's conjecture.

Theb. col. 7,27 = r. 443 Ἀπίωμεν: **F** ἀξιοῦμεν. Theb. is followed by Reardon, while Meckelnborg-Schäfer, Blake and Borgogno follow Cobet's conjecture ἐξίωμεν.

Theb. col. 8,14 = r. 449 = **F** ἀποβλέψας. ἀναβλέψας is Hercher's emendation, but Meckelnborg-Schäfer follows Theb.

Theb. col. 8,23 = r. 452 ποτὲ δ' αὖ: **F** ὁτέ. The reading of Theb., like the conjecture of Reiske, is followed by Reardon.

Theb. col. 8,26 = r. 453 ἥδιστον: **F** ἥδιον.

6.1) Other lexical variants

Theb. col. 2,13 = r. 355 ἀδυνάτου: **F** ἀμηχάνου. Editors prefer **F**. Zimmermann[28] explained: 'ἀδυνάτου vitium est natum ex antecedente ἐδυνάμην'.

Theb. col. 3,7–8 = r. 362 προσεπτύξατο (Blake, Molinié, Goold, Borgogno, Reardon): **F** προσετίθει (Zimmermann, Meckelnborg-Schäfer).

Theb. col. 3,25–26 = r. 369 Ἐ[πίσ?]θη: **F** ὑπεδήλου.

Theb. col. 4,25 = r. 377 εἰκόνας: **F** οἰκήσεις. Editors prefer Theb.

Theb. col. 7,12 = r. 439 πλούτου: **F** ὕλης τέχνης τε.

7) Cases and government

Theb. col. 1,26 = r. 350 λόγους: **F** λόγων.

Theb. col. 3,20 = 367 σου: **F** σοι.

Theb. col. 3,22–23 = r. 368 πρὸς τὴν ἀπολογίαν: **F** τῇ ἀπολογίᾳ.

---

[28] Zimmermann 1922, 340.

8) Construction

Theb. col. 2,15–18 = rr. 355–356 πρῶτον εὐεργέτην εἰ[ς] τὸν οἶκον τοῦ βασιλέως ἀναγραφῆναι (Wilcken, Reardon): **F** πρῶτος εὐεργέτης εἰς οἶκον βασιλέως ἀναγραφήσῃ (Molinié, Goold, Borgogno, Meckelnborg-Schäfer). Zimmermann regards the construction of Theb. to be 'artificiosiorem' and prefers the parataxis of **F**.

There is a greater discrepancy between the texts of Theb. and **F** in the following passages:

Theb. coll. 3,9–4,2 = rr. 362–370 (8.5.13–14)

ἐπὶ πολὺ(ν) δὲ χρόνον κατέχω(ν) αὐτὰ ἀναγεινώσκι· 'Καλλιρόη' – κατεφίλησε τοὔνομα – 'Διονυσίῳ εὐεργέτῃ' – 'οἴ⟨μ⟩μοι τῷ ἀνδρί οὐκ ἔχω' – 'χαίρειν' – 'πῶς δύναμε σοῦ διεζευγμένος;' – 'Σὺ γὰρ ἐμὸς εὐεργέτης' – 'τί γὰρ ἄξιον ἐποίησά σου;' Ησ ετο δὲ τῆς ἐπιστολῆς πρὸς τὴν ἀπολογίαν καὶ πολ[λά]κις ἀνεγίνωσκε [κα?]τὰ τὰ ῥήματα. Ἐ[πίσ?]θη γὰρ ὅτι ἄκου[σα κα]τέλιπεν. Οὕτω [δὴ?] φύσει κο]ῦφόν ἐσ[τι]ν ὁ ἔρως καὶ ἀναπί[θι] ῥα[δ]ίως ἀντερᾶσθαι.

F
καὶ ἐπὶ πολὺν χρόνον κατεῖχεν, ἀναγινώσκειν μὴ δυνάμενος διὰ τὰ δάκρυα. ἀποκλαύσας δὲ μόλις ἀναγινώσκειν ἤρξατο, καὶ πρῶτόν γε Καλλιρρόης τοὔνομα κατεφίλησεν. ἐπεὶ δὲ ἦλθεν εἰς τὸ Διονυσίῳ εὐεργέτῃ 'οἴμοι' φησὶν ⟨οὐκέτ'⟩ ἀνδρί. Σὺ γὰρ εὐεργέτης ἐμός. Τί γὰρ ἄξιον ἐποίησά σοι;'. Ἥσθη δὲ τῆς ἐπιστολῆς τῇ ἀπολογίᾳ καὶ πολλάκις ἀνεγίνωσκε τὰ αὐτά· ὑπεδήλου γὰρ ὡς ἄκουσα αὐτὸν κατάλιποι. Οὕτω κοῦφόν ἐστιν ὁ ἔρως καὶ ἀναπείθει ῥᾳδίως ἀντερᾶσθαι.

In Theb. the participle κατέχω(ν) gets around the asyndeton; also a *saut du même au même* increases the distance. In particular, I would stress the efficacy of direct speech in Theb.: it fits in a story with abundant scope for pathetic representation, with rapid narrative passing to dramatic presentation. The direct speech promotes an emotional climax: there are two levels, that of the letter and that of the verbal commentary. Dionysius weeps while reading the letter: in Theb. this emotion is absent for the *saut du même au même*. On the contrary, Theb. maintains all the *inscriptio* of the letter, spaced out by exclamations: there is room for connotation. According to Zimmermann, the differences are due to the scribe and not to a double recension, with interpolations and the results of a 'genus dicendi transformatum'.

Theb. col. 4,3–10 = rr. 370–372

[Θε]ασάμενον δὲ τὸ [π]αιδίον τὸν πατέρα ασοντα (?) προσῆλθεν αὐτῷ καὶ 'ποῦ μοι πάτερ' εἶπεν 'ἡ μήτηρ; Ἀπίωμεν πρὸς αὐτή(ν). Σὺ μὲν ἀπέλευσαι, τέκνον, εὐτυχῶς'.

F
Θεασάμενος δὲ τὸ παιδίον καὶ πήλας ταῖς χερσὶν, 'ἀπελεύσῃ ποτέ μοι καὶ σύ, τέκνον, πρὸς τὴν μητέρα'.

Theb. col. 6,8–13 = rr. 427–429:

τῶν] δὲ ἀπὸ τ[ῆς γῆς τοὺς] ἐν ταῖς τρι[ήρεσιν εὐφημίαι [τε καὶ ἔπαι]νο[ι] καὶ εὐχα[ὶ πρὸς] ἀλλήλους:
F
καὶ πάλιν ἐκείνων τοὺς ἐκ θαλάσσης, εὐφημίαι τε καὶ ἔπαινοι καὶ συνευχαὶ πυκναὶ παρ' ἀμφοτέρων πρὸς ἀλλήλους.

Theb. col. 6,23–27 = rr. 433–435

ἔδο]ξεν δὲ ὡς [ἀ]<λη>[θῶς ἔτι] καλλείων [........] νηντην (?) [ἀναδυο]μένην [ἐκ τῆς θαλάσ]σης
F
ἔδοξε δὲ ἔτι καὶ (καλλίων Reiske) αὐταῖς Καλλιρρόην (<καλλίω> Borgogno) γεγονέναι, ὥστε ἀληθῶς εἶπες ἂν αὐτὴν ὁρᾶν τὴν Ἀφροδίτην ἀναδυομένην ἐκ τῆς θαλάσσης.

The exact differences were presented earlier.

Now, if we take into account all the data mentioned here, the *modus scribendi* of Chariton can be better illustrated: the use of compound verbs, the syntax, the introduction of direct speeches and narrative forms. In some passages the text of **F** seems to water down a more concise expression, to epexegesis, in a plain register. Theb. and the papyri show a more exuberant style.

The codex Thebanus does not always deviate from Chariton's habit. Of course, not too much can be expected from a text copied on a felucca which crosses the Nile, but neither can it be undervalued. Finally, a consideration of the tradition could be added, as Sanz Morales has already shown.[29] Indeed, the discrepancies suggest two different redactions.

The no-longer-existent codex Thebanu, is also of interest as evidence for the circulation of books in the Imperial period. As Wilamowitz supposed, the text of Chariton was adapted for a less cultivated public: the codex, neglected by grammarians, would little by little could have become corrupt.[30] This could be evidence for a mixed usage of the ancient novel, with a range of book typology.[31] At the same time, the presence of the papyri, excellently written in a rather decorative literary hand, such as P.Mich. 1, in a regular and careful hand, such as P.Fay. 1, or quickly written in a semicursive hand, such as P.Oxy. 1019 and 2948, is fresh evidence for the early popularity of Chariton's romance. For example, P.Fayumensis shows a fragment of Chariton from an edition of small size and minute writing. In two pages of Hercher's Teubner edition, 72–73, Wilamo-

---

29 Sanz Morales 2006a, 129–146, and 2015.
30 Wilamowitz 1901, 34: 'Verwilderung ungeschützter Texte'.
31 Cavallo 1996, 13–46.

witz pointed out at least 13 readings that are no doubt better[32] than F. As Cavallo has suggested, the time of the papyri, 2nd-3rd centuries CE, can be assumed to be the period of diffusion for the reading of novels, and perhaps this period corresponds – or should correspond – to a moment of wider literacy. The romance of Chariton was also read in the villages of Fayum, as the papyri confirm. Two papyri from the second century, one from the third, and a parchment from the 6th/7th prove a demand for copyists over some hundreds of years. All this suggests that *Callirhoe*, with the artificial promotion that would come from being prescribed in an academic curriculum, must have enjoyed remarkable success.

The novel's structure offers recapitulatory complexes at the beginnings of the 5th and 8th books. In addition, numerous separate backward references occur in the narrative frame, such as those from the end of the first book. Reitzenstein[33] noticed that the recapitulations are placed immediately before two culminations of the action. A summary, such as the one at the beginning of the fifth book, could be an editorial proof, a clue to a division in two rolls.[34] From a codicological point of view, the chances that book five would begin on a new roll must be high. The summary of the plot calls back a story in many episodes: is it an illusionistic recall[35] to a public of readers, or of listeners, to public lectures in the theater, or rather is it a mimesis of orality? The recapitulations distributed throughout the narrative are indeed a feature of the storyteller.

And the next questions would be these: what kind of entertainment is this, what was the reception, and at last who were the owners of such books. Chariton could be pop, according to the reputation of the novels, thought of as sentimental and cheap by the literary establishment. The opinions on the readership vary widely. Perry[36] thought of a circle of uncultivated or frivolous readers, West[37] assumed that they were women. Almost everything has been suggested: teenagers, housewives, ingenuous, middle class people, etc. The study by Susan Stephens[38] investigated a causal link between wealth and education, and confirmed again the small size of the ancient population of readers: 'No evidence currently avail-

---

32 Wilamowitz 1901, 32.
33 Reitzenstein 1906, 95.
34 The sequence 2,1–3,2 occurs in the papyri in a different place than in the Byzantine tradition.
35 Cf. Fusillo 1996, 49–67.
36 Perry 1967, 100.
37 West 1973, 17. Already Rohde 1914, 67 pointed out a feminine taste. The role of women is excessively stressed by Egger 1999, 108–136. Contra, Wesseling 1988; Ruiz Montero 1989, 107–150 and 67–79; Bowie 1994, 435–459.
38 Stephens 1994, 405–418.

able allows us to construct another set of readers for ancient novels. The need to create a different audience for stories we perceive as romantic or fanciful may simply reflect our own cultural prejudices'. The novel would be entertainment for an educated élite, and not only for people to whom games and spectacles are offered in the morning, and in the afternoon, Chariton, as stated by Persius at 1,134: *his mane edictum, post prandia Callirhoen do* (to these people I offer in the morning the programme of public entertainment, and in the afternoon Callirhoe).[39]

Bibliography

Bianchi, N. 2001. 'Il codice Laur. Conv. Soppr. 627 (F): problemi e ipotesi di localizzazione', *AFLB* 44, 161–181.

Blake, W. E. (ed.) 1938. *Charitonis Aphrodisiensis de Chaerea et Callirhoe amatoriarum narrationum libri octo*, Oxford: Clarendon Press.

Borgogno, A. 2004. 'Per il testo di Caritone di Afrodisia', *Prometheus* 30, 246–252.

Borgogno, A. (ed. and trans.) 2005. *Romanzi greci. Caritone d'Afrodisia, Senofonte Efesio, Longo Sofista*, Torino: Utet.

Bowie, E. 1994. 'The Readership of Greek Novels in the Ancient World', in: J. Tatum (ed.), *The Search for the Ancient Novel*, Baltimore/London: Johns Hopkins University Press. 435–459.

Bowie, E. 1996. 'The ancient readers of the Greek Novels', in: G. Schmeling (ed.), *The Novel in the Ancient World*, Leiden: Brill. 87–106.

Cavallo, G. 1996. 'Veicoli materiali della letteratura di consumo. Maniere di scrivere e maniere di leggere', in: O. Pecere, A. Stramaglia (eds.), *La letteratura di consumo nel mondo greco-latino. Atti del Convegno internazionale Cassino, 14–17 settembre 1994*, Cassino: Università degli Studi di Cassino. 13–46.

Conca, F., De Carli, E., Zanetto, G., Beta, S. 1983–1997. *Lessico dei romanzieri greci* I-IV, Milano/Hildesheim/Zürich/New York: Olms-Weidmann.

Crawford, D.S. (ed.) 1955. *Papyri Michaelidae*, Aberdeen: Aberdeen University Press.

Egger, B. 1999. 'The Role of Women in the Greek Novel: Woman as Heroine and Reader', in: S. Swain (ed.), *Oxford readings in the Greek Novel*, Oxford: Oxford University Press. 108–136.

Fusillo, M. 1996. 'Il romanzo antico come paraletteratura? Il *topos* del racconto di ricapitolazione', in: O. Pecere, A. Stramaglia (eds.), *La letteratura di consumo nel mondo greco-latino. Atti del Convegno internazionale Cassino, 14–17 settembre 1994*, Cassino: Università degli Studi di Cassino. 49–67.

Goold, G.P. (ed. and trans.) 1995. *Callirhoe*, Cambridge: Loeb Classical Library.

Grenfell, B.P., Hunt, A. S., Hogarth, D.G. 1900. *Fayûm Towns and their Papyri*, London: The Egypt Exploration Society. 74–82.

Gronewald, M. 1979. 'Ein Fragment aus den Aithiopica des Heliodor', *ZPE* 34, 19–21.

---

[39] For a full discussion, see Reardon 1996, 316–317 n. 13.

Hägg, T. 1971. *Narrative Technique in Ancient Greek Romances. Studies of Chariton, Xenophon Ephesius, and Achilles Tatius*, Stockholm: Acta Instituti Atheniensis Regni Sueciae.
Hägg, T. 1987. *Eros und Tyche. Der Roman in der antiken Welt*, Mainz: von Zabern.
Hägg, T. 1994. 'Orality, literacy, and the "readership" of the early Greek novel', in: R. Eriksen (ed.), *Contexts of Pre-Novel Narrative. The European Tradition*, Berlin/New York: Mouton de Gruyter. 47–81.
Hercher, R. (ed.) 1858–1859. *Erotici scriptores Graeci*, Leipzig: Teubner.
Hernández Lara, C. 1994. *Estudios sobre el aticismo de Caritón de Afrodisias*, Amsterdam: Hakkert.
Hirschig, G.A. (ed.) 1856. *Erotici scriptores*, Parisiis: A. Firmin-Didot.
Hunt, A.S. (ed. and trans.) 1910. Chariton, Chaereas and Callirhoe', in: A.S. Hunt (ed.), *The Oxyrhynchus Papyri* VII, London: The Egypt Exploration Society. 143–146.
Hunter, R.L. 2006. 'The Teubner Chariton', *CR* 56, 325–326.
La Penna, A. (ed.) 1957. *Publi Ovidi Nasonis Ibis*, Firenze: Le Monnier.
Lucke, C. 1985. 'Zum Charitontext auf Papyrus', *ZPE* 58, 21–33.
Marini, N. 1993. 'Osservazioni sul romanzo di Chione', *Athenaeum* 81, 587–600.
Meckelnborg, C., and Schäfer K.H. (eds. and trans.), 2006. *Chariton. Kallirhoe*, Darmstadt: Edition Antike.
Molinié G. (ed. and trans.) 1979. *Le roman de Chaireas et Callirhoe*, Paris: Les Belles Lettres, rev. by A. Billault, 1989.
Morgan, J.R. 1998. 'On the Fringes of the Canon: Work on the Fragments of Ancient Greek Fiction 1936–1944', *ANRW* 34,4, 3291–3390.
Papanikolaou, A.D. 1973. *Chariton-Studien. Untersuchungen zur Sprache und Chronologie der griechischen Romane*, Göttingen: Vandenhoeck & Ruprecht.
Perry, B. E. 1967. *The Ancient Romances: A Literary-Historical Account of their Origins*, Berkeley/Los Angeles: University of California Press.
Reardon, B.P. 1982. 'Une nouvelle édition de Chariton', *REG* 95, 166–170.
Reardon, B.P. 1996. 'Chariton', in: G. Schmeling (ed.), *The Novel in the Ancient World*, Leiden: Brill. 309–335.
Reardon, B. P. 1999. 'Theme, Structure and Narrative in Chariton', in: S. Swain (ed.), *Oxford Readings in The Greek Novel*, Oxford: Oxford University Press. 163–188.
Reardon, B.P. (ed.) 2004. *Chariton. De Callirhoe Narrationes amatoriae*, Monachii et Lipsiae: Teubner.
Reeve, M. 1971. 'Hiatus in the Greek novelists', *CQ* NS 21, 514–539.
Rimell, V. 2007. *Seeing Tongues, Hearing Scripts: Orality and Representation in the Ancient Novel*, ANS 7, Groningen: Barkhuis & Groningen University Library.
Rohde, E. 1914. *Der griechische Roman und seine Vorläufer*, Leipzig: Breitkopf und Härtel.
Roncali, R. 1999. 'Su due varianti del Papiro Fayûm 1 di Caritone', *Bollettino dei Classici* 20, 37–44.
Ruiz-Montero, C. 1989. 'Caritón de Afrodisias y el mundo real', in: P. Liviabella Furiani, A. M. Scarcella (eds.), *Piccolo mondo antico. Le donne, gli amori, I costumi, il mondo reale nel romanzo*, Perugia: Università degli Studi di Perugia. 107–150.
Ruiz-Montero, C. 1991. 'Aspects of the vocabulary of Chariton of Aphrodisias', *CQ* NS 41, 484–489.
Sanz Morales, M. 2002. 'Textkritische Bemerkungen zum Chariton-Text auf Papyrus', *ZPE* 141, 111–115.

Sanz Morales, M. 2006a. 'Multiple Versions in the Greek Novel', *Variants* 5, 129–146.
Sanz Morales, M. 2006b. 'Dos Observaciones al Texto de Caritón Transmitido par los Papiros', *Phaos* 6, 51–56.
Sanz Morales, M. 2007. 'Konjekturen zu Chariton von Aphrodisias, Bücher I-IV', *Philologus* 151, 95–104.
Sanz Morales, M. 2009. 'Testimonio de los papiros y tradición medieval: una versión diferente de la novela de Caritón?', in: M. Sanz Morales, M. Librán Moreno (eds.), *Verae lectiones. Estudios de crítica textual y edición de textos griegos*, Anejo I de *Exemplaria Classica*, Huelva-Cáceres: Universidad de Huelva – Universidad de Extremadura.
Sanz Morales, M. 2015. 'Copyists' Versions and the Readership of the Greek Novel' (in this volume).
Stephens, S.A. 1994. 'Who Read Ancient Novels?', in: J. Tatum (ed.), *The Search for the Ancient Novel*, Baltimore/London: Johns Hopkins University Press. 405–418.
Stephens, S.A. and Winkler J.J. 1995. *Ancient Greek novels: the fragments*, Princeton: Princeton University Press.
Treu, K. 1989. 'Der antike Roman und sein Publikum', in: H. Kuch (ed.), *Der antike Roman. Untersuchungen zur literarischen Komunikation und Gattungsgeschichte*, Berlin: Akademie-Vertrag. 178–197.
Weinstein, M.E. (ed. and trans.) 1972. '2948: Chariton, *Chaereas and Callirhoe*, ii 4.5–5.1', in: G.M. Browne et al. (eds.), *The Oxyrhynchus Papyri* XLI, London: The Egypt Exploration Society. 12–14.
Wesseling, B. 1988. 'The Audience of the Ancient Novel', in: H. Hofmann (ed.), *Groningen Colloquia on the Novel*, Groningen: Egbert Forsten. 67–79.
West, M.L. 1973. *Textual criticism and editorial technique*, Stuttgart: Teubner.
Wilamowitz-Moellendorff, U. von 1901. 'Fayum towns and their Papyri, B. Grenfell, A. Hunt, D. Hogarth, London 1900', *GGA* 163, 30–45.
Wilcken, U. 1901. 'Ein neue Roman-Handschrift', *APF* 1, 227–272.
Zanetto, G. 2007. 'Review B.P. Reardon (ed.): *Chariton. De Callirhoe narrationes amatoriae* (Monachii et Lipsiae 2004)', *AN* 6, 150–158.
Zimmermann, F. 1922. 'De Charitonis codice Thebano', *Philologus* 78, 330–402.
Zimmermann, F. 1928. 'Zur Überlieferung des Chariton-Romanes', *Hermes* 63, 193–224.

Nicola Pace
New Evidence For Dating The Discovery At Traù Of The Petronian *Cena Trimalchionis*

Abstract: The date of the discovery by Marino Statileo of the long fragment of Petronius' *Satyricon* (the *Cena Trimalchionis*), at Traù in Dalmatia, has been fluctuating in a bewildering way for three centuries in Petronian scholarship. In the 20th century scholars generally agreed to fix the date around 1650, without taking into account the main documents of the time. This study aims to examine these documents, above all the historian Giovanni Lucio's report of the discovery, in relation to the recent publication of the list of Dalmatian graduates at the University of Padua, which shows that Marino Statileo graduated in law in 1644: since the discovery coincides, in the reports, with his return home to Traù soon after graduating, we can date the discovery to around 1645, about twenty years before the *editio princeps* (1664). This long interval must be explained by the widespread opposition to the printing of the new text at Traù, Padua, and Rome.

One of the most important discoveries of classical texts in the 17th century is that of the Petronian *Cena Trimalchionis* by Marino Statileo, in the small town of Traù in Dalmatia. This discovery, as is well known, gave rise to much controversy about the authenticity of the new text in the most influential European countries, above all France, Holland, and Italy, at least until 1668, when the manuscript containing the fragment of Petronius was brought to Rome and submitted to scholars for examination.

The controversy erupted following the publication of the *editio princeps* of the *Fragmentum Traguriense* by the Paduan printer Paolo Frambotti in 1664. But we have to ask: how many years intervened between the discovery at Traù and the publication at Padua? Moreover, is this uncertainty really important for the history of classical philology? If, as I hope to show in this report, at least fifteen years elapsed between discovery and publication, this surprising interval is a sign of the stiff resistance to the publication of the fragment put up by those who believed it to be a fake. What emerges is a largely unknown controver-

Nicola Pace, Università degli Studi di Milano

https://doi.org/10.1515/9781501503986-016

sy that divided scholars and politicians at Traù, Padua, Venice, and Rome before 1664, the year of *editio princeps*.[1]

Let us begin by considering 'the only detailed and, for lack of evidence to the contrary, authoritative account of the discovery'[2] and of the subsequent debates on the authenticity of the new fragment, namely a fairly well-known passage from the *Appendix* to *Memorie istoriche di Tragurio, ora detto Traù*, published by Giovanni Lucio in 1674. It should be noted that Giovanni Lucio, born at Traù, was not only the most distinguished historian of Dalmatia in the 17th century, but, as we will see in his account, also one of the protagonists of the controversy. Indeed, it was he who, through unceasing and behind-the-scenes endeavours, and the co-operation of two influential men of his time, the Ambassador of Venice at the Holy See of Rome, Pietro Basadonna, and the Second Custodian of the Vatican Library, Stefano Gradi, succeeded in printing Petronius' new fragment.[3] This undertaking is acknowledged by Lucio himself, though only privately, in a letter to the Archdeacon of Zara, Valerio Ponte, on 31 October 1665: *Conservi tra me e il Sr Cippico buona corrispondenza, interrotta per haver io stampato quel fragmento de Petronio, che era suo, contro sua voglia* ('Please, try to persuade Mr Cippico [the owner of the manuscript] to maintain good relations with me, after we broke off because I printed that fragment of Petronius, which belonged to him, against his will').[4] In the *Memorie istoriche di Tragurio* report, we see that Lucio plays down, if not actually hides, his own role and emphasizes that of Pietro Basadonna. This attitude may be explained by the gratitude that Lucio felt towards the powerful ex-Ambassador, at that time cardinal, for financing the publication of the *Memorie*.

> Il Signor Dottor Marino Statileo, ritornato dallo studio di Padova, ritrovò tra li manuscritti del Signor Nicolò Cippico un Petronio Arbitro in foglio, legato insieme con Catullo, Tibullo, e Properzio, & osservò, che la cena di Trimalchione (della quale nelli stampati si trovano alcuni pochi frammenti, & interrotti) era intiera: mi portò il libro, & io, insieme col Signor Francesco Dragazzo, lo rafrontai con lo stampato in Amsterdam, che hò in forma piccola,[5] e

---

1 Cf. Pace 2008, 374–385.
2 Rini 1937, 60.
3 A reliable biography of Lucio is Brunelli 1899–1901. As far as our research is concerned, the 4th chapter (*La vita di S. Giovanni Ursino, ed il frammento di Petronio Arbitro*, Brunelli 1899, fasc. 2, 130–139) is particularly important. For a good and up-to-date overview of Lucio's role in the controversy (and of the whole controversy in general) see Campanelli 2006.
4 Poparić 1907, 20.
5 According to the information Lucio gives us (beside this passage cf. his dedicatory epistle to Willem and Pieter Blaeu in Lucio 1671, f. A4[r]: *Quamvis autem ipse hunc codicem, cum essem Tragurii, saepe inspexissem ac perlegissem, & cum exemplo typis vestris impresso, quod apud me est, contulissem, & utriusque locos, tum congruentes, tum discrepantes in margine ejusdem editi adno-*

trovai, che tutto 'l resto di Petronio, fuori della cena, era nello stampato, ma non disposto nello stesso ordine, e nella cena verificai quello, che il signor Statileo m'haveva riferito, e nel margine dello stampato con linee, e punti notai li raffronti,[6] & esortai esso Signor Statileo, che rescrivesse la cena, come stava puntualmente con tutti gl'errori d'ortografia, & interpuntioni, e per decoro della patria lo facesse stampare: partito io dalla patria del 1654 participai questo ritrovamento a diverse persone virtuose in Padova, e Roma, che mostraron haver gran desiderio di vederlo: perciò eccitai con lettere li sopradetti Signori Statileo, e Cippico che lo stampassero; ma questi occupati nelle faccende private, e nelle publiche per l'urgenza della guerra col Turco, differivano ciò a stagione più quieta, fino a che capitato a Roma per l'Ambasciatore l'Eccellentissimo Signor Cavalier Pietro Basadonna, e saputo ciò, scrisse all'Eccellentissimo Signor General di Dalmatia che li facesse haver la copia della predetta cena di Petronio, e la ricevè, la quale da me veduta, conobbi esser di carattere del Signor Statileo predetto, e d'ordine di S. Eccellenza fattala vedere à diversi, tra questi vi furono alcuni, che dubitarono che possi essere stata finta; la maggior parte però inclinava a credere d'esser di Petronio, ricconoscendo il suo stile, & osservando, che con questo s'empivano le lacune dello stampato, & anco alcuni frammenti sparsi per lo stampato venivano ottimamente inseriti: onde S. Eccellenza diede ordine che fosse stampato in Padova ...[7]

---

tassem), he used for the purpose of collation the edition printed by Willem Blaeu in 1626, with the notes mostly by Johann von Wowern (*Lat.* Joannes Wowerius, or Wowerus): von Wowern 1626. That is, in fact, the only edition of Petronius printed by the Blaeu family (Willem, and his sons Joan and Cornelis) before that of 1669, by Michael Hadrianides (Hadrianides 1669): cf. Keuning – Donkersloot-de Vrij 1973, 31.

6 In the above-quoted passage of the epistle to Willem and Pieter Blaeu, Lucio is little clearer: *utriusque locos,* *tum congruentes, tum discrepantes* *in margine ejusdem editi adnotassem*. Lucio had marked in the margins of his edition of Petronius both the passages that matched and those that did not, but certainly could not have copied all the passages of the *Cena* in the manuscript that were not in the printed edition: the manuscript in fact had plenty of new text (Petron. 37,6 – 78,8, about 20 pages of the ms. [pp. 209, r. 7 – 229, r. 15]) that the small Blaeu edition's margins could not have held. As far as the *Cena* is concerned, it is likely that Lucio marked the small gaps in Petron. 27,1 – 37,5 (that part of *Cena* that is transmitted by the *excerpta longa*), and copied the text of the ms. in the margins: e.g. 30,7 *pariter*; 34,7 *vinum quam homuncio. quare tangomenas faciamus. vita.*

7 Lucio 1674, 531 – 532. This account corresponds generally to that ascribed to the printer Paolo Frambotti in the foreword of the *editio princeps* (*Typographus lectori*): *Marinus Statileus Traguriensis, vir diligens, et eruditus, cum olim post absolutum jurisprudentiae studium Patavio reversus in patriam, offendisset in Bibliotheca Nicolai Cippici amici omnibus officiis conjuncti sibi, antiquum volumen, in eoque una cum carminibus Horatii vulgaris exempli, Satyricon Petronii Arbitri; in quo praeter ea, quae de operis hujus auctore circumferuntur, plurima notasset nova, neque in impressis legi solita, deliberare apud se coepit de scripto publicae literatorum delectationi non invidendo, cum praeter antiquitatem codicis, ad pretium inventi conferre plurimum videretur, quod liber Hectori quondam Cippico possessus putabatur, hujus Nicolai abavo, viro longe doctissimo, magnaeque inter suos auctoritatis, et famae ... cumque idcirco satis causae habere se crederet, ne, quod invenerat contemnendum putaret, cum doctioribus quibusque suum consilium, primo in patria, deinde Venetiis, ac Patavii communicavit; sed inprimis cum Joanne Rhodio profundae*

Doctor Marino Statileo, on his return home from his studies at Padua, found among the manuscripts of Nicolò Cippico one of Petronius in folio, bound with Catullus, Tibullus, and Propertius, and noticed that it contained the whole *Cena Trimalchionis* (a few, broken fragments of which we find in the printed editions). He brought the manuscript to me, and I, together with Mr. Francesco Dragazzo, compared it to my small Amsterdam edition of Petronius, and I saw that all the other fragments, except for the *Cena*, were in this edition, but not arranged in the same order, and in the *Cena* ascertained what Mr. Statileo had told me, and in the margins of the Amsterdam edition I marked the connections by means of lines and dots, and I urged Mr. Statileo to make an exact copy of the *Cena*, reproducing all the spelling mistakes and all the punctuation marks, and to have it published, to the honour and glory of our native town. When I left Traù in 1654, I made this discovery known to many virtuous people at Padua and Rome, who showed themselves very eager to see it; therefore I encouraged, via letters, the above-mentioned Messrs. Statileo and Cippico to print it; but, since they were busy with private and public affairs (the war against the Turks was impending), they postponed it till a quieter time, until the most excellent Knight Mr. Pietro Basadonna, who had come to Rome as an Ambassador, and had got to know about it, wrote a letter to the most excellent General of Dalmatia, asking to have a copy of the above-mentioned Petronius' *Cena*, and he received it, which, since I had seen it, I recognized as written in Mr. Statileo's own hand, and, by order of His Excellency [Pietro Basadonna], I showed to many people; of these a few had doubts that it might be faked, but the majority were inclined to believe that it was Petronius' work, recognizing his style, and noticing that through it the gaps of the published work were filled, and also that some fragments, which were scattered in the published work, were very well linked up. His Excellency, therefore, ordered that it be printed at Padua ...

Here Lucio fixes the date of the *terminus ante quem* for the discovery, his departure from Traù to Rome,[8] in the year 1654, but not the *terminus post quem*, Statileo's return to Traù from Padua. For this reason many scholars were led to suppose that the discovery was made not much before 1654, in about 1650. Anthony Rini, a scholar who has studied the history of the controversy in great detail, states: 'The exact date of the discovery is not known. As Lucio tells us that he left Traù in 1654, the discovery must have been made in that year or, more probably, a few years earlier'.[9] Reliable editors and commentators of Petronius, such

---

eruditionis, & solidi judicii viro. Et quia res visa omnibus est magni inprimis momenti, propter singulare auctoris de puritate, & elegantia linguae Latinae meritum, cuius germanum hunc partum ut crederet, multis, atque indubiis argumentis adducebatur: destinavit commodiori meditationi curam vulgandi scripti, notisque, & castigationibus illustrandi ([Lucio] 1664, f. § 2^{r-v} = Burman 1709, II, 305). A detailed summary of this foreword, with useful commentary, is in Rini 1937, 63–64.

8 Lucio was never to return to his native town, and died in Rome in 1679. On the obscure reasons for his departure cf. Brunelli 1899, fasc. 2, 119–130. The date (1654) is confirmed by his testament: cf. Brunelli 1901, fasc. 4, 17.
9 Rini 1937, 60 n. 378.

as Marmorale, Smith, and Mueller, agree with dating the discovery at or around 1650.[10]

What they were unaware of (or *forgot*, as in the case of Rini) was another 17th century account, a two-fold account, not of the discovery of the manuscript but of the visit two travellers had paid to Marino Statileo at Traù in July 1675, during their voyage along the Dalmatian coast, to see the manuscript. We quote both travellers here, the Frenchman Jacob Spon and the Briton George Wheler, as their accounts do not exactly match:

> Monsieur le Docteur Statilius, dans la Bibliotheque duquel cet original se trouve, est un homme de merite, qui en auroit pû parler pertinemment, si ses maladies ne l'en eussent empêché; & Monsieur de Valois a eu tort de le prendre pour un jeune homme, puisqu'il est du moins presentement âgé de soixante ans.[11]

> The Manuscript is in the hands of Dr. *Statelius* [sic!], a man of parts and learning, but sickly; not a young man, as Monsieur Valois styles him, with more pride than good manners; for he is near Threescore years old, and a grave and sober person, who, it may be, thinks it not worth his pains to answer Monsieur Valois, whose arguments can be but of little force against the credit of sight.[12]

Apart from the different reasons for the lack of reply by Statileo to Adrien de Valois's *dissertatio*,[13] the two accounts agree in ascribing to Statileo an age of about sixty years in 1675. Having been born around 1615, he would have been almost forty when Lucio left Traù in 1654, an unusual age for a doctor who was fresh from his studies.

For this reason Anthony Rini, in another footnote to his study, proposed a much earlier date for the discovery, contradicting his previous suggestion. The discovery, he says, 'must likewise have occurred long before 1654, probably, between 1640 and 1645'.[14] Thirty years before Rini, James Anson Farrer, author of an important book on literary forgeries, had been the only scholar who had considered properly both Lucio's and Spon-Wheler's accounts, and came to the conclusion that Statileo 'must have found the manuscript about the year 1645, which

---

10 Proietti 2001, 108–119, ignores Lucio's account (as well as Spon-Wheler's) and proposes 1654 as the date of the discovery.
11 Spon 1678, I 96.
12 Wheler 1682, 23.
13 Spon ascribes Statileo's silence to his sickness, while Wheler to the evidence of authenticity given by the manuscript itself. It is surprising that Statileo did not mention at all the two apologetic learned works against Wagenseil and Valois which circulated under his name (though actually written by Pierre Petit and Stefano Gradi): Petit 1666 and Gradi 1671.
14 Rini 1937, 79 n. 503.

would leave some twenty years between its discovery and its first printed appearance in 1664'.[15] As we will see, he guessed correctly, but he weakened this conclusion by maintaining that it 'is highly incredible, and even ten years is a long time to allow for the conquest by Lucius of the modesty or the indolence of his friend and relative Statileus'. Farrer was forced by this 'incredible' interval, and by the obscure behaviour of Lucio and Gradi, 'to the suspicion ... that after all the "Supper of Trimalchio" may be a forgery',[16] a forgery that can be ascribed to Lucio, Gradi, and Statileo. But the 'incredible' interval, as well as the secretive behaviour of Lucio and Gradi, may have an alternative explanation which excludes any hypothesis of forgery: the strong and widespread opposition to the printing of the new text that Lucio and Gradi met with, first of all at Traù, from both the owner and the discoverer of the manuscript, Nicolò Cippico and Marino Statileo.

Before considering this opposition, I examine the 'new' documents which serve to fix the *terminus post quem* and a new *terminus ante quem*. Although they cannot truly be defined as new documents, since they were published in 1940 and 1992, they were ignored as far as the date of the discovery is concerned. In 1992 Michele Pietro Ghezzo published the records of academic degrees ('Atti dei Gradi Accademici') of Dalmatian students at the University of Padua in the 17th and 18th centuries: here we see that Marino Statileo obtained his degree in Law on 21 May 1644.[17]

The second document is a passage from an interesting letter by the renowned scholar Ottavio Ferrari, who taught Greek and Latin Humanities at Padua, significantly to Ottavio Falconieri, who was the archaeological consultant to Prince Leopoldo de' Medici in Rome. The eloquently written letter, sent not long after the publication of the *editio princeps*, on 22 June 1664, and published by Mario Mortin in 1940,[18] provides evidence of the stiff opposition not only of Ferrari, but also of Paduan scholars and literary circles generally to the new edition. Ferrari, who begins his letter by characterizing the fragment as *Petronius hypobolimaeus, literarum atque Italiae dehonestamentum e cella et gurgustiis emersum* ('supposititious Petronius who, emerging from the servants' rooms and from the taverns, brought dishonour upon humanities and Italy'), describes, by means of baroque metaphors, the harsh welcome it received from Paduans:

---

15 Farrer 1907, 14.
16 Farrer 1907, 19.
17 Ghezzo 1992, 42. This document was quoted in relation to the Petronian controversy by Tremoli 1995, 97, but he did not draw inferences from it concerning the date of the manuscript's discovery.
18 Mortin 1940, 238–239.

Ceteri omnes quotquot has noenias legerunt, non Gymnasii modo equestria, quique ad podium spectant, sed cavea, et cuneis spectacula totis, ordinem totius dictionis infamarunt, sibilisque ac pastoritia fistula exceperunt ('all others who have read these singsongs, not only those seated in the knights' seats of the Gymnasium and the spectators sitting in the podium, but the mass that crowds into the tiers of the cavea, have discredited the level of its entire literary style, and greeted it with hisses and with the pastoral pipe'.)[19] The profit on the sale of the book was also very disappointing for the printer Paolo Frambotti: *Summa typographi indignatione fastidiose venditatur.*[20]

In the first part of the letter, Ferrari's chief concern is to refute two statements made in the foreword of the *editio princeps:* 1) that all the Roman scholars had asserted the fragment's authenticity,[21] and 2) that Johan Rhode (*Lat.:* Joannes Rhodius), a Danish scholar and physician who spent a long period of his life at Padua[22] (where he died in 1659), was consulted by Statileo about the fragment, and advised him to publish it.[23] Ferrari was absolutely positive that both these statements were false, to the extent that he did not hesitate to summon the printer Frambotti and to rebuke him severely for having slandered the Roman scholars.[24] The printer denied being the author of the foreword and ascribed it to someone living in Rome who sent it to the Paduan promoters of the publication. It could not, I think, have been Lucio, despite its basic agreement with the account in the *Memorie istoriche di Tragurio*, because of a serious mis-

---

19 Cf. Cic. *Att.* 1,16,11 *sine ulla pastoricia fistula auferebamus.*
20 Mortin 1940, 239.
21 *Itaque tanti Legati beneficio doctissimi cuiusque in urbe censurae subiectus liber, opinionem sui, quam e Dalmatia, Venetiisque ac Patavio attulerat, facile retinere est visus* ([Lucio] 1664, f. § 3ʳ = Burman 1709, II, 306).
22 From 1622 to 1659. On Rhode see Hirsch 1932, IV, 786.
23 Cf. n. 7.
24 *Cum ego primum in praefatione legi rus merum* [Plaut. *Truc.* 269] *doctissimi cuiusque Urbanorum suffragium tulisse, tentare fidem oculorum coepi, bisque ac ter repetens, mendacium impudens detestatus, vestram vicem ingemui, quorum existimatio foede proscriberetur, et cum tu praecipue, Hesperiae lux, isthic doctorum familiam ducas, valde pertimui, ne haec fabula nomini tuo labeculam inspergeret. Bonum factum quod priores tuas elegantissimas, aliquid animo praesagiens, tanquam Cereris arcanae sacra habui. Nunc facile adducor ut credam eadem arte eruditis oculis tuis substractum fragmentum a quo me, atque Offredum, tanquam profanos submoverunt. Non enim ignorabant te, qua polles iudicii acrimonia ac libertate, nigrum theta appositurum. Accitum typographum vehementer increpui, quod ausus esset Romano nomini tantam conflare calumniam. Ille se latinae linguae rudem esse dixit: caeterum praefationem ab iis sibi traditam, qui Roma transmissam imputarent* (Mortin 1940, 238–239).

take the meticulous historian would never have made.²⁵ It is more likely to have been someone who drew on information from Lucio, partially distorting it, most probably Pietro Basadonna, the political promoter of the publication, who obliged Marino Statileo to send a copy of the fragment to Rome in the autumn of 1662,²⁶ and kept it jealously in his Roman home.²⁷

Ferrari was certainly right in challenging the statement that the Roman scholars were all firm supporters of the fragment's authenticity: Ottavio Falconieri, in his correspondence with Leopoldo de' Medici, lends clear support to a different view, even before he knew Ferrari's strong opinions on the matter. In a letter of 19 March 1663, he maintained that the fragment certainly could not be ascribed to Petronius, but that it should not be considered a forgery by moderns, but rather a medieval imitation of the Latin author.²⁸ When he received a copy of the *editio princeps* in May 1664, and was able to read it more carefully, he confirmed his rejection of the attribution to Petronius, and added that the majority of the scholars at Rome shared this position.²⁹ In their letters, Gradi and

---

25 See the mention of Horace's works as bound together with Petronius' in Cippico's manuscript (*antiquum volumen, in eoque una cum carminibus Horatii vulgaris exempli, Satyricon Petronii Arbitri*). For this reason I now reject Paolo Tremoli's assumption (Tremoli 1995, 103–104), which I was inclined to accept in Pace 2008, 385.

26 Cf. the letter sent on 11 November 1662 by Lucio to Valerio Ponte, from Rome to Zara, in Poparić 1907, 8: *Petronio è pur capitato, ma sta incognito, sino che il Sr. Abbate ritorni, riservandosi al suo giuditio la pubblicatione*. The abbé is Stefano Gradi, whose intellectual authority is acknowledged here.

27 Cf. the letter sent on 17 February 1663 by Falconieri to Leopoldo de' Medici, in Falconieri 1984, 92–93: *Ho usato ogni diligenza possibile per poter dar relazione a V(ostra) A(ltezza) in questo medesimo ordinario del manoscritto di Petronio, ma non mi è riuscito essendo detto manoscritto nelle mani dell'Ambasciador di Venezia, il quale non lo vuol dar fuori di Casa, benché questo non sia che copia di quello ch'è in Dalmazia, onde bisogna ch'io aspetti le sue comodità*. In the following letter of 19 March 1663, in Falconieri 1984, 93–94, Falconieri tells Leopoldo de' Medici he was allowed to see the manuscript for only half an hour.

28 *Scorsi l'altro giorno una parte del manoscritto di Petronio, che mi fu permesso havere in mano per lo spazio di mezz'ora, e per quello ch'io posso giudicarne così, a prima vista, non credo che la detta scrittura sia assolutamente di quell'autore, né meno aggiunta per contrafare lo stile di Petronio, ma più tosto un componimento fatto ne' secoli più infelici da qualcuno, ch'avendo inclinazione ad esso, abbia voluto imitarlo* (Falconieri 1984, 93–94).

29 Cf. the letter sent to Leopoldo de' Medici on 24 May 1664, in Falconieri 1984, 104: *Ho veduto finalmente il Petronio, o per dir meglio il frammento che si supponeva di quest'Autore, mentre in quanto a me non posso indurmi a crederlo tale, ed in ciò son conforme al Pollini et alla maggior parte di quelli che professano queste lettere in Roma*. Alessandro Pollini, a Florentine scholar who lived mainly in Rome, was engaged in linguistic studies of Tuscan. Writing to Nicolaas Heins (*Lat.* Nicolaus Heinsius) on 30 May 1664 (from Rome to Stockholm), Falconieri vehemently attacked the statement in the foreword concerning the agreement of the Roman scholars: *In qua*

Lucio also acknowledge that in 1663, particularly in the spring, there was considerable controversy in Rome concerning the fragment, and scholars were unable to reach an agreement on its authenticity.[30]

Let us return, however, to Ferrari's letter to Falconieri, and his critique of the foreword's statement concerning Rhodius.

> Quod ad Rodium pertinet, nunquam ipsi Pseudo Petronium visum, tam certo scio, quam abs te amari cupio. Sed a quodam Dalmata acceperat, hunc terrae omniparentis alumnum repente Tragurii natum, cumque id magno Scioppio communicasset, retulit ille, se de eadem re, cum Romae esset, aliquid audivisse: verum arbitrari, esse alicuius ascetae foetum infelicem, natum in culina[31] ad laevam manum.[32]
>
> As far as Rhodius is concerned, my certainty that he never saw the Pseudo-Petronius is matched only by how much I long for your love. But he heard from a certain Dalmatian that this offspring of a land that produces all kinds of things was suddenly born at Traù, and, when he made the news known to Scioppius, this scholar replied that he had heard something on the same subject when he was in Rome, but thought it was the poor product of some ascetic, brought forth in the kitchen on the left-hand side.

Kaspar Schoppe (*Lat.* Scioppius), a famous German humanist and polemicist, spent the last thirteen years of his life at Padua, and died on 19 November 1649. From this account of Ferrari, therefore, we obtain a *terminus ante quem* for the discovery which is closer to the *terminus post quem* (1644) than the date of Lucio's departure from Traù (1654). But we may go even further and con-

---

quidem re eum, qui typographi partes gerit, adeo confidenter agere perquam inique fero, qui ut privato lucro consuleret vel cum aliena jactura, nescio quam explorata eruditorum hujus urbis de Petronio illo suo sententia, liquido pronuntiare non dubitavit, id fragmentum doctissimi cujusque in urbe censurae subjectum opinionem sui, quam e Dalmatia Venetiisque ac Pataviо attulerat, facile retinuisse. Mihi vero compertum est eos, qui hic nominis hujus honorem merentur, tam fragmentum illud Petronii germanum existimare, quam Berosi monumenta, quae circumferuntur, qui criticae artis vel leviter curiosi sunt (Burman 1727, V, 493). Falconieri changed his position completely on the fragment's authenticity after 1668: cf. Pace 2007, 333–334 n. 89.

30 In the "Bilioteca Nazionale Centrale di Firenze" (Magl. VIII 1073), there is an interesting unpublished letter sent by Stefano Gradi to Antonio Magliabechi (from Rome to Florence) on 29 December 1663, a passage of which deals with the printing of the fragment: *Non è ancora finito di stampare a Padova quel fragmento creduto di Petronio e qualche savio di costà non l'ammette punto per ligitimo. Né anco qui s'è affermato francamente il contrario.* See also the letter sent by Giovanni Lucio to Valerio Ponte on 14 July 1663, which speaks of 'a long debate in Rome about Petronius', in Pace 2007, 309 n. 17. Echoes of this Roman debate reached the ears of important scholars such as Johannes Fredericus Gronovius and Nicolaus Heinsius: see the letter sent by the former to the latter (from Leyden to Stockholm) on 4 May 1663, in Burman 1727, III, 487 (cf. Pace 2007, *ibid.*).

31 Cf. Plaut. *Persa* 631 *in culina, in angulo ad laevam manum.*

32 Mortin 1940, 239.

clude, according to Lucio's account, that Statileo returned to Traù and made the discovery not long after having graduated in Padua in 1644, perhaps during the same year or the following one.

In Ferrari's account we see that the discovery of the fragment was made known to Rhodius by 'a certain Dalmatian'. Is this Statileo, as the foreword of *editio princeps* tells us? It must be said that Ferrari is very wary when he speaks of his antagonists, and never names Lucio, Gradi, or Basadonna. He is particularly afraid of Basadonna and, in a previous letter to Falconieri on the same subject,[33] states that he must only complain in private as 'it would be foolish to write against a man who can proscribe'.[34] On the other hand, Ferrari willingly names his friends, among them Statileo, described soon after as *vetus amicus*.[35] Statileo, as an old friend, revealed all his doubts about the fragment's authenticity to Ferrari, and told him that the copy he sent to Rome was 'extorted' from him.[36] Here Statileo appears very reluctant to publish the fragment.

The unnamed Dalmatian who spoke to Rhodius about the fragment cannot be Statileo, but rather an antagonist of Ferrari, almost certainly Lucio himself.

In conclusion, we have seen that the almost twenty years which elapsed between the discovery and publication of the fragment betray a bitter, often underground, dispute that placed Cippico, Statileo, and Ferrari in opposition to Lucio, Gradi, and Basadonna. The intellectual authority of Ferrari in Padua (and Venice) was so strong that only a politician of as high a rank as Basadonna could neutralize his strong resistance to the publication of the fragment.

Bibliography

Brunelli, V. 1899–1901. 'Giovanni Lucio', *Rivista Dalmatica* 1 (1899), fasc. 1, 5–24; fasc. 2, 119–139; fasc. 4, 24–51; 2 (1900–1901), fasc. 1, 32–52; fasc. 3, 271–285; fasc. 4, 17–24.

---

[33] The letter, which is not dated, was published by Mortin 1940, 236–238.
[34] *Sed te per deos deasque obtestor, ut pereat inter nos hoc qualecumque secretum. Mussandum enim mihi est, ne illius laureolam infringere videar, qui se putat Musarum facetias* [I correct the unacceptable *faccissas*, which is in the manuscript and in Mortin's edition] *reclusisse. Stultum est adversus eum scribere, qui potest proscribere, et brevi in partem regni literarii veniet* (Mortin 1940, 237).
[35] *Marinus Statilius Dalmata Fragmenti possessor*, and then: *Dalmata, vir honestus, nec literarum rudis, vetusque amicus* (Mortin 1940, 236).
[36] *Dalmata ... ingenue fatetur, se non semel de eo dubitasse, et ab invito schedas extortas* (Mortin 1940, 236).

Burman, P. (ed.) 1709. *Petronius Arbiter, Satyricôn quae supersunt cum integris Doctorum Virorum Commentariis; & Notis Nicolai Heinsii & Guilielmi Goesii nunc primum editis. Accedunt Jani Dousae Praecidanea, D. Jos. Ant. Gonsalii de Salas Commenta, Variae Dissertationes & Praefationes, quarum Index post praefationem exhibetur. Curante Petro Burmanno*, Trajecti ad Rhenum: Guilielmus vande Water.

Burman, P. 1727. *Sylloge epistolarum a viris illustribus scriptarum*, Leidae: Samuel Luchtmans.

Campanelli, M. 2006. 'Filologi "per decoro della patria": due dalmati illustri e un caso letterario del secolo XVII', in: L. Avellini and N. D'Antuono (eds.), *Custodi della tradizione e avanguardie del nuovo sulle sponde dell'Adriatico. Libri e biblioteche, collezionismo, scambi culturali e scientifici, scritture di viaggio fra Quattrocento e Novecento. Atti del Convegno internazionale di Studi, Pescara, 25–28 maggio 2005*, Bologna: CLUEB, 103–132.

de Valois, A., and Wagenseil, J. Ch. 1666. *Hadriani Valesii Histor. Regii et Ioh. Christophori Wagenseilii De cena Trimalcionis nuper sub Petronij nomine vulgata dissertationes*, Luteciae Parisiorum: Edmundus Martinus.

Falconieri, O. 1984. *Lettere di Ottavio Falconieri a Leopoldo de' Medici, a cura di L. Giovannini*, Firenze: Edam.

Farrer, J.A. 1907. *Literary Forgeries*, London: Longmans, Green, and Co.

Ghezzo, M.P. 1992. 'I Dalmati all'Università di Padova dagli Atti dei Gradi Accademici (1601–1800)', *Atti e Memorie della Società Dalmata di Storia Patria* 21, 3–210.

Gradi, S. 1671. *Apologia Marini Statilii*, in: Lucio 1671, 1–32.

Hadrianides, M. (ed.) 1669. *Petronius Arbiter, Satyricon, cum Fragmento nuper Tragurii reperto ... concinnante Michaele Hadrianide*, Amstelodami: Ioannes Blaeu.

Hirsch, A. 1932. *Biographisches Lexikon der hervorragenden Ärzte aller Zeiten und Völker. Zweite Auflage*, Berlin/Wien: Urban & Schwarzenberg.

Keuning, J., and Donkersloot-de Vrij, M. 1973. *Willem Jansz. Blaeu: a Biography and History of his Work as a Cartographer and Publisher*, Amsterdam: Theatrum Orbis Terrarum.

[Lucio, G.] (ed.) 1664. *Petronius Arbiter. Fragmentum nuper Tragurij repertum*, Patavii: Paulus Frambottus.

Lucio, G. (ed.) 1671, *Petronius Arbiter. Integrum Titi Petronii Arbitri Fragmentum, ex antiquo codice Traguriensi Romae exscriptum; cum Apologia Marini Statilii; editio secunda, quod ad Apologiam auctior & curatior*, Amstelodami: Ioannes Blaeu.

Lucio, G. 1674. *Memorie istoriche di Tragurio, ora detto Traù*, Venezia: Stefano Curti.

Mortin, M. 1940. 'Due lettere di Ottavio Ferrari sulla prima edizione della *Cena Trimalchionis*', *Aevum* 14, 231–239.

Pace, N. 2007. 'Nuovi documenti sulla controversia seicentesca relativa al *Fragmentum Traguriense* della *Cena Trimalchionis* di Petronio', in: R. Pretagostini and E. Dettori (eds.), *La cultura letteraria ellenistica. Persistenza, innovazione, trasmissione. Atti del Convegno COFIN 2003, Università di Roma 'Tor Vergata', 19–21 settembre 2005*, Roma: Edizioni Quasar. 305–336.

Pace, N. 2008. 'Ombre e silenzi nella scoperta del frammento traurino di Petronio e nella controversia sulla sua autenticità', in: P.F. Moretti, C. Torre, G. Zanetto (eds.), *Debita dona: studi in onore di Isabella Gualandri*, Napoli: M. D'Auria Editore. 373–399.

Petit, P. 1666. *Marini Statilei Traguriensis J.C. Responsio ad Joh. Christoph. Wagenseilii, et Hadriani Valesii dissertationes De Traguriensi Petronii Fragmento. Ad M. Mocaenicum P.V.*, Parisiis: Edmundus Martinus.

Poparić, B. 1907. 'Pisma Ivana Lučića Trogiranina', *Starine* 32, 1–91.

Proietti, O. 2001. 'Per la cronologia degli scritti postumi di Spinoza: Terenzio e il Petronius di M. Hadrianides (Amsterdam, 1669)', *QS* 53, 105–154.

Rini, A. 1937. *Petronius in Italy, from the Thirteenth Century to the Present Time*, New York: The Cappabianca Press.

Spon, J. 1678. *Voyage d'Italie, de Dalmatie, de Grece, et du Levant, fait aux années 1675 & 1676 par Iacob Spon Docteur Medecin Aggregè à Lyon, & George Wheler Gentilhomme Anglois*, Lyon: Antoine Cellier le fils.

Tremoli, P. 1995. 'Storia non breve di una breve storia di Traù', *Archeografo Triestino* 103, 95–109.

von Wowern, J. (ed.) 1626. *Petronius Arbiter, Satyricon, cum uberioribus, Commentarij instar, Notis*, Amsterodami: Guiljelmus I. Caesius.

Wheler, G. 1682. *A Journey into Greece*, London: William Cademan, Robert Kettlewell, and Awnsham Churchill.

Robert H. F. Carver
Bologna as Hypata: Annotation, Transformation, and Transl(oc)ation in the Circles of Filippo Beroaldo and Francesco Colonna

Abstract: Beroaldo's commentary on the *Asinus aureus* (Bologna, 1500) and the *Hypnerotomachia Poliphili* attributed to Francesco Colonna (Venice, 1499) are two of the richest legacies of the Renaissance reception of Apuleius. The enterprise of editing, annotating, reading, and imitating Classical authors such as Apuleius involved, for Beroaldo and his circle, a degree of cognitive (and moral) realignment: Lucius' metamorphosis from a donkey into a disciple of Isis serves as a metaphor for the transforming effects of the *studia humanitatis*. And the physical space of the folio page (commentary enveloping text) becomes a cultural *locus*, a site of personal and social, as well as critical and creative negotiation. Conversely, while creating an extravagant fiction of an Apuleian hero (Poliphilo) obsessed with the erotic embodiment of Antiquity (Polia), Colonna also invites his readers to re-enact the processes of Renaissance humanists as they try to reassemble the scattered fragments of the past and allow the dead to speak.

1 *Fabula ... de situ civitatis huius exorta*

At the beginning of Book Two of *The Golden Ass*, Lucius awakes after his first night in Milo's house and immediately goes out to explore the town of Hypata:

> Ut primum nocte discussa sol novus diem fecit, et somno simul emersus et lectulo, anxius alioquin et nimis cupidus cognoscendi quae rara miraque sunt, reputansque me media Thessaliae loca tenere, quo artis magicae nativa cantamina totius orbis consono ore celebrentur fabulamque illam optimi comitis Aristomenis *de situ civitatis huius exortam*, suspensus alioquin et voto simul et studio, curiose singula considerabam. (*Met.* 2,1)

> As soon as night had been scattered and a new sun brought day, I emerged from sleep and bed alike. With my anxiety and my excessive passion to learn the rare and the marvellous, considering that I was staying in the middle of Thessaly, the native land of those spells of the magic art which are unanimously praised throughout the entire world, and recalling that the story told by my excellent comrade Aristomenes had originated at the site of

Robert H. F. Carver, University of Durham

https://doi.org/10.1515/9781501503986-017

this very city, I was on tenterhooks of desire and impatience alike, and I began to examine each and every object with curiosity.[1]

Apuleius powerfully evokes the experience of the young sightseer – that vertiginous mix of anxiety and anticipation engendered by being in an unfamiliar city. In some ways, he behaves as though he is still asleep: the world that he encounters has a quality of the *somnium* about it. He cannot believe that anything is as it appears:

> *Nec fuit in illa civitate quod aspiciens id esse crederem quod esset, sed omnia prorsus ferali murmure in aliam effigiem translata, ut et lapides quos offenderem de homine duratos, et aves quas audirem indidem plumatas, et arbores quae pomerium ambirent similiter foliatas, et fontanos latices de corporibus humanis fluxos crederem; iam statuas et imagines incessuras, parietes locuturos, boves et id genus pecua dicturas praesagium, de ipso vero caelo et iubaris orbe subito venturum oraculum.* (*Met.* 2,1)

Nothing I looked at in that city seemed to me to be what it was; but I believed that absolutely everything had been transformed into another shape by some deadly mumbo-jumbo: the rocks I hit upon were petrified human beings, the birds I heard were feathered humans, the trees that surrounded the city walls were humans with leaves, and the liquid in the fountains had flowed from human bodies. Soon the statues and pictures would begin to walk, the walls to speak, the oxen and other animals of that sort to prophesy; and from the sky itself and the sun's orb there would suddenly come an oracle.

But Lucius is also reading the city in terms of the tale that he has heard from Aristomenes in the previous book (*Met.* 1,5–19). He is mapping the narrative onto the place: the heart (*media loca*) of Thessaly. Apuleius anticipates Cervantes in *Don Quixote* (1605) and Jane Austen in *Northanger Abbey* (1817), where the protagonist's perception of the world is distorted by an excessive diet of unhealthy fiction – chivalric romances in Cervantes' case, and Gothic novels in Austen's. I would also like to suggest, however, that the passage serves as a paradigm for some of the ways in which Renaissance humanists and writers engaged with Apuleius, and that the fruits of those engagements require us to enlarge our sense of the potential of, and relationship between, scholarly and literary discourses.

Petrarch begins a letter to Cardinal Giovanni Colonna (d. 1348) with an account of how he 'travelled through France, not on business [note the emphatic inversion of Apuleius' *ex negotio* in *Met.* 1,2] ... but simply out of a youthful ardour and zeal for sight-seeing' (*Gallias ego nuper nullo quidem negotio ... sed visendi tantum studio et iuvenili quodam ardore peragravi*). Lucius' encounter with

---

[1] Text and translation taken from Hanson's Loeb edition of Apuleius (1989).

Hypata (*Met.* 2,1) becomes an ironic model for the early humanist's attempt to disentangle fact from fiction on his first visit to Paris:

> *Introii non aliter animo affectus quam olim Thesalie civitatem Ypatham dum lustrat, Apuleius. Ita enim solicito stupore suspensus et cuncta circumspiciens, videndi cupidus explorandique vera ne ad ficta essent que de illa civitate audieram, non parvum in ea tempus absumpsi, et quotiens operi lux defuit, noctem superaddidi. Demum ambiendo et inhiando, magna ex parte didicisse videor quis in eadem veritati, quis fabulis locus sit.*
>
> I must have felt much the same upon entering the town [*sc*. Paris] as did Apuleius when he wandered about Hypata in Thessaly. I spent no little time there, in open-mouthed wonder; and I was so full of interest and eagerness to know the truth about what I had heard of the place that when daylight failed me I even prolonged my investigations into the night. After loitering about for a long time, gaping at the sights, I at last satisfied myself that I had discovered the point where truth left off and fiction began.[2]

Petrarch uses the term *nuper*, but this is actually the work of a mature man reflecting on his youthful past and describing his own *paideia*. And the Apuleian allusion is part of a wider discussion of the *translatio studii et imperii*, the complex negotiations between cultural 'capital' and political power which feature so significantly in *The Golden Ass* itself, most obviously in the prologue (*Met.* 1,1).

The description of Hypata also appears to have had a seminal effect on the imagination of the young Shakespeare. Apuleius supplies much of the atmosphere of deceit and confusion that pervades one of his earliest works, *The Comedy of Errors* (*c.* 1592), where Antipholus of Syracuse, newly arrived in Ephesus, resolves to 'wander up and down to view the city':

> They say this town is full of cozenage,
> As nimble jugglers that deceive the eye,
> Dark-working sorcerers that change the mind,
> Soul-killing witches that deform the body,
> Disguisèd cheaters, prating mountebanks,
> And many suchlike libertines of sin ...[3]

Looking at Hypata, Lucius observes that 'All things have been transformed (*translata*) into another shape'. In Agnolo Firenzuola's *L'asino d'oro* (begun in the 1520s but only published in 1550), Apuleius' *fabula Graecanica* (*Met.* 1,1) is transformed into *una tosca favola* ('a Tuscan tale'). Lucius becomes Agnolo him-

---

2 Petrarca 1955, I, 4, 1; Robinson 1898, 300. See Carver 2007, 124–127.
3 Act 1, sc. 2, lines 31 and 97–102. The theme of transformation recurs in the play (e.g. Luciana's remark at Act 2, sc. 2, line 202: 'If thou art changed to aught, 'tis to an ass'). For Shakespeare's use of Apuleius, see Carver 2007, 429–445, and Carver 2013, 273–306.

self, equipped with letters from Florence, and he enjoys the miserly hospitality not of Milo at Hypata, but of 'Petronio' at Bologna.[4] The choice of names and towns can hardly have been accidental: the fourth-century bishop, Petronius, is the patron saint of Bologna, and the city's most famous landmark is the 'Tower of the Little Donkeys' (*Torre degli Asinelli*) mentioned in Filippo Beroaldo's commentary on the *Asinus aureus* (Bologna: Benedictus Hectoris, 1500). Glossing *Asinium Marcellum* (*Met.* 11,27), Beroaldo observes:

> *Celebrati sunt inter oratores Asinius Pollio, & Asinius Gallus. In patria mea gens Asiniorum fuit olim florentissima opulentissimaque: à qua turris in minusculo foro constructa conuisitur, quam à conditoribus in ho[765]diernum usque cognominant turrim Asiniorum, quæ altitudine structuræque æquilibrio est Bononiæ spectatissima.* [Beroaldo (1597?), Part II, 764–765]

> Amongst the orators, Asinius Pollio and Asinius Gallus are celebrated. In my own hometown, the *gens Asiniorum* was once exceptionally successful and wealthy: the tower built by them in the tiny forum is an object of great attention; even today, on account of its builders it is known as the 'Tower of the Asinii'. In terms of height and harmony of structure, it is the most spectacular in Bologna.

2 *omnia ... in aliam effigiem translata*

But Firenzuola's description of Bologna as a city in which *tutto fusse per incanto trasmutata in quella forma* (cf. *Met.* 2,1) could be seen as a double-edged acknowledgement of the metamorphic aspects of Beroaldo's commentary. Beroaldo saw his commentary as a tool for softening and polishing any 'hardness' or 'harshness' that a reader might find in Apuleius (*In quo si quid durum uidebitur id nostrorum commentariorum expolitione emollietur*, 1500, fol. 1^v). But the whole business of editing, annotating, reading, and imitating Classical authors such as Apuleius involved, for Beroaldo and his circle, a transformation of self: Lucius' metamorphosis from a donkey into a disciple of Isis becomes a metaphor for the transformative effects of the *studia humanitatis*. In his preface (1500, fol. 2^v), Beroaldo famously identifies *inscitia* ('ignorance') as one of the drugs inducing bestiality, and *scientia* ('knowledge') as the 'roses' that restore the asinine self to human form.[5] In his commentary on *Met.* 11,13 (1500, fol. 266^r), the rose-garland is allegorized as *sapientia* ('wisdom') and Beroaldo addresses the students in his

---

4 Carver 2007, 254–256; Gaisser 2008, 275.
5 Carver 2007, 178–180 and 319–322.

audience directly: 'Do you wish to shed your bestial form?' (*Cupis exuere faciem ferinam?*).[6]

Beroaldo's immediate audience was drawn from all over Europe (when he died in 1505, he was mourned as 'the universal teacher of all nations', *communis omnium gentium praeceptor*), but the Teutonic element was particularly strong.[7] His question (*Cupis exuere faciem ferinam?*) is echoed by one of his German students at Bologna who became a notable Northern humanist. Konrad Muth (Conradus Mutianus Rufus, 1471–1526) describes the 'humanization' of German men of letters (who discarded their baptismal names for Latin identities) as an Apuleian transformation:

> *Postquam vero renatus es et pro Iheger Crotus, pro Dornheim Rubianus salutatus, ceciderunt et aures prelonge et cauda pensilis et pilus impexus, quod sibi accidisse dicit Apuleius, cum adhuc asinus esset ... restitueretur sibi, hoc est humanitati.*
>
> But after you were reborn and greeted as 'Crotus' instead of 'Jäger', 'Rubianus' instead of 'Dornheim', your enormously long ears fell off along with your drooping tail and uncombed hide, which is what Apuleius said happened to him when, having hitherto been an ass, ... he was restored to his real self, that is, to humanity.

Muth adds: 'You easily recognize the wretchedness of those who have not yet shed their barbarousness' (*facile cognoscis, quam miseri sint, qui nondum barbariam exuerunt*).[8]

3 *Comites* and *condiscipuli*

I have used the term 'circles' in my title, but this may be misleading. Instead of imagining closed communities of 'like-minded' people, it would be better to think of a complex network – a multiplicity of interconnected webs – of 'similarly able' scholars, distinguished by antiquarian appetites and linguistic hypersensitivity.[9] We should also note the word *comes* ('companion') applied to Aristomenes (*Met.* 2,1). We might set it against other sociative labels which occur in Book One: *contubernalis* (literally 'tent-mate'), used by Aristomenes of Socrates

---

6 Gaisser 2008, 219–221.
7 de Pins 1505, 125.
8 Muth 1890, 344; Carver 2007, 247. Of course, the transformational vector could easily be reversed: from the fifteenth to the seventeenth centuries, there are multiple variations on Lorenzo Valla's assertion that those who imitate the stylistic 'excesses' of Apuleius end up braying (*rudere*) like donkeys, rather than speaking like men. See Carver 2007, 262–284, esp. 263.
9 On the role of Apuleius within Renaissance sodalities, see Carver 2007, 236–262.

(*Met.* 1,6), and *condiscipulus*, used of Pythias, Lucius' 'fellow-student' at Athens (*Met.* 1,24).[10] In each case, the association proves unfruitful: Aristomenes is unable to save Socrates from the fatal effects of his congress with Meroë; and Lucius' brief reunion with Pythias will leave him 'deprived at once of [his] money and [his] supper by the strong counsel of [his] wise fellow-student' (*prudentis condiscipuli valido consilio et nummis simul privates et cena*, *Met.* 1,25). Jean de Pins, however, will apply both these terms to someone he names in his biography of Beroaldo: *Stephanus Pannonius, cognomento Brodarichus Zagroviensis contubernalis ante & condiscipulus meus* ('Stephen the Pannonian, surnamed Brodarichus of Zagreb, my fellow-student and former room-mate').[11]

Jean de Pins' description of Istvàn Brodarics (an outsider by birth, but admitted – thanks to his learning – into the sodality) is an addendum to one of the digressions or *flosculi* ('little flowers') that Beroaldo scatters amongst his commentaries, purportedly as a form of light relief to his audience.[12] A celebrated instance is the disquisition on the Bolognese artist Francesco Francia, sparked by Lucius' account of Art emulating Nature in the statue of Diana and Actaeon (*Met.* 2,4).[13] I would like to look instead, however, at the verbal portrait of someone whom Francia actually painted, Bartolomeo Bianchini.[14] It comes in Beroaldo's discussion of the virtuous and well-educated young man (*Dominus aedium habebat iuuenem filium probe litteratum atque ob id consequenter pietate, modestia praecipuum ..., Met.* 10,2) plagued by the incestuous lust of his step-mother:

> *Idolon & simulachrum huiusce iuuenis probissimi, quem Lucius noster hoc in loco describit: est Bartholomæus Blanchinus, municeps meus: qui nobili genere natus, bonis moribus ornatus, literis literatis excultus, auditor meus, mihique summa beneuolentia copulatus, effingit ac repræsentat iuuenem ex omni parte laudabilem. Dotibus animi accedunt bona corporis atque fortunæ. Diligit doctos, & me in [458] primis: contubernio proborum artificum lætatur, maximeque pictorum. Habet domi ueluti in larario nomismata ex auro & argento compluscula, quibus minutæ magnorum uirorum facies expressæ conspiciuntur: ocium & quietem literariam cumprimis probat & sectatur, modestia & probitate præcipuus uiuit in cœlibatu, quamuis eum generum optent summates: prorsusque huic Apuleiano iuueni cætera simillimus, nisi quòd nec patrem habet, nec nouercam domi: & melioribus annis natus, fortunatius degit:*

---

10 Cf. the use of the terms *sodalis*, *contubernalis*, and *parasitus* to describe the asinine Lucius at *Met.* 10,16. Lucius initially revels in the attention paid to him and the food and drink received, but his congress with the Corinthian *matrona* (*Met.* 10,19–23) leads directly to his (threatened) engagement with the condemned woman (and the beast sent to devour her) in the theatre (*Met.* 10,23).
11 de Pins 1505, 146.
12 On *flosculi*, see Gaisser 2008, 224–225.
13 Baxandall and Gombrich 1962; Warren 1999; Gaisser 2008, 225–229.
14 Bianchini's portrait is now in the National Gallery, London.

nec insidias nouercales pertimescit, quibus obnoxius fuit hic, quem Lucius noster perscribit dilectum esse à nouerca, amore incesto et infando. [Beroaldo (1597?), Part II, 457–458][15]

The image and perfect copy of this most upright young man whom our Lucius describes in this passage is Bartolomeo Bianchini, my fellow citizen. Born of a noble family, endowed with a good character, cultivated in the literary arts, a student of mine and bound to me by the greatest good will, he forges and represents a young man worthy of praise in every respect. To his intellectual gifts are added the advantages of physique and fortune. He loves learned people, and me most of all. He has at home – as though in a shrine – more than a few coins of gold and silver, in which are seen expressed in miniature the images of great men. He values and seeks, above all, leisure and quiet for literature, and, distinguished by his modesty and uprightness, he lives as a bachelor, although the most powerful men would love to have him as a son-in-law. In other respects, he is most similar to this Apuleian young man, except that he does not have a father nor a step-mother at home, and, having been born in better times, he fares more fortunately: nor does he fear a step-mother's snares to which was exposed this [young man] whom our Lucius describes as being loved by his step-mother with an unchaste and unspeakable love.

Bianchini is defined according to his relations to the city and to the person: he is Beroaldo's *municeps meus*, a 'fellow citizen' of Bologna; and he is (or has been) a student of his (an *auditor*), someone who has listened to his lectures and who loves not merely learning in the abstract, but the learned men (*docti*) who expound that learning. His collection of ancient coins (things dug up and put on display much like old words in this milieu) shows that he understands how great men should be honoured. And indeed Bianchini will go on to compose a biography of Beroaldo published in 1506 in an edition of Suetonius.[16]

What is particularly interesting about this passage is the utterly shameless way in which the commentator simply ignores the lineaments of Apuleius' plot (the incestuous step-mother) while insisting that Bianchini is the *Idolon & simulachrum* of Apuleius' young man. This is not so much Art imitating Life, as Life actually imitating Art. Alongside Apuleius' text, Beroaldo is fashioning his own para-text, and peopling it with characters taken from his immediate world, the cosmopolis of Bologna. Indeed, when we look within, and to the side of, these annotations on Apuleius, we find all sorts of quasi- or para- or meta-fictional discourses.[17]

---

15 de Pins 1505, 145–146, reproduces the passage before adding his account of Istvàn Brodarics.
16 See Bibliography.
17 For Cardano's account (1663 i, 38) of how he magically learned Latin simply by purchasing a gilded copy of Apuleius, see Carver 2007, 345. We might also note a comic account of Apuleius being hit by 'his Golden Ass' while grooming him in the stables – to the great distress of Beroaldo. See Boccalini 1656, the XCIIIrd Advertisement, 384–385.

4 *Nimis cupidus cognoscendi quae rara miraque sunt*

The opening of Book Two serves as a model for some of the other ways in which Renaissance humanists (particularly those associated with the Bolognese school) engaged with Apuleius' text. Lucius is *nimis cupidus cognoscendi* ('excessively eager to know') and the object of his lust is the class of 'unusual and marvellous things' (*quae rara miraque sunt*). In the biography published just after Beroaldo's death in 1505, another former student, Jean de Pins, describes his old master's approach:

> *Demum* ... in Lucii Apulei asinum aureum *vere aureos et pene divinos commentarios excudit: quos sic multarum & variarum rerum ubertate refersit, sic multiplici literarum cognitione ditavit, quas sæpenumero ex intimis civilis pontificiique juris, philosophiæ, sacrarum literarum ac medicinæ penetralibus eruit, ut veterem illum* Pisonem Domitium *imitatus, non tam quidem libros, quam rerum thesauros scripsisse videatur* (J. de Pins 1505, 141)

> Finally ..., he fashioned his truly golden and almost divine commentaries on *The Golden Ass* of Lucius Apuleius; he so enriched them with his manifold knowledge of literature; he stuffed them with such an abundance of many and varied items which he often dug out of the inmost recesses of civil and canon law, philosophy, scripture, and medicine, that he seems – in imitation of that ancient Piso Domitius – to have written not so much books as store-houses of things.[18]

Simon Goldhill has given us a vivid formulation of the function of handbooks in the ancient (and modern) world: 'Handbooks are ways of packaging cultures under threat.'[19] I would not wish to argue with that description. But a *thesaurus* can also be a place in which valuables are displayed: it has a performative as well as a defensive function, and it is a vital component of what we might call the *cornucopian* fictions so beloved by Renaissance humanists. It was this performative aspect of the Bolognese school – in particular, the imitation of Apuleius' language – to which so many humanists objected, especially in the sixteenth and seventeenth centuries.[20] Erasmus' Folly makes fun of this kind of philological archaeology when she talks of a perverse form of *voluptas*:

---

18 Cf. Pliny the Elder, *praefatio* to *Historia naturalis*: [17] [...] *quoniam, ut ait Domitius Piso, thesauros oportet esse, non libros* ('Since, as Domitius Piso says, it is store-houses that are needed, not books').
19 Goldhill 2008.
20 Carver 2007, 262–284.

> *Iam adde et hoc voluptatis genus, quoties istorum aliquis Anchisae matrem aut voculam vulgo incognitam in putri quapiam charta deprehenderit, puta bubsequam, bouinatorem aut manticulatorem, aut si quis vetusti saxi fragmentum, mutilis notatum literis alicubi effoderit: o Iupiter, quae tum exultatio, qui triumphi, quae encomia, perinde quasi vel Africam deuicerint vel Babylonas ceperint!*[21]
>
> Then there's this further type of pleasure. Whenever one of them digs out of some mouldy manuscript the name of Anchises' mother or some trivial word the ordinary man doesn't know, such as neatherd, tergiversator, cutpurse, or if anyone unearths a scrap of old stone with a fragmentary inscription, O Jupiter, what a triumph! What rejoicing, what eulogies! They might have conquered Africa or captured Babylon.[22]

Beroaldo gives a good deal of attention to the Apuleianism, *bubsequa* (*Met.* 8,1), but the word also turns up in one of the most important examples of humanist fiction, the *Hypnerotomachia Poliphili*, published in Venice in 1499 by Aldus Manutius and attributed (controversially) to a certain Francesco Colonna.[23] This work is in many respects a mosaic of Apuleian language and themes.[24] Conventional wisdom denies (unjustly, in my opinion) a link between the Venetian publication of 1499 and the Bolognese commentary of 1500, but it is possible to trace significant connections between the circles of Beroaldo and Aldus.[25]

We might also consider the use of another word, *rimabundus*, an Apuleian *hapax legomenon*.[26] While they are waiting for Lord Cupid, Poliphilo (an amiable but somewhat foolish neophiliac, much like Lucius himself) becomes inflamed with desire, and Polia (the beloved who combines the features of Fotis, Psyche, and Isis) distracts him by persuading him to indulge again in his passion for 'the works of antiquity'.[27] Amongst the ruins he finds a cemetery (*Polyandrion*) devoted to those who died maddened by love.

In one place, he discovers an underground chamber covered by a metal grille:

> *per laqualcosa accenso di curiosa cupidine di potere ad questa parte descendere rimabondo tra quelle fracture, & minutie & ruine perquirendo qualche meato.* (Colonna 1499, sig. p8ʳ)

---

21 Erasmus 1979, IV-3, 138.
22 Erasmus 1971, 145 [= ch. 49].
23 On *bu(b)sequa*, see Carver 2007, 188–190.
24 Carver 2007, 183–235.
25 Connecting figures include Marcantonio Sabellico and Conrad Celtis. See Carver 2007, 237–242. Beroaldo's commentary 'was already well advanced by 1496'. See Gaisser 2008, 199.
26 Carver 2007, 200–202.
27 Godwin 1999, 242.

> Possessed by an inquisitive desire to go down there, I rummaged through the debris and ruined fragments, searching for some passage.[28]

Rimabondo stands out in this passage. Apuleius seems to have coined its source, *rimabundus*, to describe Lucius' minute examination of Diana and Actaeon at the centre of Byrrhena's atrium: *Dum haec identidem rimabundus eximie delector* ('while I derive uncommon delight from examining these things again and again', *Met.* 2,5).[29] *Rimor* can mean to 'lay open', to 'rummage', but *rima* ('cleft', or 'chink') seems to give *rimabundus* the sense of 'looking into every nook and cranny.'[30] *Rimabondo* is hence the perfect term to describe both the ocular and the physical activity as Poliphilo rummages amongst the ruins on the surface in search of some 'chink' that will afford him access to the treasures below. But the resonances extend still further. The irony of *rimabundus* is that while Lucius revels in the 'sheen' (*nitore*) of the marble and the verisimilitude of the 'most skilfully polished grapes' (*uuae faberrime politae*), he is unable to assemble the delightful details into any larger meaning and hence fails to see that Actaeon, leaning towards Diana 'with an inquisitive gaze' (*curioso optutu*, *Met.* 2,4) is a warning to himself.[31] The same charge of a lack of perspective is often made against the Bolognese humanists, especially Beroaldo's pupil (and, later, rival) Giovanni Battitsta Pio, the most ardent of the so-called 'Apuleianists'.[32]

But Colonna also uses the monuments in the cemetery as a way of intercalating short but complete tales into his main narrative. He is adapting the humanist genre of *syllogai* – collections of inscriptions compiled by Cyriaco d'Ancona and his successors – to achieve the nesting effects made famous by the likes of Apuleius and Boccaccio. The woodcuts show us a succession of Latin epitaphs, among them that of P. Cornelia Anna (a virtuous contrast to Petronius'

---

28 Godwin 1999, 247.
29 Cf. Beroaldo 1500, fol. 35ʳ: *Rimabundus: Speculabundus: uehementerque contemplans: nomina enim in bundus definentia: non tam significant similitudinem ut grammatici hallucinantur: quam uim & copiam: & quasi habundantiam rei* ('Rimabundus: "on the look-out" and "observing with great intensity". For words ending in *-bundus* do not signify likeness, as grammarians wrongly imagine, so much as force and *copia*, and, as it were, abundance of material').
30 Note the description of the transgressive (and soon-to-be-punished) Psyche as she gazes upon Cupid for the first time: *insatiabili animo Psyche satis curiosa rimatur* … ('Psyche scrutinizes with an insatiable mind but sufficient curiosity', *Met.* 5,23).
31 Hence Byrrhena's laconic remark, *Tua sunt … cuncta quae vides* ('Everything you see is yours', *Met.* 2,5). Note that Lucius will be transformed into an ass after peering at the naked Pamphile through a 'crack' in the door (*per … rimam ostiorum*, *Met.* 3,21).
32 Carver 2007, 270–271, 273–275, 278–280, 293.

Widow of Ephesus) who allowed herself 'to be condemned, living, to this tomb with my dead husband'.[33]

When re-told out of context, these lapidary tales of unfortunate lovers may seem like *facetiae* – mere anecdotes or dark-humoured squibs: the lover dragged to his death by his own horse when he dismounts to meet his lady and catches his foot in the stirrup (sig. q8^v); the virgin newly-weds, killed on their wedding-night as the house collapses on them just as they clasp one another for the first time (sig. r3^r). We might compare Rabelais' long list (4,17) of unusual deaths, including those of the 'bashfull Fool who by holding in his Wind, and for want of letting out a Bumgunshot dy'd suddenly in the presence of the Emperor *Claudius*', and 'the *Italian* buried on the *Via Flaminia* at *Rome* who in his Epitaph, complains that the bite of a she-Puss on his [75] little finger was the cause of his death' (Rabelais 1694, 74–75).

But Colonna is teasing our sensibilities in far more subtle ways. Poliphilo comes across some fragments of a mosaic:

> *Ove picto mirai uno homo affligente una damicella. Et uno naufragio. Et uno adolescentulo sopra il suo dorso equitante una fanciulla, natava ad uno littore deserto. Et parte vedevasi di uno leone. Et quegli dui in una navicula remiganti. Il sequente distructo. Et ancora questa parte era in molti lochi lacerata, non valeva intendere totalmente la historia. Ma nel pariete crustato marmoreo, era intersepta una tabula aenea, cum maiuscule graecae. Tale epigramma inscripto havea. Il quale nel proprio idiomate in tanta pietate me provocava legendo sì miserando caso, che di lachryme contenirme non potui, damnando la rea fortuna. Il quale saepicule perlegendo, quanto io ho potuto cusì il fece latino.*

> Here I saw a picture of a man troubling a maiden, and a shipwreck; also a little youth swimming to a deserted shore with a girl riding on his back. And part of a lion was visible, and these two rowing in a boat, but the rest was destroyed, and even these parts were damaged in many places. One could not understand the whole story. However, let into the pavement of inlaid marble was a brass tablet with Greek capital letters that had this epigram inscribed on it, which when I had read this sad tale in my own language provoked such feeling in me that I could not contain my tears, cursing and blaming fortune. After reading it over many times, I was able to turn it thus into Latin:[34]

We are witnesses here to some highly sophisticated narrative effects. Poliphilo foregrounds the act of translation in a manner reminiscent of Apuleius' prologue – *Fabulam graecanicam incipimus* ('We begin a Greekish tale', *Met.* 1,1) – or, more specifically, of the beginning of the tale of Cupid and Psyche in Book 4, where Psyche's father goes to consult the oracle at Delphi, and Apollo, making a spe-

---

33 Colonna 1499, sig. q7r; Godwin 1999, 261 and 470.
34 Colonna 1499, sig. q5^r; Godwin 1999, 257.

cial concession to 'the author of this Milesian tale' (*propter Milesiae conditorem, Met.* 4,32), condescends to deliver his message in Latin instead of in Greek. Colonna's woodcut (sig. q5ᵛ) purports to be a faithful image of the inscription seen by Poliphilo, but the accompanying text makes it clear that the Greek has been translated (the Homeric *polystonos*, 'much-sighing, mournful', in line 2 is a teasing vestige of the supposed 'original'). So, while the author certainly eases the reader's path by turning from one learned language to another, he inserts new obstacles by making the inscription we face a Latin simulacrum of the original epitaph. The text of the epitaph (one of the longest in the cemetery) is transmitted to us not by metal type but by means of a woodcut (condensed into a single tablet on one page, Colonna 1499, sig. q5ᵛ; Godwin 1999, 258) depicting the 'brass tablet' itself (Figure 1).

Colonna's occlusive or exclusive strategies may seem perverse (or merely playful) to a modern audience, but they have a serious dimension. The author forces his reader to relive the experience of the humanists as they try to come to terms with the 'pastness' of Classical Antiquity, to reconstitue its fragments, to revivify its dead for the benefit of the living. Beroaldo (as we saw) promoted the emollient qualities of his work: 'if anything in [*The Golden Ass*] seems hard, it will be softened by the polishing of our commentaries' (1500, fol. 1ᵛ). In Colonna's case, we are forced to expend a good deal of effort to make the hard surface of the 'page' (brass set into marble) *yield* in any way. The opening lines of the inscription are particularly resistant, but the 'wayfarer' is invited to apply 'kisses' to the monument (*metallo oscula dato*).[35] And just as Pygmalion's erotic devotion to his statue causes the marble to soften into flesh (Ovid *Met.* 10,243–297), so too the scholarly reader's commitment to decoding the text of the 'Latin' inscription – inserting (or correcting) word-divisions (beginning with an easy conversion of *HEV SVIATOR* to *heus viator*), expanding contractions, filling lacunae, and translating the resulting sequence – enables the dead to tell their tales.[36] Thus, the seemingly static forms of Colonna's ecphrastic discourse can be seen as enact-

---

[35] Pozzi and Ciapponi (eds) 1980, II, 185, offer two possible expansions of the opening lines: either *Heus viator paululum inter se<pulchra> re<...> manib<us> adiurat<is>, prodi, tum ac legens*, or *Heus, viator paululum inters<is>, ere<bi> manib<us> adiurat<is>, proditam ac legens* (the latter being the text broadly followed by Godwin 1999, 469–470).

[36] Note that many of the first-person narratives on the monuments contain privileged information about the lovers which could not have been available to the person carving the inscription. This is certainly one of the 'novelistic' effects in the work.

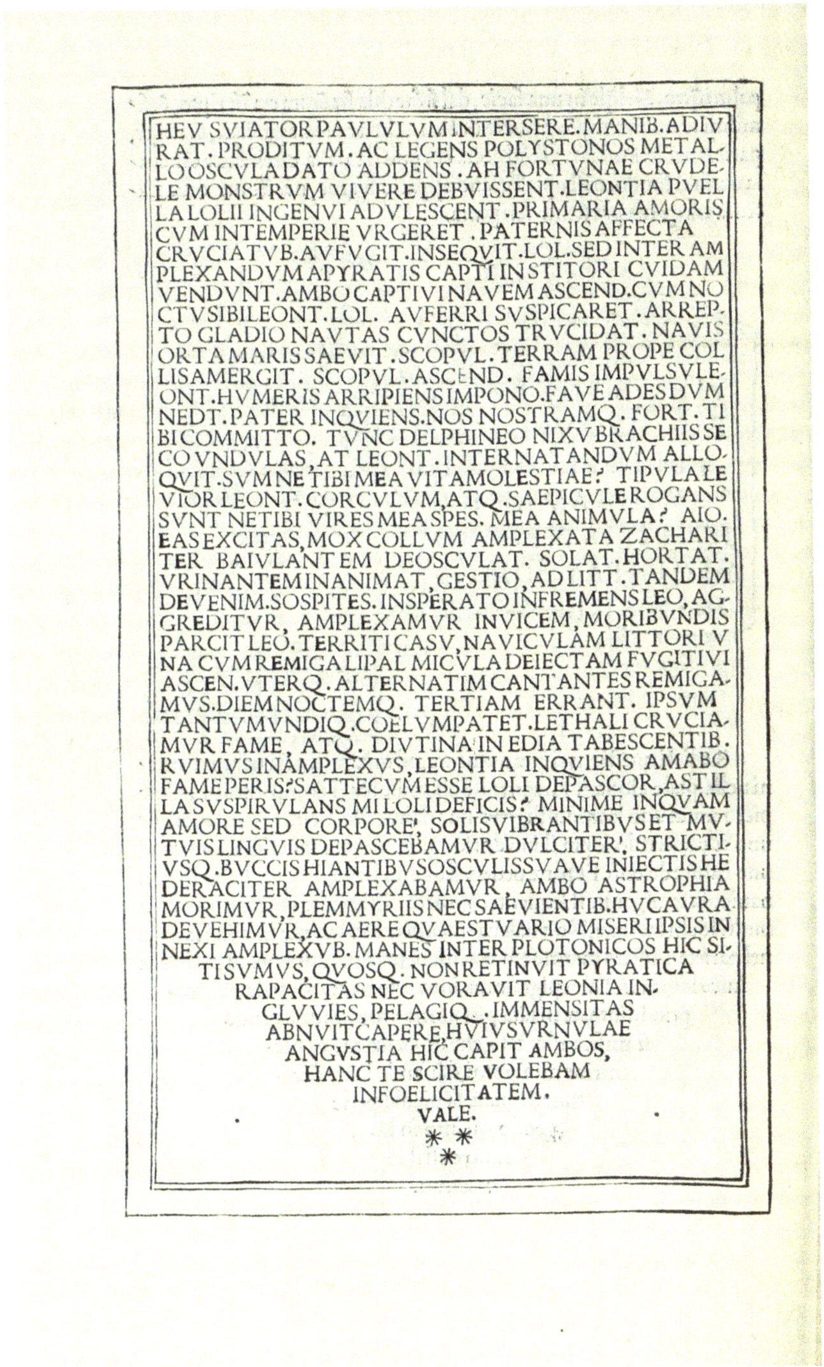

HEV SVIATOR PAVLVLVM INTERSERE. MANIB. ADIV-
RAT. PRODITVM. AC LEGENS POLYSTONOS METAL-
LO OSCVLA DATO ADDENS. AH FORTVNAE CRVDE-
LE MONSTRVM VIVERE DEBVISSENT. LEONTIA PVEL-
LA LOLII INGENVI ADVLESCENT. PRIMARIA AMORIS
CVM INTEMPERIE VRGERET. PATERNIS AFFECTA
CRVCIATVB. AVFVGIT. INSEQVIT. LOL. SED INTER AM-
PLEXANDVM A PYRATIS CAPTI INSTITORI CVIDAM
VENDVNT. AMBO CAPTIVI NAVEM ASCEND. CVM NO-
CTV SIBI LEONT. LOL. AVFERRI SVSPICARET. ARREP-
TO GLADIO NAVTAS CVNCTOS TRVCIDAT. NAVIS
ORTA MARIS SAEVIT. SCOPVL. TERRAM PROPE COL-
LISA MERGIT. SCOPVL. ASCEND. FAMIS IMPVLSV LE-
ONT. HVMERIS ARRIPIENS IMPONO. FAVE ADES DVM
NEDT. PATER INQVIENS. NOS NOSTRAMQ. FORT. TI-
BI COMMITTO. TVNC DELPHINEO NIXV BRACHIIS SE
CO VNDVLAS, AT LEONT. INTERNATANDVM ALLO-
QVIT. SVM NE TIBI MEA VITA MOLESTIAE? TIPVLA LE-
VIOR LEONT. CORCVLVM, ATQ. SAEPICVLE ROGANS
SVNT NE TIBI VIRES MEA SPES. MEA ANIMVLA? AIO.
EAS EXCITAS, MOX COLLVM AMPLEXATA ZACHARI-
TER BAIVLANTEM DEOSCVLAT. SOLAT. HORTAT.
VRINANTEM INANIMAT, GESTIO, AD LITT. TANDEM
DEVENIM. SOSPITES. INSPERATO INFREMENS LEO, AG-
GREDITVR, AMPLEXAMVR INVICEM, MORIBVNDIS
PARCIT LEO. TERRITI CASV, NAVICVLAM LITTORI V-
NA CVM REMIGA LIPAL MICVLA DEIECTAM FVGITIVI
ASCEN. VTERQ. ALTERNATIM CANTANTES REMIGA-
MVS. DIEM NOCTEMQ. TERTIAM ERRANT. IPSVM
TANTVM VNDIQ. COELVM PATET. LETHALI CRVCIA-
MVR FAME. ATQ. DIVTINA INEDIA TABESCENTIB.
RVIMVS IN AMPLEXVS, LEONTIA INQVIENS AMABO
FAME PERIS? SAT TECVM ESSE LOLI DEPASCOR, AST IL-
LA SVSPIR VLANS MI LOLI DEFICIS? MINIME INQVAM
AMORE SED CORPORE', SOLIS VIBRANTIBVS ET MV-
TVIS LINGVIS DEPASCEBAMVR DVLCITER', STRICTI-
VSQ. BVCCIS HIANTIBVS OSCVLISSVAVE INIECTIS HE-
DERACITER AMPLEXABAMVR, AMBO ASTROPHIA
MORIMVR, PLEMMYRIIS NEC SAEVIENTIB. HVC AVRA
DEVEHIMVR, AC AERE QVAEST VARIO MISERI IPSIS IN-
NEXI AMPLEXVB. MANES INTER PLOTONICOS HIC SI-
TI SVMVS, QVOSQ. NON RETINVIT PYRATICA
RAPACITAS NEC VORAVIT LEONIA IN-
GLVVIES, PELAGIQ. IMMENSITAS
ABNVIT CAPERE, HVIVS VRNVLAE
ANGVSTIA HIC CAPIT AMBOS,
HANC TE SCIRE VOLEBAM
INFOELICITATEM.
VALE.
✶ ✶
✶

Figure 1. *Hypnerotomachia Poliphili* (1499), sig. q5^v

ments of cognitive process,[37] at least for the 'erudite' *viator* (or, rather, *lector*) who was (or is) willing to tarry for more than 'a little while' (*paululum*) and reconstitute the text in something resembling the following form:

> Heus, viator paululum inters<is>, ere<bi> manib<us> adiurat<is>, proditum ac legens polystonos metallo oscula dato addens: 'Ah Fortunae crudele monstrum vivere debuissent!' Leontia puella Lolii ingenui adulescent<is> primaria amoris cum intemperie urgeret<ur>, paternis affecta cruciatub<us> aufugit; insequit<ur> Lol<ius>, sed inter amplexandum a pyratis capti institori cuidam vendunt<ur>. Ambo captivi navem ascend<imus>; cum noctu sibi Leont<iam> Lol<ius> auferri suspicaret<ur>, arrepto gladio, nautas cunctos trucidat. Navis, orta maris saevit<ia>, scopul<os> terram prope collisa mergit<ur>. Scopul<os> ascend<o>. Famis impulsu, Leont<iam> humeris arripiens impono, 'Fave, adesdum, Nept<une> pater-inquiens-nos nostramq<ue> fort<unam> tibi committo'. Tunc delphineo nixu brachiis seco undulas, at Leont<ia> inter natandum alloquit<ur>: [186] 'Sumne tibi, mea vita, molestiae?'. 'Tipula levior, Leont<ia>, corculum'. Atq<ue> saepicule rogans: suntne tibi vires, mea spes, mea animula?' aio: 'Eas excitas'. Mox, collum amplexata, zachariter baiulantem deosculat<ur>, solat<ur>, hortat<ur>, urinantem inanimat. Gestio; ad litt<us> tandem devenim<us> sospites. Insperato infremens leo aggreditur, amplexamur invicem: moribundis parcit leo. Territi casu, naviculam littori una cum remigali palmicula deiectam fugitiui ascen<dimus> vterq<ue>. Alternatim cantantes remigamus. Diem noctemq<ue> tertiam errant<es>, ipsum tantum undiq<ue> coelum patet. Lethali cruciamur fame atq<ue> diutina inedia tabescentib<us> ruimus in amplexus. 'Leontia – inquiens – amabo <te>, fame peris?' 'Sat tecum esse, Loli, depascor'. Ast illa suspirulans: 'Mi Loli, deficis?' 'Minime – inquam – amore, sed corpore'. Saviis vibrantibus et mutuis linguis depascebamur dulciter, strictiusq<ue>, buccis hiantibus, osculis suave iniectis, hederaciter amplexabamur. Ambo astrophia morimur, plemmyriis nec saevientib<us>. Huc aura devehimur, ac aere quaestuario miseri, ipsis innexi amplexub<us>, manes inter plotonicos hic siti sumus; quosq<ue> non retinuit pyratica rapacitas nec voravit leonis ingluvies pelagiq<ue> immensitas abnuit capere, huius urnulae angustia hic capit ambos. Hanc te scire volebam infoelicitatem. Vale.[38]

The modern reader may be surprised to discover that, despite its extreme compression, the 'sad tale' resembles, in many respects, a Greek ideal novel, complete with dialogue, but lacking the customary happy ending: young lovers (Lollius and Leontia), escaping parental opposition, are captured by pirates in an intimate moment, and sold to a slave-dealer. Lollius kills all the sailors but the ship sinks; the lovers swim to shore and survive the attentions of a lion, but then take to the sea again in a small boat; they attempt to sustain one an-

---

37 The quasi-macaronic language of Colonna's general narrative (a highly Latinate Italian with Greek admixtures) can also be read as an enactment of the dynamic exchanges continually taking place between past and present.
38 Pozzi and Ciapponi (eds) 1980, II, 185–186.

other other with vows and kisses, but they waste away to death and are wafted back to shore.

The pseudo-epitaph enriches our picture of the reception of the Greek novels during the early-modern period. Francesco Griffolini was able to borrow a copy of 'Eliodorus' history of matters in Ethiopia' from the Vatican Library in 1453.[39] By 1468, Cardinal Bessarion of Rome had accumulated three manuscripts of the *Aethiopica*.[40] And in 1489, Angelo Poliziano shows acquaintance not only with Heliodorus and Longus, but even with Xenophon of Ephesus, thanks to the existence at Florence of a thirteenth-century manuscript (now known as Codex Laurentianus Conventi Soppressi 627 or 'F') containing the latter two authors, as well as Achilles Tatius (up to 4,4) and Chariton.[41] But the story of 'Lollius and Leontia' provides some of the earliest evidence for the contribution of Greek prose fiction to an original literary creation in Western Europe.[42]

We might notice, in addition, verbal echoes of a non-ideal Roman novel: the phrase *hiantibus osculis* ('with eager kisses' or, more literally, 'with pretty mouths gaping wide') is one of the blandishments used by Lucius to persuade Fotis to reveal her mistress' magic arts (*Met.* 3,19), and it recurs – in reverse order, but in another manipulative context – in the description of the kiss bestowed by Venus after she has instructed Cupid to punish Psyche for her deity-defying beauty (*Met.* 4,34).

Of course, we know that many (if not most) of the purchasers of Colonna's book have not, until recently, co-operated with Poliphilo by reading and re-reading the text (*saepicule perlegendo*, sig. q5ʳ). Many of the surviving copies of the Aldine edition seem to have been possessed but little read. Girolamo Cardano even cites Colonna in a passage discussing antidotes to insomnia: 'Any time I read the *Hypnerotomachia*, I fall asleep at once' (*Ego cum audio Poliphili historiam statim dormio*).[43] The irony is that Godwin's translation (published exactly half a millenium after the original), by making the text speak so easily (one only has to turn to the appendix for an English version of the inscription) defeats that occlusive strategy – it forces the pseudo-novella of 'Lollius and Leontia' out into the open and, in so doing, exposes it as a parodic (but also emulous) compendium of early-novelistic clichés:

---

39 Reeve 2008, 282, citing Politianus, *Miscellaneorum centuria prima* (Florence, 1489).
40 Labowsky 1979, B 32, B 629, B 995; Doody 1997, 179; Carver 2007, 167.
41 Reeve 2008, 282.
42 The evidence would be even more significant if we could give any credence to the internal date recorded in the *Hypnerotomachia*: 1 May 1467 (Book II, sig. F3ʳ).
43 Cardano 1663, iii. 169. See Carver 2007, 190–191.

'Hail, wayfarer, and tarry awhile among the shades summoned here, then read with many a sigh and kiss the marble, saying: "Ah, monster of cruel Fortune! They should have lived." The girl Leontia, impelled by the first intemperance of love for Lollius, a noble youth, was tormented by her parents and fled. Lollius followed; but while embracing they were captured by pirates and sold to a slave-dealer. We both went on board as captives. When night fell, Lollius suspected that Leontia was being abducted, and seizing a sword he killed all the sailors. A rough sea arose; the ship collided with the rocks close to shore and sank. I climb the rocks. Driven by hunger, I seize Leontia, grasping her elbows: "Come hither and help us, father Neptune: I commit our fortune to you." Then with dolphin-like efforts you swim in his arms, but Leontia, while swimming, says: "Am I a burden to you, my life?" "Lighter than a water-spider, Leontia my heart." And she asks repeatedly: "Is your strength enough, my hope, my soul?" I say: "You arouse it!" Then embracing his neck she sweetly kisses her bearer, consoles and exhorts him, heartening the swimmer. I am exultant: we have finally reached the shore safely. A roaring lion comes up unexpectedly and we embrace each other; the lion spares us because we look dead. Frightened by this event, we escape by boarding a boat abandoned on the shore, with palms for oars. We row alternately, singing. After wandering for three days and nights, all that surrounds us is the sky. Tormented by mortal hunger and days of fasting, we fall in each other's arms. "Leontia," I say, "I will always love you. Are you dying from hunger?" "It is enough to be with you, Loli, for me to feed." But she sighs: "My Loli, are you weakening?" "Not at all in love," I say, "only in body." We fed sweetly with a mutual quivering of tongues and bestowed hard kisses on our open mouths, embracing like ivy. We both died by wasting away, not by the cruel seas. We were borne hither by the breeze, the miserable prey of air, caught in its embraces, and here we are laid among the Plutonian shades, whom piratical greed has not detained, nor the lion's gluttony devoured, nor the immensity of the sea captured. The narrow space of this little urn contains us both. I wanted you to know of this misfortune. Farewell.' (trans. Godwin 1999, 470–471)

Colonna's epitaph is a virtuoso display of concision, taking the conceit of *multum in parvo* ('Much in little') to its ultimate point – containing, as Christopher Marlowe might have said, 'Infinite sorrows in a little urn'.[44] But it is also an exemplification of the fact that fictional discourse, for these humanists, involves much more than simply pushing forward a plot. Indeed, the urn – a verbal and visual receptacle wrought with multi-layered and highly self-referential artifice – is in many ways even more fascinating than the narrative it contains. And much of its (peculiar) beauty is owed, I would argue, to the interdependent arts of the antiquarian, the annotator, and the proto-novelist.

---

44 Cf. Barabas in *The Jew of Malta* by Christopher Marlowe: 'Infinite riches in a little room' (1,1).

Bibliography

Baxandall, M., and Gombrich, E.H. 1962. 'Beroaldus on Francia', *JWCI* 25, 113–115.
Beroaldo, F. 1500. *Commentarii a Philippo Beroaldo conditi in asinum aureum Lucii Apulei*, Bologna: Benedictus Hectoris.
Beroaldo, F. [1597?]. *L. Apuleii Madaurensis philosophi Platonici Opera quæ quidem extant omnia. In primis verò de asino aureo libri XI. cum eruditissimis Philippi Beroaldi commentariis et Godescalci Stewichii Husdani in L. Apuleii Opera omnia Quæstionibus & Conjecturis*, Basel: per Sebastianum Henricpetri.
Bianchini, B. 1506. *Commentationes conditae a Philippo Beroaldo in Suetonium Tranquillum ... Eiusdem Philippi Beroaldi Vita per Bartholomeum Blanchinum composita*, Bologna: Benedictus Hectoris.
Boccalini, T. 1656. *I ragguagli di Parnasso, or, Advertisements from Parnassus in Two Centuries* (Henry, Earl of Monmouth, trans.), London: Humphrey Moseley ... and Thomas Heath.
Cardano, G. 1663. *Opera omnia* (C. Spon, ed.), Lyons: Jean-Antoine Huguetan and Marc-Antoine Rauaud.
Carver, R.H.F. 2007. *The Protean Ass: The 'Metamorphoses' of Apuleius from Antiquity to the Renaissance*, Oxford Classical Monographs, Oxford: Oxford University Press.
Carver, R.H.F. 2013. 'Defacing God's Work: Metamorphosis and the "Mimicall Asse" in the Age of Shakespeare', in: I. Gildenhard, A. Zissos (eds), *Transformative Change in Western Thought: A History of Metamorphosis from Homer to Hollywood*, Chapter 7, London: Legenda/Modern Humanities Research Association and Maney Publishing. 273–306.
Colonna, F. (attrib.) 1499. *Hypnerotomachia Poliphili* (Venetiis: Aldo Manuzio, 1499). Facs. ed., intro. P. Dronke, Zaragoza: Ediciones de Pórtico, 1981.
Doody, M.A. 1997. *The True Story of the Novel*, London: HarperCollins.
Erasmus, D. 1971. *Praise of Folly* (B. Radice, trans.), London: Penguin.
Erasmus, D. 1979. *Opera omnia* IV-3, Amsterdam: North-Holland.
Firenzuola, A. 1966. *L'asino d'oro d'Apuleio*, in: G. Fatini (ed.), *Opere scelte di Agnolo Firenzuola*, Turin: Unione tipogafico-editrice torinese. (Original Work Published 1550)
Gaisser, J.H. 2008. *The Fortunes of Apuleius and 'The Golden Ass': A Study in Transmission and Reception*, Princeton: Princeton University Press.
Godwin, J. (trans. and intro.) 1999. *Francesco Colonna: Hypnerotomachia Poliphili: The Strife of Love in a Dream*, London: Thames & Hudson.
Goldhill, S. 2008. 'Spreading the Word: Anecdote, and the Social Place of the Discourse of the Novel', Conference paper, ICAN IV, 21–26 July 2008, Lisbon.
Hanson, J.A. (ed. and trans.) 1989. *Apuleius. Metamorphoses*, 2 vols, Cambridge: Harvard University Press.
Krautter, K. 1971. *Philologische Methode und humanistische Existenz: Filippo Beroaldo und sein Kommentar zum Goldenen Esel des Apuleius*, Humanistische Bibliothek, Reihe 1: Abhandlungen; Bd. 9, Munich: Fink.
Labowsky, L. 1979. *Bessarion's Library and the Biblioteca Marciana: Six Early Inventories*, Roma: Edizioni di storia e letteratura.
Muth, K. 1890. *Der Briefwechsel des Conradus Mutianus* (K. Gillert, ed.), Halle: Hendel.

Petrarca, F. 1955. *Familiarum rerum libri*, in: G. Martelloti et al. (eds), *Prose*, La Letteratura Italiana: Storia e Testi 7, Milan: R. Ricciardi.

Pins, J. de. 1505. *Vita Philippi Beroaldi Bononiensis*, in: J.G. Meuschen (ed.), *Vitae summorum dignitate et eruditione virorum*, 4 vols, Coburg: Jo. Georgius Steinmarck, 1735–41. i. 123–151.

Pozzi, G., and Ciapponi, L.A. (eds) 1980. *Francesco Colonna: Hypnerotomachia Poliphili. Edizione critica e commento*, 2 vols, Padua: Antenore.

Rabelais, F. 1694. *Pantagruel's Voyage to the Oracle of the Bottle, Being the Fourth and Fifth Books of the Works of Francis Rabelais, M.D.* (P. le Motteux, trans.), London: Richard Baldwin.

Reeve, M.D. 2008. 'The Re-emergence of Ancient Novels in Western Europe, 1300–1810', in: T. Whitmarsh (ed.), *The Cambridge Companion to the Greek and Roman Novel*, Cambridge: Cambridge University Press. 282–298.

Robinson, J.H. 1898. *Petrarch, the First Modern Scholar and Man of Letters*, New York: Putnam.

Warren, J. 1999. 'Francesco Francia and the Art of Sculpture in Renaissance Bologna', *The Burlington Magazine*, 141, no. 1153, 216–225.

Saiichiro Nakatani
The First Japanese Translation of *Daphnis & Chloe*

Abstract: This paper examines the virtually unknown first Japanese translation of Longus' *Daphnis and Chloe* by Gen'ichi Yanome (1925), and reveals the historical, social, cultural, and economic contexts in which Longus was read in Japan before World War II. Yanome translates Charles Zévort's French version, but sometimes borrows Paul-Louis Courier's expression to polish his Japanese version. The most distinctive feature of this translation is *fuseji* or symbols used to replace censored words. Strongly affected by the morality of the time, the passages regarded as obscene are mutilated by the publisher's self-censorship. Yanome himself, however, does not see *Daphnis and Chloe* as pornographic, but as amorous and witty.

The importance of translation in Japan's modernization from the middle of the nineteenth century onward cannot be overstressed. During the Edo era under Tokugawa Shogunate (1603–1867), Japan basically closed itself off from the outside world. But once it opened its door to the West in the Meiji era (1868–1912), Japan insatiably absorbed Western technology and culture. In this process, Western books of every branch of knowledge were energetically translated into Japanese. Through translations, Western literature, including Greek and Latin classics, had great impact on modern Japanese culture too. Translation in modern Japan played a much more significant role than in Western countries.

In this paper, I would like to focus on the first Japanese translation of Longus' *Daphnis and Chloe* by Gen'ichi Yanome, published in 1925. I will investigate the features of his translation and explore the historical, social, cultural and economic contexts in which *Daphnis and Chloe* was read in Japan in the prewar period.

This paper was supported by JSPS KAKENHI Grant Number 23720183.

Saiichiro Nakatani, Keio University

https://doi.org/10.1515/9781501503986-018

Gen'ichi Yanome

Although there are not many studies on literary influence (except for Yukio Mishima's *The Sound of Waves* (1954), which was modelled on *Daphnis and Chloe*), it is well known that Japanese scholars and intellectuals already paid attention to ancient Greek novels in 1940s. They not only actively translated them into Japanese but also evaluated them. In ICAN 2000 held in Groningen, many Japanese translations of ancient novels were displayed at the exhibition, which might have surprised Western scholars. Unlike the West, Japanese scholars seem to have appreciated Greek romances without prejudice, probably because Japan cherished its own long tradition of romantic prose fiction, well exemplified by *the Tale of Genji*, and was freer of the western concept of the 'novel' as opposed to the 'romance.'

Regarding *Daphnis and Chloe*, three Japanese translations by Kiyoshi Eguchi (1947), Shigeichi Kure (1948), and Ryûkô Kawaji (1949) were published successively soon after World War II. And more recently, Chiaki Matsudaira's translation (1987) was issued in a more accessible Japanese paperback version. Eguchi and Kawaji's translations are based on Paul-Louis Courier's French version, and their titles clearly give the author's name as 'Courier' instead of Longus. On the other hand, Kure and Matsudaira, two of the leading pioneers of Japan's classical scholarship, translated directly from Greek editions.[1]

There is, however, an earlier predecessor. The first Japanese translation of *Daphnis and Chloe* by Gen'ichi Yanome (1896–1970) already published in Kindaisha (Tokyo) in 1925, as a part of a book titled *Sekai Tanpen-syôsetsu Taikei: Kodaimonogatari-hen* (i.e. *Library of World Short Stories: Ancient Narrative volume*). It is not listed in Ferrini's *Bibliografia di Longo*,[2] and is virtually unknown even in Japan.[3] As far as I have consulted through the internet database of Japanese university libraries (NACSIS Webcat), only five old regional universities in Japan possess this book, which must have been purchased when it was published in 1925. And it is only quite recently that this book was listed in the search

---

[1] According to the short bibliography, Kure seems to have used Seiler's edition (Leipzig, 1843). Matsudaira, on the other hand, used G. Dalmeyda's edition (Paris, 1934). It is also notable that Matsudaira translated Xenophon of Ephesus in 1948, a few months before Kure's Longus.
[2] Ferrini 1991, 253–254.
[3] As far as I know, only Masahiro Watanabe listed it in his bibliographical survey (2001–2002), and Akihiko Watanabe briefly treated it in his paper for ICAN 2008. See Watanabe 2011. I myself happened to obtain it at a secondhand bookshop in 2007.

engine of the National Diet Library of Japan. These facts prove the rarity of the book.

The translator, Gen'ichi Yanome was born into the family of an army officer in 1896. He graduated from the department of French literature at Keio University in Tokyo. He started his early career as a poet, and his poetry was characterised by its purity. However, he gradually switched over to an essayist and changed his taste to diabolism. He was also known as a translator from French, and produced famous translations of mediaeval French poetry such as Christine de Pizan and François Villon, and fin-de siècle literature of Marcel Schwob, William Beckford's *Vathek*, and Henri de Regnier's *Les Rencontres de M. de Bréot*, which indicate his extremely particular tastes. Indeed, Yanome is a unique translator. He is not an academic who belonged to a university, but a private researcher of French literature. He also had a great knowledge of Japanese classical literature and tradition. He had a full command of Japanese archaic terms, classical as well as slang, and polished his translation without too much concern for accuracy. He rather aimed at perfection as a Japanese composition. His translation is, therefore, often regarded as embodying his strong personality, and can be called a creative translation.

Yanome's translation of *Daphnis and Chloe*

Let us now consider his translation of *Daphnis and Chloe*. It is, as indicated above, a part of the book titled *Sekai Tanpen-syôsetsu Taikei: Kodaimonogatari-hen* (i.e. *Library of World Short Stories: Ancient Narrative volume*), which includes short episodes from such literary works as the Bible, Herodotus, Pliny the Younger, Apuleius, Jacobus de Voragine, Boccaccio, Chaucer, and Cervantes. Together with these works, Longus is placed in the history of short stories. It is noteworthy that, while other episodes are parts of longer literary works, only *Daphnis and Chloe* is a complete work. They are all regarded as predecessors of modern short stories, as developed by Hawthorne, Irving, Poe, Mérimée, and Maupassant.[4] Other volumes in this series contain short stories from Britain, America, France, Germany, North and South Europe, Russia and China. In other words, Japanese readers equally enjoyed ancient and modern, Eastern and Western literature in 1920s.

According to the colophon, this book is 'not for sale'. This means that it is a limited edition for registered readers. Compared with four other Japanese trans-

---

4 See the introduction to *the Ancient Narrative volume* by Ki Kimura, 1.

lations of *Daphnis and Chloe*, this one is evidently much more sumptuous. It is a large hard-covered book with a box, gilt top, and paper of good quality, which must have served as an interior adornment on the bookshelf too. About the publisher *Kindaisha*, we do not know so much. In fact we cannot identify the date of its foundation or closure. But limited information tells us that *Kindaisha* was managed by Kôzaburo Yoshizawa, and that it energetically published collected editions around 1920s. For example, the house published *Collected World Plays*, among which the first and second volumes are of selected ancient dramas including Aeschylus, Sophocles, Euripides, Aristophanes, Plautus, Terence and Seneca.

It is probable that Yanome became aware of *Daphnis and Chloe* by way of a French writer, Marcel Schwob (1867–1905). One year before his translation of Longus, Yanome had edited and translated a collection of Schwob's short stories, *Kyûketsuki* (*Vampire*) in 1924. One of the short stories titled '*Beatrice*' briefly refers to *Daphnis and Chloe* and its author Longus.[5] Furthermore, in 1929, he also translated Schwob's *Mimes*, which is the French author's attempt to reproduce Herondas' *mimiamboi*. Both in the prologue and the epilogue of the *Mimes*, *Daphnis and Chloe* is adapted effectively. Especially in the epilogue,[6] the ghosts of Daphnis and Chloe visit Lesbos together and talk about their younger days, reflecting several episodes in the Greek novel. They are not willing to drink water from *Lêthê*, a river of Underworld, so that they can keep their happy memory. Although this translation was published four years after his translation of Longus, there is a great possibility that Yanome had already read Schwob's original French book much earlier, and had been inspired by it.

What, then, was the source text for Yanome's translation of Longus? A good place to start is the names of characters. Japanese translations usually attempt to transliterate foreign proper nouns into Japanese by *katakana*, so that they can reproduce more or less similar sounds to the original nouns. For example, Daphnis is transcribed as *dafunisu*, and Chloe as *Kuroê*. In this translation, the author's name represented as *Rong'u'su* (not *Rong'o'su*), and the use of Roman gods' names such as Jupiter and Venus, show that the source of Yanome's translation was not a Greek edition, but a modern European translation. And from his career, as I mentioned above, it must have been French. However, it seems not to be based on the very popular translation by Paul-Louis Courier for several reasons.

---

5 Schwob (Yanome trans.) 1975, 95.
6 Schwob (Yanome trans.) 1929, 102–116.

Firstly, in Courier's version, the prologue of *Daphnis and Chloe* is merged into the beginning of Book 1. Yanome's translation, on the other hand, clearly separates the prologue from the first Book. Secondly, from the characters' names, we can easily determine that Yanome used a different version. For example, while Courier translated the Greek names by *Cleariste, Lycenion, Eudrome* and *Syringe*, Yanome's translation shows that his source translated them by *Clearista, Lycenium, Eudromos* and *Syrinx*.

The comparison of Yanome's Japanese and other French translations reveals that the main source of Yanome is Charles Zévort's French translation in *Roman Grecs*, vol.1. It was originally published in 1856, and republished in 1883 and 1884. Indeed Yanome's translation shows a clear correspondence to Zévort's French. Not only characters' names, but also expressions are often identical. For instance, in 1,20, when Dorkon wears a wolf-skin, its gaping jaws covered his head like 'an infantry man's helmet'. While Courier uses the words '*un homme de guerre*' for the Greek word ὁπλίτου, Zévort uses the word *hoplite*, which Yanome reproduced in *katakana* printed alongside *kanji* (i.e. Chinese characters).

Yanome even follows Zévort's misinterpretation. When Gnathon begs Astylus for the possession of Daphnis (4,16), he cries '(I) who said your chefs-de cuisine were better than all the boys in Mitylene'.[7] But Zévort mistakenly translates the place-name as '*Milet* (Miletus)', which is translated by Yanome.

Compared with his later eccentric translations, Yanome is less free in translating Zévort's French into Japanese. However, there are some parts where I cannot see the correspondence between Zévort and Yanome. He seems to have borrowed Courier's expressions too, though less frequently. In 1,1, for instance, a country estate of Dionysophanes is said to be 'about 200 stades distant city of Mitylene'. Zévort directly translated the distance '*deux cent stades*', but Courier nonliterally translated it by '*huit ou neuf lieues* (8 or 9 leagues)'. And Yanome's Japanese translation is '*hachi kyu ri* (8 or 9 *ri*)',[8] which is identical to Courier's expression. Similarly Yanome sometimes chose phrases from Courier rather than Zévort to polish his own version.

---

7 I quote from Morgan's English translation (2004).
8 '*Ri*' is a Japanese old unit of distance. 1 *ri* is about four kilometers.

Self-censorship

The most distinctive feature in Yanome's translation of *Daphnis and Chloe* is *fuseji* or symbols used to replace censored words. His translation was strongly affected by the morality of the time. Until 1945, by the Publication Law of 1893 and the Press Law of 1909, all publications were officially censored and offenders against the laws were punished in Japan. When Yanome's translation was published in 1925, it was an unstable time before Japanese-Chinese War and World War II broke out. The Japanese government tried to restrict political dissent and control people's thought and behaviour by the notorious Public Security Preservation Law issued in the same year, which strengthened the official censorship. To avoid book banning, therefore, the publisher used *fuseji*. The passages or phrases regarded as politically or morally inappropriate were replaced by dots or o-marks, and only punctuation marks are left (Fig.2). This presents quite a different appearance from censored modern translations of *Daphnis and Chloe* in Western countries, where passages are simply deleted, or suddenly changed into Latin.[9] In this Japanese version, on the other hand, we can visually trace the censored parts easily. Each circle corresponds to one Japanese letter. I must stress that it was not the translator's intention. Yanome himself translated the whole, but his text was expurgated by the publisher.

The episodes such as Lykainion's sex tutorial (3,15 ff.) and Gnathon's homosexual desire (4,10 ff.) are filled with censor marks over a much wider range than any other translation of *Daphnis and Chloe*. And even a short sentence indicating sexual desire or sexual intercourse is censored. For example, when Dorkon, wearing a wolf's skin, tries to rape Chloe, the reference to his intention to rape her (1,20: 'So he decided to make a direct assault on Chloe when she was alone!') is replaced by o-marks. In Philetas' advice to Daphnis and Chloe in 2,7, only the last phrases '(except) a kiss and an embrace and lying down together with naked bodies' are replaced by o-marks. In the final chapter of Book 4, the short phrase '[everyone escorted them] to their bedroom' is replaced by o-marks, and the whole final sentence describing the nuptial night is replaced by dots (4,40). Accordingly, this translation hides all the crucial references and allusions

---

[9] Amyot's French translation (1559) already deleted the concrete description of the sex act (3,18,3–4) from Lykainion's sex tutorial. More recently English translations by Smith 1855 and Edmunds 1916 translated some erotic passages suddenly into Latin.

to sexual desire and intercourse in *Daphnis and Chloe*, which must have left readers with a quite different impression of the Greek novel.[10]

Influence of *Daphnis and Chloe* on Yanome

Finally, I would like to treat briefly the influence of *Daphnis and Chloe* on Yanome himself. His career after World War II was somewhat bizarre. He now becomes notorious as an introducer of world amorous literature. He is also a shady expert on sexology and health management method promoted by an American nutritionist, Gayelord Hauser. In 1949, only four years after the end of World War II, he published a booklet titled *Ren'ai Style Book* (i. e. *Style Book of Love*), which was compiled and written by himself (Tokyo: Hanashi-sha). It is a collection of love poetry by poets such as Ovid and Ronsard, and also includes Italian and French amorous anecdotes along with Yanome's own. And his interest in *Daphnis and Chloe* seems to have continued after his translation. The booklet opens with the summary of *Daphnis and Chloe* with four coloured illustrations (Fig.1) by George Léonnec (1881–1940), which are reproduced from Courier's translation published in 1934 (Paris: Librairie Floury). The publisher's strong self-censorship in 1925 must have frustrated Yanome. In this brief summary, he could finally refer to some formerly censored parts such as Philetas' instruction and the nuptial night (though briefly), twenty-four years after his own translation.

However, he always claimed that amorous literature and pornographic literature are different, and that he hated the latter. According to him, amorous literature is not simply an obscene story, but always contains some wit and humour. In other words, Yanome did not see *Daphnis and Chloe* as pornographic, but as amorous and witty. Although his first translation of *Daphnis and Chloe* was mutilated by self-censorship, Yanome certainly captured the essence of *Daphnis and Chloe*.

---

10 I have investigated all the self-censored parts in Yanome's translation in my recent article (but written in Japanese). See Nakatani 2014.

1. Daphnis is piping besides sleeping Chloe (1.25).

2. Daphnis and Chloe's kissing.

3. Daphnis sees Chloe's bathing (1.32).

4. Daphnis presents an apple to Chloe (3.34).

Fig. 1: Illustrated Summary of *Daphnis & Chloe* by Gen'ichi Yanome (1949)

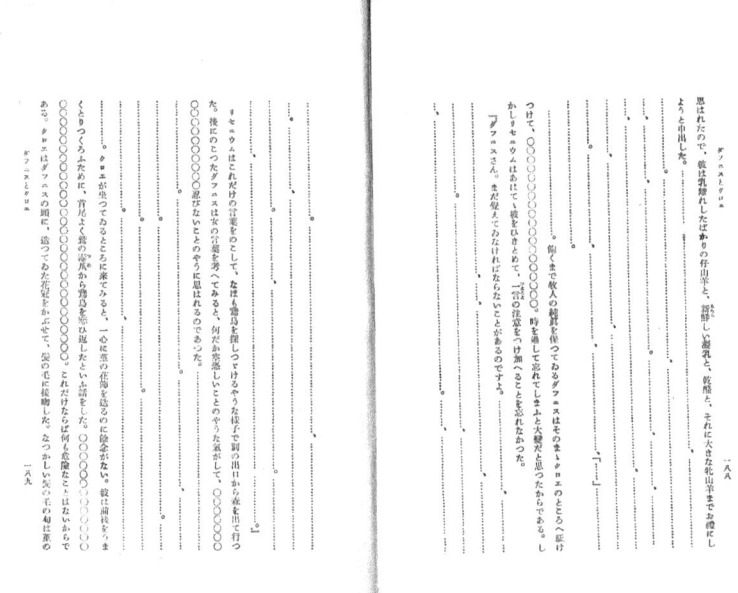

Fig. 2: Censored text (Longus 3.18–20) in Gen'ichi Yanome's translation (1925)

Bibliography

Amyot, J. (trans.) 1559. *Les Amours Pastorales de Daphnis et de Chloe: escriptes premierement en Grec par Longus, & puis traduicts en François*, Paris: Vincent Sertenas.
Barber, G. 1989. *Daphnis and Chloe: the markets and metamorphoses of an unknown bestseller*, London: British Library.
Beckford, W. 2005. *Vathek* (G. Yanome trans.), Tokyo: Gakushû-Kenkyûsha. (Original Work Published 1932)
Courier, P.-L. (trans.) 1880. *Les Amours Pastorales de Daphnis et Chloé*, Paris: Garnier Frères.
Dalmeyda, G. (ed. and trans.) 1934. *Pastorales (Daphnis et Chloé)*, Paris: Les Belles Lettres.
de Regnier, H. 2007. *Bréot-shi no Ren'ai-gyôjôki (Les Rencontres de M. de Bréot)* (G. Yanome trans.), Tokyo: Yumani-shobo. (Original Work Published 1932)
Doody, M.A. 1998. *The True Story of the Novel*, London: Fontana Press.
Edmunds, J.M. (ed.) 1916. *Daphnis & Chloe by Longus*, Loeb Classical Library, London: W. Heinemann, with English translation revised from George Thornley's 1657 translation.
Eguchi, Kiyoshi (trans.) 1947. Courier, *Daphnis to Chloe*, Tokyo: Shisaku-sha.
Ferrini, M F. 1991. *Bibliografia di Longo. Dafni e Cloe*. Edizioni e traduzioni, Macerata: E. G. L. E.
Kamei, S., and Kutsukake, Y. (eds.) 2005. *Meishi Meiyaku Monogatari (Tales of Excellent Translations of Famous Poems)*, Tokyo: Iwanami-shoten.
Kawaji, Ryûkô (trans.) 1949. Courier, *Daphnis to Chloe*, Tokyo: Nihon-kyôbunsha.
Kure, Shigeichi (trans.) 1948. Longus, *Daphnis to Chloe*, Nara: Yôtokusha.

Matsudaira, Chiaki (trans.) 1987. Longus, *Daphnis to Chloe*, Tokyo: Iwanami-shoten.
Morgan, J. R. (trans. and comm.) 2004. *Longus: Daphnis and Chloe*, Aris & Phillips Classical Texts, Oxford: Oxbow Books, with reprint of M. D. Reeve's text.
Nakatani, S. 2014. 'Yanome Gen'ichi yaku *Daphnis to Chloe* (*Daphnis and Chloe* translated by Gen'ichi Yanome)', *Jinmon* 38 (Kagoshima Prefectural College), 9–24 (written in Japanese).
Reeve, M.D. (ed.) 1994. *Longus: Daphnis et Chloe*, Leipzig: Teubner.
Schwob, M. 1929. *Kogirisha Fuzoku Kagami* (*Mimes*) (G. Yanome trans.), Tokyo: Daiichi-shobo.
Schwob, M. 1975. *Ohgon Kamen no Oh* (*Le Roi au masque d'or, The king in the gold mask*) (G. Yanome trans.), Kobe: Kobe Books. (Original Work Pulished as *Kyûketsuki* (*Vampire*) 1924)
Seiler, E.E. (ed.) 1843. *Longi Pastoralia*. Graece et Latine, Leipzig: Libraria Kuehniana.
Smith, R. (trans.) 1855. *The Greek Romance of Heliodorus, Longus and Achilles Tatius*, London: Henry G. Bohn.
Watanabe, Akihiko 2011. 'From Moral Reform to Democracy: The Ancient Novel in Modern Japan', in: M.P. Futre Pinheiro, S.J. Harrison (eds.), *Fictional Traces: Receptions of the Ancient Novel*, ANS 14.1, Groningen: Barkhuis Publishing & Groningen University Library. 227–242.
Watanabe, Masahiro (ed.), 2001–2002. *Nihon Seiyôkotengaku Bunkenshi* (*Bibliography of Classical Scholarship in Japan before 1945*), 3 vols. Kyoto: Tanaka Print.
Yanome, Gen'ichi (trans.) 1925. Longus, *Daphnis to Chloe*, in: *Sekai Tanpen-shôsetsu Taikei: Kodaimonogatari-hen* (*Library of World Short Stories: Ancient Narrative volume*), Tokyo: Kindaisha. 113–238.
Yanome, G. 1949. *Ren'ai Style Book* (*Style Book of Love*), Tokyo: Hanashi-sha.
Yoshiyuki, Jun'nosuke 2002. 'Shichihenge no Kijin', in: Yoshiyuki, J., *Collected Short Novels*, Tokyo: Kodansha. 231–250.
Zévort, Ch. (trans.) 1856. *Romans Grecs. Première série*, Paris: Charpentier.

Boundaries: Geographical and Metaphorical

Ellen Finkelpearl
Refiguring the Animal/Human Divide in Apuleius and Heliodorus

Abstract: The novels of Apuleius and Heliodorus present a deliberately scrambled paradigm of animal-human distinctions – which accompanies in both texts a scrambling of identities and categories in other respects. Apuleius' work confounds neat distinctions between rational humans and brute animals, running counter to accepted philosophical beliefs about the nature of Man and his/her distinction from 'non-human animals'. In Heliodorus, the collapse of the animal/human divide is figured somewhat differently, through the striking prominence of two vegetarian priests, Kalasiris and Sisimithres, and through the reconceptualizing of ritual sacrifice. While Heliodorus more obviously disrupts and re-draws lines of ethnic identity and Apuleius complicates human-animal distinctions, Heliodorus entwines his narrative of racial discovery with a strong strain of re-consideration of animal-human hierarchies, and Apuleius intermixes his animal-human narrative with a confusion of ethnic identity.

While the ancient novel in some respects is conventional and affirms the social institutions of family and marriage, many ancient novels challenge established social norms, categories and assumptions – about race and ethnicity, gender and sexuality, reality and illusion, class and social standing, geography and space. It is also central to some conceptualizations of the genre itself that its anomalous form resists classification.[1] At the basic level, what is most essential in the novels of Apuleius and Heliodorus is that, in the one case, a man is transformed into a donkey and, in the other, a white girl is revealed to be the princess of Ethiopia, ultimately, 'becoming black'. Both of these novels revolve around premises that break down some of the most basic categories which structure the social world, representing in different ways the fluidity of identity and 'fundamentally permeable nature of the self' (Whitmarsh's formulation) that is such

---

[1] I would like to thank the editors of this volume and the anonymous referee of my paper, but also to draw attention to the fact that this paper was written in 2008 and I have not had the opportunity to revise much in light of scholarly developments in the intervening nine years.

Ellen Finkelpearl, Scripps College

https://doi.org/10.1515/9781501503986-019

a central preoccupation of the novel.² Any solution that de-problematizes these ruptures too easily misses what is paradoxical and radical about both.³

Another arena in which these novels resist the 'fixity' of traditional categories,⁴ and the subject of the present paper, is that of animal/human distinctions, where standard definitions of humanity (and bestiality and divinity) are challenged and the accepted hierarchies most fundamental to social organization are reconfigured. Where epic constantly affirms the hierarchy of god, human and animal through the repeated representation of human performance of animal sacrifice to the gods, the novels of Apuleius and Heliodorus present a different or deliberately scrambled paradigm – which accompanies in both texts a scrambling of identities and categories in other respects. Now, obviously Apuleius' novel is *about* the breakdown of the animal/human divide, while Heliodorus' work incorporates this thematic more incidentally, and yet I hope to show that in both works the deconstruction of these fundamental categories is integral to a restructuring of the worlds in the two denouements.

In Apuleius' *Metamorphoses*, Lucius inhabits a highly ambiguous space between human and animal, the complexity of which is often glossed over.⁵ Lucius does not simply have a human mind in an animal body; the two become mixed up: he boasts of his human mental capacities at *Met.* 4,6 just after rolling in the dirt like a 'real' donkey, pretending to justify the donkey behavior by rational explanation. His narration of the behavior of his donkey doppelgänger likewise blurs the boundary between the two of them, since Lucius presents his plan to act like a natural donkey as if it were a 'bellum consilium' concocted by an intelligent human and as if the other donkey had to have guessed his brilliant idea (4,4). While comic, this episode cleverly confounds animal and human behavior: do animals think rationally about their behavior? Or do humans act instinctively and attribute their actions to intelligent thought? Lucius attributes ra-

---

2 Quotation from Whitmarsh 2002, 111.
3 So, while it is surely true that ancient belief in "maternal impression" is well-attested, it is also clear within the *Aithiopika* that it is not a belief widely enough held to prevent the suspicion of adultery in the case of a white girl born to black parents or to prevent Hydaspes from immediately denying that Charikleia could be his daughter given the color of her skin. It is also surprising how much criticism on Heliodorus (perhaps more a phenomenon of the past) says nothing at all about the central problem of race. Morgan 1989, while focusing on the ways that Heliodorus masterfully builds up to an ending, downplays the elements of unbelievability in the final scene.
4 'Fixity' is a term used repeatedly in Perkins 1999 in discussing the challenge that 'passing novels' pose to the fixity of categories (in this case of black and white).
5 See Finkelpearl 2006, with emphasis on language by and about animals. Some of the points made here appear in that essay, but I have tried to avoid overlap. Also see Shumate 1996, 62–65; Schlam 1992, Ch. 9.

tional thought to other animals at 3,26 when he says that his former horse and Milo's ass *capita conferunt* and *consentiunt* though he denies the animals in the theater rationality at 10,34. Once Lucius is an ass, he sees animal cognition differently, from the inside, and is constantly weighing the possibility that animals may be engaging in cognitive processes.

When living with the 'brothers' in Book 10, Lucius declares that he would not be *tam uere asinus* that he would eat hay when presented with human food (though he describes his consumption with an animal word *saginabar*, 10,13), but is equally pleased by the luscious grass he finds outside the theater at 10,29 (*libens adfectabam*).[6] He engages in what may or may not be interspecies sex with the *matrona* at 10,21, but he also lusts after the mares at 7,16. When mingling in Thiasus' company, drinking wine and communicating with nods, Lucius is a human trapped in the body of an animal pretending to be human, the social apparatus of human society unable to overcome the physicality of his body. The collapse of boundaries is not restricted to Lucius, but applies as well to Thrasyleon, for example, whose identity as bear seems so strong that he has almost actually become a bear by the end of the episode. At 10,33, we readers are referred to as *forensia pecora* and *togati uulturii*.

At the linguistic level, Apuleius has invented new vocabulary and forged new meanings for existing words to express the quite different relationships between animals, humans and beasts: at 5,8 and 11,14 (the latter disputed), *inhumanus* is used to mean 'divine' rather than 'bestial', a meaning unique in Latin.[7] At 5,1, Apuleius has used the word *efferauit* [*mirus prorsum homo, immo semideus uel certe deus qui magnae artis subtilitate tantum efferauit argentum* (a totally wondrous man, no really a demi-god or even a god who through the intricacy of his great art carved animals out of silver)] to mean 'shape animals out of silver' a mark of high art and skill, far from the usual meaning 'to make wild, savage or fierce'. Lucius' speechlessness is a central reality of his asinine state, and yet he can understand human speech, sometimes better than his master, and he engages willingly in ass-language more than once.[8]

The folktale/fabulistic world of *Cupid and Psyche* presents a different paradigm, in which animals and even inanimate objects speak without question. In each of Psyche's four labors, ants, the reed, water, an eagle and the tower speak and advise her. The reed is referred to as *simplex et humana* (6,13). Birds who

---

6 See Finkelpearl 2006, 207, with references.
7 See Kenney and GCA ad loc.
8 Lucius is proud of his ability to bray loudly at 7,13; see Finkelpearl 2006, 215–216. When Lucius is with the gardener confronting the Roman legionary, he understands Latin while the human does not.

seem almost humanly articulate accompany Venus and announce her arrival (*adventum deae pronuntiant*, 6,6,3). In this world, breaking the barrier of species and communicative language is not surprising, as it is explicitly a magical world, and yet this interlude, as in so many other ways, forms not quite a mirror but a background against which the 'real' world of Lucius' adventures is measured. It has been remarked that the talking animals in *Cupid and Psyche* must make Lucius in his mute ass state particularly envious as he listens, but the world also represents an extreme case of the very breakdown of species barriers occurring in the novel as a whole, and yet it is a world of no surprises and ambiguities, lending an even more nightmarish quality to the uncertain boundaries of the frame narrative.

There is the further confusion that the boundary between the now-human narrator Lucius and the ass-man *actor* is often unclear, so that the entire narrative is tinged with the uncertainty of its origin, the dual nature of its authority, man and animal.

Of course, the slippage in animal-human boundaries is comic and clever, and yet there are larger implications, philosophical and otherwise. The work confounds neat distinctions between rational humans and brute animals, running counter to accepted philosophical beliefs about the nature of Man and his/her distinction from 'non-human animals'. Plutarch, Lucius' relative on his mother's side, whose blood-relation to the text has been explained numerous ways, was the author of at least three treatises challenging Aristotelian and Stoic ideas about the irrationality and moral inferiority of animals, one framed absurdly as the argument of a man transformed into a pig by Circe, who would rather remain a pig than return to human form.[9] Apuleius, too, I submit, is framing serious reflections on the nature of humanity within apparently trivial discourse. I will have more to say about Book 11 in a moment.

In Heliodorus, the collapse of the animal/human divide is figured somewhat differently, through the striking prominence of two vegetarian priests, Kalasiris and Sisimithres, and through the reconceptualizing of ritual sacrifice.[10] Sacrifice is a symbolic ritual expression of the hierarchies of being in the world; vegetarianism is an expression of the practical consequences of a re-conceptualizing of levels of those hierarchies, so, while Apuleius and Heliodorus may seem to be

---

9 See Plutarchus, *De Esu Carnium, De sollertia animalium* and *Bruta animalia ratione uti* (or *Gryllus*) and the comparison of these works with contemporary issues in the ethical debates about animals in Newmyer 2006.
10 Baumbach discusses the priests in Heliodorus and the question of what elements make a "theios aner" in Greek thought of this period, but only briefly mentions Kalasiris' abstention from meat, which he connects with Pythagorean ideals (179).

engaged in different projects, they are both re-imagining the essential binary of human-animal.

Vegetarians, ancient and modern, draw the line between human and animal differently from mainstream (western) society.[11] While the dominant anthropocentric view of human carnivores is that animals belong to a different plane of being and may be exploited for human use, vegetarians instead make that division between animals and plants, regarding animals as thinking beings and kin.[12] In *Dumb Beasts and Dead Philosophers*, Catherine Osborne examines ancient philosophical concepts of animal-human relations, emphasizing the anormative nature of the ideas of Pythagoras, Empedocles and Plato, who 'set out to persuade us to see our fellow creatures as members of our own family...' and observing that 'their claims were based on a revised moral understanding of how the world is divided'.[13] While for the most part, this revised division of the world remains a tacit underlying principle for vegetarians, the anormative quality of that re-conceptualized division is something faced in practice daily. In Heliodorus, Kalasiris' vegetarianism is stressed as something not merely ritual and normal, but a practice that separates him from others. Most notably, at 3,11,2, Kalasiris declines a wine cup offered by Theagenes who takes it ill that he has refused: 'he glared at me angrily, supposing that my refusal was meant as a slight' (ὀξύ τε καὶ διαπυρῶν ἔνειδεν, ὑπερόρασθαι προσδοκήσας). While the social awkwardness is cleared up and Charikles explains that Kalasiris is both abstemious of wine and a vegetarian, Heliodorus, perhaps uniquely in ancient literature, has chosen to emphasize the common plight of the vegetarian who must risk impoliteness to follow moral principles. The anormative and anti-social nature of the practice is also thematized at 2,23,5—where Kalasiris' vegetarianism separates him from the dietarily normative Greek, Knemon, and 4,16,4–5, where again the priest's meatless offerings and separate cache of food occasion surprise in the Phoenician merchants, who later transport the lovers out of Delphi.

---

11 Obviously, there are vegetarians who abstain from meat for a variety of other reasons, including their own health and now environmental considerations or because of the gross mistreatment of animals in the practice of factory farming. I am here referring to a more philosophically-based vegetarianism.

12 There has been a rash of books in the past several decades, and particularly in the years since the first version of this paper, in light of a general movement toward posthumanism, on anthropocentrism and on the sense of entitlement of the human race to exploit nature and non-human animals. See e.g. the pioneering work of Peter Singer and, for example, work by Donna Haraway, Paola Cavalieri, Matthew Calarco, Cary Wolfe, Erica Fudge, J. M. Coetzee, within Classics, especially Mark Payne, and many others.

13 Osborne 2007, 61

However, it is the other vegetarian priest, the gymnosophist Sisimithres, who makes an issue directly of the slaughter of animals, when at 10,9,6, not only does he judge human sacrifice an abomination and displeasing to the gods, but wishes that 'it were possible to put an end to all animal sacrifice (θυσία τῶν ἄλλων ζῴων) as well' and (textual crux) considers that the gods would find incense and prayer sufficient. It is Sisimithres who ultimately declares that human sacrifice must be abolished, interpreting the gods' various signs, by virtue of his position as vatic priest. Thus, while Ethiopian practice had placed animals and humans sacrificially in the same position in relation to the gods, Sisimithres brings them into conformity with the Greek practice of a tri-partite division of beings. This division, however, is not only denaturalized by the divergent Ethiopian and gymnosophist beliefs, but further confused given that it is primarily through the revolt of the sacrificial animals (brought on by the gods according to Sisimithres) that human sacrifice is ended for all time. One might expect that this panic among the animals, motivated by the sight of the unfamiliar giraffe at 10,28, would have resulted in the abolition of their own sacrifice.

If Apuleius' artful confusions of the minds of metamorphosed beings and natural-born animals seem to belong to a different discussion from the lives of vegetarians in Heliodorus, I will only mention that Ovid's relentless tales of humans transformed into animals and other non-human entities creates a vision of a destabilized world whose boundaries have collapsed, and that its culmination is Pythagoras' lengthy vegetarian manifesto (Ovid, *Met.* 15,60 – 478). While there are differences, Ovid's *Metamorphoses* does suggest a strong link between the collapse of animal/human boundaries and vegetarianism.[14]

A further note: the problematization of traditional strict divisions among the hierarchies of beings in Heliodorus is nicely tied to the more prominent problematization of ethnic identity in the section about Homer's birth (3,14). Kalasiris' central point here is that Homer was actually an Egyptian – with obvious connections to Charikleia's obscured origins – but exiled from the land of his

---

14 The Pythagorean undercurrent in both Apuleius (Pythagoras is invoked at *Met.* 11,1) and in Heliodorus's Pythagorean-influenced gymnosophists, would be a fruitful one to pursue. The first of these was the subject of my paper at the Houston ICAN. Note also that Porphyry's (later) lengthy argument for vegetarianism likewise challenges the assumptions about animal rationality, language, etc. that are the underpinning of the ancient (and modern) beliefs about the ascendancy of humans that permit the consumption of animals. In general, see Haussleiter who takes the phenomenon of vegetarianism in antiquity more seriously than many contemporary critics.

birth because of his illegitimacy.[15] According to Kalasiris, Homer's father was Hermes, but the proof of his *divine* birth was that one of his thighs had a great growth of hair (3,14,3) – which would seem to make him more of an animal than god. (Incidentally, the discussion of Homer's birth follows closely on Kalasiris' declaration that when gods and spirits descend to earth, they occasionally take the form of an animal, but usually a human, 3,13,1, an explicit blurring of the three hierarchies.)

At the end of the *Aithiopika*, a new order is established in which the re-structuring of sacrifice is strangely interconnected with the establishment of Charikleia's identity: human sacrifice is abolished, Charikleia and Theagenes escape death and 'become black', qualifying them to continue the Ethiopian royal line. While the long debate over human sacrifice (along with its interruptions) is in large part a device to create suspense and to delay the long-awaited *anagnorisis*,[16] it also represents a process of remaking biological and social boundaries closely related to the process of re-thinking the obstacles to Charikleia's Ethiopian identity. Charikleia's salvation and coronation are made possible only through the awareness of a vegetarian (Sisimithres) that existential boundaries are socially constructed and re-drawable. The vegetarian who lives with the world's order differently conceived can question the Ethiopian belief that gods would effectively set humans on the same level as animals by demanding sacrifice of both.[17] That same openness to re-categorization paves the way for the re-thinking of blackness.[18] In the denouement, animal/human divisions are regularized; Theagenes has controlled the rioting animals, establishing his domination, and sacrifice–presumably animal—is about to be performed.[19] Yet while these boundaries are re-established, ethnic identity becomes more fluid and is the central focus. The same occurs in Apuleius: when Lucius regains his

---

15 On the connection between Homer's Egyptian identity and Charikleia, both of whom pass as Greeks but are actually other, see Perkins 1999, 209.
16 See Morgan 1989 on the skillful build-up to the ending of the novel.
17 Of course, human sacrifice is presented as a practice only engaged in on special occasions, so it may be argued against my thesis that Ethiopians are not creating a new division of being, but merely adding an occasional treat for the gods. Yet Sisimithres' introduction of the possibility of abolishing animal sacrifice as well speaks to the larger conceptual framework encompassing such re-drawing of lines.
18 Do Theagenes and Charikleia literally darken before our eyes at the end of the novel (cf. Doody 1997, 121), or, more probably, is blackness re-formulated as a cultural and conceptually ethnic marker rather than a physical one? See Perkins 1999, 198, with references.
19 The text is not explicit about the nature of the sacrifice, nor is it performed before the end of the novel, but is simply called θυσία at 10,41,3. The ambiguity and the silence over the many bloody hecatombs that were projected may be significant.

human form, we suddenly hear quite a bit about his mixed cultural allegiances—as if the one had been a stand-in for the other.[20]

To return to Apuleius and *his* denouement, the focus of Book 11 is, of course, on straightening out the slippage in animal-human boundaries by returning Lucius to his original human self. The culmination of the confounding of animal-human distinctions occurs early in the book, when Lucius, as I argue, speaks eloquent human language while yet a donkey (11,2).[21] After this moment, however, I see the anthropomorphizing of animals and the ruptures of species boundaries transformed and given a comfortable seat in both Lucius' prayers to Isis and the rituals of her cult. At 11,7, Lucius observes: *pecua etiam cuiusce modi et totas domos et ipsum diem serena facie gaudere sentirem* ('I could feel every sort of animal and all the houses and even the day itself rejoicing with bright faces'), an attribution of sentience even to inanimate objects and an endowing of all these with faces, expressing only joy and resolution. In the anteludia at 11,8, people appear in many disguises, but no human is dressed as an animal. Two animals are dressed like humans and, of course, an ass is dressed as Pegasus. But these are disguises and ritual mutations of identity rather than challenges to ontological categories. The theriomorphic gods of 11,11 represent perhaps a regularizing of the violation of the separation and ordering of gods, humans and animals, a somewhat alien institutionalization of an Isiac re-ordered world. In the famous pun on *esse* (to eat or to be) at 11,23, the priest, Mithras, has enjoined on Lucius 'neque ullum animal essem' meaning of course that Lucius must observe temporary vegetarianism, yet also with the resonance that Lucius is not to *be* an animal any longer. Lucius' being an animal and subsequently therefore *not* being an animal (by virtue of Isis' salvation) has led to not eating an animal (for initiation into Isis' cult). Isiac vegetarianism is part of an institutionalization of a new order of man-beast relations; vegetarian abstinence from flesh has become a substitute for *being* an animal. In short, the rupture of absolute categories embodied in Lucius' metamorphosis retains its traces in the new Isiac order, which includes theriomorphic gods and occasional abstinence from flesh; as in Heliodorus, the animal-human divide is refigured and its new shape codified.

But alongside this development, as in Heliodorus, is an outcropping of confusion over Lucius' cultural identity. Just as Heliodorus' focus on the fluidity of

---

[20] Perkins 1999, 201–202, citing Blackmer, discusses the homologous relationship of one marker of cultural difference to another, such that gender can stand in for class or race for gender. I believe that in some ways this is what is happening in Apuleius with animals and ethnicity (cf. Finkelpearl 2009), and to a lesser degree in Heliodorus. In any case, the observation of the permeability of one kind of category is closely related to that of the other.
[21] Finkelpearl 1998, 204–205.

ethnic identity is accompanied by a re-thinking of the animal/human divide, Apuleius' attention to the meaninglessness of animal/human distinctions is paired with a confusion of his ultimate ethnic identity.[22] While this confusion was introduced in the Prologue, where Lucius' various Greek origins – Athens-Sparta-Corinth, and Thessaly as mistaken birthplace of his maternal ancestor Plutarch – do not amount to any rational Greek identity, by the end of Book 11, Lucius is parading around Rome with a shaved head, looking more Egyptian than Greek, proud of his position as *pastophor*, part of a subculture marked by difference. As an immigrant, he has learned Latin and is proud to have become a successful pleader in the forum. On top of this triple identity, Lucius is notoriously designated by the priest with the animal-*nomen*, Asinius Marcellus, as 'Madaurensem' (11,27).[23] Adding to all the ink so far spilled on this crux, I think it is useful to bring into play a parallel with Heliodorus' final signature in which he (narrator or author?) identifies himself as a Hellenized Phoenician from Syrian Emesa and of the race of the Sun (10,41). Lucius' unsatisfactory assimilation, as well as his experiences as a misfit donkey, are potentially brought into the perspective of the 'Madauran' (Lucius and/or Apuleius) playing the part of the Romanized provincial. His stint as animal, then, is linked to this non-Roman, non-Hellenic identity, just as Heliodorus' 'reperspectivization' of the world, to used Whitmarsh's term, with Ethiopia now at the center, is related to the author or narrator's own non-Hellenic identity.[24] Just as Homer's Egyptian-ness is in part marked by his bestial thigh, so Lucius' non-human state seems in part a metaphor for his cultural marginality.[25]

Animals obviously appear in many texts with many functions; in an article on animals in *Daphnis and Chloe*, Ewen Bowie lays out a few – animals as actors, as figures in similes, or as dream or symbolic material. It seems to me that the animal simile, for example, represents a quite different situation, for while humans are compared to animals, the comparison works only on the assumption that animals and humans are separate entities. (However, the suckling of humans by goats does represent a crossing of the species boundary, though the

---

22 For some discussion of these issues, both in relation to Lucius and to Apuleius, see Finkelpearl 1998 and 2009; Graverini 2002; Too 2001; Alvarez 2007.
23 Notwithstanding Penwill 1990's persuasive arguments that the priest is referring to Apuleius, not Lucius, the context makes clear that those involved assume, rightly or wrongly, that Lucius is the man from Madauros.
24 Whitmarsh 1998.
25 For further thoughts on Apuleius, Lucius and ethnic identity, see Finkelpearl 2009, written after the original delivery of this paper. See also Isaac 2004, 194–215 on the identification of animals and foreigners in antiquity. Also see Lee-Finkelpearl-Graverini 2014.

genre of pastoral may make such crossover more natural.) With Apuleius and Heliodorus, on the other hand, distinctions between animals and humans (and gods) are blurred and the social uses of humans and animals are confused.

There are many disparate strands in this essay, and each of them deserves much more attention, but the aim has been to suggest some of the ways that these two very 'disruptive' novels have confounded boundaries and blurred categories. While Heliodorus more obviously disrupts and re-draws lines of ethnic identity and Apuleius complicates human-animal distinctions, Heliodorus entwines his narrative of racial discovery with a strong strain of re-consideration of animal-human hierarchies, and Apuleius intermixes his animal-human narrative with a confusion of ethnic identity.

Bibliography

Alvarez, J. 2007. 'The Coming of Age and Political Accommodation in the Greco-Roman novels', in: M. Paschalis, S. Frangoulidis, S. Harrison, M. Zimmerman (eds.), *The Greek and Roman Novel: Parallel Readings*, Groningen: Barkhuis and Groningen University Library. 3–22.

Baumbach, M. 2008. 'An Egyptian Priest in Delphi', in: B. Dignas, K. Trampedach (eds.), *Practitioners of the Divine*, Cambridge: Harvard University Press. 167–183.

Bowie, E. 2005. 'Les animaux dans le *Daphnis et Chloé* de Longus', in: B. Pouderon (ed.), *Lieux, decors, et paysages de l'ancien roman des origines à Byzance*, Lyon: Maison de l'Orient et de la Méditerranée. 75–85.

Dilke, O. 1980. 'Heliodorus and the colour problem', *PP* 35, 264–271.

Doody, M. 1997. *The True Story of the Novel*, New Brunswick: Rutgers University Press.

Dowden, K. 1996. 'Heliodoros: serious intentions?' *CQ* 46.1, 267–286

Edsall, M. 2000. 'Religious Narratives and Religious Themes in the Novels of Achilles Tatius and Heliodorus', *AN* 1, 114–133.

Finkelpearl, E. 1998. *Metamorphosis of Language in Apuleius*, Ann Arbor: University of Michigan Press.

Finkelpearl, E. 2006. 'The Language of Animals and the Text of Apuleius' *Metamorphoses*', in: W.H. Keulen, R.R. Nauta, S. Panayotakis (eds.), *Lectiones Scrupulosae, Essays on the Text and Interpretation of Apuleius' Metamorphoses in Honour of Maaike Zimmerman*, ANS 6, Groningen: Barkhuis Publishing & Groningen University Library. 203–221.

Finkelpearl, E. 2009. 'Marsyas the Satyr and Apuleius of Madauros', *Ramus* 38.1, 7–42.

Futre Pinheiro, M. 1998. 'Time and Narrative Technique in Heliodorus' *Aethiopica*', *ANRW* 2.34.4, 3148–3173.

Graverini, L. 2002. 'Corinth, Rome and Africa: a Cultural Background for the Tale of the Ass', in: M. Pascalis, S. Frangoulidis (eds.) *Space in the Ancient Novel*, ANS 6, Groningen: Barkhuis Publishing & the University Library Groningen. 58–77.

Haussleiter, J. 1935. *Der Vegetarismus in der Antike*, Berlin: Verlag von Alfred Töppelmann.

Hunter, R. 1998. 'The Aithiopika of Heliodorus: beyond interpretation?' in: R. Hunter (ed.), *Studies in Heliodorus*, Cambridge: Cambridge University Press. 40–59.

Isaac, B. 2004. *The Invention of Racism in Classical Antiquity*, Princeton: Princeton University Press.
Lee, B.T., Finkelpearl, E., Graverini, L. (eds.) 2014. *Apuleius and Africa*, New York: Routledge.
Lonis, R. 1992. 'Les Éthiopiens sous le regard d'Héliodore', in: M-F. Baslez, P. Hoffmann, M. Trédé (eds.), *Le monde du roman grec,* Paris: Press de l'École Normale Superieure. 233–241.
Morgan, J.R. 1989. 'A Sense of the Ending: The Conclusion of Heliodorus' *Aithiopika*', *TAPA* 119, 229–320.
Newmyer, S. 2006. *Animals, Rights and Reason in Plutarch and Modern Ethics*, New York: Routledge.
Osborne, C. 1995. 'Ancient Vegetarianism', in: J. Wilkins, D. Harvey, M. Dobson (eds.), *Food in Antiquity,* Exeter: University of Exeter Press. 214–224.
Osborne, C. 2007. *Dumb Beasts and Dead Philosophers: Humanity and the Humane in Ancient Philosophy and Literature,* Oxford: Oxford University Press.
Penwill, J. 1990. 'Ambages Reciprocae: Reviewing Apuleius' *Metamorphoses*', *Ramus* 19, 1–25.
Perkins, J. 1999. 'An Ancient "Passing" Novel: Heliodorus, *Aethiopika*', *Arethusa* 32, 197–214.
Selden, D. 1998. 'Aithiopika and Ethiopianism', in: R. Hunter (ed.) *Studies in Heliodorus*, Cambridge: Cambridge University Press. 182–217.
Shumate, N. 1996. *Crisis and Conversion in Apuleius' Metamorphoses*, Ann Arbor: University of Michigan Press.
Sorabji, R. 1993. *Animal Minds and Human Morals: The Origins of the Western Debate*, London: Duckworth.
Too, Y.L. 2001. 'Losing the Author's Voice: Cultural and Personal Identities in the *Metamorphoses* Prologue,' in: A. Kahane, A. Laird (eds.), *A Companion to the Prologue of Apuleius' Metamorphoses,* Oxford: Oxford University Press. 177–187.
Whitmarsh, T. 1998. 'Heliodorus and the Genealogy of Hellenism', in: R. Hunter (ed.), *Studies in Heliodorus*, Cambridge: Cambridge University Press. 93–124.
Whitmarsh, T. 2002. 'Written on the body: Ekphrasis, perception, and deception in Heliodorus' Aethiopika', *Ramus* 31.1–2, 111–125.
Winkler, J. 1982. 'The mendacity of Kalasiris and the narrative strategy of Heliodorus' *Aithiopika*', *YCS* 27, 98–158.

Mary Jaeger
Eros the Cheese Maker: A Food Studies Approach to *Daphnis and Chloe*

> Food comes first. No food, no life.
> Peter Garnsey, *Food and Society in Classical Antiquity*

Abstract: Milk, that most pastoral of foods, and its preserved and commodified form, cheese, play important structural roles in *Daphnis and Chloe*, and references to cheese offer a lens through which to examine the relationship of man and animal. The coagulation of milk by an external agent, moreover, is an important idea in ancient science: Aristotle used it to explain the action of semen on menstrual fluid in conception and the development of the embryo. Daphnis and Chloe's growing awareness of each other, their union and production of offspring, draw upon this concept. Finally, cheese is the product of both coagulation and physical pressure. The increasing restrictions placed on Chloe, and her increasing commodification, suggest cheese making as a metaphor for her transformation from a child into a commodity exchanged between men.

Writing of the artistry displayed by Longus in *Daphnis and Chloe*, Thomas Hägg says that the author 'knows what he wishes to achieve and has full control of his means of expression. The novel is carefully polished, down to the smallest detail'.[1] Inspired by Hägg's remark, this paper examines one of the smaller, if not the smallest, details of the text of *Daphnis and Chloe*, that is, its use of cheese; it suggests that the careful deployment of this foodstuff is one of the means by which the novel achieves its paradoxical effect of polished rusticity. Emily Gowers has observed that 'the significance of food in its literary representation lies both in its simple existence *and* in a bundle of metaphorical associations, a capacity to evoke a whole world of wider experience'.[2] What follows considers the cheeses of *Daphnis and Chloe* with an eye to both their simple existence in the text and their metaphorical associations.

Why cheese? Why not wine, bread, fruit, meat, or game – other products of the rustic life – which, it can be argued, also play symbolic roles in Longus'

---

[1] Hägg 1983, 37.
[2] Gowers 1993, 5.

Mary Jaeger, University of Oregon

https://doi.org/10.1515/9781501503986-020

work? There are several reasons, all interrelated, for, as the product of both a completely natural food (milk) and human intervention (the addition of rennet, the straining of curds and whey) cheese brings together several spheres of experience whose interaction is thematically important to the novel. First are those of the animal, which produces the milk, and of the human, who makes and consumes the cheese – and often consumes the offspring of the milk-giving ewe or goat as well. Every cheese thus embodies some of the structural elements of this story, in which the human infants are nursed by animals, and grow up to care for animals, milk them, and slaughter them too.³ It also lies at the intersection of nature (*physis*) and craft (*technê*), for cheese making was considered a craft in antiquity, albeit a primitive one.⁴ Moreover, in *Daphnis and Chloe* cheese plays a part in interactions between city dwellers and rustics, and between men and women, among which groups it serves as an item of exchange. Finally, and perhaps most important of all, whereas the production of grape, grain, and olive, the so-called 'Mediterranean triad', does not require animal sex (but rather hard agrarian labor), what I will call the 'pastoral triad' – milk, cheese, and meat from young animals – does.⁵ To parody Garnsey: cheese comes last. In the pastoral world food – in the form of forage – comes first, and after food comes sex. No sex, no birth; no birth, no lactation; no lactation, no milk; no milk, no cheese. Given that the very narrator of *Daphnis and Chloe* calls his work 'an offering to Eros, the Nymphs, and Pan' (Pref. 3), cheese, an end product as it were of Eros' efforts, deserves our attention.⁶

First, some context: cheese signified wealth as early as Homer, where Menelaus, in *Odyssey* 4, says that the peoples of far-off Libya have it in such quantity

---

3 Longo 1987, 295–296, observed that Longus' references to food – starting from the suckling by goat and ewe of the infants Daphnis and Chloe, moving on to their experience of 'city food' in company with Daphnis' biological parents, and concluding with the young peoples' choice of a diet heavy in fruit and milk – trace a path from nature to culture and back again. Epstein 1995, discusses extensively the interaction of the human and animal worlds.
4 Diodorus Siculus (4,81,2) credits Aristaeus with teaching mankind how to make cheese. According to Varro (R. 2,1,4), the keeping of sheep for milk, cheese, and hides was humankind's first step away from the state of nature; he also says that Greek writers devoted volumes to *tyropoiia* (2,1,28); Tibullus (2,3,14b-15) preserves the story of the invention of cheese by a lovestruck Apollo. On the ideology associated with milk and milk products, see especially Shaw 1982–1983, who points out its endurance into the late eighteenth century.
5 On the 'Mediterranean Triad' see Garnsey 1999, 13–17. Cato's *De Agricultura* does not discuss cheese making, although it contains directions for making a cheese cake, and Cicero, *Sen.* 56, has Cato include a good supply of cheese in the list of agricultural products that give satisfaction to the mature farmer.
6 On the pervasiveness of *Erôs*, see Turner 1960, 118–119.

that 'neither king nor shepherd wants for it'.[7] It is treasure and, accordingly, both something to store away, as the Cyclops does in *Odyssey* 9, and something to steal, as Odysseus and his men do, to their later discomfiture. In the opening scene of Euripides' *Cyclops*, cheese is simultaneously an object of theft and an item of exchange: the shipwrecked and hungry Odysseus, on hearing that there is food in the Cyclops's cave, including cows' milk and cheese made with fig-juice, says 'bring it out'. Silenus asks, 'how much gold will you give me in exchange (ἀντιδώσεις)?' Odysseus says, 'I bring, not gold, but the fruit of Dionysus'.[8] Delighted, Silenus trades the cheeses, which are not his to give away, for a skin of wine, and this exchange sets the drama in motion. To parody Garnsey again: on the level of dramatic action, cheese comes first. No cheese, no trade; and in this play, no trade, no plot.[9]

These ideas – cheese as wealth and cheese as trade-object in an exchange that motivates dramatic action – reappear in the pastoral poetry from which *Daphnis and Chloe* largely derives its setting and whose motifs it skillfully reworks.[10] In the bucolic singing-contest of Theocritus, *Idyll* 5, Lacon the goatherd boasts of his wealth in baskets of cheese-curd and, in a rhetorical move that reappears in *Daphnis and Chloe*, he connects this wealth to his virility.[11] In *Idyll* 1, an unnamed goatherd has given a Calydonian ferryman 'a goat and a great cheese of white milk', in exchange for which he has received the cup, which is described, in turn, in an elaborate ekphrasis.[12] This cup the goatherd proposes to give to his companion in exchange for the famous lament for Daphnis that forms much of the body of the poem. Finally, *Idyll* 11 provides a most relevant set of examples, both because it conveys the ideas of cheese as wealth and cheese as a means of exchange, and because it brings together the ideas of sex and wealth in cheese: the Cyclops Polyphemus calls Galatea 'whiter than curd, softer than a lamb'; he parades his wealth of cheese before her eyes; he invites her to live with him and to join him in the making of cheese; and his rue-

---

[7] *Odyssey* 4,87–88. For an overview of the appearances of cheese in Greek literature, mostly epic and comic, see Augerber 2000/2001, 1–41.
[8] E. *Cyc.* 96–174, especially 133–140.
[9] Gowers 1993, 81, notes that the Greek comedians used cheese making as a metaphor for plotting and contriving mischief, e.g., Arist. *Eq.* 479. Keulen 2000, 315–321, discusses Apuleius' use of it in this sense.
[10] For an overview of *Daphnis and Chloe's* intertextual relationship with Theocritus, with bibliography, see Morgan 2008, 221–224.
[11] Theocritus 5,86–87 φεῦ φεῦ, Λάκων τοι ταλάρως σχεδὸν εἴκατι πληροῖ / τυρῶ, καὶ τὸν ἀναβον ἐν ἄνθεσι παῖδα μολύνει.
[12] Theoc. 1,57–58 τῶ μὲν ἐγὼ πορθμῆι Καλυδνίῳ αἶγά τ' ἔδωκα / ὦνον καὶ τυρόεντα μέγαν λευκοῖο γάλακτος. On the adjective τυρόεντα, see Gow 1950, vol.2, 15.

ful words to himself near the poem's end admit that he would be better off making cheese-strainers than bidding for love.¹³ (Except for comparing Chloe to curds, Daphnis does some form of each of the activities mentioned above).

These topoi endure in the Latin tradition as well, as, for example, in Ovid's *Metamorphoses*, where the Cyclops dangles cheese in front of Galatea as evidence of his wealth;¹⁴ and in Vergil's first *Eclogue*, where Tityrus complains that in the bad old days he squandered the inadequate income from his cheeses on his beloved, who is also named Galatea.¹⁵ Tibullus describes a pastoral vision of pre-urban Rome, where a young girl crossing the Velabrum in a boat is 'about to please the wealthy master of the flock'. She returns with a snow-white lamb and cheese, 'gifts of the fecund countryside', says Tibullus.¹⁶ This is the most explicit representation of what is in the minds of Polyphemus and, perhaps, of Tityrus as well: the exchange, direct or indirect, of cheese for sex.

In *Daphnis and Chloe* cheeses appear frequently as items of wealth and as gifts. Indeed, Longus explicitly identifies them as such: in Book 1, Daphnis' rival Dorcon attempts to win Chloe's affection by giving her cheese; when competing with Dorcon for Chloe's admiration, Daphnis boasts of having cheese; and Dorcon gives Chloe's adoptive father Dryas cheeses as part of his campaign to win Chloe in marriage. In Book 2, Daphnis and Chloe give Philetas cheeses as thanks for his explanation of the nature of Eros; in Book 3, Daphnis promises the experienced Lycaenium cheeses, if she will only show him how to do to Chloe what he so wants to do; and in Book 4, cheeses are among the gifts that Daphnis gives to Eudromos (the master's messenger from the city), to Astylus (his own brother), and to his biological parents. Cheese, then, appears at first to be simply a marker in the system of exchange in Longus' highly idealized agrarian world.¹⁷ When, however, we consider the details of the gift giving and the descriptions of the cheeses themselves, and when we recognize the various ways in which they evoke Gower's 'world of wider experience', we can see that Longus' use of cheese

---

13 Theoc. 11,20 λευκοτέρα πακτᾶς ποτιδεῖν ἁπαλωτέρα ἀρνός. 36–7: τυρὸς δ' οὐ λείπει μ' οὔτ' ἐν θέρει οὔτ' ἐν ὀπώρᾳ, / οὐ χειμῶνος ἄκρω· ταρσοὶ δ' ὑπεραχθέες αἰεί. 65–66: ποιμαίνειν δ' ἐθέλοις σὺν ἐμὶν ἅμα καὶ γάλ' ἀμέλγειν / καὶ τυρὸν πᾶξαι τάμισον δριμεῖαν ἐνεῖσα.
14 Ov. *Met.* 13,829–830 *lac mihi semper adest niveum; pars inde bibenda / servatur, partem liquefacta coagula durant.*
15 Verg. *Ecl.* 1,31–35 *namque (fatebor enim) dum me Galatea tenebat, / nec spes libertatis erat nec cura peculi. / quamuis multa meis exiret uictima saeptis, / pinguis et ingratae premeretur caseus urbi, / non umquam grauis aere domum mihi dextra redibat.*
16 Tib. 2,5,33–38 *at qua Velabri regio patet, ire solebat / exiguus pulsa per uada linter aqua. / illa saepe gregis diti placitura magistro / ad iuuenem festa est uecta puella die, / cum qua fecundi redierunt munera ruris, / caseus et niueae candidus agnus ovis.*
17 On the 'reality' of this pastoral world, see Scarcella 1970, 103–131.

both manipulates these pastoral topoi in a manner that contributes to the sophisticated reader's enjoyment of the text, and reflects the increasing separation between the experiences of hero and heroine as they become acculturated to the gender norms of their society.[18]

The exchange of cheese for sex appears early on, when Dorcon resolves to win Chloe 'by gifts or by force' (1,15: δώροις ἢ βίᾳ). The cheeses appear in the 'by gifts' part of the program (again, δῶρα), which includes a panpipe for Daphnis, a fawnskin for Chloe and, for Chloe alone, daily gifts of flowery garlands, late-summer apples, and τυρὸς ἁπαλός, 'soft cheese'.[19] Cheese appears as wealth in the contest for Chloe's kiss, when Daphnis refutes Dorcon's accusations of poverty, saying, 'I have plenty of cheese and bread-on-a-spit, and white wine, which are the possessions of wealthy herdsmen'.[20]

Whereas Daphnis boasts of having sufficient cheese, Dorcon, who is a step ahead of the naïve hero, once again uses his cheeses economically, when he attempts to purchase Chloe as his bride. He approaches Dryas 'with certain noble little cheeses' (μετὰ τυρίσκων τινῶν γεννικῶν), which the text presents explicitly as gifts: 'he gave them [the cheeses] to be a gift' (τοὺς μὲν δῶρον εἶναι δίδωσι).[21] After Dryas refuses to agree to the marriage, and the gift-giving appears to be in vain, Dorcon decides to ambush and rape Chloe instead.[22] At this point, the narrator focalizes the narrative through Dorcon, saying, 'having failed of his hope a second time, and having lost his good cheeses, Dorcon decided to make an attempt on Chloe by force, when he found her alone'. Once 'lost', the gift cheeses that were presented so hopefully as 'noble', are still qualified as 'good' (ἀγαθούς). The adjective adds weight to Dorcon's feeling of having made a sacrifice in vain, with the result that readers see the situation for the moment from his point of view and understand the resentment that motivates the attempted ambush.

Let us give these well-bred and perfectly good cheeses a closer look. The cheese Dorcon gives Chloe is 'soft' (ἁπαλός), an adjective equally, if not more, applicable to a person: Theocritus' Cyclops called *Galatea* 'whiter than curd to

---

18 On gender-issues, see especially Winkler 1990, 101–126; Konstan 1994; Haynes 2003.
19 1,15,3 ἐντεῦθεν δὲ φίλος νομιζόμενος τοῦ μὲν Δάφνιδος ἠμέλει κατ' ὀλίγον, τῇ Χλόῃ δὲ ἀνὰ πᾶσαν ἡμέραν ἐπέφερεν ἢ τυρὸν ἁπαλὸν ἢ στέφανον ἀνθηρὸν ἢ μῆλον ὡραῖον. Passages from *Daphnis and Chloe* come from the Teubner text edited by Reeve 2001.
20 1,16,4 ἀρκεῖ δέ μοι τυρὸς καὶ ἄρτος ὀβελίας καὶ οἶνος λευκός, ὅσα ἀγροίκων πλουσίων κτήματα.
21 1,19,1.
22 1,20,1 δευτέρας δὴ διαμαρτὼν ὁ Δόρκων ἐλπίδος καὶ μάτην τυροὺς ἀγαθοὺς ἀπολέσας ἔγνω διὰ χειρῶν ἐπιθέσθαι τῇ Χλόῃ μόνῃ γενομένῃ...

look upon, *softer* than a lamb' (ἁπαλωτέρα ἀρνός).²³ To shift to a cheese an adjective that Theocritus used to describe a nymph (in terms of a lamb) is to make a very small and almost unnoticeable change; more noticeable is that the cheeses Dorcon gives Dryas are also qualified by adjectives applicable to people. They are either γεννικῶν 'noble' or 'well-born', or they are γενικῶν, 'of the clan' or 'of the family' (there is a textual problem).²⁴ Either word, however, is applicable to Chloe. The one describes her as Dorcon wishes her to be ('of the family' that is, of *his* family), the other describes her as she really is ('well-born'). In each case the adjective anticipates Dorcon's goal: soft cheeses for soft girl, and (perhaps) well-born cheeses for a well-born girl.

At the beginning of Book 2, after Philetas has described his garden and the winged boy he found frolicking in it, and has told Daphnis and Chloe what Love is and what to do about it, they give him 'some cheeses' (τυρούς τινας) and a 'kid already with horns'.²⁵ The gift of cheeses and mature kid in return for a lovely description is a variation on the pastoral exchange of a gift for a song, such as the promised cup of Theocritus 1. Daphnis and Chloe, however, give these gifts in exchange for what could have been useful information as well as a pretty story; for Philetas' discourse on Eros is, as Turner and others have pointed out, part of Daphnis and Chloe's education.²⁶ Like so many students, however, they do not immediately grasp the point of the lesson. An incident in Book 3 develops this idea of investing in education: offered private lessons in sex with the sophisticated urban matron, Lycaenium, Daphnis pledges tuition by promising her 'a weaned kid, soft cheeses from the first-flowing milk, and what's more, the she-goat herself'.²⁷ Both Philetas and Lycaenium teach: Philetas goes off with cheeses and kid after he has taught Daphnis and Chloe (τοσαῦτα παιδεύσας αὐτούς); Daphnis begs Lycaenium to 'teach him the craft' (διδάξαι τὴν τέχνην). Daphnis, moreover, offers Lycaenium the same gifts that he and

---

23 At 1,13,2, Chloe tests Daphnis' flesh to see if it is 'soft' (μαλθακή), and tries to gauge who is 'more delicate' (τρυφερώτερος).
24 Reeve follows the 1810 edition of Courier and prints γεννικῶν, 'noble', or 'well-born'. According to Reeve's apparatus, manuscripts **V** and **F** both have γενικῶν, 'of the clan' or 'of the family'.
25 2,8,1 Φιλητᾶς μὲν τοσαῦτα παιδεύσας αὐτοὺς ἀπαλλάττεται, τυρούς τινας παρ' αὐτῶν καὶ ἔριφον ἤδη καράστην λαβών.
26 Turner 1960, 119–120; Levin 1977, 5–17, points out that Philetas teaches theory, and Lycaenium practice.
27 3,18,1–2 Οὐκ ἐκαρτέρησεν ὁ Δάφνις ὑπ' ἡδονῆς, ἀλλ' ἅτε ἄγροικος καὶ αἰπόλος καὶ ἐρῶν καὶ νέος, πρὸ τῶν ποδῶν καταπεσὼν τὴν Λυκαίνιον ἱκέτυεν ὅτι τάχιστα διδάξαι τὴν τέχνην, δι' ἧς ὃ βούλεται δράσει Χλόην, καὶ ὥσπερ τι μέγα καὶ θεόπεμπτον ἀληθῶς μέλλων διδάσκεσθαι καὶ ἔριφον αὐτῇ σηκίτην δώσειν ἐπηγγείλατο καὶ τυροὺς ἁπαλοὺς πρωτορρύτου γάλακτος καὶ τὴν αἶγα αὐτήν.

Chloe gave Philetas, namely cheeses and a kid, only in his eagerness he throws in the she-goat herself.

Much of the humor in Daphnis' negotiations with Lycaenium lies in their contrast with the earlier exchange with Philetas. Daphnis feels that he is exchanging cheese with Lycaenium for knowledge about love, as he and Chloe did with Philetas; yet readers would also recognize another pastoral topos at work at the same time, that of the exchange of cheese for sex, and they might even recall specifically Theocritus' representation of the longing Polyphemus.[28] Even the description of the cheeses that Daphnis offers Lycaenium contributes to the readers' pleasure in their own superior knowledge. Expansive in his enthusiasm, Daphnis describes those cheeses as both 'soft' and 'made of the first-flowing milk'. The first expression of course, recalls Dorcon's more expert anticipation: just as he gave Chloe soft cheeses and hoped for a soft woman in return, so too Daphnis promises the same, with the same expectation. The second modifier reflects nicely Daphnis' innocence: this will be a first for him as well.

In contrast, as if to underscore the non-mercenary nature of Daphnis and Chloe's relationship, the text never shows Daphnis giving Chloe a cheese; indeed, she gives one to him. In Book 2, after Daphnis has suffered a beating at the hand of the Methymnians, and his nose is broken and bloody, Chloe wipes the blood from his face, then feeds him. This passage is unique, not in that Chloe feeds Daphnis, for she does so elsewhere, but in the nature of the food that she feeds him. Chloe gives Daphnis, not a cheese described with a multivalent adjective, nor even a complete cheese, but a slice of it (τυροῦ τμῆμά τι), together with a piece or portion of bread (ζυμίτου μέρος); and she gives him these foods without any ulterior motive of receiving something in exchange, but simply —and explicitly—for him to eat (δίδωσι φαγεῖν).[29] Here the lack of adjectives seems to imply that this food is just food, signifying nothing more. The appeal to the senses that follows underscores this simplicity by its striking contrast: Chloe's kisses taste like honey, and they, moreover, come from lips which are, like Dorcon's gift-cheeses, soft (φίλημα ἐφίλησε μελιτῶδες ἁπαλοῖς τοῖς χείλεσι). Thus the text shows Chloe as a properly 'feminine' agent playing the housewife's role of doling out portions instead of giving or trading whole cheeses, even as it

---

[28] Levin 1977, 7–11, points out that the two exchange a 'tasteful triad' of gifts: she gives him pan-pipes, honey, and a wallet; he gives her the cheese, the kid, and the she-goat.

[29] 2,18,1 διωκόντων δὴ τοὺς Μηθυμναίους ἐκείνων, ἡ Χλόη κατὰ πολλὴν ἡσυχίαν ἄγει πρὸς τὰς Νύμφας τὸν Δάφνιν καὶ ἀπονίπτει τε τὸ πρόσωπον ᾑμαγμένον ἐκ τῶν ῥινῶν ῥαγεισῶν ὑπὸ πληγῆς τινος καὶ τῆς πήρας προκομίσασα ζυμίτου μέρος καὶ τυροῦ τμῆμά τι δίδωσι φαγεῖν, τὸ δὲ μάλιστα ἀνακτησάμενον αὐτόν, φίλημα ἐφίλησε μελιτῶδες ἁπαλοῖς τοῖς χείλεσι.

parcels her out and describes her kisses and lips in terms of other items of exchange.[30]

Daphnis gives cheeses away three times in Book 4, to increasingly important people from the city: first, to Eudromos, the master's messenger, just as Eudromos is about to return to the city; then, to Astylus, the master's son and Daphnis' own blood brother; and, finally, to the master himself, his own biological father, Dionysophanes.[31] Here too, the descriptions of the cheeses may tell readers something beyond what they tell the characters. Those that Daphnis gives Eudromos are 'well set-up' (εὐπαγής).[32] On the one hand, the adjective, from a compound of πήγνυμι, the standard verb for making liquid coagulate, shows that Daphnis has mastered the craft of cheese making; on the other, εὐπαγής might also recall the similar epic adjective εὐπηγής (also from πήγνυμι), used once in Homer, of the disguised Odysseus, when Penelope argues that he should have a chance to string the bow: 'This stranger is right big and well set-up; and he claims to be the son of a noble father.'[33] If we are correct in attributing ulterior meanings to these adjectives, then the message sent by Daphnis all unknowing and conveyed by Eudromos (also all unknowing, but communicated to the reader by the cheeses), is that out on the farm there is a well set-up young man, possibly one who claims to be the son of a noble father.[34] Longus also uses a particularly apt adjective, ἀρτιπαγής, of the cheeses that Daphnis holds when facing his mother and his father for the first time: the adjective means 'recently set-up' or 'recently constructed'.[35] These, then, are particularly appropriate

---

[30] This division of labor calls to mind Ischomachus' words to his wife in Xenophon Oec., 7,33–36, which remind her that her job is to distribute foodstuffs and other household supplies. The description of Chloe's kiss also recalls, of course, Daphnis' thoughts after receiving his first kiss from Chloe (1,18,1: her lips are softer than roses, her mouth sweeter than honeycombs, but her kiss stings more sharply than a bee). Among the gifts Dorcon promises Dryas at 1,19,2, are four hives of bees. At 3,15,3, Lycaenium gives Daphnis honey. For a list of items exchanged in the novel, see Scarcella 1970, 117.

[31] 4,6,1; 4,10,3; 4,14,1.

[32] 4,6,1 μέλλοντος δὲ ἤδη σοβεῖν ἐς ἄστυ τοῦ Εὐδρόμου, καὶ ἄλλα μὲν οὐκ ὀλίγα αὐτῷ Δάφνις ἔδωκεν, ἔδοκε δὲ καὶ ὅσα ἀπὸ αἰπολίου δῶρα, τυροὺς εὐπαγεῖς, ἔριφον ὀψίγονον, δέρμα αἰγὸς λευκὸν καὶ λάσιον, ὡς ἔχοι χειμῶνος ἐπιβάλλεσθαι τρέχων.

[33] Od. 21,333–335.

[34] Such oblique glances at the truth about Daphnis' parentage appear elsewhere. When Daphnis and Chloe give Dorcon the goat to be sacrificed (1,12,5), the passage, as Cresci 1999, 222, points out, alludes to Theocritus Idyll 8, in which Menalcus tells Daphnis he may not offer a prize of a lamb because his harsh parents count the flock at night and will be angry (14–16). The irony is, of course, that in giving the goat to Dorcon, Daphnis is giving away his parents' property.

[35] 4,14,1.

cheeses for commemorating the fresh construction of Daphnis's biological family. Scholars have long recognized the 'speaking names' of many characters in Longus – Eudromus, Gnathon, Lykainion, Astylus, and the names that derive meaning from the literary tradition, such as that of Daphnis himself. Longus may also be offering his readers 'speaking cheeses', which convey meaning through their literary antecedents, and through the adjectives that describe them.[36]

When it comes to the making of cheese, *Daphnis and Chloe* continues to draw upon both an extensive literary tradition and meaningful metaphorical associations. Literary interest in the process of cheese making goes back to *Iliad* 5,902–904, where the coagulation of milk provides a simile for the clotting of blood. *Odyssey* 9 describes the Cyclops' cheeses draining in their wicker baskets in the cave. Poets after Homer remained interested in the process. We have seen the references in Theocritus; in addition, Tibullus 2,3 writes of Apollo inventing the process of cheese making through the coagulation and straining of milk; and Ovid's references to cheese in the *Metamorphoses* describe it, not surprisingly, as milk that has undergone a change.[37]

Cheese is the foodstuff that Daphnis and Chloe make, alone, together; this is intimate activity in contrast to the vintage described at the beginning of Book 2, in which they participate as part of the rustic community, and during which they find themselves exposed to the lascivious attentions of others. Cheese making is not the unpleasantly – at least for them – *public* experience that the vintage is.[38] Such privacy fits the literary antecedents for cheese making nicely: in *Odyssey* 9 the Cyclops, notoriously a loner, makes cheese alone; in Theocritus, *Idyll* 11, he invites Galatea to make it with him, and he does not want the company of a crowd.

Two passages describe cheese making: first, at 1,23,3, while Daphnis goes swimming, Chloe makes cheese by herself, a tough business in the heat, with the flies biting:

ἡ δὲ Χλόη μετὰ τὸ ἀμέλξαι τὰς ὄις καὶ τῶν αἰγῶν τὰς πολλὰς ἐπὶ πολὺν μὲν χρόνον κάματον εἶχε πηγνῦσα τὸ γάλα (δειναὶ γὰρ αἱ μυῖαι λυπῆσαι καὶ δακεῖν εἰ μὴ διώκοιντο), τὸ δὲ ἐντεῦθεν ἀπολουσαμένη τὸ πρόσωπον πίτυος ἐστεφανοῦτο κλάδοις καὶ τῇ νεβρίδι ἐζώννυτο καὶ τὸν γαυλὸν ἀναπλήσασα οἴνου καὶ γάλακτος κοινὸν μετὰ τοῦ Δάφνιδος ποτὸν εἶχε.

---

36 It is as if the novel itself engages its readers in the 'devious communication', which Winkler 1990, 110–111, shows is at play among the characters within the novel.
37 *Met.* 8,666; 13,796; 13,830; 14,274.
38 On the sexual implications of the vintage, see Zeitlin 1990, 449 and 449 n. 90.

After milking the sheep and most of the goats, Chloe worked long and hard making cheese, for the flies harassed her terribly and bit her, if they were not driven off. But afterwards she washed her face and garlanded herself with garlands of pine, tied her fawnskin about her, and having filled a pail with wine and milk, shared a drink together with Daphnis.

In Book 3,33,1–2, Daphnis announces to Chloe the promise of their marriage, and joins her in making cheese:

θᾶττον οὖν νοήματος, μηδὲν πιὼν μηδὲ φαγών, παρὰ τὴν Χλόην κατέδραμε καὶ εὑρὼν αὐτὴν ἀμέλγουσαν καὶ τυροποιοῦσαν, τόν τε γάμον εὐηγγελίζετο καὶ ὡς γυναῖκα λοιπὸν μὴ λανθάνων κατεφίλει καὶ ἐκοινώνει τοῦ πόνου· ἤμελγε μὲν εἰς γαυλοὺς τὸ γάλα, ἐνεπήγνυ δὲ ταρσοῖς τοὺς τυρούς, προσέβαλλε δὲ ταῖς μητράσι τοὺς ἄρνας καὶ τοὺς ἐρίφους. καλῶς δὲ ἐχόντων τούτων ἀπελούσαντο, ἐνέφαγον, ἔπιον, περιῄεσαν ζητοῦντες ὀπώραν ἀκμάζουσαν.

Quicker than thought, tasting neither food nor drink, he ran to Chloe, and finding her milking and making cheese, both announced the good news of their marriage and kissed her openly, because she was his future wife, and shared her work. He milked the milk into pails; he sent the cheese to curdle in its baskets, he put the lambs and kids to their mothers. When all was set in order, they washed, ate, drank, and went off searching for ripe fruit.

These two passages are similar, in part simply because they describe the same process, but also because each passage goes on to tell of the cheese maker or cheese makers washing up afterwards (ἀπολουσαμένη τὸ πρόσωπον / ἀπελούσαντο), and sharing refreshment (κοινὸν μετὰ τοῦ Δάφνιδος ποτὸν εἶχε / ἐνέφαγον, ἔπιον). The meaningful difference is that in the first passage Chloe works alone apart from Daphnis, until she shares with him a drink of wine and milk mixed together (κοινὸν μετὰ τοῦ Δάφνιδος ποτὸν εἶχε); in the second, Daphnis shares the labor (ἐκοινώνει τοῦ πόνου; note the repetition of κοιν- from the first passage); and then the two wash, drink, eat, and go off to look for ripe fruit. There is no mention of what they eat or drink in the second passage; the point is, they do it together, and they are together the subjects of the plural verbs. At the very least, the second passage aptly reflects the lovers' new hope of achieving the married state as it anticipates their future roles within an *oikos*, an economic unit distinct from others.

However, the references to the production and distribution of cheese show how those roles diverge according to gender: in Book 1, Chloe makes cheese by herself; in Book 2, she gives cheese to Daphnis, and both children give it to Philetas; but in Book 3, Lycaenium receives cheeses from Daphnis alone. Moreover, in Book 3, Daphnis 'shares the work' of cheese making with Chloe, but the verbs describing its production – milking, coagulating, tending the lambs and kids – are singular (ἤμελγε, ἐνεπήγνυ, προσέβαλλε), and thus focus attention on him as the agent. In Book 4, it is Daphnis who takes thought for laying in a better supply of milk buckets and pails and cheese-straining baskets.[39] Finally, the adjectives 'well set-up' and 'recently set-up' describing the cheeses, which Daphnis alone gives in Book 4, incorporate the process of cheese making. Thus Daphnis is the person who in the end controls the production and distribution of cheese, as he increasingly engages in gift-giving directed towards the urban sphere, an exchange that brings him closer and closer to the center of his family, and thus to his role as male head of household.[40]

When we consider the wider associations of references to cheese, we can see another way of interpreting these two descriptions, and it too points to the difference between the sexes. The medical writers connected cheese making and procreation. A text from the Hippocratic corpus calls cheese 'a thing indigestible (ἰσχυρὸν LSJ) and heating and nourishing and binding; indigestible in that it is closest to generation (ἰσχυρὸν μὲν ὅτι ἔγγιστα γενέσιος)'.[41] In his *Generation of Animals*, Aristotle compares the process of conception to the making of cheese (3,739b 21–27, A. L. Peck, Loeb tr.):

> The action of the semen of the male in 'setting' the female's secretion in the uterus is similar to that of rennet upon milk (παραπλήσιον ποιούσης ὥσπερ ἐπὶ τοῦ γάλακτος τῆς πυετίας). Rennet is milk which contains vital heat (θερμότητα ζωτικὴν ἔχον), as semen does, and this integrates the homogeneous substance and makes it 'set' (συνίστησι). As the nature of milk and the menstrual fluid is one and the same, the action of the semen upon the substance of the menstrual fluid is the same as that of rennet upon milk.

Galen too draws on these ideas when, in his commentary on the *Timaeus*, he says that the body, having its first formation from menstrual fluid and sperm, 'is brought forth nearly resembling freshly coagulated cheeses' (ἀποκυηθὲν δὲ τοῖς νεωστὶ πηγνυμένοις τυροῖς παραπλήσιον).[42]

I must speculate here, because we do not know if Longus knew the medical writers, or Aristotle's *History of Animals*, or the work of his own possible contemporary Galen; nor do we know to what degree these ideas about conception

---

39 4,4,4. Scarcella 1971, 44, notes the parallels with *Odyssey* 9,219 and 223.
40 It is meaningful that while Daphnis stands his ground, Chloe flees into the woods because she feels both fear and shame at the prospect of encountering such a crowd (4,14,1). On Chloe, see Haynes 2003, 61–67.
41 *De diaeta* (i-iv, 51, line 1). On the culinary metaphors in the medical writers, see Hanson 1995, 302–305.
42 On the ancient sources comparing cheese making, conception, and birth, see Pigneaud 1995, 3–17; on the Aristotelian ideas about the process of conception, see Dean-Jones 1994, 184–193, and Longo, 2002.

were, so to speak, in the air.⁴³ But they reinforce the link between cheese making and sex implicit both in Theocritus 5, where Lacon links his possession of twenty baskets of cheese to his virility, and especially in Theocritus 11,65–66, where Polyphemus invites Galatea to come make cheese with him; for he wants more than her company in milking the flocks and making that milk coagulate by putting rennet into it.⁴⁴

In a broad sense, the making of cheese is a nice analogy for another natural process, the increase in Daphnis and Chloe's erotic interest in one another. Like the making of cheese, it is induced by heat [the novel's action starts as the spring heats up (1,9,1)]; and it relies on the addition of a small amount of outside interference: in the case of cheese, the addition of rennet; in the case of Daphnis and Chloe, the action of the (lactating) she-wolf (1,11,1) – interference inserted by Eros himself.⁴⁵ More specifically, the cheese-making scene in Book 3 would have entertained and amused readers familiar with Aristotle's analogy for the process of conception, readers who would recognize that, here again, Daphnis and Chloe are unaware of the significance of their actions. These readers would see that Daphnis and Chloe's activities at the end of Book 3 are particularly appropriate for a couple who will be married soon, and fruitfully. Moreover, the fact that the text says Daphnis and Chloe 'shared the labor', even while the singular verbs bring Daphnis to the fore and isolate him, achieves two things: it winks at the active role of the male contribution – semen – in the Aristotelian idea of conception, and it reflects the social reality of married life, in which both partners share the activity central to the formation of a household, but the face the household presents to the outside world is that of the husband.⁴⁶

---

43 Belmont 1988, 13–28, shows how this metaphor has come down in Europe in both the scholarly and the folk tradition. Its presence in the folk tradition suggests that it may have been widely known.
44 'An image of conjugal bliss', says Hunter 1983, 63.
45 Epstein 1995, 58–59, calls the wolf 'a catalyst' and points out that 'her arrival on the scene sets Daphnis' and Chloe's love in motion'. Epstein also notes the she-wolf's ambiguous nature: 'Her predation is set against her concern to find food for her young'. The unidirectional nature of the process of curdling milk nicely reinforces the manner in which *Daphnis and Chloe* organizes its material to suggest, as Zeitlin 1990, 420, says, 'that each phase, each gesture, each transition to the next stage of the plot, is somehow a necessary, even intrinsic element in a whole evolving process'. See also McCulloh 1970, 68–69.
46 The scene comes immediately before Daphnis' climb to get the ripe apple from the tree at 3,33,4, a passage which has received extensive scholarly attention for its portrayal of eroticism and gender roles. See, e.g., McCulloh 1970, 74–77; Winkler 1990, 105 and 122–123; and Morgan 2008, 223–224.

Although cheese plays a small role in *Daphnis and Chloe*, its presence reminds us that, together with the production of wool and skins, the production of food from animals was the raison d'être of pastoral life. The care with which Longus uses it is typical of his attention to detail. As a simple food, the product of primitive craft, an item of exchange and thus a link with the urban world, cheese in *Daphnis and Chloe* marks several stages in the narrative: the first external threat to the young couple; their acquisition of erotic knowledge; their promise to each other; and Daphnis' forging of increasingly close connections with his blood-relatives from the city. With its range of wider associations, cheese provides the author with one means by which to play on the gap in understanding between his rustic characters and sophisticated readers, so as to give pleasure to the latter. Finally, it provides concrete evidence for the pervasiveness of Eros in Longus' pastoral world, a world in which this food comes both first and last: for *Daphnis and Chloe* makes it clear that, although one cannot have cheese without sex, one cannot have sex without cheese.

Bibliography

Augerber, J. 2000. 'Du prince au berger, tout Homme a son content de fromage...' *Odyssée*, 4, 87–88', *REG* 113, 1–41.
Belmont, N. 1998. 'L'enfant et la fromage', *L' Homme* 28.1, 13–28.
Cesci, L. 1999. 'The Novel of Longus the Sophist and the Pastoral Tradition', in: S. Swain (ed.), *Oxford Readings in the Greek Novel*, Oxford: Oxford University Press. 210–242.
Dean-Jones, L.A. 1994. *Women's Bodies in Classical Greek Science*, Oxford: Clarendon Press.
Epstein, S.J. 1995. 'Longus' Werewolves', *CPh* 90.1, 58–73.
Hägg, T. 1983. *The Novel in Antiquity*, Berkeley/Los Angeles: University of California Press.
Haynes, K. 2003. *Fashioning the Feminine in the Greek Novel*, London/New York: Routledge.
Garnsey, P. 1993. *Food and Society in Classical Antiquity*, Cambridge: Cambridge University Press.
Gow, A.S.F. 1950. *Theocritus, Edited with a Translation and Commentary*, 2 vols. Cambridge: Cambridge University Press.
Gowers, E. 1993. *The Loaded Table: Representations of Food in Roman Literature*, Oxford: Oxford University Press.
Hanson A. E.1995. '*Paidopoiïa*: Metaphors for Conception, Abortion, and Gestation in the Hippocratic Corpus', in: Ph. J. van der Eijk, H. F. J. Horstmanshoff, P.H. Schrijvers (eds.), *Ancient Medicine in its Socio-Cultural Context*, Amsterdam/Atlanta: Rodopi. 291–307.
Hunter, R.L. 1983. *A Study of Daphnis and Chloe*, Cambridge: Cambridge University Press.
Keulen, W.H. 2000. 'Significant Names in Apuleius: a 'Good Contriver' and his Rival in the Cheese Trade (MET. 1, 5)', *Mnemosyne*, 53.3, 310–321.
Konstan, D. 1994. *Sexual Symmetry: Love in the Ancient Novel and Related Genres*, Princeton: Princeton University Press.

Levin, D.N. 1977. 'The Pivotal Role of Lycaenion in Longus' Pastorals', *Rivista di Studi Classici* 25, 5–17.
Longo, O. 1989. 'Codici Alimentari, Rovesciamento, Regressione. Gnatone nel Romano di Longo Sofista', in: O. Longo, P. Scarpi (eds.), *Homo Edens: regimi, miti e pratiche dell' alimentazione nella civiltà del mediterraneo*, Verona. 295–298.
Longo, O. 2002. 'Latte e Formaggi Aristotelici', in: O. Longo, Ch. Cremonesi (eds.), *Lac D'Amour: Homo Edens, VII: regimi miti e pratiche dell' alimentazione nella civiltà del mediterraneo*, Padova. 227–233.
McCulloh, W.E. 1970. *Longus*, New York: Twayne Publishers.
Morgan, J.R. 1997. 'Longus 'Daphnis and Chloe': a Bibliographical Survey, 1950–1995', *ANRW* 34.3, 2208–2276.
Pigneaud, J. 1975. 'La Présure et le Lait: quelques remarques sur la reverie de la caille du lait', *LEC*, 43,1, 3–17.
Reeve, M.D. (ed.) 2001. Longus: *Daphnis et Chloe*, Bibliotheca Teubneriana, München/Leipzig: K. J. Saur (Original Work Published 1982).
Scarcella, A. 1971. 'La Tecnica dell' imitazione in Longo Sofista', *GIF*, 23, 34–59.
Scarcella, A. 1970. 'Realtà e letteratura nel paesaggio sociale ed economico del romanzo di Longo Sofista', *Maia* 22, 103–131.
Shaw, B. 1982–1983. 'Eaters of Flesh, Drinkers of Milk: the Ancient Mediterranean Ideology of the Pastoral Nomad', *Ancient Society* 13/14, 5–31.
Turner, P. 1960. 'Daphnis and Chloe: An Interpretation', *G&R* 2nd Series, 7,2, 117–123.
Winkler, J. 1990. *The Constraints of Desire: The Anthropology of Sex and Gender in Ancient Greece*, New York and London: Routledge.
Zeitlin, F.I. 1990. 'The Poetics of Eros: Nature, Art, and Imitation in Longus' *Daphnis and Chloe*', in: D.M. Halperin, J.J. Winkler, F.I. Zeitlin (eds.), *Before Sexuality*, Princeton: Princeton University Press. 417–464.

Jason König
Rethinking Landscape in Ancient Fiction: Mountains in Apuleius and Jerome

Abstract: This paper compares Apuleius' *Metamorphoses* and Jerome's *Life of Hilarion* in their representation of landscape. Apuleius' representation of mountainous landscape as a place of fear and suffering stands in contrasts with Jerome's celebration of the capacity of Christianity to transform marginal spaces into places of holiness. However, they share an interest in the difficulty of escaping from the physical realities of the world; and both of them dramatize the ultimate impossibility and inadequacy of stylized understandings of landscape, albeit to vastly different effect. Jerome's reliance on the *Metamorphoses* for his *Life of Hilarion* may be at least in part a result of the fact that he found Apuleius' conceptions of landscape and geography unusually promising as a framework for giving expression to his own exploration of the contest between conflicting conceptualizations of Christian geography.

Introduction

Distinctions have sometimes been drawn between post-romantic notions of landscape, characterized by detailed sensitivity to the social and historical specificity of particular locations, and pre-romantic, especially classical representations, where landscape tends to be presented in more stereotyped or allegorical terms.[1] Bakhtin similarly, and influentially, described the chronotope of the ancient Greek novels as geographically abstract, unconcerned with the details of place.[2] Important recent work has done much to complicate those assumptions, by drawing out the complexity and sophistication of pre-romantic landscape description.[3] This paper aims to take that process further through attention to two

---

1 E.g., see Lutwack 1984, 19, with reference amongst others to Nicolson 1997, esp. 38–42.
2 See Bakhtin 1981, 99–102, on the abstract 'adventure-time' space of the Greek novels; it is important to note, however, that he characterises the space in Apuleius and Petronius rather differently (e.g. see 120: 'space is filled with real, living meaning, and forms a crucial relationship with the hero and his fate'). Indeed, some of his insights inform my discussion later; if anything, he seems to me to overstate the degree to which Apuleius avoids abstract landscapes.
3 See esp. Lutwack 1984.

Jason König, University of St Andrews

https://doi.org/10.1515/9781501503986-021

texts: Apuleius, *Metamorphoses* (*Met.*) and Jerome's *Life of Hilarion* (*VH*), focusing, for reasons of space, on representations of hills and mountains. Both Apuleius and Jerome do indeed offer us something very different from the realism of post-romantic depictions of natural landscape, giving us descriptions which are imbued with the language of ekphrasis and allegory, repeatedly declining to reproduce a plausible vision of any particular geographical space. However, I aim also to show that they are highly self-conscious about the artificiality of their mountain scenery, using it to very deliberate effect, and furthermore that both of them comment, in different ways, on the ultimate inadequacy of these stylized conceptions of landscape. I have learnt a great deal from recent publications on novelistic landscape, in particular on landscape in Apuleius,[4] but this paper also aims to break new ground, in particular through its comparative perspective, which raises new questions about the similarities and differences between portrayal of landscape in Greco-Roman and early Christian narrative.

Apuleius

Of all the ancient novelists it is Apuleius who shows most fascination with the textures of physical landscape, especially in Books 1–10. The text is saturated with the language of rocks, peaks and precipices, steepness and jaggedness, both in its descriptive passages and in its metaphors.[5] Those images alternate with more seductive imagery of meadows and gardens, rivers and streams. And Apuleius is fascinated, too, with the often hostile landscapes through which Lucius passes.

What functions does that obsession with landscape serve? One of its functions is to contribute to a startlingly bleak vision of the territory of Roman Achaia. Fergus Millar has shown the value of the *Metamorphoses* as a source for the social history of Roman provincial life, stressing the accuracy of Apuleius' depiction of the economic and administrative realities Lucius encounters.[6] What he does not bring out, however, is the way in which that highly peopled depiction of countryside is at times in tension with ostentatiously unrealistic and stylized pictures of wild landscape, which are disorientatingly cut free from any kind of topographical markers, so that Lucius' progress through Achaia becomes ac-

---

[4] E.g., see Paschalis and Frangoulidis 2002; and on Apuleius, Zimmerman 2002, de Biasi 1990 and Trinquier 1999.
[5] See de Biasi 1990 for extensive discussion of the *Met.*'s many mountain scenes.
[6] Millar 1981.

tually very hard to map.⁷ In these scenes the sense of desertedness, the absence of both divine and human habitation, contributes to a nightmarish vision of fantastical empty territories far removed from the familiar space of provincial city life, peopled only by bandits and dangerous beasts. Pausanias, writing at roughly the same time, is an interesting point of comparison here: he too describes a landscape which is oddly devoid of living human presence, and he rarely describes his own encounters with informants or fellow travellers. And yet his version of Roman Achaia is not for that reason unrealistic or lacking in particularity. On the contrary, the land is for Pausanias imbued with the traces of Greek history and Greek myth; and his mountains, far from being anonymous spaces, are linked with the presence of particular divinities and centuries-long habits of human worship. Here, in other words, landscape is intricately tied to culture.⁸ One might draw a contrast, too, with the *Onos*. As Edith Hall has shown, that text offers a very bleak vision of the violence of a socially hierarchised society.⁹ One might view Apuleius' very hostile vision of geographical space as an extension of that rather bleak worldview. But if that is right, it is not an aspect for which the *Onos* itself gives many starting-points: the *Onos* on the whole is much more precise about topography, allowing us to track the hero's progress through identifiable parts of Achaian territory.¹⁰

Apuleius' stylized landscapes also contribute to the characterization of Lucius' state of mind and his sense of identity. Maaike Zimmerman has made that point in particular for Lucius' many road descriptions, pointing to the way in which distinctions between hard and easy terrain are often a function primarily of Lucius' pessimism or optimism at any one particular moment.¹¹ That conclusion chimes closely with theoretically informed approaches to landscape in more modern literature, which have stressed, for example, the importance of taking account of focalization – in other words, the way in which an individual's perspective determines perception and description of landscape – even in 'realistic', topographically specific post-romantic landscape description;¹² and the importance of understanding how landscape is conceptualized through an indi-

---

7 See Slater 2002, 173, and Zimmerman 2000, 11.
8 Cf. Elsner and Rubiés 1999, 10, on fascination with local culture in the travel writing of the second century CE, especially Pausanias.
9 Hall 1995.
10 See Graverini 2002, esp. 58–59.
11 Zimmerman 2002; cf. de Biasi 1990, who concludes that Apuleius is more interested in the relevance of landscape for his human characters than in nature for its own sake.
12 See Kadish 1987, esp. 5–9.

vidual's bodily experience.¹³ In the light of that latter point, it seems no accident that Lucius often describes his unfamiliar donkey's body, the alien hardness and bristliness of his new self, in landscape-like terms; in 11,13, for example, he describes his 'rocky teeth returning to their human smallness' (*dentes saxei redeunt ad humanam minutiem*). His acute awareness of the textures of physical landscape may in that sense be connected to his heightened sensitivity to his own changed body. Important also for the intertwining between landscape and identity is the status of wild landscapes – and particularly mountain landscapes – as a place for those who stand apart from normal human culture: a place for bandits and outcasts (Lucius, as a beast of burden for the band of robbers, is of course even lower in the social hierarchy than they are), and for prodigies, who overturn the normal rules of the natural world, as Lucius does in his metamorphosed state.¹⁴ The stylized, fantastical mountain spaces which recur right through the text are appropriate spaces for Lucius to inhabit, and appropriately crafted to fit into the peculiar perspective of his narrating voice, for all of these different reasons.

Still, we might feel that this does not fully explain why Apuleius carries his stylization of landscape to such extremes. One further answer, related to the points already made in the last paragraph, is the importance of allegorical connotations. In the neoplatonic (and later, Christian) writing of the later Roman Empire it becomes increasingly common for travel to be used as a metaphor for the journey to spiritual enlightenment;¹⁵ and within that complex of ideas the idea of travelling over steep or rough terrain suggests the Hesiodic distinction, much illustrated in later Greek literature, between the hard road to virtue and the easy way to vice.¹⁶ On Zimmerman's reading, those kinds of moralising connotations become increasingly important as the *Metamorphoses* goes on, although she rightly avoids suggesting that there is any simplistic moralising message here, seeing instead a playfully imprecise engagement with allegorical and moralising language.¹⁷ It may be no accident that the Cupid and Psyche story takes this imprecision of landscape further than anywhere else in the text,

---

13 See Davies 2000.
14 On links between mountainous landscapes and bandits, see Trinquier 1999, 262–267; on mountains as outside civilization, cf. Buxton 1994, 81–96.
15 See Elsner and Rubiés 1999, 8–15.
16 See Zimmerman 2000, 91–92 (on *Works and Days* 287–291); and Bakhtin 1981, 120, on the 'path of life metaphor' in the *Metamorphoses*.
17 See Zimmerman 2000, esp. 95–96.

given that this is the section of the *Metamorphoses* most saturated of all with allegorising language.[18]

Finally, and perhaps most obviously, it is clear that the stylized nature of Apuleius' landscape descriptions is intended to signal his exuberant engagement with literary tradition, drawing, for example, on traditions of ekphrasis, and weaving together elements of landscape description from a wide range of genres. That effect has been carefully charted within a series of articles and commentary discussions. To give just two examples, Alessandro Schiesaro has argued that the description of the robbers' hideout in Book 4 draws on a range of *locus horridus* traditions, inverting the conventions of the literary *locus amoenus*, and influenced in particular by Virgil and Seneca;[19] and Stephen Harrison has argued that the extravagant landscapes of the Cupid and Psyche tale are marked out as playful versions of Virgilian, epic topography.[20]

All of those explanations for the *Metamorphoses*' stylization of landscape, while not perhaps individually surprising, among them suggest that Apuleius is not simply repeating unthinkingly a general failure in classical literature to describe landscape in realistic and particularised terms; rather, he uses these tropes of anonymous space very ingeniously, to a achieve a wide range of effects.

Is there anything more to say, however? In the rest of this section, I want to suggest, perhaps more surprisingly, that Apuleius also goes out of his way to hint at the absurdities and inadequacies of the very styles of landscape description on which his work relies, even as he indulges them.

It may be useful to begin with to return to the robber's hideout. Jean Trinquier has recently taken issue with Schiesaro's reading of this passage, arguing that to align it with a *locus horridus* tradition vastly understates the complexity of the literary game Apuleius is playing here. He acknowledges the ekphrastic character of the passage, but also suggests that Apuleius/Lucius deliberately draws attention to the artificiality of the literary exercise. And he suggests, too, that the complexity of the allusions lying behind the passage deliberately undermines any clear literary or generic categorisation of it, throwing doubt on the seriousness of the exercise.[21]

I want to suggest here, however, that Apuleius's self-consciousness about the artificiality of his landscape descriptions goes beyond literary game playing. It is not simply that he sometimes chooses to break the illusion of narrative, winking, as it were, at his audience. In addition, I suggest, this acute awareness

---

[18] See Harrison 2002, 48.
[19] Schiesaro 1986.
[20] Harrison 2002, 49–52.
[21] Trinquier 1999.

of artificial landscape keys into the wider theme of false perception, which has been much discussed for the work as a whole, whereby Books 1–10 show us Lucius' inability to look beyond worldly objects, before gaining (or at least seeming to gain) access to an understanding of higher, spiritual realities. Apuleius' obsession with a style of description which is so sensitive to physical textures, reflected in the sensuous inventiveness of his Latin, and which offers us visions of landscape described almost like over-elaborate stage-sets, reflects Lucius' immersion in the things of the world, but also gives us as readers, alert to the artificiality of Apuleian style, an awareness of the illusory nature of his experience.

Here I turn to the most prominent example of self-consciousness about those patterns, and that is the description of the pantomime of Book 10. I am interested here in particular in the fake stage-set of Mount Ida.[22] The mountain is introduced in 10,30:

> *Erat mons ligneus, ad instar incluti montis illius quem vates Homerus Idaeum cecinit, sublimi instructus fabrica, consitus virectis et vivis arboribus, summo cacumine de manibus fabri fonte manante fluviales aquas eliquans.*

> There was a wooden mountain constructed with lofty workmanship on the model of that famous mountain which the poet Homer sang of, Mount Ida. It was planted with greenery and living trees, pouring out river water from a spring, made by the hands of the craftsman, on the highest summit.

The themes of fabrication are deeply ingrained here.[23] The mountain is literally brought alive through the hands of the artificer, through the living plants and trees which grow on it (in the sentence following we hear of goats grazing on the grass): that juxtaposition of life with artifice reminds us, perhaps, that even the living, peopled landscape Lucius has moved through in the last ten books may itself have been the subject of artifice despite its verisimilitude. Indeed, the mention of the stream flowing from the mountain top (*summo cacumine...fonte manante*) might prompt us to think back to the robbers' hideout, which was marked by the same feature [*de summo vertice fons affluens* (4,6)].[24] The ephemeral nature of the fake mountain becomes all the more apparent

---

22 Oddly not much discussed by de Biasi 1990.
23 See Zimmerman 1993, 148.
24 See Zimmerman 1993, 146; however, it also stands out from 4,6, as the only place in the text where a mountain is described in pleasant terms (see Zimmerman 2000, 367). In retreating from the imagery of inhospitable mountainsides, Apuleius perhaps hints at the way in which all of the landscape scenes which have come before are themselves illusionary, less intimidating than Lucius, with his materialistic view of the world, can see – it is only now, as we approach the moment of salvation, that the theatricality of Books 1–10 becomes clear.

when the dance comes to an end in 10,34 and the moment of truth for Lucius begins to be imminent:

> *Tunc de summo montis cacumine per quandam latentem fistulam in excelsum prorumpit vino crocus diluta, sparsimque defluens pascentes circa capellas odoro perpluit imbre, donec in meliorem maculatae speciem canitiem propriam liteo colore mutarent. Iamque tota suave fraglante cavea montem illum ligneum terrae vorago decepit.*
>
> Then from the highest summit of the mountain, through a hidden pipe, saffron dissolved in wine bursts up high into the air, and falling to the ground, scattering, it rains down on the goats who are pasturing all around with a sweet-smelling shower, until, dyed to a greater beauty, they swap their natural whiteness for a yellow colour. And then, when the whole theatre was filled with a pleasant fragrance, a chasm in the earth swallowed up the wooden mountain

Here, in a wonderful literalisation of the Golden Age of Virgil's fourth eclogue, the sheep become coloured by saffron, but through human, theatrical ingenuity, rather than the natural workings of nature.[25] The juxtaposition of that allusion with two distinct references to moralising discussions of theatricality in Seneca only points up all the more the theme of artificial fabrication of the scene, as well as suggesting that the narrator may here be looking back at this scene from the perspective of a later, moralising, quasi-Senecan viewpoint, rather than simply reporting his perceptions at the time.[26] Here, then, with Lucius on the brink of his conversion, the text says goodbye to theatricality, and indeed to theatrical landscapes, sweeping them – along with the sensual, voyeuristic pleasures of the 'earthly Venus' which are given such prominence in the description of the dance itself – into oblivion.[27] It may be no accident that Book 11 is strikingly uninterested in the description of movement through physical space: the mountainous scenes and metaphors, the recurring road descriptions of Books 1–10 are shunned as Lucius turns his mind to spiritual rather than physical perceptions.[28] On that reading, this theatrical destruction of the wooden mountain signals a moment of transition away from the word of illusion. And yet we may be left with a nagging doubt about that conclusion if we follow the metaphor through to its conclusions, in line with standard worries about the seriousness of Book 11. Is Apuleius' cleansing of Lucius' illusionistic, worldly viewpoint itself a conjuring trick, a piece of theatrical slight of hand, an insubstantial and temporary imitation of salvation?

---

25 See Zimmerman 2000, 404.
26 See Zimmerman 2000, 403, with reference to Finkelpearl 1991, 231–232.
27 Cf. Zimmerman 1993, 159–161.
28 See Zimmerman 2002, 80–81.

Jerome

Jerome's *Life of Hilarion* draws heavily on Apuleius' *Metamorphoses*, reshaping the resources of pagan fiction for new, Christian purposes.[29] One of the things they have most strikingly in common is their representation of social and topographical space. Like Apuleius, Jerome shows his hero coming face to face with the harsh economic realities of life in the provinces of the Roman Empire – in this case mainly Roman Palestine, where most of the work is set.[30] These repeated scenes of Hilarion's encounter with the problems and conflicts of the world around him are one of the things which makes the text so entertaining to read, full of vivid description and comic, picaresque detail. At the same time, again like the *Metamorphoses*, the *Life of Hilarion* is also full of deserted, wilderness spaces which share much of the stylized, exaggerated quality of Apuleian landscape. These are the spaces to which Hilarion longs to retreat. My aim in this section is simply to explore some of the ways Jerome uses stylized landscape, and to compare them with the picture we have seen already for Apuleius. I want to focus in particular on one passage, that is, *VH* 31, which describes the hostile mountain-top where Hilarion spends the last years of his life, and which very obviously imitates and elaborates on the mythical landscape of the *Life of Antony*,[31] but which also resembles Apuleius' extravagantly jagged and inaccessible mountains.[32]

An interest in wild landscape is of course far from unusual in early hagiographical writing, even if the *Life of Hilarion* stands out from other early Christian texts for the extravagance of its mountain descriptions. The fascination with wilderness is a vehicle for the fascination with Christianity's capacity to transform the negative into positive; it is also in many ways an act of appropriation. The saint rehabilitates the status of the outsider, and in the process also appropriates the archetypal outsider's space, the territory of mountain and desert. Space reserved before for bandits and strange animals becomes now a home for the man of god, who wins that territory against demons and hostile inhabitants. Certainly bandits and other outcasts are ubiquitous in the backdrop to Hi-

---

[29] See Weingarten 2005.
[30] See Weingarten 2005, 86 and 106–108.
[31] See Leclerc 2007, 292–293, for parallels from the *Life of Antony*; and cf. *VH* 21, on Hilarion's visit to Antony's mountain retreat; on the parallels between *VH* 21 and 31, and the way in which both look back to the *Life of Antony* and Jerome's *Life of Paul of Thebes*, see Burrus 2004, 42–45.
[32] See Weingarten 2005, 96–97 on close verbal parallels with the hostile landscape of the entrance to Hades in Apuleius, *Met.* 6,13–14.

larion's exploits. For example, in the early days of his ascetic career, Hilarion retreats into an area of the desert which was renowned for bandits (*latrociniis infamis*) (*VH* 3,1); later he is protected from robbery at the hands of men who come to steal from him in the night but are unable to find his hut (they promise to lead reformed lives when they speak to him the next day); and before he settles finally in Cyprus he expresses a desire to go to Egypt, to the area known as Bucolia (*ad ea loca quae vocantur Bucolia* (*VH* 31,1)), the home of the bandits known as *boukoloi*.[33] In addition he battles repeatedly against demons and wild beasts (for example at *VH* 14 and 28). Hilarion reclaims the desert from these creatures for the local population, but he also takes on for himself their prodigious, outsider status, turning it into something positive and beneficent.

The language of ekphrasis also contributes to that image of Christian transformation of all that is hostile and negative. It is striking, for example, that both of Jerome's extended mountain descriptions in this text combine in one space the traditions of *locus horridus* and *locus amoenus*, in a way which articulates the paradox of Christian asceticism, where the most remote and harsh landscape becomes itself a spiritual paradise. That paradoxical mixture is most obvious in Hilarion's final place of retreat in Cyprus, as described in *VH* 31,3–4:[34]

> [Hesychius] perduxit eum duodecim milibus a mari, procul inter secretos asperosque montes et quo vix reptando manibus genibusque posset ascendi. Qui introgressus contemplatus quidem est terribilem valde et remotum locum arboribusque hinc circumdatum, habentem etiam aquas de supercilio collis irriguas, et hortulum peramoenum et pomaria plurima—quorum fructum numquam in cibo sumpsit –, sed et antiquissimi templi ruinam, ex quo, ut ipse referebat et eius discipuli testantur, tam innumerabilium per noctes et dies daemonum voces resonabant, ut exercitum crederes.

> Hesychius led him to a place twelve miles from the sea, far away amongst hidden and harsh mountains, a place it was only just possible to climb up to, by crawling on one's hands and knees. Arriving there he contemplated this place which was indeed very terrible and isolated. It was surrounded here and there by trees, with water pouring down from the brow of the hill, and a delightful little garden and very many fruit trees, whose fruit he never ate. But it also had nearby the ruin of a temple from which, as he himself used to tell and as his disciples confirm, the voices of countless demons used to echo day and night, so many that you might have thought there was an army of them.

Hilarion, we hear, is pleased to be near to his enemies. This is clearly a mountain in the Apuleian tradition, with a desperately steep approach, and water flowing

---

33 For parallels in the Greek novels, see, amongst others, Heliodorus, *Aithiopika* 1,15.
34 Cf. Weingarten 2005, 97, on this passage's reversal of the most inhospitable landscape details of Apuleius, *Met.* 6,13–14.

from the top. It shares with Apuleius' landscapes the sense of being implausible and fantastical. But the odd combination of fearful steepness and idyllic garden brings out a specifically Christian paradox, where the inhospitable and the paradisiacal are combined in one space. Here, too, as for Apuleius, it is hard to miss the allegorical overtones, which further remove this landscape from realistic description. For example, it seems hardly fanciful to view the approach to the mountain-top crawling on hands and knees as a metaphor for the self-abasement and struggle which brings one close to God;[35] and the mountain-top garden itself is clearly an image of paradise.[36] The atmosphere of allegory is enhanced by Jerome's reference to the fruits of Hilarion's 'delightful garden' (*hortulum peramoenum*), which he refrains from eating. That detail casts Hilarion's self-denial in Edenic terms, while also recalling closely the Apuleian passage where Lucius refrains from eating roses in the *hortulum amoenum* of *Met.* 3,29.[37]

As for Apuleius, then, it is clear that Jerome is handling the stylized anonymity of his mountain and desert landscapes to very deliberate effect. Is there anything to match Apuleius' self-conscious exposure of the artificiality of those landscapes? I want to suggest in the final paragraphs of this paper that Jerome, too, draws attention to similar problems, not in the sense that his hero is deluded or short-sighted, as Lucius is, but rather in the sense that Jerome repeatedly exposes the difficulty Hilarion has in achieving the retreat from the world for which he strives. Both Lucius and Hilarion are hampered, in other words, by their inability to escape from the demands of the physical world. For all their differences they have that in common; indeed, Jerome may, I suggest, have been attracted to Apuleius' text precisely because of its play with that theme. Once again, Jerome is not unusual among early hagiographical writers in drawing attention to this problem. One of the driving fascinations of the early saints' lives is the way in which they draw out the paradox of ascetics, whose desire to overcome the body and the things of the physical world actually leads them to be more and more overwhelmed by bodily sensation. Fasting, after all, while it aspires to release the soul from the body, also requires obsessive bodily attention. But for all the typicality of that theme, Jerome once again takes it to extremes. Hilarion repeatedly finds it hard to escape from his admirers and supplicants. At one point we read that he longs to escape into solitude; his fasting has made him too weak to walk (paradoxically the techniques of fasting which should bring release from the world thus make release more difficult); and

---

35 Cf. Elsner and Rubiés 1999, 19, for a good parallel from Valerius letter 1a.
36 Cf. Weingarten 2005, 31–32, on similar paradise imagery in Jerome's *Life of Paul of Thebes*.
37 See Weingarten 2005, 96.

when he finally gets hold of a donkey to facilitate his escape, a crowd of 10,000 gathers to stop him from leaving; only a hunger strike finally persuades them to let him go. We see him facing a similar problem even in his mountain retreat. Very few people, we hear, were able to reach him there because of its inaccessibility (*propter asperitatem difficultatemque loci*), but one day a paralysed man turns up outside the door of Hilarion's cell, and from then on everything changes:

> Quod postquam auditum est, etiam difficultatem loci et iter invium plurimorum vicit necessitas, nihil per circuitum cunctis uillis observantibus quam ne quo modo elaberetur. (31,9)
>
> Once this was became known, the need of many overcame even the difficulty of the place and the pathless journey, and all the houses round about gave their attention to nothing other than preventing his escape.

Jerome offers us here an extraordinary picture of the world 'breaking in' on Hilarion's solitude.[38] The anonymous, harsh, solitary landscape Hilarion longs for is filled with supplicants and linked with his name, however hard he tries to avoid that.

This process is in part a reflection of the increasing Christianization of the landscape of the Roman provinces through the fourth century, as particular locations become linked with the lives of particular saints. Increasingly in the fourth century, in the decades before Jerome writes this work, we begin to see Christian pilgrimage texts emerging which chart that newly Christianized landscape, standing as Christian equivalents of Pausanias' vision of Achaia, where every town and every natural landmark is marked by its connection to significant stories.[39] The *Life of Hilarion* reflects this Christianization of landscape in particular through its account of what happens after Hilarion's death.[40] Hilarion's disciple Hesychius manages to steal away his body to Hilarion's old monastery at Maiuma in Palestine; and both Maiuma and Hilarion's garden in Cyprus become celebrated as spaces imbued with Hilarion's presence, as Jerome tells us in the very final lines of the text. In that sense Jerome dramatizes the tension between anonymous, stylized, allegorical landscape and realistic particularized topography, charting the final triumph of the latter.

---

38 See Goehring 2005 on the tension between idealised pictures of solitary desert asceticism and more realistic visions of ascetics in early hagiography, arguing that the first of those models increasingly effaces the second, while nevertheless allowing traces of it to remain.
39 See Elsner and Rubiés 1999, 15–20.
40 See Weingarten 2005, 145–152.

Conclusion

In summary: what can this brief comparison tell us about the similarities and differences between Jerome and Apuleius, and between Christian and Greco-Roman conceptions of landscape in narrative? I have argued that one of the things which makes Jerome's Christian account of landscape distinctive is the urge to celebrate Christian transformation of all that is harsh and hostile into an arena for saintly virtue, ousting the bandits from the mountains and taking on their marginal space in relation to the culture of the city, whereas for Lucius, for all his occasional bursts of ekphrastic relish, the experience of the unmarked wilderness of Achaia is always a degrading one, standing in contrast to the later release provided by the goddess Isis. That contrast is not a particularly surprising one. More unexpected, perhaps, is the conclusion that Jerome and Apuleius share an interest in the difficulty of escaping from the physical realities of the world. For Lucius, exaggerated, almost theatrical sensitivity to landscape throughout his narration in Books 1–10 is a sign that he is mired in the inferior, theatrical world of sensory perception, which he escapes from only through divine intervention in Book 11, and even then, we might feel, only partially. For Hilarion, that same awareness of landscape as anonymous stage-set comes to stand for precisely the opposite—an escape from the world of human needs and desires, which he longs to shun in part because of his modesty. But in his case, too, it is exposed as a goal which must be discarded for being unrealistic and self-defeating, thanks to the never-ending clamour of supplicants who pursue him. Both Apuleius and Jerome thus dramatize the ultimate impossibility and inadequacy of stylized understandings of landscape, albeit to vastly different effect; and in that sense they offer a valuable starting-point for rethinking the stereotype of classical landscape as unthinkingly generalised. Should we take Apuleius as typical of Greco-Roman fiction in this respect? That question would need much more space than is available here. But it is perhaps worth noting that others have commented before on the fact that Apuleius is closer to early Christian narrative in some respects than any of his Greek or Latin novelistic counterparts, because of the spiritual dimension brought to the work by Book 11. Jerome's reliance on the *Metamorphoses* for his *Life of Hilarion* may, in addition, be at least in part a result of the fact that he found Apuleius' conceptions of landscape and geography unusually promising as a framework for giving expression to his own exploration of the contest between conflicting conceptualizations of Christian geography.

Bibliography

Bakhtin, M.M. 1981. *The Dialogic Imagination: Four Essays by M.M. Bakhtin* (M. Holquist, ed.; C. Emerson and M. Holquist, trans.), Austin: University of Texas Press.
Burrus, V. 2004. *The Sex Lives of Saints: An Erotics of Hagiography*, Philadelphia: University of Pennsylvania Press.
Buxton, R.G.A. 1994. *Imaginary Greece: The Contexts of Mythology*, Cambridge: Cambridge University Press.
Davies, B. 2000. *(In)scribing body/landscape relations*, Walnut Creek: AltaMira Press.
De Biasi, L. 1990. 'Le descrizioni del paesaggio naturale nelle opere di Apuleio. Aspetti letterari', *Memorie dell' Accademia delle Scienze di Torino, Classe di Scienze Morali* 14, 199–264.
Elsner, J., and Rubiés, J.-P. 1999. 'Introduction', in: J. Elsner, J.-P. Rubiés (eds.) *Voyages and Visions: Towards a Cultural History of Travel*, London: Reaktion Books. 1–56.
Finkelpearl, E. 1991. 'The judgement of Lucius: Apuleius' *Metamorphoses* 10.29–34', *Classical Antiquity* 10, 221–36.
Goehring, J. 2005. 'The dark side of landscape: ideology and power in the Christian myth of the desert', in: D.B. Martin, P. Cox Miller (eds.) *The Cultural Turn in Late Ancient Studies: Gender, Asceticism, and Historiography*, Durham: Duke University Press. 136–49.
Graverini, L. 2002. 'Corinth, Rome and Africa: a cultural background for the tale of the ass', in: M. Paschalis, S. Frangoulidis (eds.), *Space in the Ancient Novel*, ANS 1, Groningen: Barkhuis Publishing & The University Library Groningen. 58–77.
Hall, E. 1995. 'The ass with double vision', in: D. Margolies, M. Joannou (eds.) *Heart of a Heartless World. Essays in Cultural Resistance in Memory of Margot Heineman*, London: Pluto Press. 47–59.
Kadish, D.Y. 1986. *The Literature of Images: Narrative Landscape from* Julie *to* Jane Eyre, New Brunswick: Rutgers University Press.
Leclerc, P., Morales, E.M., de Vogüé, A. (eds.) 2007. *Jérôme: trois vies de moines (Paul, Malchus, Hilarion)* (Sources chrétiennes 508), Paris: Éditions du Cerf.
Lutwack, L. 1984. *The Role of Place in Literature*, Syracuse: Syracuse University Press.
Millar, F. 1981. 'The world of the *Golden Ass*', *JRS* 71, 63–75.
Nicolson, M.H. 1997. *Mountain Gloom and Mountain Glory: The Development of the Aesthetics of the Infinite*, Seattle: University of Washington Press. (Original Work Published 1959).
Schiesaro, A. 1985. 'Il 'locus horridus' nelle 'Metamorfosi' di Apuleio, *Met*. IV, 28–35', *Maia* 37, 211–23.
Slater, N.W. 2002. 'Space and displacement in Apuleius', in: M. Paschalis, and S. Frangoulidis (eds.), *Space in the Ancient Novel*, ANS 1, Groningen: Barkhuis Publishing & The University Library Groningen. 161–176.
Trinquier, J. 1999. 'Le motif du repaire des brigands et le topos du *locus horridus*: Apulée, *Metamorphoses*, IV, 6', *RPh* 73, 257–77.
Weingarten, S. 2005. *The Saint's Saints: Hagiography and Geography in Jerome*, Leiden: Brill.
Zimmerman, M. 1993. 'Narrative judgement and reader response in Apuleius' *Metamorphoses* 10,29–34: the pantomime of the judgement of Paris', in: H. Hofmann (ed.), *Groningen Colloquia on the Novel*, vol. V, Groningen: Egbert Forsten. 143–161.

Zimmerman, M. 2000. *Apuleius Madaurensis Metamorphoses Book 10: Text, Introduction and Commentary*, Groningen: Forsten.

Zimmerman, M. 2002. 'On the road in Apuleius' *Metamorphoses*', in: M. Paschalis, S. Frangoulidis (eds.), *Space in the Ancient Novel*, ANS 1, Groningen, Barkhuis Publishing & The University Library Groningen. 78–97.

John Bodel
Kangaroo Courts: Displaced Justice in the Roman Novel

Abstract: Mock trials in the Roman novels, notably Eumolpus's defense of Encolpius and Giton aboard Lichas's ship in Petronius's *Satyrica* (107–109) and the Risus festival at Hypata in Apuleius's *Metamorphoses* (3,1–12), center on the inability of law to provide order when justice is displaced from its proper setting. In the first, an effort to regularize an impromptu trial on shipboard dissolves into brawling when declamatory rhetoric withers in the face of a judge's direct interrogation. In the second, a trial becomes a farce when the proceedings are transferred from the *forum* to the theater and the defendant absolves himself by declamation.

Roman authors of the early Empire agreed: the world they lived in was in cultural decline. Love of money and widespread moral decadence were the principal causes, but in the realm of oratory and the practice of law, the schools of declamation were equally to blame.[1] The common criticisms, voiced already in the time of Tiberius by the elder Seneca, who traced the beginning of the slide to the death of Cicero, had become hackneyed by the end of the first century CE, when Tacitus in his *Dialogus* assigns them to the orator Messala precisely in order to characterize him as somewhat old-fashioned.

> *At nunc adulescentuli nostri deducuntur in scholas istorum, qui rhetores vocantur, quos paulo ante Ciceronis tempora extitisse nec placuisse maioribus nostris ex eo manifestum est, quod a Crasso et Domitio censoribus claudere, ut ait Cicero, 'ludum impudentiae' iussi sunt. (2) Sed ut dicere institueram, deducuntur in scholas, [in] quibus non facile dixerim utrumne locus ipse an condiscipuli an genus studiorum plus mali ingeniis adferant. (3) Nam in loco nihil reverentiae est, in quem nemo nisi aeque imperitus intret; in condiscipulis nihil profectus, cum pueri inter pueros et adulescentuli inter adulescentulos pari securitate et dicant et audiantur; ipsae vero exercitationes magna ex parte contrariae. (4) Nempe enim duo genera materiarum apud rhetoras tractantur, suasoriae et controversiae. Ex his suasoriae quidem etsi tamquam*

---

[1] See in general, Williams 1978, ch. 1, 'Contemporary Analyses of Decline', 6–51. A revised version of the ICAN conference paper reproduced here was subsequently published in F. De Angelis, ed., *Spaces of Justice in the Roman World* (New York: Columbia University Press 2010) 311–329.

John Bodel, Brown University

https://doi.org/10.1515/9781501503986-022

> *plane leviores et minus prudentiae exigentes pueris delegantur, controversiae robustioribus adsignantur – quales, per fidem, et quam incredibiliter compositae! sequitur autem, ut materiae abhorrenti a veritate declamatio quoque adhibeatur. (5) Sic fit ut tyrannicidarum praemia aut vitiatarum electiones aut pestilentiae remedia aut incesta matrum aut quidquid in schola cotidie agitur, in foro vel raro vel numquam, ingentibus verbis persequantur: cum ad veros iudices ventum...(Tac. Dial. 35,1–5)*

> But nowadays our young men are led off to the schools of those who call themselves rhetoricians. These appeared a little before the time of Cicero and were disliked by our ancestors, as is clear from the fact that, when Crassus and Domitius were censors [in 92 BCE], they were ordered, as Cicero says, to close 'the school of impudence'. (2) But, as I had started to say, the young men are led off to schools in which it is hard to tell whether it is the place itself (*locus ipse*) or their fellow students or the type of studies that harms their minds the most. (3) For there is no reverence in a place in which no one enters who is not as inexperienced as the others; there is no progress among the students when boys and young men both speak and are heard with equal assurance among their peers; and indeed, the exercises themselves are for the most part detrimental. (4) For two kinds of subject-matter are treated by rhetoricians, 'persuasions' (*suasoriae*) and 'controversies' (*controversiae*). The first, being more trivial and requiring less wisdom, are given to boys; the second are assigned to older boys—but my word, how implausibly contrived they are! Consequently declaimers practice even on subjects remote from reality. (5) So it happens that the rewards of a tyrant, or the choices of violated maidens, or remedies against pestilence, or the incestuous behavior of mothers or whatever is daily dealt with in schools but rarely or never in the forum is pursued in lofty language. But when they come before real jurors <...>.

Here our manuscript breaks off, but the litany of complaints against the schools of declamation had become so predictable by the latter half of the first century CE that we can complete the thought from a similar passage that opens our fragmentary text of Petronius's *Satyrica*, in which the narrator Encolpius fulminates against declaimers who, when they enter the *forum*, in his words, 'feel that they have been transported into another world', *putent se in alium orbem terrarum delatos* (*Sat.* 1,2). In short, he continues, students become exceedingly stupid in schools, because they neither hear nor see in them anything from everyday experience but instead—and he then goes on to enumerate a list of improbable subjects of the same sort as had troubled Messalla.[2] In earlier days, according to Messalla, young orators in training had learned by accompanying their mentors to trials in the forum, attending on their speeches not only there but in the assembly, and observing not only their teachers but also their rivals engage in the thrust and parry of live debate (*Dial.* 34,1–5).

A little later in Tacitus's dialogue, another, more credible speaker, Maternus, reverts to the question of setting, deprecating the *auditoria* (recital halls)

---

2 Petr. *Sat.* 1,1–3.

and *tabularia* (records offices) in which cases were often tried and implying that within their confines the judge's dictation of points to address, the frequent interruptions for witnesses, and the virtual solitude in which the proceedings were conducted debilitate the orator's strength and deprive him of the sustenance he traditionally drew from the clamor and applause of the crowd, 'as if he were in a theater' (*velut quodam theatro*) (Tac. *Dial.* 39,1–4).

The situation described by Maternus points to the procedural context of the *cognitio extra ordinem*, a form that first appeared during the early Principate and gradually came to dominate the procedural landscape, in which the formulary procedure and private jurors were bypassed in favor of a public official representing the emperor and empowered both to adjudicate and to execute the judgment, and which might be tried almost anywhere, even in private homes.[3] The salient point in his comparison of the settings contrasts the noise and free-for-all hubbub of the forum, which the skilled advocate had to learn to rise above, with the solitary isolation of the modern orator harried by the inescapable interference of an autocratic judge. The latter setting was more suited to the controlled environment of the schoolroom, but declamation was not debate: there was no give and take, no point and counterpoint, nothing, in fact, of the peremptory interruptions and curt responses apparently characteristic of *cognitiones extraordinariae*. For that sort of interrogatory exchange, we may note the rhetorician Agamemnon in Petronius's novel, the target of Encolpius's opening diatribe, engaging with his dinner host, Trimalchio, who plays the role of the irksome *iudex*, feigning ignorance of poverty and sophistically exploiting a puerile *double entendre* to dismiss a hypothetical case as fictitious (Petr. *Sat.* 48,4–6).[4]

Students trained in such fashion lacked the stamina and concentration for public speaking in the forum, where, in the words of a rhetorician of the Tiberian period, Votienus Montanus, reported by Seneca the Elder, if nothing else, the forum itself confounded them, since they had never experienced the noise, or the silence or laughter of disapproval, or even the open air. Seneca goes on to relate the story of the master declaimer Porcius Latro, who became so flustered in defending a relative on trial in Spain that he tripped over his opening words and could not regain his confidence until he had petitioned successfully to have

---

[3] See, on *cognitiones extraordinariae*, Crook 1995, 56–57, 66–67, 133–136 with Vitruv. 6,5,2 (*privata iudicia* in aristocratic homes); further Bablitz 2007, 33–34, citing Quint. *Inst.* 11,1,47; 11,3,127, 134, 156.
[4] See van Mal-Maeder 2003, 346–347.

the proceedings moved indoors, from the forum into a basilica (Sen. *Contr.* 9, pr. 2–4).[5]

Latro's forensic 'stage-fright' notwithstanding, the proper place for a public trial was in fact in full view in the open forum. In invoking a theatrical aspect of the orator's milieu (*velut quodam theatro*), Maternus appeals to a feature of public trials remarked also by Cicero, who in *De Oratore* had characterized the speaker's platform in a public assembly as the orator's greatest stage, and in *Brutus* had described the Forum Romanum as the theater of Hortensius's talent.[6] Like Maternus, Cicero was speaking metaphorically (note the qualifiers *velut* in Tacitus, *quasi*, twice, in Cicero). The courtroom was not, in fact, a theater, and confusing the types of performance suitable to one with those appropriate to the other was one of the principal charges laid against those who trained in the declamation schools. So it had come about, according to Messalla, that speakers of the modern age imitated the style of entertainers – the speech patterns of actors, the tones of singers, and the gestures of dancers – so successfully that the shameful expression had arisen that orators of the day spoke gracefully and pantomimes danced eloquently.[7]

Three settings, then, each with its own distinctive ambience, regularly came into discussion when the decline of modern oratory was debated or decried by early imperial authors: the open space of the forum, with its multiple distractions and real-world outcomes; the close confines of the declamation schools, where artificially contrived problems found improbable solutions; and the centripetally focused stage-and-seating ensemble of the Roman theater, where solo performers fed off an attentive audience riveted on them. Counterpoised to all three of these were the variable locations and spaces of the *cognitiones extra ordinem* that increasingly came to dominate the administration of justice during

---

[5] See further for the hubbub of the public courts, in contrast to the pampered environment of the declamation schools, Quint. *Inst.* 6,4,9–11; 10,3,30; 12,5,5–6; Pliny *Ep.* 2,14,10; Dio Prus. 32,68 (catcalls to music) with Crook 1995, 135–136 and 165–166.

[6] ... *maxima quasi oratoris scaena videatur contionis esse.*, Cic. *De Orat.* 2,338 (The greatest stage, as it were, of the orator is seen to be that of the assembly.); ... *forum populi Romani, quod fuisset quasi theatrum illius ingeni...*, *Brut.* 6 (... the forum of the Roman people, which had been the theater, as it were, of his talent...).

[7] ... *laudis et gloriae et ingenii loco plerique iactant cantari saltarique commentarios suos. unde oritur illa foeda et praepostera, sed tamen frequens [sicut his clam et] exclamatio, ut oratores nostri tenere dicere, histriones diserte saltare dicantur.*, Tac. *Dial.* 26,3 (in place of praise and glory and talent, many boast that their compositions are sung and danced, whence arises that foul and absurd but nonetheless common saying that our orators speak gracefully and our actors dance eloquently.). According to Pliny *Ep.* 2,14,13, speeches in the Centumviral Court sounded sing-song (*illis canticis*).

the Empire – the *auditoria* and *tabularia* and private chambers of aristocratic households – in which, paradoxically and incongruously, the histrionic mannerisms of the stage were squandered on paltry and unappreciative audiences enveloped in the stultifying closeness of the schools.

It is against this backdrop that we must try to assess the spaces of justice depicted in the Roman novels, and more particularly the settings of trials, real and figurative, that were such a staple of the Greek novels to which they bear close, if often parodic, affinities. Chariton, Longus, Achilles Tatius, and Heliodorus all include in their fictions extended descriptions of trial scenes that advance the plot or showcase virtuoso displays of stylistic prowess.[8] In the Roman novels, on the other hand, the trial scenes serve rather to reflect, by dislocation of setting, conceptual or perceptual dislocations in the worldview of the narrator. They are out of place physically, just as the narrative is out of place rhetorically and the narrator, often, perceptually. In this they exhibit a characteristic feature of Latin literature of the empire – its tendency to convey meaning indirectly and often surreptitiously.[9] So, for example, Messalla's claim that the better apprenticeship practices of earlier days had been replaced by the declamation schools is belied by the presence in the same dialogue of the narrator Tacitus in precisely the role said no longer to exist (*Dial* 1,2). The *mise en scène* undermines the rhetorical position (and factual claims) of one of the protagonists in the debate not by direct rebuttal but by oblique refutation in substance.

Similarly, and more relevantly, the opening scene of the *Satyrica*, in which Encolpius voices the standard complaints about rhetorical education, focusing on the impractical training on subjects remote from reality, when considered in context, disproves the position it advocates and furthermore (unlike the *Dialogus*) calls into question the sincerity of its mouthpiece.[10] Indeed, declaiming is explicitly how the narrator characterizes his opening gambit (*Sat.* 3,1) a tasty package of honeyball words, as he calls them (*mellitos verborum globulos*), which the professor swallows without blinking. Encolpius's impractical modern

---

8 Schwartz 2000–2001, 94 n. 4, identifies thirteen trial scenes in the five extant Greek novels (Schwartz 2003b, 134–135), of which the most important, perhaps, are Chariton 5,4–8 (with Schwartz 2003a, 379–391); Longus 2,15–17 (with Morgan 2004, 187–188); Achilles Tatius 7,7–16; and Heliodorus 8,9–15. The fourteen trial scenes in *Acts* (Schwartz 2003b, 136–137) are constructed in the same way, as 'reflections not of reality but of mentalité': Schwartz 2003b, 105. My thanks to Saundra Schwartz for bringing this important work to my attention.
9 See Bartsch 1994.
10 See Kennedy 1978, Cosci 1978, and Salles 2002, on the role of the rhetor Agamemnon in the cultural world of Trimalchio and his friends.

rhetorical education enables him to parlay his literary learning into substantive gain for himself and his friends.

Within the insular world of the declamation schools and the houses of the wealthy with cultural pretensions, a liberal education brought its own rewards. Very different was its value outside that rarefied environment, and the next time Encolpius and his companions put the training of the declamation schools to the test, its inadequacies in the real world are exposed. After the banquet of Trimalchio, Encolpius and his boyfriend Giton fall in with the disreputable poetaster Eumolpus, who leads them on board a ship bound for points south. Only after embarking do the protagonists discover that they have inadvertently fallen into the hands of the very pair—the ship captain Lichas and the profligate voluptuary Tryphaena – whom they have previously offended and are trying to avoid. In deliberating a plan of escape, Eumolpus, momentarily nonplussed and in need of direction, has recourse to the only world he knows, the world of rhetoric and literature, and in assessing the task, he sets out the problem exactly as a rhetor would an assignment to his pupils: "Imagine that we have entered the Cyclops's cave. Some escape must be found, unless we are to stage a shipwreck and free ourselves from every danger" (Petr. *Sat.* 101,7).[11] The latter alternative – the staged shipwreck (*ponimus* must be understood in this theatrical sense) – was characteristic of mime, an entertainment known for its abrupt and ill-motivated endings (Seneca refers dismissively to a *mimicum naufragium*); it will in fact be realized at the climax of the episode, when it is the implacable Cyclops Lichas, rather than any of our heroes, who washes up dead on shore. But the series of improbable proposals that follows, each refuted in turn and eventually resulting in a misguided attempt to disguise the fugitives by shaving their foreheads and inking fake tattoos onto their brows in order to mark them as runaway slaves (*fugitivi*), evoke the competitive one-upmanship of the classroom rather than the stage. The ruse is quickly exposed, and Encolpius and Giton enlist Eumolpus in their defense in an impromptu shipboard trial presided over by Lichas (the beginning of the scene is lost in a lacuna in the manuscripts).

In the exchange that follows, Eumolpus deploys a variety of oratorical approaches, many evocative of famous Ciceronian strategies and often recalling his words, but each is ineptly applied, and each is systematically demolished by Lichas, who refutes the arguments point by point.[12] For example, Eumolpus's claim that the culprits, honorable freeborn men, have voluntarily submitted to

---

[11] *naufragium ponimus*, 'stage a shipwreck': Watt 1986, 181. Cf. Cic. *Fam.* 10,32,3; Pers. 5,3; Sen. *De Ira* 2,2,5 (*mimicum naufragium*); with Panayotakis 1995, 144–146.
[12] See Panayotakis 2006, 196–210.

the mark of runaway slaves as a sign of their contrition – a tactic based on the formal device of the *deprecatio*, a plea in mitigation of guilt, and bolstered by an appeal to the social standing of the accused, both techniques recommended by the rhetorical handbooks and deployed to good effect by Cicero – founders in the face of Lichas's demand that the points be treated individually and not confused. In fact, the tactic of the *deprecatio*, according to the anonymous late Republican rhetorical manual addressed to Herennius, seldom worked in court, but was more effective before a council or a general, when the plea could be supported by a rehearsal of the guilty party's good deeds – neither of which situations applies in the present circumstances.[13] Eumolpus knows his oratory as Trimalchio knows his mythology – only well enough to botch it. Petronius sets up a court scene and then puts into the mouth of Eumolpus a type of speech that would rarely have been heard in court. The sequence of proposition and rebuttal is brought to an end when Lichas turns to examine the accused Encolpius directly, and Encolpius, like the unfortunate declaimer constrained to plead in the forum, finds himself confused (*turbatus*) and, faced with a manifest reality (*in manifesta re*), unable to say a thing (Petr. *Sat.* 107,15–108,1).

Both the setting and the nature of the proceedings are relevant. In refuting the points individually as they arise, and especially in dictating the course of the interrogation, Lichas assumes simultaneously the roles of prosecutor and judge, and this marks the procedure as a *cognitio extraordinaria*, as was fully appropriate under the circumstances.[14] At the same time, the man of letters Eumolpus and the ineffectually well-read Encolpius, fully armed with the panoply of rhetorical tricks and steeped in literary precedents, find themselves no match for the blunt reality-check imposed on them by Lichas and, in a broader sense, by their circumstances. Ill-equipped by their education to respond to the rigors of the new legal procedure, the protagonists are metaphorically as well as literally at sea in a world in which implausible fictions are held up to the clear light of day. Petronius's point is the same one that Maternus makes in the *Dialogus* – the legal landscape has changed: isolated environments and activist judges give little space for the grand oratory of the past, and the rhetorical training pur-

---

13 *Rhet. ad Herenn.* 1,14,24, with Panayotakis 2006, 199–205, esp. 204–205.
14 A basic principle of Roman maritime law held the captain of a ship to be the sole legal authority empowered to administer justice on board so long as the vessel was not in port; issues of liability arose only when the captain – the *gubernator* or *magister navis* – had been designated by the shipowner for a specific charge – hence the important specification, when he is first introduced (101,4), that Lichas is both owner and commander of the ship: see Rougé 1981, 189; id. 1971, 178–180. Lichas's power as *iudex* of a *cognitio extra ordinem* is thus symbolically figured (and amplified) by his position as owner-captain of a ship at sea.

veyed in schools is ineffectual in the real world. The *mise en scène* of the trial at sea matches the ineffectiveness of the rhetorical strategies deployed to extricate the protagonists from a discomfiting turn in the plot with the physical displacement of the proceedings from any of their traditional venues and the restrictive procedural innovations invariably associated with the more confined physical spaces of the *cognitiones extra ordinem*.

When we turn to the other major Roman novel to come down to us, the *Metamorphoses* or *Golden Ass* of Apuleius, we encounter a similar perspective, engineered differently. When the narrator, Lucius, having arrived in Hypata, ventures into the forum to procure food for supper, he there encounters an old schoolmate from Athens, Pythias, now a local aedile invested with the trappings of office (the rods and dress of a magistrate), who offers assistance and asks how much Lucius has spent for the fish he purchased. To Lucius's reply, Pythias responds in appropriately Delphic fashion by berating the fishmonger for price gouging, ordering the fish to be trampled under foot, and, after remarking his satisfaction with having abused the old man, sending Lucius on his way (Apul. *Met*. 1,25,1–6). To this miscarriage of justice, perpetrated in the forum, Lucius reacts like Encolpius the schoolboy thrust into the limelight of judicial proceedings *in foro* – with bewilderment and stupefaction (*consternatus ac prorsus obstupidus*). In this case, however, it is not the inadequacies of his rhetorical training that leave the narrator speechless but the officious behavior of the local magistrate—not a failure of words, in other words, but an incomprehensible failure of deeds (*acta*). This reversal of the *topos*, with similar results, diverts focus away from the ineffectual and innocent 'plaintiff' onto the individual magistrate, who, empowered within his own element – the forum – both to investigate and to punish, revels in his authority but is bound by no rules of logic or sense of equity and produces no justice.

The following evening brings Lucius's hallucinogenic encounter with the robber/wineskins, followed by a fitful night of guilt and apprehension of impending arraignment in the forum (*forum et iudicia*, *Met*. 2,32). A crowd arrives the next morning to haul him off to the forum and station him before magistrates on a lofty tribunal (Apul. *Met*. 3,2,5–6). Lucius likens his role in this dismal procession to that of a sacrificial victim in a purificatory ritual of expiation ('*in modum eorum quibus lustralibus piamentis...hostiis expiant*', 3,2,5 ('in the manner of those purificatory processions in which they expiate the victims by leading them around'); '*velut quandam victimam*', 3, 2, 9 ('like a kind of sacrificial victim'), and modern scholars have been quick to recognize in the scene that follows a classic scapegoat ritual.[15] But as Stavros Frangoulidis has astutely noted, the essential orientation of a scapegoat ritual is centrifugal, whereas the trial of Lucius unfolds in a centripetal fashion, proceeding from outside of town to the forum and thence to the theater, where the ensuing spectacle results in a proposal for his integration into, rather than alienation from, the community.[16]

The location of the trial in the theater has not been fully appreciated. That Lucius is involved in a farce rather than a trial, the local Festival of Laughter, in which the murdered robbers turn out to be wineskins and the eager participants in the judicial proceedings merely actors complicit in Lucius's unwitting role in the drama, has often been noticed. Unremarked altogether, however, is the more significant incongruity between the Roman legal machinery and the Thessalian context. Whereas the theater is a perfectly plausible place for a trial in the Greek world, where verdicts in public prosecutions were rendered by popular acclaim, it was not so in the Roman west, where proceedings *in iure* were properly conducted only in the forum or areas associated with *fora*.[17] As a setting for judicial proceedings, the theater is thus pointedly at odds with the Roman context suggested by the technical legal language liberally sprinkled throughout the work that has long been recognized as somehow reflecting the author's known expertise in Roman law.[18] Among more noteworthy examples of Roman judicial proceedings before assemblies in Greek theaters and amphitheaters, the raucous accusation of the apostle Paul by the Ephesian artisans convened in unlawful assembly in the theater provides a case in point, inasmuch as the crowd on that occasion was summarily dismissed after being reminded that there were proper courts and proconsuls to try private lawsuits.[19] The theater was also in the Roman world (both east and west) a place where declamations were regularly performed as public entertainments, and thus it is unclear at the

---

15 E.g. McCreight 1993, 46–47; Habinek 1990.
16 Frangoulidis 2002, 178.
17 See Bablitz 2007, 48–50 (Rome); *Dig.* 5,1 and 13,4 with Crook 1967, 75 (provinces).
18 See Keulen 1997, rightly criticizing (203–204) the overly historicizing readings of the legal terminology by Norden 1912 and more recently Summers 1970.
19 For Roman judicial proceedings before assemblies in Greek theaters and amphitheaters see, e.g., *Acts* 19,24–41 (Paul at Ephesus) with Schwartz 2003b, 127; Tac. *Hist.* 2,80,3 (Mucianus at Antioch); *Martyr. Polyc.* 8–9 (Polycarp, before local magistrates and the proconsul at Smyrna, CE 155); Colin 1965, 342 n. 4. Note also Chariton 3,4; Heliod. 4,17–21. Roman authors remarked as Greek the custom of assembling in theaters for debates, acclamations, and receiving embassies: see, e.g. Cic. *Flac.* 16 Livy 24,39,1; Nep. *Timol.* 4,2; Val. Max. 2,2,5; Sen. *Con.* 9,4,19; Front. *Str.* 3,2,6; Juv. 10,128 with Mayor *ad loc.*

outset of the proceedings, to us as well as to the narrator, into which of these contexts he has fallen.[20]

The drama unfolds to the direction of the crier, who summons the watchman forward to assume the role of prosecutor; the watchman in turn delivers an accusation properly drawn up in accordance with the rhetorical handbooks and thus proceeds from *exordium* to *narratio* to thundering *peroratio*, in which he appeals explicitly to the xenophobia that he rightly presumes to be the dominant unifying spirit of the community and that forms such a ubiquitous feature of the local administration of justice throughout antiquity.[21]

How does Lucius respond? Initially reduced to tears, he draws inspiration from the setting and, somewhat to his own surprise, launches when bidden into a self defense that is a model of its kind, addressing point by point his accuser's argument in the same canonical order of *exordium, narratio*, here much embellished with elaborately fabricated detail, and finally a suitably expectant peroration that asserts the orator's respectability among his own people and demands of his accuser a plausible motive for the alleged crime (3,5 – 6). His formal speech concluded, Lucius again opens the floodgates of his tears and stretches his hands out in supplication theatrically. In other words, he recognizes his setting as that of a regular Greek trial before an assembly in a theater, an environment in which a defendant might win acquittal as readily by an appeal to popular mercy as by legal argumentation and persuasive rhetoric. He judges his performance suitably effective (3,7,2) – and is then surprised when his audience responds not with the anticipated absolution but with laughter and applause.

It is only in the aftermath, once he has been led forth from the theater, back through the streets by a devious route to Milo's house, avoiding encounters along the way (and thus reversing the course and circumstances of his earlier procession from the house to the forum: 3,2), that Lucius realizes that he has been applauded for his declamatory performance as an entertainer rather than acquitted for his persuasive oratory as an advocate. Place, or rather dislocation, is central to the episode, marking as distinct the physical spaces of justice and entertainment and then systematically confusing the two, so that the forum becomes the setting for a farcical enactment of *ad hoc* justice in the real world and the theater serves as the site for a fictitious trial resolved by a declamation come to life. Lu-

---

[20] For declamations in theaters, see Russell 1983, 74–77; van Mal Maeder 2003, 352.
[21] Apul. *Met*. 3,3,9, *Habetis itaque reum tot caedibus impiatum, reum coram deprensum, reum peregrinum. Constanter itaque in hominem alienum ferte sententias de eo crimine quod etiam in vestrum civem severiter vindicaretis*. (And so you have a defendant polluted by multiple murders, a defendant caught in the act, a defendant who is a stranger. So pass sentence firmly against a foreigner for a crime which you would punish severely even in the case of a fellow-citizen.).

cius, the *homo alienus* and *reus peregrinus*, resident locally only as a temporary visitor outside of town, is a foreigner to both worlds; but his failure to distinguish between them, unlike that of Petronius's narrator Encolpius, is less the product of his own perceptual failures than of the systematic deceptions perpetrated upon him by a community fully engaged in exploiting the ambivalences between the two.

Bibliography

Bablitz, L. 2007. *Actors and Audience in the Roman Courtroom*, London: Routledge.
Bartsch, S. 1994. *Actors in the Audience: Theatricality and Doublespeak from Nero to Hadrian*, Cambridge: Harvard University Press.
Colin, J. 1965. 'Apulée en Thessalie: fiction ou vérité?', *Latomus* 24, 330–345.
Cosci, P. 1978. 'Per una ricostruzione della scena iniziale del *Satyricon*', *MD* 1, 201–207.
Crook, J.A. 1967. *Law and Life of Rome 90 B.C. – A.D. 212*, Ithaca: Cornell University Press.
Crook, J.A. 1995. *Legal Advocacy in the Roman World*, Ithaca: Cornell University Press.
Frangoulidis, S. 2002. 'The Laughter Festival as a Community Integration Rite in Apuleius's *Metamorphoses*', in: M. Paschalis, S. Frangoulidis (eds.), *Space in the Ancient Novel*, ANS 1, Groningen, Barkhuis Publishing & The University Library Groningen. 177–188.
Habinek, T. 1990. 'Lucius' Rite of Passage', *MD* 25, 49–69.
Kennedy, G. 1975. 'Encolpius and Agamemnon in Petronius', *AJP* 99, 171–178.
Keulen, W. 1997. 'Some Legal Themes in Apuleian Context', in: M. Picone, B. Zimmermann (eds.), *Der antike Roman und seine mittelalterliche Rezeption*, Basel. 203–228.
McCreight, T.D. 1993. 'Sacrificial Ritual in Apuleius' *Metamorphoses*', in: H. Hofmann (ed.), *Groningen Colloquia on the Novel*, vol. V, Groningen: Egbert Forsten. 31–61.
Morgan, J.R. 2004. *Longus. Daphnis and Chloe*, Oxford: Aris & Philips.
Norden, E. 1912. *Apuleius von Madaura und das römische Privatrecht*, Leipzig: Teubner.
Panayotakis, C. 1995. *Theatrum Arbitri: Theatrical Elements in the Satyrica of Petronius*, Leiden: Brill.
Panayotakis, C. 2006. ''Eumolpus' *Pro Encolpio* and Lichas' *In Encolpium*: Petr. Sat. 107', in: S.N. Byrne, E.P. Cueva, J. Alvares (eds.), *Authors, Authority, and Interpreters in the Ancient Novel. Essays in Honor of Gareth L. Schmeling*, ANS 5, Groningen: Barkhuis Publishing & The University Library Groningen. 196–210.
Rougé, J. 1971. 'La justice à bord du navire', in: E. Volterra (ed.), *Studi in onore di Edoardo Volterra* 3, Milan: Giuffrè. 173–181.
Rougé, J. 1981. *Ships and Fleets of the Ancient Mediterranean*, Middletown: Wesleyan University Press.
Russell, D.A. 1983. *Greek Declamation*, Cambridge: Cambridge University Press.
Salles, C. 2002. 'Le professeur de rhétorique et son élève: les positions de Pétrone et de Quintilien', *Euphrosyne* 30, 201–208.
Schmeling, G. 1974. *Chariton*, New York: Twayne.
Schwartz, S. 2000–2001. 'Clitophon the *Moichos*: Achilles Tatius and the Trial Scene in the Greek Novel', *AN* 1, 93–113.

Schwartz, S. 2003a. 'Rome in the Greek Novel? Images and Ideas of Empire in Chariton's Persia', *Arethusa* 36, 375–394.

Schwartz, S. 2003b. "The Trial Scene in the Greek Novels and Acts', in: T. Penner, C. Vander Stichele (eds.), *Contextualizing Acts. Lukan Narrative and Greco-Roman Discourse*, Atlanta: Society of Biblical Literature. 105–137.

Summers, R.G. 1970. 'Roman Justice and Apuleius' *Metamorphoses*', *TAPA* 101, 511–531.

van Mal-Maeder, D. 2003. 'La mise en scène declamatoire chez les romanciers Latins', in: S. Panayotakis, M. Zimmerman, W. Keulen (eds.), *The Ancient Novel and Beyond*, Leiden: Brill. 345–355.

Watt, W.S. 1986. 'Petr. Sat. 101,7', *C&M* 37, 181.

Williams, G. 1979. *Change and Decline. Roman Literature in the Early Empire*, Berkeley: University of California Press.

Character and Emotion in the Ancient Novel

David Konstan
Pity vs. Forgiveness in Pagan and Judaeo-Christian Narratives

Abstract: There are many resemblances between the ancient Greek novels and more or less contemporary Jewish and Christian narratives that have been characterized as novels. In both traditions, the protagonists undergo various tribulations and appeal to God, or the gods, for release from their woes. But there is one crucial difference: the heroes and heroines of the Greek novels do not regard themselves as having done wrong or offended the gods, and hence, while they beseech the gods for pity, they do not ask for forgiveness. The *Life of Adam and Eve* is markedly different: here, the entire emphasis is on sin (especially Eve's), and it is God's forgiveness, rather than his pity, that the protagonists seek.

In the course of exploring the question of forgiveness in classical antiquity several years ago, I arrived at the perhaps startling conclusion that forgiveness, as the idea is understood today, did not exist in pagan Greek and Roman culture.[1] More precisely, the concept forgiveness played no role in the ethical and psychological traditions of the classical world. Forgiveness arose rather in the context of Jewish and Christian preoccupations with sin and repentance, and was part of a deep shift in the nature of human social and religious thought. Of course, pagan writers too were conscious of the problem of wrong-doing, and they discussed and illustrated ways in which one might appease or be reconciled with someone whom he or she had injured or offended. But placating another is quite a different matter from beseeching forgiveness. In this paper, I illustrate the contrast between pagan and Judaeo-Christian approaches to conciliating someone whom one has hurt or insulted by examining some novelistic narratives from both traditions. But first, I must indicate more specifically what I mean by forgiveness, and why I believe that it was not a central value, much less a virtue, in pagan civilization.

'Forgiveness' has several senses in modern English, as do the comparable terms in other languages, for example 'perdão' in Portuguese. It may mean 'par-

---

[1] See Konstan 2010; the present paper was delivered two years before the publication of my book, and presents material that was partly incorporated in the larger study.

David Konstan, Brown University

https://doi.org/10.1515/9781501503986-023

don' in the judicial sense of excusing an offense or commuting the penalty, as when the president pardons someone convicted of a crime. It may also be employed in an economic context, where it means the remission of a debt (thus Jesus' words in the Lord's Prayer: 'Forgive us our debts as we also have forgiven our debtors' [Matthew 6:12]). Sometimes 'forgive' is used in the relatively inconsequential sense of overlooking discourteous behavior, as in the formula 'Excuse me!' None of these usages captures what I take to be the essential meaning of forgiving, that is, the restoration of a moral relationship between the offender and the person who has been ill-treated. For this to happen, first and foremost the offender must admit to having done wrong: one does not forgive an innocent person or someone who steadfastly denies responsibility. But it is not enough simply to confess one's error: one must also be sorry – that is, feel remorse; and this implies a commitment not to repeat the offense. The motive for this commitment, moreover, is not fear or personal advantage – that would hardly earn forgiveness – but a deep and genuine awareness that one's previous conduct was wrong. One must repudiate the action and the values that enabled it; such a repudiation – perhaps repentance is the better word – 'is a step toward showing that one is not simply the "same person" who did the wrong', as Charles Griswold puts it in his recent and brilliant study of the topic.[2] Without such a transformation in the offender, giving up one's resentment at the injury would be tantamount to condoning it. What is more, it is not only the offender who experiences a renewal of the self; the forgiver too must undergo a change of heart, which involves, again in Griswold's words, 'seeing the offender and oneself in a new light'.[3] It is this complex of confession of guilt, remorse, and repentance, accompanied by a change of heart in both parties, that constitutes forgiveness in the rich sense I intend here. The author of a letter published in *The New York Review of Books* indicates with admirable clarity the conditions that warrant forgiveness.[4] Arguing that the German rocket scientist Werner von Braun does not deserve to be forgiven, the writer states: 'Von Braun never publicly renounced his role in the Nazi regime, of whose sadism and brutality he seems to have been fully aware. Surely confession and penitence must precede reconciliation? Amnesty yes, reconciliation maybe, but forgiveness no.'

Now, it is remarkable that the Greek and Roman thinkers paid very little attention to the ideas of remorse and repentance, just as they neglected the topic of forgiveness (clemency, which Cicero and Seneca endorse, is another matter,

---

2 Griswold 2007, 50.
3 Griswold 2007, 53.
4 14 February 2008, p. 55; the writer is Bernard Lytton, Professor Emeritus of Surgery and Urology at the Yale University School of Medicine.

since it depends entirely on the disposition of the offended person, who is understood to be in a position of power).[5] Their discussions reveal no great effort to distinguish between regret, in the sense of a wish that things had turned out otherwise, and the moral notion of remorse, that is, guilt at having harmed another.[6] This is not to say that they had no interest in winning over the goodwill of someone whom they might have offended or harmed; but confession of guilt and petition of forgiveness on the basis of a deep moral reform was not preeminent among their strategies for doing so. The emotion that an offense, whether an insult or other mistreatment, elicited was typically anger, which consisted, according to Aristotle's definition in the *Rhetoric*, in a desire for revenge. In the *Rhetoric*, indeed, Aristotle limited the causes of anger to slights, though in the *Nicomachean Ethics* he acknowledged that unjust treatment also provoked anger.[7] There were, in turn, several ways in which one might assuage the ire elicited by an offense. First and foremost, one could attempt to show that it was unintentional or involuntary. Second, one could humble oneself before the offended party, thereby demonstrating that one had no desire to devalue or demean the other. Third, one could attempt to elicit pity, a tactic that involved both self-abasement and an effort to demonstrate either one's innocence or the presence of extenuating circumstances, such as external compulsion or other diminishment of responsibility. For, as Aristotle and many other ancient writers insist, pity is felt only for those who are suffering undeservedly. What all these approaches have in common is that they seek to deny or mitigate the fault, rather than accept it. Hence, they do not entail displays of remorse or repentance, or evidence of a sincere change of heart in the offender, much less an effort on the part of the injured party to 'see the offender and oneself in a new light.'

There exist, to be sure, words in both Greek and Latin that are commonly translated as 'forgive' or 'forgiveness': in Greek, συγγνώμη and the verb συγγιγνώσκω, and in Latin *ignoscere*. But an examination of how these terms are in fact defined and used suggests that 'forgive' is not quite the right sense. Thus, in the *Nicomachean Ethics*, Aristotle remarks almost in passing that συγγνώμη is appropriate when a person has acted either under compulsion, which includes the kind of pressure that is beyond the strength of a human being to resist (1110a24–26), or else in non-culpable ignorance of the circumstances (1109b18–1111a2). But to act under force majeure or in ignorance of the relevant

---

5 See Konstan 2005 for discussion.
6 For the distinction, and a detailed study of remorse and regret in classical Greek literature, see Fulkerson 2013.
7 On Aristotle's view of anger, see Konstan 2006, ch. 2.

facts is to act involuntarily, as Aristotle himself observes (1109b30–32), and involuntary acts do not incur guilt. Thus, συγγνώμη here means something like exculpation or exoneration rather than forgiveness.[8] In *De inventione* (1,15), Cicero defines as *concessio* the situation in which 'the defendant does not argue on the basis of the facts, but asks rather to be pardoned [*ut ignoscatur*]'. This appeal takes two forms: *purgatio*, that is, when the deed is admitted, but guilt is denied (*cum factum conceditur, culpa removetur*), and *deprecatio*, when the accused admits that he did wrong deliberately (*consulto peccasse*) but nevertheless begs to be pardoned – a thing that, Cicero says, happens, and should happen, extremely rarely. In such a pass, one will want to mention past services, and insist that one acted either foolishly, or at the instigation of another, or else for some decent and upright reason (*sed aut stultitia aut inpulsu alicuius aut aliqua honesta aut probabili causa*, 2,106); once again, the defendant seeks to extenuate the guilt rather than give proof of repentance. Cicero goes on to say that one will also want to show that one has learned from the mistake, and thanks to the pardon will refrain from such conduct in the future (*postea polliceri et confirmare se et hoc peccato doctum et beneficio eorum, qui sibi ignoverint, confirmatum omni tempore a tali ratione afuturum*). This is promising as an example of remorse and a change of heart, until we read what follows immediately on this sentence (trans. Yonge): 'And besides this, he may hold out a hope that he will hereafter be able, in some respect or other, to be of great use to those who pardon him now; he will find it serviceable to point out that he is either related to the judges, or that he has been as far back as possible an hereditary friend of theirs; and to express to them the earnestness of his good-will towards them, and the nobility of the blood and dignity of those men who are anxious for his safety.' We seem to be a long way from modern conceptions of the grounds for forgiveness.

The term συγγνώμη and its cognates occur rarely in the Greek novels, save for Heliodorus, and even there they are not very frequent. Achilles Tatius offers an example that illustrates the sense. Melite, who is in love with Clitopho, begs him no longer for marriage but just for a brief affair (5,26,2): 'Extinguish just a bit of this fire in me; if I seemed urgent and overbold to you, forgive me (σύγγνωθι), my dearest: passion when it fails of its object grows mad.' Melite is excusing the explicitness of her demand, not apologizing for the desire that drives her; no repentance is in evidence here. In Xenophon of Ephesus (5,9,10), Anthia, having fallen into the possession of the pirate Hippothous, seeks his pardon (συγγώμην

---

8 Later rhetoricians sometime distinguished between the case of external compulsion, calling this *metastasis*, and inner constraint, for example under the influence of anger or passion, to which they restricted the term συγγνώμη; cf. Hermog. *Stat.* 50; Aps. *Rh.* 276; for an excellent discussion of these and many other passages, see Pirovano 2006, 93–146.

ἔχειν) for having killed one of his men, and explains that he had attempted to rape her. Once again, extenuating circumstances are alleged: there is no suggestion that Anthia believes her action to have been wrong. In Heliodorus (1,17,6), Aristippus, the father of Cnemon, has discovered that it was his wife, Demaenete, who tried to seduce the boy and tricked him into bursting into his father's bedroom with sword in hand. He attempts to drag Demaenete before the *dêmos*, but she prevents it by committing suicide en route. Aristippus then secures pardon (συγγώμη) for the boy, now that he has been shown to be innocent. Later (6,7,6), Cnemon, Calasiris, and Chariclea are guests in the home of Nausicles; as Calisiris and Chariclea are about to resume their efforts to find Theagenes, Cnemon, now in love with Nausicles' daughter, is reluctant to accompany them, though he feels duty-bound to do so. He begs their pardon (συγγώμη) and that of the gods of friendship for preferring to return home to Athens. One hardly asks forgiveness for an act one is about to commit – one cannot repent in advance of committing a sin. Cnemon is asking for leave or allowance to stay behind; repentance or a change of heart is beside the point. When Theagenes has been brought before Arsace, who has fallen madly in love with him, he greets her brazenly, as it seems to the onlookers, without the gesture of prostration. Arsace, however, bids them pardon (συγγῶτε) him, since he is a stranger and unfamiliar with their ways, and has a Greek's contempt for foreigners (10,16,7). His ignorance of local customs extenuates Theagenes' guilt, as does the habitual attitude of Greeks, for which he cannot be held individually responsible. One more illustration, from the last occurrence of the term in the *Aethiopica* (10,23,3): a servant has refrained from announcing the arrival of Meroebus, brother of the Ethiopian king Hydaspes, out of respect for protocol; when Hydaspes explodes, the servant asks for pardon (συγγνῶθι), explaining that his behavior was absolutely correct under the circumstances.

Of course, the term συγγώμη may well have a wide range of meanings, whether or not forgiveness in the modern sense is among them, without thereby authorizing us to conclude that the Greek novelists, not to mention pagan writers generally, lacked the richer concept. Yet the novels, to limit myself to those texts here, do not highlight the complex of moral ideas that constitute forgiveness, including, as we have seen, confession, remorse, and a change of disposition. Rather, they emphasize innocence and steadfastness of purpose – just the opposite of repentance, in which one regrets one's former conduct and undergoes a transformation of character, indeed of self. Novelistic protagonists may ask for pity (not quite the same thing as mercy), or humble themselves, or seek to excuse what may have seemed to be an offense – the strategies recommended by Aristotle, among others, for appeasing anger – but they do not typically admit guilt and seek a new moral relationship with the offended party. To highlight the distinction between the two conceptions, I focus on the representation of relations between mortals and the divine in two types of narrative: the Greek novels, to which I shall return in a moment, and a curious work in the Judaeo-Christian tradition called *The Life of Adam and Eve*, known also, since the first edition in the 19th century, under the rather misleading title *The Apocalypse of Moses*, which has only recently become an object of scholarly attention. I speak of it as Judaeo-Christian, because scholars are undecided as to whether it is Jewish or Christian in origin, since what is presumably the earliest version contains no certain allusions Christian themes. So too, the date of the work is in doubt: it has been placed as early as the first century BCE (which would of course exclude a Christian provenance) and as late as the seventh century CE. Versions survive in ancient Greek, which may be the original language of composition, as well as in Syriac, which also has a claim to this distinction, and in Latin, Slavonic, Armenian, Georgian and Coptic.[9] Greek and Latin manuscripts abound – the work was clearly very popular throughout the Middle Ages. There is also considerable variation among the several traditions, as is to be expected with a work of this kind, which invites abridgment or expansion according to the interests of the copyists: one thinks in this connection of the multiple recensions of the Greek *Alexander Romance* or the Latin *Story of Apollonius King of Tyre*, to which I have applied the label 'open text'.[10] The following is based on the Greek text.[11]

After the first couple was driven from Eden, Eve gave birth to Cain and Abel, and after the murder of Abel, to Seth. When Adam fell ill and was on the point of death, at 930 years of age, he gathered round him his thirty sons and thirty daughters. Seth offers to fetch him fruit from Paradise, but Adam explains the origin of the curse of death, when he, at Eve's instigation, tasted of the forbidden fruit, with the result that 'God became angry at us' (8).[12] Eve at this point laments: 'Adam, my lord, give me half your illness, and let me endure it, because

---

[9] The Coptic version is in fragmentary condition. For a handy comparison of the several versions, in five parallel columns, see Anderson and Stone 1994; for discussion of the date, contents, manuscripts, and related texts, see de Jonge and Tromp 1997; also Tromp 2005. See also Nickelsburg 1984, and especially the important collection of essays in Anderson, Stone, and Tromp 2000.
[10] Cf. Konstan 1998.
[11] I follow the recent edition by Tromp 2005, which has an extensive and important introduction; this represents a major advance over the 1866 edition of the Greek text by C. von Tischendorf, who had available only four of the 25 manuscripts now known, although the differences between the two are immaterial for my argument.
[12] The Latin version introduces a long interlude here on a vision of Adam: see Anderson and Stone 1994, 22.

this has happened to you on account of me, on account of me you are in such illness and pain' (9). Adam instructs Eve to seek out Paradise together with Seth, bidding them to weep and beg God to have pity on him. This Eve does, and groans aloud: 'Woe, woe, if I should come to the day of the resurrection, and all who have sinned will curse me, saying that Eve did not observe the commandment of God' (10). When Eve and Seth return to Adam's tent, Adam asks her to relate the story of the fall, and her responsibility for it, to their children (14). Here begins Eve's first great narrative, in which she rehearses how the devil seduced the serpent, and the serpent in turn deceived her, leading her to the forbidden fruit and even threatening to withhold it from her, having changed its mind (19), until she promises to give Adam a share as well. Having tasted the fruit, she becomes aware of her nakedness, but nevertheless fulfills her oath to make Adam eat of it as well. God then pronounces his dread judgment upon the couple, banishing them from Eden. Here, Adam begs the angels to let him beseech God's pity, since he alone sinned (27), but God is unrelenting. Adam, on his deathbed, then begs Eve to rise up and pray to God, and she, falling to the ground, says: 'I have sinned [ἥμαρτον], God, I have sinned, Father of all, I have sinned against you, I have sinned against your chosen angels, I have sinned against the Cherubim, I have sinned against your unshakable throne, I have sinned, Lord, I have sinned greatly, I have sinned before you, and all sin in creation has arisen through me' (32). At this, an angel approaches her and announces, 'Arise, Eve, from your repentance [μετάνοια]' (32).[13] He declares to her that Adam is now dead, and grants her a vision of a chariot descending to Adam, and the angels beseeching the Lord to yield (33), since Adam is made in His image. God indeed takes pity on his creation (37), and raises him to the third heaven, where he will remain until judgment day. Adam and Cain are then buried together in a secret place, as God declares that he will resurrect Adam on the final day together with all mankind. Eve supplicates the Lord to bury her next to Adam, even though she is unworthy and sinful (ἁμαρτωλόν, 42),[14] and her wish is granted. Seth is instructed to mourn for six days, and with this, the story – which is Eve's story more than anything else – is ended.

In her relation to God, Eve insists upon her own fault, and is obviously remorseful: that she was deceived by the serpent serves not as an excuse for her sin but rather as a sign that she has now perceived her error and has repented of it. This profound realization and acknowledgement of their culpability works a change in both Adam and Eve, and is the reason why God is prepared to yield to

---

[13] Much of the narrative from 27–32 is missing in the Latin and Armenian versions.
[14] The last word spelled with smooth breathing in Tromp's edition.

the petition on the part of his angels and grant the couple reprieve and resurrection. Although the term συγγώμη does not occur in this text, I believe that we can safely call God's mercy 'forgiveness' here, since all the conditions have been fulfilled – even a change of heart on the part of God himself, who had earlier manifested his sternness in expelling the couple from Paradise, despite the appeals of his angels in their behalf.

At the beginning of the *Ephesiaca*, Xenophon recounts the great physical beauty and other virtues of the protagonist, Habrocomes, which inclined the young man so to despise the attractions of others as to deny that Eros was even a god (1,1,5). This is the kind of rivalry with a deity that invariably invites punishment, even if it is not accompanied by arrogance – Venus' wrath at Psyche in Apuleius' *Metamorphoses* is a case in point. And Eros is duly furious (1,2,1) and causes the youth to fall in love with Anthia. The situation would seem to be tailor-made for a plea for forgiveness on Habrocomes' part. And yet, the first time either of the two protagonists offers supplication to a deity, it is Anthia, and she appeals to Isis rather than to Eros: she declares that she has remained chaste and kept her marriage to Habrocomes pure, and prays that she either be restored to her husband, if he is alive, or else that she remain faithful to his corpse (4,3,3–4; cf. the similar plea at 5,4,6). When Habrocomes is bound to a cross, as a result of the false testimony of Kyno, he does not hesitate to proclaim his innocence as he prays to the god of the Nile: if he has done any wrong, he declares, let him die a miserable death (4,2,4), but let the gracious Nile not look on indifferently at the death of a man who has committed no injustice. The god at once takes pity on him (οἰκτείρει, 4,2,6), since indeed his suffering is unmerited. Later, Anthia appeals to Apis as the most humane of gods (φιλανθρωπότατε), who takes pity on all strangers, and begs him to pity (ἐλεῆσον) her as well in her misfortune (5,4,10), again requesting that she either find her husband again or else die; she receives the reply that she will soon have Habrocomes. In the end, when the pair are reunited on Rhodes, they give thanks to Isis for their salvation (5,13,4). Nowhere do they suggest that they might be guilty of some offense against the gods; there is no question of repentance or forgiveness. They have proved their mutual fidelity in the course of their sufferings and now express gratitude for their deliverance. The contrast with the story of Eve is manifest.

The reason for the hostility of the gods toward Chaereas and Callirhoe in Chariton's novel is unclear: she herself blames her plight upon malicious fortune (Τύχη βασκάνη, 1,14,7; cf. 2,8,3–6; 3,3,8; 4,1,12; 4,4,2; 4,7,4; 5,1,4; 6,8,1; 8,1,2). Finally, once restored to Chaereas, Callirhoe offers thanks to Aphrodite for being reconciled with her (8,4,10), although no indication of a motive for the goddess' anger is offered, if indeed her anger is suggested at all. In the end, back home in

Syracuse, Callirhoe visits the temple of Aphrodite to give thanks once again, and adds: 'I do not blame you, mistress, for what I have suffered: it was my fate' (8,8,16). No room for forgiveness here, it is clear. Achilles Tatius is not much interested in appeals to the gods; once, Clitopho bids Aphrodite not to resent it (the verb is νεμεσᾶν) as an insult to her dignity that he and Leucippe preserved their virginity until they might be properly married (8,5,8): hardly a genuine expression of contrition. Daphnis and Chloe, for their part, are under the protection of Pan and the Nymphs and there is never any suggestion that they may have offended them. Indeed, when Chloe is carried off in a raid, Daphnis reproaches the Nymphs for betraying them (2,21,3), upon which the Nymphs appear to him in a dream and reply that they are not to blame (2,23,2), and reassure Daphnis that all will be well and that Pan is already coming to Chloe's defense.

When Chariclea and Theagenes are taken prisoner by Thyamis and his bandits at the beginning of Heliodorus' *Aethiopica*, Chariclea in her grief berates Apollo for her sufferings (1,8,2–3): 'You are retaliating too much and too harshly for our sins [ἁμαρτημάτων], and all that we have gone through does not suffice for your vengeance…. Where will you put an end to these things?' Like other novelistic heroines, she asserts that rather than suffer shame she will slay herself, and so remain chaste until death. 'But,' she adds, 'there is no judge harsher than you.' Theagenes, however, advises her to leave off such reproaches, since lamentations merely irritate the god further: 'for one must not censure but rather beseech, for the powerful are rendered propitious by prayers, not by reproofs' (1,8,4). Chariclea seems to acknowledge faults, but is certain that they do not merit such extreme chastisement; Theagenes, for his part, suggests entreaty as opposed to blame, thus finessing the question of guilt. Neither gives any hint of apology or remorse. Much later, when, thanks to the plots of the queen Arsace, Chariclea is condemned to be burnt at the stake, she, like Habrocomes in Xenophon's novel, cries out to the Sun and Earth and the spirits above and below the earth who watch over human injustice (8,9,12): 'You are witnesses that I am innocent of the charges brought against me.'

In arguing that the heroes and heroines of the Greek novels do not regard themselves as having done wrong or offended the gods, I am aware that I am not advancing any startlingly new claims. The tribulations to which the protagonists are subject are designed to test their fidelity, not to punish them for their sins. Where there is no sin, moreover, there is no place for forgiveness, and so it is unsurprising that the complex of confession, remorse, and change of heart or conversion are absent from the novels as well, in stark contrast to the story of Adam and Eve, where these motives are central to the narrative. And yet, the radical absence of forgiveness as a theme in the Greek novels is, I think, worth noting. Focusing on this concept, and the set of emotions and values associated with it, brings out the sharp distinction between pagan ethics and the sensibility characteristic of contemporary Jewish and Christian texts, and, I hope, casts some new light on both in the context of classical culture.

Bibliography

Anderson, G.A., and Stone, M.E. (eds.) 1994. *A Synopsis of the Books of Adam and Eve*, Atlanta: Scholars Press.

Anderson, G., Stone, M.E., Tromp, J. (eds.) 2000. *Literature on Adam and Eve: Collected Essays*, Leiden: Brill.

Fulkerson, L. 2013. *No Regrets: Remorse in Classical Antiquity*, Oxford: Oxford University Press.

Griswold, C. 2007. *Forgiveness: A Philosophical Exploration*, Cambridge: Cambridge University Press.

Jonge, M. de and Tromp, J. 1997. *The Life of Adam and Eve and Related Literature*, Sheffield: Academic Press.

Konstan, D. 1998. 'The Alexander Romance: The Cunning of the Open Text', *Lexis* 16, 123–138.

Konstan, D. 2005. 'Clemency as a Virtue', *Classical Philology* 100: 337–346.

Konstan, D. 2006. *The Emotions of the Ancient Greeks: Studies in Aristotle and Classical Literature*, Toronto: University of Toronto Press.

Konstan, D. 2010. *Before Forgiveness: The Origins of a Moral Idea*, Cambridge: Cambridge University Press.

Nickelsburg, G.W.E. 1984. 'The Books of Adam and Eve', in: M.E. Stone (ed.), *Jewish Writings of the Second Temple Period*, Assen: Van Gorcum; Philadelphia: Fortress Press. 113–118.

Pirovano, L. 2006. *Le* Interpretationes vergilianae *di Tiberio Claudio Donato: Problemi di retorica*, Roma: Herder.

Tromp, J. 2005. *The Life of Adam and Eve in Greek: A Critical Edition*, Leiden: Brill.

Michael Cummings
The Interaction of Emotions in the Greek Novels

Abstract: Massimo Fusillo has argued that one of the major features of psychology in the ancient Greek novels is the conflict of emotion. This paper will supplement Fusillo's work by utilising Lakoff and Johnson's theory of conceptual metaphor. It will maintain that emotions in the Greek novels are often conflicting, but also show that the metaphorical conceptualisation of emotions is integral to the depiction of this conflict. Furthermore it will show that there is an alternative model of emotion which does not necessitate conflict, an interactive one, which is as important for the understanding of emotion in the Greek novels as that of conflict.

In a paper titled 'Les conflits des émotions: un topos du roman grec érotique', Massimo Fusillo has argued that the conflict of emotions is an integral part of the portrayal of emotions in the Greek novels.[1] He discusses occurrences of multiple emotions in the novels, most often in the form of lists of emotions which involve asyndetical accumulation.[2] He also shows that these accumulated lists

---

[1] Fusillo 1990. This article was reprinted in English in the volume *Oxford Readings in the Greek Novel*: see Fusillo 1999. For articles which continue Fusillo's work on multiple emotions in the Greek Novels see Kytzler 2003 and Repath 2007. The former supplements Fusillo's analysis of multiple emotions and the later discusses the conflict of emotions in relation to Platonic psychology. In this paper all titles (of the novels) and translations are taken from Reardon 1989, unless otherwise stated. All Greek extracts and references are taken from the *Thesaurus Linguae Graecae* (TLG).

[2] Fusillo 1990, 205: 'accumulation asyndetique de substantifs abstraits'. The terms are taken from Denniston 1965, ch. 6. For an example from literature prior to the Greek novels see Plato 649d4–5: Οὐκοῦν ταὐτά ἐστι πάντα ἐν οἷς ἐσμὲν τοιοῦτοι, θυμός, ἔρως, ὕβρις, ἀμαθία, φιλοκέρδεια, δειλία. In this paper I am focusing on internal psychological metaphor, i.e. multiple emotions which take place inside one person. I am not discussing multiple metaphors among a crowd of people, in which case it is harder to say which emotion belongs to who. There is an example of this in Chariton, where emotions are flying around as Chaereas is 'resurrected' in the court scene: ἔδοξας ἂν ἐν θεάτρῳ παρεῖναι μυρίων παθῶν πλήρει· πάντα ἦν ὁμοῦ, δάκρυα, χαρά, θάμβος, ἔλεος, ἀπιστία, εὐχαί (Chariton 5,8,2,3–5,8,3,1). Fusillo 1990 discusses this passage at 205.

Michael Cummings, University of Edinburgh

https://doi.org/10.1515/9781501503986-024

utilise the antithesis of several emotion terms. This paper will argue that while Fusillo is correct in maintaining this, there are other dynamics present in the Greek novels, which display a different approach to multiple emotions. It will be seen that emotions in the novels often 'interact' in ways that are not 'conflicting', and that this feature is equally important for an understanding of psychology in the Greek Novels.

The argument of this paper will be based upon the theory of metaphor put forward by George Lakoff and Mark Johnson. Lakoff and Johnson have argued that metaphor plays an important role in language and cognition, in terms of structuring our basic understanding of experience.[3] This can be seen nowhere more clearly than in language about the emotions. In a subsequent work, Lakoff and Kövecses have shown that various metaphors are systematic in the everyday language used to describe 'anger' in American English, and that they in fact structure the concept itself and underlie folk models of the emotion.[4] For example, anger in English is often conceived of as a fire, as we can see in such common sentences as 'that kindled my ire' and 'he was consumed by his anger'.[5] When we turn to study of the emotions in ancient Greek, common metaphors become a valuable source for evidence of folk models. Folk models refer to the models of emotion used in everyday language to describe psychological experience.[6] If we are to use the term 'conflict of emotions' concerning ancient Greek emotions, which do not necessarily correspond with our own, then we must distinguish which metaphors are being used and how. The notion of conflict in English is a complex metaphor, which ranges from conceptualisation of, say, a conflict between two individuals to conflict between whole societies, such as a war. If we are to apply this metaphor to the emotions in the Greek novels, we must be careful to see that it is being applied to Greek concepts which are the equivalent of our own.

---

3 Lakoff and Johnson 1980.
4 Lakoff and Kövecses 1987.
5 Examples taken from Lakoff and Kövecses 1987, 203.
6 The term scientific model complements the term folk model. A scientific model is here defined as a model of psychology which arises from a body of knowledge which claims expertise in this area. Thus in ancient Greek literature we might term Plato or Galen's psychological models scientific, whereas the models presented in Longus, which utilise conventional metaphor, would be referred to as folk. I am not arguing that these categories are clearly distinct. For instance, in Heliodorus we see an interesting interaction between folk and scientific models in Calasiris' explanation of the evil eye (3,7,3–3,8,2): as argued by Cairns in a paper titled 'Looks of Love and Loathing', Edinburgh, 16 January 2007. Folk models can influence scientific models and scientific models can introduce new folk models.

I will do the following in this paper. First, I will outline the conflict of emotions, as it applies to occurrences of multiple emotions in the novels, and its relationship to antithesis. Secondly, I will list other metaphors used for multiple emotions, which still allow the presence of antithesis between the various emotions. Finally, I will show some examples of multiple emotions where neither conflict nor antithesis is present. I will conclude by claiming that these examples, which I have termed the 'interaction of emotions', are conceptually as important for folk models of psychology in the Greek novels as the conflict of emotions.

I

Let us begin with a passage from Heliodorus' *Aethiopica*. Calasiris' sons Thyamis and Petosiris, who have been running around the city of Memphis engaged in mortal combat like Achilles and Hector, cease when their father unexpectedly appears and supplicates them to stop. At his appearance they are overcome by various emotions. The conflict of emotions is here fittingly enacted in a literal conflict.

> πολλὰ ἅμα καὶ ἐξ ἐναντίων ἔπασχον· ἥδοντο ἐπὶ τῷ φύντι σωζομένῳ παρ' ἐλπίδας, ἐφ' ᾗ κατελαμβάνοντο πράξει καὶ ἠνιῶντο καὶ ᾐσχύνοντο, τῆς ἀδηλίας τῶν ἀποβησομένων εἰς ἀγωνίαν καθίσταντο. (Hld. 7,7,3,5–9)
>
> they experienced many contrary emotions at one and the same time: joy at the unexpected restoration of their father, sorrow and shame at the business in which he had surprised them, and finally anguish over the uncertainties of what might ensue.

The phrase ἐξ ἐναντίων marks this out as the conflict of emotions. The literal meaning is 'from the opposite side', but it is often used in a hostile sense, as enemies usually face one another on the battlefield. We can also see the antithesis of pleasure and pain, ἥδοντο and ἠνιῶντο, which is such an integral part of the conception of the emotions in Aristotle.[7] Here we definitely have a view of the emotions as contrary tensions working within the human body, fighting just as Thyamis and Petosiris were.

If we move on now to an example from Achilles Tatius, we see the same themes of conflict and antithesis.

---

[7] See Arist. 1378a20–3. Also note that pleasure and pain can co-exist in some emotions, see Konstan 2006, 42.

> πάντα δέ με εἶχεν ὁμοῦ, ἔπαινος, ἔκπληξις, τρόμος, αἰδώς, ἀναίδεια. ἐπῄνουν τὸ μέγεθος, ἐκπεπλήγμην τὸ κάλλος, ἔτρεμον τὴν καρδίαν, ἔβλεπον ἀναιδῶς, ᾐδούμην ἁλῶναι. (Ach.Tat. 1,4,5,1–3)
>
> 'I now became prey to a host of emotions: admiration, amazement, trembling, shame, shamelessness. I admired her generous stature, marvelled at her beauty, trembled in my heart, stared shamelessly, ashamed I might be caught'.

Clitophon sees Leucippe and feels many emotions. We can see antithesis in the use of αἰδώς and ἀναίδεια.[8] Clitophon feels the lover's shame in looking at Leucippe but also cannot help looking at her 'shamelessly': ἔβλεπον ἀναιδῶς. We may compare this with Medea in Apollonius' *Argonautica*, where Medea is held back (temporarily) from her attraction to Jason by αἰδώς (3,649). The erotic experience can give rise to antithetical feelings. If we stop for a moment to consider how the emotions here are metaphorically conceptualised, we see that the verb εἶχεν is used. This is a commonplace metaphor and conceptualises the emotions, πάντα, as 'holding' the person affected. This metaphor is personified, and potentially indicates conflict, although we are not told the reaction of the person affected.

A variant upon this 'holding' metaphor is the 'taking' one. In Chariton Dionysius 'takes' different sentiments: γνῶμαι.

> τούτων τῶν λόγων ἀκούσας ὁ Διονύσιος ποικίλας ἐλάμβανε γνώμας· ἥπτετο μὲν γὰρ αὐτοῦ ζηλοτυπία διότι καὶ νεκρὸν ἐφίλει Χαιρέαν, ἥπτετο δὲ καὶ φόβος μὴ ἑαυτὴν ἀποκτείνῃ· ἐθάρρει δὲ ὅμως ὅτι ὁ πρῶτος ἀνὴρ ἐδόκει τεθνηκέναι τῇ γυναικί· μὴ γὰρ ἀπολείψειν αὐτὴν Διονύσιον, οὐκ ὄντος ἔτι Χαιρέου. (Chariton 3,7,6,2–3,7,7,1)
>
> When he heard this, Dionysius was assailed by conflicting sentiments. He was seized with jealousy, that Callirhoe loved Chaereas even dead; with fear, that she would kill herself. Yet still, he was heartened by the thought that his wife thought her first husband dead, for he supposed that she would not leave Dionysius if Chaereas was no longer alive (Fusillo 1999).

These 'conflicting' sentiments are in fact 'many-coloured ones', ποικίλας.[9] The translation of ἐλάμβανε as "being assailed by" is more justified, as this is personification and 'taking' is certainly one of the actions which might be made by an assailant. However, it is actually Dionysius who is doing the taking, and therefore the emotions are not necessarily conflicting with him, as he could be taking hold of a reified emotion rather than a personified one. If we look at the emo-

---

[8] See Fusillo 1990, 207: 'en particulier, on note un gout pour l'antithèse; on voit surtout le couple αἰδώς- ἀναίδεια'. On the concept αἰδώς see Cairns 1993.
[9] Many coloured emotions, πάθη ποικίλα, appear at Chariton 3,3,4 and 4,5,10. See Kytzler 2003, 71.

tions involved we have jealousy and fear, which we might say are not obviously antithetical, and fear and courage, which are.[10]

The conflict of emotions for the most part positions the emotions or πάθη as the subjects and the person affected as the object.[11] The emotions grasp the person and treat them as a passive object. This conforms to a theory of the emotions put forward by Kövecses, who argues that folk models of emotion in English all conform to a master metaphor of Emotion as Force.[12] The notion of grasping expresses a conflict between the emotions and the person, one which the emotions usually win (at least in the Greek novels). The problem with designating whether emotions are antithetical or not resides in the relationship between them. If we have obvious opposites, such as αἰδώς and ἔρως, then antithesis is clear, but it is not so clear with other concepts, such as λύπη and φόβος. A study of the Greek emotions to determine which are antithetical or not in terms of Greek thought, and to what extent, is outside the range of this paper.[13] What we can say here is that antithesis cannot be assumed unless it is indicated in the text, for example by something like the standard Greek usage of μέν and δέ, by a culturally sustained polarity between two emotions (as seen in other contexts), or by the specific use of a metaphor, such as the conflict one. In addition, because the model of the 'grip' of emotions postulates a relationship between a group of emotions and the person affected, it offers us no evidence in itself as to the relationship between the emotions themselves. The emotions act as a group, and the conflict implied is a gang of people against the poor person affected. What I will now do is argue against the notion that multiple emotions are necessarily conflicting and even necessarily antithetical. I will do this by examining several further metaphorical conceptualisations of the emotions in the novels.

---

10 See Tyrtaeus 8,1–3 (Campbell).
11 There are other instances of the 'holding' and 'taking' of emotions at X. Eph. 5,13,3 and Chariton 1,9,3 respectively. Achilles Tatius extends this imagery of the conflict of emotions. After the metaphor of shame, grief and anger as three waves of the ψυχή he uses an image of emotions as wounds inflicted by specific utterances (2,29). The narrator in Achilles Tatius explores multiple emotions in a more explicitly philosophical way than the other novelists. For an analysis of the influence of Platonism in these instances see Repath 2007.
12 Kövecses 2000.
13 For a study of the Greek emotions which highlights many of these aspects see Konstan 2006.

II

The conflict of emotions envisions an internal conflict where the human body is the site of the action: a spatial arena. At other points in the novels multiple emotions are seen as entities in the 'container' of the human body.[14] These metaphors entail neither conflict nor antithesis.

When a character in the novels experiences multiple emotions at the same time, they are often said to contain a mixture of them. In a scene from Xenophon Manto is enraged at her rejection by Habrocomes' letter.

> Λαβοῦσα ταῦτα τὰ γράμματα ἡ Μαντὼ ἐν ὀργῇ ἀκατασχέτῳ γίνεται καὶ ἀναμίξασα πάντα, φθόνον [καὶ], ζηλοτυπίαν, λύπην, φόβον, ἐνενόει ὅπως τιμωρήσαιτο τὸν ὑπερηφανοῦντα. (X. Eph. 2,5,5,1–4)
>
> When she received this letter, Manto could not control her anger. All her feelings were confused: she felt envy, jealousy, grief, and fear, and was planning how to take her revenge on the man who was turning her down.

Manto becomes angry and mixes up, ἀναμίξασα, all the emotions she is feeling.[15] This metaphor differs from the one of 'conflict' above in the sense that the metaphor implies merely the mixing up of entities in a container. There is no notion of conflict between the person and emotions or between the emotions themselves.

A related metaphor is the filling of the human container. When the Persian King reads the letter Chaereas has sent him (written in full at 8,4,2–3), he is 'filled with countless emotions: βασιλεὺς δὲ ἀναγινώσκων μυρίων παθῶν ἐπληροῦτο.[16] Likewise in Heliodorus Calasiris is 'filled with a mixture of pleasure and sadness': ἡδονῆς δὲ ἅμα καὶ λύπης ἐνεπλήσθην.[17] Here there is definite

---

[14] Konstan 2006, 147, cites Sally Planalp, who says that the pouring out of feelings reflects an underlying conception of the human body as a container and emotions as fluids inside it. The container as an ontological metaphor is discussed in Lakoff and Johnson 1980, 29–30. As we will see, this is the case in the Greek novels, although since the verb πίμπλημι and the adjective μεστός can be used with solids as well as liquids, we cannot limit the substance of the emotion to a fluid.

[15] This metaphor of mixing also appears at X. Eph. 3,7,1 where there are πάθη συμμιγή, but in this case it is Perilaus' whole household who are experiencing the emotions.

[16] Chariton 8,5,8,1. See also the metaphor of μεστός, 'full of', at Chariton 6,6,1, which features the emotions ὀργή, λύπη, and φόβος. Here the eunuch is perturbed at Kallirhoe's deferral of his advances in the name of the king. Earlier on at 1,4,4 Chaereas' ψυχή is μεστός of ἐλπίς, φόβος and πολυπραγμοσύνη.

[17] Hld. 4,9,1,2–3.

antithesis between the two 'sensations', which are conceptualised antithetically in Aristotle.[18]

It can be argued from the above metaphors that they are just group or 'genus' metaphors for the emotions as πάθη, and retain an antithetical distinction between emotions. However, what I want to emphasise here is that antithesis does not entail conflict, and these metaphors, while they do not exclude antithesis, do not entail it either. These metaphors are alternative models of conceptualising the emotions, which do not necessitate fighting or conflict, either between the emotions themselves or the emotions and the person. The conflict of emotions, a metaphor which personifies the emotions, must take its place alongside more basic ontological metaphors, such as those which view emotions as entities in a human container. I will move on from this to show that there are examples of multiple emotions in the novels where there is not only an absence of antithesis, but where the language emphasises the purposeful interaction of emotions together. This is admittedly the interaction of the emotions together to influence the person affected forcibly, but there can be no antithesis here, as emotions cannot be antithetical to the person feeling them (the conflict of reason and emotion is a different matter).

III

In this paper space is limited, so I will restrict myself to a few important examples, mostly from Heliodorus. Three important emotions in the Greek novels are those of ἔρως, ὀργή/θυμός, and ζηλοτυπία.[19] I do not think we shall be going too far wrong if for the examples below we label them as love, anger and jealousy.

At the start of the *Aethiopica* the bandit leader Thyamis falls in love with Chariclea, the novel's heroine. Later on in chapter one, when his bandit encampment is about to be taken, he rushes to a cave where he has imprisoned her to kill her, in an action typical of a 'barbarian'.[20] His emotional state at this point is

---

18 See also n,4. Λύπη is translated as an emotion by Morgan (correctly I feel, as Calasiris goes on to say that he felt joy at the same time as crying).
19 I feel that in the novels θυμός and ὀργή represent the same concept. See Hld. 2,12,5–7: ὑπὸ μὲν θυμοῦ ληστρικοῦ καὶ βαρβαρικῆς ὀργῆς πλέον τότε δι' ἐρωτικὴν ἀποτυχίαν ἐπιτεινομένης (on the one hand he had the hot blood of all brigands and the quick temper of all savages, which, aggravated by his frustrated passion...). I assume that here Heliodorus is employing the words for variation. Certainly both concepts indicate a quick and uncontrollable anger.
20 Heliodorus tells us in the lines preceding this extract that barbarians usually kill what they love before they die, if they despair of saving themselves (1,30).

quite overwhelming, and he is 'crazed with love and jealousy and anger': ἔρωτι δὲ καὶ ζηλοτυπίᾳ καὶ θυμῷ κάτοχος (Hld. 1,30,7,3–4).²¹ The metaphor here is κάτοχος, held down, and as we have said above it can represent a conflict metaphor. But who is the conflict between? What we have here is effectively a group mugging. These three emotions have grabbed Thyamis and are holding him down. They are working together as a team against the person affected. It is also important that none of the emotion terms are necessarily antithetical with one another. If you are in love, or here more properly feel the lust of a barbarian, depending on circumstance this may lead to anger, maybe to jealousy and even to both. We have an almost identical image used later in the novel when Achaemenes, the son of the wicked nurse Cybele, takes offence at the thwarting of his plans and rides off to inform Oroondates of the intrigues taking place.

Ταῦτα εἶπε καὶ ὑπ' ὀργῆς ἅμα καὶ ζηλοτυπίας καὶ ἔρωτος καὶ ἀποτυχίας οἰστρηθείς... (Hld. 7,29,1,1)

So he spoke. Anger, jealousy, love and disappointment combined to goad him to fury...

We have no reason here, metaphorical or otherwise, to designate these emotions as conflicting or antithetical *between* one another. It is also great reductionism to equate the notion of stinging with the notion of conflict.²² In a similar way earlier in the novel Demaenete is 'maddened' by both θυμός and ἔρως.²³

To focus in upon ἔρως and ζηλοτυπία, I believe that their close conceptual relationship leads to the metaphors which show them as uniting against the person affected or even working upon one another. Arsace conceptualises the two emotions afflicting her as diseases, νόσοι, when she asks Cybele to help her effect a 'cure'. The solution she is asking for is the seduction of Theagenes.

δυεῖν δι' ἑνός μοι γενήσῃ νόσων ἰατρός, ἔρωτός τε καὶ ζηλοτυπίας, τὸν μὲν ἐμπλήσασα, τῆς δὲ ἀπαλλάξασα. (Hld. 7,10,6,2–4).

'You would cure me of two sicknesses at one stroke – love and jealousy, by satisfying the one and ridding me of the other'.

---

21 One difference is the use of conjunction here, unlike the asyndeton seen in the lists discussed by Fusillo 1990.
22 Οἰστράω can represent ἔρως: see Iamb. VP 31,195. However, its primary use is as a metaphor for madness (S. Tr. 653), and what I suspect is that it is used metonymically for the conceptualisation of emotion as madness. We often see emotion as a state of madness in the Greek novels (see following note).
23 Hld. 1,15,2,3–4 – τῷ τε θυμῷ καὶ ἔρωτι περιμανῆ: 'particularly as her fury and desire had undermined her reason'.

Although the two emotions are both conceived as νόσοι, the ontology of each metaphor is different, as one must be 'filled in', and the other 'released', and these metaphors cannot be reduced to the notion of conflict. This example details a complex process. The process of emotion here involves an initial sensation, a prolonged state, and an abatement of the emotion. The contraction (to use a fitting metaphor) of each emotion is conceptualised in the same way: both are diseases which Arsace has 'caught' and which she is 'suffering'. However, at the end of the process, the easing of the emotions or 'cure', there is a different result, in that for Arsace sex with Theagenes will complete her ἔρως but release her from jealousy. The same reference can contain multiple metaphors for the emotions, which highlight different aspects of the emotions.

This conceptual proximity of emotions explains an interesting example from book two of Heliodorus. Chariclea is a little put out at the news that Theagenes has kissed another girl (the dead Thisbe) and asks who she is. She qualifies her statement by saying she hopes that they do not think her bitten by ἔρως: Ἀλλ' εἰ μή τί με δακνομένην ἔρωτι ὑπονοεῖν μέλλετε (Hld. 2,8,2,1); 'Please do not suppose that love is making me feel pangs of jealousy'. Morgan's translation summarises the emotional experience nicely, but why does he mention jealousy when there is no word for it in the Greek? The context makes it clear that jealousy is at stake, as another (potential) rival for Theagenes is involved. What we have here is ἔρως as a metonym for ζηλοτυπία. If emotion terms can be metonymic for one another then they are not conflicting, and their models must be interacting. The model of ἔρως is superimposed onto or conflated with the model of jealousy.

Achilles Tatius goes one stage further and uses metaphor to designate the relationship between emotions.[24]

ἐμεμέριστο πολλοῖς ἅμα τὴν ψυχήν, αἰδοῖ καὶ ὀργῇ καὶ ἔρωτι καὶ ζηλοτυπίᾳ. ᾐσχύνετο τὸν ἄνδρα, ὠργίζετο τοῖς γράμμασιν, ὁ ἔρως ἐμάραινε τὴν ὀργήν, ἐξῆπτε τὸν ἔρωτα ἡ ζηλοτυπία, καὶ τέλος ἐκράτησεν ὁ ἔρως. (Ach.Tat. 5,24,3,2–5)

and she felt her soul torn apart by conflicting emotions: shame, anger, love, and jealousy – she was ashamed to face her husband; the letter made her angry, but her anger withered away before her love, which was in turn inflamed by her jealousy. In the end her love prevailed.

---

[24] There are many more of these extended explanations of emotions in Achilles Tatius, such as at 2,29 above (see also Ach.Tat. 6,19). It is outside the scope of this paper to analyse them, but they too offer interesting perspectives upon the folk models of the experience of multiple emotions.

The initial metaphor here is the division of the ψυχή: ἐμεμέριστο. Melitte is divided among her feelings. We see here a mixture of concepts which are antithetical, αἰσχύνη and ἔρως, and those which are not necessarily, such as ἔρως, ὀργή, and ζηλοτυπία. Various metaphors are used to describe the interactions between the emotions. Melitte is ashamed and angry: ἔρως extinguishes her ὀργή (ἐμάραινε), but then ζηλοτυπία lights up her ἔρως (ἐξῆπτε), and finally ἔρως takes control (ἐκράτησεν).[25] The imagery portrays emotion as fire, a common one for the Greek novels, especially in the form of ἔρως as fire. But it also portrays emotion as fire lighter and fire quencher, and therefore there is a complex state of interaction going on. Melitte's passion (ἔρως) puts out the fire of her anger, and so assuages it.[26] In this instance love is incompatible with anger, unlike the example from Heliodorus above, where it joined ἔρως in restraining Thyamis.[27] However, her jealousy ignites her passion and her passion wins out in the situation. So we have a feedback loop with the two emotions of jealousy and love. Each one can inspire the other, and each supports the other in terms of force. The final metaphor is one of the result of conflict, as ἔρως becomes master over her, another commonplace from the novels.[28]

We are now in a position to make some conclusions about the occurrence of multiple emotions in the novels. Fusillo is correct when he claims that emotions are conflicting, but it remains to be specified in what way. The most common form of conflict is between the emotions and the person affected (the group mugging mentioned earlier). However, the emotions can also be conceived of as filling the container of the human body, a metaphor which entails no conflict, and Manto even mixes up the emotions herself (see above). So there are several metaphors which depict the relationship between the emotions and the person affected. Secondly, there is a richer relationship among the emotions themselves than merely conflict or antithesis or lack of, and this is the relationship I term the interaction of emotions. They are not only related logically or grammatically, but in terms of metaphors which provide cognitive structuring, such as the master-slave relationship indicated by κρατέω above, or the action of a person lighting a fire. These examples in turn give us evidence for the folk models of emotions, and more importantly the relations between them. As a final remark I

---

[25] As Fusillo 1990, 216, notes, this marks the victory of ἔρως.
[26] Above we saw the joint action of ἔρως and ὀργή as they stung their victim (Hld. 7,29,1,1). Here they are set against one another, as they are at Ach.Tat. 6,19 where they are two competing flames.
[27] See above: Hld. 1,30,7,3–4.
[28] The metaphor of conflict gives rise to a process, with a start, a duration, and an end, and the metaphor of mastery refers to the end of this process.

would like to emphasise the depth and complexity attached to the occurrence of multiple emotions, an aspect which is submerged when we see asyndetical lists. It might be argued at this point that the examples with the interaction of emotions are not asyndetical. However, these examples show us that when emotions are used in an asyndetical list, neither conflict nor antithesis can be *assumed*, since the emotions that appear in asyndetical lists are not always antithetical.[29] The folk models of various emotions are engaged whenever we read of a person experiencing multiple emotions, and these conceptualisations underlie the surface reading.

Bibliography

Cairns, D.L. 1993. *Aidōs*, Oxford: Oxford University Press.
Denniston, J.D. 1965. *Greek Prose Style*, Oxford: Oxford University Press.
Fusillo, M. 1990. 'Les conflits des emotions: un topos du roman grec erotique', *MH* 47, 201–21, reprinted in: Simon Swain (ed.) 1999. *Oxford Readings in the Greek Novels*, Oxford: Oxford University Press. 60–82.
Konstan, D. 1994. *Sexual Symmetry: Love in the ancient novel and related genres*, Princeton: Princeton University Press.
Konstan, D. 2003. 'Before Jealousy', in: D. Konstan, K. Rutter (eds.) *Envy, Spite and Jealousy: The Rivalrous Emotions in Ancient Greece*, Edinburgh: Edinburgh University Press. 7–28.
Konstan, D. 2006. *The Emotions of the Ancient Greeks: Studies in Aristotle and Classical Literature*, Toronto: University of Toronto Press.
Kövecses, Z. 2000. *Metaphor and Emotion*, Cambridge: Cambridge University Press.
Kytzler, B. 2003. 'Der Regenbogen der Gefühle: Zum Kontrast der Empfindungen im antiken Roman', *Scholia* 12, 69–81.
Lakoff, G. and Kövecses, Z. 1987. 'The cognitive model of anger inherent in American English', in: D. Holland, N. Quinn (eds.), *Cultural Models in Language and Thought*, Cambridge: Cambridge University Press. 195–221.
Lakoff, G. and Johnson, M. 1980. *Metaphors We Live By*, Chicago: University of Chicago Press.
Reardon, B.P. 1989. *Collected Ancient Greek Novels*, Berkeley: University of California Press.
Repath, I. 2007. 'Emotional Conflict and Platonic Psychology in the Greek Novel', in J. Morgan, M. Jones (eds.) *ANS 10: Philosophical Presences in the Ancient Novel*, Groningen: Barkhuis & Groningen University Library. 53–84.

---

29 For example see X.Eph. 2,5,5,1–4 above, where none of the emotions are necessarily antithetical with one another.

Cristiana Sogno
A Critique of Curiosity: Magic and Fiction in Apuleius' *Metamorphoses*

Abstract: This paper explores the connection between curiosity and fiction, which manifests itself in Lucius' pursuit of magic and stories. Because magic is ultimately an excuse for Lucius to collect prurient and sensational stories, I argue that magic is a metaphor used by Apuleius to illustrate the magic of literature, the pleasure of fiction, and the ambition for literary success.

As every reader of Apuleius' *Metamorphoses* knows, curiosity plays a central role in the novel.[2] From a philological point of view, Apuleius can rightfully be considered the adoptive father of the word *curiositas*, which was coined by Cicero in a letter to Atticus (*Ad Att.* 2,12,2), but disappears from view in what remains of Latin literature until Apuleius' *Metamorphoses*.[3] In revisiting this well-studied theme in this paper, I have come to the conclusion that curiosity is inextricably linked with both pleasure and literary renown by way of magic, and I argue that magic is used in the novel as a metaphor for the powers, pleasures, and dangers of fiction. In order to explore and explain the complex relationship that the novel of Apuleius establishes between curiosity, pleasure, and literary renown, I have borrowed the concept of the triad of passions from the field of Augustinian studies. As the rich scholarship on the *Confessions* has shown,[4] for Augustine curiosity (*curiositas* as *concupiscentia oculorum*) is intimately connected with both pleasure (*voluptas* as *concupiscentia carnis*) and worldly ambition (*superbia* as *ambitio saeculi*), and, as such, it can be properly understood only in the context

---

[1] I am grateful to David Konstan, Marília P. Futre Pinheiro, and Bruce McQueen for including my contribution in their volume and would like to thank Jen Ebbeler, Marco Formisano, Noel Lenski, Tanya Pollard, Ron Rosenbaum, Karin Schlapbach, and the anonymous press readers for commenting on earlier drafts of the paper. Any remaining errors and infelicities are solely mine. The paper is dedicated to the memory of Gordon Williams.
[2] For a recent overview of the bibliography on *curiositas* in the *Metamorphoses*, see Leigh 2013, 137, especially note 46.
[3] For a thourough study of all the occurrences and uses in the *Metamorphoses* of *curiositas*, as well as *curiosus, curiose, curiosulus*, and *incuriosus*, see Hijmans 1995.
[4] See most recently Menn 2014, especially 95–102.

Cristiana Sogno, Fordham University[1]

of this triad of passions (*tria vitia*).⁵ The origin of Augustine's triad of passions is scriptural (1 John 2,16),⁶ but its threefold structure is clearly connected with the Platonic tripartition of the soul.⁷ It is my contention that a similar triad of passions similarly rooted in the Platonic tradition is also at work in Apuleius' *Metamorphoses*,⁸ but in this case as part of the sophisticated metafictional game that Apuleius plays with the reader.⁹

In the prologue, the author calls attention to the fictionality of the *Metamorphoses* by suggesting an intriguing connection between curiosity and the magic of sensational fiction. The promise of a pleasant story whispered to caress the reader's ears is obviously meant to tantalize the curiosity of the reader, and the whisper (*susurrus*) conveys the idea of magic in order to hint both at the literary genre of the story and the bewitching effect of this kind of literature.¹⁰ But it is the flawed protagonist of the novel who is interesting in connection between curiosity and the magic of fiction. My investigation is twofold. In the first part of the paper, I explore the role that Lucius' curiosity plays in the novel. In the second part of the paper, I examine the relationship between curiosity about magic, the pleasure of fiction, and the quest for literary renown and argue that a careful analysis of this literary rather than moral triad of passions can offer an original insight into the debated question of the nature of the Apuleian fiction.

Lucius' ancestral curiosity

The curiosity that characterizes the protagonist and main narrator of the novel is on display from the very beginning of his narrative.¹¹ When we first meet him, Lucius is riding his white steed into Thessaly, the land – we are told – of his il-

---

5 On the methodological dangers of studying these *tria vitia* in isolation in the case of Augustine, see Cipriani 1998, 157.
6 See O'Donnell 1992 at *Conf.* 1,10 and 10,41.
7 For the classical and philosophical roots of the triad, see Menn 2014, with ample bibliography in note 19.
8 For the influence of Plato and Platonism on Apuleius' *Metamorphoses*, especially with regards to the treatment of *curiositas*, see DeFilippo 1990, 471–492.
9 For the metafictionality of the *Metamorphoses*, see Winkler 1985, 39–41; Harrison 2000, 231–232; Kirichenko 2008, 368.
10 Graverini 2005, 175–196, especially 183–185 on the intertextual implications of the word *susurrus*.
11 On this passage, see Graverini 2007, 153–155.

lustrious maternal ancestors (*Met.* 1,2).¹² After a long ride he decides to take a break – ostensibly, to relieve his weariness from sitting – but, after carefully tending to the needs of his horse, he happens to spot two traveling companions and decides to follow them.¹³ Lucius' insistence on the casual nature of his encounter with the travelers is suspicious, and the reader is left with the impression that his decision to take a break is motivated by a desire to eavesdrop on a private conversation, which is exactly what happens:¹⁴

> While I try to hear what they are talking about, one of them bursts out laughing and says: "Stop telling such ridiculous and monstrous lies!" When I hear that, my thirst for novelty being what it is, I ask, "Please let me share your conversation. Not that I am a busybody, but I am the sort of person who wants to know everything, or at least most things. Besides, the delightful charm of your stories will smooth out the harshness of the hill we are climbing."'¹⁵

The weariness that Lucius attributes to sitting on the horse for too long (*fatigationem sedentariam*) seems more mental than physical, and eavesdropping is the perfect way to overcome the boredom and hardship of traveling. But the irony of Lucius' disclaimer (*non quidem curiosum*) about his painfully evident nosiness makes it difficult to tell how seriously we are supposed to take his remark.

---

12 *Thessaliam – nam et illic originis maternae nostrae fundamenta a Plutarcho illo inclito ac mox Sexto philosopho nepote eius prodita gloriam nobis faciunt – eam Thessaliam ex negotio petebam.* (I was travelling to Thessaly, where the ancestry of my mother's family brings us fame in the persons of the renowned Plutarch and later his nephew, the philosopher Sextus. 'Thessaly', I say, 'is where I was heading on business.'). All translations are from Hanson 1989. For the importance of Lucius' ancestry, see below.
13 *...duobus comitum, qui forte paululum processerant, tertium me facio., Met.* 1,2 (I made myself a third to two companions who happened to be a little ahead of me.).
14 The adverb *curiose* is cleverly exploited by Apuleius to suggest that the care with which Lucius tends to the horse's needs ultimately affords him the opportunity to indulge his *curiositas*. For other instances in which Apuleius uses this adverb 'to describe careful, painstaking, even obsessive activity' in order to indicate that these activities are 'expressions of the same impulse that elsewhere manifests itself as curiosity', see Leigh 2013, 141.
15 *Ac dum ausculto quid sermonis agitarent, alter exserto cachinno 'Parce', inquit, 'in verba ista haec tam absurda tamque immania mentiendo.' Isto accepto, sititor alioquin novitatis, 'Immo vero', inquam, 'impertite sermone non quidem curiosum, sed qui velim scire vel cuncta vel certe multa. Simul iugi quod insurgimus aspritudinem fabularum lepida iucunditas levigabit.', Met.* 1,2 (While I tried to hear what they were talking about, one of them burst out laughing and exclaimed: 'Stop telling such ridiculous and monstrous lies.' When I heard that, my thirst for novelty being what it is, I asked, 'Please let me share your conversation. Not that I am inquisitive, but I am the sort who wants to know everything, or at least most things. Besides, the charming delight of some stories will smooth out the ruggedness of the hill we are climbing.').

Read straightforwardly, Lucius's words imply a distinction between *curiositas* and the thirst for knowledge, which suggests that the former is blameworthy in a way that the latter is not.[16]

Lucius' fine distinction becomes more meaningful when read within the larger context of the novel. As several scholars have pointed out, Lucius is exceedingly keen on parading his intellectual ambitions[17] and eager to establish his literary and philosophical credentials by claiming to be a descendant of Plutarch and of Plutarch's nephew, the philosopher Sextus.[18] Such a fancy and fanciful genealogy offers 'an important frame of reference for our understanding and judging the characterization of Lucius, who poses as an intellectual',[19] but the discrepancy between Lucius' words and his behavior is bound to expose him as a poseur.

The repeated insistence on his family connection with Plutarch in particular[20] draws attention to Lucius' inadequacy as a scion of such a distinguished family and the descendant of the author of a treatise on curiosity (*Peri polypragmosyne*).[21] Plutarch condemns the tendency of curious people to pry into the lives of others and censures their desire to find out what a clearly private conversation between two 'people in a corner' was about (*Mor.* 516b-c). Moreover, he points out that this kind of misplaced inquisitiveness is usually accompanied by a propensity for gossip and chattiness, since curious people are overly eager to talk about what they enjoy hearing.[22] Plutarch's advice against this cancer of the soul[23] is to redirect attention towards 'better and more pleasant objects', such as 'the heavenly things and the things on earth, in the air, and in

---

16 Such a distinction is in keeping with the negative connotation of the adjective *curiosus* in Latin. For an overview of the semantic range of the word, see now Leigh 2013, 54–90.
17 Harrison 2000, 215–226.
18 Kirichenko 2008, especially 361–366. For the importance of these connections and the expectations that they engender in the readers of the novel, see Wlosok 1969, 83–84; DeFilippo 1990, 482–489.
19 Keulen 2003, 89. For the self-evident fictionality of Lucius's genealogy, see Kirichenko 2007, 262.
20 See *Met.* 2,3, where Lucius's aunt Byrrhena declares that both she and Lucius's mother are descendants of Plutarch (*familia Plutarchi ambae prognatae sumus*).
21 Kirichenko 2008, 351–357.
22 For the compulsive desire of the curious to divulge the shameful secrets that they discover, see Plut. *Mor.* 519c-d.
23 Plutarch defines *polypragmosyne* as 'a desire to learn the trouble of others' and as a disease intimately linked with envy and malice (*Mor.* 515d).

the sea'[24] and plants, or the unpleasant but ultimately innocuous matters that are narrated in history or novels.[25]

In direct defiance of his ancestor's advice, not only does Lucius eavesdrop on a private conversation, but his eagerness in joining such a conversation is stimulated by the very mention of 'ridiculous and monstrous lies' – a far cry from the intellectual curiosity that Plutarch endorses. There is a delightfully Apuleian ambiguity at play here, reflected in Lucius' attitude toward Aristomenes' tale. If a tale involving human suffering and death at the hands of witches turns out to be a piece of sensationalistic fiction, as the words of Aristomenes' companion suggest,[26] Lucius' eagerness to hear it would be in line with Plutarch's advice to redirect curiosity to (hi)stories no matter how gruesome or lurid (*Mor.* 517c-f). According to Lucius' 'ancestor', one can safely indulge in this kind of malicious curiosity by reading – and presumably listening to – either fiction or history because they do not involve the trouble or pain of one's associates. If, however, Lucius believed the tale to be true, he would be guilty of taking pleasure in the trouble and pain of his new acquaintance. Lucius ultimately has it both ways. By arguing that nothing can be considered impossible *a priori* and asserting his belief in Aristomenes (*huic et credo*), the ever-gullible Lucius seems driven by a 'scientific' search for knowledge akin to the Elder Pliny's,[27] but because he lacks the genuine discrimination of Pliny, he arguably ends up endorsing the truthfulness of a fantastical and sensationalistic tale of magic and witches. But by thanking Aristomenes for the 'charming story' (*lepidae fabulae*) and welcome distraction from the hardship of traveling (*sine labore ac taedio*), Lucius seems to acknowledge both the fictionality of Aristomenes' tale and the magic power of fiction.

The lowly and potentially spiteful kind of curiosity that we glimpse in Lucius at the beginning of the novel is so ingrained in his character that it survives in-

---

24 Plut. *Mor.* 517d. The contemplation of the natural phenomena advocated by Plutarch is clearly inspired by the ideal of *theoria* as the philosophical occupation par excellence. See Schlapbach 2010.
25 According to Plutarch (*Mor.* 517e-f), one can safely read about 'The deaths of men, the shufflings off of life [a quotation of Aeschylus *Suppliants*, 937], seductions of women, assaults of slaves, slanders of friends, compounding of poisons, envies, jealousies, shipwrecks of households, overthrow of empires' and enjoy him/herself without causing any trouble or pain to one's associates.
26 '*Nihil*', *inquit*, '*hac fabula fabulosius, nihil isto mendacio absurdius.*', *Met.* 1,20 ('That is the most fabulous fable, the most ridiculous lie that I have ever heard.'). The use of *fabula* and *mendacium* seems to underscore the fictionality of the account.
27 For the comparison between Pliny's and Lucius' scientific method and satire implicit in this passage, see Kirichenko 2008, 354–355.

tact even after his transformation into an ass.[28] The same expression (*familiaris curiositas*) is used to describe the 'habitual curiosity' that has the same spellbinding effect on Lucius both as a man and as an ass.[29] As a man, Lucius quickly forgets his public humiliation at the festival of Laughter under the spur of his habitual curiosity (*Met.* 3,14). As an ass, he not only forgets his own hunger and exhaustion under the spell of *curiositas*, but manages – at least at first – to derive a certain amount of pleasure (*delectatione quadam*) from the careful observation of his highly undesirable surroundings and the sufferings of his fellow slaves both human and animals (*Met.* 9,12–13).

Ultimately, the ghastly spectacle of human and animal pain does make Lucius fear for himself, and the memory of his former happiness causes him grief (*Met.* 9,13), but once again his 'innate curiosity' (*ingenita curiositas*) rescues him from his present misery. No matter how desperate his present circumstances are, Lucius finds comfort in the realization that his asinine appearance gives him unrestricted access to the private lives of people[30] and allows him to accumulate a wide-ranging 'knowledge' about matters that are normally hidden from sight.[31] In explaining to the 'careful and attentive reader' (*lector scrupulosus*) how he was able to find out about some of the most sensationalistic and horrifying tales of adultery, witchcraft, and murder narrated in novel (*Met.* 9,30), Lucius the ass admits that deep down he is the same nosy individual and collector of stories (*homo curiosus*) that we encountered at the beginning of the novel.

In addition to being the defining trait of Lucius' character both as a man and as a beast, *curiositas* is also the motivational force behind the choices of the protagonist of the novel, and, as such, it is the catalyst that propels the action of the plot.[32] The most obvious example of this twofold role of *curiositas* is the transformation of Lucius into an ass. It is his curiosity – particularly his curiosity with regard to magic – that puts in motion the concatenation of events culminating with the metamorphosis of the protagonist of the novel. This kind of curiosity, however, is closely associated with pleasure (*voluptas*), and Lucius' obses-

---

[28] Lancel 1961, 26–27.
[29] As DeFilippo 1990, 488, points out, Lucius has become 'outwardly what he had previously been inwardly, a meddlesome ass'; see also Graverini 2007, 159, who maintains that the metamorphosis into an ass exacerbates Lucius' propensity for meddling.
[30] Cf. *Met.* 9,15, where Lucius finds consolation in the fact that his 'huge ears' allow him to 'hear everything very easily, even at a considerable distance'.
[31] ...*nam et ipse gratas gratias asino meo memini, quod me suo celatu tegmine variisque fortunis exercitatum, etsi minus prudentem, multiscium reddidit.*, *Met.* 9,13 (In fact, I now remember the ass that I was with thankful gratitude because, while I was concealed under his cover and schooled in a variety of fortunes, he made me better-informed, if less intelligent.).
[32] See Scobie 1969, 72; Moreschini 1978, 43; Kirichenko 2008, 351.

sion with magic could arguably be seen as an example of a religious transgression motivated by hybris (*superbia*). I argue, however, that, because magic is for Lucius a metaphor for fiction, his pursuit of magic is motivated not by a hybristic desire to control nature (*superbia*), but by the ambition to achieve literary fame (*gloria*),[33] and I devote the rest of the essay to examine the role that this 'bookish' rather than moral triad of passions plays in the novel's exploration of the magic of literature, the pleasure of fiction, and the ambition for literary success.

The magic of fiction: curiosity, pleasure, and literary renown

The strong connection between *curiositas* and *voluptas* is evident in several episodes of the *Metamorphoses*, but the story of the ass' involvement with the matron of Corinth is perhaps the clearest example of the link that the novel establishes between curiosity and sex (*Met.* 10,19–23), since the sexual pleasures that Lucius and his mistress enjoy become the object of other people's base curiosity. A Peeping Tom with an eye for profit, the freedman in charge of Lucius spies on the two lovers and discloses their performance to his former master. His master decides in turn to stage the mating of the ass with a mass-murderess who has been condemned to die in the arena. Public spectacles are designed to arouse and satisfy the curiosity of their viewers,[34] and the novel arouses and promises to satisfy the sexual curiosity of its readers with a public pornographic show.[35]

Lucius' transformation into an ass puts an interesting spin on the connection between curiosity and pleasure, since magic and not sex turns out to be the main pursuit of our curious protagonist. In a passage that bristles with warnings against curiosity (*Met.* 2,6), Lucius admits that his aunt's words of caution against the magic skills of his hostess Pamphile have the opposite of their intended effect.[36] As soon as he hears the word magic mentioned (*artis…magicae*

---

[33] According to Graverini 2004–2005, 235, *gloria* is one of the unifying themes of the *Metamorphoses*. The noun *gloria*, adjective *gloriosus*, and verb *glorior* occur 21 times in the novel.
[34] Cf. the curiosity implicit in Socrates' pursuit of the 'pleasure of a gladiatorial spectacle' (*Met.* 1,7), which is the cause of Socrates' misadventures and gruesome death.
[35] First aroused by a hardcore peepshow and titillated by a scandalous pantomime, the reader's curiosity is ultimately frustrated, since Lucius manages to escape before his highly anticipated performance in the arena. Cf. Freudenburg 2007, 253, and Kirichenko 2008, 365.
[36] For Lucius' inability to learn a moral lesson from the sculpture group displayed in Byrrhena's house, which depicts the tragic consequences of Acteon's *curiositas*, see Wlosok 1969,

semper optatum nomen), Lucius throws caution to the winds and begins to pursue his dream to become an apprentice in the magic arts with life-changing consequences.[37]

It is at this point in the novel that Lucius' curiosity about magic makes him fall into the slavish pursuit of sexual pleasure (*voluptas veneria*).[38] Afraid to transgress the boundaries of hospitality by seducing his host's wife, Pamphile, but determined to get his hands on her potions, Lucius sets out to conquer her slave, Photis, with martial resolve. Lucius' dalliance with Photis provides extended erotic interludes in books two and three of the *Metamorphoses*, which titillate the sexual curiosity of the reader, but it is curiosity about magic that motivates Lucius to seduce Photis. Lucius remarks with pleasure that Photis is 'pretty to look at, playful in disposition, and as sharp as a needle' (*forma scitula et moribus ludicra et prorsus argutula*); and yet he decides to seduce her mainly because she has access to her mistress Pamphile's magic potions.

In the last book of the novel, the priest of Isis, Mithras, offers a Platonist reading of the *Metamorphoses* (*Met.* 11,15) that emphasizes the moral shortcomings of *curiositas* because of its close connection with *voluptas*.[39] According to Mithras' moralistic interpretation of the novel, Lucius' transformation into an ass is the 'perverse reward of (his) ill-starred curiosity' (*curiositatis inprosperae sinistrum praemium*) and a direct consequence of his fall into 'slavish pleasures' (*serviles voluptates*). Mithras' moralistic framework seems to provide the hermeneutic key to make sense of Lucius' misadventures and suggests that previous stories should be read as cautionary tales – which is exactly what Lucius has been unable to do. From the very beginning of the novel Lucius has been an exceedingly gullible listener.[40] If he had paid more careful attention to the meaning of the story told by Aristomenes and had been less distracted by the pleasure that the tale afforded him, Lucius might have learned a crucial lesson early on about the dangers that the triangle sex-curiosity-magic entails and would perhaps have avoided making an ass of himself. Following Mithras' suggestion, Ar-

---

73–74. The complex function of the cautionary tales in the novel is discussed in greater detail in what follows.

37 Graverini 2007, 159.

38 The expression *voluptas veneria*, which denotes sexual pleasure, recurs in both Aristomenes' tale (*Met.* 1,8) and in Lucius' account of his tryst with Photis (*Met.* 4,27), but *voluptas* alone can convey the same meaning (see *Met.* 2,10).

39 For the Platonic subtext of the connection between *voluptas* and *curiositas*, see DeFilippo 1990, 489–92, especially at 491.

40 As Graverini points out (2007, 158), because of his gullibility Lucius is destined to become the object of laughter.

istomenes' story about his friend Socrates (*Met.* 1,5–19) can also be read as a cautionary tale.⁴¹ There are evident and striking similarities between the story of Socrates' involvement with the witch Meroe and Lucius' involvement with Photis. Both Meroe and Photis are physically attractive,⁴² both dabble in magic,⁴³ and both have illustrious literary precedents in the *Odyssey*, such as Circe⁴⁴ and Calypso.⁴⁵ More importantly, just as in Lucius' case, Socrates' misfortunes are the consequence of curiosity and pleasure, as Socrates himself acknowledges in Aristomenes' retelling of his story (*Met.* 1,7). It is Socrates' desire to indulge in the pleasure of a gladiatorial game that leads him into the desolate and pitted valley where he is assailed by robbers and thus forced to seek refuge in Meroe's inn. Even though there is no explicit mention of *curiositas* in this passage, the very fact that Socrates appears to be dominated by his appetites (*voluptates*) suggests that, from a Platonic perspective, he is as much a *curiosus* as Lucius is.⁴⁶ The crucial difference between the two is, however, evident in their attitude toward magic. Whereas in Aristomenes' tale Socrates becomes a casualty of magic because of his love of games and sexual intemperance,⁴⁷ Lucius' curiosity about magic is a passion that far outweighs his other appetites.⁴⁸

---

41 Neither Lucius nor Aristomenes' unnamed companion seem to be aware of the deeper message of the story: Lucius is too enthralled by the pleasures of the narrative, and Aristomenes's companion is so repulsed by the story's blatant falseness that he encourages Aristomenes 'to stop telling such ridiculous and monstrous lies'.
42 The word *scitula* is used to describe both the 'old, but rather attractive' Meroe (*Met.* 1,7, *anum, sed admodum scitulam*) and the young and 'pretty to look at' Photis (*Met.* 2,6, *forma scitula*).
43 Whereas Meroe is a 'real' witch (*saga*), Photis has access to magic as assistant to her mistress Pamphyle, a first rate witch (*Met.* 2,5, *Maga primi nominis*).
44 Insofar as they are responsible for the transformation of their lovers after sleeping with them, both Meroe and Photis can be seen as Circe-like figures. Meroe in particular is responsible for a long list of bestial transformations, and by sleeping with her just once Socrates is turned into the shadow of his former self, a living ghost (*Met.* 1,6, *larvale simulacrum*).
45 Whereas the connection between Circe and Meroe/Photis is thematic, there are explicit references to the Calypso episode in the text. Meroe compares herself with Calypso (*Met.* 1,12), and Lucius describes himself as a failed Odysseus under the spell of the physical charms of Photis (*Met.* 3,19). On Lucius as a failed Odysseus, see Graverini 2007, 169–171.
46 For this definition of *curiositas*, see DeFilippo 1990, 490 n.37.
47 Aristomenes' curiosity about magic, however, is censured by Meroe, who catches him spying on her and promises to punish him for his 'previous garrulity and insistent curiosity' (*faxo eum sero, immo statim, immo vero iam nunc, ut et praecedentis dicacitatis et instantis curiositatis paeniteat, Met.* 1,12).
48 Cf. Lucius' words to Photis: '*sum namque coram magiae noscendae ardentissimus cupitor.*', *Met.* 3,19 ('I have the most passionate desire to know magic at first hand.').

Following Mithras' moralistic framework, an argument could be made that the novel draws an implicit connection between *curiositas* and *superbia*; and indeed scholars who endorse a moral reading of the *Metamorphoses* have argued that Lucius' desire to know magic is an evident sign of his hybris.[49] As Aristomenes' tale shows, magic allows the experienced practitioner to exercise complete control over nature, society, and even death or the gods. The witch Meroe can 'lower the sky and suspend the earth, solidify fountains and dissolve mountains, raise up ghosts and bring down gods, darken the stars and light up Tartarus itself' (*Met.* 1,8); moreover, she can also transform her former lovers and any other human beings into anything she pleases without fear of punishment because her powers put her above the law (*Met*, 1,9–10). Since men can overcome their natural limitations through magic and gain knowledge in areas that are precluded to humankind, the pursuit of magic can be seen as an attempt at mingling with the gods, and, therefore, as yet another instance of the kind of the 'sacrilegious curiosity' that is apparent in both the myth of Actaeon and the tale of Cupid and Psyche.[50]

There is clearly a profound Apuleian ambivalence in the novel's treatment of *curiositas*, particularly *curiositas* about magic. On the moral level, and for a *philosophus Platonicus* and a descendant of Plutarch, *curiositas* should be considered as a serious flaw. On the narrative level, however, and from the perspective of both the novel's narrator and of its author, *curiositas* is the necessary catalyst that moves the action along.[51] This ambiguity is evident in the treatment of Lucius' *sacrilega curiositas* about magic, which reveals another, far more powerful desire. When he learns from Byrrhena that his hostess Pamphile is a 'witch of the first order' (*Met.* 2,5, *maga primi nominis*), Lucius can hardly contain his excitement, but the reason that he adduces for his excitement is surprisingly modest. As an enraptured listener of Aristomenes' tale in book 1, Lucius knows that magic offers world-domination to the skilled practitioner, but he seems content with the realization that magic will grant him the opportunity to 'fill his heart with marvelous stories'.[52] Such an anti-climactic desire after his impassioned defense of supernatural phenomena (*Met.* 1,2) suggests that magic for Lucius is

---

49 For the hybris of Lucius' *curiositas* see Wlosok 1969, 74–75.
50 For the motif of sacrilegious curiosity in the *Metamorphoses*, see Kirichenko 2008, 357–360.
51 Cf. Kirichenko 2008, 367–68, who points that 'curiosity may be valued differently in ethics but, in literature, it serves as the main prerequisite of reading and, as such, is invariably a good'.
52 'Age', inquam, 'o Luci, evigila et tecum esto. Habes exoptatam occasionem, et voto diutino poteris fabulis miris explere pectus.', *Met.* 2,6 ('Come on, Lucius', I said, 'stay alert and keep in control of yourself. You have the opportunity you have been waiting for. You can have your heart's fill of marvellous stories, as you have always wanted.').

really a metaphor for fiction.[53] This conclusion is strengthened by Lucius' comments at the end of Aristomenes' tale about the magic-like power of storytelling,[54] which made him and his traveling companions forget about the hardship and boredom of a 'rough and long stretch of road'.[55]

I would like to conclude by suggesting that, because for Lucius magic is really a metaphor for fiction, his pursuit of 'magic' in the *Metamorphoses* is not inspired by a desire to control nature, but is motivated by a deep and abiding love for literary success and fame. The importance of literary success for the novel's hero is emphasized repeatedly: first by Diophanes, who predicts that Lucius will become 'a great story, an unbelievable tale, a book in several volume' (*Met.* 2,11), then by Charite, who promises that the ass's bravery will be immortalized in both literature and art, and finally by Asinius Marcellus (*Met.* 11,27) who repeats and defines Isis' prophecy.[56] These three passages 'encourage extra-textual interpretation of these predictions by alluding to the extra-textuality of the book', thus blurring the lines between Lucius' and Apuleius' reflections on their literary renown.[57] The fervid desire on Lucius' part to 'know magic' may ultimately be no more than a metaphor for the author's desire to acquire material for fiction and achieve renown through fiction, but the desire to create a fictional world is akin to a wish for divine power on the part of the author/narrator.

Apuleius' dazzling novel is neither a parable offering moral instruction nor an edifying tale of religious conversion.[58] But even though I do not subscribe to Winkler's view that Apuleius' novel is 'a philosophical comedy about religious

---

[53] I am grateful to Karin Schlapbach for pointing out other possible connections between magic and fiction by reminding me that in Schol. *Od.* 4,456 the metamorphosis of Proteus is presented as no more than an illusion created by magic, and that Lucian calls Proteus a 'mimetikos anthropos (*Salt.* 19). The adjective 'mimetikos' might simply indicate Proteus's impersonation skills, but it also might point in the direction of mimetic fiction: where other interpreters resorted to the category of 'magic', Lucian might be calling attention to 'fiction'.
[54] Cf. Graverini's remarks (2007, 47) on the prologue of the *Metamorphoses* 'che prepara il lettore ad un'opera di narrativa d'invenzione con uno spiccato carattere psicagogico, non dissimile da quello della musica e della poesia (e della magia)'.
[55] *Sed ego huic et credo hercules et gratas gratias memini, quod lepidae fabulae festivitate nos avocavit, asperam denique ac prolixam viam sine labore ac taedio evasi*, *Met*.1,20 (But as for Aristomenes, not only do I believe him, by Hercules, but I am also extremely grateful to him for diverting us with a charming and delightful story. I have come out of this rough long stretch of road without either toil or boredom.).
[56] On these predictions, see Graverini 2004–2005, 235–42.
[57] Graverini 2004–2005, 239; cf. also Kirichenko 2011.
[58] The final chapter of Harrison 2000 famously offers a brilliant reading of the novel as a work of pure entertainment and literary display.

knowledge',[59] I wholeheartedly embrace his characterization of the *Metamorphoses* as a self-consciously ambiguous text. However entertaining, the metamorphosis of a gullible consumer of fiction into an ass invites the reader to reflect upon the magic powers and subtle dangers of fiction.[60]

Bibliography

Cipriani, N. 1998. 'Lo schema dei *tria vitia* (*voluptas, superbia, curiositas*) nel *De Vera Religione*: antropologia soggiacente e fonti', *Augustinianum* 38, 157–199.

DeFilippo, J.G. 1990. '*Curiositas* and the Platonism of Apuleius' *Golden Ass*', *AJPh*. 111.4, 471–492.

Freudenburg, K. 2007. 'Leering for the Plot: Visual Curiosity in Apuleius and Others', in: M. Paschalis, S. Frangoulidis, S. Anderson, M. Zimmerman (eds.), *The Greek and the Roman Novel: Parallel Readings*, ANS 8, Groningen: Barkhuis and Groningen University Library. 238–62.

Graverini, L. 2004–2005. 'A Booklike Self: Ovid and Apuleius', *Hermathena* 177/178, 225–250.

Graverini, L. 2005. 'Sweet and Dangerous? A Literary Metaphor (*aures permulcere*) in Apuleius' Prologue', in: S.J. Harrison, M. Paschalis, S. Frangoulidis (eds.), *Metaphor and the Ancient Novel*, ANS 4, Groningen: Barkhuis and Groningen University Library. 177–196.

Graverini, L. 2007. *Le Metamorfosi di Apuleio. Letteratura e identità*, Pisa: Giardini Editori e Stampatori.

Hanson, J.A. (ed. and trans.) 1989. *Apuleius. Metamorphosis*, 2 vols., Cambridge: Harvard University Press; London: Heinemann.

Harrison, S.J. 2000. *Apuleius. A Latin Sophist*, Oxford: Oxford University Press.

Hijmans, B.L. 1995. 'Appendix III. *Curiositas*', in: B.L. Hijmans, R.Th. van der Paardt, V. Schmidt, B. Wesseling, M. Zimmerman (eds.), *Apuleius Madaurensis, Metamorphoses Book IX: Text, Introduction and Commentary*, Groningen: Egbert Forsten. 362–69.

Joly, R.R. 1961. '*Curiositas*', *AC* 30, 33–44.

Keulen, W. 2003. *Apuleius Madaurensis. Metamorphoses. Book I, 1–20. Introduction, Text, Commentary*, Ph.D. diss. Groningen.

Kirichenko, A. 2007. '*Lectores in fabula*: Apuleius' *Metamorphoses* Between Pleasure and Instruction', *Prometheus* 33, 254–276.

Kirichenko, A. 2008. 'Satire, Propaganda, and the Pleasure of Reading: Apuleius' Stories of Curiosity in Context', *HSPh* 104, 339–371.

Kirichenko, A. 2011. 'Becoming a book: divination and fictionality in Apuleius' *Metamorphoses*', *MH* 68, 182–202.

Lancel, S.S. 1961. '*Curiositas* et préoccupations spirituelles chez Apulée', *RHR* 160, 25–46.

---

59 Winkler 1985, 184.
60 Cf. Freudenburg 2007.

Leigh, M. 2013. *From* polypragmon *to* curiosus. *Ancient Concepts of Curious and Meddlesome*, Oxford: Oxford University Press.

Menn, S. 2014. 'The Desire for God and the Aporetic Method in Augustine's *Confessions*', in W. Mann (ed.), *Augustine's Confessions: Philosophy in Autobiography*, Oxford: Oxford University Press. 71–108.

Moreschini, C. 1978. *Apuleio e il Platonismo*, Firenze: Olschki.

O'Donnell, J.J. 1992. *Augustine: Confessions. 3 vols. Introduction, text, and commentary*, Oxford: Clarendon Press.

Schlapbach, K. 2010. '*Spectaculum naturae* as Theatrical Experience: New Uses of an Old Comparison', *Studia Patristica* 44, 421–426.

Scobie, A. 1969. *Aspects of the Ancient Romance and Its Heritage*, Meisenheim am Glan: A. Hain.

Van Mal-Maeder, D. 2001. *Apuleius Madaurensis Metamorphoses. Livre II, Texte, Introduction et Commentaire*, Groningen: Egbert Forsten.

Walsh, P.G. 1988. 'The Rights and Wrongs of Curiosity (Plutarch to Augustine)', *G&R* 35, 73–85.

Winkler, J. 1985. *Auctor & Actor: A Narratological Reading of Apuleius' Golden Ass*, Berkeley: University of California Press.

Wlosok, A. 1969. 'Zur Einheit der Metamorphosen des Apuleius', *Philologus* 113, 68–84.

Vered Lev Kenaan
Spectacles of a Dormant Soul: A Reading of Plato's Gyges and Apuleius' Lucius

Abstract: A comparison between Book 3,21–25 of the *Metamorphoses* and Plato's *Republic* 2,359c-360b is pivotal for understanding how Apuleius stages entry into the space of the fantastic. In both episodes, desire, sight and the forbidden collaborate in creating the passage to the world of fiction, shaping it as a dreamlike experience, a psychological event of the unconscious. But the similarity between Plato's and Apuleius' fiction can be illuminated especially through an examination of Plato's monstrous images of the soul. The essay shows that for Plato and Apuleius the entrance to the fantastic is meant to shed light on the unfamiliar sides of the soul. Comparing the two episodes from the *Republic* and the *Metamorphoses* will allow us to see that they share a motivation: the staging of that unknown part of the soul that escapes the rule of the rational.

1 Introduction

The passage depicting Lucius watching Pamphile's metamorphosis into an owl followed by Lucius' own transformation into an ass in Book 3, 21–25 of the *Metamorphoses* is pivotal for understanding Apuleius' way of staging entry into the space of the fantastic. The sequential metamorphoses of the witch and the main protagonist provide us with a programmatic case study in the affect of fiction, the psychological proceedings of the imaginary, which Andrew Laird characterizes with the help of the ancient philosophical term, *psuchagogia*.[1]

Although the episodes preceding Lucius' transformation pertain to the strange and the marvelous, Lucius' new situation determined by the events of 3,21–25 radically shifts from these fields of experience to explore other dimensions of the fantastic. In going up to Pamphile's room and seeing her transformation, Lucius' identity as an innocent, well-to-do young man is camouflaged,

---

[1] Laird 1993, 171 discusses the meaning of fiction by considering the *Met.* 3,21–22 as 'a kind of *psuchagogia* ... (Pamphile's, Lucius', ours)... *Psuchagogia* in the sense of bewitching discourse is operative throughout the *Met.*, as in all stories, causing us to construct imaginary story worlds. In the *Met.* the process is overt, either making us think we know what is going on when we do not, or confusing us by raising questions we cannot answer.'

Vered Lev Kenaan, University of Haifa

and he is then moreover deprived of his habitual appearance. In turning into an ass Lucius transgresses every aspect of trustworthiness, bringing in his wake astonished readers who, despite their situatedness in the real, follow him into his dreamland.[2] Lucius' withdrawal from the safe side of the factual needs to be contextualized. Lucius' transformation is preceded and inspired by Pamphile's metamorphosis. Yet we need to notice that what inspires Lucius is not simply the fact of Pamphile's transformation as much as the seeing, the visual experience, of that transformation. A metamorphosis takes on a visual form and it is this vision that triggers the beholder's own transformation. Moreover, Lucius' visual experience is specifically constructed as the satisfaction of his desire to see a forbidden sight. In this sense, desire, sight and the forbidden collaborate in creating the passage to the world of fiction, shaping *Met.* 3,21–25 as a dreamlike experience, a psychological event of the unconscious. In order to illuminate the psychological significance of *Met.* 3,21–25, I shall compare it with the story of Gyges in Plato's *Republic* 2,359c-360b, an episode that bears interesting similarities.

The comparison is not only interesting for its own sake, but also allows us to situate Apuleius's fiction against the background of Plato's philosophy of the fantastic and, specifically, to underscore an intimate connection that exists, in my view, between Plato's fiction and his notion of dreams. I wish to show that Apuleius, who considered himself a Platonist,[3] was influenced by the philosopher's fiction and, like him, aimed to shed light on the unfamiliar sides of the soul. Comparing the two episodes from the *Republic* and the *Metamorphoses* will allow us to see that they have the same motivation: the staging of that unknown part of the soul that escapes the rule of the rational.

The first thing to notice in our comparison is that both Gyges and Lucius undergo strange visual experiences. In both fantastic narratives, the protagonists peep through a window or a crack into an enclosed space. They eventually penetrate this space in disrespect of the laws of sacredness and witchcraft. Finally, upon their departure from the forbidden space, Gyges and Lucius experience a radical change, which includes losing their human appearance as well as gaining a new visual perspective that is in itself transgressive of the conventional boundaries of morality. For both Plato and Apuleius, the event of transformation

---

[2] For the place of dreams in Apuleius's *Metamorphoses* see Annequin 1996; Gollnick 1999; Lev Kenaan 2004; Hunink 2006; Carlisle 2008.
[3] Plato's philosophical influence on Apuleius is widely recognized, mostly in relation to his divine and daemonic conceptions, his dichotomies of body and soul, his use of metaphors of light and darkness and other issues pertaining to ethics and morality. See, for example, Penwill 1975; Schlam 1970.

is one that grows out of a private visual experience, whose grounds, I argue, are to be found in dreams. Moreover, as in dreams, the gist of this fictional visual experience consists in an astounding hidden sight, exposure to which leads to a psychological revelation.

2 Dreams and the Unconscious in Plato's *Republic* 9

Plato's notion of dreams, his understanding of the soul's condition during sleep, offers us an important prism in which to see how he constructs the philosophical tale as a fiction of the self. His theory of the tripartite soul provides important evidence for a notion of a repression mechanism, as well as recognition of a whole psychological dimension that is excluded from the boundaries of waking consciousness.[4]

In Plato's discussion of the soul, aggressive desires and instincts are never really abrogated, but remain repressed as an integral part of the soul. Even a soul ruled by its rational part accommodates, according to Plato, unwanted (suppressed) desires that he conceives as 'those desires that are awakened in sleep, when the rest of the soul – the rational, gentle, and ruling part – slumbers.' (*Rep.* 9,571c) The ancient figure of the 'beastly and savage part' of the soul prefigures the psychoanalytical understanding of the unconscious. In sleep, this savage part is uncensored by rationality and thus completely focused on finding a way to gratify itself. Plato understands the daily phenomenon of dreaming as the natural locus for the arousal of hidden desires. In a corollary manner, the disturbing and frightening affect of dreams may be understood in terms of his view that dreams reflect those aggressive aspects of our souls which we prefer not to recognize during our waking life:

> There exists in every one of us, even in some reputed most respectable, a terrible, fierce, and lawless brood of desires, which it seems are revealed in our sleep. (*Rep.* 9,572b)

The expression 'lawless brood of desires' suggests an analogy between Plato's notion of the lower part of the soul and Freud's notion of the unconscious.[5] But in contrast to the Freudian position, Plato's attitude towards repressed de-

---

[4] For a comparative analysis of Plato's and Freud's notions of the tripartite soul, see Ferrari 2000.
[5] See Simon 1973.

sires in the passage quoted above is moralistic. For Plato, dreams testify to the dreamer's impurity and, in the face of shame, the self is required to undergo a change in habits and basic attitudes. This moralizing view of dreams was still prevalent at the time Freud embarked on his *Interpretation of Dreams*. One of the unique aspects of his project lies in the manner in which he breaks away from his predecessors. Suspending judgment and moralistic sentiments is a necessary condition, according to Freud, for accessing the psychic processes that constitute the content of dreams.[6]

Yet Plato's moralistic position should not hide his deep interest in investigating the dreamer's aggressive drives. In fact, in other and no less important passages, he uses dreams as a vehicle to explore the hidden existence of erotic drives which are operative during our sleep and whose vitality he finds indispensable for understanding the nature of the human soul and even for the constitution of the philosophical life.[7] However, Plato's exploration of latent desires and hidden erotic drives goes beyond his treatment of dreams, and finds its expression in the manner in which he contrives fantastic narratives that in their own way embody the logic of dreams.[8] The question of Plato's uses of fiction is not a new one and still invites exploration.[9] For our purposes it is sufficient to note that Plato turns to the fantastic when the support of the imagination is needed in order to see that which escapes the logical rule of rational transparency. But how can fantastic narratives improve our vision?

3 Typhon: An *Eikon* of the Unconscious

Before turning to a reading of the Platonic tale of Gyges, let us recall another important source for Plato's investigation of the soul's hidden desires: myths. Plato explicitly articulates his understanding of the value of myths in the *Phaedrus* (229c-230b). For Socrates, a myth, or a fictional tale, can be interesting only

---

[6] Freud's suspension of judgment is a method for gaining knowledge, that in turn can have moral benefits.
[7] Gallop 1971.
[8] A reading of the myth of the cave (*Rep.* 7,514–517) as a dream representation of the hidden depth of the Platonic soul is offered in Lev Kenaan 2010, 173–175. It is in the psyche's dark realm, which in my view is represented by the Platonic cave, that the quest for knowledge emerges in the form of the mysterious erotic drive that impels one of the cave dwellers to leave underground existence for earth's illuminated surface.
[9] Laird 2001, who writes on the formation of fiction in Plato's *Republic*, demonstrates the various ways in which the *Republic*'s philosophical argument and fictional invention are interrelated.

under the sign of the Delphic imperative, only if it ultimately enables him to discover whether he really is 'a more complex monster (πολυπλοκώτερον θηρίον)¹⁰ and inflamed with desires (ἐπιτεθυμμένον)... than Typhon.'¹¹ Socrates expects a tale about a mythic monster such as Typhon to be of use as a mirror for self-inspection. In this respect, the fantastic tale about Typhon is not, for Plato, merely fantastic, but a tale with real philosophical significance. Typhon is a product of the soul's imagination and, as such, it also bears testimony to the nature of the soul. Plato's comparative investigation aims at explaining the difference between Socrates and Typhon: while Typhon is a strange and complex creature consisting of a bestial plurality,¹² Socrates' psyche is even more complex.¹³

In itself, however, the fact that Socrates' human psychic apparatus is different from that of the monster is not surprising.¹⁴ More intriguing is the understanding that there are grounds for an analogy between Typhon and the human soul. This Platonic analogy also occurs in the *Republic*, and while in neither text does Plato dwell on the novelty and nonconformity of his comparison, its boldness should be accounted for.

In Hesiod's *Theogony*, clearly one of Plato's sources, Typhoeus¹⁵ exhibits a hundred snakeheads with terrifying fiery tongues and eyes. His savageness, however, is found in the multiplicity of voices that simultaneously utter every sound he makes. The monster's fire represents a heathen antithesis to Zeus' lightening. Moreover, it threatens Zeus' rule because it conspires against the univocality characteristic of Zeus' institutional order. Zeus' combat with Typhon ends with the latter's final defeat after the Olympian sovereign uses his fiery thunderbolt and burns all of the monster's hundred heads. Typhon is dissolved into vapor and hurled down by Zeus to Tartaros.¹⁶

---

10 *Therion* means here a beast or an animal which is especially hostile and odious to man because of its monstrosity.
11 There are various translations of *epitethummenon*, for example, 'violent' (Rowe) and 'puffed up with pride' (Griswold 1986 following de Vries). See Rowe 1988, 140–141.
12 See Hes. *Th.* 820–834.
13 See Griswold 1986, 40, who considers this comparison hyperbolic for 'how could anything be more Typhonic, as it were, than Typhon?'
14 The analogy between the monstrous and the human points to what the bestial hybridity actually lacks: a principle of rationality. For Plato, the human soul is more complex (πολυπλοκώτερον) precisely because of its rational element. Hence in Plato's view, the myth of the Typhon is potentially enlightening, since it serves as an educational reminder of that part of the human soul – the *logikon*, without which humanity slips into bestiality. For a different interpretation of this passage, see Griswold 1986, 40–43.
15 For the different forms of the names see Fontenrose 1980, 70.
16 Hes. *Th.* 820–868.

As a figure of subversion and conspiracy against the hegemony of the logos and univocality, we can see how the Hesiodic monster offers Plato not only a suitable image of the soul's multiform essence in general, but of the soul's irrational part in particular. In the *Republic*, Socrates asks his interlocutor to fashion a symbolic image of the soul: 'One of those natures that the ancient fables tell of...[such] as that of the Chimera or Scylla or Cerberus, and the numerous other examples that are told of many forms grown together in one'.[17] Socrates expects his interlocutor to go beyond the conventional boundaries of his imagination and to contemplate an unfamiliar image of the human soul.

Although recalling the Chimera or Cerberus is specifically relevant for Plato in order to elucidate his conception of the tripartite soul, the inclusion of Scylla seems to suggest that his foremost consideration is ultimately an image of multiformity: 'many forms grown together in one' (*Rep.* 9,588c). Plato's innovation is thus twofold: it consists of a conceptualization of the human psyche in terms of a monstrous hybridity and furthermore, it uses the monster's shocking appearance as a paradigm for the effect of the human psyche on its observer. Tying the presentation of the human soul to the monster's appearance is not coincidental, since what interests Plato in depicting the soul's monstrosity is to offer the reader an essentially uncanny visual encounter with the most personal part of himself. In choosing a well-known mythological image through which the human soul can be studied, Plato grants the invisible soul visibility. Moreover, Plato uses a vivid and terrifying image to represent the soul in order to create a shocking and troubling spectacle for his imaginary reader.

> Mold, then, a single shape of a manifold and many-headed beast that has a ring of heads of tame and wild beasts and can change them and cause to spring forth from itself all such growths. It is the task of a cunning artist, he said, but nevertheless, since speech is more plastic than wax and other such media, assume that it has been so fashioned. (*Rep.* 9,588c)

Plato employs the guiding language of an art teacher. Using directed imagination, Plato assigns the reader an active role in fashioning the image. In so doing, he avoids the temptation to present his figure as an illustration for the philosophical analysis of the psyche. Instead, Plato challenges his reader. He wishes his reader to exactly follow his instructions, thus creating a powerful image of the soul's multiformity, less for the detail of the image than for the effect of awakening it can have. Following Plato's directions, the reader is confronted with an uncanny surprise: the image he himself has fashioned has a strange

---

17 *Rep.* 9,588c (The translation is by Shorey in Hamilton 1961).

effect, imposing on him a mode of self-estrangement: 'Am I really as complex as a monster?' The image, in other words, is the reader's creation but is concomitantly dictated from outside by Plato. Although Plato directs the making of the image, it is the reader's creation, and therefore in some way in his or her own idiom (and this is necessary if the image is to speak sufficiently intimately to the reader).

The image of Typhon appears in the course of Plato's attempt to lead the reader to recognize the appetitive part of the soul. Typhon is chosen by Plato to represent the most ambiguous element of the soul: 'a single shape of a manifold and many-headed beast that has a ring of heads of tame and wild beasts and can change them and cause to spring forth from itself all such growths'. In this context, Socrates evokes the hybrid image of the Typhon only for the sake of characterizing the multiform nature of the soul's appetitive part. In doing so, he completes the composition of a series of Russian dolls in the shape of a hybrid image, the image of man:

> Then fashion one other form of a lion and one of a man and let the first be far the largest, and the second in size. That is easier, he said, and is done. Join the three in one, then, so as in some sort to grow together. They are so united, he said. Then mold about them outside the likeness of one, that of the man, so that to anyone who is unable to look within but who can see only the external sheath it appears to be one living creature, the man. (*Rep.* 9,588d)

Here, in *Republic* 9, Plato begins the discussion prescribing the shaping of the monstrous image of the tripartite soul as a whole, including within it the hybrid image of Typhon, representing the lower appetitive part of the soul. Now, after specifying the appearance of the soul's three different parts consisting of Typhon as the appetitive part, a lion as the spirited part, and finally, a man as the rational part, Plato directs the molding of an external sheath representing in one guise the tripartite soul. The covering image of a man thus turns out to be a symbolic figure of its own internal hybridity.

Despite the similarities between the covering human image of the soul and the soul's internal figures, the soul's three elements remain different in character from the outer sheath. In Book 4 of the *Republic* this difference is shown to be a sign of an unhealthy soul. Showing what it means to be a just man, Plato examines the concept of a man as growing out of a psycho-philosophical process. According to the passage in Book 4, the unified image of man is a result of prolonged ethical work on the self:

> It means that a man must not suffer the principles in his soul to do each the work of some other and interfere and meddle with one another, but that he should dispose well of what in the true sense of the word is properly his own, and having first attained to self mastery

and beautiful order within himself, and having harmonized these three principles, the notes or intervals of three terms quite literally the lowest, the highest, and the mean, and all others there may be between them, and having linked and bound all three together **and made of himself a unit, one man instead of many, self-controlled and in unison,...** (*Rep.* 4,443d-e; my emphasis)

The mature person grows to become a just human as he progresses to a stage of self-mastery, adopting a beautiful internal order that harmonizes the soul's three distinctly different principles. To be an adult (a rational and just person) implies becoming 'one man instead of many, self-controlled and in unison.' Philosophical education aims to unify the soul's plural structure forcing its indiscernibility. With philosophical training the soul's inner tensions and conflicts seem to disappear. And yet, even under the guise of the self-controlled person, the soul's drives keep their potential and remain vital. Though hidden and repressed, the drives continue to be effective. And sometimes in our dreams they make an appearance and disclose their existence as an undercurrent of aggressive force (*Rep.* 9,571e-572b).

As a repressed aggressive force, the image of Typhon was extremely helpful for Plato in showing how the subversive activity of the drives continues to operate even after the soul has been unified. Pindar and Aeschylus's versions of the story of Typhon are an important source since they change the Hesiodic version of the Typhonic storm into a volcanic phenomenon. Thus, they not only place Typhon in dreadful Tartaros, but locate that abyss specifically under Etna. While Typhon loses his immediate threatening effect, he still retains dangerous vitality.

Thus they associate the eruption of Typhon with a fiery manifestation.[18] Pindar's image of the volcanic Typhon who 'hurls rocks down to the deep plain of the sea with a crashing roar'[19] surely pertains to Plato's literary horizon, a horizon that nourishes the articulation of the appetitive part in terms of the return of the repressed. One who falls asleep without attending to the 'beastly and savage part'[20] will suffer from its intensity and shamelessness, released in unhealthy dreams (*Rep.* 9,571a-d.) Like Pindar's 'deep plain of the sea,' the Platonic soul, as a symbolic space, absorbs the Typhonic outburst of the fiery instincts. Pindar describes the event of the eruption as spectacular. The monster, which Pindar

---

[18] Aeschylus *Pr.* 351–374; Pindar *P.* 1,15–25.
[19] Pindar *P.* 1,15–25.
[20] Good and healthy sleep is promised not to the one who has only 'tamed his passionate part', but to the one who also 'quieted the two elements in his soul' (*Rep.* 9,572a) namely, both the appetite and the spirited parts.

portrays as 'shooting up the most terrible jets of fire' is said to be 'a marvelous wonder to see, and a marvel even to hear about when men are present.'[21] Does the spectacle of the volcanic eruption have any edifying meaning? The way in which Plato makes room for visual experience in his philosophical fiction can be illuminating.

While the *Republic* fashions an appearance for the tripartite soul, which discloses its monstrous features in order to cultivate an awareness of its dangerous hidden potential, the appearance of the hidden in Plato's fiction is further elaborated as a story of introspection. Let us now turn to Plato's story of Gyges in order to examine its 'marvelous' spectacle, and in particular, its therapeutic meaning for Plato. How can the Typhonic spectacle be ethically valuable, and how can the uncovering of the soul's hidden parts be philosophically rewarding?

4 Gyges' Dream

It is no coincidence that the myth of Gyges appears in the second book of the *Republic*, with its famous discussion of the need to purify the mythological canon of unseemly representations. The story of Gyges with the implications it carries for censorship in the ideal state thus serves as a background for the philosophical discussion of the literary criteria for censorship.[22] The story of the naïve shepherd magically released from the public eye introduces the violence of the inner passions that the invisible Gyges experiences without shame or self-reproach. Glaucon turns to Gyges in order to show that justice is not a natural dimension of human nature. And in so doing, he attempts to problematize Socrates' claim that justice is inherent in the soul. But does Gyges' story really serve as an exemplary case in point for Glaucon's position? In my view, this is not necessarily the case. While Gyges' story indeed appears to exemplify man's innate immorality,[23] close attention to the tale reveals that the lesson of the Gyges myth may not pertain at all to what Plato sees as 'a man in his right mind,' but rather to one whose 'power of intelligence is fettered in sleep':

---

21 Pindar P. 1,20 – 25 (The translation is by Gildersleeve 1885).
22 See Laird's (2001) analysis of the story as a fictional and philosophical exercise.
23 See Davis 2000, 635 – 655. Charles Hanly (1977, 124) reads Plato's use of the myth as reflecting an unconscious conflict in Plato: "The irony is that Plato himself in the Gyges story introduces into the *Republic* a poetic fantasy, telling a disturbing psychological truth in disguised form. He unconsciously breaks his own rules of censorship.'

As for the fact that people only ever do good unwillingly out of the inability to do wrong – we would most clearly perceive this, if we made the following thought experiment (εἰ τοιόνδε ποιήσαιμεν τῇ διανοίᾳ). Suppose we grant each type of person – the just man and the unjust – the license (power, authority) to do whatever he wants, and we then follow each of them in our gaze to where desire will lead them. We would catch the just man in the act, going toward the same thing as the unjust on account of a longing for more…They'd have the kind of license I am talking about especially if they acquired the kind of power which they say belonged to the ancestor of Gyges, the Lydian. [They say] he was a shepherd in the service of the one then ruling Lydia when there was a great thunderstorm and earthquake, breaking open the earth so that there was a chasm in the place where he pastured. Looking and wondering, he went down and saw, in addition to other wonders about which [men] mythologize, also a bronze horse, hollow and having little doors, through which he peeped in and saw a corpse buried within that appeared larger than human, and this wearing nothing else than around its hand a gold ring; after stripping it off, he went out. During the usual meeting of the shepherds in order that they might bring a monthly report to the king about the herds, he came bearing the ring. While sitting with the others, he chanced to turn the collet of the ring around toward himself, to the inside of his hand. When this happened he became invisible to those with whom he was sitting, and they conversed as though about someone absent. He wondered at this, and, again feeling for the ring, he twisted the collet outward, and, in twisting it, he became apparent. Thinking about this, he brought it about that he was among the messengers to the king, and after arriving, committed adultery with his wife, and with her, setting upon the king, he killed [him] and so gained the rule.[24] (*Rep.* 2,359c-360b)

Gyges' story invites an explication in terms of its philosophical content, and yet once the strictly philosophical lesson is suspended, an unexpected psychological terrain is opened to view. 'The legend,' Charles Hanly writes, 'is made up of a series of elements and episodes which, if they occurred in a dream, could be interpreted as having unconscious significance'.[25] Indeed, once we read the story of Gyges as a dream experience, we may also explain away the apparent problem created by Glaucon's use of such a powerful example against the Socratic argument of inner justice. Read as a dreamer, Gyges is, according to Plato, not a rational agent, but a subject whose reason has been put to sleep, and whose repressed desires are momentarily freed. As such, the narrative does not merely moralize about a crooked self, but rather opens a lens through which the event of releasing a repressed desire is observed by the reader.

We need to distinguish here between waking experience and that of dreaming. Gyges' experience awake is briefly mentioned in the introductory section of the story in referring to him as one of the king's shepherds in Lydia. The dream experience begins immediately as Gyges enters the chasm. The movement down-

---

24 The translation is based on Davis 2000 and Laird 2001.
25 Hanly 1977, 120.

wards into the earth's innards metaphorically signifies the entrance to the other world, that of a sleeping consciousness. Plato constructs a different spatial order where the Typhonic Gyges could make an appearance. Inside the earth Gyges faces a marvelous spectacle, whose dreamlike dimension is emphasized by its gradual exposure and by its transgressive nature. Gyges peeps in through the doors of the bronze horse, experiencing the gratification of being exposed to a forbidden sight. The sight causes his awakening desires to take control and fulfill the dream wish inside and outside the chasm.

The story of Gyges delineates the awakening of the soul's Typhonic part within the confines of the dream. Only within these confines can the psyche's "monster" fulfill its wish and thus kill the king of Lydia, who symbolizes the Typhon's enemy, the soul's logical principle. The story of Gyges presents the dream experience as inseparable from the interpretation that it receives in waking life. The significance of the visit to the chasm becomes explicit only from the external perspective of a self who sees beyond the limits of the dream experience. The story of Gyges unites two perspectives: one internal to the dream experience and one external to it, reflecting on the dream experience.

In the *Interpretation of Dreams*, Freud argues that a dream text does not recover the dream experience as a whole. Rather, the dream text is always a product of an integration of the experience and the attempts to restore it by means of narration and interpretation.[26] Like Freud, Plato is aware of the complexity of the dream text, and in the *Timaeus*, he presents his view on the matter in the context of a discussion of the relationship between an actual dream and its interpretation. For Plato, the content of the dream and its interpretation are opposites, which are nevertheless equally important, and comprise the unity of a whole: the dream text. While the dream content is created 'when the power of...intelligence is fettered in sleep,' the dream interpretation 'belongs to a man when in his right mind.'[27]

The interplay between the irrational and the rational, which Plato understands as fundamental for the creation of the dream text, is important for our understanding of the structure of literary representations of dreams. In Plato's myth of Gyges, the reflective part of the dream depends on, and needs to be complemented by, the reader. The dream text is thus twofold. It consists in an uncensored description and a judgmental observation guided by the censoring force of

---

26 Freud 1965, Ch.7, 563.
27 Plato *Ti.* 71e (The translation is by Bury 1929).

rationality.[28] The story of Gyges, then, visualizes a psychic movement while suspending moral judgment. At the same time, and as a dream text, the story invites the reflective waking mind to adopt a critical point of view towards it.

5 Lucius' Metamorphosis

For ancient fiction writers, a protagonist who errs through the suspension of moral judgment was a real possibility of their genre: dreams provided a model for representing a subject momentarily freed from all control by shame or reason. Lucius' transformation in Apuleius' *Metamorphoses* is an exemplary case.

The understanding of dreams as the uncovering of the psyche's hidden depth is crucial for shaping narratives that deal with psychological transformation. Dream narratives release a strong affect of strangeness that instigates an urge in the dreamer to explicate the unfamiliar image of himself. Facing the possibility of becoming other than oneself is central to representations of dreams, yet it is also central to fictional episodes that do not explicitly deal with dreams, but nevertheless have dream characteristics.

Apuleius' *Metamorphoses* offers us a literary model through which we can explore the question of how an ancient fantasy unveils the unconscious at work. But how exactly does it do this? It is important to remember that the novel's protagonist is identified as the text's narrator, and that his story creates a complex temporal structure that plays with the incongruity between present and past, and between knowledge and ignorance. Moreover, Lucius' autobiographical narrative unites the internal and external perspectives discussed above. Considering how Apuleius' fiction creates a convergence of these two perspectives, we can acknowledge its affinity to a dream text.[29]

---

[28] See how Freud 1965, Ch. 2, 134, distinguishes between the parts of the twofold dream text by means of the dreamer's two roles: the self-observer and the one who reflects: 'I have noticed in my psycho-analytic work that the whole frame of mind of a man who is reflecting is totally different from that of a man who is observing his own psychical processes. In reflection there is one more psychical activity at work than in the most attentive self-observation, and this is shown amongst other things by the tense looks and wrinkled forehead of a person pursuing his reflections as compared with the restful expression of a self-observer.'

[29] The *Metamorphoses*' attraction to the illogical, the distorted and the incoherent, its fondness of exceptional deviations from narrative conventions, is essential for comprehending its unique prose, which I term 'dream poetics', namely fiction writing that absorbs the logic of dreams. The dream logic provides Apuleius with fantastic patterns and narratological strategies, but more importantly for our purpose here, it provides Apuleius the grounds for developing his psychological narrative.

I have shown elsewhere that the *Metamorphoses* narrative embodies the logic of dreams, but here I am more concerned with the question of how the ancient novel creates spaces in which the unconscious can reverberate.[30] As we shall see, the unfamiliar apparition of oneself is exposed to the 'dormant' protagonist through an uncanny visual experience which Apuleius constructs within the constraints of a secluded and private place. In the *Metamorphoses*, space is not a homogenous phenomenon. In addition to open public spaces there is a special kind of space constantly at work: a limited, restricted, forbidden space that presents an irresistible temptation for the protagonist. One of the most crucial spaces constructed by Apuleius is the setting in which Lucius' transformation into an ass takes place (3,24–25). This is the excluded place where Lucius takes the wrong potion. But it is first of all the forbidden room into which Lucius peeps, secretly observing Pamphile's arts of magic.

While on a business trip, Lucius, a well-to-do young man, finds himself in Hypata, where he lodges at a witch's house. Fascinated by the world of magic introduced to him by the witch's maid, Photis, Lucius is not able to restrain his desire to experience magic at first hand. In the middle of the night, he goes upstairs and secretly observes the witch's activities, culminating in her amazing transformation into a bird flying out of the window. The sight of the flying witch is so overwhelming that Lucius aspires to undergo just the same transformation. Acting to fulfill his wish, he takes the wrong ointment, which shockingly turns him into an ass instead of a bird.

Lucius' ambition is to fly like a bird. His proclaimed wish conceals a further ambition, to come closer to heaven, and moreover to become equal to the divine ruler whose kingdom is heaven: omnipotent Jupiter himself. As Lucius discloses his wish to Photis and begs her to grant him this opportunity, he betrays the unthinkable, forbidden wish:

> *Ut ego, quamvis ipsius aquilae sublimes volatibus toto caelo pervius et supremi Iovis certus nuntius vel laetus armiger.* (Met. 3,23)
>
> To traverse the entire sky in the lofty flight of the eagle, to become the unerring messenger and happy weapon-bearer of almighty Jupiter.[31]

All his physical and mental powers are directed towards this goal. Lucius is blinded by uncontrolled desire. He consequently describes himself in the following manner:

---

30 See Lev Kenaan 2004.
31 For the text of Apuleius, I have followed Hanson's Loeb edition (1989).

abiectis propere laciniis totis, avide manus immersi et haurito plusculo cuncta corporis mei membra perfricui. Iamque alternis conatibus libratis bracchiis in avem similis gestiebam. (Met. 3,24)

I hastily threw off all my clothes, greedily plunged my hand into the jar, pulled out a largish daub, and rubbed my body all over. Next I spread out my arms and pumped them alternately, trying hard to become a bird.

But while Lucius excitedly anticipates his transformation, his devotion to and total obsession with this wish are cruelly ridiculed by the following events. The shocking transformation is turned into a harsh experience of self-realization, in which the narrated ego becomes aware of his dangerous and unrestrained ambition. Instead of a bird, Lucius realizes that he has become an ass. He finds himself looking downward instead of upwards. Lucius' transformation is most horrifying, providing a nightmare spectacle (Met. 3,24–25). Lucius' shocking experience of disillusion is also found in dreams, and is typical of Apuleius' novel, whose protagonist often shifts rapidly and unexpectedly from one cognitive perception to another.

The protagonist's account is disturbing and funny at the same time. Lucius' self-disgust at recognizing the horrible appearance of his changed body is translated into a grotesque, even obscene, narrative. Readers respond with laughter as Lucius describes how he came to be other than himself. How can this strange sight be a source of self-illumination, and what can be the philosophical value of this grotesque description? In light of Plato's reliance on the visual in exploring the soul's tripartite structure, his insistence on providing insight into internal happenings in the form of a tantalizing vision, Apuleius' literary choices become clear. As a Platonist, Apuleius too is concerned with the interrogation of the psyche and does so in a visual framework. He thus situates Lucius' transformation as part of a series of optical episodes, carefully structuring Pamphile's transformation as the object of Lucius' gaze, and then constructing Lucius' transformation as the object of our gaze. These two events of transformation are told from the point of view of a secretive observer, since they both occur in a forbidden space penetrated by a curious and invisible eye. This mode of seeing, as Apuleius often shows, is characteristic of the dreamer. Apuleius grants Lucius' transformation the status of a dream since it is first of all constructed as a forbidden spectacle. The reader's visual experience, consisting of peeping at Lucius' transformation through a crack in the door is, in this respect, analogous to Lucius' secret experience of gazing upon Pamphile transformed. But what exactly do we see? And how does Apuleius construct this strange visual experience?

In the conversation with Photis in which Lucius implores her to help him see her mistress practicing magic, he confesses that he who has 'always disdained ladies' embraces'[32] is now possessed by an uncontrollable passion for the slave, Photis. Describing himself as the slave's slave, Lucius admits that his current psychological condition is irregular: he is away from home, and moreover, he does not miss it (3,19). This uncanny account of a servile self who is not 'at home' provides a fictional illustration of the Platonic dormant soul. Betraying a wishful thought to a servant is a gesture that releases a latent desire that Lucius would not dare express otherwise.[33]

We should remember that this story takes place in the middle of the night. Hypata is asleep, dominated by darkness and silence. Photis quietly leads Lucius on tiptoe, *suspenso et insono vestigio* (3,21) to Pamphile's room. They secretly stand behind Pamphile's door and Lucius is invited to peep through a crack in the door. He observes Pamphile secretively. Lucius' visual experience seems at first explicitly sexual. The *rima ostiorum*, the crack in the doors (3,21), grants Lucius a point of view that is not only privileged (he sees without being seen) but also gratifying. In other words, the architecture of this scene is that of a peep show: he watches Pamphile as she takes off her clothes and massages her naked body. But while this striptease seems at first to embody Lucius' secret sexual wish-fulfillment, this is in fact not the case. The next stage reveals what Lucius truly and most deeply desires, and it is certainly not the sight of Pamphile's naked body. Only now does Lucius discover the true meaning of the stimulation Pamphile's nakedness causes in him. Her secret activity prepares her for a transformation. At this stage Lucius finds deep gratification because he is gazing at a scene that uncovers the true nature of his original passion as earlier expressed to Photis: 'grant me something I clamor for with all my heart. Show me your mistress when she is working at some project of this supernatural discipline' (3,19). Lucius' desire is visual. His wish is to observe a supernatural event whose visual impact is transcendental at heart, transgressing the human boundaries of being.

In the conversation with Photis, Lucius' passion seems mere curiosity concerning the mystery of magic. Yet, at the next stage, when he actually sees Pam-

---

[32] Extreme misogyny is symptomatic of the Ovidian Pygmalion and his modern descendent, Norbert Hanold, Wilhelm Jensen's protagonist in *Gradiva* (1902), who suffers from pathological delusions.

[33] A similar release from repression is already attested to in the famous Homeric passage that tells of Penelope's dream (*Od.* 19,335–553), a dream containing the features of wish-fulfillment regarding the killing of the suitors. Penelope's dream demands an interpretation that would also take into account a repressed desire. This desire, reflected in Penelope's unconscious attachment to her suitors, is one that she would never acknowledge in her wakeful life. The exemplary case of Penelope's dream as a wish-fulfillment dream was first studied by Dodds 1951, 102–134. For a psychoanalytical approach to the phenomenon of dreams in Greek tragedy, see Devereux 1976. See also Felson-Rubin 1996, 175–179.

phile turning into a bird, Lucius' latent desire is fully revealed. And it is only by means of this revelation that his experience is explicitly presented in terms of a dream experience: 'I was outside the limits of my own mind' (*exterminatus animi*), 'amazed to the point of madness' (*attonitus in amentiam*) and finally, 'dreaming while awake' (*vigilans somniabar*) (3,22). Lucius, we should remember, is fully awake. But the experience he undergoes is similar to a dream.[34] The sight of Pamphile is rendered as a dream experience precisely because it exposes Lucius' repressed desire. In other words, Phamphile's transformation into a bird gives rise to Lucius' own secret passion. The relation of this passage to dreamlike experience should not be understood, then, only in terms of its inconceivable character. Rather, the sight of Pamphile is shaped as a dream experience precisely because it exposes Lucius to his own desire. In other words, Pamphile's transformation into a bird operates like a dream narrative because that is an appropriate form for visualizing Lucius' uncontrolled passion.

What is the psychological meaning of Lucius' transgression of Pamphile's private space? What is the significance of laying eyes upon something it is forbidden to see? Lucius' ascent to Pamphile's room leads him to face his own soul's emotive condition. Apuleius' characterization thus puts an emphasis on the protagonist's mental activity. The sight of Pamphile objectifies and visualizes Lucius' inner desire. It is interesting to note that Apuleius uses the verb *arbitror* in Lucius' narrative: 'Photis invited me to observe, through a crack in the door, the events that occurred next' (3,21). The verb *arbitror* refers to the experience of watching the naked Pamphile, yet it alludes at the same time to a judgmental form of observation. Plato, as we have seen, was the first to use this visual experience in order to construct an ethical example of a self who critically examines the unconscious parts of his soul.

We now return to the story of Gyges as a paradigmatic dream narrative for the fiction of the Platonist Apuleius. There are several similarities between the stories of Gyges and Lucius. Both protagonists find themselves in isolated and distant places. Gyges enters a deep chasm in the earth while Lucius climbs upstairs to the uppermost level of Milo's house. Both also have similar clandestine visual experiences. Lucius watches Pamphile through a crack in the door, while Gyges looks through the doors of the bronze horse. Both are overwhelmed and captivated by the visuality of the event. In Gyges' case, things are not separate from their appearance as the eye's objects of desire: they are described as *idonta*, seen, and as *thaumasanta*, causing wonder (359d). In the case of Lucius, the sight of the naked Pamphile is a symbolic manifestation of the convergence be-

---

[34] See Laird 1993's discussion of the episode's hallucinatory aspects.

tween desire and sight. In fact, it is not only Lucius who sees a naked body; Gyges too happens to see a dead man's naked body. The vision is uncanny: the woman is a witch practicing her magic while, in the case of Gyges, it is a corpse of unusual size with a magic ring. In both stories the protagonists assimilate the point of view of the figure each has just seen: following Pamphile's transformation, Lucius loses his human appearance and acquires (like Pamphile) an animal perspective. Gyges, on the other hand, experiences death as he overhears his friends talking about him as if he were absent. Finally, Lucius resembles Gyges in that he turns into an invisible observer. As an ass, Lucius has the presence of a radical outsider – he becomes a witness to events, though his testimony is not recognized by others. In this form he is not required to follow public codes of morality. Moreover, typical of the ass' status in human society, Lucius is considered to be no more than a mere body housing lowly appetites.

But does Lucius' transformation into an ass expose him as being entirely immoral? Likewise, do the consequences of Gyges' invisibility define his soul merely as the place of wayward desires? As suggested, these narratives should not be regarded as telling the story of a wakeful soul, but rather of one asleep. Both stories are situated in a chthonic darkness, the nocturnal space which Hesiod identifies as being the domain of *Nyx*. Night plays a most important role within this cosmogony as the parent of all hidden thoughts, latent intentions, and concealed passions. Night is also the mother of death, sleep, and of the dream.[35] Night, we might add, is the place that in Hesiod's mythological language prefigures the repressed, the uncensored, and the unconscious. It is interesting that Hesiod's *Theogony* insistently portrays darkness as the regulative principle that governs the world of simple shepherds, controlled by the appetite of their bellies.

Read as dream experiences, the stories of Gyges and Lucius can be redeemed from the authorial accusation of immorality. We should remember that the Platonic shepherd desires to be a tyrant. Once he becomes invisible, he is able to fulfill this desire. The *Republic* considers the will to power a form of wishful thinking typical of dreams. In Book 9, Plato examines the figure of the tyrant. For Plato, the tyrant's outspoken and shameless behavior is an extreme expression of human instinct that is usually restricted by rationality. In sleep, Plato argues, tyrannical desire is awakened. Dreams reveal the existence of such tyrannical elements in each one of us, and make extreme aggression an ordinary, if concealed, phenomenon.

The fact that dreams often disturb and frighten us can be thought of, in Platonic terms, as reflections of the aggressive aspects of our souls that are not com-

---

[35] *Th.*, 211–32.

pletely repressed by our rationality. If we agree to read the story of Gyges as a depiction of dormant life, we may also want to consider the workings of a dream poetics in Apuleius' depiction of Lucius. Apuleius' dream poetics offers us a spectacle of a dormant soul, a spectacle whose philosophical aim is to awaken the reader. Gyges and Lucius are not simply exposed to their aggressive desires. The narratives we are dealing with create extraordinary events, fantastic spectacles, which the protagonists are driven to watch. The protagonists, attracted to the unfamiliar side of their soul, are uncontrollably drawn to seeing what lies beyond the horizon of ordinary vision.

Bibliography

Annequin, J. 1996. 'Rêve, Roman, Initiation dans les Métamorphoses' d'Apulée', *DHA* 22, 133–201.
Bury, R.G. 1929. *Plato: Timaeus, Critias, Cleitophon, Menexenus, Epistles*, Cambridge: Loeb Classical Library.
Carlisle, D.P.C. 2008. '*Vigilans somniabar*: Some Narrative Uses of Dreams in Apuleius' *Metamorphoses*', in: W. Riess (ed.), *Paideia at Play: Learning and Wit in Apuleius*, ANS 11, Groningen: Barkhuis Publishing and Groningen University Press. 215–233.
Davis, M. 2000. 'The Tragedy of Law: Gyges in Herodotus and Plato', *The Review of Metaphysics* 53, 635–655.
Devereux, G. 1976. *Dreams in Greek Tragedy: An Ethno-Psycho-Analytical Study*, Berkeley: University of California Press.
Dodds, E.R. 1951. *The Greeks and the Irrational*, Berkeley: University of California.
Felson-Rubin, N. 1996. 'Penelope's Perspective: Character from Plot', in: S. L. Schein (ed.), *Reading the Odyssey*, Princeton: Princeton University Press. 163–183.
Ferrari, G.R.F., 2000. 'The Three-Part Soul', in: G.R.F. Ferrari (ed.), *The Cambridge Companion to Plato's Republic*, Cambridge: Cambridge University Press. 165–210.
Fontenrose, J. 1980. *Python: A Study of the Delphic Myth and its Origins*, Berkeley: University of California Press.
Foucault, M.1988. *The Care of the Self: The History of Sexuality*, Vol. 3 (R. Hurley, trans.), New York: Vintage Books.
Freud, S.1965. *The Interpretation of Dreams*, New York: Avon Books.
Gallop, D. 1971. 'Dreaming and Waking in Plato', in: J.P. Anton, G.L. Kustas, (eds.) *Essays in Ancient Greek Philosophy*, Albany: State University of New York Press. 187–201.
Gollnick, J. 1999. *The Religious Dreamworld of Apuleius' Metamorphoses: Recovering a Forgotten Hermeneutic*, Waterloo: Wilfrid Laurier University Press.
Gildersleeve, B. L. 1885. *Pindar: The Olympian and Pythian Odes*, New York: Harper and Brothers (edited for Perseus).
Griswold, C.L. 1986. *Self-knowledge in Plato's Phaedrus*, New-Haven: Yale University Press.
Hamilton, E. (ed.) 1961. *The Collected Dialogues of Plato*, Princeton: Princeton University Press.

Hanly C. 1977. 'An Unconscious Irony in Plato's *Republic*', *The Psychanalytic Quarterly* 46, 116–147.
Hunink, V. 2006. 'Dreams in Apuleius' *Metamorphoses*', in: A. Lardinois, M. van der Poel, V. Hunink (eds.), *Land of Dreams: Greek and Latin Studies in Honour of A.H.M. Kessels*, Leiden: Brill. 18–31.
Laird, A. 1993. 'Fiction, Bewitchment and Story Worlds: The Implications of Claims to Truth in Apuleius', in: C. Gill, T.P. Wiseman (eds.), *Lies and Fiction in the Ancient World*, Austin: University of Texas Press. 147–174.
Laird, A. 2001. 'Ringing the Changes on Gyges: Philosophy and the Formation of Fiction in Plato's *Republic*', *JHS* 121, 12–29.
Lev Kenaan, V. 2004. 'Delusion and Dream in Apuleius' *Metamorphoses*', *CA* 23 (2), 247–284.
Lev Kenaan, V. 2010. 'The Ancient Road to the Unconscious', in: E. Scioli, Ch. Walde (eds.), *Sub Imagine Somni: Nighttime Phenomena in Greco-Roman Culture*, Pisa: ETS. 165–184.
Penwill, J.L, 1975. 'Slavish Pleasures and Profitless Curiosity: Fall and Redemption in Apuleius' *Metamorphoses*', *Ramus* 4, 49–82.
Price, S.R.F. 1986. 'The Future of Dreams from Freud to Artemidorus', *P&P* 113, 3–37.
Rowe. C.J. 1988. *Plato: Phaedrus with translation and Commentary*, Warminster: Aris & Phillips.
Schlam, C.C. 1970. 'Platonica in the *Metamorphoses* of Apuleius', *TAPA* 101, 477–487.
Simon, B. 1973. 'Models of Mind and Mental Illness in Ancient Greece: II. The Platonic Model', *Journal of the History of the Behavioral Sciences* 9, 3–17.
Simon, B. 1978. *Mind and Madness in Ancient Greece: The Classical Roots of Modern Psychiatry*, Ithaca: Cornell University Press.
Walde, C. 1999. 'Dream Interpretation in a Prosperous Age? Artemidorus, the Greek Interpreter of Dreams, in: D.D. Shulman, G.G. Stroumsa (eds.), *Dream Cultures: Explorations in the Comparative History of Dreaming*, Oxford University Press. 121–142.

Edmund P. Cueva
Why doesn't Habrocomes run away from Aegialeus and his Mummified Wife?: Horror and the Ancient Novel

Abstract: Scholarship on the ancient novel does not engage what the novelists, or, for that matter, other ancient authors, considered or thought of as 'horror'. This essay examines novel passages that may be said to stir horror in the reader and relies on modern horror theory to determine if the ancients wrote what we would call 'horror'. For example, in Xenophon 5,1–2 Habrocomes does not react with disgust/revulsion when introduced to the mummified body of Thelxinoe, he does not run away or show any discomfort with what is unmistakably a weird state of necrophilia. Why do these circumstances not horrify Habrocomes? Did they elicit horror in the ancient reader? Do they horrify the modern reader?

The scholarship on horror in the ancient novel does not specifically engage what the novelists considered or thought of as 'horror.' This paper examines those sections in the novels that may evoke this emotion in order to initiate a dialogue on the formation of a theory on the ancient literary use of horror. My investigation relies on modern horror theory. The examination begins with the Aegialeus passage in Xenophon (5,1–2) and seeks to answer why Habrocomes did not react with disgust and revulsion when introduced to the body of the mummified Thelxinoe. Why do these circumstances not horrify Habrocomes? Did they elicit horror in the ancient reader? In order to answer these questions this analysis first examines modern theorists on horror. Secondly, it reviews passages in the ancient novel that have key words, cues, locations, reactions, and configurations that alert the reader to the fact that they are supposed to be scared by the text.

---

[1] This is an edited version of the paper presented at the International Conference on the Ancient Novel IV.

Edmund P. Cueva, University of Houston-Downtown[1]

The Theorists

Lovecraft calls fear the 'oldest and strongest emotion of mankind...the oldest and strongest kind of fear is fear of the unknown.' Moreover, the horror tale was established on a multifaceted, yet straightforward principle that had to have a tone of 'breathless and unexplainable dread of outer, unknown forces.'[2] Penzoldt comments that it is not until the Graeco-Roman period that the supernatural 'short tale...finds its place in fiction' (Petronius' werewolf story and Apuleius' grisly passages).[3] The model for the supernatural story is short, dramatic, and without a plot (11). The horror narratives that we examine fit this pattern: they lack a plot, are dramatic, and make a brief appearance within the larger structure of the novels in which they find themselves. Kristeva posits that one can find horror's origin in a theorized pre-Oedipal stage, where an infant undergoes a crisis during which it 'breaks away from its mother and seeks to define its own identity.'[4] The mother during the crisis is viewed by the infant as 'horrific'—'in the sense of being all-engulfing, primitive, and impure or defiled by bodily fluids....Kristeva uses the term "abjection" to designate the psychic condition inspired by this image of the mother.'[5] Horror is the violation of boundaries, their transgression, and the 'need to do so';[6] we are thus repelled and attracted to the horrific.[7] One needs to go through abjection, and abjection has suffering as its intimate expression and horror as its 'public feature'.[8]

Twitchell use the term 'horror art' to label an assortment of patterns, predictably sequenced so as to produce 'a specific physiological effect – the shivers.'[9] It is artificial horror sought by an audience that can be produced verbally or visually,[10] supplies a frisson without exhaustive cogitation or complexity, and, most importantly, requires that the audience participate in a conspiracy or encounter a paradox.[11] Twitchell notes that 'horror' is a difficult word to analyze because we

---

[2] Lovecraft 2005, 106 and 107–108. Cf. King 1982, 62.
[3] Penzoldt 1965, 3.
[4] Kristeva 1982, 13.
[5] Freeland 1996, 197.
[6] Freeland 1996, 197; see also Freeland 2000, 3 and 273–276.
[7] Cf. King 1982, 31.
[8] Kristeva 1982, 140. Freeland 1996, 198, refutes Creed 1986 and 1993. Cf. Creed 2000, 64.
[9] Twitchell 1985, 8.
[10] See Walton 1973, 284 and Ellis 1994, 67.
[11] See Vorobej 1997, 219, who succinctly summarizes the paradox. Cf. Todorov's 1973 study of the fantastic.

think we know what it means.[12] He narrows the definition to the 'rather specific effect of...fright,' supplies the Latin verb *horrēre*, and designates it to be that shiver that we experience when we have the 'creeps'.[13] The hormone corticotropin triggers the shiver response,[14] which is clinically known as 'horripilation'.[15] Moreover, he differentiates horror from terror because the latter is external, transitory, real, and objectifiable, while horror is 'more internal and long-lasting'.[16] Horror attracts in three ways: '(1) as counterphobia or the satisfaction of overcoming objects of fear'; (2) as 'the return of the repressed'[17] or the compulsive projection of objects of sublimated desire; and (3) as part of 'a more complicated rite of passage from onanism to reproductive sexuality'.[18] These three items seem to be psychological in nature, which is not unusual since a good amount of scholarly analysis of horror literature or film uses psychology as a basis.[19]

Carroll suggests in Aristotelian fashion[20] that horror creates a paradox: how can one be horrified by reading what one knows to be fiction?[21] Walton, a predecessor of Carroll in this field of study, declares that fictional 'characters cause real people to shed tears, lose sleep, laugh, and scream.'[22] Neill attempts to solve the paradox with his 'quasi-fear' hypothesis,[23] which states that the spectator is in a state of shock rather than in a state of real or make-believe fear. The spectator 'describes himself as afraid because the feelings and sensations that typically go with being shocked and startled can...very much feel like some of the feelings and sensations characteristic of fear.'[24] Robinson can perhaps help resolve this problem: the form of the genre not only dominates the 'initial affective appraisals made by the reader, but can also serve the function of "reappraisal" or "coping"...one's experience is controlled by the form of the work, so that...

---

12 Cf. Tudor 1997, 456, who advises against the 'fallacy of generic concreteness.'
13 See Chamberlain 1899, 304, on the etymology of 'horror.'
14 Twitchell 1985, 10. See also Levy 1985; Heller 1987, viii; Bartholomew 1994, 206–207; Schneider 1993, 7–8; and Holland-Toll 2001, 6, 10, 15, and 25.
15 Twitchell 1985, 11. On horripilation and the 'startle' effect see Robinson 1995, 53; 56–57. Cf. Vrana and Lang 1990; Lang et al. 1990, 386–387; and Baird 2000, 15–20.
16 Twitchell 1985, 16. On the difference between horror and terror also see Heller 1987, 19; Rockett 1988, 45–47; and Schneider 1993, 133.
17 Cf. Tudor 1997, 449.
18 Twitchell 1985, 65. See also Twitchell 1985, 66, and Tudor 1997, 461.
19 Cf. Hills 2005, 61; see also Grixti 1989, 78 ff. and Jancovich 1992, 9–13.
20 On the linking of horror and art see White 1971.
21 Cf. Carroll 1987, 56 and Levison 1990, 79.
22 Walton 1978b, 12. For more information on cognitive theory see Morreall 1993, 359, and Leffler 2000, 217–222.
23 Cf. Walton 1978a, 22; Skulsky 1980, 7; and Morreall 1993, 359–363.
24 Neill 1991, 54.

even one with painful subject matter, the form will organize the experience into a harmonious whole that brings pleasure.'[25] Authors assemble the proper design elements and readers arrange the coping strategies.[26]

Carroll labels the emotion produced when reading horror as 'art-horror,' which parallels the emotions of the certain fictional characters, and is caused by a monster in the narrative.[27] The monster/monstrous is a menace that is compounded by 'revulsion, nausea, and disgust'.[28] The entity is so 'unwholesome that its very touch causes shudders' and is described in terms of or associated with filth, decay, deterioration, slime, and so on. Carroll's conception of the monster and horror is formulaic: the reader/spectator (R) is 'art-horrified' if and only if (1) R is in 'some state of abnormal physical agitation (shuddering, tingling, screaming, etc.) which (2) has been *caused* (sic)' by (a) R's thought that the monster (M) could possibly exist, and R's evaluative beliefs that (b) said M 'has the property of being physically (and perhaps morally) threatening in the ways portrayed in fiction, and that (c) said M is impure, where (3) 'such beliefs are accompanied by the desire to avoid the touch of things like' M (54). The figure of the monster is important for the realization of Carroll's hypothesis.[29] It is interstitial in nature, 'contradictory…incomplete, and/or formless'.[30] The interstitial is that which crosses 'the boundaries of the deep categories of a culture's conceptual scheme' and are 'primary candidates for impurity'.[31] Horror, therefore, is a result of the 'categorical transgression or jamming plus fear' (156–157).[32]

Neill notes that people like horror as a genre because '*horror horrifies*';[33] it supplies a pleasure inseparable from horror that cannot be found in other types of fiction.[34] Carroll rejects Neill's conclusion: 'Disgust, shock and edgy anticipation are inter-related affects that attend the consumption of horror fictions. Being in these states is discomforting'.[35] It is the structure of the horror narrative that causes pleasure and the negative emotions that arise are the price paid.[36]

---

25 Robinson 2004, 156.
26 Baird 2000, 18, to some extent argues the contrary.
27 Carroll 1990, 14–16. See Gelder 2000, 81–82, on the meaning of 'monster,' teratology, and teratogeny. Cf. Wells 2000, 8, and King 1982, 39.
28 Carroll 1987, 53.
29 See also Carroll 1999, 147–152. On the contrary, see Holland-Toll 2001, 251.
30 Carroll 1987, 56.
31 Carroll 1999, 152.
32 Cf. Carroll 1981, 24.
33 The italics are Neill's; Neill 1992, 57.
34 Neill 1992, 59; 63. Cf. Leffler 2000, 250–273.
35 Carroll 1992a, 73.

Gaut links David Hume's 'Of Tragedy' to Carroll's paradox and notes three similarities: '(1) Some of us enjoy horror fictions. (2) Horror fictions characteristically produce fear and disgust in their audience. (3) Fear and disgust are intrinsically unpleasant emotions.'[37] We can enjoy fear and disgust, and, therefore, there is no paradox. Gaut wants to substitute Carroll's 'art-horror' with her own 'enjoyment theory,' which is similar to Feagin's views because 'horror attracts because people enjoy being scared and disgusted', and as a genre it has its 'self-conscious aim the production of fear and disgust in the audience' (336). Indeed, Gaut is clear that the fear and disgust produced are true 'physiological' (340)[38] reactions based on the evaluation or disvaluations of these emotions (341). Carroll critiques Gaut's 'no paradox' evaluation by observing that Gaut does not leave room for the 'possibility that *sometimes* (sic) being horrified may not be pleasant.'[39] There is no doubt that authors of the horror genre are deliberate in their aims to cause apprehension and discomfort in their audiences. They purposefully create, as Hantke notes, 'staged collisions' that cause the audience' to shudder rather than to think.'[40] What then can be classified as truly horrific? And, why is does the genre attract?[41]

Leffler focuses on the paradox and notes that fictional horror must portray horror with the aim of eliciting 'pleasurable emotions'.[42] Unlike most of the other scholars who have worked on the paradox, Leffler significantly redirects attention to the importance of seeing and horror: 'either seeing too little and therefore not knowing, or seeing too much, or so much that it leads to trauma or madness' (125). Visualization allows the reader to become aware of the internal viewpoints of the fictive characters and their reactions. If we use Carroll's approach, we can then start to be cued in to the reactions of the characters to the horrific event. Carroll's monster, Leffler argues, is frightening because of the setting in which the character encounters the monster – 'the representation of the surrounding space and main character's perception of it' (150–151). While the identification with the fictive character can lead to a momentary experience of the fictional

---

36 Cf. Feagin 1992, 80–81, on horror and pleasure. Carroll 1992b, 85, disagrees with what he calls Feagin's 'affect/attraction principle.'
37 Gaut 1993, 333.
38 See also Lang *et al.* 1983 on the psychophysiological responses caused by fear elicited through reading (in particular, 302). Cf. Vrana *et al.* 1989, 189–190.
39 Carroll 1995, 70. Cf. Gaut 1995, 287.
40 Hantke 2002, 5.
41 For a possible answer see White 1971, 7. See also Rockett 1988, xiii-xiv; Des Pres 1983; and Wells 2000, 7–10.
42 Leffler 2000, 23.

world, the reader is also privileged with an outsider's view of the horrific event (258).

The Novelists

Of the five canonical Greek novels, the first example of what may be considered a horror narrative is found in Chariton 1,9,4–5 where we read of one of the robbers making their way into Callirhoe's tomb. The robber 'was terrified and jumped back. Shaking with fear, as cried to his fellows: "Let's get out of here! There's some sort of spirit on guard in there who won't let us come in!" Theron laughed scornfully at him and called him a coward and deader than the dead girl. Then he told another man to go in; and when nobody had the courage to do so, he went in himself, holding his sword ready before him.'[43] In this passage the reader does not experience any horror since he is aware that Callirhoe is alive and that the fear of the robbers is caused by their belief that they are plundering the tomb of a dead person (as would be expected; graves are meant for the dead and not the living). However, the robber who first encounters Callirhoe does feel fear, is terrified, and is startled: κἀκεῖνος φοβηθεὶς ἐξεπήδησε. Τρέμων δὲ πρὸς τοὺς ἑταίρους ἐφθέγξατο…,1,9,4,3–5 (…he was terrified and jumped back. Shaking with fear, he cried out to his fllows…).[44] He, and his comrades to a lesser extent, does experience horror, but that horror is not shared by the audience. Perhaps, Carroll is correct in arguing that a monster is necessary for 'art-horror' to be experienced. The robber who initially enters the tomb may experience a shiver due to his belief that there is a monster (an unusual entity) in the tomb, but, as noted, the audience knows better.

In book 5,1 Xenophon writes that Habrocomes on his way to Italy from Egypt was blown off course and arrived at the port of Syracuse, where he runs into Aegialeus. He and Habrocomes become friends and he tells our hero about the one love of his life, Thelxinoe, with whom he had spent his life in Sicily. Thelxinoe died not long ago, but Aegialeus had not buried her but has her with him. He concludes his story by saying that 'I always have her company and adore her (5,1,9,3).'[45] He then takes Habrocomes into the inner room of the house to introduce him to his dead wife, who had been embalmed in the Egyptian style. In fact, the fisherman still talked to her, slept beside her, and shared meals with

---

[43] The English translation is from Reardon 1989a.
[44] The Greek text is from Molinié 2002.
[45] The English translation is from Anderson 1989.

her. The sight of her consoled him after a long and tiring day of fishing. The normal and sane reaction to an encounter of this type would be one of shock, repulsion, and fright. After all, we have just been presented with a case of absolute unnatural, insane, and disgusting behavior. There just is no way to make pretty a case of necrophilia. However, our hero does not act as would be normally expected. Instead, he breaks out into lament about his won plight. He is not afraid and the audience parallels this lack of fear and expresses puzzlement.

Achilles Tatius supplies the reactions of Clitophon when he sees his beloved sacrificed in what unknown to him and the reader was not a real slaughter. He and reader experience the stabbing of the victim in the heart, the sawing of the victim from stern to abdomen, the leaping out of her viscera, the removal of her entrails, which were then cooked and eaten. The hero 'just sat there staring,' he was in shock, he was thunderstruck[46] (Τὸ δὲ ἦν ἔκπληξις· μέτρον γὰρ οὐκ ἔχον τὸ κακὸν ἐνεβρόντησέ με, 13,5,6).[47] The hero decides to kill himself, but he is saved by Menealos and Satyros. They bring him to the coffin in which Leukippe had been placed and tap on its lid and from within comes a voice that makes the hero tremble. The lid is opened and within there is a 'frightening...and blood-chilling sight.' The dead Leukippe then falls into Clitophon's arms, both embrace and then collapse. Our hero, one imagines from fright, faints. Once our hero regains consciousness and asks what the dickens was going on, Menealos continues the supernatural tone of the moment by telling him that he will cure Leukippe, recover her innards, and seal the gash caused by the stabbing. He proceeds to tell Clitophon to cover his eyes, and then moves on to some hocus-pocus and the speaking of magical words in order to summon Hecate to help in this endeavor. He tells Clitophon to open his eyes, but he is somewhat 'slow and fearful' in doing so. Leukippe, of course, is fully restored and this causes even more amazement in Clitophon. The heroine then bids Menelaos to stop frightening Clitophon and tell him the truth.

What is important to note here are the words used in this narrative: καὶ κάτωθεν φωνῆς ἀκούω καὶ πάνυ λεπτῆς. Τρόμος οὖν εὐθὺς ἴσχει με, 3,17,6 (... and I heard a delicate voice from under the lid. I began to tremble all over...); φοβερὸν θέαμα...καὶ φρικωδέστατον, 3,17,7 (...a frightening... and blood-chilling sight...); Καὶ ἐγὼ μόλις μὲν καὶ φοβούμενος—ἀληθῶς γὰρ ᾤμην τὴν Ἑκάτην παρεῖναι, 3,18,4 (I was very slow and fearful about doing so, for I did indeed think Hecate was there...); Ἔτι μᾶλλον οὖν ἐκπλαγείς, 3,18,5 (Still more amazed...); Παῦσαι...δεδιττόμενος αὐτόν, 3,18,5 ('...stop frightening him.'). All

---

46 The English translation is from Winkler 1989.
47 The Greek text is from Garnaud 2002.

these words are indicative of the fact that Clitophon actually experienced fear and horror. Secondly, and more importantly for this paper, is that the reader, too, did not know that a trick had been played and that Leukippe had not been killed and cannibalized. The reader would have been cued into experiencing 'art-horror.'

In *Daphnis and Chloe* 2,25 – 26, the author relates the fright that the Methymneans experienced the night after the capture of Chloe: 'suddenly the whole earth seemed to blaze with fire, and they heard the noise of splashing oars, as though a huge fleet was sailing against them. Someone shouted out that they should arm themselves; someone else called for the general; someone looked as if he had been wounded; and someone else lay there looking like a corpse. You would have thought you were seeing a night attack—but there was no enemy there.'[48] Of course, this would be scary enough for the sailors, but Longus charges the supernatural atmosphere even more by writing that the day was even more terrifying: the goats had flowering ivy in their horns, the rams and ewes looked like wolves, Chloe was wearing a pine garland in her head, the anchors were stuck to the seabed, the oars broke when placed in the water to be rowed, dolphins launched an attack on the ship, a piping was heard coming from the mainland, which terrified the folks on board, who became panic-stricken and took up arms against an invisible enemy. Once again, the Greek is important here: … σχῆμά τι ἔκειτο νεκροῦ…, 2,25,4 (…and someone else lay there looking like a corpse…); Ἠκούετό τις καὶ ἀπὸ τῆς ὀρθίου πέτρας τῆς ὑπὲρ τὴν ἄκραν σύριγγος ἦχος· ἀλλὰ οὐκ ἔτερπεν ὡς σῦριγξ, ἐφόβει δὲ τοὺς ἀκούοντας ὡς σάλπιγξ., 2,26,3 (Above the steep cliff that lay under the headland a sort of piping sound was heard; but it did not give pleasure to those listening, as pipes usually do, but terrified them, like a war trumpet.).[49] The people on the boat are frightened and the reader is left to wonder what is taking place. 'Art-horror' is not evident in this passage, because, I suspect, Carroll's monster is not present and the entire incident has more of the uncanny than the horrific and marvelous (to borrow from Todorov's vocabulary).

In Heliodorus' novel we find instances where bandits are frightened at the sight of Charikleia, who is presented to the bandits and reader as an unknown, unidentified girl: … ὑπὸ θαύματος ἅμα καὶ ἐκπλήξεως ὥσπερ ὑπὸ πρηστῆρος τῆς ὄψεως βληθέντες…, 1,2,5 (Thunderstruck with wonder and terror at the sight…); Knemon faints when he finds out the body in the tomb is that of Thisbe and not Charikleia (ὑπέβη τε εἰς τοὐπίσω καὶ τρόμῳ συσχεθεὶς ἀχανὴς εἱστήκει., 2,5,4 (He

---

[48] The English translation is from Gill 1989.
[49] The Greek text is from Vieillefond 2002.

reeled backwards and stood shivering in dumb amazement); an old woman, who is a witch and has lost a son in a recent battle, performs a necromantic ritual in order to find out if of her one surviving son would return home (6,14–15). The necromantic scene is quite horrific and full of ghastly and scary detail. The observers of this scene, Charikleia and Kalasiris, are alarmed at what they are seeing. Charikleia's 'horror at this appalling ritual became so great that she began to tremble with fear':

> Ἡ Χαρίκλεια δὴ οὐδὲ τὰ πρῶτα ἀδεῶς κατοπτεύουσα τότε δὴ καὶ ὑπέφριττε καὶ πρὸς τῶν γινομένων ἀήθων ἐκδειματωθεῖσα τὸν Καλάσιριν ἀφύπνιζέ τε καὶ θεατὴν γενέσθαι τῶν δρωμένων παρεσκεύαζεν. (6,14,5)
>
> Even before this Charikleia had been somewhat alarmed by the scene she was observing, but now her horror at this appalling ritual became so great that she began to tremble with fear. She shook Kalasiris awake so that he was able to see with his own eyes what was taking place.

Nevertheless, the heroine wants a close look at the ritual, but Kalasiris prevents her from getting close and states that 'the mere sight of such things was unclean' (ὁ δὲ παρῃτεῖτο φάσκων καὶ τὴν θέαν οὐκ εὐαγῆ…, 6,14,7). Moreover, the power to accomplish such abominations was obtained 'literally by crawling upon the ground and skulking among corpses' (τοῖς δὲ βεβήλοις καὶ περὶ γῆν τῷ ὄντι καὶ σώματα νεκρῶν εἰλουμένοις…, 6,14,7). Here we do have the monster and fear that is felt by a fictive character and paralleled by the reader. Of course, we have two monsters in the narrative, the old witch and the reanimated corpse. A double thrill.

Carroll would find the Roman novel narratives more in line with his theory.[50] Petronius has two passages that may fit his definition of horror. The first is the werewolf story (61–62), and the other is Trimalchio's horror story of the death of his former master's favorite (63). In the first story Niceros relates the account of the very brave soldier that joined him in his trip to Melissa of Tarentum. When they came to a cemetery by the roadside, the soldier went to look at the tombs and then proceeded to strip and to lay the clothing on the road. Niceros' reaction was: '*Mihi anima in naso esse; stabam tanquam mortuus.*', 62,5 ('My heart was in my mouth, I stood there like a corpse.'). The soldier then urinated around his clothes and suddenly turned into a wolf, howled, and ran off into the woods. Niceros tried to pick up the soiled clothing to no avail since they had been turned to stone. Once again, it is important to note Nicero's reaction:

---

[50] The Latin texts of Petronius and Apuleius come from The Latin Library (http://www.thelatinlibrary.com/). The translation of Petronius is from Sullivan 1986.

> *Ego primitus nesciebam ubi essem.... Qui mori timore nisi ego? Gladium tamen strinxi et <in tota via> umbras cecidi, donec ad villam amicae meae pervenirem. In larvam intravi, paene animam ebullivi, sudor mihi per bifurcum volabat, oculi mortui; vix unquam refectus sum.* (62,8,10)
>
> At first I didn't know where I was....If ever a man was dead with fright, it was me. But I pulled out my sword, and I fairly slaughtered the early morning shadows till I arrived at my girl's villa. I got into the house and I practically gasped my last, the sweat was pouring down my crotch, my eyes were blank and staring—I could hardly get over it.

After he makes his way to Melissa's house, she tells him that a wolf had attacked her sheep, but it had been stabbed through its neck by a slave. The next day Niceros goes back to the spot where the lycanthropic transformation had taken place only to find a pool of blood. He then returns home, where he finds the brave soldier being treated by a doctor for a neck wound. Here we have the requisite monster, the expected reactions, and the separation from normal to abnormal space that is necessary for 'art-horror' to occur. It can only be expected that someone reading this passage for the first time would have emotions parallel to those of Niceros, and, most importantly, to those of Trimalchio and the dinner guests: *Attonitis admiratione universis: 'Salvo,' inquit, 'tuo sermone', Trimalchio, 'si qua fides est, ut mihi pili inhorruerunt.',* 63,1 ('Everyone was struck with amazement. "I wouldn't disbelieve a word", said Trimalchio. "Honestly, the way my hair stood on end..."').

Trimalchio, not to be outdone, wants to tell his own horror story: *'Nam et ipse vobis rem horribilem narrabo.',* 63,2 ('Now I'll tell you a horrible story myself.'). After describing the circumstances of the death of his master's favorite, he jumps into the mourning caused by the death. All of a sudden '*<stridere> strigae coeperunt; putares canem leporem persequi.',* 63,4 ('...when the witches started howling—you'd think it was a dog after a hare.'). One of the household, a slave, runs out and stabbed one of the witches. They heard a groan, but saw nothing. The slave came back with his body bruised, where the 'mala manus' had touched him. When they all got back to where the boy's corpse had been, they found a straw changeling in its place. Evidently, the witches had carried off the corpse. The slave died a few days later. Trimalchio's story also meets Carroll's criteria.

Aristomenes' (1,9–20) and Thelyphron's (2,20–31) stories may also fulfill the requirements of Carroll's thesis.[51] In book 1 Aristomenes tells the story of his friend Socrates, who while in Aristomenes' company, was killed after becoming sexually involved with a witch. Aristomenes, at the start of the story told by

---

[51] The translation for Apuleius is from Kenney 1998.

his friend, gives his initial reaction: *'Denique mihi quoque non parvam incussisti sollicitudinem, immo vero formidinem.'*, 1,11 ('You really have made me uneasy— no, you've terrified me.'). Indeed, Aristomenes is so truly frightened of what he had heard that when they settle down to sleep and his friend has slumbered off: *'Ac primum prae metu aliquantisper vigilo.'*, 1,11 ('At first my fear kept me awake for a time...'). When the witches appear, we get further insight into what are the natural responses caused by fear:

> *Tunc ego sensi naturalitus quosdam affectus in contrarium provenire. Nam ut lacrimae saepicule de gaudio prodeunt, ita et in illo nimio pavore risum nequivi continere de Aristomene testudo factus.* (1,12)
>
> Then I discovered that some emotions naturally express themselves by their opposites. Just as one very often weeps tears of joy, so then, terrified I was, I couldn't help laughing at the idea of myself as a tortoise.

After the threats have been made by the witches, we get more information on the narrator's emotions:

> *Haec ego ut accepi, sudore frigido miser perfluo, tremore viscera quatior, ut grabattulus etiam succussu meo inquietus super dorsum meum palpitando saltaret.* (1,13)
>
> Hearing this I was in agony, drenched in an icy sweat and shaking all over, so that the bed too was convulsed by my shudders and heaved up and down on top of me.

We get even more information once the witches leave:

> *At ego, ut eram, etiam nunc humi proiectus inanimis nudus et frigidus et lotio perlutus, quasi recens utero matris editus, immo vero semimortuus, verum etiam ipse mihi supervivens et postumus vel certe destinatae iam cruci candidatus.* (1,14)
>
> As for me, I remained where I was, grovelling on the floor, fainting, naked, cold and drenched in piss, just like a new-born child—or rather half dead, a posthumous survivor of myself, an absolutely certain candidate for crucifixion.

Later in the story we find out that Socrates is the walking-dead, and that a sponge in his throat is the only thing keeping him alive. When Socrates sits down to eat a meal he starts to die, and Aristomenes cannot eat:

> *frustulum panis quod primum sumpseram quamvis admodum modicum mediis faucibus inhaereret ac neque deorsum demeare neque sursum remeare posset.*
>
> ... and the first piece of bread I'd taken, not a very big one, lodged right in my throat and refused either to go down or come back up.

When Socrates proceeds to have a drink, he finally dies. Aristomenes' reaction is fear: *'Ipse trepidus et eximie metuens mihi per diversas et avias solitudines aufugi.'*, 1,19 ('Then panic-stricken and in fear of my life, I made my escape through remote and pathless wildernesses...'). Oddly, his story is rejected as a fable, untrue, and unbelievable. However, the reader, according to Carroll, would have experienced 'art-horror' since all the elements to create such an affect are present.

Thelyphron tells the story of how he was disgraced and disfigured by unwary dealings with witches at Larissa. Thelyphron had been assigned to keep watch over a corpse and keep it from any witchery harm; the one proviso given was that he not fall asleep. When left alone with the deceased and in dead of night, he begins to experience fear: *'Mihique oppido formido cumulatior...'*, 2,25 ('My fear was at its height...'). Eventually, Thelyphron did fall asleep and awoke terrified [*'nimio pavore perterritus...'*, 2,26 ('with my heart in my mouth')] thinking that something may have happened to the corpse. It eventually turns out that the corpse, which has been unmolested, is reanimated by his uncle to tell the truth: his wife had poisoned him. There had been bodily mutilation, but it was Thelyphron who had been maimed. The witches, the fear experienced by Thelyphron, the reanimation of a corpse, and the bodily mutilation would cause 'art-horror.'

In conclusion, it can be argued by using Carroll's 'art-horror' theory that the ancient authors, at least the ancient novelists, did write horror. This paper is meant to get the conversation started on producing a universal theory on horror in Graeco-Roman antiquity. Modern horror theory on literature and film can help us come to some understanding on why narratives like the Aegialeus passage in Xenophon do not cause horror, but Achilles Tatius' tale of human sacrifice and cannibalism and Petronius' werewolf story do.

Bibliography

Anderson, G. (trans.) 1989. *An Ephesian Tale*, in: B.P. Reardon, *Collected Ancient Greek Novels*, Berkeley/Los Angeles/London: University of California Press. 125–169.

Baird, R. 2000. 'The Startle Effect: Implications for Spectator Cognition and Media Theory', *Film Quarterly* 53.3, 12–24.

Bartholomew, D. 1994. 'The Horror Film', in: G. Crowdus (ed.), *The Political Companion to American Film*, Chicago: Lakeview Press. 205–213.

Carroll, N. 1981. 'Nightmare and the Horror Film: The Symbolic Biology of Fantastic Beings', *Film Quarterly* 34.3, 16–25.

Carrol, N. 1987. 'The Nature of Horror', *The Journal of Aesthetics and Art Criticism* 46.1, 51–59.

Carrol, N. 1990. *The Philosophy of Horror, or, Paradoxes of the Heart*, London/New York: Routledge.
Carrol, N. 1992a. 'A Paradox of the Heart: A Response to Alex Neill', *Philosophical Studies* 65, 67–74.
Carrol, N. 1992b. 'Disgust or Fascination: A Response to Susan Feagin', *Philosophical Studies* 65, 85–90.
Carrol, N. 1995. 'Enjoying Horror Fictions: A Reply to Gaut', *The British Journal of Aesthetics* 33.4, 67–72.
Carrol, N. 1999. 'Horror and Humor', *The Journal of Aesthetics and Art Criticism* 57.2, 145–160.
Chamberlain, A.F. 1899. 'On the Words for "Fear" in Certain Languages. A Study in Linguistic Psychology', *The American Journal of Psychology* 10.2, 302–305.
Colavito, J. 2008. *Knowing Fear: Science, Knowledge and the Development of the Horror Genre*, Jefferson/London: McFarland & Company, Inc.
Colavito, J. 1993. *The Monstrous Feminine: Film, Feminism, Psychoanalysis*, London: Routledge.
Colavito, J. 2000. 'Kristeva, Femininity, Abjection', in: K. Gelder (ed.), *The Horror Reader*, London: Routledge. 64–83.
Crowdus, G. (ed.) *The Political Companion to American Film*, Chicago: Lakeview Press.
Des Pres, T. 1983. 'Terror and the Sublime', *Human Rights Quarterly* 5.2, 135–146.
Ellis, B. 1994. '"The Hook" Reconsidered: Problems in Classifying and Interpreting Adolescent Horror Legends', *Folklore* 105, 61–75.
Feagin, S.L. 1992. 'Monsters, Disgust and Fascination', *Philosophical Studies* 65, 75–84.
Freeland, C.A. 1996. 'Feminist Frameworks of Horror', in: D. Bordwell, N. Carroll (eds.), *Post-Theory: Reconstructing Film Studies*, Madison: University of Wisconsin Press. 195–218.
Freeland, C.A. 2000. *The Naked and the Undead: Evil and the Appeal of Horror*, Boulder: Westview Press.
Garnaud, J. 2002. *Achilles Tatius d'Alexandrie: Le Roman de Leucippé et Clitophon*, Paris: Les Belles Lettres.
Gaut, B. 1993. 'The Paradox of Horror', *The British Journal of Aesthetics* 33.4, 333–345.
Gelder, K. (ed.). 2000. *The Horror Reader*, London: Routledge.
Gill, C. (trans.) 1989. *Daphnis and Chloe*, in: B.P. Reardon (ed.), *Collected Ancient Greek Novels*, Berkeley/Los Angeles/London: University of California Press. 285–348.
Grixti, J. 1989. *Terrors of Uncertainty: The Cultural Contexts of Horror Fiction*, London/New York: Routledge.
Hantke, S. 2002. 'Shudder As We Think: Reflections on Horror and/or Criticism', in: S. Hantke (ed.), *Horror*, Vashon, WA: Paradoxa. 1–9.
Heller, T. 1987. *The Delights of Terror: An Aesthetics of the Tale of Terror*, Urbana/Chicago: University of Illinois Press.
Holland-Toll, L.J. 2001. *As American as Mom, Baseball, and Apple Pie: Constructing Community in Contemporary American Horror Fiction*, Bowling Green: Bowling Green State University Popular Press.
Hills, M. 2005. *The Pleasures of Horror*, London/New York: Continuum.
Jancovich, M. 1992. *Horror*, London: B. T. Batsford, Ltd.
Kenney, E.J. 1998. *The Golden Ass, or, Metamorphoses*, London: Penguin Books.

King, S. 1982. *Stephen King's Danse Macabre*, New York: Berkeley Book. (Original Work Published 1981)

Kristeva, J. 1982. *Powers of Horror: An Essay on Abjection* (L. S. Rodriguez, trans.), New York: Columbia University Press.

Kristeva, J. 1995. 'The Enjoyment Theory of Horror: A Response to Carroll', *The British Journal of Aesthetics* 33.4, 284–289.

Lang, P.J., Levin, D.N., Miller, G.A., Kozak, M.J. 1983. 'Fear Behavior, Fear Imagery, and the Psychophysiology of Emotion: The Problem of Affective Response Integration', *Journal of Abnormal Psychology* 92.3, 276–306.

Lang, P. J., Bradley, M.M., and Cuthbert, B.N.. 1990. 'Emotion, Attention, and the Startle Reflex', *Psychological Review* 97.3, 377–395.

Leffler, Y. 2000. *Horror as Pleasure: The Aesthetics of Horror Fiction* (S. Death, trans.), Stockholm: Almqvist & Wiksell.

Levison, J. 1990. 'The Place or Real Emotion in Response to Fictions', *The Journal of Aesthetics and Art Criticism* 48.1, 79–80.

Levy, R.I. 1985. 'Horror and Tragedy: The Wings and Center of the Moral Stage', *Ethos* 13.2, 175–187.

Lovecraft, H.P. 2005. 'Supernatural Horror in Literature', in: C. Miéville (intro.), *At the Mountains of Madness: The Definitive Edition*, New York: The Modern Library. 103–173. (Original Work Published 1965)

Molinié, G. 2002. *Chariton: Le Roman de Chairéas et Callirhoé*, Paris: Les Belles Lettres.

Morgan, J.R. (trans.) 1989. *An Ethiopian Story*, in: B.P. Reardon (ed.), *Collected Ancient Greek Novels*, Berkeley/Los Angeles/London: University of California Press. 349–588.

Morreall, J. 1993. 'Fear Without Belief', *The Journal of Philosophy* 90.7, 359–366.

Neill, A. 1991. 'Fear, Fiction and Make-Believe', *The Journal of Aesthetics and Art Criticism* 49.1, 47–56.

Neill, A. 1992. 'On a Paradox of the Heart', *Philosophical Studies* 65, 53–65.

Penzoldt, P. 1965. *The Supernatural in Fiction*, New York: Humanities Press.

Reardon, B.P. (trans.) 1989a. *Chaereas and Callirhoe*, in: B.P. Reardon (ed.), *Collected Ancient Greek Novels*, Berkeley/Los Angeles/London: University of California Press. 21–124.

Reardon, B.P. (ed.) 1989b. *Collected Ancient Greek Novels*, Berkeley/Los Angeles/London: University of California Press.

Robinson, J. 1995. 'Startle', *The Journal of Philosophy* 92.2, 53–74.

Robinson, J. 2004. 'The Art of Distancing: How Formal Devices Manage Our Emotional Responses to Literature', *The Journal of Aesthetics and Art Criticism* 62.2, 153–162.

Rockett, W.H. 1988. *Devouring Whirlwind: Terror and Transcendence in the Cinema of Cruelty*, New York: Greenwood Press.

Schlobin, R.C. 1992. 'Prototypic Horror: The Genre of the Book of Job', *Semeia* 60, 23–38.

Schneider, K.J. 1993. *Horror and the Holy: Wisdom-Teachings of the Monster Tale*, Chicago: Open Court.

Skulsky, H. 1980. 'On being Moved by Fiction', *The Journal of Aesthetics and Art Criticism* 39.1, 5–14.

Sullivan, J.P. (trans.) 1986. *The Satyricon. The Apocolocyntosis*, Harmondsworth, Middlesex, England: Penguin Books.

Todorov, T. 1973. *The Fantastic: A Structural Approach to a Literary Genre*, Cleveland/London: The Press of Case Western Reserve University.

Tudor, A. 1997. 'Why Horror?: The Peculiar Pleasures of a Popular Genre', *Cultural Studies* 11.3, 443–463.
Twitchell, J.B. 1985. *Dreadful Pleasures: An Anatomy of Modern Horror*, New York/Oxford: Oxford University Press.
Vieillefond, J. 2002. *Longus: Pastorales: Daphnis et Chloé*, Paris: Les Belles Lettres.
Vorobej, M. 1997. 'Monsters and the Paradox Horror', *Dialogue* 36, 219–246.
Vrana, S.R., Cuthbert, B.N., Lang, P.J.. 1989. 'Processing Fearful and Neutral Sentences: Memory and Heart Rate Change', *Cognition and Emotion* 3.3, 179–195.
Vrana, S.R., and Lang, P.J. 1990. 'Fear Imagery and the Startle-Probe Reflex', *Journal of Abnormal Psychology* 99.2, 189–197.
Walton, K.L. 1973. 'Pictures and Make-Believe', *The Philosophical Review* 82.3, 283–319.
Walton, K.L. 1978a. 'Fearing Fictions', *The Journal of Philosophy* 75.1, 5–27.
Walton, K.L. 1978b. 'How Remote Are Fictional Worlds from the Real World?', *The Journal of Aesthetics and Art Criticism* 37.1, 11–23.
Wells, P. 2000. *The Horror Genre: From Beelzebub to Blair Witch*, London: Wallflower.
White, D.L. 1971. 'The Poetics of Horror: More than Meets the Eye', *Cinema Journal* 10.2, 1–18.
Winkler, J.J. (trans.) 1989. *Leucippe and Clitophon*, in: B.P. Reardon (ed.), *Collected Ancient Greek Novels*, Berkeley/Los Angeles/London: University of California Press. 170–284.

List of Contributors

Ashli J. E. Baker is an assistant professor at Bucknell University in Lewisburg, Pennsylvania with special interest in Roman Imperial literature – especially the Greek and Roman novel – and ancient magic. She is currently writing a monograph on Apuleius' *Metamorphoses*, *Florida*, and *Apology*.

H. Christian Blood holds a BA in Liberal Arts from St. John's College, New Mexico, and a PhD from UC Santa Cruz, and is now an Assistant Professor of Comparative Literature and Classics at Yonsei University. Currently his research focuses on the intersections of transgender studies and classics, as well as the receptions of Greco-Roman antiquity in the Republic of Korea.

John Bodel is W. Duncan Macmillan II Professor of Classics and Professor of History at Brown University. He studies ancient Roman social, economic, and cultural history and Latin literature of the empire and has a special interest in the Roman novels of Petronius and Apuleius.

Shannon N. Byrne is a Professor of Classics at Xavier University in Cincinnati, Ohio. Her research interests include late republican and early imperial literature, in particular the status of poets, literary patronage, and the image of Maecenas as the ideal patron, as well as the ancient novel. Her recent publications include "Maecenas and the Battle of Actium – Again," in Apis Matina: *Studi in onore di Carlo Santini*, ed. Aldo Setaioli (Trieste 2016) 106–117, and the co-edited *A Companion to the Ancient Novel* (Wiley-Blackwell, 2014).

Andrea Capra has recently joined Durham University as Reader in Greek Literature after holding a tenured position as Assistant Professor at the University of Milan. He has been a residential fellow of the Scuola Normale Superiore of Pisa, the Harvard Center for Hellenic Studies and the Princeton Seeger Center for Hellenic Studies. His research interests include Plato's dialogues, Aristophanes, lyric poetry, the Greek novel and the Italian reception of Greek literature. Besides numerous articles, he is the author of three monographs (on Platos' *Protagoras*, *Phaedrus* and Aristophanes' *Assemblywomen*).

Robert Carver is an Associate Professor in Renaissance Literature in the Department of English Studies at the University of Durham. His publications include *The Protean Ass: The 'Metamorphoses' of Apuleius from Antiquity to the Renaissance* (Oxford: Oxford University Press, 2007), articles on Sir Philip Sidney and the reception of Heliodorus, and the chapter on 'English Fiction and the Ancient Novel' in the first volume of the *Oxford History of the Novel in English*, ed. Thomas Keymer (Oxford: Oxford University Press, 2017).

Catherine Connors is Professor of Classics at the University of Washington, Seattle and is the author of Petronius the Poet: Verse and Literary Tradition in the Satyricon (1998) and articles on Chariton, Apuleius, and the reception of the ancient novels in the work of John Barclay. Her current research focuses especially on representations of nature and geography in Roman and Greek literature.

Michael Cummings has completed a PhD at the University of Edinburgh, titled 'Metaphor and Emotion, Eros in the Greek Novel', out of which this article emerged. His research interests are emotions and metaphorical conceptualisation in ancient Greek. He currently works at the University of Edinburgh.

Ellen Finkelpearl is Professor of Classics at Scripps College, Claremont, CA. She has published primarily on Apuleius, including *Metamorphosis of Language in Apuleius*, a *Lustrum* bibliography on the *Metamorphoses* (with Carl Schlam), *An Apuleius Reader*, and the co-edited *Apuleius and Africa* with Ben Lee and Luca Graverini. She is currently working on animals and art/music in Imperial Greek and Latin texts.

Pilar Gómez is Professor of Greek Studies at the University of Barcelona, where she has been teaching and conducting research in 1981. She obtained a PhD in Classical Philology in 1987, with a thesis on the iambic tradition and fable (La Vida d'Isop entre el iambe, la faula i la novel·la), and is the author of numerous articles and book chapters on the Greek literature of the Roman Imperial period. Her research interests are mainly directed to the Second Sophistic, the novel and writers like Lucian (collaborating in the edition and translation of his works into Spanish for the Alma Mater collection), Plutarch and Aelius Aristides. She is a member of the research group Graecia Capta of the University of Barcelona.

Mary Jaeger is Professor of Classics at the University of Oregon. Her interests include Roman historical narrative, Republican and Augustan authors, and the use of food in Greek and Latin literature. She is the author of *Livy's Written Rome* and *Archimedes and the Roman Imagination*, in addition to articles on Livy, Horace, and Vergil. Other food-related publications include "Blame the Boletus? Demystifying Mushrooms in Latin Literature," *Ramus* (2011), and "Why is there no Cheese in Horace's Satires?" *AJP* (2015).

Gottskálk Jensson holds a Ph.D. in classics from University of Toronto (1997). He is Associate Professor at University of Copenhagen, Denmark, and Affiliate Professor at University of Iceland. Among his publications is The Recollections of Encolpius: The Satyrica of Petronius as Milesian fiction, ANS 2, Groningen: Barkhuis Publishing & Groningen University Library, 2004.

Dimitri Kasprzyk is Maître de conférences at the University of Brest. He has published several articles on Greek imperial literature (Greek novel, Philostratus, Artemidorus, Dio of Prusa); he is also co-author, with C. Vendries, of a book on Dio's *Alexandrian Oration*, (*Spectacles et désordre à Alexandrie: Dion de Pruse, Discours aux Alexandrins*. Rennes: PUR, 2012) and has edited (with J.-P. Guez) *Penser la Prose dans le monde gréco-romain* (Poitiers: La Licorne, 2016).

Jason König is Professor of Greek at the University of St Andrews. He works broadly on the Greek literature and culture of the Roman Empire. His books include Athletics and Literature in the Roman Empire (2005) and Saints and Symposiasts: The Literature of Food and the Symposium in Greco-Roman and Early Christian Culture (2012). His current research includes a Leverhulme-funded project on 'Mountains in ancient literature and culture and their post-classical reception' (2017–2020).

David Konstan is Professor of Classics at New York University. Among his publications are *Greek Comedy and Ideology* (Oxford, 1995); *Friendship in the Classical World* (Cambridge, 1997); *Pity Transformed* (London, 2001); *The Emotions of the Ancient Greeks: Studies in Aristotle and Classical Literature* (Toronto, 2006); *Before Forgiveness: The Origins of a Moral Idea* (Cambridge, 2010); and *Beauty: The Fortunes of an Ancient Greek Idea* (Oxford, 2014). He is a past president of the American Philological Association (now the Society for Classical Studies), a fellow of the American Academy of Arts and Sciences and an honorary fellow of the Australian Academy of the Humanities.

Christoph Kugelmeier, Born 1965 in Leverkusen (Germany). Doctoral thesis at Cologne University in 1995 on lyrics and Ancient Comedy. Habilitation at the University of Saarbrücken in 2002 on Senecan drama. Since 2010 professor of Classical Philology at the University of Saarbrücken. Several publications on Greek and Latin drama, ancient historiography, theory and practice of translation and the forming of philosophical terminology in antiquity and renaissance and on the terminology of the Septuagint and the Vulgate.

Sophie Lalanne is an Associate Professor in Ancient History at Paris 1 University Panthéon-Sorbonne. She is also a member of the research center ANHIMA (UMR 8210) where she leads a working group on Greek society and culture in the Roman Empire. She is a former student of the Ecole Normale Supérieure (Paris) and of Paris 4 University Paris-Sorbonne, where she has prepared a Master's Degree in Greek studies and an Agrégation in Classics. She got her PhD in Ancient History at Paris 1 University. She is the author of a book and many other publications, mainly on the Greek novel.

The relationship between myth, textuality, gender and psychoanalysis is a central focus of **Vered Lev Kenaan**'s work. In *Pandora's Senses: The Feminine Character of the Ancient Text* (Wisconsin UP 2008) she has shown how various mythical aspects of the feminine, such as beauty, ambiguity, voice and the art of weaving, are indispensable for studying the ancient literary canon. Her various articles on emotions, ancient dreams and dream poetics open up a new hermeneutical perspective that she develops in her forthcoming book on *The Ancient Unconscious*. Lev Kenaan teaches Comparative Literature at the University of Haifa, and lives in Tel Aviv.

Marina F.A. Martelli, PhD in Classical Philology at University of Milan, has extended her research training at Institut für Klassische Philologie, Humboldt Universität, Berlin, under supervision of prof. Lehnus and prof. Rösler. Her research fields are Hellenistic Literature and History of Tradition, in particular Callimachos *Ibis* and *Pinakes*.

Francesca Mestre is Professor of Greek Philology at the University of Barcelona. In 1991 she published her PhD thesis (defended in 1985) on essay, as literary genre, in Greek literature of the imperial period. Her main field of research is the literature and culture of the hellenophone part of the Roman Empire. She works on authors like Dio Chrysostomus and Philostratus (she has also published translations of these in Catalan and Spanish), and Lucian, the editing and translating of whose complete works she has been working on since 2000. She has published several articles and chapters of collective books, and coordinates the work of the 'Graecia Capta' research group at the University of Barcelona. Recently she published (as editor with P. Gómez) the books *Lucian of Samosata. Greek Writer and Roman Citizen* (2010), and *Three Centuries of Greek Culture under the Roman Empire* (2014).

Martina Meyer earned her PhD in Art History from the University of Toronto and has a second degree in museology. She currently lectures in both art history and gender studies. She held a Postdoctoral Fellow in the Humanities at Stanford University and is currently completing a book entitled *Household Names: Mythic Imagery in the domestic Sphere*, which investigates the decoration of feminine spaces with Greco-Roman mythic subject matter from ancient to contemporary appearances.

Saiichiro Nakatani is Associate Professor of Greek at Keio University in Tokyo and Yokohoma, Japan. He studied classics in Tokyo (BLitt, MLitt), Cambridge (MPhil), and Swansea (PhD). His interest covers literary interpretation as well as reception history of the ancient novel. He is founder member of KYKNOS Centre for Research on the Narrative Literatures of the Ancient World, and a Japanese translator of Achilleus Tatios' Leucippe & Clitophon (2008).

Nicola Pace is Associate Professor of Classical Philology at the StatebUniversity of Milan. He studied Latin translations of Greek authors (Origen and Polybius), Epicurean poetics in Philodemus of Gadara, and the unpublished Byzantine Lexicon Ambrosianum. He is currently working on the history of the Petronian controversy in the XVIIth century and on humanistic commentaries on Horace.

Janelle Peters holds degrees from the University of California, San Diego, University of Chicago, and Emory University. Her revised dissertation on Paul's statecraft is forthcoming with the University of Pennsylvania Press. She has written a dozen articles and chapters on Esther, Daniel, Paul's letters, the historical Jesus, 1 Clement, and Daphnis and Chloe.

Manuel Sanz Morales (born 1961) is Professor of Ancient Greek at the Universidad de Extremadura (Cáceres, Spain). His research interests include Greek textual criticism and the transmission of classical texts, as well as Greek lyric poetry and the Greek novel. His book *El Homero de Aristóteles* (Amsterdam: Hakkert, 1994) studies the text of Homer as transmitted by Aristotle. He will publish (with Prof. Manuel Baumbach, Bochum) at the end of 2017 the first volume of a commentary on Chariton's *Callirhoe* (Heidelberg: Winter Verlag). He is also preparing for Winter a critical edition of the novel, to be published in 2018. Other areas of interest in his research are the classical tradition and the history of the Classical Studies. He is the coordinator of the Spanish and Latin-American section of the Catalogus Philologorum Classicorum.

Cristiana Sogno is Associate Professor of Classics at Fordham University. She has worked on the correspondence of Symmachus and has recently co-edited a volume on Late Antique letter collections together with Bradley Storin and Edward Watts.

Index nominum et rerum

Abjection 362
Achaia 278f., 287f.
Achilles 2, 52f., 55, 57–61, 97, 109, 113–115, 118f., 317
Achilles Tatius 51f., 61, 83, 94, 96, 184–186, 188, 190, 235, 295, 308, 313, 317, 319, 323, 367, 372
Afranius Burrus (commander of the Praetorian Guard under Nero) 85
Agamemnon 118, 293, 295
Agrippina (mother of Nero) 2, 79–81, 83, 85f.
Ajax 97, 114, 118f.
Ajax the Locrian 118
Ajax the Telamônian 118
Alexander 9, 31, 42f., 46, 48, 154, 190
Alexander Romance 185, 187, 310
Alexander Severus 108
Alkyoneus 111
Allegory 278, 286
ambulatio 157
Amphiaraos, 113
Amphilokhos 113
Anahita 32
Anecdotes 83, 231, 245
Anthia 9, 21, 24f., 96, 98, 101f., 308f., 312
Antilokhos 114, 118
ἁπαλός 267,
Aphrodite 22, 30, 32f., 44, 47, 128f., 312f.
Apollo 19, 24, 26, 43, 97, 128, 231, 264, 271, 313
ἀπόλογος Ἀλκίνου 13
Apuleius 2–4, 11f., 14, 163f., 166, 168, 172–174, 176f., 187, 221–225, 227f., 230f., 241, 251–254, 256–260, 265, 277–282, 284–286, 288, 291, 298, 327–329, 337, 341f., 352–354, 356, 358, 369f.
Arados 29
Ariosto 24f.
Aristippus of Cyrene (Greek philosopher, founder of the hedonistic Cyrenaic school) 6 83
Artemis 19, 26, 97, 101, 128

Artyactes 112
Asclepius 32
Asinius Marcellus 259, 337
Asinus aureus / *The Golden Ass* / *Metamorphoses* 221, 223f., 228, 232, 291, 298, 312, 327f., 333f., 336–338, 341f., 352f.
Astylos 99f.
Audience 23f., 26, 65f., 75f., 130, 148, 167, 169f., 173, 187, 189f., 206, 225f., 232, 281, 294f., 300, 362, 365–367
auditoria 292, 295
Augustus 67–71, 74, 81, 173
Austen, Jane, *Northanger Abbey* 222
Authorial variants 184, 191
Autobiography 12

Bakhtin 2, 125, 163f., 166–169, 171f., 178, 277, 280
Bandits 279f., 284f., 288, 313, 368
βασιλεύς 60
Beroaldo, Filippo 3, 221, 224–230, 232
Bessarion, Cardinal 235
Bianchini, Bartolomeo 226f.
Bibliotheca, cod. 129 48, 187, 211
Bierl, Anton 19f., 26
Boccalini, Traiano 227
Bochoris / Bocchorus / Borochus 35
Body 9, 56, 82, 110, 127–129, 136–138, 167f., 174, 177, 233, 236, 252f., 265, 273, 280, 286f., 317, 320, 324, 342, 354f., 357, 361, 368, 370
Bologna 221, 224f., 227
Boscoreale 144, 157
Boscotrecase 144, 153–156, 158
Brodarics, István / Stephanus Brodarichus 226f.
Bucolic 138, 154f., 265
Bürger, Karl 18

Caesar, C. Iulius 13, 86
Caligula 79, 81
Callimachus 83

Callirhoe   31, 40, 87, 94, 96–99, 136, 195, 205f., 312f., 318, 366
Callisthenes   98f.
Cambyses   87
Caracalla   82, 115
Cardano, Girolamo   227, 235
Cassius Dio   79f.
Celsus   115
Celtis, Conrad   229
Cena   71f., 75, 211f.
Cervantes, Miguel de, *Don Quixote*   222, 241
Chariton   3, 10, 17, 29, 40, 87, 94, 184f., 188, 190, 195–201, 204–206, 235, 295, 299, 315, 318–320, 366
Chloe   3, 96, 98, 123–137, 139f., 239, 242, 244, 246, 263, 266–274, 313, 368
Christian, Christianity   1, 3, 11, 111, 115–117, 119, 129, 145, 163, 277f., 280, 284–288, 305, 310, 314
Cicero   11, 264, 291f., 294, 297, 306, 308, 327
– *De Oratore*   294
Cilicia   21, 102, 113
clementia   84
clementia Caesaris   84
codex Thebanus   195–197, 204
cognitio extra ordinem   293, 297
Colonna, Cardinal Giovanni   221f., 229–232, 234–236
Colonna, Francesco   3, 221, 229–232, 234–236
constitutio textus   195–197
consuetudo   8
Conversion   109f., 117, 166, 172, 174, 176, 232, 283, 313, 337
Cornelius Gallus   86
Corticotropin   363
Crateia (mother of Periander)   82f.
Credibility   35, 81f., 88
Cult   1f., 10, 47, 97, 107f., 109, 111–117, 119, 129, 174–176, 258,
curiositas   327–330, 332–336
Cyprus   22, 285, 287
Cypselus (tyrant of Corinth)   85
Cyriaco d'Ancona   230

Dalmatia – Traù – XVIIth century   209f., 212–214, 217f.
Daphnis   9, 96, 100, 123f., 126–140, 239, 242f., 246, 264–275, 313
Daphnis and Chloe   2f., 96, 99f., 123–129, 131, 133–135, 138f., 143–149, 158, 239–246, 259, 263–271, 274f., 313, 368
Death   32, 34, 36, 47–49, 59, 66f., 69f., 75, 83, 87, 110f., 113, 118f., 132, 136, 167–169, 228, 231, 235, 257, 287, 291, 310–313, 331, 333, 336, 357, 369f.
Debaucheries   81
Declamation   33, 291–296, 299f.
δείκνυμι   55
Dialogus   291, 295, 297
– Maternus   292–294, 297
– Messalla   292, 294
διδάσκω   268
Digression   33
Diomedes   118
δορυφόροι   60
Doulamis, Konstantin   19f.
dramatic elements   33
Dream   126, 343f., 349, 351f., 357
Dream Poetics   352, 358
Dream Text   351f.,
δῶρον   267

Egypt   21f., 24, 51, 59f., 175, 285, 366
Ekphrasis   53
Elaious   109
Elite   98
Encolpius   1, 3, 7–12, 14, 71f., 291f., 295–298, 301
ἐπιείκεια   84
Erasmus, Desiderius, *Encomium Moriae*   228f.
Eros   25, 56, 71, 126, 134, 139, 175, 263f., 266, 268, 274f., 312
ἐρωμένη   55
ἐρωτικός   54f.
eugeneia   93, 95f., 98
Eumolpus   3, 7, 13f., 296f.
Euphorion (Hellenistic poet)   86
Euphrates   29–31, 39f., 42f., 46–48
exul   9, 12

Fabius Rusticus (biographer of Seneca) 86
facetiae 231
Fantastic (Imaginary) 20, 176, 341 f., 344 f., 358
Fasting 286
Ferrari, Ottavio 187, 214–218, 343
Fiction 277, 327
Ficus Ruminalis 85
Film 363, 372
Firenzuola, Agnolo, *L'asino d'oro* 223 f.
Flowers 131
Focalization 169, 279
Forgiveness 305
Fortunata 2, 65 f., 71–76
Forum 170, 294
Francia, Francesco 226
Fratricide 81
Freud 343 f., 351 f.

Galatea 155 f., 265–267, 271, 274
Galen 115, 273, 316
Garden 143 f., 150–153, 157
Garmos 32, 36, 40, 46–48
Gender 1 f., 57, 123, 127, 129, 139, 251, 267, 272,
Geta (brother of Caracalla) 82
gloria 294, 329, 333
Goatherd 93, 101, 130, 265
God 3, 117, 286, 305, 310–312
Golden Age 59, 94, 143 f., 146, 148, 283
Gradi, Stefano 210, 213 f., 216–218
Griffolini, Francesco 235
Grotto 126, 130, 134
Gyges 4, 341 f., 344, 349–352, 356–358

Habrocomes 9, 20 f., 24 f., 96, 98, 101, 312 f., 320, 361, 366
Hadrianus 59–60
Hägg, Thomas 18, 25, 116, 184, 189 f., 263
Hall, Edith 279
Harrison, Stephen 147, 281, 328, 330, 337
Hektor 114
Heliodorus 3, 10, 24, 34, 36, 48, 52, 94, 97, 186, 195, 235, 251 f., 254–256, 258–260, 285, 295, 308 f., 316 f., 320 f., 323 f., 368
Helios 19, 25, 98, 101

Hellenicity 109
Hellenism 117
Hephaistos 115
Hermippus of Smyrna (Hellenistic biographer and philosopher) 83
Hero 107, 110, 119
Herodes Atticus 88
Herodotus 34 f., 39, 45, 49, 52, 84–87, 89, 241
Heroikos 2, 107–109, 111, 114–119
Hesiod 22, 114, 345, 357
Hippothoos 21, 24
History 36, 47, 51, 273
– of Classical Philology – XVIIth century 209,
Homer 22 f., 89, 109 f., 112–115, 118, 173, 256 f., 259, 264, 270 f., 282
Horace 65–67, 74–76, 127, 152
Horror 361–365
Hôtel de Lauzon 148
Hyllos 111
Hypata 11, 14, 169–172, 221, 223 f., 291, 298, 353, 355
Hypnerotomachia Poliphili 3, 221, 229, 233

Iamblichus 2, 29 f., 34–36, 39–41, 43–49, 52
Ideal novel 93, 102, 234
Identity 97, 107, 109, 116, 118 f., 128, 130, 152, 157, 166, 176, 251, 253, 256–260, 279 f., 341, 362
Idomeneus 118
Incest 82 f., 86 f., 226 f., 292
Initiation 108, 110, 112, 115, 137, 174 f., 177, 258
ira 11, 80, 296
Isis 19, 26, 97, 163 f., 172, 174 f., 177, 221, 224, 229, 258, 288, 312, 334, 337
Island 24
Isthmus of Corinth, canal 85
Iulia Domna (wife of Septimius Severus, mother of Caracalla) 82
Iunius Silanus (Roman politician, murdered by Agrippina) 80

Jerome 3, 277 f., 284, 286–288
– Life of Hilarion 3, 277 f., 284, 287 f.

- Life of Paul of Thebes 284, 286
Jesus 115–117, 119
Jewish 1, 116–118, 126, 305, 310, 314
Judaism 117

καινὴ διδαχή 116
καινόν 52, 61
κάλλος 54–56
König, Jason 19–21, 113, 277
Konstan, David 1, 21, 124, 130, 135, 137–139, 267, 305, 307, 310, 317, 319f., 327
Kore 32, 46

Lacedemon 34
Lampon 101
Landscape 143, 152, 156f., 277
– early Christian responses to 284–287
– post-romantic representations of 277–283
– wild 19, 134, 143f., 150–152, 253, 278, 280, 284f., 346f.
Laodameia 112
Laplace, Marcelle 19f., 186
Law, maritime 214, 244
λειμῶν 56
Lesbos 2, 9, 21f., 100, 123, 125, 147, 242
Lichas 3, 7–9, 11f., 296f.
Life of Aesop 187f.
Life of Antony 284
Lives of Greek poets 88
Livia 68, 144, 150–153
locus horridus 281, 285
Longus 2f., 94, 123–125, 127–131, 133, 136–140, 143f., 146–150, 155, 157f., 184, 187, 191, 235, 239–242, 247, 263f., 266, 270f., 273, 275, 295, 316, 368
Love / Eros 25, 56, 71, 126, 133f., 138f., 166, 175–177, 264, 266, 268, 274f., 312
Lucian 9, 36, 42, 45, 111, 115, 187, 337
Lucio, Giovanni 209–218
Lucius 4, 11f., 166, 168–172, 174–177, 187, 214, 221–224, 226–230, 235, 252–254, 257–259, 278, 280–283, 286, 288, 298–301, 327–337, 341f., 352–358
Lucius or The Ass 187
Lykainion 126, 129, 131, 133–139, 244, 271

Maecenas 2, 65–72, 74–76
Maenad 125, 136
Magic 4, 14, 34, 47, 166, 170, 235, 327f., 333–337, 353–355, 357, 367
Maiuma, Palestine 287
Marcus Aurelius 43f., 81
Marôn 113
Martyr, Martyrdom 299
μέλι 45
Melissa (wife of Periander) 87, 369f.
Menelaos 118, 367
mentula 11
Merkelbach, Reinhold 18f., 32, 116, 187
Meroe 30, 97, 335f.
Mesopotamia 29–31, 35f., 39–44, 46–48
Metamorphoses 2–4, 12, 14, 163f., 166–168, 170–178, 187, 252, 256, 266, 271, 277f., 280f., 284, 288, 291, 298, 312, 327f., 333f., 336–338, 341f., 352f.
Millar, Fergus 40f., 94, 278
Monster 345–348, 351, 364–366, 369f.
Moon 26
Mother Earth (motif) 84, 86
multiple versions 2, 183f., 186, 188–191
Muses 23
Muth, Konrad / Conradus Mutianus Rufus 225
μῦθοι Μασσαλιωτικοί 13
Myrtale 137
Mysia 114
Myth 116
Myth of the Cave 344

Name 10, 17f., 22, 31, 34f., 44f., 47, 56, 75, 102, 107–109, 133, 145, 218, 224–226, 229, 240, 242f., 266, 271, 287
Narrative 17, 81, 240f., 305
Nauplios 119
ἡδονή 109
Necrophilia 361, 367
Nero 2, 13, 42f., 65, 76, 79–83, 85–88, 170, 173
Nestor 118
Nilus / Nile 2, 21f., 31, 51f., 58, 60f., 95, 204, 312,
Ninyas (son of Semiramis) 83f.

Index nominum et rerum — **385**

Novel 1, 39, 51, 79, 93, 107, 132, 183, 195, 291, 315f., 361
Novelistic passages of earlier historiography 88
Nymphs 124–131, 134, 139f., 143f., 264, 313

Octavia Praetexta (anonymous Roman drama about Nero, Agrippina, and Seneca) 81
Odysseus 13f., 32, 109, 113, 117–119, 128, 132, 135, 157, 265, 270, 335
of Greek novel 94
Olympia 115, 345
Oratory 291, 294, 297, 300
Orestes 85, 111
Orpheus 114
Osiris 19
O'Sullivan, James 19, 23, 25, 157, 184
otium 157
Ovid 40, 68, 125, 129, 132, 137f., 152, 232, 245, 256, 266, 271

paideia 35, 97, 102, 116, 223
παιδεύω 133
Palamedes 109, 113f., 117–119
Pamphile 230, 333f., 336, 341f., 353–357
Pan 123, 130, 135, 139f., 264, 313
Paradox 10, 145, 148, 285f., 362f., 365
φαρμακός 10f.
Parrhasius 143
Parthenius 83–87
Pastoral 149
Paul, the Apostle 145, 148, 239f., 242, 299
paupertas 11
Pausanias 138, 279
peregrinus 8, 301
Periander (son of Cypselus, tyrant of Corinth) 83–87
Peripatetic tradition 83
περιπέτεια in the rule of Nero 79–89
Perseus 155
Persuasion 54, 110, 292
Petronio, patron saint of Bologna 9f., 210f., 216f., 224

Petronius Arbiter 7, 10–12, 14, 65f., 74–76, 209–212, 214, 216, 224, 297, 369, 372
– *Cena Trimalchionis* 3, 209, 212
– *Satyrica* 1, 3, 7–14, 163, 291f., 295
Phaedrus 344
pharmacus 12
Pharsiris 33
Philoktêtês 118
Phoenician 20, 56, 58, 101, 107–113, 115, 119, 255, 259
Photis 169–171, 175–177, 334f., 353–356
Photius (Byzantine philologist) 29f., 33–36, 40, 45f., 48f., 84, 187
Pilgrimage 287
Pins, Jean de 225–228
Pio, Giovanni Battista 230
πιστεύω 110
πίστις 110, 112, 114, 118
πιθανός 110
Pity 305
Plato 4, 65, 86, 255, 315f., 328, 341–351, 354, 356f.
Plato's notions of 343
Pliny the Elder 143, 228
Pliny the Younger 115, 241
φοῖνιξ 56, 58
Political defamation 81
Political interpretation of sexual innuendo 84
Poliziano, Angelo 235
Polynices 85
Polyphemos 156
Poppaea (mistress and wife of Nero) 85, 87
Porcius Latro 293
Power 80
πραότης 84
Protesilaos 107, 109–115, 117f.
Ps.-Lucian, Onos 279
Psüchagogia 341
Pythias 226, 298

quinquennium Neronis 85

Rabelais, François 231
Re 19, 245
Readership 183

Religion 19
Remorse 306–309, 313
Representation 31, 39, 41, 93, 129, 146, 152, 154f., 165, 203, 252, 263, 266, 269, 277f., 284, 310, 349, 351f., 365
Republic 341–347, 349, 357
Resurrection 32, 311f.,
Rhêsos 113
Rhianus (Hellenistic poet and grammarian) 86
Rhodanes 9, 32, 34, 40, 44–48
Rhodes 21–26, 29, 98, 101, 312
Rhododendron 45, 47
Rhone 31
rimabundus (Apuleius, *Met.* 2,5) 229f.
River 31
Roads 44, 171, 369
Rohde, Erwin 17f., 23, 46, 205
Roman Empire 2, 35, 40, 88, 93–97, 103, 107f., 116, 280, 284
Rubicon, crossing of the 86
Ruiz-Montero, Consuelo 19f., 23, 184, 188
Rumours 80, 87f.

Sabellico, Marcantonio 229
sacer 9f.
Sacro-idyllic 144, 152–154, 157f.
Sailors 93, 100f., 234, 368
Sarapis 19
Schiesaro, Alessandro 281
Second Sophistic 20, 53, 94, 124, 147, 158
Semiramis (queen of Babylon) 39f., 83f., 86
Seneca the Elder 293
Seneca the Younger 13, 65–76, 163–177, 283
Septimius Severus 81
Seven Sages 82f., 85
Severans 119
Sinonis 9, 30, 32, 40, 44–46, 48
Sleep 33, 46, 68, 76, 101, 126, 137, 221f., 235, 343f., 348–351, 355, 357, 363, 371f.
Society 93, 183, 263
Socrates 225f., 333, 335, 344–347, 370–372
Soraichos 29f., 33f., 46, 48

Soul (Tripartite Soul, Psyche) 223, 341
Spasinou Charax 43, 46f.
Spectacle 341
Spring 123, 125, 127, 132, 134, 138
Statileo, Marino 209–216, 218
Sthenelos 113, 118
Story of Apollonius, King of Tyre 188, 310
Subjectivity 80, 171
Suetonius 67, 79–81, 85–87, 165, 167, 227
Sun 24–26, 58, 259, 313
superbia 327, 333, 336
syllogai 230

Tacitus 2, 43, 79–81, 85–88, 115, 291, 294f.
Tale of the unknown lover 83
Tanais 33–35
θέαμα 51f., 61
Techne 127, 130, 149, 264
Temple 126, 139
Terentia 2, 65–72, 74–76
τέχνη 55
The Georgics 152
The Unconscious 4, 341–344, 352f., 356f.
Theaters 176, 299
Theatricality 283
Theocritus 147, 155, 265, 267–271, 274
Theodorus Prodromus 24
Theory 3f., 17–20, 23, 25, 31, 191, 315f., 319, 343, 361, 365, 369, 372
Thrace 9, 113
Thrasybulus (tyrant of Miletus) 85
Tiberius 86, 291
Tigris 29–32, 34, 39, 42f., 46–49
Timaeus 273, 351
Tlepolemos 23
Tomb 46, 57, 98, 111, 115, 119, 136, 231, 366, 368f.
Topoi 81, 136, 139f., 157, 266f.
Tragic elements 33
Tragic historiography 89
Trajanus 40–47
Transformation (Metamorphsis) 221
Trials 3, 176, 291f., 294f.
Trimalchio 2, 65f., 71–76, 214, 293, 295–297, 369f.
Trinquier, Jean 278, 280f.

Trompe l'oeil   150
Troy   9, 12 f., 108, 110 f., 113, 115, 117, 119, 173
Tryphaena   7 f., 296
τυρός   57, 266 f.
Tyndareus   23
Typhon (Typhoeus)   344 f., 347 f., 351
Tyrant   82–85, 87 f., 292, 357

Unknown (clandestine) paramour   83
Unterhaltungslektüre   190

Vergil   86, 266
Villa of Livia   150
Vinedresser   107–113, 116 f.
Virgil   9–11, 152, 281
Vision (Visual Experience)   342 f., 349, 353–356

voluptas   228, 327, 332–334
Votienus Montanus   293

Wandering motif   88
Wandering novel   83
Wealth   71, 93, 95 f., 98, 102, 205, 264–267
Worship   101, 135, 154, 175, 177, 279

Xenophon   10, 17–26, 29, 36, 44, 84, 101, 127, 132, 184 f., 191, 270, 312, 320, 361, 366, 372
Xenophon of Ephesus   1, 17, 52, 184, 187, 235, 240, 308

Zeuxis   143
Zimmerman, Maaike   163, 185, 197, 199–203, 278–280, 282 f.

Index locorum

Achilles Tatius
- *Leucippe and Clitophon*
  - 1.3.1   57, 96, 101
  - 1.4.2   55
  - 1.4.5.1–3   318
  - 1.7   138
  - 1.15.2   53
  - 1.16.1–2   54–55
  - 1.16.2–3   54, 56
  - 1.17.3–5   56
  - 1.19.1–2   55–56
  - 2.1.2   60
  - 2.2.2   186
  - 2.15.4   60
  - 2.29   319, 323
  - 3.24   57
  - 3.25.1–6   57, 60
  - 3.17.6   367
  - 3.17.7   367
  - 3.18.4   367
  - 4.11.3–4.12.1   51
  - 5.24.3.2–5   323
  - 6.19   323–324
  - 8.6.14–8.7.6   186
- *Act. Ap.*
  - 7,54–60   118
  - 17,19   116
  - 17,22–31   111

Ammianus
- 23.6.11   48
- 23.6.24   44
- 23.6.32–36   41

Apollonius
- *Argonautica*
  - 3.649   318

Apuleius
- *Met.*
  - 1.1   223, 231
  - 1.1–3.24   166
  - 1.2   222, 329, 336
  - 1.2–3.24   168
  - 1.5–19   222, 335
  - 1.6   226, 335
  - 1.7   333, 335
  - 1.8   334, 336
  - 1.9–10   336
  - 1.9–20   370
  - 1.12   335
  - 1.20   331
  - 1.24   226
  - 1.25   226
  - 1.25.1–6   298
  - 2.1   221–225
  - 2.20–31   370
  - 2.3   330
  - 2.4   226, 230
  - 2.5   230, 335–336
  - 2.6   333, 335–336
  - 2.10   334
  - 2.11   337
  - 2.32   168, 298
  - 3.1–12   11, 291
  - 3.2.5–6   298
  - 3.3.9   300
  - 3.5–6   300
  - 3.7.2   300
  - 3.14   332
  - 3.19   235, 335, 355
  - 3.21   230, 355–356
  - 3.21–25   341–342
  - 3.22   356
  - 3.23   353
  - 3.24   354
  - 3.24–25   353–354
  - 3.25–11.13   166, 170
  - 3.26   253
  - 4.4   252
  - 4.6   252
  - 4.27   334
  - 4.32   232
  - 4.34   235
  - 5.1   253
  - 5.8   253
  - 5.23   230
  - 6.13   253
  - 6.13–14   284–285
  - 7.16   253
  - 9.11   171

– 9.12 171
– 9.12–13 332
– 9.13 171, 332
– 9.15 332
– 9.30 332
– 10.16 226
– 10.19–23 226, 333
– 10.21 253
– 10.22 171
– 10.29 253
– 10.30 282
– 10.33 253
– 10.34 253, 283
– 10.35 172
– 11.2 258
– 11.7 258
– 11.8 172, 258
– 11.11 258
– 11.13 172, 224, 280
– 11.14 253
– 11.15 334
– 11.27 174, 259, 337
– 11.14–30 166
– 11.18 174
– 11.23 258
– 11.24 175
– 11.26 175
– 11.27 174, 224, 259, 337
– 11.28 174
Aristid.
– *Aeg.*
 – p.353 (Jebb) 13
 – p.354 (Jebb) 13
Aristophanes
– *Eq.*
 – 479–265
– *Pax*
 – 440 124
– *Ec.*
 – 661 135
Aristotle
– *EN*
 – 1109b18–1111a2 307
 – 1109b30–32 308
 – 1110a24–26 307
– *GA*
 – 3.739b 21–27 273

– *MM*
 – 2.1.1 p. 1198b26 84
– *Rh.*
 – 1378a20–3 317
Arrianus
– *An.*
 – 5.13.2 31
 – 7.7.3 30
 – 7.16.5–17.6 42
Athenaeus
 – 1.20d 74
 – 1.20e 76
 – 12.25 13
Augustine
 – *C.D.* 18.18 12
 – *Conf.* 1.10 328
 – *Conf.* 10.41 328
Aurelius Victor
 – 5.2 85
Cassius Dio
 – 44.6.3 85
 – 46.55 31
 – 54.3.4 67
 – 54.3.5 67
 – 54.17.5 74–75
 – 54.19.1–3 68
 – 54.30.4 69
 – 54.6.5 70
 – 62.27.4 87
 – 63.1–6 43
 – 63.16 85
 – 68.26–30 43
 – 68.28.4 30
 – 68.28–31 43
 – 68.31.4 43
 – 68.33.2 43
 – 68.33 43
 – 71.2 43
 – 71.3 40
 – 78.16.7 115
Chariton
 – 1.1.16 201
 – 1.4.4 320
 – 1.4.12 86
 – 1.9.3 319
 – 1.9.4–5 366
 – 3.2.10 198

– 3.3.4	318	– 2.11	46
– 3.4	299	– 2.20.1–3	84
– 3.7.6.2–3.7.7.1	318	– 2.29.4–6	49
– 4.2.3–4.3.2	195	– 2.29–31	41
– 4.5.10	31–8	– 3.8.1	31
– 5.4–8	295	– 4.81.2	264
– 5.8.2.3–5.8.3.1	315	**Diogenes Laertius**	
– 6.6.1	320	– 1.94	87
– 8.4.2–3	320	– 1.96	82
– 8.5.8.1	320	– 1.99	85
– 8.5.9–8.6.1	195	– *Elegiae in Maecenatum*	
– 8.6.8–8.7.3	195	– passim	

Cicero
– *Att.*

Euripides
– 13.49.2	69	– *Cyc.* 96–174	265
– 2.12.2	328	– *Hel.* 767	119
– 1.16.11	215	– *Hel.* 1122–1131	119

– *Brut.*
– *Ev. Marc.*

– 6	294	– 1,27	116

– *De Orat.*
Heliodorus

– 2.338	294	– 1.2.5	368

– *Fam.*

– 7.24.1	69	– 1.8.2–3	313

– *Flac.*

– 16	299	– 1.8.4	313
– 63 12		– 1.15.2.3–4	322

– *Inv.*

		– 1.30	321
– 1.15	308	– 1.30.7.3–4	322
– 2.106	308	– 2.5.4	368
– Codex Laurentianus		– 2.8.2.1	323
Conventi Soppressi		– 2.12.5.5–7	321
627 *(Florence)*	184, 195, 235	– 2.23.5	255

Conon
		– 3.7.3–3.8.2	316
– *FGrHist* 26 F 1,9 7	84	– 3.11.2	255

Ctesias
		– 3.13.1	257
		– 3.14	256
– *FGrHist* 688 F 1,20 7	84	– 3.14.3	257

Demetrius Phalereus
		– 4.9.1.2–3	320
		– 4.16.4–5	255

– *Eloc.*
		– 6.14–15	369
		– 7.7.3.5–9	317
– 120	118	– 7.10.6.2–4	322

Digest
		– 7.29.1.1	322
– 5.1	299	– 8.9–15	295
– 13.4	299	– 8.16.6–7	186
– 24.1.64	69	– 8.17.3–4	186

Diodorus Siculus
		– 10.5.1	31
– 2.7	84	– 10.9.6	256
– 2.7.5	42	– 10.16.7	309
– 2.11.1–3	39	– 10.23.3	309

– 10.41	259	– *Carm.*	
– 10.41.3	257	– 2.10	66
Herodianus		– *S.*	
– 4.8.3	115	– 1.5.38	67
Herodotus		– 1.2.64	75
– 1.108	47	– 2.8	65
– 1.140	45	**Hyginus**	
– 2.121–123	35	– *Fab.* 253	83
– 3.32.4	88	**Iamblichus**	
– 3.50.1	87	– *Babyloniaka*	
– 5.46	34	– 74b1	46
– 5.92 ζ 1	85	– 75a34	30, 34
– 7.33	112	– 75a36	33
– 9.120	112	– 75a37–8	46
Hesiod		– 75a41	32
– *Op.*		– 75b1–8	35
– 287–91	280	– 75b1	33
– *Th.*		– 75b8	33
– 211–32	357	– 75b12	35
– 820–868	345	– 75b19	34
Hippocrates		– 75b20	34
– *De diaeta* i-iv,		– 75b27–41	35
51, line 1	273	– 75b28	34
Hipponax		– 75b29	35
– Frs. 5–11 (West)	10	– 75b36	35
– *Historia Augusta*		– 75b37–38	36
– 7.3.7	82	– 76a3–6	34
– 7.5.8–11	82	– 76a4	32
– 8.1–2	43	– 78a15	36
– 10.21.7	82	– *VP*	
– 13.3	44	– 31.195	323
– 13.10.1	82	**Jerome**	
Homer		– *Life of Hilarion*	
– *Il.*		– 3.1	285
– 2.645–680	23	– 14	285
– 2.695–702	110	– 21	284
– *Od.*		– 28	285
– 6.229–235	32	– 31	284
– 6.231	122	– 31.1	285
– 4.87–88	265	– 31.3–4	285
– 9.219	223–273	– 31.9	287
– 19.335–553	355	**Justin**	
– 21.333–335	270	– *Epitome*	
– 23.157–162	132	– 1.12	83
Horatius		– 43.5.3	13
– *Epod.*		– *Life of Adam and Eve*	
– 14	74	– 8–10	310–311

– 14	311	– 4.32.3	100
– 19	311	– 4.40	244
– 27	311	– 4.40.3	133
– 32–33	311	**Lucian**	
– 37	311	– *Hist. conscr.*	
– 42	311	– *Salt.*	
Livy		– 19	337
– 24.39.1	299	– *VH*	
– 37.54	12	– 1.26	111
Longus		– *De Dea Syria*	
– *Daphnis and Chloe*		– 17–18	42
– 1.9.1	274	**Lucan**	
– 1.12–13	126, 128, 131	– 3.340	12
– 1.13.2	128, 268	**Macrobius**	
– 1.15.3	267	– *Sat.*	
– 1.16.4	267	– 1.11.21	67
– 1.18.1	270	– 2.4.12	68
– 1.19.1	267	– 2.7	74
– 1.19.1–2	55–56	**Marlowe, Christopher**	
– 1.19.2	270	– *The Jew of Malta*	
– 1.20	243–244	– 1.1	236
– 1.20.1	267	**Martial**	
– 1.21.4	126	– 12.30	72
– 1.23.3	127, 271	**Ovid**	
– 1.32	126	– *Fast.*	
– 2.7	244	– 4.133–160	129
– 2.8.1	133	– *Met.*	
– 2.18	126, 130	– 8.666	271
– 2.18.1	269	– 10.243–297	232
– 2.20	135	– 13.796	271
– 2.23.1	126	– 13. 829–30	266
– 2.25–26	368	– 13.830	271
– 3.15 ff.	244	– 14.274	271
– 3.15.3	270	– 15.60–478	256
– 3.17.1	126	**Parthenius**	
– 3.18.1–2	268	– 17.1	84
– 3.24.2	126, 131	– 17.4	83
– 3.26.4	137	– 17.7	84
– 3.33.1–2	272	– *test.* 3 Lightfoot 11	
– 4.1.3	126	= Suetonius *Tib.* 70	86
– 4.4.1	126	– *test.* 4 Lightfoot 11	86
– 4.6.1	270	– *test.* 9 (a) Lightfoot 10	
– 4.10 ff.	244	= Macrobius 5.17.18	86
– 4.10.3	270	**Pausanias**	
– 4.14.1	270, 273	– 5.12.8	115
– 4.16	243	– 5.25.8	115
– 4.26.4	131	– 5.26.3	115

Persius
- 1.134 — 206

Petrarca, Francesco
- *Familiarum rerum libri*
- 1.4.1 — 223

Petronius
- 1.1–3 — 292
- 3.1 — 295
- 10.4–6 — 14
- 27.1–37.5 — 211
- 29.6 — 72
- 30.7 — 211
- 31.7 — 74
- 34.7 — 211
- 37 — 71
- 37.6 — 78.8
- 43.7 — 72
- 47.5 — 73, 76
- 48.4–6 — 293
- 52.8 — 75
- 52.10 — 73
- 54.2 — 72
- 55.3 — 72
- 57.1 — 73
- 58.1 — 73
- 61–62 — 369
- 63 — 369
- 67.1–3 — 72, 75
- 67.11 — 72
- 67.12 — 75
- 68.7–8 — 74
- 69.1–2 — 74
- 69.9 — 8
- 70.10 — 75
- 73.5 — 72
- 74.1 — 72
- 74.10–12 — 73
- 74.13 — 73
- 76.7 — 73
- 77.2 — 73
- 77.4 — 73
- 77.6 — 73
- 80.6 — 8
- 80.8 — 8
- 81.3 — 7–8, 12
- 83.6 — 10
- 89 — 13
- 100 — 7
- 100.4 — 8
- 101 — 7
- 101.7 — 296
- 104.2 — 8
- 105.9 — 11
- 107.15 — 12
- 107–109 — 291
- 107.15–108.1 — 297
- 108.1 — 12
- 113.3 — 7
- 117.3 — 10
- 125.4 — 11
- 139.2.14–15 — 11

Philostratus
- *Vitae sophistarum*
  2.1.8 — 88

Philostratus
- *Her.*
  - 6.3–7 — 110
  - 7.2 — 110
  - 7.3 — 110
  - 8.10 — 111
  - 8.12 — 111
  - 8.18 — 112
  - 14.2–3 — 113
  - 16.6 — 113
  - 18.1 — 113
  - 21.6 — 117
  - 23.20–23 — 118
  - 24.14 — 118
  - 25.2 — 109, 114
  - 25.3–4 — 114
  - 25.13 — 114
  - 25.13–17 — 118
  - 25.18 — 118
  - 26.1 — 109
  - 27.12 — 114
  - 29.6 — 109
  - 33.1–34.7 — 118
  - 33.31–33 — 118
  - 33.36 — 119
  - 33.37 — 119
  - 33.47 — 119
  - 33–34 — 109
  - 34 — 109
  - 34.4 — 109

Index locorum — **395**

– 43.2	109
– 43.3	111
– 43.3 – 44.4	114
– 43.4	114
– 43.10 – 16	109
– 43.16	114
– *VA*	
– 4.13	117

Pindar
– *P.*
– 1.15 – 25	348
– 1.20 – 25	349

Plato
– *Lg.*
– 649d4 – 5	315

– *R.*
– 4.443d-e	348
– 9 p. 571 c f.	86
– 9.571a-d	348
– 9.571c	343
– 9.571e-572b	348
– 9.572b	343
– 9.588c	346
– 9.588d	347

Plautus
– *Cas.*
– 963	13

– *Per.*
– *Truc.*
– 269	215

Pliny the Elder
– *Nat.*
– 6.27	42
– 6.96	46
– 6.130	48
– 6.135	46
– 8.81	137
– 10.5	59
– 13.7	57
– 13.9	58
– 16,79	45
– 18.152	47
– 21.38.4	132
– 21.74	45
– 21.77	45
– 24.90	45
– 29. 93 – 94	47
– 29.93 – 97	47
– 30.1	41
– 30.16 – 17	43
– 31.36	46
– 35	143

Plutarch
– *Ant.*
– 19.1	31

– *Alex.*
– 73.1	42

– *Caes.*
– 32	86
– 57.4	84

– *Cim.*
– 8.5 – 7	111

– *Crass.*
– 19.4	47
– 18.4	42
– 21	42
– 22.4 – 6	42

– *Demet.*
– 38	42

– *Mor.*
– 146d	83
– 384d-394c (*E ap. Delph.*)	115
– 394d-409d (*Pyth. or.*)	115
– 409e-438d (*Def. orac.*)	115
– 515d	330
– 516b-c	330
– 517d	331
– 517e-f	331
– 519c-d	330
– 759 – 760f	68

– *Thes.*
– 36.2	111

Polybius
– 3.42.7	31
– 5.46.9	30

Ps. Acro
– ad Horace Odes 2.12	75

Ps. Apollodorus
– 3.10.3	34

Ps. Plutarch
– *Proverb. Alex.* 60	13

Quintilian
- *Inst.*
  - 5.9.14 — 128
  - 6.5.9–11 — 294
  - 9.4.18 — 87
  - 10.3.30 — 294
  - 11.1.47 — 293
  - 11.3.127 — 293
  - 11.3.134 — 293
  - 11.3.156 — 293
  - 12.5.5–6 — 294
- *Rhetorica ad Herennium*
  - 1.14.24–297
- *Scholia in Homeri Odysseam*
  - Od. 4.456 — 337

Seneca the Elder
- *Contr.*
  - pf. 10.8 — 74
  - pf. 9.2–4 — 294

Seneca the Younger
- *Apoc.*
  - 1.1–2 — 165
  - 3–4 — 167
  - 4–11 — 173
  - 4.3 — 165
  - 4.37–42 — 168
  - 4.39–4 — 167
  - 5.1–11.6 — 172
  - 9.3 — 173
  - 11.1 — 170
- *Brev. vit.*
  - 4.5 — 67
- *Cl.*
  - 1.9.6 — 67
  - 1.15.2 — 13
- *Ep.*
  - 12.8 — 66
  - 18.4 — 71
  - 27.5–8 — 66
  - 114.3 — 71
  - 114.6 — 70
- *Prov.*
  - 3.10 — 70, 76

Servius
- ad Aen. 3.57 — 9

Shakespeare, William
- *Comedy of Errors*
  - 1.2 — 223
  - 2.2 — 223

Sidonius Apollinaris
- *Carm.*
  - 23.157–160 — 68
  - 28.145–7 — 11
  - 28.155–7 — 11

Silius Italicus
- 15.168–72 — 12

Stephanus of Byzantium
- Ethnica, s.v. Syrbanè — 30

Strabo
- 12.3.18 — 44
- 14.5.4 — 67
- 15.1.68 — 41
- 15.3.13–15 — 41
- 15.3.22 — 46
- 16.1.6 — 41
- 16.1.20 — 47
- 16.1.21 — 46
- 16.4.1 — 42
- 17.1.2 — 31

Suda
- epsilon 499 — 13
- epsilon 3161–13

Suetonius
- *Aug.*
  - 19.1 — 87
  - 56.4 — 67
  - 66.3 — 67
  - 69 — 68
- *Cal.*
  - 23–24 — 81
- *Cl.*
  - 44 — 167
- *Jul.*
  - 7 — 86
- *Nero*
  - 19 — 85
  - 28.2 — 86
  - 35.3 — 87
- *Tib.*
  - 8 — 67

Tacitus
– Ann.
- 1.1   80
- 1.10.4   67
- 1.54   75
- 1.54.2   74
- 13.1   80
- 13.13.2   80–81
- 13.45.1   85
- 13.58   85
- 14.2   86
- 14.2.1   83
- 14.52.1   85
- 15.28–30   43
- 16.6.1   87

– Dial.
- 1.2   295
- 26.3   294
- 34.1–5   292
- 35.1–5   292
- 39.1–4   293

– Hist.
- 2.80.3   299

Theocritus
- 1.57–58   265
- 5.86–87   265
- 11.20   266
- 11.65–66   274

Tibullus
- 2.3   271
- 2.3.14b-15   265
- 2.5.33–38   266

Tyrtaeus
- 8.1–3   319

Sophokles
- *Tr.* 653   322

Varro
– R.
- 2.1.4   264
- 2.1.28   264

Velleius Paterculus
- 2.91.2   68

Vergil
– Ecl.
- 1.31–35   266

– G.
- 4.111   11

Xenophon
– Oec.
- 7.33–36   270
- 10   127

Xenophon of Ephesus
- 1.2.3   101
- 1.3.1   101
- 1.10   25
- 1.10.4   101
- 1.10.8   101
- 1.11   371
- 1.11.6   101
- 1.13.5–14.3   101
- 1.14   371
- 2.5.5.1–4   320
- 2.9.1   101–102
- 2.9.4   102
- 2.11.1   102
- 2.11.2   102
- 2.11.3   102
- 2.11.4   102
- 2.11.9   102
- 3.7.1   320
- 4.2.4   312
- 4.2.6   312
- 4.3.3–4   312
- 5.1   366
- 5.1–2   361
- 5.4.6   312
- 5.4.10   312
- 5.9.10   308
- 5.13.3   319
- 5.13.4   312
- 5.15   25
- 5.15.2   19
- 5.13.3   312